# Thomas F. Torrance

## Theologian of the Trinity

PAUL D. MOLNAR
*St John's University, New York, USA*

ASHGATE

© Paul D. Molnar 2009

All rights reserved. No part of this publication may be reproduced, stored in a retrieval system or transmitted in any form or by any means, electronic, mechanical, photocopying, recording or otherwise without the prior permission of the publisher.

Paul D. Molnar has asserted his right under the Copyright, Designs and Patents Act, 1988, to be identified as the author of this work.

Published by
Ashgate Publishing Limited
Wey Court East
Union Road
Farnham
Surrey, GU9 7PT
England

Ashgate Publishing Company
Suite 420
101 Cherry Street
Burlington
VT 05401-4405
USA

www.ashgate.com

**British Library Cataloguing in Publication Data**

Molnar, Paul D., 1946–
    Thomas F. Torrance: Theologian of the Trinity. -- (Great Theologians series)
    1. Torrance, Thomas F. (Thomas Forsyth), 1913–2007. 2. Trinity – History of
    doctrines – 20th century. I. Title. II. Series
    231'.044'092–dc22

**Library of Congress Cataloging-in-Publication Data**
Molnar, Paul D., 1946-
    Thomas F. Torrance: Theologian of the Trinity / Paul D. Molnar.
        p.    cm. – (Great Theologians series)
    Includes bibliographical references and index.
    1. Torrance, Thomas F. (Thomas Forsyth), 1913–2007. 2. Theology, Doctrinal –
    History – 20th century. 3. Trinity – History of doctrines – 20th century. I. Title.
    BX4827.T67M65 2009
    230'.044092–dc22                                                        2009007666

ISBN    9780754652281 (hbk)
ISBN    9780754652298 (pbk)
ISBN    9780754696322 (ebk)

**Mixed Sources**
Product group from well-managed forests and other controlled sources
www.fsc.org Cert no. SA-COC-1565
© 1996 Forest Stewardship Council

Printed and bound in Great Britain by
MPG Books Group, UK

# Contents

*Acknowledgements*                                                          vii

1    Introducing T. F. Torrance                                               1
2    T. F. Torrance, Theologian of the Trinity: The Centrality of
     the Doctrine of the Trinity in Torrance's Theology                      31
         The Deposit of Faith                                                36
         Dualism                                                             39
         Arius/Arianism                                                      44
         Imageless Thinking of God                                          48
         *Homoousion*                                                        54
         Onto-relational Understanding of Person                            59
         *Perichoresis*                                                      61
         The *Filioque*                                                      65
         Torrance's View of the Relationship of the Immanent and
         Economic Trinity                                                    67
         Conclusion                                                          70
3    God the Father Almighty, Maker of Heaven and Earth                     73
         Understanding Creation through the Incarnation                     85
         Torrance's New Natural Theology                                    93
4    Jesus Christ, the Incarnate Word, *Homoousion* with the Father
     and with Us in our Humanity                                           101
         Torrance's Rejection of Ebionite and Docetic Christology          105
         The Incarnation as an Act of Love                                 111
         The Incarnation as an Act of Life                                 117
         Jesus' Vicarious Humanity                                         119
         The Incarnation Means Light, Truth                                120
         The Receptacle or Container Concept of Space and Time             124
5    Atonement: Incarnation and Reconciliation Are One
     in Jesus Christ                                                       137
         Atonement as a Personal Act                                       142
         Divine Impassibility                                              147
         Cross, Sin and Evil                                               159
         Torrance's View of Justification                                  168
         John Knox and the *Scots Confession*                              174
6    Torrance's Pneumatology                                               187
         The Interrelationship between Incarnation, Atonement
         and Pentecost                                                     189
         Torrance's Understanding of *Theosis*                             197

The Holy Spirit in the Life of the Trinity 201
The Holy Spirit and God's Self-Communication 206
The Holy Spirit Who Proceeds from the Father through the Son 209
The Procession of the Holy Spirit and the *Filioque* 212
The Problem with the Cappadocian Solution to the *Filioque*
and Torrance's Solution 214
7 Resurrection and Ascension: Implications for Humanity in Light of
Redemption and Eschatology 219
Resurrection and Faith 221
Effects of Dualism on Understanding the Resurrection 223
The Resurrection and the Person of Jesus 226
Resurrection, Incarnation and Atonement 227
Passive Obedience 229
Active Obedience 230
Resurrection and Virgin Birth 234
The Nature of the Resurrection 239
The Ascension and Eschatology 246
The Nature of the Ascension 250
God's Time 253
Christ's Second Coming 259
8 Torrance's Trinitarian Understanding of the Church, Sacraments
and Ministry 265
The Church Grounded in the Trinity and its Existence in Israel 266
Rejection of Dualism and Legalism 269
The Spirit and the Church 273
The Church as a Body of Justified Sinners 275
The Church as a Community of Reconciliation 279
Torrance's View of Grace in Relation to the Roman
Catholic View 282
Prophet, Priest and King and the Sacraments of Baptism and
the Lord's Supper 287
Torrance's Understanding of the Sacraments 295
Baptism 295
The Lord's Supper 306
9 Considering Some Criticisms of T. F. Torrance's Theology 325

*Conclusion* 351
*Selected Bibliography* 353
*Name Index* 361
*Subject Index* 365

# Acknowledgements

I would like to thank John Webster, first for suggesting that I contribute this volume and then for helping me by reading the manuscript as it progressed and as it began to reach its final form, offering very helpful comments along the way—comments that ultimately I believe made this a much better book. His support, encouragement, friendship and assistance not only enabled me to complete this work but made the whole process much easier than it otherwise would have been. John generously gave of his time and expertise with his unparalleled insight and sense of humor and I am most grateful to him for that. I would especially like to thank Iain R. Torrance for his assistance. From the very beginning Iain made available to me all of his father's papers, letters and documents that were in the process of being transferred to Princeton Theological Seminary. And he personally helped me in many ways, not only with information that I had difficulty acquiring; any time I needed to clarify important material, Iain was there to assist me in concrete ways in spite of his own very rigorous and busy schedule. I am extremely grateful to him also for reading parts of the manuscript and offering encouragement as the book progressed, and for his constantly reliable friendship throughout the writing of this book. In addition, I am indebted to him for enabling me to secure the photo of his father for use on the cover of this book. And it is to him that I owe the pleasure and honor of first meeting his father when he helped arrange a visit by T. F. Torrance to St. John's University in 1997 to speak on Einstein and God. A thank you is due to Alasdair I. C. Heron who graciously gave his time to speak with me about T. F. Torrance and his years at Edinburgh as I was preparing certain portions of the book. Alasdair's very keen wit and thorough knowledge of T. F. Torrance's work were very helpful to me. Thanks are also due to my good friend, George Hunsinger, for providing material from his recent book, *The Eucharist and Ecumenism* (Cambridge, 2008), which I was able to use in connection with Chapter 8 long before the book was published.

Also, I would like to thank Christopher A. Kuczewski for helping me prepare the bibliography and for compiling information required in obtaining permissions. I am grateful as well to Clifford B. Anderson, Curator of Special Collections, Princeton Theological Seminary, for his help in enabling me to acquire necessary texts written by T. F. Torrance. Thanks are also due to I. John Hesselink for sending me copies of articles on Torrance that I found helpful. I am appreciative that St. John's University provided a one-semester research reduction to assist the writing of this book. I must also express my gratitude to John J. McCormick for reading each chapter of this work and offering critical and editorial comments that helped me improve the manuscript at every stage. His input and support throughout the writing of this book were, as always, invaluable. I am indebted to Luke Watson of

Edinburgh who was very generous in tracking down the photo of T. F. Torrance that he had taken back in 2003, setting it up for use on the cover, giving permission for its use and sending it to me. I am grateful to the *Scottish Journal of Theology* for a grant to secure permission to use Luke Watson's photograph of Thomas F. Torrance at the age of 90. Scottish Journal of Theology Ltd is a Charity registered in Scotland, SC000435.

Further, I would like to thank T&T Clark/Continuum International Publishing Group for permission to reprint previously published material: Karl Barth, *Church Dogmatics* Volumes I–IV (1958–1981); Thomas F. Torrance, *Divine and Contingent Order* (1998); *Divine Meaning: Studies in Patristic Hermeneutics* (1995); *God and Rationality* (1997); *Karl Barth, Biblical and Evangelical Theologian* (1990); *Royal Priesthood: A Theology of Ordained Ministry* (1993); *Scottish Theology: From John Knox to John McLeod Campbell* (1996); *Space, Time and Incarnation* (1997); *Space, Time and Resurrection* (1998); *The Christian Doctrine of God, One Being Three Persons* (1996); *The Trinitarian Faith: The Evangelical Theology of the Ancient Catholic Church* (1988); and *Trinitarian Perspectives: Toward Doctrinal Agreement* (1994). I would also like to thank Robin Baird-Smith, Publishing Director of Continuum International Publishing Group, London, for his generosity and special assistance in securing these permissions.

A thank you is due to the members of the Executive Board of the T. F. Torrance Theological Fellowship, especially Gary Deddo and Elmer Colyer, with whom I have had the pleasure of working as a board member, friend and now as President. Their interest in the theology of T. F. Torrance and our theological exchanges are always helpful and uplifting. In addition, I would like to thank Sarah Lloyd of Ashgate Publishing for her patience and assistance throughout the writing of this manuscript. Without her support this book could never have reached its final form.

Finally, I would like to thank Thomas F. Torrance himself. When I had the privilege of getting to know him during his visit to St. John's and my subsequent visit with him at his home in Edinburgh, as well as through correspondence, I experienced one of those rare opportunities where I actually was able to discuss theology in depth with a man whom I regarded then and now to be one of the truly great theologians of the twentieth century. His thinking has been a very positive influence on my own thought for many years now. As anyone will see from this book, Torrance not only was a masterful systematic theologian, but he was a truly humble minister of the Christian Gospel. His one compelling drive was to preach and teach about the centrality of Jesus Christ and thus also of the Triune God, in order to stress how important it is for people to lift up their minds and hearts toward God in grateful joy and happiness for the one who, in his Word and Spirit, loves us more than he loves himself. It is to Thomas F. Torrance and to his memory that I dedicate this book.

# Chapter 1
# Introducing T. F. Torrance

There is little doubt that Thomas Forsyth Torrance (1913–2007) is one of the most significant English-speaking theologians of the twentieth century. According to Alister McGrath, those outside of Great Britain generally regard Torrance "as the most significant British academic theologian of the twentieth century"[1] and, in his view, "one of the most productive, creative and important theologians of the twentieth century".[2] In the estimation of George Hunsinger, Torrance's understanding of the sacraments in particular represents a new synthesis of Calvin and Barth which improves on both and embodies "the most creative Reformed breakthrough on the sacraments in twentieth-century theology, and arguably the most important Reformed statement since Calvin".[3] Stanley Grenz notes that as early as 1984 the editors of the *Reformed Review* praised Torrance as "the leading Reformed theologian today in the Anglo-Saxon world" and "one of the most brilliant and seminal thinkers of our time".[4] Elmer Colyer believes there is a "growing consensus that Thomas F. Torrance is one of the premier theologians in the second half of the twentieth century".[5] Kye Won Lee calls Torrance "the most

---

[1]  Alister E. McGrath, *Thomas F. Torrance: An Intellectual Biography* (hereafter: *An Intellectual Biography*), (Edinburgh: T&T Clark, 1999), p. xi.

[2]  McGrath, *An Intellectual Biography*, p. 107.

[3]  George Hunsinger, "The Dimension of Depth: Thomas F. Torrance on the Sacraments of Baptism and the Lord's Supper" in the *Scottish Journal of Theology* (hereafter: *SJT*) Vol. 54, No. 2: 155–76, 160. See also George Hunsinger, "The Dimension of Depth: Thomas F. Torrance on the Sacraments", pp. 139–60 in *The Promise of Trinitarian Theology: Theologians in Dialogue with T.F. Torrance*, ed Elmer M. Colyer (Lanham, Maryland: Rowman & Littlefield Publishers, Inc., 2001), and Torrance's glowing response in the same volume (pp. 318–21). Hunsinger dedicates his recent book *The Eucharist and Ecumenism: Let Us Keep the Feast* (Cambridge: Cambridge University Press, 2008) to T.F. Torrance, noting that, of all the many important influences that have led him to write his book with a view toward ecumenical agreement on the Eucharist, T.F. Torrance towered above them all in providing him with many of the important themes that helped him move "from Karl Barth to something like the Catholic Evangelical Orthodox center" in his thinking (p. x).

[4]  Stanley J. Grenz, *Rediscovering the Triune God: The Trinity in Contemporary Theology* (Minneapolis: Fortress Press, 2004), p. 201.

[5]  Elmer M. Colyer, *How to Read T.F. Torrance: Understanding His Trinitarian & Scientific Theology* (Downers Grove, Illinois: InterVarsity Press, 2001), p. 11 and *The Promise of Trinitarian Theology*, p. ix.

consistent evangelical theologian in our times".[6] Most people today recognize that Torrance has made significant contributions to the discussion between theology and science. Daniel Hardy, for example, writes that Torrance "is virtually unique amongst theologians in the depth of his knowledge of the philosophy of the natural sciences".[7] And P. Mark Achtemeier believes Torrance's contributions to the study of science and religion "are magisterial and highly original".[8] Alister McGrath also notes that Torrance authored, edited or translated a massive amount of material—more than 360 pieces before his retirement in 1979 and over 250 more after that date.

While Torrance's writing covers a wide range of topics, he is perhaps best known for his study of science and Christian theology. McGrath notes wryly that many of those theologians he has studied did not seem bothered by the fact that they had no first-hand knowledge of the method and norms of natural science, but wrote about science nonetheless! But it is different with Torrance. "Torrance's writings were, quite simply, of landmark significance."[9] While this book will consider Torrance's contribution to the discussions between science and theology later in this chapter in order to give the reader some indication of his massive contribution to that area of study, we shall not focus on that contribution but will instead call attention to his dogmatic theology and how that theology informs all other aspects of his thought. Of course, even his dogmatic theology shows signs of his commitment to the scientific method, since every aspect of this dogmatic theology is marked by his belief that accurate thinking can only take place as thought conforms to the unique nature of the object being investigated. As the title of the book suggests, Torrance's thinking is deeply structured around his understanding of the triune God. Not only all other doctrines, but even Torrance's work toward ecumenical understanding between Orthodox and Protestants and Protestants and Roman Catholics is informed by his understanding of the Trinity. Interestingly, although he did not formally teach courses in the doctrine of God at the University of Edinburgh,[10] he did write three very important books on the

---

[6]   Kye Won Lee, *Living in Union With Christ: The Practical Theology of Thomas F. Torrance* (New York: Peter Lang Publishing, Inc., 2003), p. 1.

[7]   Daniel W. Hardy, "Thomas F. Torrance" in *The Modern Theologians: An Introduction to Christian Theology in The Twentieth Century, Volume I*, ed David F. Ford (Oxford: Blackwell Publishers, 1993), pp. 71–91, 71.

[8]   P. Mark Achtemeier, "Natural Science and Christian Faith in the Thought of T. F. Torrance" in *The Promise of Trinitarian Theology*, pp. 269–302, 269.

[9]   McGrath, *An Intellectual Biography*, p. xii.

[10]   Because John Baillie and later John McIntyre taught the doctrine of the Trinity, Torrance was denied that possibility at Edinburgh and was very disappointed about that (McGrath, *An Intellectual Biography*, p. 91). Nonetheless, in his honors courses in dogmatics, Torrance was able to emphasize Christological and trinitarian themes, including the fact that the Trinity was the "ground and grammar of theology" in a dynamic and engaging fashion. He thus impressed upon his students the importance of the doctrine. I am

Trinity after his retirement and he personally was most pleased with his important book *The Trinitarian Faith*, which was published in 1988.[11] But before we get into the dogmatic material that will comprise the heart of this book, let us finish introducing the man himself.

T. F. Torrance was born of missionary parents in Chengdu, in the province of Sichuan, West China, on August 30, 1913, and was named after his great-grandfather, Thomas Forsyth Torrance. From 1920 to 1927 he attended a school established by Canadian missionaries "at Lan Tai Tze on the campus of the West China Union University",[12] which, according to Alister McGrath, was not quite up to British standards but was good enough for Torrance to dream of entering the University of Edinburgh to prepare himself for missionary work in Tibet. Because of growing hostility to missionaries in China, all women and children had to leave in 1927, and so Torrance returned to Scotland in the middle of the Depression. When things stabilized in China, his father returned there in 1928 and left his wife Annie to raise the family in Scotland. His father finally returned home to Scotland after retiring late in 1934 and lived there until his death in 1959. T. F. Torrance eventually attended the University of Edinburgh to study classics and philosophy and began to formulate some of his own realist views of philosophy, theology and morality; he also studied the philosophy of science.[13] He began the formal study of theology in New College in the fall of 1934. At that time he read and was disappointed by Schleiermacher and developed an interest in the theology of the early church. In Torrance's own words:

> I was captivated by the architectonic form and beauty of Schleiermacher's method and his arrangement of dogmatics into a scientific system of Christian

---

grateful to Professor Alasdair I.C. Heron of the University of Erlangen, Germany, for this information regarding Torrance's teaching about the Trinity while at Edinburgh.

[11] The three books are: Thomas F. Torrance, *The Christian Doctrine of God, One Being Three Persons* (hereafter: *The Christian Doctrine of God*), (Edinburgh: T&T Clark, 1996); Thomas F. Torrance, *Trinitarian Perspectives: Toward Doctrinal Agreement* (hereafter: *Trinitarian Perspectives*), (Edinburgh: T&T Clark, 1994); and Thomas F. Torrance, *The Trinitarian Faith: The Evangelical Theology of the Ancient Catholic Church* (hereafter: *The Trinitarian Faith*), (Edinburgh: T&T Clark, 1988). Torrance's remark about *The Trinitarian Faith* appears in Michael Bauman, *Roundtable Conversations with European Theologians* (hereafter: *Roundtable Conversations*), (Grand Rapids, MI: Baker Book House, 1990), p. 117. For an excellent brief introduction to Torrance's realist theology noting its trinitarian shape, see Robert J. Palma, "Thomas F. Torrance's Reformed Theology" in *Reformed Review*, Autumn 1984, vol. 38, no. 1: 2–46.

[12] McGrath, *An Intellectual Biography*, p. 13.

[13] Torrance studied philosophy with Norman Kemp Smith, who was an authority on Kant and Hume, and A. E. Taylor, who taught moral philosophy and was an expert on Plato. According to his own recollections, he "had a very powerful training in philosophy". See I. John Hesselink, "An Interview with Thomas F. Torrance" in *Reformed Review*, Autumn 1984, vol. 38, no. 1: 47–64, 52.

doctrine, but it was clear to me that the whole conception was wrong, for due to its fundamental presuppositions Schleiermacher's approach did not match up to the nature or content of the Christian Gospel, while the propositional structure he imposed upon the Christian consciousness lacked any realist scientific objectivity.[14]

Under the influence of his mother,[15] his view of Scripture was both Christ-centered and opposed to any crude fundamentalism. Indeed, his mother had given him a copy of Barth's *Credo* that encouraged him to oppose not only rationalistic liberalism but fundamentalism and deterministic sorts of Calvinism as well.

Two professors at New College were to have a lasting influence on Torrance. Hugh Ross Mackintosh (1870–1936) stressed the centrality of Christ for the doctrines of revelation and salvation and also emphasized the connection between theology and mission,[16] and Daniel Lamont (1869–1950), who succeeded Alexander Martin in 1927 and held the chair of "Apologetics, Christian Ethics and Practical Theology", was interested in the relationship between Christianity and scientific culture.[17] Mackintosh's thought was so influential for Torrance that he took extraordinarily detailed notes. Mackintosh's books, *The Doctrine of the Person of Christ* (1912) and *The Christian Experience of Forgiveness* (1927), remained the basic texts for divinity students at the University until the 1970s. Interestingly, two key points emphasized by Mackintosh were to be of long-lasting influence in Torrance's own thought. First, "No one knoweth the Son, save the Father; neither doth anyone know the Father save the Son, and he to whomsoever the Son willleth to reveal him" (Matthew 11:27). This classic text indicated for Torrance that our knowledge of God comes only in and through Christ himself and that "What Jesus was on earth God is for ever".[18] As we shall see, Torrance would later develop this into his important position that what God is toward us in Jesus Christ, he is eternally in himself. Second, Mackintosh was quite convinced

---

[14]  Thomas F. Torrance, *Karl Barth, Biblical and Evangelical Theologian* (hereafter: *Karl Barth*), (Edinburgh: T&T Clark, 1990), p. 121. See also Thomas F. Torrance, "My Interaction with Karl Barth" in *How Karl Barth Changed My Mind* (hereafter: *My Interaction with Karl Barth*), ed Donald K. McKim (Grand Rapids, MI: Eerdmans, 1986), pp. 52–64, 52, and Hesselink, "Interview with Torrance": 53.

[15]  Torrance once stated that, of the seven ministers in his family, including sons and brothers-in-law, his mother was "the best preacher" (Hesselink, "Interview with Torrance": 50).

[16]  See David W. Torrance, "Thomas Forsyth Torrance: Minister of the Gospel, Pastor, and Evangelical Theologian" in *The Promise of Trinitarian Theology*, pp. 1–30, 7.

[17]  See David F. Wright and Gary D. Badcock (eds), *Disruption to Diversity: Edinburgh Divinity 1846–1996* (hereafter: *Disruption to Diversity*), (Edinburgh: T&T Clark, 1996), p. 140.

[18]  Torrance's own recollections as quoted in McGrath, *An Intellectual Biography*, p. 31.

that the most important issue facing the Church in his time was the same truth that was central during the time of Nicaea, namely, "the cardinal truth of the Deity of Christ, the incarnate Son of God".[19] This same thought was repeated by Torrance many years later in his book *The Christian Doctrine of God*: "The Deity of Christ is the supreme truth of the Gospel, the key to the bewildering enigma of Jesus ...."[20] And, of course, Torrance developed this insight into his own insistence on the centrality of the Nicene *homoousion* for all theological loci.

Daniel Lamont helped to generate Torrance's interest in science and in applying the scientific method to theology in the sense that knowledge was perceived to take place when thinking was conformed to the unique nature of the object being investigated. Some of this was presented in Lamont's important book *Christ in the World of Thought*, published in 1934. This scientific thinking was to dominate Torrance's thought in all areas, as we shall see. During his time as a student at Edinburgh, he had contact with John and Donald Baillie who were both critical of Barth in a way that Torrance considered inappropriate. He himself believed that John Baillie's thinking in particular suffered from what he called an epistemological dualism. This meant that Baillie tried to establish "a method of inquiry apart from the subject-matter of his inquiry" on the one hand, and, on the other, "he worked out a theory of religion from its roots in the human soul and the moral claims of God upon it, without really taking divine revelation into account".[21] It is certainly not too much to say that Torrance became a lifelong opponent of subjectivism because such an approach to objective knowledge essentially cut one off from the truth as it exists independent of the subject. At this point in his career, he was following the thought of his teachers Mackintosh and Lamont and argued that "it is impossible for man to gain knowledge of God 'by digging into himself'".[22] Barth's theology was becoming popular in Scotland in the mid 1930s and Torrance became more interested in Barth's thinking at that time. H. R. Mackintosh had introduced him to Barth's "Theology of the Word" and Torrance himself read Barth's *Church Dogmatics* I/1 as soon as the translation by G. T. Thompson appeared in 1936. Torrance was particularly intrigued by Barth's understanding of dogmatics as a science, by his view of the objectivity of God's self-revelation and by his trinitarian doctrine.[23] It is no wonder that Torrance was to become famous as the key person to introduce Barth's theology to the English-speaking world. Torrance's book *Karl Barth: An Introduction to His Early Theology, 1910–1931* was to dominate the received view of Barth in the English-speaking world until 1995 when Bruce

---

19  Torrance's own recollections, cited in McGrath, *An Intellectual Biography*, p. 31.
20  Torrance, *The Christian Doctrine of God*, p. 46.
21  Torrance's own recollections, cited in McGrath, *An Intellectual Biography*, p. 37.
22  Torrance's own recollections, cited in McGrath, *An Intellectual Biography*, p. 37.
23  Torrance, *Karl Barth,* p. 121.

McCormack questioned his thesis that Barth turned from dialectic to analogy after reading Anselm.[24]

In 1936 Torrance was awarded the Blackie Fellowship which allowed him to study in the Middle East. He traveled to Egypt, Syria and Lebanon as well as Bethlehem, Nazareth and Iraq. When he arrived at Basra, the city was still under martial law because a revolt had recently taken place against the Baghdad government. He was accused of being a spy and actually sentenced to death by hanging. Happily, he was able to persuade the authorities that he was just a theological student from Edinburgh and was allowed to travel to Baghdad and on to Damascus. Interestingly, Torrance retained some Arabic throughout his life. He also remained fluent in Chinese, Greek, Latin, German and French. When he returned to Scotland he graduated *summa cum laude* having specialized in systematic theology. It was at this time that he was awarded the Aitkin Fellowship which allowed him to engage in postgraduate study at Basel with Karl Barth. After studying German in Berlin and Marburg, he enrolled in Barth's seminar for the academic year 1937–1938. There were about fifty students in the seminar, but Barth also selected around twelve students to meet once a week at his home, based on the results of an examination he gave them. Torrance was among them. During the semester, in addition to the weekly meetings at Barth's residence where the group studied Wollebius' *Compendium Theologiae*, Torrance heard Barth lecture four times a week on what would later become *Church Dogmatics* II/1. They were studying Vatican I's teaching on natural theology at that point. Even as late as 1990 Torrance indicated that he considered *Church Dogmatics* II/1 and II/2—Barth's Doctrine of God—to be the high point of Barth's dogmatics. As far as Torrance is concerned, the second volume of the *Church Dogmatics* "surely ranks with Athanasius, *Contra Arianos*, Augustine, *De Trinitate*, St Thomas, *Summa Theologiae*, and Calvin, *Institutio*, as a supremely great work of Christian theology".[25] Torrance originally wanted to write his doctoral thesis

---

[24]    See Bruce L. McCormack, *Karl Barth's Critically Realistic Dialectical Theology: Its Genesis and Development 1909–1936* (Oxford: Clarendon Press, 1995). McCormack also claims that Barth himself was mistaken when he attributed his own theological change to his encounter with Anselm and thus to his Anselm book as when he wrote that in his book on Anselm [*Fides Quaerens Intellectum: Anselm's Proof of the Existence of God in the Context of his Theological Scheme*, trans. Ian W. Robertson (London: SCM Press, 1960)] he was "working with a vital key, if not the key, to an understanding of that whole process of thought that has impressed me more and more in my *Church Dogmatics* as the only one proper to theology" (*Fides Quaerens*, p. 11). See McCormack, pp. 421–2. McCormack's downplaying of the importance of Barth's Anselm book for his thinking has now been questioned by Timothy Stanley ("Returning Barth to Anselm" in *Modern Theology* 24:3, July 2008: 413–37, especially 426ff).

[25]    Torrance, *Karl Barth,* p. 124. In an interview in 1990, Torrance said that Barth was "perhaps the most powerful theological mind we've had for many centuries. He was steeped in the Bible, and he was able to put things so clearly, ontologically and dynamically. He also had such a light-hearted godliness about him. I am persuaded that his *Doctrine of God*

on "the scientific structure of Christian dogmatics" but Barth told him he was too young for that and he settled on "The Doctrine of Grace in the Apostolic Fathers".[26] Because other events intervened, he was not actually able to finish his doctoral dissertation and take his doctoral exam until 1946, the year he became engaged to and married Margaret Edith Spear. It was during his engagement that he finished his doctoral requirements and was awarded his doctorate *magna cum laude*.[27] Torrance's dissertation was published that same year and established his reputation in historical theology.

From 1938 to 1939 Torrance taught theology at Auburn Theological Seminary, a Presbyterian seminary in upstate New York. He was actually recommended for the job by John Baillie who was not exactly thrilled with Torrance's theology but nevertheless respected him personally and as a theologian. Baillie had received an urgent request for help from the President of Auburn, a school with a reputation for being liberal, after one of their key professors suddenly departed for the Pacific School of Religion in California. Torrance initially had preferred to return to Basel to complete his doctorate but eventually agreed. As a new professor, he worked hard on his lectures at Auburn. They showed the influence of both Mackintosh and Barth, stressing the fact that one cannot really understand the person of Christ apart from his work and also emphasizing that what God reveals in Christ and the way in which he reveals it can never be separated. At this stage of his career Torrance basically agreed with Barth's critique of natural theology. Later he formulated his own "new" natural theology which he viewed as a bridge between theology and natural science in the sense that both sciences operated in ways that undermined dualistic ways of thinking about reality and tended to reinforce the idea that accurate thinking could only occur when ideas were thought in accordance with the nature of the reality being investigated. Torrance's "new" natural theology was, of course, controversial. We shall consider Torrance's "new" natural theology and his divergence from Barth on this subject in its proper place.[28] Other areas where Torrance eventually disagreed with Barth concerned 1) Barth's view of the

---

is simply the best thing of its kind" (T.F. Torrance in Bauman, *Roundtable Conversations*, p. 112).

[26]   McGrath, *An Intellectual Biography*, p. 46. Interestingly, both Mackintosh and a retired professor at New College named H.A.A. Kennedy strongly influenced his view of grace. See Hesselink, "Interview with Torrance": 53.

[27]   Interestingly, Torrance's oral exam at Basel was difficult because he was put through "a terrible ordeal", partly because Martin, the son of his examiner, Karl Ludwig Schmidt, was being examined at the same time, as was Christoph Barth, Karl Barth's son. Torrance believes that K.L. Schmidt wanted his son to do better than Christoph and him. As it turned out, both Christoph and T.F. Torrance were awarded their degrees *magna cum laude* while Martin Schmidt received his degree *insigne cum laude*. Karl Barth wrote to Torrance telling him he was disappointed in the outcome and that if he had been present he would have received his degree *summa cum laude*. See Hesselink, "Interview with Torrance": 57.

[28]   See below, Chapter 3.

sacraments, which Torrance considered to be a reversion to a dualism that Barth had rejected earlier in the *Church Dogmatics*; 2) Barth's failure to emphasize sufficiently Christ's high priestly mediation later in the *Church Dogmatics*, which for Torrance accounted for difficulties in Barth's treatment of the ascension in the *Church Dogmatics* IV/3, "in which Christ seemed to be swallowed up in the transcendent Light and Spirit of God, so that the humanity of the risen Jesus appeared to be displaced by what he called 'the humanity of God' in his turning toward us";[29] 3) what he deemed to be an "element of 'subordinationism' in his doctrine of the Holy Trinity"[30] which was linked to the *filioque* clause because, for Torrance, the addition of the *filioque* and the Eastern emphasis on the procession of the Son from the Father alone were responses to an "incipient subordinationism in the Cappadocian doctrine of the Trinity" which should never have arisen and could easily be overcome if theology were to stick to the teaching of Athanasius, Gregory Nazianzen and Cyril of Alexandria and admit that the Spirit proceeds from the being of the Father and not just the person of the Father and thus through the Son; 4) Torrance also wondered whether Barth's treatment of creation was as thoroughly trinitarian as it might have been; he was also critical of the fact that Barth limited his treatment of creation to "*man* in the cosmos" and did not treat the cosmos itself except in his discussions of time and providence.[31] According to Alister McGrath, Torrance regarded Barth's most serious weakness as his "failure to engage with the natural sciences", and, for McGrath, this fact "offers a significant criterion of dissimilarity between Torrance and Barth".[32] It is interesting that McGrath links this issue to the interpretation of natural theology offered by both Torrance and Barth. We shall consider this in its proper place in Chapter 3.[33]

Torrance also accentuated the importance of the doctrine of the atonement and eschewed any superficial attempt to explain atonement with some sort of liberal "moral influence theory". Some students reacted interestingly; one strongly objected to belief in Christ's divinity and let Torrance know about it—Torrance

---

[29]   Torrance, *My Interaction with Karl Barth*, p. 62.

[30]   Torrance, *Karl Barth*, pp. 131–2. See also Paul D. Molnar, *Divine Freedom and the Doctrine of the Immanent Trinity: In Dialogue with Karl Barth and Contemporary Theology* (hereafter: *Divine Freedom*), (New York/London: T&T Clark/Continuum, 2002), pp. 323–4.

[31]   Torrance, *Karl Barth*, p. 132.

[32]   McGrath, *An Intellectual Biography*, p. 198.

[33]   According to Alister McGrath, Torrance was also critical of Barth's reading of Calvin's doctrine of election, Barth's treatment of the Holy Spirit and at an earlier point in Barth's theology what he considered to be Barth's failure to emphasize our living union with Christ. See McGrath, *An Intellectual Biography*, p. 197. It might be mentioned that Torrance presents an essentially positive treatment of Barth's doctrine of the Holy Spirit in *Karl Barth* (pp. 208–12) and that he also believed that Barth finally did properly emphasize our union with Christ: "Barth's own thinking was governed by the dimension of the union of God and man in Christ" (Torrance, *Karl Barth*, p. 22).

informed him that it was not the case that he *could* not believe in Christ's divinity but that he chose not to. The student spent three days and nights without sleep and finally returned to tell Torrance that he was right, that is, if Jesus really is the Son of God, then one has no alternative but to follow and obey him. They had dinner together and all was quiet again. In addition to lecturing on Christology, Torrance lectured on grace, theology and philosophy, theology and psychology, theology and science, the doctrine of God and especially the doctrine of the Trinity. During his stay in the United States, Torrance was offered a job at McCormick Theological Seminary in Chicago but declined because he hoped a better offer might come from Princeton University. And it did. But that it did was somewhat surprising to Torrance because during the interview he was told that at Princeton they did not want theology taught in a confessional way but in "a dispassionate way as one of the liberal arts, rather than as in a theological seminary", without proselytizing.[34] Torrance indicated that he would teach theology as science and explained that such thinking would not be based on free choice but would take place under the compulsion of the nature of the object being investigated. For Torrance, the rigorous method of scientific inquiry understood in this way could be applied also to Christian theology with due respect, of course, to the fact that the object of Christian faith is an utterly unique object that cannot be directly observed within the created realm. Torrance did not say that he would be dispassionate and also indicated that he could not guarantee that no one would be converted through his lectures. To his surprise, he was offered the job, but because of the impending war in Europe he decided to return home to Scotland immediately and had to decline the offer. That was one of the two most difficult decisions of his life. The other one, as we shall see, was when he turned down the offer to succeed Barth in Basel.

When Torrance returned to Scotland he enrolled at Oriel College, Oxford, from 1939 to 1940, where he continued to work on his dissertation. He became involved in student life while there and also got involved in discussions of philosophy and theology with other well-known figures at Oxford including Austin Farrer, Raymond Kilbansky, Eric L. Mascall and Donald MacKinnon. Torrance had finished his ministerial studies while at Edinburgh and only needed a call to a local parish at this point to become a minister. He was ordained as minister at Alyth Barony Parish Church on March 20, 1940. His father attended and presented him with a full set of Calvin's commentaries which proved useful to Torrance in preparing his sermons.

His sermons during his time at Alyth were both pastoral and theological in emphasis. For instance, in explaining the meaning of "grace", Torrance said, "GRACE, from its very nature, has only one direction which it can take. Grace always flows down." He was, of course, referring to the love of God revealed in the incarnation of God in Jesus Christ: "Grace is the love of God in princely

---

[34]   McGrath, *An Intellectual Biography*, pp. 57–8. See also Hesselink, "Interview with Torrance": 54.

condescension. It is the love of God to those who do not deserve his love, the indifferent and disloyal, whose only claim is their need."[35] This thinking is certainly in line with the main ideas expressed in his doctoral dissertation as when Torrance writes:

> Grace means the primary and constitutive act in which out of free love God has intervened to set our life on a wholly new basis, but also means that through faith this may be actualised in flesh and blood because it has been actualised in Jesus Christ, who by the Cross and the Resurrection becomes our salvation, our righteousness, and our wisdom. Thus any attempt to detach grace in a transferred sense from the actual embodiment of God's grace in Jesus Christ is to misunderstand the meaning of the Pauline *charis* altogether ... Paul deliberately avoided using *charis* in the sense of an energising principle, though that is the way in which *charis*, due to Hellenistic influences, came to be used in later Christian literature.[36]

For Torrance,

> Christ Himself is the objective ground and content of *charis* in every instance of its special Christian use ... [in the New Testament] *charis* refers to the being and action of God as revealed and actualised in Jesus Christ, for He is in His person and work the self-giving of God to men ... Grace is in fact identical with Jesus Christ in person and word and deed ... neither the action nor the gift is separable from the person of the giver.[37]

The ideas expressed here were so decisively important that they were to affect all of Torrance's theology throughout his career. In particular, because Torrance emphasized that grace is identical with the Giver (Jesus Christ) he opposed all attempts to detach grace from Christ acting among us and locate it within experience as a moral quality or something within our religious consciousness. It would not be too much to say that the doctrine of justification by grace and through faith is so decisively important for Torrance that one can easily see how the doctrine shaped much of what he thought and said as a theologian throughout his career. And, as we shall see, this doctrine takes shape in relation to Christology and the doctrine of the Trinity.

Torrance's preaching placed Jesus Christ at the center, as when he insisted that "When you look into the face of Jesus Christ and see there the face of God, you

---

[35]    Torrance, sermon on 2 Corinthians 13:14, preached November 1940 as quoted in McGrath, *An Intellectual Biography*, pp. 63–4.

[36]    Thomas F. Torrance, *The Doctrine of Grace in the Apostolic Fathers* (Pasadena/Eugene OR: Wipf and Stock Publishers, 1996), p. 33.

[37]    Torrance, *The Doctrine of Grace*, p. 21.

know that you have not seen that face elsewhere, and could not see it elsehow". [38] Torrance's stress upon the once-for-all atoning act of God in Christ was disturbing then, as it is today. A number of his parishioners were upset enough to wonder whether or not Torrance meant by that doctrine that their own church work did not actually put them right with God. That is indeed what Torrance meant. Years later one could see the same issue occupying Torrance when he insisted that "the subtle Pelagianism of the human heart ... comes under the judgment of Christ's unconditional forgiveness", so that if divine forgiveness was thought of as "conditional on our responses, we would never be saved". That is why Torrance emphasized that "the gospel of unconditional grace is very difficult for us, for it is so costly. It takes away from under our feet the very ground on which we want to stand, and the free will which we as human beings cherish so dearly becomes exposed as a subtle form of self-will". [39]

Torrance's work as a pastor did not keep him from writing and publishing journal articles and from getting involved in theological debate. He was invited to respond to a paper by H. A. Hodges that had been presented to a group of philosophers and theologians who regularly gathered for discussion, in which Hodges argued that it was the task of Christians to focus on those impulses in humanity that Christianity was meant to satisfy in order to demonstrate Christianity's relevance. Naturally, Torrance's response was critical because he saw Hodges espousing the idea that Christianity was somehow generally available within the range of human ideas and could be understood easily by understanding humanity and its ideas. For Torrance, of course, Christian truth was not so easily available, as it comes to us through an act of God revealing himself to us and justifying and sanctifying us. For Torrance, "Christian truth is not something that we already have, and to be looked for along the converging lines of human thinking; it is something which must be brought TO our thinking". [40] Torrance also strongly opposed any attempt to grasp Christianity by analyzing the human subject. Naturally Hodges was not thrilled with Torrance's paper; others who were involved found his style difficult as well. The group was pretty much dismissive of Torrance.

Although he wanted to become a chaplain, in 1943 Torrance took a position as head of "Huts and Canteens" which focused on providing pastoral and practical support to Scottish soldiers engaged in wartime service. [41] His service brought

---

[38] Torrance's sermon on 2 Corinthians 13.14, quoted in McGrath, *An Intellectual Biography*, p. 64.

[39] Thomas F. Torrance, *Preaching Christ Today: The Gospel and Scientific Thinking* (Grand Rapids, Michigan: William B. Eerdmans, 1994), pp. 36–7. See also Thomas F. Torrance, "Preaching Jesus Christ" in Gerrit Dawson and Jock Stein (eds), *A Passion For Christ: The Vision that Ignites Ministry*, (Edinburgh: The Handsel Press and PLC Publications, 1999), pp. 23–32, 30.

[40] Torrance, cited in McGrath, *An Intellectual Biography*, p. 67.

[41] Daniel Lamont, one of Torrance's professors in Edinburgh, held this position in World War I. Lamont also was Moderator of the Church of Scotland in 1936.

him back once again to North Africa where he was involved in delivering needed supplies to soldiers in Tobruk and Tripoli who were preparing to invade Italy. As he later made his way through Italy providing food for the soldiers, he met a chaplain named J. K. S. Reid, in Rome, where they toured some important sites and Torrance was able to borrow some books from a college library and purchase sets of Thomas's *Summa Theologiae* and *Summa Contra Gentiles* for his brothers back home. Reid later joined Torrance as an editor of the *Scottish Journal of Theology* which was founded by Torrance in 1948. Torrance's service in Italy was not without its dangers. His brother David tells us that on one occasion he was with a forward patrol that crossed the German line and entered a farmhouse occupied by the Germans. After coming under fire, only he and one other returned. In another incident he was being shelled while in a ditch between two others. Both of them were killed but Torrance miraculously escaped unscathed.[42]

He relished ministering to soldiers in the front line and telling them of the Gospel. One particular incident stuck with Torrance for life. In October 1944 after an assault on San Martino-Sogliano during which he served as a stretcher bearer under fire, he came upon a mortally wounded 20-year-old soldier named Private Philips who was lying on the ground and clearly did not have much time to live. As Torrance bent over him he said, "Padre, is God really like Jesus?" Torrance assured him that he was and while he prayed with the man he passed away.[43] But this question raised an important issue for Torrance himself: what had gone wrong in Christian theology that could lead someone to think in such a way that a wedge was driven between Jesus and God? This was the damage done by natural theology because it left the impression that there was a God "behind the back" of Jesus himself. Years later, Torrance's wonderment was only confirmed once again when an elderly lady in his parish in Aberdeen asked a similar question to that of the soldier on the battlefield: "Dr Torrance, is God really like Jesus?" And again Torrance was troubled and asked, "What have we been doing in our preaching and teaching in the church, to damage in the faith of our people the relation between their faith in Jesus Christ and God?"[44]

Just before Torrance was to give a series of lectures at Assisi, the war ended. One of his surviving lectures gives a clue to the centrality for Torrance of the atonement in its connection with the incarnation.. He observed:

> Put God in heaven and Jesus on the cross allowed to die, and you destroy your faith, for you cannot believe in a God who allowed that ... *But* (and this is the gospel) *put God on the cross* and you alter the whole situation, for then the cross is not the picture of God's unconcern or careless disregard. Rather it is the

---

[42]  David W. Torrance, *The Promise of Trinitarian Theology*, pp. 16–17.

[43]  Torrance, cited in McGrath, *An Intellectual Biography*, p. 74.

[44]  Torrance, cited in McGrath, *An Intellectual Biography*, p. 74.

picture of God's utmost concern, nay, a picture of his actual intervention in the affairs of men ...[45]

Years later Torrance would tie the atonement together with the incarnation in a decisive way that would exemplify why it is so important to him to respect Christ's uniqueness in all areas of theology:

> After all, it was not the *death* of Jesus that constituted atonement, but Jesus Christ the Son of God offering Himself in sacrifice for us. Everything depends on *who* He was, for the significance of His acts in life and death depends on the nature of His Person ... we must allow the Person of Christ to determine for us the nature of His saving work, rather than the other way round.[46]

This led Torrance to oppose any idea that Jesus' death should be seen as "an example of heroic self-giving love, the kind of behaviour which he intended to inspire in his followers".[47] Any such thinking would undermine the real significance of the cross which was that God himself in his sovereign love had condescended to experience our sin and alienation in order to redeem us from them.

After the war Torrance returned to his parish at Alyth, even though he had an opportunity to become the minister at St Columba's Church in Oxford. On his way home he stopped, prayed and gave thanks at St Martin-in-the-Fields in London, a place he would visit later whenever he was in London. In addition to founding the *Scottish Journal of Theology*, Torrance founded the Scottish Church Theology Society in 1945 and the Society for the Study of Theology in 1952. In 1949 Torrance's book on Calvin's theological anthropology,[48] which represented his attempt to mediate between Barth and Brunner, was published. Barth himself said he wished he could agree with him but could not because, in Barth's view, Calvin did not allow his understanding of sin to be exclusively dictated by what was revealed in Christ himself.[49]

In 1947 Torrance became minister at Beechgrove Church in Aberdeen where the first minister had been his former professor, Hugh Ross Mackintosh. Beechgrove paid almost twice what the parish at Alyth paid and this was helpful since his family was growing. Thomas Spear Torrance, who is now an economist and philosopher of science at Heriot-Watt University in Edinburgh, was born

---

[45]    Torrance, cited in McGrath, *An Intellectual Biography*, p. 75.

[46]    Thomas F. Torrance, *God and Rationality* (London: Oxford University Press, 1971; reissued Edinburgh: T & T Clark, 1997), p. 64.

[47]    McGrath, *An Intellectual Biography*, p. 76.

[48]    Thomas F. Torrance, *Calvin's Doctrine of Man* (London: Lutterworth Press, 1949; reissued Wipf and Stock, Eugene, OR, 2001).

[49]    See Karl Barth, *Church Dogmatics*, 4 vols in 13 pts (hereafter: *CD*). Vol. IV, pt 1: *The Doctrine of Reconciliation*, trans. G.W. Bromiley, ed. G.W. Bromiley and T.F. Torrance (Edinburgh: T&T Clark, 1974), p. 367.

July 3, 1947. Iain Richard Torrance, now the President of Princeton Theological Seminary and Professor of Patristics, was born January 13, 1949. Alison Meta Elizabeth Torrance, born on April 15, 1951, is a medical doctor in general practice in Edinburgh.

Torrance was happy at Beechgrove and firmly believed that his pastoral work helped him in his theological pursuits, but it was also clear that his calling was to an academic career in theology. And when a position opened in 1950, he became Chair of Ecclesiastical History at the University of Edinburgh. This was not his chosen field, but within two years he succeeded G. T. Thomson as the Chair of Christian Dogmatics, a position once held by his beloved teacher, Hugh Ross Mackintosh. Moving to the area of dogmatics was not without its intrigue since, as we have seen, John Baillie was not exactly in sympathy with Torrance's theology, which was strongly influenced by Karl Barth, and realized that Torrance could be more influential at Edinburgh teaching dogmatics than he was teaching church history. Torrance made the transition in spite of Baillie and then became just as influential in the 1960s and 1970s as Baillie was in the 1940s. Because Baillie continued to teach courses in "divinity", which included the doctrine of God, while Torrance taught Christology, soteriology, ecclesiology and sacraments, Torrance was unable to teach the doctrine of the Trinity. This was a major disappointment to him but one which was certainly remedied by the publication of his two books on the Trinity during his retirement. Torrance also lectured on Barth's theology and the theology of science.

As noted above, one of the two most difficult decisions of his life faced Torrance when he was invited to succeed Barth at Basel in 1961. Barth himself wanted Torrance to succeed him, and Oscar Cullmann wrote to him asking him to consider taking the chair that would become vacant upon Barth's retirement at the end of the summer term in 1961. Both Torrance and his wife loved Switzerland and certainly Torrance considered it a privilege to succeed Barth at Basel. While he was proficient in German, he would have had to lecture four times a week in German and that was a demanding task. And his school-age children did not speak German. Torrance felt that their education would suffer from such a move and with sadness he declined the offer which eventually was accepted by Heinrich Ott. Life certainly would have been different had he succeeded Barth at Basel. He may never have become Moderator of the Church of Scotland and he may never have had the opportunity to pursue his special interest in studying the natural sciences. In any case, Torrance never regretted staying at Edinburgh and he never gave serious consideration to other positions for the rest of his career there. According to McGrath, Torrance was offered the position of Principal and Dean of New College but because he saw himself as a scholar and teacher he declined the offer which was later accepted by John McIntyre. But this account is misleading because it could suggest that McIntyre was a kind of second choice as Principal whereas, according to Iain R. Torrance in his review of McGrath's book, his father "loathed academic administration" and never would have seriously considered the position in the first instance.[50] While Alister McGrath claims that McIntyre moved the school more toward religious studies and away from traditional Christian dogmatics,[51] this is decisively rejected by Iain R. Torrance.[52] In any case, the Department of Christian Dogmatics eventually became the Department of Theology and Religious Studies. According to McGrath, T. F. Torrance was not happy with these developments which he believed tended to undermine the sense that the University of Edinburgh had become a center for the study of Christian theology under his leadership. And there is evidence in Torrance's own writing that he did not want to see Christian theology subordinated to religious studies.[53] Even so, after Torrance's retirement in 1979, James Mackey, "a radical Roman Catholic"[54] and a "laicized priest",[55] was appointed to the new Thomas Chalmers Chair of Theology and in effect succeeded Torrance at the University. Mackey's theology could reasonably be said to have been shaped more by a religious studies perspective than by a strictly theological perspective formed by the Nicene faith of the Church.[56] In that sense, one could conclude that the chair once occupied by T. F. Torrance had taken a turn away from what it had been under Torrance. According to McGrath, Mackey's appointment led to controversy within the school and in the Church of Scotland. And McGrath insinuates that, as University Principal, John McIntyre used his influence in the matter of Mackey's appointment. This too, however, Iain Torrance notes, is something that John McIntyre vehemently rejected. In any case, it should also be

---

[50]    See Iain R. Torrance, review of *Thomas F. Torrance. An Intellectual Biography* by Alister McGrath, (T&T Clark, Edinburgh, 1999), in *The Evangelical Quarterly*, Vol. 73, pt 3 (2001): 285–88.

[51]    McGrath, *An Intellectual Biography*, p. 104.

[52]    According to Iain Torrance, John McIntyre himself had seen an earlier draft of his review and rejected as erroneous Alister McGrath's suggestions that he pursued an agenda that would steer Edinburgh away from Christian dogmatics and toward religious studies. Torrance helpfully notes that a number of Scottish Universities (Aberdeen, Glasgow, St Andrews and Edinburgh) moved toward religious studies in those years because funding was no longer determined by block grants but rather by student numbers. So this was not a singular pursuit arranged by McIntyre at Edinburgh for philosophical or theological reasons. It also should be noted here that Iain Torrance thinks highly of Alister McGrath's biography of his father and is only critical of his treatment of that episode at New College.

[53]    Years later in *Speaking the Christian God: The Holy Trinity and the Challenge of Feminism*, ed Alvin F. Kimel, Jr (Grand Rapids: Eerdmans, 1992), "The Christian Apprehension of God the Father", pp. 120–43, Torrance traced attempts to substitute some different formula such as "Creator, Redeemer and Sustainer" for "Father, Son and Holy Spirit" to what he called "the lapse from definitely Christian theology into what is called 'religious studies', in which Christianity is robbed of its uniqueness through being subjected to interpretation in terms of timeless universal religious ideas" (pp. 142–3).

[54]    McGrath, *An Intellectual Biography*, p. 105.

[55]    Wright and Badcock, *Disruption to Diversity*, p. 181.

[56]    See, for example, James P. Mackey, *Jesus the Man and the Myth: A Contemporary Christology* (New York: Paulist Press, 1979), pp. 190ff.

mentioned here that, as Iain Torrance remarked, Reformed doctrine continued to be taught "without a break" at the University of Edinburgh "by such distinguished players as David Fergusson, Bruce McCormack and Gary Badcock". And both John McIntyre and T. F. Torrance were delighted that David Fergusson "now succeeds them both in the new single chair of Divinity".[57]

T. F. Torrance has been very influential in ecumenical relations. After the formation of the World Council of Churches in 1948 he represented the Church of Scotland in conversations with the Church of England between 1949 and 1951. He also wrote a number of important works that explored the kind of theology necessary for ecumenical dialogue. He addressed issues concerning atonement, ministry, sacraments and order and disorder in the church.[58] Torrance addressed issues with Anglicans concerning ministry and catholicity, explaining what Presbyterians think; he offered what he called a "new approach" to unity which sought to avoid the Docetic idea that the two Churches could have a mere "spiritual" unity without visible unity.[59] Torrance stressed the need for "Intercommunion" and insisted on practical moves toward unity, so that, for example, Episcopalians and Presbyterians "both are to seek together fuller obedience to Christ in the light of what He has taught and now teaches both of them".[60] Neither church would be asked to give up its order or structure but both would be open to elements of difference such as the episcopate and would incorporate these in ways that would not compromise their own received view of the church.

Torrance also addressed specific problems with regard to Roman Catholicism such as the doctrines of the Immaculate Conception and the Assumption. Torrance rejects the former doctrine on Christological grounds: "The Roman Church repudiates the idea that in the Incarnation the Son of God assumed our fallen humanity, and it has barricaded itself behind this aberration from the Apostolic and Catholic faith by the dogma of the immaculate conception."[61] He linked the issue of Intercommunion with the Roman Catholic teaching concerning Mary's assumption, arguing that "The physical assumption of the virgin Mary means that she is taken up into the divine sphere, and that it is there that she belongs rather than to the Church that waits to see its Lord ...."[62] This breach of biblical eschatology means not only that Mary can be seen as "co-redeemer" with the One Mediator, Jesus himself, but it means a denial of the need to await Christ's second advent. And this, in Torrance's view, has ominous implications for the Roman Catholic view of priesthood because it implies that the priest has the power over the Eucharist,

---

[57]   Iain R. Torrance, review of *An Intellectual Biography*.

[58]   See Thomas F. Torrance, *Conflict and Agreement in the Church, Vol. I, Order and Disorder*, (hereafter: *Conflict and Agreement I*), (Eugene, OR: Wipf and Stock, 1996). This was originally published in 1959.

[59]   Torrance, *Conflict and Agreement I*, p. 138.

[60]   Torrance, *Conflict and Agreement I*, p. 140.

[61]   Torrance, *Conflict and Agreement I*, p. 149.

[62]   Torrance, *Conflict and Agreement I*, p. 160.

whereas, for the Evangelical Church, the ministry respects the fact that it is the Holy Spirit alone, over whom no one has control, who "makes Christ present in its midst".[63] Torrance's ecumenical stress was on the eschatological nature of the church and upon the fact that when sacraments and ministry in particular are understood within a dualistic perspective, then either God is excluded from the picture by those who would focus exclusively on the human element of the church, sacrament or ministry, or God is brought under control of the church in such a way that the those in authority become the criterion of truth in place of the coming Lord who is present now in his Holy Spirit.[64] Because the nature of the church's unity had to be understood eschatologically, Torrance insisted that while it was understandable that when the early church faced the danger of Gnosticism it might appeal to "an actual succession of bishops to attest the historicity of its claims", this could not mean that this "chronological precedent can be transmuted into a theological principle".[65] Torrance also applied this eschatological thinking with great effect to the Eucharist.[66]

He was also in dialogue with Roman Catholicism with respect to the doctrines of justification and the Trinity. For Torrance, justification is central to the whole of the Reformation itself but not as a principle because the primary function of the doctrine is to direct "us to Jesus Christ and his mighty acts"[67] as the one who determines the truth of all theology. Torrance believes there is no separate article on justification since it does not stand alone, but rather it belongs "to the inner texture of the Gospel and becomes evident as its cutting edge".[68] Justification illuminates

---

[63]   Torrance, *Conflict and Agreement I*, p. 161. This issue is discussed in Chapter 8.

[64]   In his discussion of eschatology, Torrance rejects what he calls the Copernican world-view that anticipates only an earthly future and he also rejects the Roman Catholic view that the church was impregnated with the Kingdom so that its real existence can be read off its earthly pattern. For Torrance, "it is by thinking election and eschatology into each other that the Reformers found their answer to Romanism on the one hand and to Copernicanism on the other. Predestination does not mean that there is a predetermined pattern which can be read off the structure of the Church on earth, but that the whole of the story of the Church like nature is contingent on the will of God, and that while the pattern is discernible in principle, as it were, in Christ in the Word of The Gospel, it remains essentially a *mysterium* and cannot be known in advance, but only from the final end, by apocalyptic manifestation at the advent of Christ." Thomas F. Torrance, *Kingdom and Church: A Study in the Theology of the Reformation* (Eugene OR: Wipf and Stock, 1996), pp. 4–5.

[65]   McGrath, *An Intellectual Biography*, p. 98.

[66]   See Thomas F. Torrance, "Eschatology and the Eucharist", *Conflict and Agreement Vol. II, The Ministry and the Sacraments of the Gospel* (hereafter: *Conflict and Agreement II*), (Eugene OR: Wipf and Stock, 1996), pp. 154–202.

[67]   Torrance, "Justification: Its Radical Nature and Place in Reformed Doctrine and Life", *Theology in Reconstruction*, pp. 150–68, 150. This was originally the Presidential address delivered to the Scottish Church Theology Society on January 18, 1960, and printed in *SJT* 13.3, 1960.

[68]   Torrance, "Justification", *Theology in Reconstruction*, p. 150.

the essence of the Gospel of salvation by grace. Here Jesus Christ is central as the one in whom God became one with us and enabled our unity with him. "Therefore it is only in and through our union with him, that all that is his becomes ours. It is only as such, that is in the Name of Christ, that we appear before God, and as such that he regards us—in Christ."[69] As we shall see later in Chapter 5, Torrance associates justification with Christ's resurrection and ascension, arguing that it is not only forgiveness of sins but the conferral of a genuine righteousness "that derives from beyond us". Yet, it is "not the beginning of a new self-righteousness, but the perpetual end of it, for it is a perpetual living in Christ, from a centre and source beyond us".[70]

This important point of seeking our righteousness only in Christ also became determinative for Torrance's view of the Trinity itself, as when he argued, following Athanasius, that "It would be more godly and true to signify God from the Son and call him Father, than to name God from his works alone and call him Unoriginate".[71] To be sure, this vital point led Torrance to argue, with great effect, that we must think from a center in God and not from a center in ourselves if we are to think accurately about God in his relations with us, as those relations have been established and are maintained by God himself in the incarnation and the outpouring of the Holy Spirit. That is why Torrance will typically insist that "we are summoned to live and act ... not out of a centre in ourselves but out of a centre in the Lord Jesus"[72] in order to stress that we must begin with the economic Trinity (God's actions as Creator, Savior and Redeemer in history) to know of our relations with the immanent or ontological Trinity (God as he exists eternally in himself as Father, Son and Holy Spirit and as he would have continued to exist even if he had not loved us and acted graciously toward us in Christ and the Spirit) as these have been established and maintained by God's self-communication in grace. Torrance was hopeful that "the Nicene–Constantinopolitan Creed and the Trinitarian Faith it proclaims" could help bring the Church of Scotland closer to both the Roman Catholic Church and to the Greek Orthodox Church.[73] Torrance saw the Christocentric emphasis of the Second Vatican Council and the distinction between the "substance of Faith and dogmatic expressions of it" together with the idea of "a hierarchy of truths" that would consign some truths to the periphery as occasions for closer relations between the Church of Scotland and the Roman Catholic Church.[74]

With respect to the doctrine of justification, Torrance insisted that the expression "by grace alone" protects the Gospel from distortion by "Evangelicals", "Liberals"

---

[69]   Torrance, "Justification", *Theology in Reconstruction*, p. 151.

[70]   Torrance, "Justification", *Theology in Reconstruction*, pp. 151–2.

[71]   Torrance, *The Trinitarian Faith*, p. 49.

[72]   Torrance, *The Christian Doctrine of God*, p. 88.

[73]   The Very Rev. Professor T.F. Torrance, "The Deposit of Faith" in *SJT*, 36, 1 (1983): 1–28, 28.

[74]   Torrance, "The Deposit of Faith": 28.

and Romans alike.[75] We will not go into the details of Torrance's view here but it is worth mentioning his attempt to dialogue with Roman Catholic theologians. Torrance did not set the Reformation exclusively against Roman Catholicism but insisted that because justification is by grace and thus in and through Christ alone, therefore the Word had to be acknowledged as supreme over all tradition. This called for "repentant rethinking of all tradition face to face with the revelation of God in Jesus Christ" and this "applies no less to the Reformed and Evangelical tradition; to our Presbyterian tradition as well as to the Roman tradition".[76] In this regard, Torrance expressed astonishment at how close the Church of Scotland itself actually had come to the Roman position at the time that he wrote *Theology in Reconstruction*. This was especially the case with respect to the fact that tradition rather than Scripture was allowed to function as the criterion of what was thought and said.[77] He spoke forthrightly of the fact that the Reformed quarrel with Rome concerned the centrality of Christ himself, which he considered to have become obscured by "Roman doctrines of merit and tradition, and above all by Mariology".[78] He also opposed what he called "Roman sacerdotalism" because the doctrine of justification teaches that "Jesus Christ is our Sole Priest".[79] This must be the center for ecumenical discussion; all questions concerning mutual recognition of "orders" must be subordinated to this. Torrance insisted that whenever Christ's true humanity is obscured or depreciated, "then the need for some other human mediation creeps in" with the result that the human priesthood came to displace the sole Priesthood of Christ representing us before God.[80] Torrance also criticized

---

[75]    Torrance, "Justification", *Theology in Reconstruction*, p. 162.

[76]    Torrance, "Justification", *Theology in Reconstruction*, p. 164.

[77]    Torrance argues against allowing the Westminster Confession to function as a criterion of biblical truth because he believed in the primacy of Scripture over all tradition. For Torrance, this confession "constituted a *system of doctrine* organised on extraneous lines in which sets of statements were put forward for belief, but they were statements governed by the specific form in which they were cast" ("The Deposit of Faith": 23–4).

[78]    Torrance, "Justification", *Theology in Reconstruction*, p. 165.

[79]    Torrance, "Justification", *Theology in Reconstruction*, p. 166. Torrance's book, *Royal Priesthood: A Theology of Ordained Ministry* (hereafter: *Royal Priesthood*), (Edinburgh: T&T Clark, 1993) first published in 1955, presents a powerful biblical and patristic argument for the idea that ministry consists in participating by way of service in the Priesthood of Jesus Christ himself. Torrance argued for a theology of ordained ministry that included women. In the new 1993 edition, he noted the changes in the Roman Catholic Church since Vatican II and he approved its economic and patristic understanding of the Eucharist, together with its linking its celebration with Christ's High Priesthood with the words "through whom, *with* whom and in him" (p. xiii). Still, he continued to note that unfortunately both the Anglican and Roman Catholic Churches continued to distort the true meaning of ordained ministry with their "sacerdotalisation of the priesthood", which to him meant the confusion of Christ's sole Priesthood with the activity of the church's ordained ministers.

[80]    Torrance, "Justification", *Theology in Reconstruction*, p. 166.

what he called "Protestant sacerdotalism" which allows the minister to become the focus of the congregation in its worship and in the whole life of the community. Both sacramental and psychological sacerdotalism obscure the fact that Christ alone is the one who mediates between us and the Father; for Torrance, it is neither the personality of the minister nor the sacramental *res* or *potentia* that does this mediating.

As we shall see, Torrance forthrightly addressed Roman Catholic theology on these issues.[81] He opposed impersonal notions of grace, together with the idea that grace was "a detachable quality which could be made to inhere in creaturely being".[82] He was hopeful that Reformed and Roman Catholic theology could find agreement on a Christological basis: by applying the *homoousion*—that is, the doctrine that Jesus is one in being with God the Father from eternity by nature as the Son, and with us by virtue of the incarnation—one could see that grace cannot be in any way detached from Christ himself as God communicating himself to us. Yet this is exactly what happens with the concept of *created grace*, according to which there are many different kinds of graces. Torrance is particularly helpful in his discussion of the sacraments, especially the Lord's Supper, by showing that much of the disagreement between Reformed and Roman Catholic theology lay in terminological misunderstanding, which he believed could be cleared away by properly focusing on Christ himself and by seeing that true ecumenical theology must find its basis and meaning in Christology and the doctrine of the Trinity. This can happen, Torrance believed, when "each side is ready to let itself be called into question by the other, and each is ready to examine itself to see whether what it holds to be error in the other may not have a place within itself even if under quite a different guise".[83] We will, of course, discuss these details in their proper place. At present it is important to note that Torrance himself served on the Reformed–Roman Catholic Study Commission on the Eucharist which met at Woudshoten, in the Netherlands, in 1974[84] and forged a personal relationship with Yves Congar in the process. Torrance was also present at the World Council of Churches meeting in Evanston, Illinois, in 1954.

With respect to the doctrine of the Trinity, Torrance led a colloquy in Switzerland in March 1975 which discussed Karl Rahner's work on the Trinity[85] because he believed that Rahner's work offered "the possibility of some real ecumenical convergence between East and West, Catholic and Evangelical Christians".[86] He believed that Rahner's basic approach to understanding God from God's saving

---

[81]    See Torrance, "The Roman Doctrine of Grace from the Point of View of Reformed Theology", *Theology in Reconstruction*, pp. 169–91.

[82]    Torrance, "The Roman Doctrine of Grace", *Theology in Reconstruction*, p. 182.

[83]    Torrance, "The Roman Doctrine of Grace", *Theology in Reconstruction*, p. 191.

[84]    McGrath, *An Intellectual Biography*, pp. 101–2.

[85]    Karl Rahner, *The Trinity*, trans. Joseph Donceel (New York: Herder and Herder, 1970).

[86]    Torrance, *Trinitarian Perspectives*, p. 77.

revelation of himself as Father, Son and Holy Spirit in the economy made the economic Trinity the criterion for all speech about God. This, Torrance thought, helped to overcome the isolation of the treatise on God's oneness from the treatise on his triunity so that there could be agreement between: 1) systematic and biblical theology; 2) Latins and Greeks by shifting away from abstract thinking to thinking that is bound up with piety shaped by the biblical message; and 3) Roman Catholic and Evangelical theology, especially as represented by Karl Barth and Karl Rahner with their emphasis on God's self-revelation in Christ. Torrance was certainly optimistic that real agreement could be reached between Reformed and Roman Catholic theology and between Reformed and Eastern Orthodox theology with respect to the doctrine of the Trinity. He was aware of difficulties in Rahner's thought, but he nonetheless believed that if those difficulties were cleared away, then perhaps there might be real agreement.[87] Torrance, however, was not naïve and so he also left open the possibility that Rahner might still be a "prisoner of a scholastic metaphysical framework" to a certain extent. Still, he hoped that Rahner intended the same as did Athanasius and Barth, namely, that all theological thinking would begin with God's self-communication in Christ and thus would recognize that what God is toward us in the economy of salvation he is eternally in himself. We will not get into the specific areas of agreement and disagreement between Rahner and Torrance here. We simply note in this context that Torrance saw the *homoousion* as the basis for genuine agreement between Reformed and Roman Catholic theology as it is tied to Christology and the doctrine of the Trinity.

Torrance was also instrumental in the development of the historic agreement between the Reformed and Orthodox Churches on the doctrine of the Trinity when a joint statement of agreement on that doctrine was issued between the World Alliance of Reformed Churches and the Orthodox Church on March 13, 1991. This was the culmination of discussion initiated by Torrance himself in 1977 when he proposed to the Ecumenical patriarch and others that the Reformed and Orthodox should enter into discussions toward agreement concerning the doctrine of the Trinity. This was truly historic because, as Torrance himself noted, it "overcomes the entrenched divisions of the Orthodox and Reformed Churches".[88] There was in fact basic agreement on three key issues. First, the formula "one Being, three Persons" must be understood in a completely personal way in order to avoid the idea that the one Being of God that is common to all three Persons is not personal. Any such notion rests on a preconceived idea of God's oneness and not on his self-revelation and obscures the fact that "the 'One Being' of God does not refer to some abstract divine essence, but to the intrinsically personal 'I am' of God".[89] Second, concerning God's monarchy, it was agreed that all three divine Persons share equally as the one ultimate principle of Godhead so that any idea of subordination at all is totally excluded. This includes any notion of degrees of Deity "such as

---

[87]   Torrance, *Trinitarian Perspectives*, p. 80.

[88]   Torrance, *Trinitarian Perspectives*, p. 111.

[89]   Torrance, *Trinitarian Perspectives*, p. 112.

that between the 'underived Deity of the Father', and the 'derived Deities of the Son and the Spirit'".[90] Third, relying on the twin doctrines of the *homoousion* (the identity of Being of the three Persons) and *perichoresis* (the fact that the three Persons interpenetrate each other within the indivisible eternal Being of the Trinity), the agreement affirms that the procession of the Spirit from the Father must be understood "in the light of the indivisible unity of the Godhead in which each Person is perfectly and wholly God. The effect of this is to put the doctrine of the procession of the Spirit on a fully Trinitarian basis".[91] The result is an advance beyond the disagreement over the *filioque* because it can then be seen that the Holy Spirit ultimately proceeds from "the Triune Being of the Godhead"[92] and not from the Father in a way that could open the door to some sort of subordinationism. By stating that the Spirit proceeds from the Being of the Father and not simply from the Person of the Father, the agreement effectively overcame the Western need to say that the Spirit proceeds from the Father and the Son and the Eastern need to stress that the Spirit proceeds only from the Father. An indication of the high regard in which Torrance was held by the Orthodox Church is the fact that in 1973 he was consecrated a Protopresbyter in the Patriarchate of Alexandria by the Archbishop of Axum at a commemoration of the death of Athanasius the Great in 373 and a celebration of an agreement between Chalcedonian and non-Chalcedonian Christians which was initiated by Torrance in 1954.[93]

Torrance was also Convener of the Church of Scotland Commission on Baptism from 1954 to 1962. He was instrumental in publishing the interim reports from 1955 to 1959 and the final report in 1960. The Secretary of the Baptism Commission was John Heron. He was one of the original directors of the *Scottish Journal of Theology* and his son Alasdair Heron, Professor Emeritus of Reformed Theology at Erlangen, was for many years co-editor of the journal with T. F. Torrance's son Iain. Torrance established a reputation as a leading representative of the Reformed tradition. From 1976 to 1977 he was Moderator of the Church of Scotland—a position later held by his son Iain from 2003 to 2004 prior to becoming President of Princeton Theological Seminary. Iain Torrance continues as co-editor of the *Scottish Journal of Theology* with Bryan Spinks of Yale University.

In recognition of his extraordinary contributions to the study of the relationship of science and Christian theology, Torrance received the Templeton Foundation Prize for Progress in Religion in 1978. As noted above, Torrance is highly regarded for this area of scholarship. Few in the twentieth century can claim to have contributed to this subject as much as Torrance himself. In the words of Christopher B. Kaiser, "If Einstein is the 'person of the century' in the judgment of secular media, Torrance's interest is enough to qualify him as 'theologian of

---

[90]   Torrance, *Trinitarian Perspectives*, p. 112.
[91]   Torrance, *Trinitarian Perspectives*, p. 112.
[92]   Torrance, *Trinitarian Perspectives*, p. 113.
[93]   McGrath, *An Intellectual Biography*, p. 102.

the century' in the eyes of many science-minded people".[94] Torrance was well aware of the fact that natural science could not tell us about the ultimate origin of the world of nature and that it was limited to studying nature "out of itself" as it were. He maintained that it was the Christian doctrine of *creatio ex nihilo* that allowed scientists to "understand nature only by looking at nature and not by looking at God". In fact, "God means us to examine nature in itself ... We know God by looking at God ... But we know the world by looking at the world ..."[95] Hence, there is a distinct difference between a philosophy of religion and a philosophy of theology. In his groundbreaking book *Theological Science*, Torrance argued that theological and natural science held in common the same need to understand reality *through* our thoughts by pointing beyond ourselves and not letting our subjective experiences and knowledge distort the objective reality we are attempting to conceptualize.[96] Theology and science should be seen as "allies in a common front where each faces the same insidious enemy, namely, man himself assuming the role of Creator ..."[97] As long as the dialogue is conceived to be between *science* and *religion*, Torrance contended, "we shall not escape from romantic naturalism". Instead, he insisted that we must focus on the dialogue between *science* and *theology* and thus between the "philosophy of natural science" and the "philosophy of theological science" because these two methods have in common the "struggle for scientific method on their proper ground and their own distinctive fields".[98] Hence, as Torrance himself indicated in an address given on March 11, 1978, upon his reception of the Templeton Prize for Progress in Religion at Guildhall, London:

---

[94]   Christopher B. Kaiser, "Humanity in an Intelligible Cosmos: Non-Duality in Albert Einstein and Thomas Torrance" in *The Promise of Trinitarian Theology*, pp. 239–267, 240.

[95]   Torrance, *God and Rationality*, p. 39.

[96]   For an extremely clear and instructive account of just how limited human reason is when it comes to knowing God and why the rationality of faith requires allowing God in Christ to be the one who enables such knowledge, which is the opposite of "irrationality", see the very interesting exchange of letters between Thomas F. Torrance and Brand Blanshard in *The Scotsman* from April 1952. Blanshard was a Yale philosopher and at the time the Gifford lecturer addressing the theme of natural theology, who accused Torrance, Barth and Brunner of "irrationalism" because they refused to allow human reason independent status in determining what could be regarded as true. Torrance responded claiming that Barth was simply arguing, with Anselm, that human rationality must find its true meaning outside itself and neither in any sort of idealism such as the one apparently espoused by Blanshard nor any sort of existentialism which he believed was espoused by Rudolf Bultmann, whose interpretation of the Bible Torrance regarded "as a menace to the Christian Gospel" (Torrance's letter to Brand Blanshard of April 11, 1952, published in *The Scotsman* on April 14, 1952).

[97]   Thomas F. Torrance, *Theological Science* (New York: Oxford University Press, 1978), p. xiii.

[98]   Torrance, *Theological Science*, p. xiii.

... theological science and natural science have their own proper and distinctive objectives to pursue, but their work inevitably overlaps, for they both respect and operate through the same rational structures of space and time, while each develops special modes of investigation, rationality, and verification in accordance with the nature and the direction of its distinctive field. But since each of them is the kind of thing it is as a human inquiry because of the profound correlation between human knowing and the space–time structures of creation, each is in its depth akin to the other ... natural science and theological science are not opponents but partners before God, in a service of God in which each may learn from the other how better to pursue its own distinctive function ...[99]

Torrance read widely in the area of science, both ancient and modern. He believed that the physicist and theologian John Philoponos (490–570), who was mistakenly labeled a "monophysite" and was condemned as a heretic in 680, properly held a non-dualist /non-monist view of science and theology and so offered a worthy critique of Plato and Aristotle that has proven valuable to modern scientists in their unitary thinking of the universe. Torrance believed that when, in the ninth century, Photius confirmed the anathema against John Philoponos based on his own "Aristotelian rationalism", he "retarded scientific development for a thousand years and contributed to the domination of Aristotelianism in the West. That was one of the greatest tragedies in the history of thought".[100] The tragedy, in Torrance's mind, lay in the assimilation of Aristotelian notions of space and the unmoved mover along with Neoplatonic ideas, which had been theoretically demolished by Philoponos, into Christian doctrine.[101] Influenced by the thought of James Clerk

---

[99] Thomas F. Torrance, *The Ground and Grammar of Theology* (hereafter: *The Ground and Grammar*), (Charlottesville: The University Press of Virginia, 1980), pp. 6–7. Torrance was very clear that while ancient materialism was obsessed with "perceptible and tangible magnitudes as the exclusively real" as opposed to "the imperceptible, intangible magnitude of the space–time metrical field, in which structure and substance, form and being, are inseparably fused together", that did not mean that what is experienced as imperceptible in natural science could or should be identified with "the experienced imperceptible in theology" since that reality is identical with the triune God who transcends space and time as "the source of all form and being". Thomas F. Torrance, *Theology in Reconciliation: Essays towards Evangelical and Catholic Unity in East and West* (hereafter: *Theology in Reconciliation*), (London: Geoffrey Chapman, 1975), p. 282.

[100] Thomas F. Torrance, "John Philoponos of Alexandria—Theologian & Physicist", pp. 1–18, 2, a paper sent to me by T.F. Torrance in 1997. See also Torrance, *The Ground and Grammar*, p. 61ff., and Thomas F. Torrance, *Theological and Natural Science* (Eugene, OR: Wipf and Stock, 2002), Chapter 6, "John Philoponos of Alexandria: Sixth Century Christian Physicist", pp. 83–104, and Chapter 7, "The Relevance of Christian Faith to Scientific Knowledge with Reference to John Philoponos and James Clerk Maxwell", pp. 105–11.

[101] We shall see below how the container concept of space, for instance, adversely affected both Christology and the church's view of the sacrament.

Maxwell, Albert Einstein and Michael Polanyi, Torrance argues that just as there would be no real science without belief in God the Creator and thus belief in a genuine contingent universe with its own created intelligibility, so theology can learn from contemporary and ancient scientists to think in unitary ways that do not separate the spiritual from the material or the intelligible from the sensible.

Torrance is especially indebted to Einstein for re-establishing a unitary view of reality that cuts across Kantian and Cartesian dualist conceptions; this also affects biblical interpretation, because when Einstein overcame epistemological dualism with his relativity theory, he cut the ground out from under those who separated form and being in their interpretation of Scripture. That is to say, those who think proper scriptural interpretation is based solely on observation of phenomena as they appear to us, and thus on our deductions from those phenomena, are forced to argue for a kind of interpretation that leaves out theological observation based on the deep reality that is before us.[102] In Christology, for instance, it is assumed, from within the Kantian dynamic, that "it is impossible for us ever to know anything of Jesus Christ as he is in himself, for we are restricted to Jesus as he appeared to his contemporaries—and indeed to the impression he made upon them as it is mediated through the structures of their consciousness, by which they made him an 'object' of their faith and knowledge".[103]

Any such thinking, of course, not only opens the door to a type of Ebionite Christology, in which Christ's authentic and definitive Deity is grounded in the experience of the community and thus stripped of its reality, but leads to the idea that the task of historical criticism is to clarify how Jesus made this impression on

---

[102]    Torrance gives a very clear and succinct understanding of his approach here by distinguishing three interrelated modes of thought, namely, 1) the way of the Greeks which means the way of vision or seeing things or observation; 2) the way of the Romans which stressed law and order and emphasized also control and management of "resources, armies and supplies, and of public life. These Latin modes of thought have left their mark in the legal structures, and social and political institutions of the West"; and 3) the way of the Hebrews which primarily involved hearing, especially hearing the Word of God and "letting it speak out of itself and upon obedience of the mind in response to it". This was later applied to science in an effort to let nature offer its own secrets without "attempting to force our own patterns upon it" (Torrance, "Theological Education Today", *Theology in Reconstruction*, pp. 13–29, 14–15). Each of these ways of thinking needs to be held together and allowed to operate while understanding that the emphasis changes when the object of knowledge changes. Thus, in some types of knowledge, observation and description are paramount, while in others control is important. And yet these approaches could cause problems in our knowledge of God since God cannot be controlled and certainly cannot be directly seen or observed since, as noted above, God is "imperceptible" to phenomenological observation. See also Torrance, "The Church in the New Era of Scientific and Cosmological Change", *Theology in Reconciliation*, Chapter 6, pp. 267–93. See Chapter 2 below, pp. 44ff. for an application of these insights to Torrance's trinitarian thinking.

[103]    Torrance, *The Ground and Grammar*, pp. 28–9.

his followers, and use that clarification as a basis for biblical truth.[104] For Torrance, this undercuts the theological content of the New Testament because the one who gives meaning to the New Testament witness is Jesus himself and thus all biblical statements have to be rooted in him as he was and is, namely, as the incarnate Son of God. Torrance thus relies on the kind of scientific thinking employed by Einstein in order to stress that our knowledge must be governed by reality distinct from our own knowledge and experience.[105] Consequently, Torrance opposed "existentialism" and "nominalism" or any philosophy of linguistic science that does not allow the underlying reality, namely, the reality that gives meaning to language to determine thinking. Hence,

---

[104] Torrance therefore firmly opposed any attempt to base Christology on a "scientific investigation of the historical Jesus" because this involved and involves "a phenomenalist bracketing off of the evangelical material from any realm of things in themselves or their internal relations, so that it is approached merely as a collection of appearances relative to observers and detached from any objective sub-structure" (Torrance, "The Church in the New Era", *Theology in Reconciliation*, p. 280). Translation: Jesus cannot be understood properly by starting only from his humanity or only from his divinity because he is the Word of God incarnate and must be understood "conjunctively … as God and man in the one indivisible fact of Jesus Christ" (Torrance, "The Church in the New Era", *Theology in Reconciliation*, p. 281). And this is grounded neither in the community's experiences nor in its ideas about Jesus but only in Jesus himself as he really was and is and is to come.

[105] In fact, Torrance follows Einstein's account of knowledge given in his essay *Physics and Reality* to elaborate what he calls the "stratified structure" of our knowledge as it begins in experience and proceeds in different levels until it reaches the highest level. This applies both to science and to theology. And Torrance explains how applying this to theology leads from an experiential encounter with Jesus Christ in the community to the theological level where we come up with our basic concepts of Father, Son and Holy Spirit based on God's self-revelation in Jesus Christ, and finally to the higher level of scientific knowledge of God, that is, to knowledge of the immanent Trinity. Torrance makes the all-important point that while we may speak of moving from lower to higher levels of knowledge from an epistemological perspective so that the higher level (the immanent Trinity) actually controls our thinking, "in reality the Economic Trinity and the Ontological Trinity are identical, for there is only one divine Reality of God in himself and in his saving and revealing activity toward us in this world … In the strictest sense the doctrine of the Holy Trinity is *theologia*, that is, theology in its purest form, the pure science of theology, or *episteme dogmatike*. I myself like to think of the doctrine of the Trinity as the *ultimate ground* of theological knowledge of God, the *basic grammar* of theology …" (Torrance, *The Ground and Grammar*, pp. 158–9). Torrance gives a detailed account of this matter in his important book *The Christian Doctrine of God* (pp. 84ff.) and indicates that he is also indebted to the thought of M. Polanyi in his book *The Study of Man* for this way of thinking. It must be remembered, however, that Torrance does not use the thought of Einstein or Polanyi prescriptively for his theology, but only insofar as their thinking enables him to clarify the object of theology which he believes can be known with clarity only from revelation and through faith.

... while scientists have moved on, far beyond the narrow mechanistic determinisms of the Laplacians or the Marxists, to a profounder and more unitary grasp of the intelligible connections in the contingent order of the universe, theology tends, for the most part, to remain stuck in obscurantist modes of thought that have their roots in the radical dualisms of the past.[106]

This was no abstract insight for Torrance because he saw in the dialogue between natural science and Christian theology the possibility for theology to overcome "dualist, phenomenalist and mechanistic habits of thought"[107] in a way that would be helpful toward dialogue between Reformed and Roman Catholic theology on the substance of the Christian faith. As Torrance saw it, the Roman Catholic Church faced a "strange impasse" after Vatican II. While there was a genuine deepening of its understanding of the "heart and substance of the Christian faith" in the areas of Christology and soteriology and their impact on liturgy and mission, still the Roman Catholic Church, according to Torrance, "remains trapped in obsolete dualist structures of thought which derive from mediaeval roots but still govern its epistemology and canon law".[108] Unless this is cleared away, Torrance thinks, the renewals of Vatican II will be met by resistance and misunderstanding which is evident in the thought of Edward Schillebeeckx and Hans Küng, "both of whom appear to be still tied to dualist and phenomenalist, if not also mechanist, habits of thought, and who therefore are unable to integrate empirical and theoretical ingredients in their understanding of Jesus Christ at the very heart of the Faith".[109] Translation: Schillebeeckx and Küng were unable to present a unified view of Jesus Christ as truly divine and human and thus as the One Mediator because their thinking was not consistently determined by who Jesus really was in the depth of his being as the incarnate Word. And this is important because they are not alone in being unable to distinguish the substance from the formulations of the faith without themselves falling into the relativistic idea that all doctrinal formulations of our knowledge of God are relative.

The error here, in Torrance's view, is one that is widespread also in the social sciences: "relativity is confounded with relativism". Torrance believes that theological misunderstanding can be cleared away easily with the help of natural science with its emphasis on unified thinking in accordance with the nature of reality. And, ultimately, if such misunderstanding can be cleared away, this would open the door to basic agreement between Evangelical and Roman Catholic theology. Hence, he insists that in both natural science and in theological science "we must be faithful to the reality we seek to know and must act and think always

---

[106] Torrance, *The Ground and Grammar*, p. 20.

[107] Thomas F. Torrance, *Transformation & Convergence in the Frame of Knowledge: Explorations in the Interrelations of Scientific and Theological Enterprise* (hereafter: *Transformation & Convergence*), (Grand Rapids: Eerdmans, 1984), p. xii.

[108] Torrance, *Transformation & Convergence*, p. xiii.

[109] Torrance, *Transformation & Convergence*, p. xiii.

in a relation of relentless fidelity to that reality".[110] For that reason, theological and natural science cannot be opposed to one another but must be seen as "applying the one basic way of knowing faithfully to their respective fields".[111] Torrance's conception of the relationship between science and theology today can be summarized in his own words expressed when he received the Templeton Prize:

> ... the new science gives ample room for the human sciences and the sciences of the spirit, and for all sciences concerned with living connections, within the framework of an open-structured dynamic universe in which the human person is not suffocated, but can breathe freely transcendent air, and yet be profoundly concerned with scientific understanding of the whole complex of connections that make up our universe ... It is more and more clear to me that, under the providence of God, owing to these changes in the very foundations of knowledge in which natural and theological science alike have been sharing, the damaging cultural splits between the sciences and the humanities and between both of these and theology are in the process of being overcome, that the destructive and divisive forces too long rampant in world-wide human life and thought are being undermined, and that a massive new synthesis will emerge in which man, humbled and awed by the mysterious intelligibility of the universe that reaches far beyond his powers, will learn to fulfill his destined role as the servant of divine love and the priest of creation.[112]

Although Alasdair Heron has observed that Torrance's vision of science and theology working together as expressed here may or may not be fully realized in the future, however desirable it may be in principle, and that it may appear to some to be utopian, while to others he may place too much stress on pure science or understanding,[113] the truth is that, in the years since that address, Torrance did much to move theology and science closer together without confusing the distinctive tasks of each as prescribed by the unique nature of the objects investigated by natural science and theological science. And he did so precisely by emphasizing what theology and science have in common: "... they operate within the same rational structures of space and time and have in common the basic ideas of the

---

[110] Torrance, *The Ground and Grammar*, p. 10.

[111] Torrance, *The Ground and Grammar*, p. 10.

[112] Torrance, *The Ground and Grammar*, pp. 13–14. See Thomas F. Torrance, *Divine and Contingent Order* (Edinburgh: T&T Clark, 1998), "Man's Priestly and Redemptive Rôle in the World", pp. 128–42, for a full understanding of what Torrance means by the phrase "priest of creation".

[113] Alasdair I. C. Heron, *A Century of Protestant Theology* (Philadelphia: The Westminster Press, 1980), p. 213.

unitary rationality of the universe—its contingent intelligibility and contingent freedom, contributed by Christian theology to natural science ..."[114]

The purpose of this chapter was to present not only a biographical sketch of T. F. Torrance but also a survey of the broad theological landscape to which he dedicated his life, teaching, preaching and writing. As noted above, the emphasis of this book will be on Torrance the theologian of the Trinity, in order to show how his dogmatic theology is deeply shaped by his view of trinitarian theology and why that must be considered a scientific theology. We will not specifically concentrate on Torrance's contributions to the discussions of natural science and the relation of natural science to theology; that is one reason why, as mentioned above, my account of Torrance's thinking on this subject moves a bit beyond introduction to exposition. His view of natural science affected his view of theological science, but always with a view toward distinguishing the unique objects of reflection that determine each. Therefore, Torrance's keen insight that theology must be scientific as it allows itself to be conformed to the unique nature of the object being investigated will continue to illuminate the chapters ahead. It is important here to note that Torrance pursued this scientific theology within a particular context.

The historical context within which Torrance developed his scientific approach to nature also shaped his scientific approach to theology. Scientifically, his goal always was to "discern the nature of what is being investigated", by adapting both his questions and the manner of posing his questions to nature so that all preconceptions might be set aside in order to "know what is there as it ought to be known".[115] Torrance therefore strongly opposed the thinking of John Wren Lewis who believed that it was the task of the scientist to move from pure science to technology and thus to impose some order upon nature rather than discovering the order created by God that is in nature itself.[116] In Torrance's mind, such thinking ignored the doctrine of creation and confused God with nature, thus obscuring any possible scientific understanding of the world as created by God.

Torrance saw the thinking of John A. T. Robinson as the theological and therefore the "artistic" corollary to this unscientific approach to understanding nature. Instead of allowing God the Creator and Redeemer to be God in his own right and to act for us within nature and history, Robinson, in his famous

---

[114] Torrance, *The Ground and Grammar*, p. 107. For a clear and illuminating discussion of just how Christian theology contributed these ideas to science, see *The Ground and Grammar*, Chapter 3. For further information about Torrance's understanding of the relationship between natural science and theology, see also McGrath, *An Intellectual Biography*, Chapter 9; P. Mark Achtemeier, "Natural Science and Christian Faith in the Thought of T.F. Torrance," in *The Promise of Trinitarian Theology*, pp. 269–302; and Colyer, *How To Read T F. Torrance*, Chapter 9.

[115] Torrance, "Theological Education Today", *Theology in Reconstruction*, p. 15.

[116] See Torrance, "Theological Education Today", *Theology in Reconstruction*, pp. 16ff. and "Epilogue: A New Reformation?", *Theology in Reconstruction*, pp. 259–83, 275ff.

book *Honest To God*, imposed his own creative and pictorial images "upon God", understood vaguely as the "ground of being", and then portrayed God as "helplessly involved in the toils of our own processes of life and thought".[117] This God, Torrance insisted, was "unable by definition to stoop down to us and to intervene creatively and redemptively in our need and condition". Consequently, "Like the God of Schleiermacher, he is a God without pity and mercy, and like the God of Bultmann, he is present and active in the death of Jesus Christ in no other way than he is present and active in a fatal accident in the street".[118] Here we see that Torrance's scientific theology was aimed at overcoming the sort of projectionism he saw in the work of someone like John A. T. Robinson, as well as the existentialism he saw in the work of Bultmann and the Protestant modernism he perceived in Schleiermacher. Torrance just as strongly opposed the thinking of Paul Tillich for similar reasons.[119] We shall see specific examples of this as the work proceeds. All of Torrance's thinking, including his approach to the Bible, as already mentioned, depended on this scientific understanding of theology which refused to allow creatures to set the agenda for the truth of theology precisely because God alone was the one who set that agenda by his own actions as Lord, Creator, Reconciler and Redeemer. In a very similar way, Torrance turned to the early church fathers for theological reasons and not merely for historical ones, and so he also found himself opposed to those who, like Maurice Wiles, used history at times to undermine the very theology Torrance sought to espouse. For instance, as we have already noted, Torrance insisted on the deep ontological meaning of history which was tied to the fact that God himself was active in the incarnation, death and resurrection of Jesus within the structures of space and time reconciling the world to himself, justifying the world by his grace as is evidenced in the miracle of Jesus' resurrection. Maurice Wiles, however, rejected the idea that God himself could intervene within world history and saw biblical miracles as symbolic of Christian life rather than as signs of God's direct actions within history.[120]

Our special concern in the rest of this book will deal with just how one must approach the triune God, and how a properly conceived trinitarian theology must therefore inform every other theological pursuit for T. F. Torrance. Though formally unable to lecture on the Trinity at Edinburgh, the doctrine shaped all that Torrance taught then and thereafter. As we shall see, for Torrance, the theology of the Trinity was always shaped by that unique object to which all theology must conform itself in acts of free obedience. We turn our attention now to this task.

---

[117]   Torrance, "Epilogue", *Theology in Reconstruction*, p. 277.

[118]   Torrance, "Epilogue", *Theology in Reconstruction*, p. 277.

[119]   See, for example, Chapter 5, below, pp.172ff.

[120]   See Maurice Wiles, *The Remaking of Christian Doctrine* (Philadelphia: Westminster Press, 1978).

Chapter 2

# T. F. Torrance, Theologian of the Trinity
## The Centrality of the Doctrine of the Trinity in Torrance's Theology

For T. F. Torrance, the doctrine of the Trinity is *the* central doctrine around which all other Christian doctrines gravitate and become comprehensible. That is why he can declare:

> It is not just that the doctrine of the Holy Trinity must be accorded primacy over all the other doctrines, but that properly understood it is the nerve and centre of them all, configures them all, and is so deeply integrated with them that when they are held apart from the doctrine of the Trinity they are seriously defective in truth and become malformed.[1]

But Torrance offered no shallow economic trinitarianism in the form of a model for his view of society or of the human psyche, or of the church and the world for that matter; a model which we then use in our theological reflections to suggest the kind of church or world we would want to build and shape. For Torrance, "it is finally in our understanding of the trinitarian relations in God himself that we have the ground and grammar of a realist theology".[2] In other words, while much contemporary theology is interested merely in an economic Trinity, Torrance insisted that the ground and grammar of theology that takes shape within the economy is rooted in God's eternal Being which would remain entirely unknown

---

[1]    Torrance, *The Christian Doctrine of God*, p. 31. Following Athanasius, Torrance insists that we do not know God in "disjunction" from the world by distinguishing natural and supernatural, nor do we know God by way of some logical inference "from the world". Rather, we know God as Creator who transcends the world in and through the world as the medium of his self-communication in the incarnation and outpouring of his Spirit. We thus know God in his internal trinitarian relations through the incarnation; that is what "makes the doctrine of the Holy Trinity absolutely basic and essential in the Christian understanding of God" (Torrance, "Athanasius: A Study in the Foundations of Classical Theology", *Theology in Reconciliation*, pp. 215–66, 222). This same piece appears in Thomas F. Torrance, *Divine Meaning: Studies in Patristic Hermeneutics* (hereafter: *Divine Meaning*), (Edinburgh: T&T Clark, 1995), pp. 179–228, 186.

[2]    Torrance, *The Ground and Grammar*, p. xi.

to us without the incarnation of God in Jesus Christ and the outpouring of the Holy Spirit at Pentecost. In his own words:

> I myself like to think of the doctrine of the Trinity as the *ultimate ground* of theological knowledge of God, the *basic grammar* of theology, for it is there that we find our knowledge of God reposing upon the final Reality of God himself, grounded in the ultimate relations intrinsic to God's own Being, which govern and control all true knowledge of him from beginning to end.[3]

That, of course, is the key to understanding Torrance's thinking here—unless theology begins from a center in God himself and unless it is controlled by the reality of God himself throughout, it becomes little more than mythology, or the projection of our human wishes based on experience on to reality, resulting in fantasy and not perception of reality. And it is perception of reality that Torrance is after with his "realist theology". Yet such perception must respect the fact that in thinking about the triune God we are bound to God's trinitarian self-revelation in such a way that we must acknowledge that it "confronts us as a 'primitive all', to be understood primarily and completely in terms of itself". Thus, unlike those who suppose that Eastern theology begins with the three Persons and moves toward God's oneness whereas Western theology begins with God's oneness and moves toward the three Persons, Torrance quite properly insisted that trinitarian theology "takes its rise *ab initio* from God's indivisible wholeness as one Being, three Persons, and proceeds in accordance with what is revealed of God's internal *homoousial* and *hypostatic* interrelations as Father, Son and Holy Spirit".[4] What Torrance meant by this will become evident as the chapter proceeds.

Still, we must ask how exactly are we to begin with the reality of God, given that God himself transcends all our human experience and reflection and indeed we human beings tend toward idolatry since, in light of the Fall, we are inclined toward self-centeredness rather than God-centeredness? Without seeming simplistic, the answer for Torrance lies in Jesus Christ himself as we know him through the apostolic testimonies of the New Testament and subsequently through the teaching of the Councils of Nicaea (325) and Constantinople (381).[5] It is because he is who he is that we have knowledge of God at all. And that means acknowledging the fact that determines all true theology, namely, that Jesus Christ himself is the eternally begotten Son of the Father present in history as our advocate, helper and friend. But this indicates that theology can only begin and end in faith and prayer. That is why Torrance insisted that the Council of Nicaea

---

[3]  Torrance, *The Ground and Grammar*, pp. 158–9.

[4]  Torrance, *The Christian Doctrine of God*, p. 29.

[5]  Reference to these two Councils should not be taken to imply that other Councils such as the Council of Chalcedon, among others, were not considered extremely important by Torrance as well.

accorded primacy to faith.[6] While there were, of course, "negative determinations" (to avoid heresy—primarily the heresy of Arius) and while there were "formal rules" that were expressed, in the main the Nicene Creed was "an evangelical declaration of saving faith which the Church found itself obliged to make under the constraint of the divine truth mediated to it through the Holy Scriptures".[7]

Following Hilary of Poitiers (312–367/8), who was unique among Western theologians with his wide knowledge of Eastern theology and was familiar with the thinking of Origen and Athanasius as well as being a strong opponent of Arianism, Torrance insisted that faith is objectively and not subjectively grounded. By this he means that the basis and meaning of faith is found in its object and not at all in the knowing and believing subject: "in faith a person takes his stand on the ground of God's own being (*in substantia dei*)".[8] This, for Torrance, is the epitome of scientific knowledge precisely because it is knowledge that must take place in accordance with the unique nature of the object that is being investigated.[9] Torrance relied heavily on the fathers who frequently cited the Septuagint, saying, "If you will not believe, you will not understand", and so he believes with Irenaeus that "faith rests on things that really are" and that faith is "produced by the truth" so that only as we believe in things as they really are can we stay confident in them. Likewise, he followed the thinking of Augustine: "We do not seek to understand what we believe ... we believe that we may understand".[10] All of this means that for Nicene theology, faith was not seen as some "non-cognitive or non-conceptual relation to God" but involved "acts of recognition, apprehension and conception,

---

[6] See Torrance, *The Trinitarian Faith*, p. 19.

[7] Torrance, *The Trinitarian Faith*, pp. 18–19.

[8] Hilary, *De. Trin.*, 1.18 cited in Torrance, *The Trinitarian Faith*, p. 19. It is worth noting here that for Torrance it was Athanasius in the East and "Hilary, his later contemporary in the West, who, more than any other Christian theologians" known to Torrance "gave the most serious attention to the nature of the change that language and technical terms must undergo when they are appropriately employed in the service of knowledge and speech about God" (Torrance, "Athanasius", *Theology in Reconciliation*, p. 217).

[9] "Scientific knowledge," writes Torrance, "was held to result from inquiry strictly in accordance with the nature (κατὰ φύσιν) of the reality being investigated, that is, knowledge of it reached under the constraint of what it actually and essentially is in itself" (*The Trinitarian Faith*, p. 51). Such knowledge, Torrance believed, "had long prevailed in Alexandria" and was employed by Origen to develop a way to know God "strictly in accordance with the nature of God as he has revealed himself to us" (*The Trinitarian Faith*, p. 38). This was the epitome of "godly" thinking. Its opposite, of course, was ungodly or heretical thinking which involved a rationalizing and mythologizing "perversion of the Gospel" (*The Trinitarian Faith*, p. 29). For a particularly clear expression of this understanding and how it can lead beyond the errors inherent to the receptacle or container notions of space and toward ecumenical agreement, see Torrance, *God and Rationality*, pp. 114ff.

[10] Torrance, *The Trinitarian Faith*, p. 20.

of a very basic intuitive kind" that Torrance believed takes place when the human mind assents to God's self-revelation in Jesus Christ.[11]

It is important to realize here that Torrance in no way desired to ground true knowledge in human intuition. He simply wished to note that human knowledge takes place always with concepts and always under the constraint of an object distinct from the human subject. That is why he insisted, in another context, that

> Even though God transcends all that we can think and say of Him, it still holds good that we cannot have experience of Him or believe in Him without conceptual forms of understanding—as Anselm used to say: *fides esse nequit sine conceptione.*[12]

Hence, faith was a kind of "listening obedience" in which faith is founded upon God himself and not at all upon the church's confession as such. Here again Torrance follows Hilary in two important respects by insisting that: 1) "God cannot be apprehended except through himself"[13] and 2) the biblical statements through which we understand God must "be interpreted in the light of the matters or realities (*res*) to which they refer".[14]

Torrance was not only in agreement with Hilary here but was also in accord with the thinking of Karl Barth, who was so insistent, with respect to the Trinity and to all doctrine, on the importance of following Hilary's maxim "*quia non sermoni res, sed rei sermo subjectus est*" (the reality is not subject to the word, but the word must be subject to the reality) that he could declare that "he who does not adopt this statement as his own methodological axiom is no theologian and

---

[11]   Torrance, *The Trinitarian Faith*, p. 20. For Torrance's own explanation of this, see Thomas F. Torrance, *The Hermeneutics of John Calvin* (Edinburgh: Scottish Academic Press, 1988), pp. 89ff. and 129–30. He clearly wished to follow Calvin and move away from any subjective basis for knowledge and language in order to allow our intuitive knowledge and language to be shaped by the objective reality of God's self-revelation in Christ and through his Spirit.

[12]   Torrance, *God and Rationality*, p. 170. For a detailed explanation of how Torrance relates Anselm's statement to forms of "non-conceptual" knowledge and to "direct and intuitive apprehension of reality" by claiming a type of "implicit conceptuality" controlled by reality itself, see *God and Rationality*, pp. 21ff. See also Thomas F. Torrance, "Truth and Authority: Theses on Truth" in *The Irish Theological Quarterly* 38 (1972): 215–42, 220–28.

[13]   Hilary, *De. Trin.* 5. 20–21, cited in Torrance, *The Trinitarian Faith*, p. 21. This is also a theme that appears in Irenaeus. See Irenaeus, *Adversus haereses*, 4.11 as cited in Torrance, *The Christian Doctrine of God*, p. 13. See also Irenaeus, *Adversus haereses* 4.8.1, as cited in Torrance, *The Christian Doctrine of God*, p. 77.

[14]   Torrance, *The Trinitarian Faith*, p. 22. See also Torrance, *The Christian Doctrine of God*, p. 117.

never will be".[15] Torrance very definitely adopted this axiom for his doctrine of the Trinity and for all his theology, not least when he claimed that Calvin himself followed Hilary when he "laid it down that we must not subordinate things to the words that indicate them but the words to the things they indicate, for it is of the things themselves that we think rather than the words used of them".[16]

And so he insisted that Nicene faith excludes belief in any other god than the Father Almighty or any other revelation than the revelation of his only-begotten Son.[17] Consequently, there simply is no access to God except through Jesus Christ his only Son and by means of the power of his Holy Spirit. In that sense we know God in very human ways without leaving the sphere of human experience and knowledge; but we know God only because of the grace that God has shown us by becoming incarnate in Jesus Christ and uniting us to Christ in faith through the Holy Spirit so that we may actually think from a center in God provided by God himself in the incarnation and outpouring of the Holy Spirit.[18] All of this, however, demands "unconditional obedience" to the truth of God which seizes hold of us in Jesus Christ and over which we have no control. Unconditional obedience here means that faith is tied to revelation in such a way that any alternative way of knowing is set aside and a judgment is made

> which excludes divergent belief, and endorses an affirmation of truth which thereby rejects other affirmations as false. The objective pole of the Church's faith is the truth of God … which makes it free and establishes it in the love

---

[15]   Barth, *CD* I/1, p. 354. In presenting the thought of John Major, the Scottish philosopher and theologian, by way of background for presenting Calvin's theology, Torrance rejected the idea that Major was a nominalist and insisted that he was influenced by Hilary, Lombard and Anselm especially as they argued that "in theological understanding the *res* must not be subordinated to the *sermo* but the *sermo* to the *res*" (*The Hermeneutics of John Calvin*, p. 36). See also Torrance, "Knowledge of God and Speech about him according to John Calvin", *Theology in Reconstruction*, pp. 76–98, 92, where he insists this thinking led Calvin to reject nominalism. Torrance repeats this in *God and Rationality*, p. 37, and *Karl Barth*, p. 188. And, in *Royal Priesthood*, Torrance responds to criticism of James Barr by accusing Barr of a kind of nominalism and citing this text as employed by Greek and Latin Fathers (p. x). See below, Chapter 9, for a brief discussion of Torrance's view of James Barr's approach to the Bible. Torrance held that "human statements in the Scriptures direct us beyond themselves to God, so that … the divine reality they mediate, the very Word of God himself, is not to be subordinated to the human word, but the human word to the divine reality to which they refer" (Torrance, *Theological and Natural Science*, p. 106). Although Torrance does not refer to Hilary here, it is clear that Hilary's maxim has influenced his view of Scripture.

[16]   Torrance, *God and Rationality*, p. 37.

[17]   See Torrance, *The Trinitarian Faith*, pp. 22–3.

[18]   This is why Torrance insisted that it is through the Spirit that "we are converted from ourselves to thinking from a centre in God and not in ourselves, and to knowing God out of God and not out of ourselves" (Torrance, *God and Rationality*, p. 174).

of God … the Church cannot but confess its faith in God, before God, with an unreserved endorsement of belief in the truth of Christ and his Gospel …[19]

Everything, including knowledge of God as well as salvation and redemption, therefore hinges on the oneness in being and agency between God and his self-revelation in Christ. It is at this point that we meet an oft-repeated but pivotal assertion of Torrance's trinitarian theology taken over from Athanasius: "It would be more godly and true to signify God from the Son and call him Father, than to name God from his works alone and call him Unoriginate."[20] Here faith and "godliness" go together because

> Faith itself is an act of godliness in humble worship of God and adoring obedience to him, and godliness is a right relationship to God through faith which gives a distinctive slant to the mind and moulds life and thought in accordance with "the word and truth of the Gospel".[21]

Torrance cites a number of biblical texts such as 1 Timothy 1:4; 4:7; 6:3–6; 2 Timothy 4:4; Titus 1:14; and 2 Peter 1:3, 6; 3:11 to stress that faith, godliness and truth go together and that godliness is based on "sound doctrine" that is diametrically opposed to any "rationalising and mythologising perversion of the Gospel".[22] Godliness, then, was associated with belief and truth whereas ungodliness was associated with unbelief and error. Following Origen, but, of course, criticizing the dualist framework of thought that misled Origen, especially when he tended to relativize the historical Jesus,[23] Torrance believed that *theologia,* which "is properly knowledge of the Holy Trinity", and *eusebeia* (godliness) mutually condition each other "in the course of deepening theological inquiry".[24] It was this thinking that led the church to struggle against heresy over the next three hundred years.

## The Deposit of Faith

In fact, for Torrance, the only proper way to understand Christian teaching and preaching is to correlate faith, godliness and truth correctly as Irenaeus did within

---

[19]   Torrance, *The Trinitarian Faith*, p. 23.

[20]   Athanasius, *Con. Ar.* 1.34 and *De decretis*, 31, cited in Torrance, *The Trinitarian Faith*, p. 49. See these important statements in *A Select Library of Nicene and Post-Nicene Fathers of the Christian Church Second Series*, trans. and ed Philip Schaff and Henry Wace (Edinburgh: T&T Clark, 1987), pp. 326 and 171. Hilary holds a similar position in *De Trin.*, 1.17; 3.22. See also Torrance, *The Christian Doctrine of God*, p. 117.

[21]   Torrance, *The Trinitarian Faith*, p. 28.

[22]   Torrance, *The Trinitarian Faith*, p. 29.

[23]   See Torrance, *The Trinitarian Faith*, pp. 37, 41.

[24]   Torrance, *The Trinitarian Faith*, p. 38.

the concept of the "deposit of faith" but without making that apostolic deposit primarily a set of doctrinal statements to be accepted. Rather, the deposit was to be seen as:

> a body of objective evangelical truth which through the power of the Holy Spirit constantly rejuvenates the Church by renewing its bond with the creative source of its being in the Gospel, and structures its continuing life and mission in accordance with the image of Christ the incarnate Son of God and the pattern of divine truth embodied in him.[25]

Torrance adamantly opposed making the "deposit of faith" a "compendium of doctrines formulated in definitive statements which were regarded as themselves identical with the truths they were meant to express"[26] because such thinking would then prescriptively be imposed on the life and faith of the church in a way that no longer would allow the church's existence to be governed, as it should be, by its relation to the Truth itself, namely, the risen Lord who, through the power of the Holy Spirit, continues to guide the church *through* the deposit of faith and not in identity with it.

Torrance traced this approach to Tertullian's rather legalistic understanding of the deposit while supporting Irenaeus' more evangelical view of the matter which came to be embodied in the Nicene–Constantinopolitan Creed. In fact, according to Torrance, it was just this divergent way of reading the "deposit of faith" that distinguished Roman Catholic and Evangelical understanding of the apostolic teaching and led to differing views of tradition and differences regarding the *sola scriptura* as well as the eventual stress by the Roman Catholic Church on the infallible role of "the Papacy as the supreme Teaching Office in the Church, and the irreformable nature of officially proclaimed dogmatic pronouncements" which "came to a head in the First Vatican Council of 1870, when dogmatic propositions about the truth were identified with the truth itself".[27] According to Torrance, this "reactionary" view of the "deposit" was replaced with the more Irenaean view at Vatican II when Pope John XXIII said, "The Deposit of Faith is one thing; the way it is presented is another. For truths preserved in our sacred doctrine can retain the same substance and meaning under different forms of expression."[28] Indeed, Torrance noted that when the Decree on Ecumenism stated that "if the influence of events or of the times has led to deficiencies of doctrine (which must be carefully distinguished from the Deposit of Faith itself), these should be appropriately rectified at the proper moment",[29] this signaled a change in emphasis from Vatican I to Vatican II so that "the primacy accorded to the divine Revelation in Holy

---

25    Torrance, *The Trinitarian Faith*, p. 31.
26    Torrance, "The Deposit of Faith": 16.
27    Torrance, "The Deposit of Faith": 17.
28    Torrance, "The Deposit of Faith": 18.
29    Torrance, "The Deposit of Faith": 18.

Scripture and to the substance of the Faith over all the Church's expressions or formulations of their truth" place the Roman Catholic Church once again on the Irenaean side of the divide. For Torrance, it would be a serious mistake for theologians to take doctrinal propositions and connect them in a "logico-deductive system of thought" because then it would be human logic and not the object of faith that determined their truth. Any such approach to doctrine would be akin to the creature substituting itself for the creator. What is more, such an approach to doctrine would make the fatal assumption that these propositions "have their truth in themselves" whereas in reality their truth comes from beyond themselves "in that supreme truth to which they refer ..."[30] This is the constant temptation facing theology: will theologians think in a faithful and godly way, allowing their thoughts to point beyond human logic and experience to the truth inherent in the triune God himself from all eternity, or will they think in a dualist way which stops short of God himself in his self-revelation and identifies revelation with the product of one's own thought or experience?

In this sense, Torrance insisted that there is an open range to faith so that terms are seen to refer away from themselves and toward God; they are imperfect and always need revision in light of further knowledge of God himself that may come through the apostolic deposit. That is in fact how the non-biblical term ὁμοούσιος (*homoousios*) came to be used by the fathers at Nicaea. They were compelled by circumstances to use this term clearly to express biblical and evangelical truth in face of Arius' dualistic view that called into question the unity of the Trinity by asserting creatureliness of the Son. Following Athanasius, Torrance believed it was irrelevant that a non-biblical term was used to clarify the faith. What mattered was that the person who used the term had a "godly" mind. But that meant a mind shaped by the unique revelation of God that took place in Jesus Christ, the Word of God incarnate, and through his Holy Spirit. That meant further that the person using the term was not thinking mythologically "from a centre in the human mind" but rather theologically "from a centre in God".[31]

Here we have three crucial terms that constantly reappear in Torrance's trinitarian theology: dualism, Arius (Arianism) and the *homoousion*. These terms in turn are connected with several other expressions that structure Torrance's thought as well: his onto-relational view of the divine persons, his rejection of subjectivism and agnosticism, his emphasis on *perichoresis* rightly understood and his groundbreaking understanding of the *filioque*. Let us begin seeing how Torrance's opposition to dualism affects his view of the Trinity.

---

[30]  Torrance, *The Trinitarian Faith*, p. 34. See also Torrance, *The Christian Doctrine of God*, pp. 76–7 and 73. The same applies to statements of the biblical authors (p. 43).

[31]  Torrance, *The Trinitarian Faith*, p. 47.

## Dualism

It is a mark of Torrance's thinking that he can summarize a thousand years of thought in one paragraph. A good example appears in *The Trinitarian Faith* where Torrance notes that when the Christian church spread from Judaea into the Mediterranean world, the Gospel came up against "a radical dualism of body and mind that pervaded every aspect of Graeco–Roman civilisation, bifurcating human experience and affecting fundamental habits of mind in religion, philosophy and science alike".[32] In his mind, Aristotle took over from Plato the separation between the sensible and the intelligible world and hardened it into a disjunction between "action and reflection, event and idea, becoming and being, the material and the spiritual, the visible and the invisible, the temporal and the eternal" in a way that hampers philosophy and theology up to this very day; he also believed that Ptolemy built this dualistic thinking into a scientific cosmology that "was to dominate European thought for more than a millennium". "The combined effect of this all-pervading dualism was to shut God out of the world of empirical actuality in space and time."[33] This is a crucial insight because it is just here that the Gospel was in conflict with Greek thought, that is, between thinking mythologically from a center in one's own experience and thinking objectively from a center in God himself provided by God in the incarnation. But that is the great difficulty—within a dualistic frame of thought the idea of the incarnation of God within space and time was an absurdity. Hence, for Torrance, it is dualism, the chasm between God and the world which dualist thought posits, that marked Gnosticism and Arianism in particular. Gnosticism, by its very nature, denied the central importance of the humanity of Jesus Christ as the incarnate Word, while Arianism denied his true Deity by insisting that Christ belonged only to the creaturely side of the universe created by God.[34]

---

[32] Torrance, *The Trinitarian Faith*, p. 47.

[33] Torrance, *The Trinitarian Faith*, p. 47. For an excellent explanation of what Torrance means by the dualistic disjunction of the sensible and intelligible realms and how this leads to a type of idealism, see Torrance, *Divine Meaning*, Chapter 5, "Early Patristic Interpretation of the Holy Scriptures", pp. 93–129, especially pp. 93–6. It is clear that Torrance himself follows Irenaeus' approach to the truth as it is embodied in the Scriptures since for Irenaeus the starting point cannot be "words and expressions but … the truth itself" (p. 110) and that truth is identical with the Word of God who became flesh in Jesus of Nazareth. That is why Irenaeus and Torrance both reject any dichotomy between "the Redeemer God and the Creator God" since such a distinction "gives the interpreter of the Scriptures an excuse for taking off into realms of fancy and imagination uncontrolled by the observable, tangible world in which we have our existence" (p. 114).

[34] Torrance, *The Trinitarian Faith*, p. 48. Torrance astutely sees Arianism and Sabellianism as approaches to the doctrine of the Trinity that are the "heretical successors" of Ebionite and Docetic Christologies which disjoin Christ's divinity and humanity and thus threaten the integrity of the faith. See Torrance, *The Christian Doctrine of God*, p. 115.

It is his rejection of all forms of dualism that led Torrance to criticize Origen: "… unlike Irenaeus he worked with a dualist framework of thought, the Platonic or Philonic disjunction between the sensible world (αἰσθητὸς κόσμος) and the intelligible world (νοητὸς κόσμος)."[35] What was the result for his theology? It led him to conclude that "the invisible and incorporeal things in heaven are true, but the visible and corporeal things on earth are copies of true things, not true themselves".[36] This disjunction not only affected Origen's way of interpreting Scripture but it affected his view of Christ himself: "the historical Christ was to be regarded as a time-conditioned form in which the eternal truth is mediated to fallen creatures, but that once the eternal truth is known the historical medium will be relativised".[37] This dualism also affected Origen's view of God's relation with the world because it led him to blur the distinction between the eternal generation of the Son from the Father and the creation of the world by the will of the Father through his eternal Word or Son. In other words, Origen "was unable to think of God except in a necessary eternal conjunction with all things … creation had to be regarded as concomitant with the being of God and as eternally coexisting with him".[38] In essence, Origen's failure at this point was to give the required priority to the Father/Son relation over the Creator/cosmos relation because he tended to think that the generation of the Son and the creation of the world were both due to the Father's will. In a sense, as we shall see, Origen's failure at this point is the precursor of the contemporary failure to distinguish without separating the economic and immanent Trinity, while simultaneously acknowledging that what God is toward us in Christ and the Holy Spirit he is eternally in himself.

Of course, the whole point of Nicene theology, based on the *homoousion*, was to insist that the Son was begotten of the *being* of the Father and therefore was eternally Son by nature. This is the significance of Athanasius' speaking of God's activity "as inherent in his Being (ἐνούσιος ἐνέργεια) in precisely the same way in which he could speak of the Word of God as inherent in his Being (ἐνούσιος λόγος)".[39] By tying together God's being and act in this way, Athanasius, Barth and Torrance could then insist that what God is toward us in his saving acts he is eternally in himself in such a way as to cut out any other approach to God than that which takes place in faith through the Son by the Holy Spirit and toward the Father. Torrance makes this assertion so often it would take pages to document each reference. But that does not mean one should let it slip by as merely repetitious or unimportant. For Torrance, the *homoousion* of the Son and Father and again of the Spirit with the Son and the Father was decisive because it stressed their indivisible

---

[35]   Torrance, *The Trinitarian Faith*, p. 34.

[36]   Origen, quoted in Torrance, *The Trinitarian Faith*, p. 35.

[37]   Torrance, *The Trinitarian Faith*, p. 37.

[38]   Torrance, *The Trinitarian Faith*, p. 85. For an especially clear explanation of the errors of Origen, see Torrance, "Athanasius", *Theology in Reconciliation*, p. 220 and *Divine Meaning*, p. 184.

[39]   Torrance, *The Christian Doctrine of God*, p. 120.

union and distinction as three co-equal Persons within the Godhead. Following Athanasius, Torrance stressed the

> simple, uncompounded and undivided nature of the Being of God, in sharp opposition to the Arian separation of the Son from the Father, and of the semi-Arian separation of the Spirit from the Godhead. For Athanasius, then, *ousia* refers to the Being of God in the inner reality and unity of his coinherent trinitarian relations.[40]

In Torrance's view, the Nicene *homoousion* led to a profound reconstruction of Greek thought in two ways. First, it ended "the menace of the dualist structure of thought that in different ways lay behind the modalist and tritheist conceptions of God". Modalism, of course, denied the distinction of persons within the Trinity and thus the divinity of the Son and Spirit whereas tritheism denied the unity of persons and opened the door to polytheism. Second, it changed the understanding of *ousia* and *hypostasis* by the way the economic and immanent Trinity were related. In Torrance's words:

> The doctrine of the *homoousion* was as decisive as it was revolutionary: it expressed the evangelical truth that what God is toward us and has freely done for us in his love and grace, and continues to do in the midst of us through his Word and Spirit, he really is *in himself*, and that he really is *in the internal relations and personal properties* of his transcendent Being as the Holy Trinity the very same Father, Son, and Holy Spirit, that he is in his revealing and saving activity in time and space toward mankind, and ever will be.[41]

This is also the significance of the emphasis by both Torrance and Barth on the fact that God is the Subject of his own internal and external activities. This is extremely important because it rules out any notion whatsoever of a relation of mutual dependence between the triune God and creation, whether it be conceived in terms of pantheism, panentheism or some other way. It is the "I am who I am/I will be who I will be" (Exodus) that informs their thinking here: "the Lord God is the Subject ... and the sole Subject of all he is and will be, and of all his ways and works".[42]

Torrance frequently asserts that God never surrenders his transcendence because creation and incarnation are not necessary for his trinitarian existence; rather, they are new acts that freely flowed from his love—the incarnation in particular "took place in the sovereign ontological freedom of God to be other in his external relations than he eternally was, and is, and to do what he had never

---

[40]  Torrance, *The Christian Doctrine of God*, p. 130.

[41]  Torrance, *The Christian Doctrine of God*, p. 130.

[42]  Torrance, *The Christian Doctrine of God*, p. 120.

done before".[43] God did indeed freely choose not to live alone as he might have, but he freely created us for fellowship with himself and became incarnate out of love for us, "yet in such a way that he remains undiminished in the transcendent Freedom, Nature and Mystery of his eternal Being".[44] That is why Torrance stresses that Athanasius used to insist that "God was not always incarnate any more than he was always Creator, the incarnation and the creation are to be regarded as new even for God, although they result from the eternal outgoing movement of his Love".[45] And here is the point that distinguishes Torrance's thought from much contemporary reflection that fails to note God's freedom at this point:

> All this warns us that we cannot think of the ontological Trinity as if it were constituted by or dependent on the economic Trinity, but must rather think of the economic Trinity as the freely predetermined manifestation in the history of salvation of the eternal Trinity which God himself was before the foundation of the world, and eternally is. Hence when we rightly speak of the oneness between the ontological Trinity and the economic Trinity, we may not speak of that oneness without distinguishing and delimiting it from the ontological Trinity—there are in any case ... elements of the incarnate economy such as the time pattern of human life in this world which we may not read back into the eternal Life of God. On the other hand, the fact that the ontological Trinity has ontological priority over the economic Trinity, does not preclude us from saying that the ontological Trinity is essentially and intrinsically evangelical, for it is precisely the ontological Trinity that God has made known to us in his self-giving and self- revealing as Father, Son and Holy Spirit ...[46]

What needs to be stressed at this point is that while God's eternal being as Father, Son and Spirit is not in any way *constituted* or *determined* by his relation to others, nevertheless he is free to love others and thus to be "God in the highest and God with us".[47] Errors arise today as they arose in the early church in connection with Origen's failure to distinguish God's internal and external relations by neglecting to distinguish "the eternal generation of the Son and the creation of the world, between the ontological and cosmological dimensions".[48] That is why Torrance connects Origen's error here, which Athanasius naturally opposed, with "process theology according to which the external relations of God are held in some measure to be constitutive of what he is as God".[49]

---

43  Torrance, *The Christian Doctrine of God*, p. 108.
44  Torrance, *The Christian Doctrine of God*, p. 108.
45  Torrance, *The Christian Doctrine of God*, p. 108.
46  Torrance, *The Christian Doctrine of God*, pp. 108–9.
47  Torrance, *The Christian Doctrine of God*, p. 132.
48  Torrance, *The Christian Doctrine of God*, p. 208.
49  Torrance, *The Christian Doctrine of God*, p. 208.

Origen's thinking, then, in effect opened the door both to monism (the idea that the world was eternal and necessary for God) and dualism (the idea that the historical incarnation was only a transitory symbolic representation of the eternal Gospel). It was this failure to distinguish between God's internal and external relations that Arius exploited with his own dualism. Arius' prime error was to include the Son among the works that God brought into being by his creative will: "for him God was primarily Creator and not the Father", whereas for Nicene theology, the theology Torrance himself adopted, it is imperative to realize that although God was always Father, he was not always Creator, and that although God was always the Son, he was not always incarnate.[50] This is no small issue and the very recognition of this fact shows quite clearly that Torrance intended to acknowledge God's eternal existence as Father, Son and Holy Spirit and further intended to distinguish clearly between God's internal and external activities in his economic trinitarian actions *ad extra*. It is in this context that Torrance continually emphasized the priority of the Father/Son relation over the Creator/creature relation. This destructive and abstract dualistic thinking Torrance later identified as the "Latin Heresy", which Karl Barth himself did much to combat. Barth opposed "the Augustinian, Cartesian and Newtonian dualism built into the general framework of Western thought and culture" which tended to damage and even cut "the ontological bond between Jesus Christ and God the Father, and thus introduce an oblique or symbolical relation between the Word of God and God himself". Much of this dualistic thinking is traceable to abstractive thinking in formal terms in ways that were reinforced by Kant's denial that we can know things in their internal relations. Thinking exclusively in terms of external relations is what Torrance called "the Latin Heresy" because its roots can be traced to "a form of linguistic and conceptual dualism that prevailed in late patristic and mediaeval Latin theology".[51]

---

[50] Torrance, *The Trinitarian Faith*, pp. 85ff. See also Thomas F. Torrance, "The Atonement: The Singularity of Christ and the Finality of the Cross: The Atonement and the Moral Order" in *Universalism and the Doctrine of Hell: Papers presented at the Fourth Edinburgh Conference in Christian Dogmatics, 1991*, Nigel M. De S. Cameron (ed), (Carlisle, UK: The Paternoster Press; Grand Rapids: Baker Book House, 1992), pp. 225–56, 233ff. See also Torrance, *The Ground and Grammar*, p. 66, where he writes, "God was not eternally Creator. Athanasius rejected the idea that God is eternally Creator and its attendant idea that the creation eternally exists in the mind of God ... Nor was God eternally incarnate, for in Jesus Christ he became what he never was eternally, a creature, without of course ceasing to be the eternal God."

[51] Torrance, *Karl Barth*, pp. 215–16.

## Arius/Arianism

As we have seen, then, for Torrance, the doctrine of the Trinity is central because through it we are able to describe within due limits the eternal, dynamic and relational being of God himself as Father, Son and Holy Spirit. Torrance helpfully notes the differences between Christianity and Judaism and between Christianity and Hellenism in this perspective. Torrance contends that, for the Jews, God remained utterly transcendent and unnamable, even though he made himself known to Moses, the prophets and psalmists through his saving activity. Still, before the incarnation, according to Torrance, "the faithful were not brought into such a close personal relation with God that they came to know him directly in himself as he became known in Jesus Christ".[52] It is here that the revolution in knowledge of God articulated at Nicaea took place: "God in himself is no longer closed to us, but has opened himself to our knowledge in his own being as Father, Son and Holy Spirit."[53] That, for Torrance, is the epistemological function of the doctrine, namely, "that we may really know God the Father Almighty in a positive way", so that, in contrast to Judaism, "in some real measure we may have a conceptual grasp of God in his own internal relations".[54] Yet, here Torrance adds an extremely important point. Although Nicene theologians did indeed know God in himself, they remained "Hebraic" with their horror of presumption when it came to knowing the triune God so that they imposed upon themselves a "disciplined reserve". While they realized they could know God accurately and devoutly in his divine nature through his incarnate Son and in the Holy Spirit, they also knew that "If even the holy cherubim or seraphim cover their faces in the immediate presence of God, how much more must human beings, for how can they look upon God, really know God as he is in himself and live?"[55] In other words, because

---

[52]　　Torrance, *The Trinitarian Faith*, p. 66.

[53]　　Torrance, *The Trinitarian Faith*, p. 67.

[54]　　Torrance, *The Trinitarian Faith*, p. 67.

[55]　　Torrance, *The Trinitarian Faith*, p. 67. Torrance therefore follows Barth and insists that "we can no more offer an account of the 'how' of these divine relations [Fatherhood, Sonship and Procession] and actions than we can define the Father, the Son and the Holy Spirit and delimit them from one another" (Torrance, *The Christian Doctrine of God*, p. 193). See also Karl Barth, *CD* I/1, pp. 475–6. For Torrance, when we speak of the begetting of the Son or the proceeding of the Spirit "we have to suspend our thought before the altogether inexpressible, incomprehensible Nature of God and the onto-relations of the Communion of the Father, the Son, and the Holy Spirit, which the Holy Spirit eternally is. To cite Athanasius once again, 'Thus far human knowledge goes. Here the cherubim spread the covering of their wings'" (Torrance, *The Christian Doctrine of God*, p. 193). That is why, while Torrance insists that we cannot remain agnostic when it comes to knowing the triune God, still we must use the concepts we have "with apophatic reserve and reverence" (Torrance, *The Christian Doctrine of God*, p. 194). On this point see also Torrance, "Athanasius", *Divine Meaning*, p. 202 and "Athanasius", *Theology in Reconciliation*, p. 224. Torrance rejects false forms of apophaticism ("Athanasius", *Theology in Reconciliation*, p. 221).

our knowledge of God is grounded in God's revelation to us and not at all in our own experiences of fatherhood and sonship, we must admit that what we know of God's inner relations is partial and that the inner relations of the Trinity are "ineffable relations and refer to ineffable realities".[56]

Torrance's thinking is extremely revealing and interesting with regard to the differences he sees between Christianity and Hellenism. He certainly did not agree with Harnack that Christianity itself had become Hellenized; rather, Torrance insisted that while making use of Greek thought forms, Christianity expressed ideas that were fundamentally alien to Hellenism. Hence, one of the most significant features of Nicene theology was "not the Hellenising of Christianity but the Christianising of Hellenism".[57] This Christianizing was most evident in connection with three important categories: *image*, *word* and *activity*. Because Hellenism gave priority to sight over other senses, it developed "an essentially *optical* model of thought"[58] with the result that terms such as "idea", "form" and "theory" tended to refer to modes of seeing or to what is seen. Names or words were held to image what they signified and since, for Greeks, vision was thought to occur through a beam of light aimed from the eye to the object, "it is understandable that in Hellenism the habit of thinking in images ... projected by human beings beyond themselves in the form of myths, should have had such a predominant role in religion and philosophy alike".[59]

It is precisely here that the conflict between Christianity and Hellenism developed in the Arian crisis. The issue, of course, concerned the relation of the Father and Son. And the key question was: should we understand the terms "father" and "son" "as visual, sensual images taken from our human relations and then projected mythologically into God"?[60] If that is the approach taken, then Torrance believed, quite rightly, that we could hardly avoid "projecting creaturely gender into God, and thinking of him as grandfather as well as father, for the only kind of father we know is one who is son of another father".[61] Any such approach to knowledge of God, however, inevitably leads to polytheism and idolatry, that

---

[56]   Torrance, *The Christian Doctrine of God*, p. 193.

[57]   Torrance, *The Trinitarian Faith*, p. 68.

[58]   Torrance, *The Trinitarian Faith*, p. 69.

[59]   Torrance, *The Trinitarian Faith*, p. 69.

[60]   Torrance, *The Trinitarian Faith*, p. 69.

[61]   Torrance, *The Trinitarian Faith*, p. 69. Very importantly this includes the idea that terms such as πνευμα are not to be governed by the gender which they have in Greek because of linguistic convention either. See Torrance, *Trinitarian Perspectives*, pp. 129–30. Additionally, while the Greek terms for being (οὐσία and ὑπόστασις) are "linguistically feminine and conceptually impersonal, when used theologically to speak of the Being of God and of each of the divine Persons, are neither feminine nor impersonal, for they were radically changed through the mighty acts of God in Jesus Christ and were given an intensely dynamic and personal significance in the service of God's self-revelation, unlike anything that they had in secular Greek" (Torrance, *Trinitarian Perspectives*, p. 130).

is, to our creating God in our own image rather than accepting the fact that God created us in his image. It is exactly in connection with the Arian crisis that biblical thinking, with its emphasis on faith and obedience to the Word of God revealed, contrasts most sharply with Greek thinking, which tends toward projection. Here we meet Torrance's often repeated and extremely important insight that a biblical approach thinks from a "centre in God as he reveals himself to us through his Word incarnate in Jesus Christ" so that "we know him [God] as Father in himself *in an utterly unique and incomparable way*, which then becomes the controlling standard by reference to which all notions of creaturely fatherhood and sonship are to be understood".[62]

This rules out any strictly agnostic viewpoint which Torrance believed necessarily neglects revelation itself because it leaves open who God is, when in reality God has named himself to us in Jesus Christ and through the Holy Spirit as the eternal Father, Son and Holy Spirit. This God is no myth invented by human beings who can be changed at will. This is the one true and eternal God who has his existence from himself alone and who created us and sustains us in his Word and Spirit. By basing his theology on the Father/Son relation, Torrance undercuts all forms of agnosticism and subjectivism (grounding truth in the human subject) and thus any attempt by us to create God in our own image which would then leave us separated from the true God (dualism). The counter question as to whether or not these are names governed by the fact that the "Unique Fatherhood and unique Sonship in God mutually define one another in an absolute and singular way",[63] so that our thinking about God as Father and Son is grounded in God's naming himself to us in revealing himself to us in his incarnate Son Jesus Christ and through his Holy Spirit, is the one that shaped Nicene theology and still should shape theology today. Athanasius rejected mythologizing with these words: "Just as we cannot ascribe a father to the Father, so we cannot ascribe a brother to the Son."[64] It is here, Torrance contends, that the Hebraic element in Nicene theology most clearly conflicts with Hellenism because it is here that there is uncompromising rejection of projecting sensual images in an effort to understand God himself, as actually occurred in "heathen worship of the *Baalim* and *Astaroth*, the nature and sex deities of the old Semitic world".[65] In this context, one can perhaps understand why Torrance so adamantly refused to engage in the contemporary feminist call for renaming God in order that women and men might achieve equality. In Torrance's view, they have equality because of who God is in Jesus Christ—but that God named himself to us as the eternal Father, Son and Spirit and that name is no mere projection. Consequently, equality is not something we must create; it is something we recognize as God's gift to us in the Giver, from whom the gift may not be separated.

---

[62]  Torrance, *The Trinitarian Faith*, p. 69; emphasis mine.
[63]  Torrance, *The Trinitarian Faith*, p. 70.
[64]  Athanasius, quoted in Torrance, *The Trinitarian Faith*, p. 70.
[65]  Torrance, *The Trinitarian Faith*, p. 70.

In directly addressing this issue, Torrance insisted that "There is no other God than this God who has revealed himself in this way, and there is no other way for us to conceive of the one being of God in accordance with his divine nature except as Father, Son and Holy Spirit".[66] Everything here turns upon the fact that God eternally exists as Father, Son and Holy Spirit and that this particular God is not remote from us but enables us to know him as he really is in and through his condescension to us by uniting us to himself in his Son and through his Spirit. But this means respecting God's freedom in faith and obedience and not attempting to define God by projecting human images of fatherhood or of anything else into God. Torrance was very convinced, with Barth, that we cannot come to know God by means of our thinking, but only by means of God's grace enabling us to do so. Hence, for Torrance, the ability to know God is not part of our human nature marked by the Fall but must come to us through God's Spirit. We ourselves really can know God without leaving the sphere of human experience and of our relations to created objects used by God to relate with us. It is because God has mediated himself to us historically through the Old and New Testaments that we may know him:

> we know that it is through God's knowing of us that we are enabled to know him … Thus our knowing of God rests not on a center in ourselves but on a center in God, not on the ground of our own being but on the free ground of God's being. Our ability to know him is grounded not in some capacity of our own but in the activity of God in opening himself to our knowing and in actually making himself known to us through his Word.[67]

Torrance insisted that we "can know nothing of God apart from God and without being sustained by God through his self-revealing activity in Word and Spirit".[68]

It is, of course, the incarnation that plays a central role here. Since Jesus *is* the Word of God incarnate, we think from a center in God present among us in history when we begin our thinking in faith with him; he provides the divine approach to us and the human response required of us in our two-way relation with God from within our human experience. Because of the incarnation there is an "anthropomorphic component" to our relationship with God grounded in God's act of revelation. This component, however, is no merely cultural "inheritance" "that we may replace as we choose" because "it is not something defined by what we human beings are of ourselves and projected by us onto God in our conceiving of him".[69] Because the image of God is not something that "inheres in man's nature" but is the relation established between God and us in Christ and through the Spirit,

---

[66]   Torrance, "Apprehension of God the Father": 121.

[67]   Torrance, "Apprehension of God the Father": 123. See also Torrance, *Calvin's Doctrine of Man*, pp. 123, 146-7.

[68]   Torrance, "Apprehension of God the Father": 123–4.

[69]   Torrance, "Apprehension of God the Father": 124.

Torrance insisted that "any self-projection of the human into God—*eristis sicut Deus*—is ruled out". Yet he also maintains that "a real man–Godward relation is given an integral place in the Creator/creature relationship" so that there has to be an "anthropomorphic element" in the way we know and speak of God.[70]

## Imageless Thinking of God

How, then, does Torrance answer the crucial question of how we know God with our human views and concepts (which are, of course, anthropomorphic) without projecting them into God? Torrance's answer is simple but with profound implications: "In Jesus we encounter the very EGO EIMI of God, so that in him we are summoned to know God in accordance with the way in which he has actually objectified himself for us in our human existence and communicated himself within the structure and modes of our human knowing and speaking."[71] But there is an important proviso here: just because it is we who know God in Christ as he is in himself, that does not mean we can read back any of our human characteristics into God. It is here that Torrance relied upon the patrisitic notion that we must think of God imagelessly. This concept is not as odd as it might first appear. By this expression Torrance means that although our human images are in no sense descriptive of God since they only point to human relationships and experience, they are used by God to point beyond their usual meaning to who God is in himself. If we renounce any sort of reliance on ourselves and our concepts, as we must if we are following Christ, then precisely by relying on him and through the power of his Holy Spirit, God himself enables us to know him as he really is "imagelessly", that is, in a way that does not project our human experiences and images into God but allows God to define himself to us through our human images. In another context, Torrance explains what he means here by linking the *homoousion* of the Son with the *homoousion* of the Spirit insisting that as Father, Son and Spirit are coinherent in one God, so one cannot separate the *homoousion* of the Son from that of the Spirit. If such a separation were to occur, then we would project our images into God and "subordinate him in our thought to, the creaturely representations in our conceiving of him" because to focus merely on the *homoousion* of the Son without that of the Spirit would inevitably end in projection and prohibit us from actually knowing God in his internal relations. Still, if we merely focused on the *homoousion* of the Spirit abstracting from that of the Son, then "we would have no conceptual content in our reference back to God apart from what we might derive from our own subjective states".[72]

---

[70]   Torrance, "Apprehension of God the Father": 125.

[71]   Torrance, "Apprehension of God the Father": 126–7.

[72]   See T.F. Torrance, "Theological Realism", pp. 169–96 in *The Philosophical Frontiers of Christian Theology: Essays presented to D. M. MacKinnon*, Brian Hebblethwaite and Stewart Sutherland (eds), (Cambridge: Cambridge University Press, 1982), pp. 191–2.

For Torrance, all our knowing is "humanly conditioned" and we should not even want to escape that in light of the incarnation. There has to be an "anthropomorphic element" in our knowledge of God for without it God becomes no more than an abstraction or a "negative borderline concept empty of living content".[73] Nonetheless, theology must be self-critical because of the constant danger of projection as just noted. It is in this sense that Torrance emphasizes that the early church adopted the Hebraic form of thought that held that "all images properly used in speech and thought of God refer to him away from themselves *without imaging him*".[74] What exactly does this mean? Given what was just said, it certainly does not mean that we do away with our images. What it does suggest is that we must think of God "in a 'see-through' way and *not* in any mimetic or descriptive way".[75] In other words, we must allow God to reveal himself to us in and through our concepts or images and not without them, while at the same time we must not attempt to project our human experience and thoughts into God, limiting him to what we think God can or cannot be. Our images do not mimic God as in Greek thought. Rather, Nicene theology followed the Hebraic idea that "all images properly used in speech and thought of God refer to him *without imaging him*".[76] That indeed was exactly the error of Arius. He did not realize that "the Father/Son relation is essentially a relation in the Spirit, and that does not allow us to read material images back into God".[77] Thinking mythologically is what Arius did and, for Torrance, that constituted an attempt to understand God from a center "in the human self and its fantasies" and thus it failed to acknowledge that God's inner being is not "dumb" but "eloquent" because, as Hilary held, God's Word is a reality and indeed his Word is part of the eternal reality of the triune God.

At this point it is important to realize that the crucial differences between Nicene and Hellenic thought included the concepts of *word* and *activity* in addition to the notion of *image*. Word (λόγος) was Christianized so that, in contrast to the Greek view of logos as "an abstract cosmological principle", Christians stressed that the Logos inheres in the very being of God (ἐνούσιος λόγος) and is identical with the

---

[73]  Torrance, "Apprehension of God the Father": 128.

[74]  Torrance, "Apprehension of God the Father": 129. See also, Torrance, *The Trinitarian Faith*, pp. 71ff.

[75]  Torrance, "Apprehension of God the Father": 129.

[76]  Torrance, *The Trinitarian Faith*, p. 71.

[77]  Torrance, *The Trinitarian Faith*, p. 72. This is why Torrance insisted that "God is to be acknowledged as eternally Father in himself, as Father of the Son, before the foundation of the world and apart from the creation, and so is Father in a sense that is absolutely unique and transcendent" (Torrance, *The Christian Doctrine of God*, p. 57). While Jesus' teaching appealed to the Pentateuch, the Prophets and the Psalms in ways that compared God's power and compassion to the characteristics of human fathers and mothers, in no way did he read these human conceptions "into the Nature of God, as was common with the heathen notions of Deity abhorred in the Old Testament" (Torrance, *The Christian Doctrine of God*, p. 55).

Person of the Son.[78] God is thus "intrinsically eloquent, speaking being".[79] God is not dumb in his inner being. In reality it is this ontological concept of *Logos* that set the Christian view of revelation apart because, for Christians, such revelation is identical with God's objective self-communication in his Word with the result that *theologia*, or thinking about God "from a controlling centre in his Word, was sharply differentiated from all *mythologia*, thinking of God from a centre in the human self and its fantasies".[80] This is why Torrance so adamantly opposed trying to understand God by negating human experience. He believed that such an approach to God meant that in the end we are flung back upon ourselves to verify our knowledge of God, and, for Torrance, that is exactly what must not happen because it opens the door directly to fantasy instead of to genuine knowledge of the reality of God who speaks his eloquent Word in the very person and work of Jesus of Nazareth.[81]

And this thinking has profound implications for the doctrine of the Holy Spirit. Since the Spirit is the Spirit of the Father and the Son (Word) from all eternity, we can only understand the Spirit through his Word and inseparably united with his Word. That is why Athanasius also "turned sharply away from any conception of the Logos as a cosmological principle (or of *logoi spermatikoi*, 'seminal reasons', immanent in the universe) occupying an intermediate status between God and creation".[82] Instead, "Athanasius developed the doctrine of the Spirit from his essential relation to the one God and his undivided co-activity with the Father and the Son, and specifically from his inherence in the being of the eternal Son".[83] In this way, Athanasius preserved the unity of the Trinity by arguing that "The Father does all things through the Word and in the Holy Spirit".[84] In addition, "The Holy Spirit does not bring to us any independent knowledge of God, or add any new content to God's self-revelation".[85] "Thus, knowledge of the Spirit as well as of the Father is taken from and is controlled by knowledge of the Son".[86] In addition, the Christian doctrine of *creatio ex nihilo* through God's Word and Spirit altered the Greek view of *logos* in relation to created being so that Christians could emphasize that all creation has a contingent intelligibility endowed by God that could not be confused with God's self-sufficient intelligibility; this eventually opened the door to the development of empirical science, according to Torrance.

The Greek notion of activity (ἐνέργεια) was also radically transformed. Although, for Aristotle, God was characterized by an "activity of immobility" and

---

78   Torrance, *The Trinitarian Faith*, p. 72.
79   Torrance, *The Trinitarian Faith*, p. 73.
80   Torrance, *The Trinitarian Faith*, p. 73.
81   See Torrance, *The Trinitarian Faith*, p. 51.
82   Torrance, *The Trinitarian Faith*, p. 201.
83   Torrance, *The Trinitarian Faith*, p. 201.
84   Torrance, *The Trinitarian Faith*, p. 202.
85   Torrance, *The Trinitarian Faith*, p. 203.
86   Torrance, *The Trinitarian Faith*, p. 203.

one who moves the world only as "the object of the world's desire", [87] Athanasius envisioned both activity and movement as intrinsic to the very being of God. Hence, God was not at all inactive in his inner being; he was instead able to move, energize and act. Nicene theologians therefore thought of Jesus Christ "as one with God the Father in *act* as well as in *being*, for he incarnated the *active presence* of God himself in human history, and constituted in all he was and did the free outgoing movement of the divine being in condescension and love toward mankind".[88] This divine saving love spoken of by Athanasius contrasted sharply with Aristotle's notion of *eros* which meant "the immanent desire for itself by which the unmoved Mover timelessly affects the world".[89] This Aristotelian view meant that there could be no idea of *creatio ex nihilo* and also meant that time could only be thought of as eternal; on these two points Christianity and Hellenism found themselves opposed once again.

It is in this context in which the Greek concepts of *image*, *word* and *activity* were so changed that Torrance understands the church's use of the terms "Father" and "Son". For Torrance, "the concepts of fatherhood and sonship do not derive from any analogy or inherent likeness between the creature and Creator".[90] Rather they are used by God to point away from all creaturely content to God's transcendent and eternal reality as Father "apart from and altogether antecedent to any relation with us".[91] God is our Father as well, but only because he has freely loved us in and through his Son Jesus Christ. For Torrance, human fatherhood cannot be the standard for understanding God's Fatherhood. This would amount to a reversal of the Creator/creature relationship. We must, according to Torrance, think of God's Fatherhood in a spiritual way (because God is Spirit, John 4:24) and we must think of him in an *imageless* way, which means "without ever reading back descriptively

---

[87]   Torrance, *The Trinitarian Faith*, p. 73.

[88]   Torrance, *The Trinitarian Faith*, p. 74.

[89]   Torrance, *The Trinitarian Faith*, p. 74.

[90]   Torrance, "Apprehension of God the Father": 129. This is an enormously important point and it distinguishes Torrance's thinking about analogy most clearly from that of much feminist thought as articulated for example by Elizabeth Johnson who thinks in exactly the opposite way: "… analogy … means that while it [human naming of God] starts from the relationship of paternity experienced at its best in this world, its inner dynamism negates the creaturely mode to assert that God is more unlike than like even the best human father …" [Elizabeth A. Johnson, *She Who Is: The Mystery of God in Feminist Theological Discourse* (New York: Crossroad, 1992), p. 173]. For Torrance, "God is not to be understood on the analogy of our finite creaturely being" (Torrance, *The Christian Doctrine of God*, p. 236). Nor is God to be understood by negating our creaturely experience because if that is thought possible, then in reality we are thinking from a center in ourselves and negating that in order to achieve knowledge of God instead of actually relying in faith on God's disclosure of himself.

[91]   Torrance, "Apprehension of God the Father": 129.

into God the creaturely content or finite imagery of human fatherhood", since, according to Exodus 20:4, we may not make any image or likeness of God.[92]

The ultimate issue here concerns whether or not one will accept revelation on its own terms. Revelation, as understood at Nicaea, is identical with the person and work of Jesus Christ himself. That is why, as we shall see shortly, the *homoousion* was so important to them and should be so for us. Because Torrance will not allow his thinking to deviate from Jesus Christ even slightly, he resolutely maintains that "We cannot go behind the incarnation, for there is in fact no God behind the back of Jesus Christ, and no God apart from his own self-revelation".[93] But it is just at this point that the crucial questions in trinitarian theology arise. Did God become incarnate in Jesus Christ in such a way that he is man without remainder? Did God, in other words, hand himself over to us conceptually in a certain sense in the incarnation? In this perspective, Torrance very carefully distinguishes his thought in a way that is not usually the case among contemporary theologians. He argues that although it is truly the eternal God whom we know in Jesus Christ and only in him, that neither means that God does not continue to have his own life in himself nor does it mean that his freedom as God has been reduced to his life for us. It is here that the question of agnosticism becomes acute.

Although many react to this predicament by explicitly retreating to an agnostic position and then thinking mythologically from a center in human experience, Torrance sticks to the revelation of God in Jesus Christ and asserts that whereas we may apprehend God in Jesus Christ through faith, "we cannot comprehend him".[94] Following patristic thought here, Torrance holds that

> Only God can comprehend himself, and only God can name himself—hence his unique self-revelation and ineffable self-naming to us as *Yahweh, I am who I am, I shall be who I shall be.* What God ultimately is in the essence of his eternal being we cannot know, but we are given by God to know *who* he is.[95]

---

[92]   Torrance, "Apprehension of God the Father": 130.

[93]   Torrance, "Apprehension of God the Father": 136. See also Torrance, *Karl Barth*, p. 201.

[94]   Torrance, "Apprehension of God the Father": 136.

[95]   Torrance, "Apprehension of God the Father": 136. Following Athanasius, Torrance repeats this idea in *The Trinitarian Faith*: "To know God in this way [through his self-revelation in his Word and Spirit] does not mean that we can know *what* the being of God is, but it does mean that we are given knowledge of God that is directly and objectively grounded in his eternal being" (p. 67). That is the function of the doctrine of the Trinity— through Jesus Christ and in the Holy Spirit we may really have a "conceptual grasp of God in his own internal relations" in spite of the fact that we do not know God as God knows himself. That limitation in our knowledge of God remains and it must be respected always.

Torrance therefore maintains a proper apophaticism and not an agnostic view at this critical point. And the possibility and limit of his thinking at this juncture crucially revolves around the person of Jesus Christ himself. Here Torrance emphasizes the fact that it is through the Holy Spirit alone that we may hear the Word of God who remains hidden even in his self-revelation:

> ... the Holy Spirit confronts us with the sheer mystery, unnameability and ultimate incomprehensibility of the Lord God ... Through the presence of Holy Spirit we ... are enabled to apprehend him [the Holy Trinity], yet only in such a way that what he is as God (τί ἐστι θεός) is completely veiled from us.[96]

The Holy Spirit follows the work of the incarnate Son and cannot be separated from the Word in any way. It is indeed the Holy Spirit, who is *homoousion* with the Father and Son, who enables us to know God within our creaturely conditions, through our thoughts and in our speech, but, as Torrance emphasizes, following Athanasius: "without any compromise of his sheer Godness or any diminution of the mystery of this transcendent Being. 'Thus far human knowledge goes. Here the cherubim spread the covering of their wings.'"[97] Because God is Spirit, God must be known in a "spiritual way" in accordance with his nature and thus "in a completely genderless way".[98] The term "Spirit" therefore has a double meaning: it means first that God himself is Spirit, as it says in John 4:24, and in this way it refers absolutely to the being of God without adverting to the distinction of persons; and second it means that the Holy Spirit is the distinct person within the Trinity, so that considered "relatively" the Spirit is distinct from and together the Father and Son from all eternity.[99] Torrance will even say that just as the Son is the image of the Father, the Spirit is the image of the Son in the sense that the Spirit himself is imageless. This means that since Father, Son and Spirit are of the same nature, they must be understood in an "imageless and wholly spiritual way". That implies that God is and remains ineffable in his eternal relations and also in his relations with us. Citing Basil, Torrance writes, "We confess that we know what is knowable of God and yet what we know reaches beyond our comprehension."[100]

Torrance also stressed that this same Holy Spirit which "guards the ultimate unknowableness of God" takes us into communion with himself and thereby opens himself to be known and enables us to know him by including us in his self-revelation. God is not only free in himself but he is free to impart himself to us without ceasing to be God. The Holy Spirit thus actualizes in us our reconciliation with God and God's reconciliation with us that was effected by God in Christ. Hence, Torrance can say at one and the same time that God remains hidden in

---

[96]   Torrance, *The Christian Doctrine of God*, p. 151.
[97]   Torrance, *The Christian Doctrine of God*, p. 151.
[98]   Torrance, *The Christian Doctrine of God*, p. 158.
[99]   Torrance, *The Christian Doctrine of God*, p. 148.
[100]   Torrance, *The Christian Doctrine of God*, p. 158.

himself and revealed to us in the communion he establishes in and through his Son and the Holy Spirit. So, while God dwells in unapproachable light, he is revealed to us through the "shining of his Light upon the face of Jesus Christ and through the enlightening presence of his Spirit who leads us into the truth as it is in Jesus",[101] so that the *homoousion* enables us to recognize that Father and Son are of one nature and that they exist in a *relation* beyond what is ascertainable in our ordinary language, for the truth signified in the terms "lies beyond the limits of the terms used to signifiy it".[102] Still,

> This does not mean that God is in himself in the depths of his eternal Being, other than what he has revealed of himself in the Gospel as the Father of the Son, but rather that we are unable to pierce behind what God has revealed of himself apart from his self-revelation to us.[103]

### Homoousion

We have already seen how the *homoousion* (the oneness in being and act of the Father, Son and Holy Spirit) enabled Torrance to oppose all forms of dualism as well as subjectivism, agnosticism and Arianism in order to present the truth of the Gospel in a trinitarian way that is faithful to who God is *in se* and *ad extra*. Now let us briefly note how this important concept structures much of what Torrance says throughout his doctrine of the Trinity and Christology in such a way that without it not only would there be no true knowledge of God, but there would be no true knowledge of creation, salvation and redemption either. Everything quite literally hinges on the fact that Father, Son and Spirit are one in being and action. As Torrance himself asserts in connection with the incarnation:

> The *homoousion* crystallizes the conviction that while the incarnation falls within the structures of our spatio-temporal humanity in this world, it also falls within the Life and Being of God … Jesus Christ is not a mere symbol … detached from God, but God in his own Being and Act come among us … the *homoousion* is the ontological and epistemological linchpin of Christian theology.[104]

Even the doctrine of creation itself, Torrance insisted, "hinges upon the *homoousion*, that is, upon whether it was through Jesus Christ who is of one substance with the

---

[101]   Torrance, *The Christian Doctrine of God*, p. 159.
[102]   Torrance, *The Christian Doctrine of God*, p. 159.
[103]   Torrance, *The Christian Doctrine of God*, p. 159.
[104]   Torrance, *The Christian Doctrine of God*, p. 95.

Father that 'all things were made'".[105] And "the *homoousion* applied to the Spirit as well as the Son".[106]

In trinitarian theology proper, Torrance viewed the *homoousion* as a "bulwark against Sabellianism and Arianism, against Unitarianism and polytheism, alike".[107] Of course, during the Arian crisis the issue arose as to whether or not such a term was appropriate at all since it is was not a biblical term. But that was no problem for Athanasius since his main concern was not the actual biblical words or terms themselves but rather their meaning and the realities to which they referred. According to Torrance, terms such as *ousia* and *homoousios* "applied to God in the Council of Nicaea were not employed with the sense commonly given them in Greek textbooks, but only with the new meaning given them under the transforming impact of God's self-revelation in Jesus Christ".[108] It is in this sense that, according to Torrance, "the Nicene ὁμοούσιος τῳ Πατρί was a *hermeneutical* as well as a *theological* instrument".[109] When Scripture was read in such a way that the oneness in being and act of the Father and Son was allowed to govern the meaning of the text, then the church was engaged in properly interpreting the Scriptures. But what exactly does the *homoousios* refer to?

First, as noted above, the *homoousion* conveys the all-important notion that

> ... what God is "toward us" and "in the midst of us" in and through the Word made flesh, he really is **in himself**; that he is in the **internal relations** of his transcendent being the very same Father, Son and Holy Spirit that he is in his revealing and saving activity in time and space toward mankind.[110]

Second, *ousia* was distinguished from *hypostasis* and given a personal meaning in line with who God is in his internal relations and different from the usual meaning they had in classical Greek. Thus, *homoousios* refers to the "immanent personal relations in the Godhead", whereas *hypostasis* refers to the persons of the Trinity in their inner *enhypostatic* or consubstantial relations in which each is fully God yet the Father is the Father and not the Son, and the Son is the Son and not the Father or the Holy Spirit. Father, Son and Spirit, then, are one and equal in such a

---

[105]  Torrance, *The Trinitarian Faith*, p. 109.
[106]  Torrance, *The Trinitarian Faith*, p. 216.
[107]  Torrance, *The Trinitarian Faith*, p. 125.
[108]  Torrance, *The Trinitarian Faith*, p. 129.
[109]  Torrance, *The Trinitarian Faith*, p. 129.
[110]  Torrance, *The Trinitarian Faith*, p. 130. Also, Torrance, *The Christian Doctrine of God*, p. 130. What Torrance had in mind here is the revolutionary character of the *homoousion* formulated at the Council of Nicaea. Because the council stressed that what God is toward us he is in himself, the ground was cut out from under dualism, modalism and tritheism.

way that God was to be understood as "one Being, three Persons".[111] For Torrance, both *ousia* and *hypostasis* describe "'being' as such" in the expression "one Being, three Persons". Yet, Torrance makes a further important distinction: "Being or οὐσία is being considered in its internal relations, and Person or ὑπόστασις is being considered in its otherness, i.e. in the objective relations between the Persons".[112] This is a difficult point and Torrance offers another helpful distinction to clarify what he means here. He distinguishes between the Father "considered absolutely, as he is in himself" and "the Father considered relatively to the Son". It is, of course, one and the same being of the Father being considered in both cases. Yet, the term "Father" has this double reference. The Father is God *in se* as *ousia* (being) and at the same time the Father is *ad alium* (for others) as *hypostasis* (person). This distinction is crucial because it allows Torrance to say that while the three persons exist in relation to each other, they have in common only one Being. For Torrance, God is not to be thought of as "isolated in himself" but rather as a "*Being for others (ad alios)*". Hence, God's being for others is actually grounded in his own internal and transcendent freedom: "God lives and moves and has his Being *for us* as well as for himself."[113] Torrance does not blur the distinction between the immanent and economic Trinity here. He simply wishes to stress that because God is inherently one Being, three Persons, therefore what God is in himself is "onto-personal", that is, the three Divine Persons are "*for one another*" so that God is "inherently altruistic, *Being for others, Being who loves*".[114] Again, Torrance is very clear here in distinguishing without separating the immanent and economic Trinity, as when he says that while God does indeed seek and create communion between himself and us, that relation with us should not be seen "as something necessary for his existence as God, but as flowing freely from the ground and will of his transcendent Self-being".[115]

Third, the oneness in being, act and word between Jesus Christ and God the Father concerned the integrity of the Gospel itself. Therefore, the primary intention of the Councils of Nicaea and Constantinople in formulating the *homoousion* was to be faithful to the Gospel and to offer an authoritative confession "that enshrines at its heart the supreme evangelical truth by which the Church stands or falls".[116] It is here that Torrance clarifies his thinking about the wide-ranging implications of the *homoousion* by asking what exactly would be implied if there were no oneness in being between the incarnate Son and the Father. In reality, Torrance insists that the main point of the *homoousion* is to assert "that Jesus Christ is *God*". When Arius denied this by thinking of Jesus merely as a creature, that denial allowed

---

[111]   Torrance, *The Trinitarian Faith*, p. 131. Also, Torrance, *The Christian Doctrine of God*, pp. 130–131.

[112]   Torrance, *The Christian Doctrine of God*, p. 131.

[113]   Torrance, *The Christian Doctrine of God*, p. 131.

[114]   Torrance, *The Christian Doctrine of God*, p. 131.

[115]   Torrance, *The Christian Doctrine of God*, p. 132.

[116]   Torrance, *The Trinitarian Faith*, p. 132.

Arius to assert that God remains "utterly unknowable". Cutting the ontological bond between Jesus, the incarnate Son, and the Father meant "there would be no identity between God and the content of his revelation" and thus no access to God the Father through the Son and in the Spirit: "Hence we would be left completely in the dark about God. God would be for us no more than an absolute blank, of which we can neither think nor speak."[117] This is the kind of thinking that then opens the door to mythology and to projecting images of God from our own experience instead of actually knowing God objectively and in truth through his own self-revelation in his Word and Spirit. What is more, the *homoousion* "grounds the reality of our Lord's *humanity*" and thus of all that Jesus did for us "in an indivisible union with the eternal being of God".[118] Jesus, the incarnate Son is not only *homoousion* with the Father from all eternity, he is *homoousion* with us in our humanity so that the heart of the Gospel consists in the fact that "God himself came among us precisely as man".[119] God meets us in this man and shares our complete humanity.

The *homoousion* also affected the way salvation and grace were understood. According to Athanasius, creatures could never be saved by other creatures. If Jesus Christ is not understood correctly as the very incarnation of the eternal God himself acting as our Savior, then he is utterly incapable of helping us divinely as only God can. Jesus Christ heals, forgives, reconciles and redeems lost humanity precisely because he, the incarnate Son of the Father, is one in Being with the Father in such a way that the Father Almighty acts for us and our salvation in what Jesus is and does for us. Hence, "Unless Jesus' words and acts of forgiving love are completely backed up by the sheer being and reality of God, they do not finally amount to anything".[120] The cross of Christ is itself the reconciling act of God in history exactly because God himself was immediately and directly active in Christ's suffering and death for us. Torrance cites Gregory Nazianzen to stress that "We were put to death together with him, that we might be cleansed; we rose again with him, because we were put to death with him; we were glorified with him, because we rose again with him".[121]

Moreover, because God is the content of his revelation and activity in the incarnate Son, therefore "In Jesus Christ the Giver of grace and the Gift of grace are one and the same, for in him and through him it is none other than God himself who is savingly and creatively at work for us and our salvation".[122] That is why it is only through union with Christ in his true humanity that we can be saved.

---

[117]  Torrance, *The Trinitarian Faith*, p. 133.

[118]  Torrance, *The Trinitarian Faith*, p. 135.

[119]  Torrance, *The Trinitarian Faith*, p. 136.

[120]  Torrance, *The Trinitarian Faith*, p. 142.

[121]  Torrance, *The Trinitarian Faith*, p. 142.

[122]  Torrance, *The Trinitarian Faith*, p. 138. See also Torrance, *The Christian Doctrine of God*, pp. 21, 63, 100. For Torrance, "The Holy Spirit is no less than the Son the self-giving of God, for in him the divine Gift and the divine Giver are identical. This is why the

Rejecting any notion that grace is "a created medium between God and man", Nicene theologians understood grace as God's self-giving "in his *incarnate* Son in whom the Gift and Giver are indivisibly one".[123] Because grace is "governed by the oneness of the Father and the Son, grace cannot be regarded as a detachable and transferable divine quality which may inhere in or be possessed by the human being to whom it is given in virtue of which he is somehow 'deified' or 'divinised'".[124] This is an extremely important point in Torrance's thought because it is just the union of the Father and Son that precludes any search for knowledge of God except in and through the grace of God revealed, namely, Jesus Christ himself. That is the significance of his often repeated assertion that we must think from a center in God provided by God himself (Jesus Christ) and not from a center in ourselves. That is what it means to live by grace. Whenever grace is detached from Christ himself as its active agent either theoretically or practically, then theology will be searching in the wrong places to understand who God really is and who we are in relation to God. Following the thinking of Athanasius in his letters to Serapion, Torrance stresses that just as "The Holy Spirit is always the same, and does not belong to those who partake, but all things partake of him",[125] so grace is God's very own self-gift in Jesus Christ and thus it cannot be separated from him in any way whatsoever: "This self-giving of God in grace is no more divisible than the one being and activity of the Holy Trinity".[126]

Finally, the *homoousion* also affects the way redemption is understood. It is because Jesus Christ is true God of true God that the ultimate destiny of the human race is not some "utterly unknown, arbitrary Deity who bears no relation to Jesus Christ or all he stood for".[127] Precisely because Jesus Christ experienced judgment on our behalf as the Mediator, therefore we know that it is through him that God will judge humanity on the last day. Thus the *homoousion* makes an enormous difference in our understanding of divine judgment because it stresses that "The judgment of Jesus and the judgment of God are one and the same".[128] When the Nicene creed says that Christ's Kingdom will have no end, what is being emphasized is that "the incarnation does not finally vanish away but remains on into eternity".[129]

It is in these ways, then, that the *homoousion* was seen as the main point of Christian orthodoxy and godliness because, as Gregory Nyssen believed, to reject it meant to reject the message of salvation which was the content of the Gospel

---

*homoousion* was applied to the understanding of the nature and identity of the Holy Spirit" (p. 147).

[123]   Torrance, *The Trinitarian Faith*, p. 140.
[124]   Torrance, *The Trinitarian Faith*, p. 140.
[125]   Athanasius, *Ad Ser.*, 1.27 cited in Torrance, *The Trinitarian Faith*, p. 140.
[126]   Torrance, *The Trinitarian Faith*, p. 141.
[127]   Torrance, *The Trinitarian Faith*, p. 143.
[128]   Torrance, *The Trinitarian Faith*, p. 143.
[129]   Torrance, *The Trinitarian Faith*, p. 143.

message. There were far-reaching implications to the *homoousion* because it meant that what Jesus Christ "experienced, said, and undertook for us and our salvation, is grounded in God and has been assumed into God as his very own", so that his fully human life "for ever belongs to the innermost being and life of the Godhead".[130] The Nicene *homoousion* was a decisive and irreversible step in the history of Christian theology because it was "a giant step forward ... in grasping the inner ontological coherence of the Gospel as it had been mediated through the apostolic Scriptures".[131] This is the case, as we have seen, because the *homoousion* applies not only to the relation of the Father and Son in eternity but also to the incarnate Son and the Father, so that it is just as important to stress Jesus' oneness in being with us, for, without that, the Gospel loses its essential meaning, which is that unless Christ is fully human as well as fully divine, it is not we human beings who are truly saved in him. We will consider that aspect of Torrance's thought when we come specifically to the atonement and how Torrance's understanding of that is structured by his trinitarian theology.

A brief consideration of several more important concepts will bring to an end our discussion of Torrance's trinitarian theology and open the door to our reflections on his important understanding of the doctrine of creation as that doctrine is also shaped by his understanding of the Trinity. Let us begin with Torrance's "onto-relational" understanding of the concept of persons.

## Onto-relational Understanding of Person

What is revealed in our encounter with Jesus Christ, the Word of God incarnate, and through the power of his Holy Spirit is the fact that by nature God is "a Communion in himself" and that he freely loves us in such a way that, while his Being is in no way "constituted" by his relation to us, his free movement of love toward and for us reveals the nature of his transcendence and immanence. God's presence is his being and his presence is to be seen as "*personal, dynamic and relational Being*".[132] Torrance has not now shifted his thinking into an abstract consideration of being as relational and dynamic. Rather, his very concept of being is determined by the being of the immanent and economic Trinity as the activity of the living God, so that he insists that God's being is both "fellowship-creating or communion-constituting Being" toward us and "ever-living, ever-dynamic *Communion* (κοινωνία) in the Godhead".[133] His thinking is grounded simultaneously in the Old Testament emphasis on God's naming himself without resigning his transcendence or glory as the covenant partner of Israel, so that in spite of Israel's unfaithfulness he holds on to them with "unswerving fidelity ... in

---

[130]  Torrance, *The Trinitarian Faith*, p. 144.
[131]  Torrance, *The Trinitarian Faith*, pp. 144–5.
[132]  Torrance, *The Christian Doctrine of God*, pp. 123–4.
[133]  Torrance, *The Christian Doctrine of God*, p. 124.

order to heal them of their unfaithfulness and restore them to true fellowship with him in his love".[134] When God revealed himself as *Yahweh* or *I am who I am/I will be who I will be*, he revealed himself as at once the Lord of the covenant and the one who renews and maintains the covenant in the face of sin. This understanding of God is quite different from the static metaphysical notion of essence or substance offered in Greek philosophy. Torrance explicitly connected his understanding of the Old Testament *I am* with the New Testament *I am* articulated by Jesus as recounted in John's Gospel: "'I am the Light of the World', 'I am the bread of life', 'I am the Resurrection and the life', 'I am the Vine', 'I am the Way, the Truth and the Life', 'I am with you', etc."[135] in order to stress that Jesus' *I am* is "grounded in the indwelling of the Father and the Son in one another, in the eternal Communion which belongs to the inner Life of God as Father, Son and Holy Spirit", as echoed in John 14:10 in the statement that "I am in the Father and the Father is in me".[136]

It is also worth mentioning in this context Torrance's repeated stress upon Matthew 11:27 and Luke 10:22 to which the Nicene Fathers often appealed: "All things have been delivered to me by my Father; and no one knows who the Son is except the Father; and no one knows who the Father is except the Son and any one to whom the Son chooses to reveal him."[137] This mutual knowing itself involved "a mutual relation of *being* between them as well". And this relation of being applies not only to the immanent trinitarian relation of the Father and Son but also to the incarnate Son's relation to the Father in such a way that "we are given access to the closed circle of divine knowing between the Father and the Son only through cognitive union with Christ, that is only through an interrelation of knowing and being between us and the incarnate Son, although in our case this union is one of participation through grace and not one of nature".[138] Here Christocentrism and Theocentrism coincide and are properly understood in and through the activity of the Holy Spirit uniting us to Christ and through him to the Father. Torrance was adamant that any prior knowledge must be completely reconstructed through our "sharing in the mutual knowing of the Father and the Son".[139] Two other scriptural passages were important here as well: 1 Corinthians 2:10 and John 14:6, so that Torrance stresses, on the one hand, that we cannot possibly understand the things

---

[134]   Torrance, *The Christian Doctrine of God*, p. 123.

[135]   Torrance, *The Christian Doctrine of God*, p. 124.

[136]   Torrance, *The Christian Doctrine of God*, p. 124.

[137]   Torrance, *The Trinitarian Faith*, p. 58. See also Torrance, *The Christian Doctrine of God*, pp. 77–8; T.F. Torrance, *Reality and Evangelical Theology* (Philadelphia: The Westminster Press, 1982), p. 111; Thomas F. Torrance, *The Doctrine of Jesus Christ* (Eugene, OR: Wipf and Stock Publishers, 2002), p. 44 (this volume represents Torrance's lectures at Auburn given in 1938–39); "The Christian Apprehension of God the Father", p. 120; Torrance, "Athanasius", *Theology in Reconciliation*, p. 223; Torrance, "Athanasius", *Divine Meaning*, p. 187; Torrance, *Karl Barth*, p. 214.

[138]   Torrance, *The Trinitarian Faith*, p. 59.

[139]   Torrance, *The Trinitarian Faith*, p. 60.

that God has prepared for those who love him without the Spirit of God enabling it, while, on the other hand, he can stress that because Jesus is the Way and the Truth and the Life no one can come to the Father except through him. A trinitarian perspective is here determined by the fact that our knowledge of and relationship with God the Father almighty takes place only in and through the Spirit uniting us conceptually and existentially to the Son and thus to the Father.

The upshot of all this is Torrance's onto-relational understanding of the term "Person". When the Old Testament and New Testament concepts just described were coupled together during the church's formulation of the doctrine of the Trinity, this led to the idea that God is fully personal and relational in the very structure of his inner being since "the three divine Persons in their Communion with one another *are* the Triune Being of God, and there is no other God but he who is Father, Son and Holy Spirit".[140] Here there is union in distinction and distinction in union between the Father, Son and Spirit. By onto-relational, Torrance means to stress that God is three Persons in the heart of his being and that as such God is dynamic, relational and personal as the living God who loves *in se* and *ad extra*. That is why Torrance can emphasize that "the ontic relations between the divine Persons belong to what they are as Persons", so that "No divine Person is who he is without essential relation to the other two, and yet each divine Person is other than and distinct from the other two".[141] Each of the Persons is wholly and completely God but each is hypostatically interconnected with the other in such a way that together they constitute the indivisible unity of the Trinity. This leads to Torrance's all-important point that the Godhead is complete not in the Father only but also in the Son and Spirit. "These ontic and holistic interrelations between the three divine Persons in virtue of which they are what and who they are as Persons are substantive relations (οὐσιώδεις σχέσεις) or onto-relations."[142] Because the divine Persons are who and what they only in relation to each other from all eternity, Torrance calls them onto-relations: "That is to say, the relations between the divine Persons belong to what they are as Persons—they are constitutive onto-relations. 'Person' is an onto-relational concept."[143] It is here that Torrance's conception of *perichoresis* can be understood in its connection with the *homoousion*.

## *Perichoresis*

This is a term which will arise throughout this book. Here it is sufficient to note that for Torrance this concept helps to clarify the onto-relations of the three divine Persons. In a refined form, the term *perichoresis* (περιχώρησις) illuminates "the biblical teaching about the mutual indwelling of the Father and the Son and the

---

[140]  Torrance, *The Christian Doctrine of God*, p. 124.
[141]  Torrance, *The Christian Doctrine of God*, pp. 156–7.
[142]  Torrance, *The Christian Doctrine of God*, p. 157.
[143]  Torrance, *The Christian Doctrine of God*, p. 157.

Spirit and thus about the Communion of the Spirit". *Perichoresis* originates from a combination of two words *chora* (χώρα), the Greek word for "space" or "room", and *chorein* (χώρειν), which means "to contain", "to make room" or "to go forward", and means that there is a kind of "mutual containing or enveloping of realities" which can be described as a type of *"coinherence* or *coindwelling"*.[144] Torrance is adamant that this concept, for which Athanasius himself offered a theological basis when he explicated certain statements such as "I am in the Father and the Father in me" from John's Gospel,[145] and which Hilary himself was familiar with, means to "make room for" and to "go to" or "to contain" in deliberate distinction from those who confuse the term χωρέω with χορεύω, which means to dance as in the Greek word χορός or chorus.[146] This is an extremely important clarification because when these terms are confused, a pantheistic perspective that sees communion as an umbrella concept encompassing both divine and human being replaces the clear trinitarian doctrine. In such perspective, the conceptual distinction between divine and human being and communion is lost with the result that theology is reduced to a variation of anthropology and Arian projection once again becomes the only viable option.[147]

*Perichoresis* was first explicitly employed by Gregory Nazianzen with reference to Christ's two natures and how they remain fully what they are (divine and human in the Person of the Son) while also coinhering in one another in such a way that Christ's human nature did not interpenetrate the divine Nature.[148] Then it was applied to the way the three divine Persons of the Trinity "coinhere or inexist in one another while nevertheless remaining other than one another and distinct from one another".[149] As applied to the trinitarian Persons, the meaning of *perichoresis* was refined and changed so that it came to refer to "the complete mutual containing or interpenetration of the three divine Persons, Father, Son and

---

144    Torrance, *The Christian Doctrine of God*, p. 102.

145    Torrance, *The Christian Doctrine of God*, p. 168.

146    Torrance, *The Christian Doctrine of God*, p. 170, n. 8.

147    See, for example, Catherine Mowry LaCugna, *God For Us The Trinity and Christian Life* (San Francisco: Harper San Francisco, 1991), who mistakenly believes that *perichoresis* refers to "the divine dance" and argues that the term should not refer to God's inner life but rather to "divine life as all creatures partake and literally exist in it" (p. 274). Hence, "The exodus of all persons from God and the return of all to God is the divine dance in which God and we are eternal partners" (p. 304).

148    Torrance, *The Christian Doctrine of God*, pp. 102, 170. According to Torrance, the first actual extant use of the term perichoresis was found in the work of an unknown theologian writing on the Trinity which was attributed to Cyril of Alexandria and then used by John of Damascus. While John of Damascus properly understood the way the divine persons had their being in and with the others, he was guilty of having applied its Christological use to the trinitarian in a confusing way so that he actually thought of Christ's divine and human natures, following Maximus, as interpenetrating each other in a way that "easily slips into a Eutychian conception of Christ's humanity" (p. 170, n. 9).

149    Torrance, The *Christian Doctrine of God*, p. 102.

Holy Spirit, in one God". Once this change had taken place, *perichoresis* could no longer be used Christologically to refer to the hypostatic union (the union of natures in the Person of Christ) without gravely damaging our understanding of Christ himself. Torrance contends that whenever this has been attempted in the modern era it has led to some form of "docetic rationalising and depreciating of the humanity of Christ".[150] One of the key functions of this category, however, is to enable us to recognize that the coinherent relations of the Father, Son and Holy Spirit are not temporary manifestations of God's nature but "are eternally grounded in the intrinsic and completely reciprocal relations of the Holy Trinity. In this way, the concept of *perichoresis* serves to hold powerfully together in the doctrine of the Trinity the identity of the divine Being and the intrinsic unity of the three divine Persons."[151] It is precisely here that the close relation of *perichoresis* and the *onto-relational* notion of the divine Persons can be seen since the ontic relations (relations on the level of being) of three persons of the Trinity "belong to what they essentially are in themselves in their distinctive *hypostases*". According to Torrance, a wholly new concept of person "unknown in human thought until then, according to which the relations between persons belong to what persons are" developed with the doctrine of the Trinity.[152] Here the *homoousion, perichoresis* and the *onto-relational* concept of persons function together with the result that God is understood as fully three distinct persons in communion with one another within the eternal Godhead. But that is not the end of it. This onto-relational notion of "person", which developed through the doctrines of Christ and of the Trinity, also could be applied to human persons in ways appropriate to their created nature and reflective of the uncreated way in which God exists as three Persons, one Being. All of these categories were refined and changed through encounter with the revelation of God in Christ and through the Holy Spirit, so that while they had one meaning when applied to human relations and experience, they had quite another when applied to the divine relations and activities *ad intra* and *ad extra*.

In sum, then, we can say that the category *perichoresis* not only helps us clarify and deepen our understanding of the onto-relations of the three divine Persons, but it helps us clarify the threefold yet distinct way in which God has acted and acts toward us in history as Creator, Savior and Redeemer. It also has several other crucial implications as well.

First, when it comes to knowing God, none of the three may be known without the other two:

> No one Person is knowable or known apart from the others. Due to their perichoretic onto-relations with one another in which they have their Being in one another, the Father is not truly known apart from the Son and the Holy

---

[150] Torrance, *The Christian Doctrine of God*, p. 102.

[151] Torrance, *The Christian Doctrine of God*, p. 102.

[152] Torrance, *The Christian Doctrine of God*, p. 102. See also pp. 124, 133, 157 and 163.

Spirit, the Son is not truly known apart from the Father and the Holy Spirit; and
the Holy Spirit is not truly known apart from the Father and the Son.[153]

As we have seen and shall see again, this insight has far-reaching consequences
both for our knowledge of God and our relations with God and each other in all
areas of dogmatic theology.

Second, the divine monarchy (the location of supreme power) cannot be limited
to the Father alone. Because each of the divine Persons is fully God and Lord, the
divine monarchy must be understood to reside in the being of God as one and three.
Here Torrance is critical of some of the Cappadocians, namely, Basil and Gregory
(not Nazianzen), because they made too sharp a distinction between the immanent
and economic Trinity and because they never referred to the Holy Spirit as God.
Further, they thought of the Father as the *archē* and this implied degrees of deity,
thus opening the door to subordinationism which, of course, Torrance strongly
opposes because any such thinking undermines the Deity of the Son and Spirit
and thus calls into question God's actions *ad extra* as Savior and Redeemer.[154]
Torrance objected to the main thrust of their argument which suggested that it
was the first Person of the Trinity who was the "sole Principle or Cause or Source
of Deity" because this weakened Athanasius' view that "whatever we say of the
Father we say of the Son and the Spirit except 'Father'".[155]

Third, there is an order between the divine Persons disclosed in revelation and
"governed by the irreversible relation between the Father and the Son",[156] such
that the Father is first, the Son is second and the Spirit is third. Hence, "there can
be no thought of one Person being ontologically or divinely prior to another or
subsequent to another".[157] What this implies is that the Father is not the "Deifier
of the Son" because in his own eternal Being the Father is not the Father without
the Son, just as the Son is not the Son without the Father. The Father is not to be
seen as the cause of the divine Being but only as first in the order of the persons.[158]
The Son is not less than the Father but wholly God. Since each Person is fully
God, the order within the Trinity does not apply to the Being of the divine Persons
or to their Deity; "they are distinguished by position and not status, by form and

---

[153]    Torrance, *The Christian Doctrine of God*, p. 174.

[154]    See, for example, Torrance, *The Trinitarian Faith*, p. 222, where he writes,
following Epiphanius, "There is no suggestion of any subordinationism in God, for
whatever the Father is, this the Son is and this the Spirit is in the Godhead ... There never
was when the Spirit was not." Further, Torrance insists, following Athanasius, that "there is
a coinherent relation between the Holy Spirit and God the Son, just as there is a coinherent
relation between the Son and the Father" (p. 233).

[155]    Torrance, *The Trinitarian Faith*, p. 241.

[156]    Torrance, *Trinitarian Perspectives*, p. 135.

[157]    Torrance, *The Christian Doctrine of God*, p. 180.

[158]    Torrance, *The Christian Doctrine of God*, p. 180.

not being, by sequence and not power, for they are fully and perfectly equal".[159] According to Torrance, although there are variations of order in Scripture that still point to the indivisible nature and equality of Being of the Persons of the Trinity, Athanasius and Basil warned against changing the traditional order just noted and as embodied in the baptismal formula because of the Sabellian and Eunomian heresies.[160] A change in order would suggest once more that the eternal God was somehow different from what was revealed in his Son and Spirit, or that God is ultimately one and not three in such a way that the deity and power of the Son and Spirit acting for us would be called into question, perhaps in some Arian subordinationist sense. In this context, Torrance notes that Jesus' statement that "My Father is greater than I" (John 14:28) should be understood soteriologically, that is, economically in the way Gregory Nazianzen, Cyril of Alexandria and Augustine did, and not ontologically.[161]

Fourth, with his criticism of the Cappadocians on this important point and his return to Athanasius' thinking about the monarchy residing in the whole Trinity, Torrance offers a most interesting understanding of the procession of the Holy Spirit that actually avoids the difficulties that led to the divisions between East and West over the *filioque* (the procession of the Spirit from the Father *and* the Son). A brief discussion of this issue together with a clear statement about where Torrance stands on the relation of the immanent and economic Trinity will conclude this chapter.

## The *Filioque*

With a proper understanding of the divine monarchy in place alongside a suitable view of *perichoresis* and the *homoousion*, Torrance returns to Athanasius' position on the procession of the Holy Spirit from the Being of God the Father which is common to the Son and Spirit. It will be recalled that if a simple distinction is made between understanding the Father absolutely as referring to the Being of the Godhead and relatively as referring to the Father in relation to the Son and Spirit, as the Person of the Father, then it is easy to avoid the difficulty that led to the *filioque* in the first instance. As far as Torrance was concerned, the Cappadocians failed to make this distinction in their thinking so that for them the unity of God derived from the Person of the Father and not from the Being of the Father in the Nicene sense. This not only opened the door to subordinationism within the Trinity but it also undercut the *homoousion* of the Spirit with the Father and Son,

---

[159]  Torrance, *Trinitarian Perspectives*, p. 136.

[160]  See Torrance, *Trinitarian Perspectives*, p. 136, and *The Christian Doctrine of God*, p. 180. An example of such a variation is given in 2 Corinthians 13:14 where Paul writes, "The grace of the Lord Jesus Christ, and the love of God and the communion of the Holy Spirit be with you all" (*Trinitarian Perspectives*, p. 136).

[161]  Torrance, *The Christian Doctrine of God*, p. 180.

although the Cappadocians firmly rejected the Arian and Macedonian heresies that denied the divinity of the Spirit.[162] Unfortunately, however, the idea that the Spirit proceeds from the Person of the Father and not from the Being of the Father is exactly what precipitated the reaction of the Western Church so that the "*ex Patre filioque*" clause was "unecumenically" introduced into the Creed, thus creating the problematic relations between the East and West.

Since the Spirit proceeds from the Father and is sent by the Son, theologians in the West were trying to avoid any idea that the Son could be seen as subordinate to the Father, perhaps as an adopted creature, and thus were rejecting Arianism with the *filioque*. But Eastern theologians saw the idea that the Spirit proceeds from the Father *and* the Son as implying that there were two ultimate principles in the Godhead and that is why they stressed that the Spirit proceeds from the Father only. The Eastern theologians made a further distinction between the eternal procession of the Spirit from the Father and the historical mission of the Spirit as sent by the Son. Torrance thinks this latter point undercuts the homoousial relation between the Spirit and the Father and Son within the immanent Trinity. In fact, Torrance argues that the Basilian and Palamite understanding of this distinction led to the distinction between God's being and energies in such a way that our knowledge was restricted to the latter with the result that we had no real knowledge of God's inner being. This, Torrance believes, reflects a dualism inherited from the Origenistic tradition which drove a wedge between what God is in himself and what he is for us in his saving actions within history. Torrance rejects this thinking because he insists that the immanent and the economic Trinity cannot be separated without calling into question our true knowledge of God and salvation and without calling into question the *homoousion* with the idea that God's saving activity is only "like" what God is in himself when in fact there is an identity of being between God's actions in history and what God is in himself. Torrance wants what he calls a "realist doctrine of the Holy Spirit" and "a realist conception of the homoousial and perichoretic interpenetration of the three divine Persons in one another in accordance with which each Person is whole God and all three are together the one Triune God".[163] The Constantinopolitan Creed ruled out any disparity or disjunction between the Father and the Spirit by stressing that, in the Spirit, God communicates himself and not just something of himself in the form of his uncreated energies. That is why this creed stressed that the Spirit proceeds from the Being of the Father as well.

Torrance's solution to this long-standing dilemma was to suggest a return to Athanasius' view that since the Spirit and the Son coinhere in one another and since the Spirit "is ever in the hands of the Father who sends and the Son who gives him as his very own, and from whom the Spirit on his part receives", therefore "The Spirit is from the Father but from the Father in the Son". And since the Spirit, like the Son, is of the Being of God "he could not but proceed from or out of the

---

162    Torrance, *The Christian Doctrine of God*, p. 186.
163    Torrance, *The Christian Doctrine of God*, p. 187.

Being of God inseparably from and through the Son".[164] Further, the procession of the Spirit from the Father is bound up with the generation of the Son from the Father and both exceed and transcend human thinking. Here Torrance appeals to the eschatological reserve that properly marks his understanding of the mystery of the Trinity by insisting with Athanasius that "it would not be reverent to ask *how* the Spirit proceeds from God".[165] Any such attempt to explain how this could take place would represent an improper intrusion into the mystery of the Godhead.

This, then, is the solution to the "problem" of the *filioque*. If the Spirit is seen to proceed from the Father in the Son and not from the person of the Father only, then the difficulties noted above that led to the insertion of the *filioque* into the Creed would never have arisen in the first instance. Additionally, since the Son and Spirit are both of the Being of the Father, then "the idea that the Spirit derives from the *Being* of the Son just did not arise and could not have arisen".[166] Thus, for Torrance, if theologians had kept closer to Athanasius' thinking and hence also to the thinking of the Councils of Nicaea and Constantinople, this division between East and West would never have arisen.[167] Relying further upon the thought of Epiphanius, Torrance believes that today we should say that "the Holy Spirit proceeds from the one Monarchy of the Triune God".[168] Since God is thus seen as a Unity in Trinity and Trinity in Unity, Torrance thinks it is acceptable to say both that the Spirit proceeds "from the Father and the Son" and "from the Father through the Son", as long as these expressions are: 1) *not* understood in such a way that the monarchy is limited to the Father (as has happened in the churches of both East and West); 2) *not* understood in the framework of thinking that suggests that there is an "underived Deity of the Father" and a "derived Deity of the Son and Spirit"; and 3) *not* in the framework of thought that fails to acknowledge that the Holy Spirit belongs "equally and completely homoousially with the Father and the Son in their two-way relation with one another in the divine Triunity".[169]

## Torrance's View of the Relationship of the Immanent and Economic Trinity

By now it should be obvious that Torrance's thinking about God and about our relations with God is grounded in God's economic trinitarian self-revelation in such a way that he thinks consistently from a center in God and not from a center in human experience. Within that perspective, Torrance insists, as we have seen,

---

[164] Torrance, *The Christian Doctrine of God*, p. 188.

[165] Torrance, *The Christian Doctrine of God*, p. 188. Also, Torrance, *The Trinitarian Faith*, p. 235.

[166] Torrance, *The Christian Doctrine of God*, p. 188. See also Torrance, *The Trinitarian Faith*, p. 244.

[167] See, for example, Torrance, *The Trinitarian Faith*, p. 246.

[168] Torrance, *The Christian Doctrine of God*, p. 190.

[169] Torrance, *The Christian Doctrine of God*, p. 190.

that what God is toward us in the economy of salvation is what he is eternally. But he also maintains that we must respect God's mystery and not attempt to read back our experiences of God into God's eternal being in any inappropriate way. Perhaps the best way to see clearly what Torrance wishes to affirm and deny with regard to the relation of the immanent and economic Trinity is to see just how his thinking is in agreement with and differs from the thinking of Karl Rahner with his famous axiom that the immanent Trinity is strictly identical with the economic Trinity.

There is, of course, a perfectly non-controversial way of understanding Rahner's axiom that "the immanent Trinity is strictly identical with the economic Trinity and vice versa".[170] It may simply be interpreted to mean that what God is in the economy, he is eternally in himself.[171] And if that is how this axiom is interpreted, then Torrance and Rahner would be saying the same thing and there would be good grounds for ecumenical agreement. That is why Torrance himself adopted Rahner's axiom in a monograph he wrote expressing the conclusions of a colloquy considering Rahner's doctrine of the Trinity held in Switzerland in March, 1975. Torrance read the axiom as suggesting that all knowledge of God had to proceed from God's saving activities in the economy and thus from God's self-communication in the incarnation so that the economic Trinity would be the "norm for all our thought and speech about God".[172] This reformulation of traditional Roman Catholic theology offered by Rahner meant that: 1) there would be a closer connection between biblical theology and systematic theology which would connect more closely the presentation of Jesus Christ in the New Testament and the church's worship and proclamation of the Trinity; 2) there would be a rapprochement between East and West concerning the Trinity as theology shifted from a more abstract or scholastic framework to one bound up with the piety, worship and experience of the church and thus with what Athanasius called "a pious and reverent use of reason";[173] and 3) there could be some genuine ecumenical agreement "between Roman Catholic theology and Evangelical theology, especially as represented by the teaching of Karl Barth in his emphasis upon the self-revelation and self-giving of God as the root of the doctrine of the Trinity".[174] With his early enthusiastic endorsement of Rahner's axiom, however, Torrance did not see the full implications of the problems he himself already noticed in Rahner's thought even as he expressed these positive views in 1975. Torrance criticized Rahner for "expressing the Economic Trinity as immanent, that is, as it

---

[170]   Karl Rahner, "Theology and Anthropology", *Theological Investigations* (23 vols) (hereafter: *TI*), Vol. 9, trans. by Graham Harrison (New York: Herder and Herder, 1972), pp. 28–45, 32. See also Rahner, "Observations on the Doctrine of God in Catholic Dogmatics", *TI*: 9, pp. 127–44, 130, and *The Trinity*, pp. 22ff.

[171]   See J.A. DiNoia, O.P., "Karl Rahner", *The Modern Theologians*, Vol. 1, David F. Ford (ed.), (Oxford: Blackwell, 1989), p. 197.

[172]   Torrance, *Trinitarian Perspectives*, p. 78.

[173]   Torrance, *Trinitarian Perspectives*, p. 78.

[174]   Torrance, *Trinitarian Perspectives*, p. 78.

is in God, in such a way that it precinds from God's free self-communication",[175] so that he believed Rahner introduced a logical necessity (a necessity of thought) into the doctrine in such a way that it is his thinking rather than the economic Trinity that becomes normative for what he says about God *in se* and *ad extra*. Torrance believed that, while Rahner may still be a "prisoner of a scholastic metaphysical framework",[176] if this difficulty in Rahner's thought could be cleared away, then there could be ecumenical convergence because what he intended was the same as Athanasius and Karl Barth intended. Torrance praised Rahner for intending to unite the treatises on *De Deo Uno* and *De Deo Trino* but also criticized him for not seeming to realize that the real reason for their separation was due to an epistemological and cosmological dualism. Still, he applauded Rahner's argument that one could not speak of the one God apart from historical experience of him and thus (in Torrance's mind) apart from the trinitarian self-revelation.

While Rahner apparently wished to ground his theology in God's economic trinitarian self-revelation, his transcendental method, which begins with our experiences of self-transcendence and posits the existence of God as the nameless, silent whole or horizon surrounding us, effectively allows God's oneness to be defined and understood without specific reference to God's self-communication in Christ and the Spirit. The result is that God's self-communication becomes for Rahner a universal element of human experience in the form of the "supernatural existential" (a concept that Torrance would never countenance) and Rahner ends up allowing his rather abstract idea of God's oneness to determine his thinking about God in ways that Torrance would most certainly reject. I have made this clear by comparing the way each theologian thinks both about the resurrection and Christology, and I have tried to show that the differences remain irreconcilable as long as Rahner and those who follow Rahner remain unwilling to accept the methodological axiom that Torrance repeatedly stresses, following Athanasius, namely, that "It would be more godly and true to signify God from the Son and call him Father, than to name God from his works alone and call him Unoriginate".[177]

The upshot of all this is that for Torrance the identity of the immanent and economic Trinity meant simply that what God is toward us in his Word and Spirit he is eternally in himself so that there could be no epistemological or cosmological dualism because of the incarnation and the outpouring of the Spirit. Rahner's axiom, with its vice versa, unfortunately allows for the possibility of thinking about our relations with God as mutually conditioned and mutually conditioning. But again Torrance consistently insists in his writing and more so in his last book on the Trinity, *The Christian Doctrine of God*, that no such mutual conditioning is possible if the economic Trinity is and remains normative, as it should, throughout the theological enterprise. That is why Torrance consistently distinguished the

---

[175]   Torrance, *Trinitarian Perspectives*, p. 79.

[176]   Torrance, *Trinitarian Perspectives*, p. 81.

[177]   Torrance, *The Trinitarian Faith*, p. 49. I have discussed the implications of these differences in Chapters 3 and 6 of *Divine Freedom*.

immanent and economic Trinity in ways that Rahner did not. For instance, Torrance insists that God's omnipotence as demonstrated in the death and resurrection of Jesus Christ "is so unique that we cannot describe it by analogical reference to any other kind of power", and it must be understood by us "only out of its own uniqueness, and the incredible acts of God Almighty in incarnation, atonement and resurrection".[178] But for Rahner, because grace is already part of human experience in the form of a supernatural existential, one already experiences the power of Christ's resurrection when one has a transcendental experience of hope.[179] And Rahner insists that "The *a priori* transcendental subjectivity of the knower … and the object of knowledge … are related to one another in such a way that they mutually condition one another …".[180] For Torrance, of course, it is the fact that the economic Trinity is and remains normative for all that is said about God and us that precludes any such mutually conditioned conception of our knowledge of God. Such a view would invalidate Athanasius' dictum about knowing the Father through the Son and open the door to a knowledge of God as the Unoriginate that is not dictated by God's own trinitarian self-revelation. It would ultimately mean that in some sense we could rely on our self-knowledge to know and relate with God instead of thinking only from a center in God on the basis of grace, faith and revelation. That is why, as seen above, Torrance insisted that "when we rightly speak of the oneness between the ontological Trinity and the economic Trinity, we may not speak of that oneness without distinguishing and delimiting it from the ontological Trinity".[181] It is imperative, then, that the key differences between Torrance and Rahner in their respective understanding of knowledge of God be seen if Torrance's conception of the relation between the immanent and economic Trinity is to be understood correctly.

## Conclusion

It has been noted often that, with the theology of Karl Barth and Karl Rahner, trinitarian doctrine has been revived as an important factor in twentieth-century theology. In concluding this chapter we should observe that T. F. Torrance also did much to revive the doctrine in British theology and beyond during the twentieth century. This can be seen most especially in his influence on the thinking of Colin Gunton whom Torrance himself praised when he described him as "one of the leading theologians in Britain" and as a noted authority on the doctrine of the Trinity.[182]

---

[178]   Torrance, *The Christian Doctrine of God*, p. 215.

[179]   See Molnar, *Divine Freedom*, pp. 182, 185, 190.

[180]   See Rahner, "Reflections on Methodology in Theology", *TI:* 11, pp. 68–114, 87.

[181]   Torrance, *The Christian Doctrine of God*, p. 109.

[182]   "Thomas Torrance Responds" in ed Elmer M. Colyer, *The Promise of Trinitarian Theology: Theologians in Dialogue with T.F. Torrance*, (Rowman & Littlefield Publishers,

Gunton offers two important memories he had of Torrance. First, when he and others heard Torrance speak in Bristol in 1963 along with a number of other theologians, including Lesslie Newbigin, Torrance stressed the nature of scientific theology, emphasizing the need to allow reality to dictate their understanding. Second, he recalled the gathering in 1975 when Torrance led the colloquium on Rahner mentioned above.[183] On one particular evening Gunton recounted that he was one of a number who met with Torrance at the end of the conference to express their "profound disquiet with some of Rahner's theology".[184] Torrance placed their concerns within a wider context in a "magisterial" response to the conference that he wrote that evening and later published as "Towards an Ecumenical Consensus on the Trinity".[185] Important here is the fact that, when Gunton himself entered the theological profession, many leading figures were mainly critical of the doctrine of the Trinity, if not actually dismissive of it. He notes that Maurice Wiles, for instance, expressed doubt about the biblical basis of the doctrine.[186] To Torrance, Gunton says, "must go much of the credit for refusing to succumb to the loss of confidence in mainstream Christian theology after the last war and for maintaining steadily and faithfully the vision of the classic doctrine of God".[187] And, in reading Gunton's works on the Trinity, one certainly can see evidence that Torrance's scientific and patristically grounded trinitarian theology has influenced him, especially since he, like Torrance, sought to show that "everything looks different" in light of the Trinity.[188] Such a view is the very opposite of that of John A. T. Robinson who thought of the doctrine as of no interest to or relevance to the modern world.[189] While Gunton had his criticisms of Torrance's trinitarian theology, as we shall see in Chapter 9, it is clear that much of his own development took place in reliance upon and in dialogue with the magisterial work of Torrance himself.

One also can see the influence of Torrance on John Webster who is today one of the leading theological figures in Great Britain. For instance, in his important work *Word and Church*, Webster explicitly relies on Torrance's formulation of the Trinity in his own reading of Scripture.[190] And one also can see Torrance's influence on the American theologian Stanley Grenz, who uses Torrance's trinitarian

---

Inc., 2001), p. 314.

[183]   See above, Chapter 1.

[184]   Colin Gunton, "Being and Person: T.F. Torrance's Doctrine of God" in *The Promise of Trinitarian Theology*, pp. 115–37, 115.

[185]   This later became Chapter 4 of *Trinitarian Perspectives* cited above.

[186]   Colin Gunton, "Being and Person", p. 134.

[187]   Colin Gunton, "Being and Person", p. 134.

[188]   Colin E. Gunton, *The Promise of Trinitarian Theology*, second edition (Edinnburgh: T & T Clark, 1997), p. 7.

[189]   Gunton, *The Promise of Trinitarian Theology*, pp. 2–3.

[190]   See John Webster, *Word and Church: Essays in Christian Dogmatics* (Edinburgh: T&T Clark, 2001), pp. 28ff.

theology as a contemporary instance of one who seeks to return the doctrine of the immanent Trinity to its rightful place of importance in understanding the economy of salvation.[191] All of this shows that Torrance's thinking on this important subject has been and continues to be influential on a worldwide basis.

---

[191]  See Grenz, *Rediscovering the Triune God*, pp. 200–215.

## Chapter 3

# God the Father Almighty, Maker of Heaven and Earth

Torrance's view of God the Creator was strictly determined by his trinitarian theology so that, in order to understand his explication of the doctrine of creation, it is important to realize that his thinking remains structured by Athanasius' insight that it is better to "signify God from the Son and call him Father, than to name God from his works alone and call him Unoriginate".[1] What this means is not only that, following the Council of Nicaea, Athanasius stressed the centrality of the Father/Son relation for understanding God the Father Almighty who is the Creator, but that he wanted to stress that this same relation must have "primacy over the Creator/creature relation. The latter is to be understood in the light of the former and not vice versa".[2] Or, to put it another way, "while God is always Father he is not always Creator" and "it is as Father that God is Creator, not vice versa".[3] What are the implications of these important insights for a properly conceived doctrine of creation?

To speak of God from within the perspective of the Creator/creature relation or the Unoriginate/originate relation allows us only to speak of him "in vague, general and negative terms" marked by our distance as creatures from God the Creator. But, for Torrance, following the Nicene Fathers and Hilary in particular, to think of God this way does not allow us to "know God as he is in himself … in accordance with his divine nature" but only "in his absolute separation from us, as the eternal, unconditioned and indescribable".[4] In these circumstances, what happens is that we attempt to know God from what he has made (his works) instead

---

[1]  Torrance, *The Trinitarian Faith*, p. 49. Torrance repeats this important Athanasian insight when he develops his understanding of God the Almighty Creator (p. 76). He frequently cites this text as the proper way of knowing God in accordance with God's own self-revelation. See also, for example, Torrance, *Karl Barth*, p. 213. He carries through this insight in his chapter on the "Sovereign Creator" in *The Christian Doctrine of God*, pp. 203–34, by insisting that belief in God as Creator is "presented within a trinitarian structure" so that "our knowledge of the Sovereign Creator may not be abstracted from the incarnate power of the saving love of the triune God mediated to us and activated among us in salvation history or from the creative power of the Holy Spirit poured out upon all flesh" (pp. 203–4).

[2]  Torrance, *The Trinitarian Faith*, p. 49.

[3]  Torrance, *The Christian Doctrine of God*, p. 207.

[4]  Torrance, *The Trinitarian Faith*, p. 50.

of allowing our knowledge of him to be shaped by who he is in Jesus Christ, the Son or Word of God incarnate. Because such thinking, however, cannot "tell us anything about who God is or what he is like in his own nature", as Athanasius also emphasized, it is "entirely lacking in accuracy or precision".[5] Torrance insists that Nicene thinking about God the Creator is markedly different from the kind of Gnostic thinking advanced by Basileides of Alexandria who relied on Plato's idea that "God is beyond all being" so that "we cannot say anything about what God is, but can only say something about what he is not".[6] In opposition to such agnosticism, which opens the door to the idea that we can know God by negating what we experience in this world, Torrance follows Gregory Nazianzen who claims that the inability to say anything positive about what God actually is means that we "really cannot say anything accurate about what he is not".[7] Hence, a negative theology that is not determined by the revelation of God in Jesus Christ is every bit as arbitrary and useless as is a positive one that is not grounded in that same revelation. Any such thinking leads both toward Arianism and Gnosticism. Torrance also follows Athanasius' doctrine of creation quite explicitly because Athanasius worked "within the Origenist reversal of the Aristotelian–Stoic relation of the human reason to God" (which means that God was to be found beyond the world of created intelligibility) by bringing "faithful expression and articulation to the Hebraic–Christian understanding of God" as "beyond all *created* being and all human devising … [who] nevertheless remains Being in his own transcendent way and in accordance with his own transcendent nature as Creator of all other being".[8] This is important because in Greek thought it was supposed that anything beyond this world would be unintelligible. Torrance wants to say that "God creates all things through the Logos, his own eternal Son, and continuously maintains them

---

[5]   Torrance, *The Trinitarian Faith*, p. 50.

[6]   Torrance, *The Trinitarian Faith*, p. 50. Torrance notes that in Greek philosophy it was thought that we could know only that which was limited; anything unlimited is beyond our grasp and thus would be considered irrational. Such thinking implied, then, that knowledge of God was knowledge of a "finite, limited and intra-mundane deity" (Torrance, "Athanasius", *Theology in Reconciliation*, p. 218). Origen reversed that thinking with his view of the doctrine of creation from nothing by claiming that God created the universe and gave it an order accessible to rational knowledge, an order different from God himself. But because Origen too embraced the dualist disjunction of the intelligible and sensible realms, "he was forced to speak of God as finally beyond being". This thinking, according to Torrance, eventually had a damaging effect in Greek theology, even when it was held in a "modified form" by John of Damascus, because in reality God is not beyond all being and knowing and God is not nameless, but God's being and knowing is the unique being and knowing of the Trinity. See also "Athanasius", *Theology in Reconciliation*, pp. 221ff., and *Divine Meaning*, pp. 181f. and 372f.

[7]   Torrance, *The Trinitarian Faith*, p. 50. See also Torrance, *The Trinitarian Faith*, p. 78.

[8]   Torrance, "Athanasius", *Theology in Reconciliation*, p. 218.

in their created being so that they do not lapse back into nothing" through his grace and thus through his Word and Spirit.[9]

This implies that we must first think about the Father in his *perichoretic* and *homoousial* relation to the Son if we are to have an accurate perception of God the Creator. If, instead, we were to think only of the Creator in relation to creatures, then "we inevitably come to think of the Son himself as one of God's created works". Were this to happen, we would then be thinking of God in a way that is not at all grounded in who God eternally is and we would end up referring to God in an impersonal way "far removed from what he is in himself".[10] Furthermore, any attempt to reach knowledge of the triune God "from some point outside of God" would mean that we would not have any point within God himself by which we could evaluate our conceptions of him. We would, in other words, be "flung back upon ourselves" and in essence we would be unable to avoid "using ourselves as some sort of measure for what we think and say of him". Any such approach, however, is exactly what the Arians were accused of doing with their arbitrary way of knowing God by projecting images based on their experience into God and "dreaming up conceptions of him with no ground in reality".[11] Such thinking is neither scientific nor precise because instead of allowing the unique nature of the triune God to determine what is said, it is self-willed and indeed it represents a form of self-justification in face of God's justification by grace recognized through faith. It is in this sense that, although Torrance recognizes the existence of natural theology and natural human goodness, he still insists that we cannot rely on that natural knowledge or our innate goodness, because we are required by the nature of revelation, namely, our justification by faith and thus our relation with Jesus Christ himself, to recognize that "man with his natural goodness is called in question".[12] Torrance therefore rightly insists that because Jesus Christ "died for the whole man (with his good and his evil) not for part of him, the evil part, but for the whole man" and indeed "for all men, the good and the bad", we must be completely born again according to the Gospel. And this suggests that

---

[9]   Torrance, "Athanasius", *Theology in Reconciliation*, p. 219.

[10]   Torrance, *The Trinitarian Faith*, p. 50.

[11]   Torrance, *The Trinitarian Faith*, p. 51.

[12]   Torrance, "Justification", *Theology in Reconstruction*, p. 162. In *The Christian Doctrine of God*, Torrance notes that because the Holy Trinity is "incomparable and non-derivable", theism itself is called into question. So while Christians respect the fact that God has made himself known to people "from the beginning of the creation", trinitarian thinking forces upon us the fact that any way of thinking about God apart from the incarnation or "behind the back of Jesus Christ" actually falsifies the truth of the created order because of our alienated and "inturned" human minds, so that all conceptions of God are called into question by the knowledge of God provided by God in the incarnation and outpouring of the Spirit. Justification thus reveals we are in the wrong in ourselves so that we cannot even rely on our own goodness to know God accurately (pp. 24–7).

Justification by the grace of Christ alone, does not mean that there is no natural knowledge—what natural man is there who does not know something of God even if he holds it down in unrighteousness or turns the truth into a lie? But it does mean that the whole of that natural knowledge is called in question by Christ who when he comes to us says: "If any man will come after me, let him deny himself, take up his cross and follow me". The whole man with his natural knowledge is there questioned down to the root of his being, for man is summoned to look away from all that he is and knows or thinks he knows to Christ who is the Way the Truth and the Life; no one goes to the Father but by him.[13]

As in his doctrine of the Trinity proper, Torrance stressed that because "there is no likeness between the eternal Being of God and the being of created reality, God may be known only out of himself".[14] What this means in this context is that those who would try to know God from the works of creation are really no better off than the Greeks who do not know the revelation of God in Jesus Christ because then, in that approach, God is not known as the Father of his Son Jesus Christ. But God is known accurately in accordance with his nature when the Father is known through the Son or Word of God, for it is through that very same Word that the Father created the universe. It is here, then, in the doctrine of creation that Torrance emphasizes once more that we must think from a center in God himself provided by God alone in the incarnation and in our creaturely existence (in and through the man Jesus who is God incarnate) if we are to think accurately here. Relying on the fathers, who themselves relied upon that important statement in Matthew's Gospel mentioned above, that "no one knows who the Son is except the Father; and no one knows who the Father is except the Son and any one to whom the Son chooses to reveal him", Torrance insists that, as the Word of God incarnate, Jesus Christ includes us in God's self-knowledge in and through the sending of the Holy Spirit so that "it was by reference to the inner relation of the Son to the Father in the centre of its faith that the Church formulated its understanding of everything else: creation, salvation, the Church, the resurrection of the dead and the life of the world to come".[15]

---

[13]   Torrance, "Justification", *Theology in Reconstruction*, p. 163. Torrance consistently opposes transposing the doctrine of justification by grace from being an "objective act in Christ on our behalf and apart from us, to justifying faith interpreted to modern man in terms of his own existential decision detached from any objective act of Christ in history" (Torrance, *God and Rationality*, p. 121). In this context, Torrance is keen to point out how disregard for the doctrine of justification, rightly understood, has led the church into doctrinal disagreement. It is also worth noting that Torrance's position on natural knowledge explicated here follows the pattern he presented in his book *Calvin's Doctrine of Man*, pp. 20, 85, 154–68, 180–3.

[14]   Torrance, *The Trinitarian Faith*, p. 52.

[15]   Torrance, *The Trinitarian Faith*, p. 56.

Within this perspective, one can perhaps understand why Torrance insisted that the Council of Nicaea gave primacy to the Fatherhood of God, since for the Nicene theologians "knowledge of God as Creator is taken from knowledge of God as Father, and not the other way round".[16] In this respect, the Nicene–Constantinopolitan Creed offers us a trinitarian picture of God the Creator: "belief in God the Sovereign Creator is presented within a trinitarian structure: one God the Father Almighty, Maker of heaven and earth and of all things visible and invisible, one Lord Jesus Christ through whom all things were made, and the Holy Spirit the Lord and Giver of life."[17] The concept of God the Creator developed by Judaism was "radicalised through the New Testament teaching"[18] about creation having taken place through the Word of God, namely, Jesus Christ. What, then, are the specific details of Torrance's presentation of the doctrine of creation? Following Athanasius once again and as already noted, Torrance argues that while God was always Father of his Son, he was not always the Creator. Several implications follows from this.

First, the relation between God and creatures is of an altogether different kind from the relation between the Father and Son; because the Father and Son are one in nature "there is a unity of activity between them: what the Father does the Son does, and the works of the Son are to be regarded as works of the Father".[19] While the term "Father" refers absolutely to God and relatively to the Father in his relation to the Son and Spirit and while the Father is seen as the source of all being, only he is eternally the fount of being "in his very nature as God".[20] Hence none of this implies that "God is the Fount of created beings in the same way as he is the Fount of the eternal Son", but rather suggests that because he is generative within his own being, he can be the source of the created world as well;[21] this, however, does not mean that the origin or principle of being (the ἀρχή) is to be found in the Father alone because the Father, Son and Holy Spirit are each wholly God and God together in virtue of their *perichoretic* relationship—thus the ἀρχή is to be found in the whole Trinity.[22] It is just this thinking that distinguishes Torrance's approach from that of the Cappadocians, as seen in the last chapter.[23] The weakness of their position is that they considered the Father as Person the ἀρχή and so introduced a note of subordinationism into the doctrine of the Trinity which Torrance opposed for both ontological and soteriological reasons. What is implied here is a rejection of any idea that one might stress the notion that

16  Torrance, *The Trinitarian Faith*, p. 76.

17  Torrance, *The Christian Doctrine of God*, p. 203.

18  Torrance, *The Christian Doctrine of God*, p. 203.

19  Torrance, *The Trinitarian Faith*, p. 78.

20  Torrance, *The Trinitarian Faith*, p. 79.

21  Torrance, *The Trinitarian Faith*, p. 79. See also Torrance, *The Christian Doctrine of God*, p. 209.

22  Torrance, *The Trinitarian Faith*, pp. 80–82.

23  See above, Chapter 2.

person is more basic than substance or nature when it comes to understanding God the Father as Creator. Any such thinking could easily open the door to subordinationism, modalism and pantheism, as well as to a confusion of nature and grace. This would obscure the fact that it is the one God who is three Persons who is the free and sovereign Creator of all that is distinct from and dependent upon him; it might even imply that God needed to create in order to be a person in relation. Torrance wanted to stress that by knowing God in his internal relations as Father, Son and Holy Spirit and thus as the Father Almighty and not just as a kind of originating person, we will understand ourselves as in a genuine relationship with God that undermines neither his nor our freedom, but instead sees human freedom established and renewed by God's own free actions of love on our behalf. Furthermore, Torrance was wary of any idea that we become "divinized" by virtue of the incarnation because this blurs the distinction between divine and human freedom exercised by God the Father in the incarnation of his Son.[24]

---

[24] Torrance rejects the idea that grace could be regarded as "a detachable and transferable divine quality which may inhere in or be possessed by the human being to whom it is given in virtue of which he is somehow 'deified' or 'divinised'" (Torrance, *The Trinitarian Faith*, p. 140). Torrance considers the Platonising translation of θέωσις as "deification" misleading because it suggests a change in human nature that he rejects and he prefers to translate 2 Peter 1:4 to say that we are "partners of the Deity" rather than "partakers of divine nature" (Torrance, *The Christian Doctrine of God*, p. 95). Torrance wants to understand this phrase in a Christological and trinitarian way because he believes it is through our personal union with Christ that we share in his humanity and thus, because of the unique hypostatic union of natures in him, we then also share in his divinity and thus are "partakers of the divine nature" (Torrance, *Conflict and Agreement I*, p. 110). He also considers Athanasius' remark that "He [the Word] became man in order to make us divine" inopportune and even embarrassing because there can never be any suggestion of us becoming divine. Still, if the expression is understood in terms of our personal relations with God in which our existence is "permeated by the Divine Presence", Torrance finds this acceptable (Torrance, *The Christian Doctrine of God*, p. 96). Torrance, however, emphatically rejects notions of "divinization" or "deification" insofar as they tend to confuse the Creator and creature "and to think of grace as deifying man or heightening his being until he attains the level of a supernatural order appears to do docetic violence to creaturely human nature" (Torrance, "The Roman Doctrine of Grace", *Theology in Reconstruction*, p. 180). What Torrance opposes is the idea that grace is "a transferable quality infused into and adhering in finite being, raising it to a different gradation where it can grasp God by a connatural proportion of being" (Torrance, "The Word of God and the Nature of Man", *Theology in Reconstruction*, pp. 99–116, 114). Ultimately, Torrance's positive point is to assert that "Grace is not something that can be detached from God and made to inhere in creaturely being as 'created grace'" (Torrance, "The Roman Doctrine of Grace", *Theology in Reconstruction*, p. 182). Instead, grace is identical with Christ himself, the Giver of grace. That is why the Gift and the Giver must not be separated as in the thinking that detaches grace from Christ and makes it inhere in creaturely being. See, for example, Torrance, *The Trinitarian Faith*, pp. 24 and 140–141, and *The Christian Doctrine of God*, p. 147.

Second, for these reasons a sharp distinction must be made between the eternal generation of the Son from "the *nature* of God" which takes place eternally without beginning or end and the creation of the world "by the *will* of God, who in accordance with his good pleasure has freely brought it into existence out of nothing and given it a finite beginning"[25]. Just as it is not necessary for God to have created the world since "God does not need the world to be God, so the Fatherhood of God is in no way dependent on or constituted by relation to what he has created outwith himself".[26] Nonetheless, the God we know from the self-revelation of the incarnate Word and through the power of his Holy Spirit is not a God who is totally locked up within himself but a God who freely interacts with us out of love.

Third, it is important to realize that the Christian doctrine of *creatio ex nihilo* (creation from nothing) does not imply that the creation of the universe took place "out of something that is nothing, but out of nothing at all", so that it came into being by a "sheer fiat of God's Word" with the result that while there was nothing in existence outside of God before, there came into being the whole universe.[27] And there is no internal or external need on God's part to act as Creator. Moreover, the act of creation does not refer to any emanation of God, that is, to "something which is in God or part of God, or created out of God".[28] These are all extremely important qualifications, because Torrance's trinitarian view of creation as expressed here is to be sharply distinguished from the thinking offered by Jürgen Moltmann.

For instance, whereas Moltmann actually interprets the "*creatio ex nihilo*" to mean God's creating the world from something called nothing and thus by asserting that creation takes place through a shrinkage process in his eternal being, Torrance is quite clear that any such explanation compromises the sheer miracle of creation itself as God's fiat and thus not only calls into question God's freedom to act in a completely new way, but blurs the distinction between what is going on internally within God and externally outside God. It would also undermine any true notion of contingence which, of course, refers to the fact that creation is simultaneously distinct from and dependent upon God.

---

[25]  Torrance, *The Christian Doctrine of God*, p. 206.

[26]  Torrance, *The Christian Doctrine of God*, p. 207.

[27]  Torrance, *The Christian Doctrine of God*, p. 207. Following Athanasius, Torrance insists that the *creatio ex nihilo* "does not mean that God created the universe out of some 'stuff' called 'nothing', but that what he created was not created out of anything" (*The Trinitarian Faith*, p. 99). Creation receives its existence and stability from the Word through whom it was made by an act of power and will on the part of God.

[28]  Torrance, *The Christian Doctrine of God*, p. 207. Torrance rightly insists that the fathers made no attempt to explain *how* the universe was created out of nothing because they recognized that this was a mystery grounded in God's free action *ad extra*. But he insisted that when Gregory Nyssen spoke of creation as "genesis from God" this was not to be understood "as an emanation from God's being, but as the product of his will and the activity of his love" (Torrance, *The Trinitarian Faith*, p. 92).

Following the Jewish kabbalistic doctrine of God's self-limitation or zimsum (sometimes spelled *zimzum*), Moltmann thus contends that *nihil* is something that actually comes into being as a condition for God's creating the world:

> God makes room for his creation by withdrawing his presence. What comes into being is a *nihil* ... which represents a partial negation of the divine Being, inasmuch as God is not yet Creator. The space which comes into being and is set free by God's self-limitation is a literally God-forsaken space. The *nihil* in which God creates his creation is God-forsakenness, hell, absolute death ...[29]

Following this notion of the *zimsum*, Moltmann can actually refer to the nihil as "something" exactly in the manner rejected by Torrance: "The *nihil* for his *creatio ex nihilo* only comes into being because—and in as far as—the omnipotent and omnipresent God withdraws his presence and restricts his power."[30] Unfortunately, however, the result of making the *nihil* something, rather than the symbol that God is truly free in relation to all that is distinct from him and dependent upon him (contingent), is the incorporation of *nihil* itself directly into the Godhead. While Moltmann undoubtedly intends to oppose dualism, this thinking introduces the dualistic ideas that God-forsakenness, hell and absolute death are part of God before creation.

Ultimately, Moltmann ends up conceiving of creation as an emanation of the divine Being because, according to the doctrine of the *zimsum*, creation refers to a shrinkage process in God himself and only then to his "issuing" outside himself.[31] Following Isaac Luria, Moltmann then thinks of creation as a "contraction" or "concentration" of the divine Being such that "the existence of the universe was made possible through a shrinkage process in God".[32] This thinking is of a piece with Moltmann's panentheism which ultimately collapses back into pantheism because for Moltmann the relationship of reciprocity that exists between God and creation means ultimately that God needs the world in some sense: "God 'needs' the world and man. If God is love, then he neither will nor can be without the one who is his beloved".[33] What is more, according to Moltmann, God makes himself in need of redemption.[34] When this thinking is coupled with statements such as "Creation is part of the eternal love affair between the Father and the

---

[29]   Jürgen Moltmann, *God in Creation: A New Theology of Creation and the Spirit of God* (hereafter: *Creation*), trans. Margaret Kohl, (New York: Harper and Row, 1985), p. 87.

[30]   Moltmann, *Creation*, pp. 86–7.

[31]   Jürgen Moltmann, *The Trinity and the Kingdom, The Doctrine of God* (hereafter: *Trinity and Kingdom*), trans. Margaret Kohl (New York: Harper & Row, 1981), pp. 109–10. See also Moltmann, *Creation*, p. 87.

[32]   Moltmann, *Trinity and Kingdom*, p. 109.

[33]   Moltmann, *Trinity and Kingdom*, p. 58.

[34]   See Moltmann, *Trinity and Kingdom*, p. 29.

Son"[35] and "the idea of the world is already inherent in the Father's love for the Son",[36] it seems clear both that Moltmann is unable to distinguish God's internal and external actions of love and that he has incorporated creation into the divine Being in a mutually conditioning way that bespeaks a pantheistic or emanationist understanding of the doctrine.

Torrance carefully notes that creation was indeed in God's mind before he created,[37] but he is also very clear that he brought creation into being by a definite act of will so that he was under no constraint to do so.[38] Hence, following Athanasius, Torrance rejects not only the notion that God is eternally Creator but also "its attendant idea that the creation eternally exists in the mind of God, for the creation of the world out of nothing meant that it had an absolute beginning".[39]

---

[35]   Moltmann, *Trinity and Kingdom*, p. 59.

[36]   Moltmann, *Trinity and Kingdom*, p. 108.

[37]   See Torrance, *The Trinitarian Faith*, p. 87, where he notes that while God was always Father and therefore not always Creator, nonetheless creation was in the mind of God before he actually created, but "he brought it into being by a definite act of his will and thereby gave it a beginning" (p. 87). The main issue in Torrance's mind here is that the limitations of our time relations may not be read back into God. That would end by confusing God's creative act with his eternal act of begetting his Son. See also Torrance, *The Christian Doctrine of God*, p. 208. Torrance places the doctrine of creation in an interesting historical context in "Epilogue", *Theology in Reconstruction*, pp. 272–9, rejecting, among other things, the Thomist modification of the Augustinian tradition which envisioned a "sacramental universe in which the visible and the sensuous world was held to be the counterpart in time to the invisible and eternal realities of the spiritual world" (p. 272). This led to the idea that nature had no importance in itself but only as we look through it to the eternal world. The Thomist modification meant that the world of nature was "impregnated with final causes". But that meant that "nature was inevitably controlled by prior understanding of the eternal ideas in the mind of God". This, unfortunately, carried with it "the difficult notion of the eternity of the world" (p. 272). Duns Scotus attacked this thinking with the idea that "creation was not causally related to timeless ideas in the mind of God but rather to creative ideas which God freely produced along with the created realities themselves" (p. 273). Hence, the doctrine of creation together with the doctrine of justification by grace led to a truly accurate view of the contingence of nature and our dependence upon God in such a way that God was not confused with nature and creatures could not be confused with God but were seen to exercise dominion over nature under God. Nature was studied out of itself and not by seeking something beyond it while God was understood to be creatively able to interact with nature.

[38]   Although Moltmann is strongly opposed to thinking of God in Aristotelian terms, he does not seem to realize that by holding that the idea of the world is already inherent in the Father's love for the Son, he has indeed fallen prey to the thinking of Aristotle. Torrance clearly distinguishes the Christian understanding of the matter from Aristotle's here arguing that "to regard the Creator as the First Cause from which the universe took its rise appears to imply 'the eternity of the world' if only in the mind of God who knows himself as its First Cause" (Torrance, *Divine and Contingent Order*, p. 6).

[39]   Torrance, *The Ground and Grammar*, p. 66.

By contrast, for Moltmann, God is constrained by the very nature of his "suffering love" to bring creation into existence both because God cannot find bliss in his eternal love and because it is impossible to conceive of a God who is not a creative God. In Moltmann's own words:

> ... it is impossible to conceive of a God who is not a creative God. A non-creative God would be imperfect ... if God's eternal being is love, then the divine love is also more blessed in giving than in receiving. God cannot find bliss in eternal self-love if selflessness is part of love's very nature.[40]

Fourth, creation and incarnation are something *new* even for God. That is the significance of Torrance's remark that while God was always Father, he was not always Creator. He could recognize and maintain God's freedom in a way that preserved God's distinction from the world together with the idea that the world is truly contingent and not in any sense necessary to God for his own existence. Beyond that, he could then insist that when God created the world "he acted in a way that he had not done before, in bringing about absolutely new events". Creation of the world from nothing then means that creation "is something *new even for God*".[41] Torrance insists that the same thinking applies to the incarnation and Pentecost. Just as God was always able to create, become incarnate and pour out his Spirit in a new way, he chose by definite acts of will to do so in each instance at particular points in time and his relations with the world.[42] Thinking this way, Torrance sharply distinguishes his view of the divine freedom from static ideas about God that refer to an "unmoved mover".[43] The triune God is not only a living and moving God but one who reveals himself as "absolutely free to do what he had never done before, and free to be other than he was eternally: to be Almighty Creator, and even to become incarnate as a creature within his creation, while nevertheless remaining eternally the God that he always was".[44] What all of this implies is that God's being is "always *new* while always remaining what it ever was and is and ever will be". This is the significance of understanding creation in a trinitarian way.

God is ever the Father, Son and Holy Spirit but, since he is a living God, he is also free to act in new and surprising ways, as just indicated. But his power is

---

[40]   Moltmann, *Trinity and Kingdom*, p. 106. For a full treatment of how Moltmann's panentheistic interpretation of the Trinity and of creation leads him into emanationism and pantheism, see Molnar, *Divine Freedom*, Chapter 7.

[41]   Torrance, *The Christian Doctrine of God*, p. 208. Torrance clearly is following the thought of Athanasius and John of Damascus here. See Torrance, "Athanasius", *Divine Meaning*, p. 187, and "Athanasius", *Theology in Reconciliation*, p. 223.

[42]   For a full description of Torrance's thinking on this issue, see Torrance, *The Trinitarian Faith*, pp. 88–9.

[43]   Torrance, *The Christian Doctrine of God*, p. 208.

[44]   Torrance, *The Christian Doctrine of God*, p. 208.

not exhausted in what he has done and it is perfectly appropriate to speak of a "before" and "after" with respect to God's activity because God is not to be seen as "timeless" but rather as having time in his own unique manner that differs from the way we have time. In this sense, however, the limitations of our created time may not be read back into God without once again denying God's actual eternal freedom. In this sense, Torrance follows Athanasius once more and maintains that "for God to create is secondary, and to beget is primary"[45] in order to distinguish the Father/Son relation and its primacy from the Creator/creature relation which is always secondary; the former belongs to God's nature and is internal to God whereas the latter comes into existence outside of God by a definite act of his will and in accordance with his wisdom and love. Torrance notes that words like "was", "before", "when", and "beginning" are time-related and cause problems when used to refer to God because "the time-relations they imply may not be read back into God",[46] since they have one meaning when they refer to God and another when they refer to creaturely being. So when Scripture says, "in the beginning God created", Torrance notes this must be understood in two ways: 1) with reference to God's creative act and 2) with reference to his works, namely, that which he has created. Thus, "Behind the beginning of creation there is an absolute or transcendent beginning by God who is himself eternally without beginning".[47] It is in the interest of maintaining this distinction that Torrance then insists that something "baffling" and "astonishing" takes place in creation and incarnation:

> It is not only that something absolutely new has begun to be, new even for God who created it by his Word and gave it a contingent reality and integrity outwith himself, but that in some incomprehensible way, to cite Athanasius again, "the Word himself *became* the Maker of the things that have a beginning". God was always Father, not always Creator, but now he is Creator as well as Father.[48]

Similarly, "The Son was always Son of God, but now he is Man as well as God. 'He was not man previously, but he became man for our sake'".[49] Both creation and incarnation, then, are "something new to the eternal being of God", though, of course, they are neither unforeseen events nor arbitrary ones, since God planned them in eternity and willed them and indeed, as his acts, they are expressions of his eternal knowledge and love. Still, "They tell us that he [God] is free to do what he had never done before, and free to be other than he was eternally: to be the Almighty Creator, and even to become incarnate as a creature within his creation, while remaining eternally the God that he is".[50]

---

45    Torrance, *The Trinitarian Faith*, p. 87.
46    Torrance, *The Trinitarian Faith*, pp. 87–8.
47    Torrance, *The Trinitarian Faith*, p. 88.
48    Torrance, *The Trinitarian Faith*, p. 88.
49    Torrance, *The Trinitarian Faith*, p. 88.
50    Torrance, *The Trinitarian Faith*, p. 89.

Moltmann also opposes thinking of God as the "unmoved mover". But the crucial difference between him and Torrance is that Torrance makes a clear and sharp distinction between the immanent and economic Trinity and thus between God's internal relations of love and his external relations with us in history. And so Torrance opposes any idea that God needs the world or that God needs redemption.[51] For Torrance, "the universe ... is not a necessary emanation of the divine".[52] He also opposes any idea that God is not free in his choices. In Torrance's words: "The world needs God to be what it is, but God does not need the world to be what he is ... the Creator was free not to create ..."[53] So whereas Moltmann holds that God's love "is a self-evident, unquestionable 'overflowing of goodness' which is therefore *never open to choice at any time*",[54] Torrance insists that since the love of God manifest in the economic Trinity "directs us back to the Love that God eternally is in himself in the ontological Trinity apart from his relation to the world",[55] we must recognize the freedom of God's grace in creating and becoming incarnate.[56] This is, of course, exactly the very opposite of Moltmann's view of the eternal Trinity, since Moltmann contends that contemporary trinitarian thinking cannot allow for "an immanent Trinity in which God is simply by himself, without the love which communicates salvation".[57] And he argues, in accordance with his panentheistic perspective, that he must surrender the traditional distinction between the immanent and economic Trinity and affirm Rahner's thesis of identity, but only with the proviso that "The economic Trinity not only reveals the immanent Trinity; it also has a retroactive effect on it".[58] It is this thinking, together with the ideas that God's love and overflowing goodness are never open to choice— which stem from Moltmann's failure to acknowledge the freedom of the immanent Trinity—that contrasts with Torrance's view that creation is the result of God's free choice and act of will. God's choice is free and thus he is not constrained to love us by creating us; but because "God loves us better than he loves himself" or even "loves us more than he loves himself",[59] he does indeed freely choose to love us even to the point that he willingly sacrificed his own Son for our benefit. Unlike Moltmann, however, Torrance will never say God needs to become incarnate to be God or that creation represents a self-limitation on God's part. Instead, he believes that even in the incarnation, where God humiliates himself on our behalf, God's

---

[51]  For Torrance, "There is, therefore, no necessary relation between God and the created cosmos, as if God needed relation to what is not himself in order to be what he eternally is in himself as Father Almighty" (*The Trinitarian Faith*, p. 90).

[52]  Torrance, *Divine and Contingent Order*, p. 71.

[53]  Torrance, *Divine and Contingent Order*, p. 34.

[54]  Moltmann, *Trinity and Kingdom*, p. 55. Emphasis mine.

[55]  Torrance, *The Christian Doctrine of God*, p. 210.

[56]  See also Torrance, *Divine and Contingent Order*, pp. 34ff.

[57]  Moltmann, *Trinity and Kingdom*, p. 151.

[58]  Moltmann, *Trinity and Kingdom*, p. 160.

[59]  Torrance, *The Christian Doctrine of God*, pp. 209–10 and 215.

action is not to be understood as "the self-limitation of God or the curtailment of his power, but the staggering exercise of his power within the limitations of our contingent existence in space and time".[60]

How, then, did Torrance think about God's relation with the universe? That relation, he insisted, "is neither a necessary relation, nor an arbitrary relation. God was *free* to create the universe, but he was also free not to create it".[61] Creation was not the result of any random accident, but was an act of God's Word and Wisdom. As such it only could be understood properly through God's Son or Word and not by considering it in itself. Furthermore, the universe "did not come into existence through any inner compulsion in God's being" since "God has no need of the universe".[62] Nonetheless, because God created the world out of his love and grace, he gave it a rationality that was grounded in his own eternal triune knowledge and love so that, as Barth himself believed, the universe could be seen as a "created correspondence" to the Holy Trinity. The important point in Torrance's mind here is that a proper understanding of creation can make sense only in light of what God himself has revealed in and through his incarnation and the outpouring of the Holy Spirit. And what he has revealed is this:

> The whole *raison d'être* of the universe lies in the fact that God will not be alone, that he will not be without us, but has freely and purposely created the universe and bound it to himself as the sphere where he may ungrudgingly pour out his love, and where we way enjoy communion with him.[63]

## Understanding Creation through the Incarnation

It is no wonder, then, that when Torrance spells out the history of the doctrine of the *creatio ex nihilo* he argues, following Athenagoras, that the starting point for the doctrine was the resurrection of Christ himself because it was in that event that God's power over being and non-being was uniquely evident.[64] But, of course, the resurrection never would have occurred unless, as Athanasius put it, "the Lord became man and did not come into man".[65] Hence, for Torrance, the Christian view of creation proceeds properly when creation is understood in and through the doctrines of the incarnation, atonement and redemption. While we have already seen that in the early part of the fourth century there was serious confusion between the eternal generation of the Son and God's creative act, stemming from Origen's failure to distinguish clearly between God's internal and external activities; there

---

[60]  Torrance, *The Christian Doctrine of God*, pp. 214–15.
[61]  Torrance, *The Trinitarian Faith*, p. 92.
[62]  Torrance, *The Trinitarian Faith*, p. 93.
[63]  Torrance, *The Trinitarian Faith*, pp. 94–5.
[64]  See Torrance, *The Trinitarian Faith*, p. 97.
[65]  Torrance, *The Trinitarian Faith*, p. 104.

was also confusion regarding God, Christ and the world, stemming from Arian thinking. Origen could only think of God as almighty "in a necessary eternal conjunction with all things".[66] In this way, he failed to give priority to the Father/Son relation over the Creator/creature relation. In addition, he tended to think of the generation of the Son and creation of the cosmos as both due to the Father's will; indeed, Origen was critical of the idea that the Son was begotten of the Father's being. By assuming the world is eternal, Origen made external relations necessary to God, and needless to say, as we have seen, Athanasius, Irenaeus and others rightly opposed such thinking, insisting that creation is in no way necessary for God because it comes into existence by an act of his will and as an act of love and grace.

Further, Arius approached creation in dualist fashion, dissolving the connection in being between the Incarnate Son and the Father, and so he included the Son as one of the works of God created by God's will. In this way, Arius restricted knowledge of God to his external relations with creation. "Hence for him God was primarily Creator and not Father, and it is only as Creator that he was Father, not the other way around".[67] And, as we have already seen, Athanasius helpfully overcame both of these erroneous forms of thought by insisting that the Father/Son relation has priority over the Creator/creature relation, so that although God was always Father of the Son, he was not always Creator. Hence the world is neither eternal nor could it be seen as in any way necessary to God. According to Torrance, all of this had the effect of forcing theologians to understand more clearly both the *creatio ex nihilo* and the created nature of the universe by thinking through the doctrine "in the light of the relation of the incarnate Son to the Father", as well as attempting to understand the world of space and time in light of God's own becoming incarnate within it. In fact, Torrance spells out three important implications that follow from an interpretation of creation by starting from the incarnation: 1) creation is contingent; 2) creation has a "contingent intelligibility"; and 3) creation is genuinely free in a limited sense. After a brief discussion of these concepts we will look at Torrance's "new natural theology" before drawing this chapter to a close.

*Creation Is Contingent*

Once more Torrance follows Athanasius who reflected upon the relation between the only begotten Word of God who is "unchanging, unlimited and not composite in his being and nature" and creation which is indeed "changing, limited and composite" because it was created out of nothing. By reflecting on the incarnation itself, Athanasius concluded that although the created universe was "weak and mortal" as well as "fleeting" and in "a state of flux" and finally "subject to dissolution", when it was seen in light of the incarnation one could see that it was

---

66    Torrance, *The Trinitarian Faith*, p. 85.
67    Torrance, *The Trinitarian Faith*, p. 85.

"maintained in being by the creating and ordering activity of the Word of God, and thus preserved by divine grace from lapsing back into nothing".[68]

For Athanasius, the universe was "framed by the Word of God" and was made out of nothing, which means, as seen above, it was not created out of anything but was brought into being and held in being by God through his Word. Thus, creaturely events were neither necessary, accidental nor did they come about by chance; rather they came into existence and existed as contingent events. Torrance attributes this idea of contingence to Christian reflection on the incarnation as a wholly new idea that differed from Greek philosophy and science which saw the contingent as accidental and as the antithesis of "what is necessary or logical" and to that extent as lacking "rational order".[69] In fact, for Greek thinking, contingence was a "surd" and even seen as a form of evil that was unthinkable and impossible. Such thinking, then, was antithetical to the Christian concept of contingence advocated by Athanasius and explicated by John Philoponos. It is, of course, in this context that Torrance argues that both ancient and modern science by themselves "could not come up with the notion of contingence", because although this idea is necessary for scientific exploration of nature in its difference from God, it originally came from Christian faith.[70]

Torrance admits that contingence in the Christian sense is not at all an easy concept. It first presupposes the creation of the world out of nothing, so that the world is to be seen as "utterly distinct from God" while at the same time having a "measure of genuine independence". This thinking was "radicalised and reinforced by the doctrine of the incarnation" with the result that two important ideas were held simultaneously: on the one hand, by virtue of its contingence, creation was totally dependent on God for its existence, while, on the other hand, it was given a measure of independence by God as well. In other words, "the very reality of this independence of nature is itself dependent, or contingent, upon God".[71] All of this means that the universe is not "self-supporting or self-explaining" and it is no mere appearance "for it is ontologically grounded beyond itself on God", who has given it a reality outside himself. And if God were to withdraw his presence from creation, it would slip back into nothing. Since the universe has its meaning outside itself in the goodness, love and wisdom of God, we can say that "the universe may be thought of as 'in God', embraced within the power and presence of the Creator Word and Spirit".[72] Torrance obviously does not mean this in Moltmann's panentheistic sense but in the sense of true contingence, namely, that the universe which is "in God" is at the same time "by God" and therefore exists in utter difference from God by his grace and love alone.

---

[68] Torrance, *The Trinitarian Faith*, p. 98.

[69] Torrance, *The Trinitarian Faith*, p. 100.

[70] Torrance, *Divine and Contingent Order*, p. 76.

[71] Torrance, *The Trinitarian Faith*, p. 100. For the scientific implications of this double sense of contingency, see Torrance, *Divine and Contingent Order*, pp. 74ff.

[72] Torrance, *The Trinitarian Faith*, p. 101.

The incarnation also shed light on the fact that creation is marked by "deficiency" in the sense that when creatures turn away from God they "waste away into non-existence" and "fall under the condemnation of death".[73] What was revealed by the incarnation, then, was that beyond the natural contingence and corruptibility of the created order there was a "deep-seated corruption (φθορά) ... which worked for their utter dissolution", which could be seen as the "corruption of evil".[74] It is in this sense that the reason for the incarnation was seen as the "restoration of God's creation" by God's eternal Word taking on our corruptible and alienated human nature in order to redeem our human being in himself. It was by "transferring our contingent existence into himself in whom ... divine and human, uncreated and created, realities and natures are indissolubly united, Jesus Christ has secured its origin and end in his own eternal being". It is in this sense that creation is thought of "as proleptically conditioned by redemption".[75] Indeed, it is precisely the incarnation of God in time and space that leads us to respect the empirical world.[76] This is one of the reasons why Torrance insists upon the fact that human beings have a unique place in the universe. "In that it is redeemed man who is established at the head of the whole system of inter-level interaction throughout the created order, man's priestly function in the universe now takes on the pattern of a redemptive mission to nature."[77] In this priestly function, human beings become scientists and bring to light the intelligibility of nature. But they also become the instruments, under God, "whereby physical evil and disorder are rectified and are made, contrary to what they may actually be, to serve the whole created order ... it is only as man himself is healed of his own inward split and disorder that he may exercise a truly integrative and reordering role in the world around".[78]

## Creation's Contingent Intelligibility

If the Christian idea of contingence was difficult for the Greek mind, the idea that the created order had a "contingent intelligibility" was even more difficult. The universe does indeed have an immanent rational order but it is an order given by God and totally dependent on God for its existence and rationality. Just as there is "an absolute distinction between the uncreated being of God and created being, so there is an absolute distinction between the uncreated rationality of

---

73   Torrance, *The Trinitarian Faith*, p. 101.

74   Torrance, *The Trinitarian Faith*, p. 101. For an interesting discussion of how human sin and evil relate to natural evil embedded in the cosmos and why Torrance insists that God did not directly intend these as part of his good creation, see Torrance, *Divine and Contingent Order*, pp. 139ff.

75   Torrance, *The Trinitarian Faith*, p. 102.

76   Torrance, *Divine and Contingent Order*, p. 33.

77   Torrance, *Divine and Contingent Order*, p. 138.

78   Torrance, *Divine and Contingent Order*, p. 138.

God and the created rationality of the world".[79] It is here that Torrance relies on Athanasius' rejection of Greek dualism between the intelligible and sensible which posited a notion of the "divine *logos* as an immanent cosmological principle and of 'seminal reasons' (λόγοι σπερματικοί), or eternal rational forms embedded in nature, that often went with it".[80] It is the distinction between incarnation and creation that "shattered the Greek idea that the intelligible order of the world is to be understood as a general embodiment of the divine Logos immanently within it, i.e. as its necessary, inner cosmological principle".[81] While the *Logos* through whom God created the world gives creation an intelligibility that depends upon God's transcendent rationality, the two are not to be confused. Understanding God's transcendent intelligibility through the incarnate Word led theologians to comprehend the fact that when God created time and space, and yet came to exist within time and space in the incarnation without being contained and conditioned by time and space, Christians found it necessary to develop "*relational* conceptions of space and time" which could be applied to God in a way that did not restrict his transcendent nature and to creatures in another way that did justice to their contingent nature. They therefore rejected the container notion of space and time which took shape along Platonic, Aristotelian and Stoic lines in Greek philosophy and which we will discuss in detail in a later chapter. Here it is important to note that by developing relational conceptions of space and time on the basis of revelation, Christian theologians were able to escape the usual necessitarian and deterministic notions that dominated Greek thought. This led to a view of natural laws that are understood as "orderly sequences and enduring structures in nature that arise under the commanding voice of the Creator" and as such they were seen as "dependent on the Word of God as their source and ground".[82] What this finally meant was that such natural laws could be understood properly only when creation was seen as pointing beyond itself "to a transcendent ground of rationality in the *Logos* of God the Creator".[83]

---

[79]   Torrance, *The Trinitarian Faith*, p. 103.

[80]   Torrance, *The Trinitarian Faith*, p. 103. See also Torrance, "Athanasius", *Theology in Reconciliation*, p. 217. Here Torrance notes that the idea of "seminal reasons" is a Stoic notion, while the idea of the Logos as an impersonal cosmological principle, with its inherent dualistic implications of the separation between the intelligible and sensible realms so damaging to Christian theology, was embraced by "Hellenism, Gnosticism and Origenism". Athanasius rejected these concepts, along with the Platonic idea that God is "beyond knowledge and being". It is this idea, Torrance notes, that was combined in Alexandria with "a transcendentalist Judaism in its notion of the 'namelessness' of God and an intellectual mysticism such as we find in Neoplatonism", which Athanasius rejected but which later caused problems for Greek theology.

[81]   Torrance, *Divine and Contingent Order*, p. 33.

[82]   Torrance, *The Trinitarian Faith*, p. 104.

[83]   Torrance, *The Trinitarian Faith*, p. 104.

*The Free Creation*

In the final analysis, the complete notion of contingence means that "God is related to the universe, neither arbitrarily nor necessarily, but through the freedom of his grace and will".[84] What this means is that "God was absolutely free both to create and not to create the universe, which means the universe might not have come into existence at all."[85] God was thus under no constraint of any kind to create and he might well have allowed the universe to cease to exist. We might never have existed or might have existed differently if God so willed it. Nonetheless, creation is a rational act of God and so God did not act arbitrarily. While the prevailing Greek thinking was dominated by the equation of necessity and rationality, the new Christian thinking opposed this and rejected notions of "an all-controlling impersonal fate" and "the superstitious hold of astrology and divination".[86] In light of the incarnation, Christians could see that by becoming man in Jesus Christ, God set all creation free from sin, corruption and death. In Christ, God "established and secured a new relation between creation and himself in which creation is given a freedom grounded in the transcendent and unlimited freedom of God".[87] This emphasis on the redemption and renewal of the whole of creation was stronger in the East than in the West because the West was more influenced by the dualistic separation of the intelligible and sensible realms as this was understood by Augustine. In the East, the incarnation and resurrection of Jesus Christ meant that "the whole universe is ontologically bound to the incarnate and risen Jesus, and therefore that the whole universe is brought to share in the freedom of the Creator".[88] What sort of freedom is it, then, that creation as a contingent reality has?

It is, of course, a "limited freedom". Any idea of an unlimited freedom applying to a contingent reality would in fact be a contradiction in terms. Contingent freedom means that the universe is "limited only by that transcendent Freedom in God which is its very ground precisely as contingent freedom".[89] What this means to Torrance is that created freedom is at once dependent on God and thus limited and also independent in such a way that it is also "correlated to the unlimited and inexhaustible freedom of God" with the result that it is "continuously open to his creative power" and it actually mirrors the freedom of God. There are then "unlimited, and inexhaustible possibilities in the created universe".[90] This, Torrance believes, is basic to the idea of contingence. Just because the universe has a measure of God-given independence, it can be investigated scientifically and

---

84   Torrance, *The Trinitarian Faith*, p. 105.
85   Torrance, *The Trinitarian Faith*, p. 105.
86   Torrance, *The Trinitarian Faith*, p. 106.
87   Torrance, *The Trinitarian Faith*, p. 106.
88   Torrance, *The Trinitarian Faith*, p. 107.
89   Torrance, *The Trinitarian Faith*, p. 107.
90   Torrance, *The Trinitarian Faith*, p. 107.

in fact we have a duty to do so.[91] Indeed, the goal is to allow nature to reveal itself to us "without imposing upon it the presuppositions hidden in our questions".[92] What we learn from the doctrine of creation interpreted through the incarnation, and thus interpreted in a trinitarian way, is that the universe is "endowed with an openness, spontaneity and freedom which will always take us by surprise".[93] God's ways and works in nature have a surprising quality to them and "defy any anticipation on our part". We are thus unable to anticipate certain structures and patterns in the universe *a priori*.[94] Yet there is also an amazing constancy and reliability to nature in a way that mirrors God's freedom and constancy.

Of all the early church fathers, John Philoponos of Alexandria grasped this best with his distinction between the uncreated light of God and the created light of the universe as a reflection of God's uncreated light. Torrance spells this out in detail in his important book *Divine and Contingent Order*. Since God is light, as recounted in the Gospel of John, there is in him no darkness. According to Torrance, the idea that God's light shines in the world from its incarnation in Jesus Christ and thus illumines all of nature was new and had to be learned in conflict with the idea that

> the world is determined by blind inexorable fate or sheer irrational chance, or that human existence imprisoned in the darkness of irrational matter is the prey of inscrutable occult powers that are to be feared and appeased, conceptions which lent themselves readily to magic, superstition, and astrology.[95]

Even rational Greek thought diverged from the Christian view because it operated on the assumption that there was an intelligible light native to human reason that could comprehend the eternal forms embedded in the cosmos, as in Plato's idea of *reminiscence*. Torrance notes that, according to this view, "all learning is ultimately a kind of recalling from within of a truth which we brought with us from a previous existence".[96] According to the fathers, however, genuine learning meant "discovering of the truth of things which we did not know before but which we come to know for the first time as we make actual contact with the realities concerned and know them out of their own intelligibilities".[97] In other words, truth comes to us from the object of inquiry and not from any preconception of the inquiring subject. What this means is that the distinction between God's uncreated light and created light imparted by God to the universe enables us to know things

---

91  See Torrance, *Divine and Contingent Order*, p. 72.

92  Torrance, *The Trinitarian Faith*, p. 107.

93  Torrance, *The Trinitarian Faith*, p. 108. See also Torrance, *Divine and Contingent Order*, pp. 22–3.

94  See Torrance, *Divine and Contingent Order*, p. 22.

95  Torrance, *Divine and Contingent Order*, p. 65.

96  Torrance, *Divine and Contingent Order*, p. 66.

97  Torrance, *Divine and Contingent Order*, p. 66.

as they really are. Just as the sun cannot be looked at directly, so God cannot be looked at directly, but can only be known through the shining of his light upon creation; that indeed is what happens in the incarnation: "Bathed in the Light of God that shines in concentrated form in Jesus Christ, the universe took on a radically different aspect".[98]

Importantly, then, Torrance's understanding of creation was dictated by his view of the incarnation and ultimately by his view of the immanent Trinity. Indeed, he insisted that we may only grasp something of the combination of "freedom and constancy, spontaneity and reliability, unpredictability and order" in nature as we allow our minds to come under the influence of God's self-revelation in Jesus Christ himself. In Torrance's words:

> Everything hinges, however, upon what we understand of the love, constancy and faithfulness of Jesus Christ as Lord and Saviour, and whether what he reveals of the nature of God is really true of God the Father Almighty, Creator of heaven and earth and all things visible and invisible, in his own essential nature. Is there a relation of absolute fidelity between the self-manifestation of God in the incarnation and what he is in his own eternal being? If there is such a relation of utter fidelity and constancy, then Jesus Christ in his redeeming love and liberating grace is the divine pledge for our understanding of the freedom, integrity and reliability of the creation even in its physical order and behaviour.[99]

Here we have the full-blown picture of contingence that was thought through in the early church by reflecting on God the Creator through his incarnate Word: a world with genuine independence, with a rationality all its own, but a rationality grounded beyond itself in God's love and freedom—a world that might never have come into being at all or might have been quite different than it actually is. This world is nonetheless stable, reliable and constant, and indeed it is open to God's providential care and his loving purposes as revealed in the incarnation and resurrection of Jesus himself. All of this was accomplished in the early church in face of the Greek tendency to identify God with nature and to think in terms of determinism and fatalism and the "necessity" of nature. Thus, as far as Torrance was concerned, even the doctrine of creation "hinges upon the *homoousion*, that is, upon whether it was through Jesus Christ who is of one substance with the Father that 'all things were made'".[100] Unless God's creative act is understood in this Christological and trinitarian sense, the danger of pantheism and dualism will always threaten and thus the true contingence of creation inevitably will be undermined. And we might say the ultimate reason for this would be the failure to acknowledge God's freedom both to have existed without us and actually to

---

[98]   Torrance, *Divine and Contingent Order*, p. 67.

[99]   Torrance, *The Trinitarian Faith*, pp. 108–9.

[100]  Torrance, *The Trinitarian Faith*, p. 109.

become incarnate within creation to enable our contingent existence and to renew it. It is within this context that we will close the chapter with a brief consideration of Torrance's "new" natural theology.

## Torrance's New Natural Theology

It is quite obvious from what has been said above that Torrance did not think we can know God with any accuracy apart from revelation. That is the import of his trinitarian understanding of the doctrine of creation. So it may come as a surprise to discover that Torrance would want to discuss natural theology at all. What must be stressed here is that, in Torrance's two major works on the Trinity, even his "new" natural theology hardly makes an appearance. So I think it is fair to say that the issue of natural theology only arises in his attempt to set Christian theology into dialogue with natural science. That, of course, as we noted at the outset, will not be the main theme of this book because my goal here is to see how all of Torrance's dogmatic thinking is structured by his understanding of the Trinity. Still, it is important to see what he said and what he intended with his "new" natural theology and how that fits within his theology as a whole.

A good deal of Torrance's discussion of his "new" natural theology initially takes place in relation to Barth's thinking on the subject.[101] As is well known, Barth unequivocally rejected natural theology in all its forms because for him such thinking always manifested the human attempt to construct idols. Even the most innocuous forms of natural theology were problematic from Barth's perspective because, although they may seem to treat revelation with respect and even with reverence, apparently allowing a proper place for revelation in the church, they were after all attempting to *find a place* in their thinking for revelation. But that is exactly the problem. A theology that has to find a place for revelation is already idolatrous precisely because revelation by its very nature claims human thinking and human being in all its dimensions for itself in such a way that it has unequivocal and irreversible priority over human reason and experience. In other words, thinking that takes place in faith in the Word of God through the Holy Spirit is thinking that is obedient to the Word. And such thinking never deviates for a moment from the authority and freedom that comes solely from God's Word and Spirit.

---

[101]    In this regard Torrance provides us with an interesting discussion of these issues in "The Problem of Natural Theology in the Thought of Karl Barth" in *Religious Studies* 6 (1970): 121–35. This article was republished in Thomas F. Torrance, *Transformation & Convergence*, Chapter 9, "Natural Theology in the Thought of Karl Barth", pp. 285–301. For a full discussion of Torrance and Barth on the issue of natural theology, see Paul D. Molnar, "Natural Theology Revisited: A Comparison of T.F. Torrance and Karl Barth" in *Zeitschrift für dialektische Theologie* Vol. 20, No. 1, December 2005: 53–83.

Torrance, of course, agreed with Barth that natural theology cannot function independently of faith, grace and revelation and believes that what Barth was rejecting in disallowing natural theology was that it could function in any way epistemologically prior to actual knowledge of God that takes place in faith.[102] Torrance also thought that Barth's critics misunderstand him on this issue because of their own dualist presuppositions, with the result that they mistakenly think Barth rejected natural theology because of some sort of deistic separation of God and the world or because of some Marcionite denigration of the natural world or because of some sort of fideism.[103] Nonetheless, Torrance also believed there should be a proper natural theology that is neither independent nor antecedent to "actual or empirical knowledge of God upon which it is then imposed".[104] Whereas theological science deals with God and thus looks "*through* the rational structures of the universe to the Creator", natural science looks "*at* the universe and its natural order". [105] Yet, for Torrance, within his unitary rather than dualistic view of reality,

> there is a necessary and inescapable connection between theological concepts and physical concepts, spiritual and natural concepts, positive and natural theology, or rather between theological science and natural science, for it is in that connection that the changed status of natural theology has its place.[106]

---

[102]   See, for example, Thomas F. Torrance, *Space, Time and Resurrection* (hereafter: *STR*), (Edinburgh: T&T Clark, 1998), pp. ix–x. According to Torrance, "instead of rejecting natural theology *tout court*, Barth has transposed it into the material content of theology where in a changed form it constitutes the epistemological structure of our knowledge of God" (Torrance, *STR*, p. x). In his important book *The Ground and Grammar*, Torrance notes that what Barth objects to epistemologically in traditional natural theology "is not any invalidity in its argumentation, nor even its rational structure, as such, but its *independent* character" which abstracts from "the active self-disclosure of the living and Triune God—for that can only split the knowledge of God into two parts, natural knowledge of the One God and revealed knowledge of the Triune God, which is scientifically as well as theologically intolerable". Accordingly, Barth did not reject "the place of a proper rational structure in the knowledge of God, such as natural theology strives for ... That is why Barth claims that, properly understood, natural theology is included *within* revealed theology" (pp. 90–1). In Torrance's view, then, Barth objected to natural theology as an independent undertaking "antecedent to the rise and formulation of actual knowledge of God" (p. 92).

[103]   Torrance, *The Ground and Grammar*, pp. 87ff.

[104]   Torrance, *STR*, p. 1. See also Thomas F. Torrance, *Reality and Scientific Theology* (Eugene, Oregon: Wipf & Stock Publishers, 2001), p. 40.

[105]   Torrance, *Reality and Scientific Theology*, p. 70.

[106]   Torrance, *Reality and Scientific Theology*, p. 69. It is perhaps interesting to note here that on the one hand Torrance sees an intrinsic connection between what he calls positive and natural theology, while on the other hand he immediately seems to modify this by saying that this relation is "rather" between "theological science and natural science". This nuance makes a world of difference because he may simply mean that theological

Whether or not Torrance intended to construct a theology of nature in his dialogue with the natural sciences, his belief that there is room for what he calls a new kind of natural theology led him to conclude that

> If natural theology is to have a viable reconstruction even in something like its traditional form, it can be only on the basis of a restored ontology in which our thought operates with a fundamental unity of concept and experience, or of form and being, within a contingent but inherently intelligible and open-structured universe.[107]

There is little doubt that even in this statement, where Torrance mentions that his reconstructed natural theology could exist "in something like its traditional form", he is after something more than just a theology of nature. And there are a number of other remarks that he makes that confirm this judgment. For instance, Torrance believes natural theology can be bracketed from revelation artificially and temporarily "for purposes of clarification".[108] But, even according to Torrance's own analysis, what exactly is it that could possibly be clarified by such thinking when by definition it ignores the revelation of God in his Word and Spirit? In addition, Torrance says, in a manner reminiscent of more traditional natural theology, that "the combination of unpredictability and lawfulness in nature found in its capacity spontaneously to generate richer and more open-structured forms of order in the constantly expanding universe may be regarded as something like the

---

science, like natural science, is not dualistic and seeks to understand reality in accordance with its nature. That might explain why, after noting that "Torrance's reconstruction of natural theology is one of the most difficult aspects of his theology", Elmer Colyer mentions that "There is reason to believe that Torrance may regret calling this reformulated version 'natural theology'" (Colyer, *How To Read T.F. Torrance*, pp. 192, 194). Perhaps, Colyer suggests, he really meant to call it a theology of nature. This is an especially important point since I believe Alister McGrath's attempt to construct a natural theology within the ambit of revelation, while claiming to follow Torrance, falters precisely because of its apologetic intent and goes beyond anything Torrance himself would countenance especially when McGrath turns to Pannenberg to present a "public theology" that appeals to those with or without faith in the Christian God [See Alister E. McGrath, *A Scientific Theology: Volume I Nature* (Grand Rapids, Michigan: William B. Eerdmans Publishing Company, 2001), pp. 264–305]. Strangely, McGrath actually argues that the apologetic value of a "legitimate natural theology" will allow us to see that "the Christian evangelist will have a number of 'points of contact' for the gospel within the created order" (p. 299), and he believes that all acts of understanding are based upon some pre-understanding (p. 298) so that "the human mind possesses the capacity to recognize this work of creation as such, and to draw at least some reliable conclusions concerning the nature and character of God from the created order" (p. 299). Torrance rejects all three of these ideas in his theology.

[107]    Torrance, *The Ground and Grammar*, pp. 86–7.
[108]    Torrance, *Reality and Scientific Theology*, p. 42.

signature of the Creator in the depths of contingent being".[109] Statements such as this only encourage the motives behind traditional natural theology to search for an understanding of God the Creator by focusing on his supposed signature within the created order instead of pointing us firmly and consistently to revelation, as Torrance certainly does in his trinitarian doctrine, as the source of our knowledge of God the Creator. Further, although Torrance quite properly insists that there is no possibility of building a logical bridge between the world and God or between our thoughts and God's being,[110] and while he insists that his new natural theology will never function independent of its material content (revelation),[111] he also believes that since created intelligibility does not carry its own ultimate explanation within itself, it must therefore point beyond itself "with a mute cry for sufficient reason" so that "the fact that the universe is intrinsically rational means that it is capable of, or open to, rational explanation—from beyond itself".[112] The fact that the universe is indeed comprehensible in this way

> *suggests*, or directs us to, a transcendent ground of rationality as its explanation.
> It is the objective depth of comprehensibility in the universe that projects our
> thought beyond it in this way ... To be inherently reasonable the universe
> requires a sufficient reason for being what it is as an intelligible whole.[113]

In the process of reasoning, then, "we are aware of coming under an imperious constraint from beyond".[114] All of this "would seem to *suggest* that there is an *active agency* other than the inherent intelligibility and harmony of the universe, unifying and structuring it, and providing it with its ground of being".[115] When one compares this thinking to Torrance's explicit statements about God which

---

[109]   Torrance, *Divine and Contingent Order*, p. 73.

[110]   Torrance, *The Ground and Grammar*, pp. 75ff., 79, 80–82, 86, 99. See also *Reality and Evangelical Theology*, pp. 24–5, 32. Torrance regards Anselm's argument as a scientific one rather than a logical one. Within this method intelligibility and being are not separated, but created intelligibility operates under the compulsion of God's uncreated intelligibility.

[111]   Thus, for example, Torrance insists that his "new" natural theology "must be brought within the body of positive theology, where it is integrated with its material content and pursued in indissoluble unity with it. But now the whole character of natural theology becomes transformed, for pursued within the actual inquiry of scientific theology, where we must think rigorously in accordance with the self-disclosure of God in his own intelligible relations, it will become *natural* to the material content of theology and will fall under the determination of its inherent intelligibility" (Torrance, *The Ground and Grammar*, pp. 92–3). This is repeated in Torrance, *Karl Barth*, p. 149.

[112]   Torrance, *Reality and Scientific Theology*, p. 52.

[113]   Torrance, *Reality and Scientific Theology*, p. 53.

[114]   Torrance, *Reality and Scientific Theology*, p. 54; cf. Torrance, *Reality and Evangelical Theology*, p. 26.

[115]   Torrance, *Reality and Scientific Theology*, p. 56.

appear in the context of his trinitarian doctrine, one can easily observe that this reference to God is not a reference primarily to God the Father in his relation with the Son (although that may well have been in the back of his mind and guiding his thought). Still, this is where Torrance and Barth remain separated. Barth insisted that natural theology in any form must lead to idolatry, as when he wrote: "Quite apart from grace and miracle, has not man always had what is in relation to the being of the world the very 'natural' capacity to persuade himself and others of a higher and divine being? All idols spring from this capacity."[116]

But Torrance even will go so far as to suggest that just as geometry cannot function properly independent of physics, it still can be bracketed from physics, and that by analogy our human understanding of God "apart from the divine side of the bi-polar relationship which knowledge of God involves" amounts to an artificial methodological separation akin to "converting four-dimensional geometry back into three-dimensional Euclidean geometry, or physical geometry back into *a priori* geometry".[117] Such an enterprise, Torrance insists, only can have "quasi-validity" because of the artificially imposed limits.[118] Nonetheless, Torrance does insist that, properly understood, geometry would not function independent of physics and would instead function as the "epistemological structure in the heart of physics, although considered in itself it would be incomplete without physics".[119] In this thinking, Torrance believes that natural theology simply refers to natural human thinking taking place within revelation so that he can say it is incomplete without revelation but still offers us a sense that there is an imperious constraint from beyond which commands our attention. Indeed, in his consideration of Barth's thinking, he can argue that independent natural theology does not terminate upon the Trinity but upon "some being of God in general".[120] And Torrance claims that an independent natural theology misses the mark "by abstracting [God's] existence from his act, and so by considering one aspect of his being apart from other aspects".[121] But it is just this assumption, that natural theology actually can know an aspect of God's being, that Barth will not accept. It is just this thinking, then, that Barth himself would reject in spite of Torrance's belief to the contrary. The key difficulty in Torrance's thought concerns his willingness to bracket his "new" natural theology from its material content (revelation) at all.[122] This is certainly

---

116 Barth, *CD* II/1, p. 84.

117 Torrance, *Reality and Scientific Theology*, p. 59.

118 Torrance, *Reality and Scientific Theology*, p. 60.

119 Torrance, *Reality and Evangelical Theology*, p. 33; also see Torrance, *Reality and Scientific Theology*, p. 39.

120 Torrance, *Karl Barth*, p. 151.

121 Torrance, *Karl Barth*, p. 151.

122 See Torrance, *Reality and Scientific Theology*, pp. 59–60. Torrance insists that while methodologically we can bracket our natural knowledge of God from revelation, this must not be taken too seriously and cannot be allowed to harden. But he does maintain that natural theology might be "artificially bracketed off from the material content of actual

in tension with his own insistence that such bracketing cannot lead to accurate knowledge of God and is just as certainly in conflict with Barth's thinking. Very simply put, Barth was not at all convinced that a philosophical understanding of the intelligibility of the universe would lead us to God and made a point of this when, in response to a question about Karl Heim's thinking in connection with the relation of science and philosophy to theology, he asked, "is the presupposition true, that at the end of our thoughts we will always meet God? After all, it may be the devil!"[123] It is Torrance's belief, then, that the intelligibility of the universe "does more than raise a question for it seems to *cry silently* for a transcendent agency in its explanation and understanding". Indeed, for Torrance, "there strikes at us through the blank face of the universe a mysterious intelligibility which takes us under its command in such a way that we feel we have to do with an undeniable and irreducibly transcendent reality". [124] How can the universe cry silently for an explanation? How can we speak of a mysterious intelligibility from the "blank face" of the universe? Do those questions not come from those who are reflecting on the universe rather than from the universe? And if so, are those not the perennial questions of natural theology? The difference here between Torrance and the more traditional natural theologies—and it is an important one—is that Torrance here refuses to build a logical bridge from the contingent universe to God the Creator. But the real question in the context of this discussion is what use is it to know of some "mysterious intelligibility" or some "irreducibly transcendent reality" when knowledge of the triune God leads to quite a specific and different content according to Torrance's own estimation throughout the rest of his dogmatic theology and especially in his trinitarian theology? It seems that what Torrance really wanted to say was that if we see the world in its true contingent

---

knowledge of God, and could be accepted only as a temporary methodological device for purposes of clarification" (Torrance, *Reality and Scientific Theology*, p. 42), although such a natural theology "still retains the imprint of its empirical origins and foundations, which means that in our clarificatory analysis of it we cannot in truthfulness forget its correlation with revealed theology" (p. 43). See also Torrance, *Karl Barth*, p. 158, where he claims that when Henri Bouillard believed that he could "envisage an aspect of God's being apart from the Trinity made known in his work of revelation and reconciliation", Bouillard believed this was a "legitimate 'methodological abstraction' provided that we do not simply rest in it". In this context, however, Torrance explicitly says that he did not consider this defense by Bouillard of his position against Barth to be a sufficient answer to Barth. Yet, the issue between Torrance and Barth still remains because, for Barth, such an abstraction is completely unacceptable in any form or at any time. And any such abstraction will never clarify our knowledge of the triune God but only obscure it. And the claim that natural theology might "retain the imprint of its empirical origins" avoids the problem here, namely, that no reflection on creation apart from faith in God's Word and Spirit will lead to knowledge of the triune God.

[123]   John D. Godsey (ed.), *Karl Barth's Table Talk* (Richmond: John Knox Press, 1962), p. 20.

[124]   Torrance, *Reality and Scientific Theology*, p. 58.

intelligibility, then we will have to admit that for the world to make ultimate sense it would have to be explained by reference to God the Creator. And he also wanted to say that modern science, since Einstein, has been moving away from the kind of phenomenalism involved in Kantian thinking, which would deny that we can know reality in itself, and toward a more realistic view that maintains that we can really know creation in its intrinsic intelligibility and that that objective reality indeed should be the factor governing all our thought about nature. But neither of these two goals, laudable in themselves, is really served by the pursuit of a natural theology that can be bracketed from revelation even momentarily. And to call the epistemological structure of our knowledge of God that takes shape in revelation "natural theology" just confuses the issue, since any epistemological structure of ours that may faithfully present knowledge of the triune God is already transformed by its encounter with grace such that it is no longer operating according to nature but rather is operating according to the dictates of grace, faith and revelation.

Our purpose in this chapter has been to see that, for Torrance, our knowledge of God the Father who is the Creator comes through the Son and by means of the Holy Spirit and that such knowledge precludes any attempt to reach a proper understanding of God abstractly by reflecting on God's works. We have seen why it was extremely important to Torrance to stress the primacy of the Father/Son relation over the Creator/creature relation and why it is important to avoid the errors of Origen and Arius. We have also seen why a proper view of the world's contingency is critical for a clear understanding of the Creator/creature relation. Finally, we have seen why Torrance formulated his "new" natural theology and how that understanding stands in tension to a certain degree with his own insistence that accurate thinking about God the Creator can only take place, as Athanasius himself taught, as knowledge of the Father through the Son and not by reflection on the universe itself. Now we will specifically consider Torrance's Christology which is certainly the key to understanding his vision of the Trinity, with a view toward seeing how his understanding of the incarnation leads him to reject Ebionite and Docetic Christology along with all forms of dualism that distort our view of space and time. We will consider his revolutionary discussion of the receptacle or container notion of space in order to see whether or not there could be some ecumenical agreement if and to the extent that these problematic notions are overcome in light of a clearer Christology.

# Chapter 4

# Jesus Christ, the Incarnate Word, *Homoousion* with the Father and with Us in our Humanity

Even the most cursory exploration of Torrance's theology will disclose the centrality of the *homoousion* for understanding who Jesus is as the incarnate Word and as the revelation of God present in history. We have already seen the importance of this concept in connection with Torrance's view of the Trinity because it signifies that it is only from within the Father/Son relation "that we are given access to know God as he is in himself" precisely because the Son, as God's action *ad extra*, is one in being with the Father and as such is God himself present in history, enabling us to know God "in accordance with his divine nature".[1] We have also seen how the *homoousion* shaped Torrance's understanding of creation as the act of the eternal Father that took place through his Son and in his Spirit and how he considered this the "linchpin" of Christian theology. In this chapter we shall explore Torrance's understanding of the incarnation and of the person and work of Jesus Christ as the revealer and reconciler. We will not discuss Torrance's view of reconciliation in any detail in this chapter since that will be the subject matter of the next chapter. But, as will be seen, it is impossible to reflect on Torrance's concept of revelation without at once realizing that reconciliation is an intrinsic part of the discussion.

For Torrance, the New Testament holds together Jesus' humanity and divinity from the start so that any implication of adoptionism (the idea that Jesus was a man who became God) with "an approach from below upwards" (Ebionite Christology, which saw in Jesus an extraordinary human being who was adopted into divine sonship)[2] or any implication of Apollinarianism (the idea that the Logos replaced Jesus' human mind and soul to save us) with "an approach from above downwards" (Docetic Christology, which undercut Jesus' humanity)[3] inevitably meant that neither approach

> had really started from the fundamental datum of the Gospel: that in Jesus Christ, who was born of Mary and suffered under Pontius Pilate, God himself has come

---

[1]   Torrance, *The Trinitarian Faith*, p. 110.

[2]   Torrance, *The Trinitarian Faith*, p. 112. See also Torrance, *The Christian Doctrine of God*, pp. 114–15. We will discuss Ebionite and Docetic Christology more extensively below.

[3]   Torrance, *The Trinitarian Faith*, p. 113.

to be with us and reveal himself to us, and that in the one Person of Jesus Christ God and man are inseparably united for us and our salvation.[4]

Torrance's view of the incarnation is clearly expressed in his important book *Space, Time and Incarnation*:

> By the Incarnation Christian theology means that at a definite point in space and time the Son of God became man, born at Bethlehem of Mary, a virgin espoused to a man called Joseph, a Jew of the tribe and lineage of David, and towards the end of the reign of Herod the Great in Judaea. Given the name of Jesus, He fulfilled His mission from the Father, living out the span of earthly life allotted to him until He was crucified under Pontius Pilate, but when after three days He rose again from the dead the eyes of Jesus' disciples were opened to what it all meant: they knew Him to be God's Son, declared with power and installed in Messianic Office, and so they went out to proclaim Him to all nations as the Lord and Saviour of the world.[5]

And it is important to see that Torrance's understanding of the incarnation is trinitarian in nature since it is by the Holy Spirit that the Word became incarnate: "Through him [the Holy Spirit] the Word of God became flesh and dwelt among us, but he was not himself that Word. Through him the Son of God became incarnate, but he did not incarnate himself among us."[6] And the incarnation is also a sending of the Son to become incarnate for the sake of our salvation. With this understanding of the incarnation in place, we may begin by noting that, for Torrance, "The Deity of Christ is the supreme truth of the Gospel, the key to the bewildering enigma of Jesus, for it provides it with a central point of reference consistent with the whole sequence of events leading up to and beyond the crucifixion".[7] Yet in light of his understanding of the incarnation already given, this statement by no means should be taken to indicate that Torrance in any way weakens Christ's humanity as the touchstone for God's approach to us in the sphere of creation. Rather, for Torrance,

---

[4]     Torrance, *The Trinitarian Faith*, pp. 114, 163–4.

[5]     Thomas F. Torrance, *Space, Time and Incarnation* (hereafter: *STI*), (Edinburgh: T & T Clark 1997), p. 52.

[6]     Torrance, *The Trinitarian Faith*, p. 212.

[7]     Torrance, *The Christian Doctrine of God*, p. 46. In his Auburn lectures of 1938–1939 Torrance put it this way: "Because the Deity of Christ is denied, people are not sure of what they believe. How do you know you are right and not wrong? ... Such is the uncertainty engendered through relativism so characteristic of the modern mind, because the one rock of certainty which anchors the faith of men and women, the Deity of Christ, the actual presence of God among us is struck out of their faith. When that goes the bottom drops out of Christianity. Hence we see today the enormous emphasis on ethical and human values, on personality and social relations, in which man tries to find a foundation for his feet." (*The Doctrine of Jesus Christ*, p. 143; text slightly altered)

the humanity of Christ is *enhypostatic*,[8] that is, it has its reality in and through the eternal Word becoming incarnate for us and for our salvation in the history of the particular man, Jesus of Nazareth.

The word *enhypostatic* has two senses for Torrance, as does the word *homoousion*. First, it refers to the fact that the persons of the Trinity are consubstantial within the Godhead so that each is fully God and each together inhere in the one being of God. And as Torrance himself indicates:

> The term *homoousios* (ὁμοούσιος) … refers to immanent personal relations in the Godhead. Within the one being of God, Father, Son, and Holy Spirit, who are each distinct … from one another, are all consubstantial, yet in relation to one another they are *hypostatic* … or *enhypostatic* …[9]

Second, it refers to the fact that the second person of the Trinity has become incarnate in the humanity of Jesus of Nazareth and so is *homoousion* with us in our humanity. Consequently, "it is specifically in Jesus Christ, the incarnate Son, that God has communicated himself to us … Thus it is only in him who is both ὁμοούσιος with the Father and ὁμοούσιος with us, that we may really know God as he is in himself".[10] That is why Torrance can say "through the *homoousion* the incarnational and saving self-revelation of God as Father, Son and Holy Spirit was traced back to what God is enhypostatically and coinherently in himself, in his own eternal being as Father, Son and Holy Spirit".[11] The important point for Torrance here is that because Jesus is one in being with the Father *and* with us, he not only can reveal God to us as only God can, but he can reconcile us to God as only God can. Therefore, Torrance rightly insists that "the human nature of Jesus was personalised or given enhypostatic (ἐνυπόστατος) reality in the Person of the

---

[8]     That is why in *The Doctrine of Jesus Christ* Torrance stressed that: 1) "the Word became united to a particular man, the man Jesus of Nazareth" (p. 132); 2) "There is no sense in universalising or deifying the humanity of Christ in itself apart from the fact that it is united to the eternal Word or Son of God" (p. 132); 3) following H.R. Mackintosh, "If the manhood of Christ is unreal, at any remotest point, God has not stooped to unity with man" (p. 133); 4) "Thus both these truths, the Divinity and the Humanity of Christ, must be held inseparably together … If Jesus Christ is not God, then God has not reached us, but has stopped short of humanity; then God does not love us to the uttermost. But the fact that Christ is God, really God, that Christ is perfectly human flesh of our flesh, bone of our bone, means that God has stopped short of nothing… Thus the humanity of Christ is the objective actuality of God to us in revelation and redemption; it guarantees a veritable Incarnation of God 'in all points made like unto his brethren', as the writer of the Epistle to the Hebrews expressed it" (p. 133).

[9]     Torrance, *The Trinitarian Faith*, p. 131.

[10]    Torrance, *The Trinitarian Faith*, p. 203.

[11]    Torrance, *The Trinitarian Faith*, p. 199.

Son of God become man. That took place in Jesus in an utterly unique way."[12]
Furthermore, this meant that

> Far from the presence of the Deity of the Son overwhelming or displacing the
> rational human person of Jesus, his human mind and human soul, the exact
> opposite took place. And so it must be said that no human being has such a full
> and rich personal human nature as Jesus.[13]

That is why Torrance insists that, when reading the Scriptures, we must "take our
stand on the supreme truth of the Deity of Christ, and therefore interpret them in
the light of the epistemic and ontological relation between the historical Jesus
Christ, the incarnate Son, and God the Father".[14]

What Torrance means here is that Jesus, the incarnate Word, is not the revealer
in his humanity as such. Consequently, he maintains, "It was not flesh and blood
that revealed Christ and the true significance of his Person, not even the flesh and
blood of Christ himself. What constitutes the revelation is not his personality in the
historical and psychological sense or at that level, but the Divine within Christ—
*God in Christ*".[15] Even more clearly expressed, Torrance writes in connection with
the incarnation, that "While the Incarnation means that God is revealed to us in a
human form, it does not mean that God is human; or to put it the other way around,
that human creatures as such can reveal God".[16] Ultimately, for Torrance, there is a
dialectic at work here that he terms the "logic of grace" and the "logic of Christ".
The former is signified by the technical term *Anhypostasia* because this describes
"the unconditional priority of Grace, that everything in theological knowledge
derives from God's Grace, while all truths and their relations within our thinking
must reflect the movement of Grace".[17] And this, for Torrance, means that in all
theology there is an

> unconditional priority of the Truth as Grace and the irreversibility of the
> relationship established between the Truth and us. The Logic of Grace is the
> way the Truth has taken in His disclosure to us. Because He does not cease to be
> Grace in our knowing Him, all our thoughts and their interrelations must reflect
> the movement of Grace.[18]

The latter is signified by the technical term *Enhypostasia* which asserts that "God
does not override us but makes us free. In merciful and loving condescension He

---

[12]   Torrance, *The Trinitarian Faith*, p. 230.
[13]   Torrance, *The Trinitarian Faith*, p. 230.
[14]   Torrance, *The Christian Doctrine of God*, p. 48.
[15]   Torrance, *The Doctrine of Jesus Christ*, p. 35.
[16]   Torrance, *The Doctrine of Jesus Christ*, p. 100.
[17]   Torrance, *Theological Science*, p. 217.
[18]   Torrance, *Theological Science*, p. 214.

gathers us into union with Himself, constituting us as His dear children who share His life and love".[19] The doctrine of "*enhypostasia* asserts the full unimpaired reality of the humanity of the historical Jesus as the humanity of the Son of God" and thus "it affirms in our theological knowledge full and unimpaired place for human decision, human response, and human thinking in relation to the Truth of God's Grace".[20]

## Torrance's Rejection of Ebionite and Docetic Christology

Paramount, then, in Torrance's understanding of the incarnation is the fact that Jesus Christ as attested in the New Testament must be understood as God and man. In other words, his divinity and humanity never can be separated in any way, either theoretically (epistemologically) or in reality (ontologically). This, of course, is connected with the fact that from very early on Torrance saw that the incarnation was a miracle, that is, it was an act of God coming into history from outside in order to heal our estranged humanity in its relation with God. Torrance therefore opposed the idea that history could or should be seen as "a vast human progress which will end up in a fulfilment of creation".[21] Such a conception ignores the fact that when eternity enters time, that has to mean "time cannot save itself. It means that if Eternity *does really come to and into* time, then time is not in touch with Eternity; it means that time is discontinuous with Eternity".[22]

Torrance's thinking here stands in contrast with Karl Rahner's view of the relationship between time and eternity. For Rahner, "Eternity is not an infinitely long mode of pure time, but rather it is a mode of the spiritual freedom which has been exercised in time, and therefore it can be understood only from a correct understanding of spiritual freedom".[23] Consequently, "eternity comes to be in time as time's own mature fruit" through the human exercise of freedom:

---

[19]   Torrance, *Theological Science*, p. 217.

[20]   Torrance, *Theological Science*, p. 218.

[21]   Torrance, *The Doctrine of Jesus Christ*, p. 79.

[22]   Torrance, *The Doctrine of Jesus Christ*, p. 79. Torrance's thinking is here in line with Karl Barth's rejection of Schleiermacher's view that "[He saw in Christ] the preservation 'of the receptivity implanted in human nature from the beginning and continuously evolving, a receptivity which enables it to take up into itself such an absolute potency of the God-consciousness' ... The Word of God is not seriously regarded by him as the Subject of the redeeming act, but as one of the factors in the world-process" (*CD* I/2, pp. 134–5 and 150ff).

[23]   Karl Rahner, *Foundations of Christian Faith: An Introduction To The Idea of Christianity* (hereafter: *Foundations*), trans. William V. Dych (New York: Seabury, 1978), p. 437.

wherever a free and lonely act of decision has taken place in absolute obedience to a higher law, or in a radical affirmation of love for another person, something eternal has taken place, and man is experienced immediately as transcending the indifference of time in its mere temporal duration.[24]

Rahner thinks eternity is implied both by history and by our thinking process, but most of all by our free decisions.[25] Hence, "Eternity is experienced in time itself most clearly when the intellectual subject in man makes a free decision which concerns and involves the one and entire person".[26] Indeed "ultimate personal decisions, at least when they involve a life in its totality, are irrevocable, they are truly eternity coming to be in time ... Here time really creates eternity and eternity is experienced in time".[27] Absent from Rahner's discussion of eternity here is Jesus himself as the one eternal God incarnate among us, that is, as eternity present within time and without being defined *by* time. Absent also is the sense advocated by Torrance that eternity and time are "discontinuous". That is why Rahner can speak of time and eternity in this reciprocal fashion. Because Torrance will not detach eternity from Jesus himself as the incarnate Word, that is, from the person of the Son, he insists that the relation between eternity and time is an irreversible one that can be understood only from Jesus himself as God's self-communication to us and among us. That is why Torrance writes:

> We cannot therefore properly think of the Incarnation apart from the Atonement, or the Atonement apart from the Incarnation. Nor may we separate the work from the Person of Christ for they are one, and it is the work of the Person and the Person who does this work, that together make the whole life and work of Jesus of Nazareth significant as fraught with saving Power, as pregnant with Eternity ... The Incarnation of the Living Word means that he Jesus is the Way, the Truth, and the Life.[28]

Torrance's thinking on this subject is extremely important because it clearly demonstrates that he takes the incarnation seriously as an act of God coming into history from outside, as a free act of love and one that cannot be read off the processes of history itself because of the predicament of sin and evil as well as the continuing distinction between Creator and creature. Indeed, because the incarnation is "a real coming of God to the world", it therefore cannot be conceived

---

24  Rahner, *Foundations*, p. 439.
25  See Rahner, "Eternity from Time", *TI*: 19, pp. 169–77, 172ff.
26  Rahner, "Eternity from Time", *TI*: 19, p. 174.
27  Rahner, "Eternity from Time", *TI*: 19, p. 175.
28  Torrance, *The Doctrine of Jesus Christ*, p. 85.

in any sense as a "flowering of humanity toward God".[29] Accordingly, Torrance maintains that

> Were that not so, the movement would not be from God to man, but one from man to God! It is thus that Ebionite Christology like all philosophy, starting from man, ends by denying man, and making history and time merely docetic! The Incarnation means that the Divine is not present in the world in any natural fashion, is not immanent within the world *as* the world would like to have it.[30]

Rejecting Ebionite and Docetic Christology is not at all incidental to Torrance's view of the incarnation. These deviations that appeared early in church history and had to be rejected in the fourth century were due to differences between Hellenistic and Hebraic starting points as well as a kind of dualism that sharply distinguished between God and the world. Each in its own way distorted the New Testament picture of the mystery of Jesus Christ because they separated the "divine Christ from the man Jesus".[31]

Torrance traces Ebionite Christology to an early community of Jewish converts who were known as "the poor". They held that Jesus was elected to special divine Sonship through the descent of the Holy Spirit upon him at his baptism. "They did not think of him as begotten of the Father, but as created. Far from being God become man, he was rather like a prophet indwelt by God."[32] In this thinking, the Ebionites were basically rejecting any internal relation between Jesus and the Father in favor of a mere external and moral relation which depended on his fulfilling his vocation as messiah. In Torrance's words:

> Through an approach from below upwards, ebionite Christology sought to explain *how* God was in Jesus Christ in such a way as to give full value to his unique place within Christian faith, and yet in such a way as not to compromise the absolute oneness and transcendence of God. However, Jesus Christ was placed quite definitely on the creaturely side of the radical difference between God and the creation, and as such could not be regarded as embodying in his

---

[29] Excluded here are all attempts to make revelation comprehensible by exploring the processes of evolution. Those who would ask about the meaning of revelation in terms of the evolutionary nature of the cosmos miss the crucial point that revelation is so utterly unique that there is no vantage point apart from or beyond Jesus himself from which we may rightly understand it. See, for example, John F. Haught, *The Revelation of God in History* (Wilmington, Delaware: Michael Glazier, 1988), pp. 24–5. See also Rahner's view of Christology within an evolutionary context, "Christology Within An Evolutionary View of the World" in *TI* :5, pp. 157–92, and his discussion of these matters in *Foundations*, pp. 181ff.

[30] Torrance, *The Doctrine of Jesus Christ*, p. 80.

[31] Torrance, *The Trinitarian Faith*, p. 111.

[32] Torrance, *The Trinitarian Faith*, p. 112.

own person the real presence or saving activity of God himself among men. It was not Jesus Christ, therefore, who was the focus of faith, but only "the heavenly Father" to whom he directed mankind in his teaching.[33]

It will be noticed how Torrance's view of the incarnation is conceived in strictly trinitarian terms and that such a conception is pivotal to a proper understanding of the matter. First, Torrance continues to oppose an approach from "below" because such method misses the main ingredient in the doctrine, namely, that, in Jesus, God has come into the world from outside. Second, this is an insight that can be seen and understood only from within faith—faith in the eternally begotten Son of the Father who became incarnate for the sake of our salvation. Third, by thinking of God as "absolutely one" and by not acknowledging that God is one Being in three Persons, such thinking necessarily envisions Jesus as a "mere" man indwelt by God and cannot by definition see him as he really is, that is, as truly divine and human—as the incarnate Son of the Father. Hence, thinking which does not begin with faith in Jesus as the incarnate Word actually is dualistic in the end because it must insist that Jesus can be no more than a man, perhaps an extraordinary man, but still no more than a man. Such thinking, of course, strips the meaning both from the incarnation and from trinitarian doctrine by its failure to acknowledge the oneness in being in eternity of the Father and the Son. Ultimately, as Torrance himself notes, such thinking is agnostic because, for the Ebionites, God was thought to be related to the world "only in a tangential way" so that "he remained for them essentially the hidden, unknowable God of Judaism who does not give human beings access to any knowledge of himself as he is in his own eternal being".[34] Although Torrance acknowledges that this approach to understanding Jesus needed to "present him as divine" in some sense, in reality it did not start with his humanity and so ended where all Docetic Christology ends, namely, with its idea of divinity which is precisely what kept the Ebionites from acknowledging the truth of the incarnation of the eternal Word.[35]

Certainly, Torrance sees the connection between Ebionite and Docetic Christology and in fact argues that they often run into each other.[36] In particular, he traces Docetic Christology to what he calls "spiritualistic sects" which denied

---

[33]   Torrance, *The Trinitarian Faith*, p. 112.

[34]   Torrance, *The Trinitarian Faith*, p. 112.

[35]   Torrance believed Christology should begin neither from above nor from below but "from below and from above at the same time"; dualist ways of thinking led to Ebionite and Docetic types of Christology which "tended inevitably to pass over into each other" (*The Christian Doctrine of God*, pp. 114–15).

[36]   See Torrance, *The Trinitarian Faith*, p. 133, where he writes that because of their dualist presuppositions that separated both God from the world and idea from reality, these two forms of thought "tended inevitably to pass over into each other". Torrance notes that Athanasius seemed to be aware of this dialectic and that he saw the Nicene Creed as a defense against it.

that Christ's body was real, claiming instead that it only "seemed" to be real. According to Torrance, there were already warnings against Docetism in the New Testament itself for instance in 1 John 2:22; 4:2–3 and 2 John 7. Nonetheless, this erroneous way of understanding Jesus Christ became dominant in the second and third centuries among the Gnostics. Instead of beginning from below where Ebionite thinking started, they began from above and then attempted to explain "on a dualist basis *how* God became man in Jesus Christ in such a way as not to compromise his eternal immutability and impassibility through union with the flesh".[37] The end result was an understanding which insisted that Jesus' suffering and death only appeared to be real and a way of thinking that undermined the historical reality of Jesus. It also undermined the reality of our salvation which was tied to his human reality as the incarnate Word. Such thinking conceived the incarnation as little more than an instrument in God's hands which allowed "divine truth" to enter the world; but for this very reason the need for the incarnation ended once divine truth actually entered the world. Docetic thinkers had in view an "ideal Christ" and not the real Jesus of Nazareth who was the Christ attested in the New Testament. Hence, in Torrance's estimation,

> docetic Christology regularly cut itself off from its starting point in the Divinity of Christ, and tended to transmute itself into human speculations or mythological constructs projected into God from below. For a docetic Christology the Divinity of Christ was finally no more than a divinised human idea.[38]

Crucial to Torrance's Christology, then, is his belief that neither the approach from below nor the approach from above begin with Jesus Christ himself as attested in the Gospel. Neither accepts the fundamental datum of the Gospel, namely, that in the man Jesus, who had his own particular history, God himself has entered history to reveal himself to us, and to inseparably unite divine and human being in the Person of Jesus Christ for the salvation of the world.[39] For the New Testament, and for us, it is imperative that Jesus be seen and acknowledged for who he is at the outset in the "undivided wholeness of his divine–human reality as God become man".[40] It is in this sense that Torrance's emphasis on both Jesus' divinity and his humanity support his ideas of Christian revelation and salvation. For unless Jesus *is* God incarnate, he could not reveal God to us and we would indeed remain uncertain as to God's eternal nature; indeed, he could not save us either "for only as one with us would God be savingly at work within our actual human existence".[41]

---

[37]   Torrance, *The Trinitarian Faith*, p. 113.

[38]   Torrance, *The Trinitarian Faith*, p. 113.

[39]   See Torrance, *The Trinitarian Faith*, p. 114. For the same ideas, see Torrance, *The Christian Doctrine of God*, p. 115.

[40]   Torrance, *The Trinitarian Faith*, p. 114.

[41]   Torrance, *The Trinitarian Faith*, p. 114.

For Torrance, then, the central evangelical truth reaffirmed at Nicaea concerned the simple fact "That Jesus Christ *is* God's Son or Word, and that God's Son or Word *is* Jesus Christ".[42] This is an ultimate that cannot be circumvented even for a moment if one is to think rightly about the incarnation and about Christology, Soteriology and the Trinity. And what Torrance means by referring to Jesus as ultimate is that "There is no authority for believing in Jesus outside of Jesus himself".[43] Even as stated, this remark might need some clarification. What Torrance means is that since Jesus is God himself incarnate in human history, there is no authority above him or beside him that anyone could appeal to in order to assess his claims and then make a decision to believe in him or not. For Torrance, the Jewish leaders wanted another authority outside of and higher than Christ before they would believe in him "so that they would not have to submit to him but could control relation to him from a superior position". What Jesus himself revealed to them, however, was the fact that any question "about the ultimate authority is irresponsible and self-contradictory, for it is an attempt to find some authority above the highest authority".[44] Torrance therefore insists that we must not ask questions like that "about the Ultimate for they are not genuine, but we may address our questions *to* the Ultimate".[45] Hence Torrance believes

> that the incarnation and the resurrection really are *ultimates* which must be accepted, or rejected, as such, for they cannot be verified or validated on any other grounds than those which they themselves provide. Thus regarded, the incarnation and the resurrection are the basic and all-embracing miracles upon which the Christian Gospel rests, miracles which, by their nature, are not verifiable in terms of the kind of evidence and argument which obtain within the natural sciences where we are concerned only with natural processes and the natural order of things. If they were verifiable in that way, they would not be miracles, far less ultimates.[46]

We must, in other words, allow ourselves to be directed in our questioning by the ultimate and never seek to find an authority beyond it, because there really is no such thing. It is this factor which obviates all forms of ancient and modern subordinationism as well as Arianism and Sabellianism, together with Ebionite and Docetic Christology which Torrance considers to be their successors. Unless Jesus is seen as fully divine, then "there was no divine reality in anything he said

---

[42]   Torrance, *The Trinitarian Faith*, p. 115.

[43]   Torrance, "Questioning in Christ", *Theology in Reconstruction*, pp. 117–27, 121.

[44]   Torrance, "Questioning in Christ", *Theology in Reconstruction*, p. 121.

[45]   Torrance, "Questioning in Christ", *Theology in Reconstruction*, p. 121. Torrance relies heavily on this same thinking to illustrate that the starting point for a proper understanding of the resurrection as well as the incarnation is Jesus himself. See, for example, Torrance, *STR*, pp. 20–25.

[46]   Torrance, *STR*, p. 22.

or did", and unless he is seen as fully human, then "what God did in him had no saving relevance for human beings".[47]

What all of this means, of course, is that today, just as in the early church, we must allow both the incarnation and the resurrection to "force themselves upon our minds" because when we are confronted with the ultimate self-revelation of God in Jesus Christ we are confronted with a truth about which "there is no way of penetrating from what we already know or believe we know, far less of establishing or verifying it on grounds that are outside of it. It confronts us as an objective reality which must be accepted or rejected on its own ground".[48] In other words, our only possible response to the incarnation and resurrection is one of faith and obedience—not a blind faith separated from any "recognition of credibility, for the reality of the incarnation or of the resurrection is the kind of objectivity which makes itself accessible to our apprehension, creating the condition for its recognition and acceptance, that is, in such a way that belief on our part is the subjective pole of commitment to objective reality", which itself is grounded in God's own intelligibility revealed in these events and which is grasped only through "repentant rethinking and structural recasting of all our preconceptions".[49] It might be helpful to spell out some implications of Torrance's view of the incarnation before concluding the chapter with a discussion of why he rejects the container notion of space and time. Torrance thinks of the incarnation in a three-fold way, namely, as 1) an act of love, 2) an act of life and 3) an act of light or truth. Let us briefly explore these.

## The Incarnation as an Act of Love

This act, Torrance notes, is the "Way from Eternity into Time, the way which God takes in becoming flesh".[50] In the incarnation, Torrance insists we have "something that never happened before". While God was certainly close to Abraham, Moses and the prophets, he never before actually descended "in *Person* out of his Eternity in this fashion and don the garb of man".[51] As an act of love, the incarnation means that God personally bestows himself—he loves us; but this cannot mean that God is "resolved into Love". Hence, Torrance insists that "we may not construe the Incarnation simply in terms of love; rather must we construe our idea of love in terms of the Incarnation".[52] In this sense, Torrance insists that "Christianity reverses all our values". And the example he gives here is instructive. We do not

---

[47]  Torrance, *The Trinitarian Faith*, p. 115.
[48]  Torrance, *STR*, p. 18.
[49]  Torrance, *STR*, pp. 18–19.
[50]  Torrance, *The Doctrine of Jesus Christ*, p. 85.
[51]  Torrance, *The Doctrine of Jesus Christ*, p. 86.
[52]  Torrance, *The Doctrine of Jesus Christ*, p. 86.

know God's Fatherhood except through the Fatherhood of God revealed in Jesus Christ. This thinking leads Torrance to make a number of interesting points.

First, God is himself the subject of the incarnation. That means that the origin of the act of incarnation "lies outside time altogether, quite apart from our world". As an act of grace, the incarnation is not an event that arises out of history at all. It is rather "an invasion of history and an interruption of history and takes place in the midst of history. It upsets history!"[53] What this means is that God does not wait for us to seek him or to try to be good; instead, it means that he has sought us out in love in order to enable us to be good. God's love is not caused by anything in us. Since the initiative here lies completely with God, we cannot say that God loves us because we are valuable or even because we are worth loving. Our love therefore differs from God's love in the fact that we respond to his love as his creatures; he is the uncreated one who creates us and enables our love by loving us first while we were still sinners. In Torrance's words:

> His Love is grounded in itself, in the Holy Trinity, and does not depend on our being fit or good or having value. Thank God for that! Were it not so, there would be no salvation for any of us! And yet man in his pride dares talk about the infinite value of the human soul![54]

God's love is not in any way "forced", not even by the fact that "we are of infinite value". Any suggestion here that "God ought to love" immediately obscures the fact that God's love is free and sovereign love and thus obliterates the distinction between divine and human love disclosed in the incarnation. That is why in his 1938-39 Auburn Lectures, which are as applicable today as they were 70 years ago, Torrance insists that "There is nothing so perverted today in our Christianity as a false cheap view of the Love of God and consequently there has rarely been such a perverted view of Christianity as there seems to be today".[55] Consequently, any thought that there is a "Law in the Divine nature which makes God love, is to misunderstand it quite as much as to think of something in man which demands that God love him".[56] This is what distinguishes the Christian religion from all others, says Torrance.

In Christianity the emphasis is completely Theocentric and therefore simultaneously Christocentric, so that we should not be asking how God can come to us but instead we should recognize the fact that he has actually done so in Christ. Yet, since it is *God* who has come to us, his loving action must be acknowledged as free and spontaneous and as a real coming of God to us, so that it is what God himself actually says and does that saves us. Torrance thus rejects the twin ideas that it is the duty of a Christian either "to save his own soul" or to

---

53   Torrance, *The Doctrine of Jesus Christ*, p. 86.
54   Torrance, *The Doctrine of Jesus Christ*, p. 87.
55   Torrance, *The Doctrine of Jesus Christ*, p. 87.
56   Torrance, *The Doctrine of Jesus Christ*, p. 87.

"cultivate Christian personalities". Both of these errors, which Torrance identifies with the Roman Catholic and Neo-Protestant approach respectively, undercut the meaning of the incarnation as God's act of movement toward us, because both mistakenly assume that in some sense the meaning of Christianity consists in our human movement toward God. Following Brunner, Torrance notes that in every other religion it is a question of how *we* can come to God. But in Christianity the direction is reversed, so that it is a question of God coming to us in his revelation to overcome this particular religious activity of ours to our benefit. Because God has come in the Person of Jesus Christ, all ethical standards and institutions are now reversed. "That is why Jesus always points men to himself: *I am*. This is Love, this self-grounded Love, God's giving of himself to men. He, as coming from the Father, is Love. We have to do with him alone."[57] It is worth noting that this simple yet profoundly important point is what so many contemporary Christologies from below contend against.

Second, what happens by way of God loving us in the incarnate Word is something that is "utterly new" in the sense that God's relations with humanity are no longer mediated by anything or anyone other than God himself. The kind of love that meets us in Christ is new because it establishes a new relation between us and God and transforms us by enabling us to surrender to God himself and thus to love him. Thus, Torrance asserts, "It is not just to love that we are called in Christianity, but to *this* divine kind of Love."[58] Here the priority of the divine love must be acknowledged and maintained. Because God has drawn near to us on his own initiative, this love expressed in the incarnation must come first and everything else second. It is at this point that Torrance very interestingly contends that

> I cannot love God through loving my neighbour. I can love my neighbour truly and only through loving God. To love God through loving my neighbour is to assert that the Incarnation is not a reality, the reality it is, that relation to God is still a mediated one. To love God through my love to my neighbour is to move toward God. It does not know a movement of God toward man.[59]

Notice how Torrance is quite consistent in carrying through his initial argument here. The incarnation is an utterly new event in which God moves toward us in love and enables our love of God and neighbor. But this movement in the incarnation is the direct movement of God mediated only through the incarnate Word himself and therefore it is recognizable as divine love only in faith in Christ himself which we cannot and do not control. And here is the point. To claim that we can love God in Christ merely by loving our neighbors is to ignore this gracious movement on the part of God to us that has already taken place in the incarnation and that meets

---

57   Torrance, The *Doctrine of Jesus Christ*, p. 88.

58   Torrance, *The Doctrine of Jesus Christ*, p. 88.

59   Torrance, *The Doctrine of Jesus Christ*, pp. 88–9.

us now in the power of his Holy Spirit and in its place to set up a mediated relation with God, namely, a relation mediated once again by someone or something other than the one Mediator.

That is a rather large statement. But, in my view, it is a true and accurate one and one that needs to be very clearly demarcated once again from the quite different view advanced by Karl Rahner, who argues that "Love of God and love of neighbor stand in a relationship of mutual conditioning",[60] so that love of neighbor is not only called for by God's love but "it is also in a certain sense its antecedent condition".[61] Torrance opposes any such thinking in the interest of maintaining the freedom of grace and the distinction between Christ and us in order to underscore the fact that God's distinctive love, active and revealed in the incarnation, is quite different from what we might discover as love in human relations. Rahner even goes so far as to say that "the one [love of God] does not exist and cannot be understood or exercised without the other [love of neighbor], and that two names have really to be given to the same reality if we are to summon up its one mystery, which cannot be abrogated".[62] In arguing for what he calls "a radical identity of the two loves",[63] Rahner basically damages the distinction between divine and human love and the distinction between us and Christ. In the end, Rahner actually argues "that wherever a genuine love of man attains its proper nature and moral absoluteness and depth, it is in addition always so underpinned and heightened by God's saving grace that it is also love of God, whether it be explicitly considered to be such a love by the subject or not".[64] But if Torrance is right, and I think he

---

[60] Karl Rahner, *The Love of Jesus and the Love of Neighbor*, trans. Robert Barr, (New York: Crossroad, 1983), p. 71.

[61] Rahner, *The Love of Jesus and the Love of Neighbor*, p. 71. In an interview documented in *Karl Rahner in Dialogue: Conversations and Interviews 1965–1982* (hereafter: *Karl Rahner in Dialogue*), ed Paul Imhof and Hubert Biallowons, trans. and ed Harvey D. Egan (New York: Crossroad, 1986), p. 183, Rahner insists that love of neighbor is "a precondition for our relationship with God". But, of course, given what Torrance has said, any such thinking ignores the incarnation of God in Christ, and in reality throws the weight of salvation back on us, so that instead of pointing us to the love of God in Christ as the enabling condition of our love of God and neighbor, such thinking inevitably confuses our love of others with the love of God which alone can save us in this or any circumstance.

[62] Rahner, "Reflections on the Unity of the Love of Neighbour and the Love of God", *TI*: 6, pp. 231–49, 232.

[63] Rahner, *TI*: 6, p. 236.

[64] Rahner, *TI*: 6, p. 237. In an interview in 1981, Rahner insisted that in an ultimate sense his theology should not be characterized as "anthropocentric" since his main concern was with God and God's sovereignty. We must, says Rahner, "surrender ourselves with Jesus, the crucified" to this God who does not depend on us. Rahner believes the world vanishes into God, not where theologians talk about it or pastors and the pope preach about it but "in a quite unannounced, almost anonymous way. Wherever a person does manage to be selfless, to love selflessly ... there something takes place that I regard as the most

is, Rahner's analysis disregards the incarnation in its newness as an act of pure grace.[65] His thinking transfers the weight of salvation from God's unique action in the incarnate Word to our activities in relation to our neighbors, thus placing the burden of salvation back on us and obscuring the gracious love of God in the incarnation which has already freed us from the need for any such unnecessary behavior. In addition, such behavior leads to anxiety and not to the joy associated with the love of God in Christ.

By contrast, Torrance insists on deliberately and unequivocally putting Christ at the center. He argues that true love to neighbor, true goodness and true religion can only follow as "by-products" of our specific relation to Christ himself. Hence, he contends that we can neither be truly good, religious or loving by *trying* to do so; that is only to cultivate our own personality in a supreme act of selfishness. We only rightly engage in these activities, Torrance believes, when they happen spontaneously out of our relationship with Jesus himself. In any event, it is the incarnation itself that cuts behind all these self-centered attempts to make ourselves good, religious and loving and removes from us the need to do so. Christians obviously will engage in these activities spontaneously, as Torrance says, because such activities will reflect the glory of God revealed in the love that is active in the incarnate Word. Thus, "True love of others is generated in the heart of the believer by the Holy Spirit; but the Holy Spirit operates in that way in and through us only as our eyes are fixed unselfishly on the Lord Jesus Christ".[66]

Torrance's thinking here is of monumental importance, especially today, when so many theologians seem unwilling or unable to allow Christ himself to occupy the center in a way that prevents us from thinking or saying that our point of reference for theological inquiry should be our self-experience (transcendental or other), including our experience of our neighbor or the state or society. While less careful thinkers patently confuse the actions of Christians toward others with the Kingdom of God that is present uniquely in Jesus himself, Torrance quite clearly asserts, against such confusion, that

> It is not the giving of the cup of cold water to the thirsty that counts, it is not the
> kindly behaviour of a good Samaritan that is of value, nor even martyrdom, the

---

fundamental thing a person can do ... Only when we love each other can we love God. Love of neighbor is not just one among various commandments of God; it is the actual way in which human beings can encounter God" (*Karl Rahner in Dialogue*, p. 268). Torrance, by contrast, is saying that 1) we cannot equate selfless love with the love of God; 2) we cannot make our love for each other the condition for our love of God; and 3) human beings encounter God in Jesus Christ and therefore they obey God precisely by loving their neighbors.

[65]  For more on this issue see Paul D. Molnar, "Love of God and Love of Neighbor in the Theology of Karl Rahner and Karl Barth", vol. 20, no. 4, October 2004 of *Modern Theology*: 567–99.

[66]  Torrance, *The Doctrine of Jesus Christ*, p. 89.

giving of my body to be burned, but *all that for Christ's sake alone*. Unless this love takes hold of us; unless we see through Christ's eyes, unless we exercise our will through the Will of Christ … we do not live Christian lives at all … salvation is *his* act of love and grace, and the fruits of it as well.[67]

Torrance's thinking here is in line with the important reflections of Martin Luther which Karl Barth relied on to make the point that apologetics and polemics can never be a program but can only be an event:

> If we do not uphold the Gospel with its own strength, but rather with our own resources, all will be lost, so that no matter how well we defend it, it will crumble to pieces. Let us have no anxiety that the Gospel needs our help. It is sufficiently strong of itself, and may be committed to God alone, whose it is … It is thus settled that the Word of God can have no other master, judge or protector than God Himself. It is his Word, and therefore, as He utters it quite apart from human merit or counsel, so He Himself will uphold and defend it without human help or strength. If any man seek human protection or comfort in this respect, he will undoubtedly fall and miss both, being abandoned by both God and man.[68]

Finally, for Torrance, as an act of love the incarnation means that God became man in one specific man, Jesus of Nazareth. It would almost seem that such an obvious statement is not worth mentioning until one realizes how many contemporary theologians have completely lost sight of this. A number of contemporary theologians wonder why we have to assume that the incarnation happened only once.[69] Torrance argues that because eternity has come into time in this one unique historical event in a way that is absolutely decisive for history, it is wrong to think of the incarnation as something mythological that might run in cycles. It is also wrong to think of it as a necessary event. It is instead an absolutely unique historical event that happened at one point in time when "Eternity enters directly into time" and so cannot be read directly from history itself but only can be seen and understood in faith. This event cannot be accounted for by examining history because it "fits into nothing". Because here Eternity comes into time and does not at all derive its meaning or reality from time, one can grasp this unique occurrence only as an event that cannot be repeated; an event that calls for decision on our part. Thus, "The Incarnation of God in one man, a Man who has no existence apart from the Incarnation means that to this one Man we must turn and nowhere else. It is another way of asserting the absolute Theocentricity, and the Christocentricity,

---

[67]    Torrance, *The Doctrine of Jesus Christ*, p. 90.

[68]    Martin Luther, *Sermon vom Glauben und guten Werken*, 1522, *W.A.*, 10/3: 354, 1.15 and *Fastenpostill*, 1525, *W.A.* 17/2: 108, 1.26, quoted in Barth, *CD* I/1, p. 31.

[69]    For a discussion of this issue, see Paul D. Molnar, *Incarnation and Resurrection: Toward a Contemporary Understanding* (Grand Rapids: William B. Eerdmans Publishing Company, 2007), especially Chapters 5 and 7.

which uniquely characterises the Christian Gospel and Christian Faith".[70] Here we are confronted with the truth of God himself and this calls for an absolute decision in face of which there can be no neutrality. It is because Roger Haight believes there must be an analogy in our experience by which we can make sense of Jesus' resurrection that he is led to undermine the uniqueness of the incarnation and then suggest that the incarnation may well have happened more than once.[71]

## The Incarnation as an Act of Life

For Torrance, the incarnation cannot be understood as a natural event. That would confuse this act of gracious love on God's part in and for a sinful world with something in the world itself. Instead, the incarnation brings life from death because in that event God has come to restore life in the midst of death and sin. He has, in Torrance's words, "come to resurrect man, to remake him".[72] In fact, Torrance believes that we do not even really see the true meaning of our alienation from God until we are enabled to do so by Christ himself in the life that he brings to us: "It is the Word of God which tells us that we are rebels against his Grace ...".[73] That is why Torrance sees the incarnation as intrinsically linked with reconciliation. Yet, he believes that we cannot understand the incarnation as reconciliation *eo ipso* because what happens in the incarnation is not completed until the cross and resurrection. Christ forgives our sins and that is, as Torrance puts it, validated by new life which is fellowship with God himself.

We were created in God's image. In other words, we were created for fellowship with God; but to be in the image of God now, after the Fall, is to become sons and daughters of God in and through Christ his Son and the Holy Spirit conforming our lives into the image of Christ himself. For Torrance, "Our life is hid with Christ in God, bound up with the Word of God".[74] Because our relations with God have been broken by sin, which consists in our attempts to exist autonomously and apart from God in selfishness and self-affirmation, we are in reality cut off from God who seeks and creates fellowship with us. Our relations with God are cut off by our unwillingness to give ourselves to God and by God's wrath, namely, God's opposition to our sin and unbelief. In Torrance's words: "Thus relations with God are closed from both sides—man is cut off from God in his sin, and his sin is confirmed in its being sin by the divine opposition or resistance to it, that is, God's wrath! *And yet God loves us in spite of that.*"[75] And that means that God becomes incarnate in Jesus in order to forgive our sins and thus to have fellowship once

---

[70]   Torrance, *The Doctrine of Jesus Christ*, p. 90–1.
[71]   See Molnar, *Incarnation and Resurrection*, p. 237.
[72]   Torrance, *The Doctrine of Jesus Christ*, p. 91.
[73]   Torrance, *The Doctrine of Jesus Christ*, p. 91.
[74]   Torrance, *The Doctrine of Jesus Christ*, p. 92.
[75]   Torrance, *The Doctrine of Jesus Christ*, p. 93.

more; sin, Torrance insists, must be dealt with and the way it is dealt with by God in the incarnation is by forgiveness—God in Christ overcomes our unbelief and all our attempts at autonomy and in reality restores us to a new life in which we are renewed by the divine love and nourishment, so that the Holy Spirit restores the lost image of God by conforming us to Christ his Son who is the image of the Father.[76]

We are guilty not only in the sense that we are subjectively aware of our alienation from God but in the sense that God himself by nature opposes our sin; God opposes our attempts to exist apart from him. God does not, as Torrance says, "wink at evil". Rather he takes it seriously in a way that does not just erase it but in a way that maintains his holiness and love. And that is the way of the incarnation in which God in Christ demonstrates that he hates sin but loves the sinner, simply because, in Christ's vicarious humanity, Jesus Christ himself pays our debt to God by blotting out the "handwriting of the ordinances that are against us" (Colossians 2:14).[77] Before explaining how the incarnation manifests God's holy love by opposing sin and reconciling us to himself, it might be helpful to state clearly just what Torrance means when he frequently refers to the *vicarious humanity* of Christ.

---

[76] It is at this point that one might pose the so-called Scotist question of whether or not God would have become incarnate had there been no sin. Torrance's answer is somewhat ambiguous. On the one hand, he says, "we cannot and may not try to press our thought speculatively behind that Love [the incarnation] to what might have happened, had not the fall taken place ... We can no more do that than we can think beyond the ultimate Being of God in his inner divine Life". But, on the other hand, he also says, "while clapping our hands upon our mouth, without knowing what we say, we may nevertheless feel urged to say that in his eternal purpose the immeasurable Love of God overflowing freely beyond himself which brought the creation into existence would have become incarnate within the creation even if we and our world were not in need of his redeeming grace" (Torrance, *The Christian Doctrine of God*, p. 210). Nonetheless, it seems quite clear that Torrance does not really want to go beyond the love of God actually revealed in the incarnate Word and so he does not in fact speculate about matters as they "might have been". He really sticks to the love of God revealed in the incarnation and that is why for him incarnation and atonement are inseparably related. It is not at all unusual therefore for Torrance to say that "The purpose of the incarnation, revealed above all in the passion and resurrection of Christ, was to penetrate into the innermost centre of our contingent existence, in its finite, fragile and disrupted condition, in order to deliver it from evil ... healing and re-ordering it from its ontological roots and entirely renewing its relation to the Creator" (Torrance, *Divine and Contingent Order*, p. 134). Indeed, "The only contingence we actually know is a disordered contingence, so that the work of the incarnation within it is at once a creative re-ordering of our existence in which the passion and resurrection of Jesus Christ play an absolutely essential and climactic part. Thus the incarnation represents the almighty condescension and self-humiliation of the Son of God to be one with us in our contingent being in which we are menaced by nothingness—this is the import of the Pauline concept of *kenosis* ..." (p. 135).

[77] Torrance, *The Doctrine of Jesus Christ*, p. 94.

## Jesus' Vicarious Humanity

This expression plays a pivotal role in much of Torrance's theology, especially his view of atonement, as we shall see, because it eliminates any idea that Jesus' humanity only played an "instrumental role" in our atonement so that atonement was seen as "something done over our head", instead of "as something made to issue out of the depths of our actual existence through the incredible oneness which Christ forged with us in his vicarious humanity".[78] In connection with the incarnation, Torrance explains that we must say that Christ was both "completely *like* us, in all things, in our frail, feeble and corrupt and temptable humanity, yet without being himself a sinner". In other words, the Word assumed our sinful flesh in order to heal and redeem us. But Torrance also insists that Christ was "completely *unlike us* in that by taking our fallen human nature upon himself, he condemned sin in it; he overcame its temptations, resisted its downward drag in alienation from God, and converted it back in himself to obedience toward God, thus sanctifying it". [79] Since he is both completely like us and also completely unlike us in this way, Torrance maintains that in his humanity "there took place a vicarious sanctification of our human nature and lifting of it up again into fellowship with God", so that it is only in him that human nature is "pure and perfect, for human nature was made for fellowship with God, and it is always less than human when it withdraws from or alienates itself from that divine fellowship, while in Christ it is restored to fellowship".[80] It is just here that Torrance himself gives a very clear definition of what he means when he refers to Christ's vicarious humanity:

> "Standing in our place" (Lat, *vicarius*, substitute). Christ in his humanity stands in our place and represents us, and hence the term the *"vicarious humanity"* of Christ in which the humanity of Christ takes our place and represents us, so that what is true of him is true of us, and what he did in his (our) humanity is ours.[81]

This is an all-encompassing category for Torrance because in Christ's humanity (from his birth, through his ministry, death, resurrection and ascension) and only in his humanity, as the humanity of the Word, our humanity is changed once for all and we are thus enabled to live as those who are now free for God and for our neighbors; by being baptized into Christ's own death and resurrection, we now live the life of the new creation since we also share in Christ's faith and obedience

---

[78]   Torrance, "The Atonement: The Singularity of Christ and the Finality of the Cross", p. 239.

[79]   Thomas F. Torrance, *Incarnation: The Person and Life of Christ*, ed Robert T. Walker (Downers Grove, IL: InterVarsity Press, 2008), p. 205.

[80]   Torrance, *Incarnation*, p. 205.

[81]   Torrance, *Incarnation*, p. 205.

as well as his risen and ascended humanity which is no longer subject to sin, suffering, evil and death.[82] All of this, of course, takes place now in faith and in hope with due eschatological reserve. While we may inexplicably bypass Christ and thus bypass our forgiveness and new life in relation to God, it is nonetheless a reality in him.

It is precisely in God's act of incarnation in Christ, then, that "Jesus bears our sin, takes our sin away, and nails the judgment against us on the Cross. It is in that very act of God in the crucified Lord Jesus"[83] that we can see both our guilt and God's mercy. That, Torrance says, is God's amazing grace. That was indeed the purpose of the incarnation. God became "God with us" in order to vicariously bear our sin and guilt and remove them. It is really in his death that all have died and been restored to fellowship with God in a very real sense. That, Torrance insists, is the objective side of reconciliation: "The curse of sin that we should bear he has taken upon himself."[84] It is unimaginable that anyone would still oppose the love of God revealed and effective in the incarnation, life, death and resurrection of Jesus. But the fact that this still occurs is part of the "very irrationality of evil and sin".[85] Subjectively, our minds must be cleared of enmity through the forgiveness of the cross. It is by being united with Christ that we "partake of eternal life in Christ".[86] And yet the predicament of sin inexplicably still keeps some people from Christ and thus leaves them exposed to final judgment.

## The Incarnation Means Light, Truth

Torrance declares that the incarnation not only brings revelation and forgiveness but knowledge and light and, indeed, he believes the incarnation cannot really be effective in our lives without a real understanding of it or "apart from an actual initiation into the Mind of Christ".[87] This light, however, that comes to us can do so only through the reconciliation that reaches us through the cross. It is impossible, then, to know God correctly until we actually realize that in Christ we are forgiven

---

[82]    For an especially helpful summary statement of how Christ's vicarious humanity occupies a unique place and fulfills a representative and substitutionary role for us, see Torrance, *God and Rationality*, p. 145.

[83]    Torrance, *The Doctrine of Jesus Christ*, p. 94.

[84]    Torrance, *The Doctrine of Jesus Christ*, p. 94. "That is the amazing grace", Torrance says, "of the Lord Jesus Christ, who though he was rich, for our sakes became poor, that we through his poverty might become rich" (*Incarnation*, p. 227).

[85]    Torrance, *The Doctrine of Jesus Christ*, p. 95.

[86]    Torrance, *The Doctrine of Jesus Christ*, p. 95. For a full discussion of how Torrance works these insights out in his view of Atonement, see Chapter 5 below, pp. 149–61.

[87]    Torrance, *The Doctrine of Jesus Christ*, p. 95. That is why Torrance repeatedly insists that "we have no other source of knowledge than that given us in Christ" (Torrance, *The Christian Doctrine of God*, p. 211).

sinners. Without Christ, Torrance contends, we have "a very distorted view of God, which is not of God". But in Christ and through the Holy Spirit, as we "take on the Image of God", we "become like God" and can know God. There is, of course, objective revelation, forgiveness and reconciliation. But we may indeed ignore this and pass Christ by. Here Torrance follows Barth and stresses that we can only know the Word of God as God himself enables it in and through our obedience of faith. Because Torrance is so adamant that it is only through God that we may know God with accuracy, he actually believes that "the philosopher *qua* philosopher cannot be a Christian, cannot accept revelation" because what we learn through revelation in the incarnation is that all other knowledge about God is invalid.[88] Because the incarnation as an act of grace provides knowledge of God for us, any attempt by us to rely on reason and thus on philosophy to know God amounts to a denial of grace. Torrance is thinking of Kant in this context and actually contends that "To be a consistent philosopher like Kant is *eo ipso* to repudiate grace and revelation. To become a Christian, Kant would have had to become converted and become a little child, as Jesus said".[89] Humility is what is required in face of the incarnation, because we must admit that here God has moved toward us and what is here revealed is not attainable elsewhere or in any other way. Repudiating philosophy in this sense, however, is not at all to repudiate using human reason—it is in no way to espouse any sort of anti-intellectual position. Rather, Torrance wishes to reject any idea that human reason can and should act on its own without submitting to the truth of revelation made known in Christ and through his Holy Spirit. While philosophy has its rightful place, it can never usurp the place of the one who is the Way, the Truth and the Life. In Torrance's words:

> Now that we have the reality there is no sense in speculating about what we could or would naturally conceive God to be. Our business is to look at Jesus Christ and trust him ... Philosophy is said to be man speaking in a loud voice about himself, and that must be silenced in the courts of the Christian sanctuary![90]

That is why the doctrine of the Trinity is central to Torrance's understanding of the incarnation and of our knowledge of God. Torrance rightly insists that in light of what actually happened in Jesus Christ it is impossible to entertain any other alternatives such as the possibility that the Father or Holy Spirit might have become incarnate. In reality, the Father and Holy Spirit did not become incarnate; only the Son did. This exclusive incarnation "decides the hypothetical question whether the incarnation of another divine Person was a possibility".[91] Also excluded is any idea that there "may still be a *Deus absconditus* behind the back of Jesus

---

88  Torrance, *The Doctrine of Jesus Christ*, p. 96.
89  Torrance, *The Doctrine of Jesus Christ*, p. 96.
90  Torrance, *The Doctrine of Jesus Christ*, p. 98.
91  Torrance, *The Christian Doctrine of God*, p. 199.

Christ or some hidden God for which Jesus Christ does not stand surety".[92] Any argument from what God has actually done in Jesus Christ to what he might have done basically operates on the agnostic assumption that there ultimately is no connection between the incarnate Son and the Father so that God would have to remain ultimately unknown. But since God is really the content of his revelation in Christ and we may know this through the Spirit, no such agnostic position is possible. It is in this connection that Torrance also stresses that although only the Son became incarnate, that did not mean that the Father and Spirit had no part in that event. Rather, because the whole Trinity is perichoretically One and Three and Three and One, the whole Trinity was also involved in each of the events of salvation. In this regard, Torrance notes that the doctrine of appropriation, which traditionally assigned certain actions to the Father, the Son or the Holy Spirit, was "brought in by Latin theology to redress an unbalanced essentialist approach to the doctrine of the Trinity from the One Being of God".[93] But Torrance thinks that the problem addressed by the doctrine of appropriation should never have arisen in the first place because all the acts of God toward us "cannot but be acts of the Trinity in Unity and of the Unity in Trinity, while in all these acts each person who is himself whole God acts without any surrender of his distinctive hypostatic properties as Father, Son or Holy Spirit".[94] In the end, therefore, "Far from being some cold metaphysical deduction, or second-order construction the doctrine of the Holy Trinity gives supreme theological expression to the evangelical truth that through Christ Jesus and his Cross we have access by one Spirit to the Father".[95]

Finally, then, the incarnation says two important things concerning our knowledge of God. First, because God has come to us in the incarnation and made himself personally knowable to us in our own human language, we know we do not have to (and cannot) leave the human sphere to know him. But we also know "there can be no analogy to him through the creature".[96] Here Torrance follows Athanasius in his *De Incarnatione* to argue that while people sought God in nature and constructed idols thereby, God made himself knowable in human form and human language in the incarnate Word. The real revelation of God to us in his Word can only be mediated to us in our human forms of thought. But this takes place in a way that is the opposite, say, of a kind of Socratic method which encourages

---

[92]   Torrance, *The Christian Doctrine of God*, p. 199. For this reason, Torrance repeatedly insists that "God is not one thing in himself and another thing in Jesus Christ— what God is toward us in Jesus he is inherently and eternally in himself ... There is thus no God behind the back of Jesus Christ, but only this God whose face we see in the face of the Lord Jesus. There is no *deus absconditus*, no dark inscrutable God, no arbitrary Deity of whom we can know nothing but before whom we can only tremble ..." (Torrance, *The Christian Doctrine of God*, p. 243).

[93]   Torrance, *The Christian Doctrine of God*, p. 200.
[94]   Torrance, *The Christian Doctrine of God*, p. 200.
[95]   Torrance, *The Christian Doctrine of God*, p. 254.
[96]   Torrance, *The Doctrine of Jesus Christ*, p. 98.

people to ask questions and think for themselves because it is thought that no new knowledge can actually be imparted by professors to students. Torrance claims Christianity is the opposite of this: it declares that new knowledge is given us in the Word—knowledge which we cannot get for ourselves and which was not there before. Torrance rejects any idea that incarnation and communion with God can be understood in any other way than through a faith which, as St Paul says, comes by hearing and hearing which takes place through the Word of God. For that reason, it is foolish to focus on "man as such, because God assumed man's form—for that would be to think that the humanity of Christ as such was the Word of God and to think of God only in human terms or in terms of humanity!"[97] In order to know God, then, we must turn to the Bible which, for Torrance, in a certain sense is the "intellectual Incarnation of the Word of God in Christ".[98] But Torrance immediately adds that we must not make the mistake of assuming the Bible is God; rather, the words of the Bible "are the vehicles of the Word, but *really* the vehicles of the Word ... we cannot separate the humanity of Christ from his Divinity for his humanity as such has no separate existence or self-existence".[99] Still, he insists that all anti-intellectualism must be opposed because the Holy Spirit "does not work in sub-rational ways or non-intelligible ways in the hearts of men". Citing Brunner, Torrance maintains that "God's Spirit is no magical stream of power, but always speaking Spirit", that is, the Spirit who speaks the Word of Christ which is found in the Bible.

Second, it is important to realize that Torrance takes seriously the incarnation in such a way that he does not reduce the divinity of Christ to his humanity but rather sees the divinity as active in and through Christ's true humanity: "While the Incarnation means that God is revealed to us in a human form, it does not mean that God is human; or, to put it the other way around, that human creatures as such can reveal God."[100] In this connection, once again, Torrance stresses the all-important fact that just as in Christ his divinity cannot simply be equated with his humanity, so in the Bible we cannot just equate the human words with the Words of God. All of this is true because in the incarnation "the new act of the eternal God whereby God himself becomes man without ceasing to be God, the Creator becomes creature without ceasing to be Creator, the transcendent becomes contingent without ceasing to be transcendent, the eternal becomes time without ceasing to be eternal".[101] Just as we cannot separate the humanity of Christ from his divinity and focus on his humanity as such, so we do not worship his humanity

---

[97]   Torrance, *The Doctrine of Jesus Christ*, p. 100.

[98]   Torrance, *The Doctrine of Jesus Christ*, p. 100.

[99]   Torrance, *The Doctrine of Jesus Christ*, p. 100.

[100]   Torrance, *The Doctrine of Jesus Christ*, p. 100.

[101]   Torrance, *The Christian Doctrine of God*, p. 214. That is why Torrance contends that *kenosis* "does not mean the self-limitation of God or the curtailment of his power, but the staggering exercise of his power within the limitations of our contingent existence in space and time" (pp. 214–15).

as such or the Bible as such. It is the Holy Spirit who reveals the truth to us here; it is the Spirit who brings the objective revelation to light for us as human subjects. It is the Spirit who enables us to relate personally with Jesus Christ as a Subject who is objectively the revelation of God in history. Once more, Torrance emphasizes in his Auburn lectures what he later stressed in his trinitarian writings, namely, that while we cannot "know God as he is in himself but only in his act of self-manifestation in Christ", still there is no God hidden behind his revelation in Christ and what God makes known in Christ God is in himself antecedently from all eternity. Hence, Torrance here stresses that in Christ "we have a real knowledge of the very heart of God, for God and Christ are *One*".[102]

Now that we have seen roughly what Torrance means by the incarnation and how his view is structured by his understanding of the *homoousion* and ultimately by his trinitarian theology, together with his rejection of Ebionite and Docetic Christology, it will be important to see exactly how Torrance's view of the incarnation of the Word into time and space offer to contemporary theology a revolutionary approach to all aspects of dogmatic theology that actually may prove helpful, especially in connection with sacramental theology, in overcoming long-standing misunderstanding and conflict between Reformed and Roman Catholic theology. It is with this in mind that we will explore Torrance's understanding of and rejection of what he calls the receptacle or container notion of space and time.

## The Receptacle or Container Concept of Space and Time

At the start of his book *Space, Time and Incarnation*, Torrance made a very important distinction between symbolic knowledge of God's presence as a "personal Agent within the space and time of our world" confessed in the Nicene–Constantinopolitan Creed and what he calls "significative" knowledge of that divine presence. The former type of knowledge employs "aesthetic, non-conceptual forms of thought" that are not actually rooted in the self-revelation of God in Jesus Christ and thus are not grounded in the nature and activity of God himself within history. As such their meaning and justification come "through coordination with the religious imagination and self-understanding of the Church".[103] The latter

---

[102]  Torrance, *The Doctrine of Jesus Christ*, p. 101.

[103]  Torrance, *STI*, p. 1. See also Torrance, "The Relation of the Incarnation to Space in Nicene Theology", *Divine Meaning*, Chapter 10, pp. 343–73, 345–6. Here Torrance speaks of "signitive" rather than "symbolic" use of language in order to make the same point. In this very interesting chapter, Torrance explores the thinking of Origen who refused to think of the incarnation using a "container view of space defined in terms of its immovable limits, and any receptacle view of the self-emptying or *kenosis* of the Son that involves an emptying however partial of material content out of him" (p. 361). Torrance notes that despite the fact that "there was not a little in his teaching that was unacceptable" (p. 363),

kind of knowledge uses concepts "that are intended to refer us to God in a direct and cognitive way and that have their meaning and justification precisely in that objective and operational reference".[104] In other words, a significative use of language in contrast to a symbolic one allows the reality in question to dictate the meaning and truth of our concepts; such a view demands that true understanding is not at all grounded in the language itself or in the imaginations of those using the language. Thus, the Nicene approach allowed the reality of God the Creator who became incarnate in his Son Jesus Christ to reveal himself to us in such a way that the objective reality of God himself present and active within time and space, and not the subjective concepts of those doing the reflecting, controlled the manner and mode of thought. Hence, significative thinking would not allow the basic theological conceptuality to change in accordance with people's "own devising" but rather was controlled "by the reality intended".[105]

With this important distinction in place, Torrance notes that if we think of space in simply symbolic terms, then the spatial language of the Creed can be interpreted in "a merely metaphorical or tropical sense".[106] In that case there can be no definite knowledge of God himself acting within space. But if this language is understood in a significative way, then the concepts used in the Creed have some genuine reference to God himself in his own nature and activity within history. It is in this perspective that Torrance reflects upon exactly how we should understand the spatial concepts used in the Creed. In the first instance, it is clear that because God is the Father Almighty who is the maker of heaven and earth and of all things visible and invisible, he transcends all of space and time which he created or brought into being out of nothing. From this "It follows that the relation between God and space is not itself a spatial relation".[107] What if one were to think of God's relation to space and time as itself a spatial relation? The answer is simple and profound. Athanasius himself argued with the Arians about this very issue, claiming that it was "nonsensical to ask of God whether He is without place … or whether He is in place".[108] Any such question imagines that God exists in a manner comparable to the way we exist in time and space and manifestly ignores the truth that God exists in a creative not a spatial relation to time and space.

---

he "prepared the ground for a scientific theology which could meet the Church's need" (p. 363). That theology "emerged at Nicaea and was defended and advanced most formidably by Athanasius in the East and Hilary in the West" (p. 363). Torrance spends the rest of the chapter discussing Athanasius' view of space and time with regard to the incarnation.

[104]  Torrance, *STI*, p. 1.

[105]  Torrance, *STI*, p. 2.

[106]  Torrance, *STI*, p. 2. See also Torrance, "The Relation of Incarnation to Space", *Divine Meaning*, p. 345. It should be clear from what was said above in Chapter 1 that Torrance finds this patristic approach to the matter to be precisely the antidote to the kind of thinking advanced by John A.T. Robinson in his book *Honest to God*.

[107]  Torrance, *STI*, p. 2.

[108]  Torrance, *STI*, p. 2.

This is an extremely important insight with far-reaching consequences. For instance, to speak of the Son coming down from heaven for us and for our salvation does not refer, as Torrance himself notes, to "a journey through space",[109] because such a creedal statement must be understood the same way as statements that refer to the fact that the Son is "God from God" and "Light from Light". These references to God and to the incarnate Son's relation to the Father cannot be understood spatially but only theologically so that "even if we could conceive of a heaven of heavens we could not think of this as containing God".[110] What Torrance opposes here is the mythological conception of God and the cosmos that incorrectly confused God's presence with "upper space" in the manner portrayed in the anonymous *De mundo* which was incorrectly attributed to Aristotle and was popular in the second and third centuries. According to Torrance, this corrupted any proper view of Ptolemaic cosmology and led to the distorted idea that there was some intervening space "between God and man".[111] This thinking, which is far removed from the significative thinking of Nicene theology, has caused great difficulty for the church, both in connection with the incarnation and the sacraments, as we shall see in Chapter 8. Here, however, it is important to give one specific example that will illuminate how very important Torrance's rejection of the container or receptacle notions of time and space is when it comes to Christology in particular.

In the West, Latin Christianity incorporated the idea of the "receptacle" into its theology so that "Supernatural grace was widely thought of as contained in ecclesiastical vessels and capable of being handed on in space and time by means of them".[112] When this receptacle notion of space was shaped by Aristotle's philosophy in the twelfth and thirteenth centuries, space was conceptualized in terms of substance and accidents, instead of from a consideration of the relationship between creation and incarnation as in Eastern theology. The outcome was that attention was focused on Christ's real presence in the Mass and on cosmology with the result that God's presence was conceived mainly in terms of space and *"apart from time"*,[113] and this opened the door to static notions of God's relations *in se* and *ad extra* and led to a lack of attention to eschatology. It cannot be overstressed that when space is separated from time, magical conceptions of the sacrament and of God's relations with us in history develop. Indeed, whenever our spatial relations with God are conceptualized without including time, the genuine historical foundations of the Christian faith are jeopardized. In the end, as natural theology developed independently of revelation, the Aristotelian notion of space led to the idea that "there is a relation of interdependence between the

109   Torrance, *STI*, p. 2.

110   Torrance, *STI*, p. 3. This thinking has a profound effect upon Torrance's notion of the ascension as well. See Torrance, *STR*, pp. 123ff. and below, Chapter 7.

111   Torrance, *STI*, p. 3. See also Torrance, *STR*, p. 110 n.3.

112   Torrance, *STI*, p. 25.

113   Torrance, *STI*, p. 25.

containing vessel and what it contains", so that "this receptacle notion of space cannot but exercise conceptual control over whatever is conceived by means of it".[114] We will not go into the details of how this thinking caused great difficulty for the way Christ's real presence in the Eucharist was conceived since that will be treated in Chapter 8. What is important to note here is how this faulty concept of space affected Christology. The difference can be seen clearly by noting certain key distinctions between Reformed and Lutheran Christology. Luther adopted the receptacle notion of space in order to assert the "reality and actuality of the Son of God in our human and earthly existence". Thus, for Luther, "the whole Son and Word of God is contained in the infant of Bethlehem and communicated to us in the sacrament of the Lord's Supper".[115] Torrance contends that Reformed and Anglican theology, as typified in the thought of Calvin and Hooker, stood much closer to Patristic thinking. And this can be seen in three important ways: 1) with respect to the "*extra Calvinisticum*", 2) with respect to the location of Christ's body in heaven and 3) with respect to the Eucharistic *parousia*. Here, as I have already noted, we will only consider the Christological differences and leave the discussion of the Eucharist until later.

Torrance stresses that when Reformed theologians spoke of the incarnation they saw the Son of God "as having descended from heaven without leaving heaven, or as living and acting on earth without abandoning His government of the universe".[116] Consequently, they intentionally adopted the Nicene rejection of any sort of container or receptacle notion of space that would envision "the enclosure or confinement of the Son of God in a human body". Indeed, they also rejected "any local or spatial connection between the divine and human natures of Christ".[117] By contrast, the Lutherans operated with a receptacle or container notion of space and concluded that the Reformed position kept something of the Son of God "outside" the created sphere, and this they described as the Calvinist "extra". The same difficulties could be seen in relation to the ascension. When the Reformed theologians described Christ's ascent to the right hand of the Father which transcends created space and time, their thinking was not governed by the receptacle notion, so that they could at once insist that Christ genuinely retained his risen body but was yet located in heaven. In Torrance's words:

---

[114]    Torrance, *STI*, p. 26. For a particularly enlightening discussion of how this receptacle view of space has hindered ecumenical theology and how we might advance toward theological union if this is overcome, see Torrance, *God and Rationality*, pp. 123ff.

[115]    Torrance, *STI*, p. 30.

[116]    Torrance, *STI*, p. 31. Torrance traces this particular thinking back to Origen ("The Relation of Incarnation to Space", *Divine Meaning*, p. 356) and to Athanasius ("The Relation of Incarnation to Space", *Divine Meaning*, p. 365).

[117]    Torrance, *STI*, p. 31.

> As the Incarnation meant the entry of the Son into space and time without the
> loss of God's transcendence over space and time, so the Ascension meant the
> transcendence of the Son over space and time without the loss of His incarnational
> involvement in space and time.[118]

The importance of this insight can scarcely be overstressed. The Reformers'
concept of space allowed for the differences between divine and human activity in
such a way that God was free to act within space and time without being limited or
conditioned by space and time. The Lutherans unfortunately could only interpret
the Reformed theologians to be saying that somehow after the ascension, Christ
was "confined" in heaven in accordance with their container view of space and
place which had already dictated their view of the incarnation. Similar difficulties
arose in connection with the sacrament of the Lord's Supper, as we shall see.
In addition, Luther transferred the meaning of *perichoresis* from the Trinity to
Christology and, according to Torrance, developed a notion of coinherence with
respect to Christ's divine and human natures that "risked deification of Christ's
humanity".[119]

But here we have said enough to indicate the revolutionary nature of the early
church's rejection of the container or receptacle concept of space. Wherever such
a notion is employed, difficulties are created for understanding Christ's activity as
divine and human within space and time, and this inevitably leads to a compromise
of either his divinity or his humanity with the result that the union between God and
creatures that took place in the incarnation is undermined. This is why Torrance
correctly insists that the Nicene theologians rejected

> the idea that the human creature is able to make room ... for God in its nature and
> is able to grasp or comprehend ... the infinite, and so insisted that the receptacle
> ... notion cannot be used to interpret the Incarnation as the emptying of the Son
> of God into a human vessel, for the creature is not ... *capax infiniti*.[120]

This way of conceptualizing the matter led to two further Christological difficulties:
1) using the receptacle notion led theologians to think of the incarnation "as the
self-emptying of Christ into the receptacle of a human body" and this led to the
idea that in some sense Christ renounced certain properties of his divine nature in
the incarnation;[121] 2) when thinking of Christ's human nature as a receptacle that

---

[118]  Torrance, *STI*, p. 31.

[119]  Torrance, *STI*, pp. 32–3.

[120]  Torrance, *STI*, p. 35.

[121]  It is worth noting the parallels between this thinking and Karl Rahner's view of the
incarnation as the symbolic self-expression of the Logos so that Jesus, as the Real Symbol
of the Logos, is "full of the reality symbolized"; Rahner insists that there is a "mutual
causal" relation between the humanity and divinity of Christ and in the sacraments between
grace and the sacramental signs. Both of these problematic ideas, according to Torrance,

housed his divinity, the idea of his human nature had to be enlarged "and so it was held that the Son of God communicated to the humanity of Christ an infinite capacity enabling it to be filled with the divine fullness".[122] Although Lutheran intentions of preserving both divine and human freedom were the best, this receptacle concept of space eventually led to dualism: a divinization of Christ's humanity meant that there was no genuine union of two distinct natures. In other words, "it was held that the Son of God communicated to the humanity of Christ an infinite capacity enabling it to be filled with the divine fullness".[123] The Calvinists eventually were led to wonder what kind of humanity it was that could have divine attributes. Torrance notes that in this context Christ's own "capacity" for the divine (the infinite) was regarded only as "a special and exemplary instance of man's own capacity for the divine".[124] And this thinking obliterated the need to rely on the historical Jesus to relate with God epistemologically and ontologically.

Sir Isaac Newton's thinking exemplified the dualism that follows from adopting the receptacle notion of space. He applied the concept to God and concluded that if God "is the infinite Container of all things He can no more become incarnate than a box can become one of the several objects that it contains".[125] This thinking, however, represents exactly what the Nicene theologians rejected with their doctrine of the incarnation because it prevents God from actually entering into time and space while remaining the Lord he always was and is, in order to save the world. No wonder Newton set out to defend Arius![126] The key point here is that it is the receptacle notion of space, introduced into Christology by the Lutherans, that led to the deism advanced by Newton and later on to different forms of dualism advanced by Lessing (with his stress on the fact that there is a historical gap between Christ and us that simply cannot be bridged) and Kant (with his dualistic separation of idea and reality—of the noumenal and phenomenal realms). Without going into all the historical and theological details of the matter, it might

---

stem from the receptacle or container notion of space. For more on this, see Molnar, *Divine Freedom*, pp. 57, 90, 116, 158, 161, 164 *et passim*, and Paul D. Molnar, *Karl Barth and the Theology of the Lord's Supper: A Systematic Investigation* (New York: Peter Lang, 1996), pp. 27ff. and 88ff.

[122]   Torrance, *STI*, p. 36.

[123]   Torrance, *STI*, p. 36.

[124]   Torrance, *STI*, p. 41.

[125]   Torrance, *STI*, p. 39.

[126]   Torrance spells out the implications of this issue in patristic theology by explaining that "The relation between the Son and the Father cannot be thought out in terms of a receptacle ... notion of room or space. That would mean that we think out the problem simply in terms of bodies and containers, which was precisely what the Arians were guilty of, a material approach, in which they thought of the Father and the Son as each filling the emptiness of the other" ("The Relation of Incarnation to Space", *Divine Meaning*, pp. 366–7). Moreover, "a receptacle notion of space can only lead to a false kenoticism which does not do justice to the 'fullness' and 'perfection' of either the Father or the Son, for it fails to think of them in accordance with their natures" (p. 367).

be worth mentioning just one more instance of how the receptacle concept of space introduced into Christology by Luther affected modern theology. That is the case of Rudolf Bultmann.

Torrance notes that Bultmann's program of demythologizing is "the most radical attempt in our day to think away space and time" in relation to Christian faith. He believes Bultmann actually employed a Newtonian conception of God which was essentially "objectivist, rigid and closed". By making space timeless, that is, by eliminating time from his conception of space, Bultmann fell into an old mistake. Whereas Luther insisted that Christ acting for us was an objective event outside of us, Bultmann argued that "the objective reference must be dropped altogether in order to get the meaning out of it 'for me'", so that, in a manner similar to Lessing, Bultmann abandoned history as the place where Christian faith is grounded in the first instance. This dualism and deism is consistent with Bultmann's belief that we can only speak of God's relations with the world in "terms completely detached from creaturely and this-worldly content or treat language about God as the paradoxical obverse about our self-understanding in this world".[127] Furthermore, by cutting the connection between space and time, Bultmann was led to focus exclusively on one's own experience of faith in the present with the result that the past can have no meaning for us now because it has vanished; that thinking eliminates the historical Jesus as the foundation of faith and since all now is thought of in timeless fashion in relation to one's own experience of faith, the future "offers us no existence" either and so any hope for the resurrection is also eliminated. In this way, eschatology is also undermined. The important point to be noted here is that, in Torrance's eyes, Bultmann, like Tillich, still retains the old receptacle notion of space in his own effort to flee from time and space in attempting to explain Christian faith. The end result is that both Bultmann and Tillich reject the "*extra Calvinisticum*" and in the process they both end up mythologizing the incarnation since they assume the doctrine means that "the Son of God is received and contained within the dimensions of a human body".[128] But what makes the incarnation of God in space and time mythological for Bultmann in the first instance is his dualistic and deistic belief that God cannot interact with this world. This example shows the revolutionary nature of Torrance's analysis with regard to the receptacle or container concept of space. His contention is that if theology had stuck to the relational thinking advanced at Nicaea and not adopted the receptacle or container concept, then much of the deism and dualism that followed from such thinking might have been avoided. There is no doubt that Torrance's analysis and conclusions on this issue represent a major historical and theological contribution especially to the doctrine of the incarnation because clearing away the receptacle notion of space means allowing Christ's incarnate presence within history to determine our thinking, rather than ideas or experiences that are not grounded objectively in God's own actions *ad extra*.

---

[127]   Torrance, *STI*, pp. 48–9.
[128]   Torrance, *STI*, p. 49.

In any case, what was intended by the Nicene Creed was that the Son of God actually came to be present within space and time but in such a way that he remained fully divine and thus *homoousion* with the Father and yet he condescended to be one with us for the purpose of saving us. His oneness with us, then, is not "an indication of finite imperfection in Him" but an indication of his love which was expressed in his incarnate condescension.[129] The central point to be made here is that even in the incarnation his eternal being was never merely creaturely nor "space-conditioned". Rather, "He humbled Himself to be one with us and to take our finite nature upon Him, all for our sakes".[130] This thinking sounds simple enough until you compare it to the thinking of either those who are unaware of the significative thinking advocated by Torrance or those who reject it and who thus envision God's relation with us in the incarnation as circumscribed by time and space instead of properly seeing it as a creative relation with us in time and space.[131] Whereas Torrance insists that our significative thinking must be governed by the incarnate Word himself in his personal interaction with us as attested in Scripture and recognized by the Nicene theologians, Ted Peters turns toward social psychology and the experience of human relationality to understand God's life. He uses the human person as his criterion and actually makes God himself dependent on time and limited by space, and thus in reality makes God indistinguishable from time and space so that God himself can then be defined *by* time and space; God is incorporated into time and space by virtue of this starting point in human experience: "What has been happening is that the relational understanding of the human person is becoming a tool used by an increasing number of theologians for interpreting the relations of the three persons of the Trinity."[132] And he concludes, following Hegel's thinking, that we should understand God's life "as one in which the divine undergoes self-separation", so that we must then conclude that God needs "an eschatological reunion" which involves more than just Jesus; it includes all of creation. Hence, according to Peters, "The trinitarian life is itself the history of salvation. To put it most forcefully: the fullness of God as Trinity is a reality yet to be achieved in the eschatological consummation".[133] In these few remarks, Peters has not only undone the entire doctrine of the Trinity by denying that God is who he is from eternity to eternity as the Father, Son and Holy Spirit, as one who

---

[129]  See Torrance, "The Relation of Incarnation to Space", *Divine Meaning*, p. 344.

[130]  Torrance, *STI*, p. 3.

[131]  For example, Ted Peters, *God as Trinity: Relationality and Temporality in Divine Life* (Louisville: Westminster/John Knox Press, 1993), p. 15, instead of allowing his thinking to be shaped by the trinitarian self-revelation of God in Christ and through the Spirit, argues that "Relationality—a social-psychological concept so important for understanding human personality in our time—is becoming the key for unlocking newer understandings of the divine life".

[132]  Peters, *God as Trinity*, p. 15.

[133]  Peters, *God as Trinity*, p. 16.

does not need us to be who he is, but he has in reality enclosed God into time in exactly the way Torrance claims the Nicene theologians deliberately rejected.

At any rate, Torrance notes that the words of the Creed that state "whose Kingdom shall have no end" stressed that when the Son of God assumed our bodily existence, it was not a temporary episode or a purely economic involvement of God in space and time, but that his involvement in our human existence and being "even after His resurrection, ascension, and *parousia,* must be maintained without reserve".[134] This is an enormously important point in Torrance's thinking because it is Christ's continued High Priestly mediation of God to us and us to God that takes place in the sacraments that is of decisive importance, as we shall see in Chapter 8. For now it is enough to note that Torrance stresses the fact that Nicene theologians were forced to develop a properly relational conception of time and space in order to understand the incarnation and creation in ways that would avoid the problems caused by Greek philosophy and science, which tended to understand time and space according to what he calls "a *receptacle* or a *container* notion of space" that was traceable as far back as the Pythagoreans and Atomists and influenced the thinking of Plato, Aristotle and the Stoa.[135]

Plato himself spoke of space as a "receptacle" in a metaphorical sense. He also believed that there was a sharp disjunction between the intelligible and sensible realms so that our thought had to be directed to an objective ground beyond subjective experience by tracing the line of thought to a reality beyond. The problem Plato faced with regard to space was that he wanted to speak of a realm beyond space but needed to use spatial concepts in order to do it. Unfortunately, however, he could not simply project a spatial concept beyond the gulf that separated the intelligible and sensible realms. Therefore, Plato left unanswered how far we need to discard these concepts in order to speak of an objective ground beyond them that gives them their meaning. According to Torrance, this became a serious problem with Arianism. And in Chapter 2 we saw that the Arians projected their sensual images into God, instead of thinking imagelessly as Athanasius insisted they must.

When we turn to Aristotle, the real issue regarding the receptacle notion of space comes to the fore because Aristotle misunderstood Plato in two ways which led to difficulties in the early church: 1) "he misconstrued the Platonic separation (χωρισμός) as a local or spatial separation", and 2) "he mistook the Platonic 'receptacle' or 'matrix' for the original stuff or substrate from which bodies are derived".[136] Aristotle was thus led to develop a "predominantly volumetric conception of space" so that he thought of space as a vessel through which things pass; a vessel that "not only contains them but exercises a certain force or causal activity ... in relation to them". Aristotle's "receptacle notion of space" therefore

---

134   Torrance, *STI*, p. 4.
135   Torrance, *STI*, p. 4.
136   Torrance, *STI*, pp. 6–7.

visualized a "relation of interdependence between the container and its contents".[137] According to Torrance, this led Aristotle to think of place as the "immobile limit within which a body is contained". But, importantly, this approach led to serious conceptual difficulties. First, Aristotle ended up offering a static notion of space that saw the "unmoved Mover" as the place of absolute rest. Second, he equated volume with spatial magnitude. This not only had the effect of separating space from time but also led to a "highly artificial disjunction of substance from accidents" which led to endless difficulties in Western mediaeval theology.[138]

The Stoics offered a rather different approach. They were concerned with the distinction between space and void and so some argued that "the notion of space must be thought out not so much from the side of any container as from the side of the body contained".[139] They therefore thought of the universe as held together not by some exterior upper sphere but by some immanent reason so that they could speak of the material universe as a "rational animal" and of God as the soul of the cosmos. They actually thought of God and body together as part of the content of the universe. Hence, for the Stoics to think of God as transcendent would be to relegate him to "the infinite void beyond space" which would be a meaningless thought for them. But to think of God as existing within space would mean that the universe "could not provide any account of itself" or offer any rational explanation of its existence. In Torrance's view, the Stoic notion of space as "room forged for itself by an active agency" represented an advance beyond the prevalent receptacle notion in Greek thought. But the Stoic approach also made it too easy to "confound God with nature" and "theology with cosmology".[140]

It is in this context that Torrance explains how Nicene theology forged its new understanding of God in relation to time and space. According to Torrance, Aristotle's view "found no place at all in the Nicene theology".[141] This is important for a number of reasons. First, following the Nicene view, the incarnation meant that when the Son became incarnate he became the "place" where the Father is to be known and believed. But he became this place by assuming a body and thus making "room for Himself in our physical existence, yet without being contained, confined or circumscribed in place as in a vessel".[142] This is in fact how Origen understood the incarnation: while the active agent of the event was the eternal Word, "He was wholly present in the body and yet wholly present everywhere, for He became man without ceasing to be God".[143] And so while the Word occupied a definite space or place on earth and in history, he still occupied his position as Lord of the universe so that Aristotle's notion of place or space was, in the words

---

137  Torrance, *STI*, p. 7.
138  Torrance, *STI*, pp. 8–9.
139  Torrance, *STI*, p. 9.
140  Torrance, *STI*, p. 10.
141  Torrance, *STI*, p. 11.
142  Torrance, *STI*, p. 13.
143  Torrance, *STI*, p. 13.

of Torrance, "sprung wide open".[144] While Origen certainly introduced other difficulties, he did indeed lay the ground for a better relational conception of space developed by Athanasius who emphasized that the God who is fully present with us in space and time "remains present with the Father. He was certainly 'outside' all things in respect of his essence, but 'in' all things and events in respect of his power".[145] Even while he was incarnate, however, he continued to rule the universe as its Lord; thus the spatial aspect of the incarnation was not allowed to define who Jesus was as the eternal Word/Son, but he himself *acting* within space and time remained the only one to do that. For that reason, "He cannot, therefore, have the same space-relation (χώρα) with the Father as we creatures have, otherwise He would be quite incapable (ἀχώρητος) of God".[146] Athanasius never accepted the dualistic notion that the intelligible and sensible worlds were separated; for him the doctrines of incarnation and creation were linked together and actually prevented that, since these two realms were seen to intersect in Jesus Christ himself. Here the all-important point to be observed is that *kenosis* must not be understood in accordance with the receptacle notion of space; such a view would obviate the vital connection between the incarnation and creation and call into question the incarnation as an act of Lordship in our favor.

In other words, when we think of the relation of the incarnate Son to the Father, their *perichoretic* relation, discussed above in Chapter 2, must be allowed to control our thinking about the Father/Son relation so that we must "think of the whole being of the Son as proper to the Father's essence, as God from God, Light from Light".[147] Hence, while creaturely realities can be divided by place, the Father can never be divided from the Son. Consequently, when the Son became the place where God is to be known and encountered in history in the incarnation, the word place in this instance must be understood in accordance with the nature of God's actions *ad extra* and also in accord with the nature of created space, time and being. In this way, the ordinary concepts of place and space changed as God himself, who had become incarnate in Jesus Christ, enabled concepts to point beyond themselves toward his own transcendent reality. It is therefore the relation between the Father and the Incarnate Son that must be allowed to control our conceptions of space, time and meaning, and when that happens—when in reality we think from a center in God (as Torrance puts it elsewhere) and not from a center in ourselves (as the Arians did)—then we actually can appreciate God's eternal nature as Father, Son and Spirit without trying to circumscribe him by limiting him to or by our own human conceptions of time and space or our human experiences of him in time and space. Space is here defined "in accordance with the interaction between God and man, eternal and contingent happening" between the "horizontal dimensions" of space and time and the one "vertical dimension,

---

144  Torrance, *STI*, p. 14.
145  Torrance, *STI*, p. 14.
146  Torrance, *STI*, p. 15.
147  Torrance, *STI*, p. 15.

relation to God".[148] Thus, the Son who had become incarnate in Jesus of Nazareth could never be seen or understood as "one who had become so confined within the limits of the body that the universe was left empty of his government".[149]

What all of this means, then, is that our very human concepts, which are obviously limited by the space and time of creation, can never be projected from us in an effort to understand God's relations with us in time and space. That will always result in some idea that God is contained in and by the space he supposedly created and some relation of mutual conditioning between God and the world will be posited. Any such notion, however, will obscure the reality of grace and the meaning and power of the incarnation itself as a divine act for the benefit of humanity. Any such projection is mythology and will never lead to a genuine view of reality. Any use of human concepts to speak accurately here of God in his relations with us can only happen by an act of God from above. It is in this perspective that patristic theology importantly recognized a second key point, namely, that the incarnation did not represent an "intrusion" of God or an "abrogation of space and time" but rather his chosen way of relating with us. Here patristic theologians rejected the idea of space as that which "receives" and "contains" God as in a material body and so they sharply opposed Aristotle's notion of space in order to articulate the meaning of the incarnation in relational terms. Unfortunately, according to Torrance, Western theology adopted the receptacle idea and then proceeded to think of sacraments as containing grace in exactly the wrong way—the way opposed by Athanasius.[150]

We now have seen how the failure to think from a center in God provided in the incarnation and outpouring of the Holy Spirit led to many errors historically and today. And the key point to be stressed as we conclude this chapter is that such errors are the direct result of uncritically adopting the receptacle or container notion of space and thus separating space from time in an attempt to understand the significance of the incarnation. Repentant thinking is what is required; but such thinking will only occur when the incarnation is seen in its essential connection with the vicarious activity of the Son in his act of reconciling us to the Father. We have already noted several times that the atonement is intimately connected with the incarnation. Now let us explore the atonement in more depth to see how Torrance's doctrine of the Trinity and how his rejection of the receptacle notion of space lead him to a plausible explanation of atonement that does justice to the fact that in the incarnation God indeed suffered and died for us, but without ceasing to be God and thus without actually being defined by suffering.

---

[148]  Torrance, *STI*, p. 18.
[149]  Torrance, *STI*, p. 18.
[150]  Torrance, *STI*, pp. 25ff.

# Chapter 5

# Atonement: Incarnation and Reconciliation Are One in Jesus Christ

In the previous chapter we saw what Torrance meant by the incarnation and why it is important to realize that when God really did become human in Jesus Christ, he was not just a human being participating in God but he himself was essentially one in being with God the Father, and so Jesus was not simply a prophet but God himself present among us *as* that particular human being. Or, as Torrance frequently insists, "In the incarnation God did not just come into man but actually made our human nature his own in such a way that he came among us precisely *as Man*, without ceasing to be God".[1] But God became human in the sense that he assumed a complete body, soul and mind without ceasing in any way to be God the Son begotten of the Father before all worlds. In this way, he could both save us from sin as only God could by forgiving our sins, and he could obey God humanly and thus represent us before God in a way that no other human being could precisely because he was the Son of God incarnate. That is why we stressed that for Torrance the purpose of the incarnation was soteriological: God became incarnate for our sakes; he did something therefore that was new, new even for himself, since he was not eternally incarnate.[2] He was eternally the Son of the Father but chose to become incarnate for us and for our salvation. This is a very important insight because unless it is true that the incarnation is new even for God, then the incarnation, like creation, will be seen as in some sense necessary to God and this would deny his eternal existence as Father, Son and Holy Spirit in such a way that incarnation and creation could no longer be seen as free and decisive divine actions of the triune God, creating a world that is truly different from him and acting for us within history without being confused with history itself. In addition, Torrance insisted that Jesus' humanity was not simply an instrument used

---

[1]  Torrance, *The Christian Doctrine of God*, pp. 40–1. See also Torrance, *The Trinitarian Faith*, pp. 55 and 136, and "The Mind of Christ in Worship: The Problem of Apollinarianism in the Liturgy", *Theology in Reconciliation*, pp. 139–214, 157–58 and 227–28.

[2]  Torrance repeatedly stresses this important point not only in his books on the Trinity but elsewhere when speaking of atonement as well. Hence, for instance, Torrance writes, "Just as the incarnation was a new event, new even for God, for the Son of God was not always incarnate; so the atonement was a new act, new even for God" [Thomas F. Torrance, *The Mediation of Christ*, (Colorado Springs: Helmers & Howard, 1992), p. 114]. See also Chapter 2 above. See also Torrance, "The Atonement: The Singularity of Christ and the Finality of the Cross", pp. 225–56, 232ff.

by God to accomplish our salvation. Rather, "the human life and activity of Christ must be understood from beginning to end in a thoroughly personal and *vicarious* way".[3] It is Christ's vicarious representation of us before the Father that makes the atonement what it is, as we shall see.

When Jesus' full humanity was challenged by Docetic interpretations of the incarnation and atonement, especially in the thinking of Apollinaris of Laodicea with his idea that the divine mind replaced Jesus' human mind, Torrance notes that Athanasius wrote to Epictetus of Corinth to defend Christ's true and complete humanity while simultaneously stressing that "he was not changed into flesh".[4]

> "The Saviour having in very truth become man, the salvation of the whole man was brought about ... Truly our salvation is no myth, and does not extend to the body only—the whole man, body and soul, has truly received salvation in the Word himself."[5]

The Nicene theologians adamantly defended Christ's complete historical humanity for soteriological reasons; that is, they understood that even the slightest compromise of Christ's true humanity meant that we were not actually saved by his sacrifice for us on the cross. That is why Athanasius emphasized that Christ did not lack a human soul or mind or any other aspect of human being; in his thinking, Jesus' entire life was one of vicarious representation in which human nature itself and as a whole was saved in the sense that our sin and self-will were overcome in and through his entire sinless life of obedience to the Father. In the incarnation, God "condescended" to become one of us by assuming our sinful flesh into union with the Word in order to heal our sin and restore us to communion with God as only God could. We shall explore this further later in this chapter, explaining why Torrance thinks it is so important to see that the Word assumed our sinful, fallen and alienated flesh in the incarnation. But here it is worth mentioning that, as Gregory Nyssen declared, "Our faith staggers at the thought that God, the infinite, inconceivable and ineffable reality, who transcends all glory and majesty, should be clothed with the defiled nature of man, so that his sublime activities are abased through being united with what is so degraded".[6] Following Paul's idea of *kenosis* (κένωσις), Torrance asserts that this was not construed in a metaphysical fashion "as involving a contraction, diminution or self-limitation of God's infinite being"

---

[3]   Torrance, *The Trinitarian Faith*, pp. 150–51. See also *The Christian Doctrine of God*, pp. 40–1; Torrance, "The Mind of Christ in Worship: The Problem of Apollinarianism in the Liturgy", *Theology in Reconciliation*, pp. 156ff. and 228; Torrance, *Incarnation*, p. 205; and above, Chapter 4.

[4]   Torrance, *The Trinitarian Faith*, p. 151.

[5]   Athanasius, *Ad Epict.*, 7, cited in Torrance, *The Trinitarian Faith*, p. 152.

[6]   Gregory Nyssen, cited in Torrance, *The Trinitarian Faith*, p. 153.

but rather as an "abasement, which he freely took upon himself in what he became and did in Christ entirely for our sake".[7]

This vital point stands in sharp contrast with those who speak of God's incarnation as necessary to God in the sense that he had to suffer in order to love or that he had to become one of us in order to be the eternal God he is. Eschewing all forms of panentheism, Torrance stresses the freedom of grace in God's act of *condescension* so that God's eternally free love is never collapsed into his acts of incarnation and atonement. Because Torrance is not encumbered by any panentheistic logic, he quite properly insists, on the one hand, that Christ's humanity has no independent existence, in accordance with the patristic notion of *anhypostasis*. Yet, on the other hand, he also insists that Christ's genuine humanity has a real and full existence of its own "*in* the hypostasis of the eternal Son of God" in accordance with the patristic notion of *enhypostasis*. Hence, "Instead of discounting human nature the downright act of God's grace incarnate in Christ creates and upholds human nature".[8] And the singularity of incarnation and atonement in the life of Jesus himself means that these events took place once for all and are not repeatable. Still, the incarnation and atonement have actual meaning and reality here and now because God "did not and does not cease to be free and sovereign but remained and remains the free sovereign Lord of his becoming flesh".[9] Thus, while the Word does not surrender his being as the eternal Word and was not eternally incarnate, and while the incarnation took place once and for all, that does not mean it is just a past event because God "remains God incarnate for ever and is unceasingly present and active as God incarnate".[10]

Because Torrance makes a clear and sharp distinction (without separation) of the immanent and economic Trinity, whenever he discusses incarnation and atonement he will say something like this:

---

[7]    Torrance, *The Trinitarian Faith*, p. 153. Torrance provides a very interesting discussion of this in *God and Rationality* (pp. 144ff.) by stressing that in Jesus' human response to God we have the "divinely provided response" in Jesus' vicarious humanity which provides the creative ground for our response to God. Because the incarnate Son acted humanly for us as our reconciler, we may trust and obey, understand and know and love and worship God rightly. Christ freely offered "what we could not offer and offering it in our stead, the perfect response of man to God in a holy life of faith and prayer and praise, the self-offering of the Beloved Son with whom the Father is well pleased" he acted in our name before God (*God and Rationality*, p. 145).

[8]    Torrance, "The Atonement: The Singularity of Christ and the Finality of the Cross", p. 230.

[9]    Torrance, "The Atonement: The Singularity of Christ and the Finality of the Cross", p. 231.

[10]    Torrance, "The Atonement: The Singularity of Christ and the Finality of the Cross", p. 232.

... we must remind ourselves right away that the Father/Son relation subsists eternally within the being and life of God. This means that we cannot but think of the incarnation of the Son as *falling within the being and life of God*—although, as we have had occasion to note, the incarnation must be regarded as something "new" even for God, for the Son was not eternally man any more than the Father was eternally Creator.[11]

With this distinction, Torrance can say that in the incarnation and atonement God freely acts to become one of us in order to overcome the sin and evil that mark our humanity from within his divine person acting humanly in history for our sakes. And because Torrance respects God's freedom to become incarnate and to save the world in his only begotten Son, he is not forced into a position where he has to deny God's impassibility in order to affirm his passibility. The ultimate reason why Torrance can make sense of these matters in a clear and consistent manner, and in a way that preserves God's freedom, upholds human freedom and therefore also distinguishes divine and human activity, is because he holds together Christ's person and work in a way that those who embrace panentheistic versions of divine activity do not. No less than everything here hinges on the fact that God did not have to become incarnate and did not have to save us from sin but that he *freely* chose to do so out of his love for us. For Torrance,

> the doctrine of the Deity of Christ is basically and really the same as the doctrine of election—for the fact that the eternal God himself has chosen to become Man in the Lord Jesus Christ means that the salvation of man rests on that *divine* choice or decision. Election is what it ultimately is, and means therefore, because God has chosen and willed to become man in the Lord Jesus Christ.[12]

Like Barth, Torrance stressed that the doctrine of election is and has been misunderstood in deterministic ways when it is not thought of in Christ. But when it is acknowledged that God unites us to himself in spite of our sin and evil and in a way that we could neither actualize nor cooperate with, then we also may see that "in a basic and all-important sense we are all elected in Christ—but as a matter of fact in Christ too we are all damned, for he received on himself the sentence of death for every man!"[13] From all of this it follows that affirming and

---

[11]  Torrance, *The Trinitarian Faith*, p. 155.

[12]  Torrance, *The Doctrine of Jesus Christ*, p. 144.

[13]  Torrance, *The Doctrine of Jesus Christ*, p. 144. See Torrance's interesting response to an article by John A.T. Robinson, "Universalism—is it Heretical?" in *SJT*, 2, 1949: 139–55, advocating universalism with his own article, "Universalism or Election?" in *SJT*, 2, 1949: 310–18. Torrance claims that universalism "rationalises sin" (314) and ends up denying that atonement is the only way out of the surd-like character of sin and evil. For Torrance, we must suspend our judgment in face of what God actually did for humanity on the cross, so that while God wills the salvation of all, "Whether all men will *as a matter*

never letting go of Christ's Deity, even as we emphasize the importance of his humanity, means

> that God himself is actually and actively present in the Person of the historical Jesus Christ; that the death of Christ on the Cross and his Resurrection were personal acts of the eternal God himself; that therefore our salvation in Christ is a salvation by the very hand of God.[14]

Even the slightest failure to notice this fact theoretically or practically always results in some form of moralism or legalism by which people displace the saving actions of God in Christ by their own sinful attempts to be righteous on their own and in their own way.

God has accomplished the work of our salvation in Jesus Christ so that in that sense God's work is finished. In fact,

> The resurrection shows us that it was very God himself who had been suffering in and with his beloved Son on the Cross and it was God himself who had come in the Lord Jesus to break through sin and death. In dogmatic language the significance of the Cross lay in the Deity of the One who died there.[15]

But *we* must enter into this work through the activity of the Holy Spirit. And that takes place precisely by recognizing the Deity of Christ and its significance for our salvation. Yet that very recognition can only occur in and through God's own activity in the power of his Spirit, as Torrance frequently stresses: "The Spirit is so intimately one with Christ in his being and activity as the incarnate Son of God that he is, as it were, Christ's *Other Self* through whose presence in us Christ himself is present to us."[16] Consequently, "Salvation is thus of Grace and not of

---

*of fact* be saved or not, in the nature of the case, cannot be known" (314). Torrance insists that it is precisely the biblical doctrine of election that establishes our personal choice and decision, whereas universalism takes these away. God's election of grace is in fact his justification of the ungodly in Christ and that is the Gospel.

[14] Torrance, *The Doctrine of Jesus Christ*, p. 144.

[15] Torrance, *The Doctrine of Jesus Christ*, p. 147. Importantly, Torrance stresses that "Our best cue for understanding the power of the Spirit must surely be taken from the bodily resurrection of Jesus Christ from the grave, which was at once a pure act of the Spirit and an event that took place in space and time" (Torrance, *The Christian Doctrine of God*, p. 229). It is in the bodily resurrection of Jesus that "the final immobility of death, or the immobility which is death, was utterly vanquished", so that it is there that we may see the "dynamic nature of God's unchangeableness or constancy" (Torrance, *The Christian Doctrine of God*, p. 244).

[16] Torrance, *The Mediation of Christ*, p. 117. Torrance is quite consistent in this. See Torrance, *The Trinitarian Faith*, pp. 56, 61, 64. Importantly, Torrance insists that "The Holy Spirit so works that saving exchange within our lives that He produces from our side its counterpart in the renunciation of ourselves for Christ: I am crucified with Christ (as St

works—no works of ours can bring us to God. It is the work of God in Christ alone which brings us to God and God to us". Torrance illuminatingly puts it this way:

> On the one side, in the humanity of Christ we have the great *Anknüpfungspunkt*, or the all-important point of contact, between man and God, and on the other side, in the Deity of Christ we have the great *Anknüpfungspunkt* between God and man: both are bound up together in the act of God in which the Word assumed flesh and united himself hypostatically for ever with Jesus Christ.[17]

Let us now explore the meaning of the atonement in Torrance's thought as it relates to the incarnation and the Trinity in detail.

## Atonement as a Personal Act

We begin by noting that, for Torrance, atonement is a personal act on the part of Jesus himself as God incarnate. One must therefore keep in mind that Christ is both divine and human and so he can represent us in his redemptive work; his redemptive activity is truly universal in scope precisely because of who he is. Here Torrance's trinitarian theology and Christology are intimately connected. While the Arians searched the Scriptures for passages that would indicate Christ's weakness, mortality and creatureliness in order to show how different he was from God the Father in his transcendence, Athanasius actually focused on those same passages to show how Jesus *as God* incarnate came to act as God among us in order to save us by acting humanly in a way that is the very opposite of our selfish and self-willed activity marked by sin. Important here is the Pauline notion that Christ was both servant and priest and so he could act before God the Father on our behalf (divinely from God's side and humanly from ours). It is exactly because "he who by nature is internal to the being of God has embodied the creative source and ground of all human being in himself as man"[18] that Jesus could act on behalf of all as mediator. What does all this mean?

Torrance rejected the so-called physical theory of redemption, according to which it is sometimes thought that it is merely through the physical union of the Logos with our "decaying humanity" that salvation automatically takes place. Any such thinking seriously misconstrues the fact that it is not the incarnation by itself that establishes our redemption. Rather, it is because Christ, the incarnate Logos, "acts *personally* on our behalf, and that he does that from within the ontological

---

Paul expressed it), nevertheless I live, yet not I but Christ lives in me" (Torrance, *God and Rationality*, p. 174). In this sense, for Torrance, the Holy Spirit "is at work to realize the Godward side of our life" and to direct us away from ourselves and toward Christ as the one who alone enables us to know and love God truly.

[17]    Torrance, *The Doctrine of Jesus Christ*, p. 145.

[18]    Torrance, *The Trinitarian Faith*, p. 155.

depths of our human existence which he has penetrated and gathered up in himself" that redemption has meaning.[19] This is a particularly key point that needs to be underscored. Torrance rightly opposes what he calls an "external" view of the atonement, namely, one which would merely see Jesus as a human being external to God who then was seen to act as a moral representative of the human race in somehow placating God (which, of course, is neither necessary nor possible within the Christian view).[20] Such thinking would construe Christ's atoning sacrifice "only in terms of some kind of superficial socio-moral or judicial transaction between God and mankind which does not penetrate into the ontological depths of human being or bear savingly upon the distorted and corrupt condition of man's actual human existence".[21] Herein lies the significance of affirming and allowing Jesus' true divinity to determine the way one thinks about the atonement. Because he *is* the eternally begotten Son of the Father, begotten of the Father before all worlds, and because he now exists in the flesh as the Reconciler acting in our place to change humanity from its fallen sinful condition, we can see that "atoning reconciliation must be understood as having taken place within the personal being of Jesus Christ as the one Mediator between God and man".[22] The early church's notion of atonement was in fact nurtured by Christ's own view of his passion enshrined in the eucharistic liturgy.[23] But, just as propitiation cannot be understood in some socio-moral and legal sense, so the New Testament references to the fact that Jesus was a "ransom" for many[24] must not be understood, as Gregory Nyssen did, as a ransom paid to the devil. This view, Torrance insists, is morally repugnant, utterly unbiblical and was decisively rejected by Gregory Nazianzen as well as by

---

[19]    Torrance, *The Trinitarian Faith*, p. 156. Interpreting Melito of Sardis, Torrance insists that the atonement does not just take place "in some impersonal physical way, but in an intensely personal and intimate way within the incarnate Lord and his coexistence with us in our fallen suffering condition as sinners. Incarnation is thus intrinsically atoning, and atonement is essentially incarnational, for the saving act and divine-human being of the Saviour are inseparable" (Torrance, "Dramatic Proclamation of the Gospel: Melito of Sardis, Homily on the Passion", *Divine Meaning*, pp. 75–92, 84).

[20]    As Torrance puts it, "The Christian doctrine of salvation is no pagan doctrine of placation or propitiation. Man cannot propitiate God or in any way make amends for the sin he has committed against the infinite Majesty of God" (*The Doctrine of Jesus Christ*, p. 146). Torrance rightly insists that "the atonement is not something done by God outside of Christ as if in some external relation to the Incarnation or in addition to it, but is something done within the ontological depths of the Incarnation, for the assumption of the flesh by God in Jesus Christ is itself a redemptive act and of the very essence of God's saving work" (Torrance, "Dramatic Proclamation", *Divine Meaning*, pp. 83–4). See also Torrance, *The Mediation of Christ*, pp. 80–81.

[21]    Torrance, *The Trinitarian Faith*, p. 158.

[22]    Torrance, *The Trinitarian Faith*, p. 158.

[23]    Torrance, *The Trinitarian Faith*, p. 168.

[24]    Mark 10:45 and Matthew 20:28. See Torrance, *The Trinitarian Faith*, pp. 169ff.

Augustine and was always kept to the margins of the church's tradition.[25] The proper view is that Christ sacrificed himself for us and thus substituted himself for us out of pure love for us.

It is in this sense that atonement is not some act that God does "*ab extra* upon man, but an act of God become man, done *ab intra*, in his stead and on his behalf; it is an act of God as man, translated into human actuality and made to issue out of the depths of man's being and life toward God".[26] Consequently, the fact that Christ suffers only has serious importance for Christian faith because of the person who does the suffering. That person is the eternal Son of God, the one Word of God. In that sense, Jesus is the one who, as Torrance puts it, is "the *personalising Person*".[27] Because of the Fall we are "imprisoned in a self-centred individualism which cuts us off from genuine relations with others, so that the very personal relations in which persons subsist as persons are damaged and twisted".[28] Into this situation

> the personalising Person of the Son of God became incarnate, but, instead of becoming insincere and hypocritical himself, he healed the ontological split in human being through the hypostatic and atoning union which he embodied within it, thereby reintegrating image and reality in and through a human life of perfect sincerity, honesty and integrity in the undivided oneness of his Person as Mediator.[29]

In this way, God in Christ overcomes all that is "depersonalising" in humanity and establishes us as persons in relation to him and through that relation as those who are free to relate with our fellow humans in ways that are no longer self-centered and hypocritical. "He is the Truth of God in the form of Personal Being, Word of God identical with His Person."[30] Since Jesus is both Person and Word, the knowledge that arises in us must be both personal and verbal or propositional. Or, to put it in Torrance's own words: "Since He is Person of God, the personalising

---

[25]    Torrance, *The Trinitarian Faith*, pp. 178–9.

[26]    Torrance, *The Trinitarian Faith*, p. 158.

[27]    Torrance, *The Mediation of Christ*, p. 67. Interestingly, Torrance notes that two frequently discussed Christological "problems"—namely, how can the person of the Son become incarnate without there being two persons in him, the divine and human, "which would make him schizoid", and how can the incarnation not lead to the idea that his human person is just "an empty mask of the divine Person which would make the Incarnation unreal"—should never have arisen and never would have arisen except for the fact that these two problems stem from a dualist way of thinking about the Person of Jesus Christ (p. 67).

[28]    Torrance, *The Mediation of Christ*, p. 68.

[29]    Torrance, *The Mediation of Christ*, p. 69.

[30]    Torrance, *Theological Science*, p. 207.

Person, personal forms of reflection are begotten in us as we are obedient to Him."[31]

What this means, to Torrance, is simply that we must allow our minds to be shaped by our relationship with Jesus Christ established and maintained by God in his free grace. As we think about Christ, then "we are adapted to personal thinking and gain true subjectivity. He [Christ] certainly communicates truths to us, but they are truths that inhere in His Personal being and are not detachable from Him."[32] Because he is the eternal Son of the Father he personalizes us who are created persons; all his actions are personal actions in that he basically recreates us in his image, overcoming our self-will and self-centeredness. The twin ideas that the person of the Son might overwhelm the human Jesus or that the human Jesus might just be a mask of the divine person making the incarnation unreal both arise only because theologians refuse to accept the fact that Jesus is both personalizing Person and personalized Person in one and the same being. Hence, "As an act of reconciling at-onement, it is simultaneously an act from God to man and an act from man to God".[33] Suffering in and of itself, then, is not redemptive as one might be led to think by Jürgen Moltmann's emphasis on the idea that suffering is the principle which illuminates all theology even to the point that he can say, with Unamuno, that "only that which suffers is divine".[34] It is rather the case that "it is *God*, really *God in Christ*, who suffers and bears the sin of the world—that is

---

[31]   Torrance, *Theological Science*, p. 207.

[32]   Torrance, *Theological Science*, p. 207. See also Torrance, *Theological Science*, pp. 210ff. We thus understand the truth that Christ reveals to us in what Torrance calls a "'personalogical' relation with Him" (Torrance, *Theological Science*, p. 208). This means that in his love for us he establishes a personal relationship between us and the triune God and his love for us therefore involves personal union with him. That, for Torrance, is the logic of love which corresponds to what he terms the logic of grace, namely, we would not know God in truth and scientifically if it were not for the fact that in Christ "God has condescended to objectify Himself for us in time and within our own humanity, freely giving Himself to us as the Object of our knowledge, reconciling and assimilating us to Himself as the Truth" (Torrance, *Theological Science*, p. 203). Theology can only take place in faith because it is in faith that we recognize that we know the truth and live in relation to God only by this particular activity of grace on God's part. So the logic of grace means that we must always respect the unconditional priority of God's action in relation to us "and the irreversibility of His relationship to us may be called *the Logic of Grace*" (Torrance, *Theological Science*, pp. 206–207). God never ceases to be the subject in this relationship with us as those who know him because he never hands over control to us but always remains Lord in that encounter. We certainly know God, but that knowledge is "grounded in His divine freedom and nature" and we experience this only "on the ground of divine Grace" itself. We must always respect the fact that when we know God in a personal way it is the result of an act of reconciliation on God's part as well.

[33]   Torrance, *The Trinitarian Faith*, p. 159.

[34]   See Moltmann, *Trinity and Kingdom*, pp. 33–4, 38, and Molnar, *Divine Freedom*, pp. 203, 209 and 219. For an important critique of Moltmann on this issue as it relates to

the particle of truth, the *particula veri*, as Karl Barth once said, in the Patripassian heresy".[35] For that reason, Torrance rightly points out that "it was not the *death* of Jesus that constituted atonement, but Jesus Christ the Son of God offering Himself in sacrifice for us. Everything depends on *who* He was".[36]

Nonetheless, Torrance has no use whatever for any sort of dualism that might suggest that God somehow remained aloof from our suffering. In fact, he argues that it is precisely God's nearness to us in Christ and on the cross that reveals not only our sin but that the only possible solution to our sin is God's reconciling act in Christ. Avoiding Patripassianism and any idea that the relationship between the Father and Son breaks off on the cross so that God himself might be said to need redemption, Torrance insists upon the unbroken unity of the Son and Father, even in the midst of Christ's vicarious experience of hell on our behalf in his cry of dereliction: "My God, My God, why have you forsaken me?" For Torrance, Christ must descend into hell, namely, "the gulf which separates man and God ... a gulf whose reality has been produced by man [as a black abyss in his fallen nature] and is under the divine judgment upon sin"[37] in order to save and redeem us. And he unequivocally rejects Patripassianism while arguing that God suffers God-forsakenness, hell, sin and evil all out of love for us. In his words:

> What Christ did and suffered for us God himself did and suffers as the Father of the Son ... only God can bear the wrath of God, and if the Atonement really means anything at all it must mean that it is God who suffers there in Jesus Christ—if the divinity of Christ is denied the Christian doctrine of atonement becomes immoral—that is why spurious ideas of atonement go along with weak faith in the Deity of Christ ...[38]

---

the thinking of Barth and Balthasar, see David Lauber, *Barth on the Descent into Hell: God, Atonement and the Christian Life* (Aldershot: Ashgate, 2004), pp. 127–52.

[35]   Torrance, *The Doctrine of Jesus Christ*, p. 146. See Barth, *CD*, IV/2, p. 357. Torrance explicitly cites this text in *The Christian Doctrine of God*, p. 249.

[36]   Torrance, *God and Rationality*, p. 64. See also T.F. Torrance, *The Incarnation: Ecumenical Studies in the Nicene–Constantinopolitan Creed* (hereafter: *The Incarnation*), (Edinburgh: The Handsel Press, 1981), pp. xiv-xv.

[37]   Torrance, *The Doctrine of Jesus Christ*, p. 163.

[38]   Torrance, *The Doctrine of Jesus Christ*, pp. 146–7. See also Torrance, *The Mediation of Christ*, where he says, "the suffering of Christ on the cross was not just human, it was divine as well as human, and in fact is to be regarded as the suffering of God himself, that is, as the being of God in his redeeming act, and the passion of God in his very being as God" (p. 113). And Torrance even offers some less well-known patristic evidence for this same position when he refers to Melito of Sardis' "Homily on the Passion": "it was God himself in Christ who was condemned and judged in our place; and God himself who came down to us and acted for us and our salvation in this immediate way" (Torrance, "Dramatic Proclamation", *Divine Meaning*, p. 83).

What Torrance means when he says that the doctrine of atonement would become immoral unless Jesus really is God with us is that, apart from his divinity, the cross could only represent a pagan human attempt to appease God through human sacrifice or self-justification. What makes Christ's forgiveness real is the fact that it is an act of God himself as the subject of incarnation and atonement. With this in mind, Torrance very carefully notes that it was not the Father who became incarnate and was crucified "for it was the Son in his distinction from the Father who died on the cross". Rather, "the suffering of Christ on the cross was not just human, it was divine as well as human, and in fact is to be regarded as the suffering of God himself, that is, as the being of God in his redeeming act, and the passion of God in his very being as God".[39]

Here Torrance's trinitarian theology, which simultaneously emphasizes God's unity and trinity, enables him to maintain that *God* truly suffers our dereliction and sinfulness in order to overcome them on our behalf. He can say that both the Father and the Spirit, in virtue of the perichoretic unity of the three Persons of the Trinity, also are involved in Christ's atoning death on the cross. But he can say it without collapsing the single activity of the Godhead in his reconciliation of the world to himself in Christ into a modalistic claim that it is part of God's nature to suffer and that he cannot love if he does not suffer. God loves eternally as Father, Son and Holy Spirit and did so love before creating and would so love even without us. But in his merciful and holy love and in accordance with the "logic of grace", he seeks us and reconciles us to himself at great cost to himself in his Son and through his Spirit. It is in connection with the doctrine of the atonement, not only in its unity with the doctrine of the incarnation but also in its essential unity with the doctrine of the Trinity, that Torrance sees the future of Israel and the church. He argues that it is precisely the God of Israel, the one and only God, "the *I am who I am*, or *I shall be who I shall be*" revealed in the Old Testament who is revealed in the New Testament and has become incarnate in Jesus Christ.[40] Because true knowledge of God involves cognitive union with God, we can see that the doctrine of atonement is pivotal to any true conception of God. We are at enmity with God because of sin and need to be reconciled by God himself in order to have cognitive union with him. That is what happened in Christ.

## Divine Impassibility

Here the important question concerning God's impassibility needs to be discussed in more detail. As we have just seen, it is because Torrance conceives the atonement as internal to the incarnate Word that he believes that God not only can suffer but that he did so *as* God *for us* in order to act within history as our savior, helper and

---

[39]  Torrance, *The Mediation of Christ*, p. 113. See also Torrance, *The Trinitarian Faith*, p. 182.

[40]  Torrance, *The Mediation of Christ*, pp. 101ff.

friend. Torrance insists that God "had no need for others to be able to love" since "God's love knows no *why* beyond itself—there is no reason for God's love apart from his love … What God did, therefore, in creating fellowship between himself and others, he did in the sheer freedom of his overflowing love".[41] Following St Paul's statement that "He who spared not his own Son but delivered him up for us all, how shall he not with him also freely give us all things?" (Romans 8:32), Torrance says that "God loves us more than he loves himself".[42] While we have already seen that Torrance repeatedly and rightly stresses that what God is toward us in the economy he is eternally in himself as the God who loves and indeed the God who *is* love, he also emphasizes that God's love is manifest in the incarnation and atonement as free love. Hence, "God does not love us because of the atoning propitiation enacted in the sacrificial death of Christ. Rather does that propitiation flow freely from the consistent self-movement of the Love that God himself is".[43] It is specifically in the blood of Christ that God draws near to us and brings us near to himself by overcoming all sin, hostility and fear between us and God. But this love of God demonstrated in the incarnation and atonement in their essential unity is "characterised by a total freedom from rigid immutability or inflexibility and by an infinite range of variability and mobility". God's love is dynamic and not static and it is not encumbered by what we think God can and cannot do. In fact, when the atonement is seen from within the moral order as it is apart from the cross, "the substitutionary death of Christ would be judged morally wrong" since an innocent man taking the place of others is morally inexplicable.[44] This makes it clear that the whole moral order needed to be redeemed and placed on a whole new basis as it was in God's justifying action in Christ. Still, God's love "will never be other than it eternally is, so that it always acts faithfully and appropriately with the just and the unjust, the merciful and the froward alike". In this sense, God's love functions "unreservedly and equably as love even in the judgment of the sinner".[45] It is in this context that the question of God's impassibility arises.

---

[41] Torrance, *The Christian Doctrine of God*, p. 244.

[42] Torrance, *The Christian Doctrine of God*, p. 244. See also, Torrance, "The Atonement: The Singularity of Christ and the Finality of the Cross", pp. 234–5, where Torrance notes that this was an expression used by H.R. Mackintosh.

[43] Torrance, *The Christian Doctrine of God*, p. 245. In another context, Torrance writes that atoning propitiation means that "God draws near to us and draws us near to him through the blood of Christ. Propitiation has nothing to do with propitiating God as though he needed to be placated in order to reconcile us to himself, but with the two-way movement on the part of God who in his prevenient love freely draws near to us in order to draw us near to himself on the ground of the atoning self-sacrifice of Christ offered for us" (Torrance, "The Atonement: The Singularity of Christ and the Finality of the Cross", p. 242).

[44] Torrance, "The Atonement: The Singularity of Christ and the Finality of the Cross", p. 252.

[45] Torrance, *The Christian Doctrine of God*, pp. 245–6.

Because Torrance makes a careful distinction in arguing that what God is toward us in the economy he is antecedently or eternally in himself as the triune God who is love, he can say with conviction and force not only that Christ's Deity means that in the incarnation his life as the "one Mediator between God and man falls within the life of God" but that "his passion belongs to the very Being of God, and thus of God the Father and God the Spirit as well as God the Son".[46] Further, he can say that it is through Christ's resurrection and ascension that all he "has done for us in his historical life and death in offering himself for the sins of mankind has not only been accepted by the Father but has been taken up into God and is anchored in his eternal unchangeable reality".[47] Notice the very important difference between Torrance and Ted Peters on this issue. Ted Peters claims that "the immanent Trinity is consummated eschatologically, meaning that the whole of temporal history is factored into the inner life of God. God becomes fully God-in-relationship when the work of salvation—when the economic Trinity—is complete".[48] Clearly this image of the Trinity is one which ignores the freedom of God's love as espoused by Torrance and instead supposes that God needs the world to be in relationship to himself. In Peters' reasoning, the line between divine and human being and action is also blurred with the idea that all of history is "factored into the inner life of God". Such analysis fails to make the important distinctions deployed by Torrance. It fails to reflect the fact stressed by Torrance that: 1) God's love is free and not at all dependent on his relations with us in history; 2) in the incarnate Word, Jesus' human history and not the whole of temporal history is taken up into God and is anchored in God's eternal life so that we may relate with God in and through the humanity of Jesus as our eternal High Priest. Peters' thinking fails to distinguish what happened uniquely in the life of Jesus for our benefit and what happens in history as such; and 3) God is fully in relationship within the immanent Trinity with or without loving us in creation, incarnation and atonement. That is why God opposes our sin and then actually steps into that relation of opposition in order to forgive our sin by becoming incarnate in the man Jesus. For that reason he can act decisively and therefore divinely in our favor to overcome sin, suffering, evil and death.

Torrance not only relies on biblical testimony for his understanding of these issues but on such theologians as Gregory Nazianzen who spoke of "'God crucified', as a downright 'miracle'". Gregory said, "'We needed an incarnate God, a God put to death, that we might live. We were put to death with him, that we might be cleansed ...'" And, according to Athanasius, the crucified who was

---

[46]   Torrance, *The Christian Doctrine of God*, p. 246.

[47]   Torrance, *The Christian Doctrine of God*, p. 247. Torrance here remarks that one of the merits of Moltmann's book *The Crucified God* (London: SCM Press, 1974) was exactly this emphasis. Still, he also notes that "his somewhat tritheistic understanding of the unity, rather than the oneness of the Father, the Son and the Holy Spirit, in spite of what he intends, damages this insight" (p. 247).

[48]   Peters, *God as Trinity*, p. 181.

dishonored and suffered was indeed God. Cyril of Alexandria insisted that "If the Word did not suffer for us humanly, he did not accomplish our redemption divinely; if he who suffered for us was mere man and but the organ of Deity, we are not in fact redeemed".[49] All of this is summed up in the important Patristic soteriological principle that "*the unassumed is the unredeemed*" developed by the aforementioned Greek fathers: Athanasius, Cyril and Gregory.[50] As Gregory Nazianzen said, rebutting the Apollinarian denial that Christ had a human soul:

> "The unassumed is the unhealed ... but what is united to God is saved. If only half Adam fell, then what Christ assumes and saves may be half also; but if the whole of his nature fell, it must be united to the whole nature of him who was begotten, and so be saved as a whole".[51]

And, in refuting Eunomius, Gregory Nyssen noted that when, according to the Gospel parable, Christ sought out the lost sheep, he carried home "the whole sheep, not just the fleece, that he might make the man of God complete, united to God in body and soul ... [he] left no part of our nature which he did not take up into himself".[52] But what of the divine impassibility?

*First*, Torrance insists that it was in Jesus himself that the "whole human race, and indeed of the whole creation", is "already redeemed, resurrected and consecrated", because in him, within his divine-human being as the Mediator, salvation is a reality. But it is a reality that applies to all ages, past and future, and thus reaches forward to the advent of Christ when salvation will be complete for all creation. But because salvation has taken place in Christ for all, it is just as eternal as he himself is as the eternal Son. Our creaturely existence is now "as securely anchored in the very being and life of God as Jesus Christ himself ... in him our humanity, in spite of its temporal changeable nature, is given a place in God, and is thus grounded in his eternal unchangeable reality".[53]

For Torrance, there is a very practical implication to this understanding of atonement in its essential unity with the incarnation and it is this: because God in Christ assumed our fallen human nature, as is commonly espoused in Eastern theology, and began to heal, sanctify and redeem it, and because he did not assume some neutral humanity or some humanity thought to be untouched by sin and guilt, as has been commonly assumed in Western theology, Torrance is able to promote the Greek rather than the Latin view of atonement. Accordingly,

---

[49]   Torrance, *The Christian Doctrine of God*, p. 247.

[50]   Torrance, *The Christian Doctrine of God*, p. 250. See also Torrance, *The Trinitarian Faith*, pp. 163ff. and Torrance, "The Atonement: The Singularity of Christ and the Finality of the Cross", p. 237.

[51]   Torrance, *The Trinitarian Faith*, p. 164.

[52]   Torrance, *The Trinitarian Faith*, p. 164.

[53]   Torrance, *The Trinitarian Faith*, pp. 183–4.

It is the whole incarnate life of Christ vicariously and triumphantly lived out from his birth to his crucifixion and resurrection in perfect obedience to the Father within the ontological depths of his oneness with us in our actual fallen existence, that redeems and saves us and converts our disobedient alienated sonship back to filial union with the Father ... the *vicarious humanity* of Jesus Christ as Lord and Saviour of mankind ... carries with it a rejection of any idea that the humanity of Christ played a merely instrumental role in some kind of external legal transaction ... and gives it an essential and integral place in indivisible oneness of agency with that of the Father and the Holy Spirit.[54]

But this means that incarnation and atonement cannot be separated from each other. When they are, some sort of legalism and self-justification follow, thus undermining the actual atoning act of Christ on behalf of all humanity. Here, then, is the intensely practical implication of atonement for our moral relations: no account of atonement offered in merely moral or legal terms will do justice to the doctrine of justification as St Paul understood it, because both our moral and legal frameworks are external to the incarnate life of the Mediator and therefore these very domains must be set right by God himself in the atoning action of Christ.

While the moral and legal orders are what they are by God's will and action, they are used by sinful creatures to hide from God and so they too need to be redeemed. Hence, there is a difference between what we *are* and what we *ought* to be—a difference that we can never bridge because of our sinful natures marked by the Fall. That is why Torrance notes that our "free will is finally a form of our self-will".[55] Hence, even our good behavior needs to be "cleansed by the blood of Christ". Because the moral *ought* has been freely lived by Christ in his obedience to the Father on our behalf, we no longer have to fulfill the law because that has been done for us by him and in him. Therefore, instead of legalistically attempting to save ourselves through the law and its observance by means of obeying a moral imperative, we are now freed to allow our lives to be ruled by "the indicatives of God's love rather than externally governed by the imperatives of the law".[56] This has very practical implications because it means that whenever the atonement or incarnation are interpreted in terms of the moral order or legal order as it stands under judgment, then we will inevitably find Christ's vicarious representation of us on the cross to be an immoral action. Yet, as seen above, it can only be viewed in that way if it is viewed as an action of the man Jesus externally related to God. However, if Jesus is seen as God acting for us and among us for our sakes, then it will be seen that what we have here is a "soteriological suspension of ethics"

---

[54] Torrance, "The Atonement: The Singularity of Christ and the Finality of the Cross", pp. 238–9.

[55] Torrance, "The Atonement: The Singularity of Christ and the Finality of the Cross", p. 251.

[56] Torrance, "The Atonement: The Singularity of Christ and the Finality of the Cross", p. 253.

because we now have a "new moral life" that flows "from grace in which external legal relation is replaced by inner filial relation to God the Father".[57]

By making our God-forsakenness his own, Jesus also embraces our agnosticism and atheism, that is, our attempts to know God by natural theology within the context of what we claim to know "without God", and re-orients our thinking to a center in God which we ourselves are incapable of securing but which God in his grace gives us in the cross and resurrection of Jesus. By actually experiencing our dereliction in face of God the Father, Jesus the incarnate Son reconstructs our existence from within and recasts our questions so that they may actually come from a center in God and find their answers in that same center in God and thus truly speak of the Father, through his Son and in the Spirit.[58]

*Second*, suffering itself is redeemed in Christ's suffering. To understand this, Torrance insists that we must first acknowledge that when God became incarnate in Jesus "he did not cease to be God".[59] And we must also recognize that in Jesus Christ, God brought his own holiness to bear upon our sinful humanity which Jesus assumed in order to heal in such a way that "He was made sin for us that we might be made the righteousness of God in him".[60] How, then, should we understand the issue of divine *possibility* and *impassibility* in this context?

Torrance says, "There is certainly a sense in which we must think of God as impassible (ἀπαθής), for he is not subject to the passions that characterize human and creaturely existence …".[61] Indeed God is "intrinsically impassible for in its own divine Nature he is not moved or swayed by anything other than himself or outside of himself". And God is actually "opposed to all suffering and pain".[62] It should be noted here that it is precisely Torrance's trinitarian understanding of this issue, with its intrinsic opposition to modalism, subordinationism and tritheism, that enables him to say at once that suffering is alien to God and yet in his free love God takes our suffering to himself and makes it part of his nature in the sense that he overcomes this for us on the cross and through Christ's resurrection from

---

[57]   Torrance, "The Atonement: The Singularity of Christ and the Finality of the Cross", p. 252.

[58]   Torrance, "Questioning in Christ", *Theology in Reconstruction*, pp. 125–6.

[59]   Torrance, *The Trinitarian Faith*, p. 184. See also Torrance, *STI*, p. 53, and Torrance, "The Atonement: The Singularity of Christ and the Finality of the Cross", p. 231.

[60]   Torrance, *The Trinitarian Faith*, p. 184. See also Torrance, "The Atonement: The Singularity of Christ and the Finality of the Cross", pp. 236–7, where Torrance writes: "He assumed from the virgin Mary our actual human nature in such a way as to make our sin, our guilt, our death and our judgment, our plight and our agony his own. He took upon himself our twisted, lost and damned existence … and substituted himself for us … he expiated our guilt in taking our just judgment upon himself, wiped away our sin and debt in making the restitution which we are utterly unable to make, thereby cancelling all our debt and blotting out all accusations against us and justifying us in himself."

[61]   Torrance, *The Trinitarian Faith*, pp. 184–5.

[62]   Torrance, *The Christian Doctrine of God*, p. 248.

the dead. Torrance is well aware of the fact that ancient and mediaeval theology often stressed God's impassibility in ways that were inappropriate because instead of thinking soteriologically such theology was influenced by metaphysical notions of God's being as unmoved. This unquestionably applies to certain contemporary thinking as well. But Torrance unequivocally insists on a theology based on God's economic trinitarian self-revelation and follows Isaiah 63:9 to affirm both that God is "afflicted in all the afflictions of his people" and God is not "untouched by their sufferings",[63] so that "What Christ felt, did and suffered in himself in his body and soul for our forgiveness was felt, done, and suffered by God in his innermost Being for our sake".[64]

Following Athanasius, Torrance insists that because atonement is something that takes place within the personal constitution of the Mediator on behalf of creation, therefore

> we cannot think of the sufferings of Christ as external to the Person of the Logos. It is the very same Person who suffered and who saved us, not just man but the Lord as man; both his divine and his human acts are acts of one and the same Person.[65]

This thinking exhibits what one might call Torrance's anti-Nestorian Christological stance in connection with both incarnation and atonement. And it further illustrates that, for Torrance, incarnation and atonement can never be separated. Any time they are in fact separated that has to mean that "the atonement is inevitably thought of as an external transaction between God and man and between Christ and man, in which divine and human agency in Christ are held apart".[66] In reality, it is through the incarnation itself that "atonement is established and anchored in our human existence". But it is also "anchored in the transcendent being and love of God from whom it derives and to whom it restores us in the communion of his reconciling love".[67] In this way, atonement is also intrinsically connected with the doctrine of the Trinity because it is only on the basis of the cross "that the Holy Spirit is mediated to us, and it is only as Christ himself is mediated to us through the presence of the Spirit that we may be united to Christ in his vicarious humanity and participate in the fruit of his saving and redeeming work".[68] Torrance insists that "Calvary and Pentecost belong integrally together, for the pouring out of

---

[63]   Torrance, *The Trinitarian Faith*, p. 185.

[64]   Torrance, *The Christian Doctrine of God*, p. 249.

[65]   Torrance, *The Trinitarian Faith*, p. 185.

[66]   Torrance, "The Atonement: The Singularity of Christ and the Finality of the Cross", p. 239. See also Torrance, *The Trinitarian Faith*, p. 160.

[67]   Torrance, "The Atonement: The Singularity of Christ and the Finality of the Cross", p. 242.

[68]   Torrance, "The Atonement: The Singularity of Christ and the Finality of the Cross", p. 243.

the Holy Spirit upon us belongs to the fulfilment of God's reconciliation of the world to himself".[69] Indeed, it is only because of the atonement in Christ that we have a proper understanding of God as Father, Son and Holy Spirit. This very knowledge

> takes place only within the movement of atoning propitiation whereby God himself draws near to us and draws us near to himself and thereby enables us to have communion with him in his inner trinitarian relations … Through Christ and his cross alone do we have access by one Spirit to the Father, and so our reconciliation and communion with God through the atoning mediation of Christ are ultimately grounded in the triune being of the one eternal God.[70]

Consequently, it is in Christ's own suffering—that is, in experiencing our passion, hurt, violence and our human condition that stands under judgment as captured in his cry on the cross "My God, my God, why hast thou forsaken me?"—that Jesus vicariously "brought his eternal *serenity* or ἀπάθεια to bear redemptively upon our passion". As a result, Torrance maintains that it is just because the incarnation and atonement in their intrinsic unity uniquely disclose Christ's divine-human Person and action that we cannot offer a logical explanation of divine *passibility* or *impassibility* any more than we can offer a logical account of *how* God can be human and divine at the same time.[71] According to human logic, it is an either/or issue: either God is passible *or* impassible; either Jesus is God *or* man; either God is changeable *or* unchangeable. But on the ground of what actually happened in the life, death and resurrection of Jesus himself—thus on the basis of soteriology and on the basis of God's economic trinitarian self-revelation—Torrance insists that we must think soteriologically and not logically. We must think in faith, according

---

[69]    Torrance, "The Atonement: The Singularity of Christ and the Finality of the Cross", p, 243. Torrance insists that the Spirit received by Jesus in the Jordan at his Baptism enabled us to become sanctified in him by that very action. "This twofold movement of the giving and receiving of the Spirit actualised within the life of the incarnate Son of God *for our sakes* is atonement operating within the ontological depths of human being. It constitutes the 'deifying' content of the atoning exchange … Pentecost must be regarded, not as something added on to atonement, but as the actualisation within the life of the Church of the atoning life, death and resurrection of the Saviour" (*The Trinitarian Faith*, p. 190).

[70]    Torrance, "The Atonement: The Singularity of Christ and the Finality of the Cross", p. 243.

[71]    See, for example, Torrance, *The Mediation of Christ*, where Torrance notes that those who think that it is difficult to think of God becoming man in Christ without his divinity overwhelming his humanity are thinking of what happened in the incarnation in terms of human logic: either he was divine *or* human. Soteriologically, we know that he was both in accordance with the faith that knows his divinity and humanity are "neither separated from one another nor confounded with one another, and in such a way that neither nature suffers loss or change through relation to the other" (p. 69).

to what Torrance describes as the logic of grace,[72] and allow God in Jesus Christ to disclose to us something quite new and unexpected here.

Consequently, Torrance says, "logically impassibility and possibility exclude one another",[73] and we cannot get the right understanding here thinking about impassibility in the Stoic sense either. Rather, we must understand that God in his impassibility has "stooped down" to us and has overcome our suffering, pain and guilt in the Mediator out of sheer divine love. By sharing our passion, then—by experiencing in mind, heart, soul and divinity our God-forsakenness as exemplified in his cry of dereliction in Mark 15:34, a passage repeatedly cited by Torrance when discussing the incarnation and atonement—Christ enables us to share in his "imperturbability".[74] In fact, it is just at this point that Torrance shows how a proper trinitarian understanding of this issue shows the way forward. Torrance stresses Mark 15:34 but at the same time links Jesus' cry of God-forsakenness on the cross with John 13:46 and says that his cry of dereliction is followed by his cry "Father, into thy hands I commend my spirit".[75] This is the epitome of Christ's vicarious humanity at work in human history for our benefit. Jesus Christ not only experienced our passibility or God-forsakenness, even though he himself was not a sinner, but he answered to God for us by experiencing God's own opposition to our self-will and sin in a complete life of obedience which consisted in a renewed relationship between Creator and creatures exemplified in his obedience to the will of God: "not my will, but thine be done" (Mark 22:42).[76]

In this perspective, Torrance says, we should apply this same thinking to Christ's ignorance and wisdom. While the Arians made much of the fact that the Gospels say that Christ grew in wisdom and was lacking in knowledge in order to make their case that he was fully human and divine only in a sense that placed him on the creaturely side of the divide between Creator and creature, Torrance says Athanasius maintained that while Jesus continued to have his unique relation of knowing with the Father as Son, he nonetheless condescended for our sakes "really to make our ignorance along with other human limitations his own precisely in order to save us from them".[77] While some fourth-century theologians downplayed Christ's ignorance or even denied it, Torrance notes that others such as Gregory Nazianzen and Gregory Nyssen insisted "on the reality of our Lord's ignorance as essential to his humanity". And, according to Torrance, Cyril of Alexandria carried

---

[72]     See Chapter 4 above. See also Torrance, *Divine and Contingent Order*, pp. 136–8. According to Torrance, we have no analogy for the power of grace by which God undoes our sin within the person of the one Mediator—God does not impose himself on us from above but works as man from below in order to resolve the sorrow, pain and agony of the universe "through his own eternal righteousness, tranquility, and peace" (p. 138).

[73]     Torrance, *The Trinitarian Faith*, p. 185.

[74]     Torrance, *The Trinitarian Faith*, p. 186.

[75]     Torrance, *The Christian Doctrine of God*, p. 251.

[76]     Torrance, "Questioning in Christ", *Theology in Reconstruction*, p. 126.

[77]     Torrance, *The Trinitarian Faith*, p. 186.

through Athanasius' thinking most fully when he argued that Christ's ignorance was part of his *kenosis*—his sharing in our human condition with all its limitations and imperfections. Hence,

> It was an economic and vicarious ignorance on our Lord's part by way of a deliberate restraint on his divine knowledge throughout a life of continuous *kenosis* in which he refused to transgress the limits of the creaturely and earthly conditions of human nature.[78]

So, just as it is imperative to stress that in Christ our minds as well as our bodies have been healed and reconciled with God, so it is important to stress that Christ really shared our human ignorance so that we might share his divine wisdom. Torrance insists that this is not just an appearance, for if that had been the case, then our salvation too would only be an appearance. Unless Christ assumed the whole person, including our human ignorance, salvation would not be a reality. God in Christ therefore took upon himself in the incarnation and atonement the whole of human nature including

> the sin, alienation, misunderstanding, and darkness that had become entrenched within it. Jesus Christ came among us sharing to the full the poverty of our ignorance, without ceasing to embody in himself all the riches of the wisdom of God, in order that we might be redeemed from our ignorance through sharing in his wisdom. Redemption was not accomplished just by a downright *fiat* of God, nor by a mere divine "nod", but by an intimate, personal movement of the Son of God himself into the heart of our creaturely being and into the inner recesses of the human mind, in order to save us from within and from below ...[79]

Perhaps the immense strength of this insight can be seen even more clearly when it is seen against the background of what has become such a consuming question of contemporary Christology for the last twenty or more years: how can Jesus be truly one of us, as Chalcedon emphasized, if he is thought to have a super-human consciousness as well? For example, Canon A. T. Hanson argues that only the Synoptics give us an accurate historical view of Jesus. Thus, he thinks we must bracket John and Paul to achieve a proper view of the historical Jesus in his true humanity. Therefore, in the interest of not giving Chalcedon "equal status" with Scripture, Hanson concludes:

> I am far from ignoring the tradition of the Church, which tells me that in Jesus God was uniquely present. *But I do not admit that this necessarily involves elaborating a christology according to which God is substantially present in Jesus* ... I know the Fathers would have said that we have no justification in

---

[78]   Torrance, *The Trinitarian Faith*, p. 187.

[79]   Torrance, *The Trinitarian Faith*, pp. 187–8.

making this complaint ... *But we cannot think in these terms today.* If it can be said with any meaningfulness that Jesus enjoyed a superhuman consciousness, *then he was not sufficiently one of us.*[80]

But on what basis can we not think in these terms today? Clearly, for Hanson, we cannot think this way based on anthropological considerations. And, from the perspective of human anthropology, it would indeed be ridiculous to suppose that any human being could be divine and concurrently possess a superhuman consciousness while still remaining fully and completely human. Yet that is precisely Torrance's point: we cannot separate John and Paul from the Synoptics because together they attest the unique revelation of God in the Person and work of Jesus Christ who, as inseparably divine and human, acted both divinely and humanly in vicarious representation of us once and for all on the cross and in his resurrection from the dead. Instead of accepting this truth on soteriological grounds as Torrance does, Hanson clearly thinks about this matter logically and concludes that *if* Jesus enjoyed a superhuman consciousness, *then* he could not be fully human, fully one of us. Torrance consistently and rightly opposes any such thinking, arguing soteriologically that it is just because the man Jesus from Nazareth was and is the Word of God himself present among us in space and time that he is humanly one of us, sharing to the full our humanity, ignorance and sinful alienation from the Father in order to overcome all this passibility from within as our representative. Not only does logical thinking compromise a proper understanding of the incarnation, but here it can be seen that it also endangers a proper conception of the atonement, as well as true knowledge of God himself as one who does not in any way cease being fully divine as he acts for us from within the limitations of our creaturely existence.

*Third*, we need to discuss the proper understanding of *theopoiesis* (θεοποίησις). Succinctly put, it is because God became man in Jesus Christ that we are able to participate in his divine knowledge, loving and in his own eternal life itself. We are, in Torrance's words, "admitted into an intimate sharing of what is divine".[81] It is in this context that Athanasius' rather unfortunate remark that "He became man in order to make us divine" is to be understood. Following Georges Florovsky, Torrance thinks that when *theosis* is understood in some ontological way it is indeed embarrassing, for no one of us could ever become divine without obliterating the all-important distinction between God and us. But if *theosis* is understood in personal terms, as indeed Torrance believes the fathers did, then "Theosis means a personal encounter. It is the ultimate intercourse with God, in which the whole of human existence is, as it were, permeated by the Divine Presence".[82] While one might be slightly taken aback by Torrance's explicit support of Florovsky's

---

[80]    Revd Canon A.T. Hanson, "Two Consciousnesses: The Modern Version of Chalcedon", *SJT*, vol. 37, no. 4, 1984: 471–83, 481; emphasis mine.

[81]    Torrance, *The Christian Doctrine of God*, p. 96.

[82]    Torrance, *The Christian Doctrine of God*, p. 96.

remark that *theosis* should be understood to mean that our human existence is "permeated" by God's presence and wonder whether or not he is indeed confusing divinity and humanity after all, it would be important to remember that Torrance has no thought of this. He insists that Jesus acts as our reconciler because he is God acting *as* man and not merely God acting in a man. This means that his whole human life as the life of God with us is itself to be seen as a dynamic action of God in human form. But Torrance utterly refuses to confuse divine and human being and action, as when he says that

> there is no suggestion that this interaction between Christ's deity and our humanity, results in any change in divine or human being (οὐσία), for as he is not less divine in becoming man, so we are not less human in being brought under the immediate presence and power of his divine being.[83]

While Torrance adopts Athanasius' term by saying we are made "divine" and also speaks of our "deification" here, it is clear that he does not in any way wish to think of human nature becoming anything more than human, and he certainly does not wish to diminish the sovereignty of God's free actions *in se* or *ad extra*. In fact, he wants to say that our humanity becomes fully human only in and through Christ's atoning actions on our behalf because in Christ we are lifted up "to enjoy a new fullness of human life in a blessed communion with divine life".[84]

For Torrance, it is through the Holy Spirit that we are enabled to have eternal life in and through Christ. Our *theopoiesis* consists in our encounter with the Word of God himself in Jesus Christ. Properly understood, our "deification" (a word which Torrance generally does not want to use but will use occasionally in the sense just described) consists in the recreation of our humanity in Christ himself through union and communion with God the Father. The Holy Spirit makes us "partakers of God beyond ourselves".[85] Just as the Holy Spirit descended upon

---

[83]   Torrance, *The Trinitarian Faith*, pp. 188–9.

[84]   Torrance, *The Trinitarian Faith*, p. 189. For Torrance, following Athanasius, "'Deification' did not mean, of course, any change in the nature of human essence, but that without being less human we are by grace made to participate in divine Sonship" ("The Relation of Incarnation to Space", *Divine Meaning*, p. 369).

[85]   Torrance, *The Trinitarian Faith*, p. 189. Torrance also tends to want to shy away from the word "divinization" as when he says, "The Greek Fathers used to speak of that experience [of our mutual indwelling with God in Christ] as *theopoiesis* or *theosis* which does not mean 'divinization' as is so often supposed, but refers to the utterly staggering act of God in which he gives *himself* to us and *adopts us* into the communion of his divine life and love through Jesus Christ and in his one Spirit, yet in such a way that we are not made divine but are preserved in our humanity" (Torrance, *The Mediation of Christ*, p. 64). See also Torrance, "Athanasius", *Divine Meaning*, p. 198, where he notes that "*theopoiesis* (or *theosis*) through the Spirit … does not import any inner deification of our human nature" because in our union with Christ "we find our real life hid with Christ in God". Elmer Colyer makes this important point as well, noting that "*Theosis or theopoiesis is not the*

Christ in the Jordan, so the Spirit descends on us because Christ bore our body. This, of course, did not take place "for the promotion of the Word himself, but for our sanctification". Pentecost, then, is not something that is added on to the atonement but rather is "the actualisation within the life of the Church of the atoning life, death and resurrection of the Saviour".[86] That indeed is how Torrance thinks of the apostolic foundation of the church itself: "that which was atoningly wrought out in Jesus Christ on our behalf is now through the Spirit subjectively actualized in the apostolic foundation of the Church".[87]

## Cross, Sin and Evil

Now, in order to fill out Torrance's understanding of the atonement in its essential connection with the incarnation, it will be important to understand just what he means by the cross and by sin and evil. Without a full understanding of these three factors that loom large in any theory of atonement, it will be impossible to understand fully what it was that actually happened in Christ's death and resurrection. The most important point to note is that one cannot genuinely appreciate the meaning of sin apart from the revelation of God himself in Jesus Christ. Torrance follows Barth's thinking here and remarks that "There is, so to speak, an unfruitful knowledge of sin, of evil, of death and the devil, that succeeds in making it hard for a man to have happy and confident faith in the Almighty Father and Creator". Such unfruitful knowledge is any attempted knowledge of sin and evil that fails to recognize that "We cannot in ourselves know what our misery and despair, our guilt and punishment really are" because we can only discern these in truth "in the fact that Christ has taken them upon himself and borne them".[88] It is from within this perspective that Torrance asserts that "the Cross itself [is] the background in which sin is shown up and the despair of man is exposed to which the Cross is the answer and the remedy".[89] We can see what Reformed theology following Calvin means by our "depravity" only in the light of grace. This, of course, can be misunderstood, as both Calvin and Torrance assert. But what this means is not that God takes delight in the degradation of

---

divinizing or deification of the human soul or creaturely being, Torrance contends, but rather is the Spirit of God humanizing and personalizing us by uniting us with Christ's vicarious humanity in a way that both confirms us in our creaturely reality utterly different from God, and yet also adapts us in our contingent nature for knowledge of God, for communion with God and for fellowship with one another" (*How to Read T.F. Torrance*, pp. 178–9). For how this plays out in Torrance's thinking with respect to 2 Peter 1:4, see Chapter 3 above.

[86] Torrance, *The Trinitarian Faith*, p. 190.

[87] See Torrance, "The Place of Christology in Biblical and Dogmatic Theology", *Theology in Reconstruction*, pp. 128–49, 137ff.

[88] From Karl Barth, *Credo*, cited in Torrance, *The Doctrine of Jesus Christ*, p. 157.

[89] Torrance, *The Doctrine of Jesus Christ*, p. 157.

humanity. Instead, it means that "Apart from the judgment of grace there can be only an unhealthy knowledge of human depravity which is not only misanthropic but an insult to the Creator".[90] Grace shows us that even the sinner who stands in contradiction to God's grace is "maintained in being by the same grace" so that "all his endowments and virtues are themselves directly due to the Spirit of God".[91] Hence the fact that humanity stands under God's total judgment does not mean the annihilation of the "natural man", but it does mean that all that human beings do is marked by their inclination toward self-will and autonomy.

What exactly does human sin look like in light of the cross? First, "The Cross alone exposes for the first time the real condition of mankind; it strips a person of the external mask that covers his wretchedness and exposes him to view".[92] Second, what is exposed to view is the fact that since the Fall there is no way to escape the dark aspect of human nature that led to the cross. Romantic–idealists hate the shadow cast by the cross. But the shadow remains nonetheless. And that shadow is the simple fact that the cross represents judgment not only pronounced by human beings themselves in the crucifixion of Jesus but also pronounced by God against them in his own submission to that action in Christ. This means there is no place to hide. Humanity cannot protect itself from judgment by embracing human values, no matter how dear or noble they may be. What the cross reveals to us is not only the reality of sin but the fact that we *are* sinners so that, whether or not we do good or ill, all of our activities are marked by our inherent attempt to be autonomous, that is, to be free of God. That is why Torrance accepts Calvin's judgment that the very essence of sin is ingratitude, so that while we should exist in the image of God by obediently and thankfully accepting grace as grace, the reality is that we do not and instead we exercise our pride and self-will by acting as if we belonged to ourselves.[93] But nothing can change the fact that we were made for relationship with God and we really have no life at all without relation to him. We are, in other words, dependent upon God for life itself and yet as sinners we live as those who rely only on ourselves, exercising self-will over against God. We are therefore rebels against God. And that rebellion reaches its climax at the cross:

> The Cross is the supreme revelation of the sin of mankind. Man is so utterly sinful that nothing will suffice, but that the very Son of God must be plucked

---

[90] Torrance, "The Word of God and the Nature of Man", *Theology in Reconstruction*, p. 106. Torrance follows Barth in this. See also Torrance, *Calvin's Doctrine of Man*, p. 182.

[91] Torrance, "The Word of God and the Nature of Man", *Theology in Reconstruction*, p. 106.

[92] Torrance, *The Doctrine of Jesus Christ*, p. 158.

[93] See Torrance, "The Word of God and the Nature of Man", *Theology in Reconstruction*, pp. 108–9. Torrance spells this out in detail in his important book *Calvin's Doctrine of Man*.

from his bosom to sacrifice himself for mankind … man is so bad that he rose up and slew the very Son of God.[94]

What is revealed on the cross is that sin is not something neutral but actually is an "attack upon God".[95] In the words "My God, My God, why have you forsaken me?" we see that sin means guilt and guilt is defined according to Colossians 2:21 as "The handwriting of God against us".[96] It is extremely important to understand Torrance at this point. He explains that from the incarnation we know that because God in reality had to come to us, we already recognize that there is a gulf between God and us; we are cut off from relationship with God by our self-will, by our attempts at autonomy. Our distance from God, then, can only be seen by and through God's nearness to us in Christ. And what we see in that particular nearness is the fact that this distance cannot be thought of as a metaphysical distance but rather as a "clash of wills".[97] It is exactly God's immediate presence to humanity in the person of Jesus Christ that causes us to say, "Depart from me, O Lord, for I am a sinful man. I am not worthy that Thou shoudest come under my roof".[98] These words signify that in God's approach to us in the person of Jesus Christ we are judged and condemned. Here we see that in our mind and heart, while we were originally created in God's image to be in relation and fellowship with him, we

---

[94]   Torrance, *The Doctrine of Jesus Christ*, p. 158. See also Torrance, *Incarnation*, pp. 246ff. In an unpublished manuscript entitled "Atoning Justification", Torrance speaks forcefully of the cross as "the supreme crime of mankind" which God used in order to redeem us (17). This was a supreme act of justification on God's part because the atonement meant that God had restored to humanity its original righteousness by undoing the past, and simultaneously it was made to serve the purpose of the cross. In other words, God took our punishment upon himself on the cross, in Christ's descent into hell and burial, so that "God has given Himself to man in his sin and corruption and lost estate, in such a way as to take the course, the punishment, the corruption of sin upon Himself, to slay the old sinful and perverted Adamic existence and bury it … to raise it out of the grave a new humanity in the resurrection of Jesus Christ …" (17).

[95]   Torrance, *The Doctrine of Jesus Christ*, p. 158.

[96]   As noted above, Torrance frequently cites Mark 15:34—"My God, My God, why have you forsaken me?"—not only to stress Jesus' true humanity but to stress the fact that Jesus made the words of Psalm 22 his own on the cross in order to reveal that he had taken our human despair and God-forsakenness upon himself in our place; he made our questions his own, "in order both to ask them in truth and in truth to receive the answers" (Torrance, "Questioning in Christ", *Theology in Reconstruction*, p. 117). Jesus' cry of dereliction indicated his "descending into the hell of our darkness and godlessness. He was asking the ultimate question from the point of identification with man in his ultimate need" (pp. 117–18).

[97]   Torrance, *The Doctrine of Jesus Christ*, pp. 158–9. See also Torrance, "The Word of God and the Nature of Man", *Theology in Reconstruction*, p. 107.

[98]   Torrance, *The Doctrine of Jesus Christ*, p. 159.

are now at enmity with him.[99] For Torrance, it is imperative to realize that to be a creature is, through God's Spirit, to be in relation to God: "The creature in order to be a creature requires relation to the Creator. That relation is given by the Holy Spirit who upholds the existence of the creature ..."[100] But the creature is also distinct from God and dependent on God. So there is a double relation here: God gives us life and we depend on God for that life. In other words: "The creature requires the Creator in order to live. He thus requires relation to Him. But this relation he cannot create. God creates it through His presence to the creature, i.e. in the form of a relation of Himself to Himself."[101]

This is why Torrance insists that the Spirit is "God Himself in His freedom to be present to the creature, and so to create this relation, and thereby to be the life of the creature".[102] While all of this can be said of any creature, Torrance notes that the distinctive thing about human beings is that they were "created in order to enjoy this relation in a conscious and intelligent fashion", so that for us to be creatures we need to hear the Word of God and obey it—that hearing and acknowledgment makes our lives different and in that sense we are created in the image of God. We can, Torrance says, retain this life in the Word "only by a continuous thankful acknowledgment of this gracious calling of God which carries with it the confession of creaturehood",[103] that is, our complete dependence upon God himself.

---

[99]     For a full description of what Torrance means by the fact that we were created in God's image, see *Theology in Reconstruction*, pp. 102–110. For Torrance, following Calvin, the *imago dei* in Reformed theology means that we must admit that our human lives are pure gift from God and so we can arrogate nothing to ourselves. Hence the *imago dei* "is not a doctrine about man's being in himself, but rather an acknowledgment that he depends entirely upon the will of Another, whose grace and truth he images in a knowledgeable and obedient relation to the Word of grace" (pp. 104–5). Objectively, then, the *imago dei* is the grace of God revealed and active in Jesus Christ, and subjectively it is the Holy Spirit conforming a person to Christ through faith. Subjectively, the *imago dei* is the witness of the creature to the glory of God. For this reason, Reformed theology completely rejected Augustine's idea that "in the mind itself, even before it is a partaker of God, his image is found" (p. 105). Torrance notes that Barth, following Calvin, called this the thinking of the antichrist because it is the very attempt on the part of human beings to claim the image of God as a natural possession that was "the very root motion of original sin" (p. 106). What is at stake here, according to Torrance, is the biblical view of grace and of the dynamic relation between God and us. For a full discussion of these matters, see Torrance, *Calvin's Doctrine of Man*, especially pp. 35-113.

[100]     Torrance, *The Doctrine of Jesus Christ*, p. 159.

[101]     Torrance, "The Word of God and the Nature of Man", *Theology in Reconstruction*, p. 104.

[102]     Torrance, "The Word of God and the Nature of Man", *Theology in Reconstruction*, p. 104. See also Torrance, *Incarnation*, p. 247.

[103]     Torrance, "The Word of God and the Nature of Man", *Theology in Reconstruction*, p. 104.

Everything that Torrance says here in his Christology fundamentally reflects his understanding of humanity as he grasped it in his presentation of Calvin's theological anthropology in his 1957 book *Calvin's Doctrine of Man*. In that work, Torrance repeatedly stresses that to understand Calvin we must realize that humanity, as created in the image of God, fallen in Adam and re-created in Christ who is himself the very image of God in the truest sense, can only be understood from what he calls the "downward motion of grace".[104] Hence, he understands Calvin's stress upon our total depravity to be a rhetorical device meant to point us in humility toward our complete dependence upon grace both to know God and to live in and from Christ and thus to be in the image of God. That is why Torrance opposes later Calvinism which detached the notion of total depravity from this rhetorical context and distorted the positive nature of Calvin's theological anthropology by considering the Fall and depravity of human beings "apart from the context of grace" and instead interpreted "grace as God's answer to human depravity". This incorrectly makes Calvin out to be "the author of a thoroughly pessimistic view of man".[105] Torrance stresses that to be in the image of God does not mean that humanity possesses something that enables some sort of human structural resemblance of God,[106] although there are places where Calvin does indeed speak of our differences from the beasts in that we retain intelligence and the ability to distinguish good from evil. Torrance believes that Calvin actually is inconsistent in this since, on the one hand, he speaks of the total annihilation of the image of God in us by virtue of the Fall, while, on the other hand, he speaks of the fact that a spark of that image remains intact in spite of the Fall.[107] Nonetheless, what Torrance adamantly maintains is that Calvin, even in that inconsistency, always insisted that we could never rely on that image by relying on ourselves either to know God or to relate with God in any true and proper way. Torrance himself maintains that "Reformed theology cannot but talk in terms of total depravity or perversity, and, to be consistent, cannot talk about there remaining in fallen man, as such, any portion of the *imago dei*".[108] And this is said because our total salvation takes place only in Christ. Any notion of a partial remainder of the *imago dei* in us could open the door to some sort of self-reliance, which is the very opposite of what it means to live by grace alone.

Torrance's discussion of how Calvin dealt with natural theology captures his whole conception of the image of God as something that can only be rightly grasped in a dynamic and not some static way, precisely as our relation to God in Christ established and maintained by God himself in grace, through Christ

---

[104]    Torrance, *Calvin's Doctrine of Man*, p. 14. This is especially true of our knowledge of God (pp. 174–5).

[105]    Torrance, *Calvin's Doctrine of Man*, p. 20.

[106]    See Torrance, *Calvin's Doctrine of Man*, pp. 109–110.

[107]    See, for example, Torrance, *Calvin's Doctrine of Man*, p. 93.

[108]    Torrance, "The Word of God and the Nature of Man", *Theology in Reconstruction*, p. 108.

and thus through his atoning act of reconciliation on the cross and so through revelation and faith.[109] While he says that all have some natural knowledge of God, he also believes that, in light of the cross, we cannot depend on that at all because we must rely on our being created anew in Christ through the Spirit in order to have true and saving knowledge of God.[110] All such capability therefore comes only from God's Word and Spirit and thus only through grace. That is why Calvin always spoke of our knowledge of God as taking place in the obedience of faith. But perhaps the most important factor to note in this context is that Torrance's understanding of the *imago dei* is heavily dependent upon Calvin's presentation of the image of God. In other words, the image of God as properly understood means that God actually sees himself through us as in a mirror, and thus the image of God in us refers to the fact that in our obedient knowing and loving of God in Christ we mirror the glory of God as Creator and Reconciler.[111] As already noted, it must be understood only from and in Christ in a spiritual way and only in a relational fashion.[112] To summarize: for Calvin and for Torrance, human beings were created to find their happiness in God—they were called to live in thankful obedience to God's loving kindness, upon which they depend every moment of their lives. Even creation itself testifies to this. But the human ability to relate with God and thus to know God through creation, which is indeed the theater of his glory, was lost because of Adam's sin. That ability and thus the image of God was restored only in Christ and consequently it is only in Christ, and therefore only by grace and in faith, that we live as those who are now reconciled with God through God alone—as those who are truly joyous and thankful. That is why even when we can know that creation glorifies God, that very knowledge comes only from the Word of God and through faith.

---

[109]  It must therefore be seen as "a continuous relation of man's mind and will in response to God" (*Calvin's Doctrine of Man*, p. 64) and not "in terms of a static analogy of being" (p. 65). Torrance insists that Calvin stressed "the dynamic character of the image of God which is maintained in man by continuous conformity to God, by continuous obedience to the claim of the divine will upon him. In other words, the *imago dei* is interpreted teleologically as above and beyond man in terms of man's destiny which is made known in the Word of God, and in the claim of the divine Will thus revealed upon man's life" (pp. 65–6).

[110]  See Torrance, *Calvin's Doctrine of Man*, pp. 154–83.

[111]  Thus Torrance refers to a wider sense of the image that describes how the universe mirrors God but he insists that can be interpreted correctly only through the narrower spiritual view that sees the meaning of the universe through God's Word and Spirit, and thus through faith, and leads us to joy and gratitude. Still, Torrance writes, "there can be no image where there is not one beholding ... Primarily, it is God Himself who beholds His own glory in the works of His hand, or rather who images Himself in these works" (*Calvin's Doctrine of Man*, p. 39). He then notes that "man looks into the mirror of creation, too; and he also beholds the image of God there, only he does it through the Word, which, properly speaking, is the image of God" (p. 40).

[112]  Torrance, *Calvin's Doctrine of Man*, pp. 80–82

Seen in this perspective, sin must be understood as a fatal contradiction in our relationship with God—a relationship which, as we have just noted, is essential for our very existence. Because sin in this sense means rebellion against the Creator on whom creatures depend, it represents a kind of "suicide": "by rebelling against the Creator and asserting his independence the creature is acting against the innermost relation which constitutes his very being and existence; and so sin is as such, it has been said, an impossible possibility!"[113] This contradiction introduces into the notion of sin a double factor. First, all sin means that the creature is *against* the Creator by acting in such a way as to suggest that he or she does not *actually* depend upon God the Creator for all things. Second, even existence itself and the Creator are against the creature because God does not let go of his creatures but still loves them and seeks to create fellowship between himself and them. While God in his mercy maintains creatures in existence in spite of their sin (their turning their backs on God who is the sole source of life and truth), God nevertheless is against us in our rebellion so that there is a drastic change in our relations with God. Our situation has changed from one of life to one of death. As sinners, creatures are no longer positively related to God but are instead "negatively related to God".[114] Rightly understood, sin must be thought of from the human side as well as from God's side:

> Sin is not simply the perversion of man's mind and attitude toward God but affects man in the ontological depth of his being; and it also entails a real "change", as it were, in God's mind and attitude towards his disobedient and rebellious creatures or children; and it is that which constitutes the innermost nature and therefore gravity of sin, the guilt of man before God.[115]

The gravity of sin and our guilt can be seen even more clearly when seen against the background of God's holiness. In the book of Exodus, God is revealed as one who tells Moses "I am that I am", so that we see that God's very nature as the one and absolute Being and Creator of all that is distinct from him shows that he alone is "the universal norm of life".[116] Because God alone is self-sufficient, his holiness is reflected in the fact that he is this norm. Understood within that context, sin is in reality seen as "a contradiction of that in virtue of which God is thus God ... Sin is thus an attack upon the very Godness of God and God to be God must and

---

[113]   Torrance, *The Doctrine of Jesus Christ*, p. 159. Though he does not here identify his source, it seems clear that Torrance takes that expression "impossible possibility" from Barth. What this means is that it is possible for creatures to rebel against God as they actually have and continue to do. But it is impossible for them actually to be what in their sin they attempt to be, namely, equal to and independent of God himself.

[114]   Torrance, *The Doctrine of Jesus Christ*, p. 160.

[115]   Torrance, *The Doctrine of Jesus Christ*, p. 160. See also Torrance, *Incarnation*, pp. 248ff.

[116]   Torrance, *The Doctrine of Jesus Christ*, p. 160.

does in his Being, precisely by his Being God, reject and resist sin."[117] This is an enormously important point because it is essential to understand the meaning of what happened on the cross and through Christ's resurrection from the dead. The atonement was necessary because the very nature of God as one who loves and is good is such that he must oppose evil and sin; hence God would not be God if he acquiesced in human sin. It is in this sense that God unequivocally resists the creature's attempt to be God by means of self-assertion and false autonomy. As Torrance says, "God would cease to be God if he were to condone sin or overlook it."[118] That is why God's grace meets us in the form of judgment after the Fall. Unless this is properly understood, Torrance believes we will not understand the cross or the person of Jesus Christ correctly.

Here Torrance clarifies his notion of sin even more. Sin, he says, is not just an act against goodness or love but an act against God himself. He has in mind Psalm 51:4, where it is said that "Against Thee, Thee only have I sinned".[119] There are, then, two aspects of sin. On the one hand, sin is rebellion against God so that if God did not resist it, then the actual distinction between good and evil would disappear. On the other hand, sin is disclosed precisely as rebellion against God just because God resists and opposes it. That is the wrath of God. God's wrath indicates God's personal opposition to sin. And sin so marks our human existence that there is, in a certain sense, a "constitutional" change in human nature which means that we as creatures are wholly involved in sin and have nothing within ourselves that we can rely upon to extricate ourselves from this situation. So sin is not just this or that evil action on our part; sin involves our entire human existence before God which is at enmity with God. Hence, Torrance follows Paul who says, "Whatsoever is not of faith is sin" (Romans 14:23) in order to emphasize that sin is the very opposite of our positive relation with God that can only take place in faith. Torrance makes things crystal clear when he says that we do not really understand evil when we equate it with something we might have done wrong and then think that before that we were either good or neutral. Following Brunner, Torrance says evil is rooted in our very nature so that "man does not only *do* wrong, he does not only commit sinful acts, but he *is* bad, he is a sinner. A sinner is not a human being who has sinned a certain number of times; he is a human being who sins whatever he is doing".[120] Sins merely manifest the fact that our whole existence is at enmity with God.

This leads to Torrance's final point in understanding human sin. Exactly because sin determines our entire existence and cannot be reduced to the sins we commit, Torrance stresses that sin is not something we are capable of changing. No matter how much a person tries to save himself or herself, that person sins all the more because all human actions are so deeply rooted in our attempts at

---

[117]   Torrance, *The Doctrine of Jesus Christ*, pp. 160–61.

[118]   Torrance, *The Doctrine of Jesus Christ*, p. 161.

[119]   Torrance, *The Doctrine of Jesus Christ*, p. 161.

[120]   Torrance, *The Doctrine of Jesus Christ*, p. 162.

being autonomous in relation to God—which, of course, is in itself the impossible possibility. In other words: "As fallen human beings, we are quite unable through our own free-will to escape from our self-will for our free-will is our self-will."[121] This is what Torrance identifies as guilt. Guilt means that our past as sinners powerfully determines our present. Guilt is further identified with our "in-turned nature" as those who put ourselves first instead of putting God first as we really need to do. We have not only turned away from God by turning to ourselves as the criterion of truth, if you will, but God has turned away from us as he must in his holiness since it is that holiness that we have contested. People are in fact caught in a "guilty tension" in which they boldly and self-righteously dare to claim that God's reaction to sin, which they think they are aware of in their consciences, is actually their own better selves. In thinking this way we just cover up our existence as it is enmeshed in sin. And it is this "hypocrisy" that is "exposed at the Cross where man sees himself for the first time in the true light".[122] Guilt, then, also has a twofold determination: it involves our autonomy and the divine wrath against this attempt at independence from relationship with God which is the only possibility of life. In Torrance's view, it is an incomprehensible mystery that God does not allow his relationship with us to cease altogether. But the fact that God does not do so indicates his patience and love. Even though we *are* sinners, God still seeks and creates fellowship with us as one who must also maintain his holiness. When this is grasped, then the nature of the atonement in all its depth can be seen. God assumes our twisted humanity into union with his Word. He assumes a humanity that is maintained by relation to God but a humanity that is marked by our own rebellion against God and by God's reaction against that rebellion. That explains why the cross is so terrible. It is because guilt itself is so dreadful. What makes guilt so terrible, according to Torrance, is that behind it is the full force of

> the divine resistance to sin. The gulf which separates man and God in the very nature of fallen man is a black abyss, a gulf whose reality has been produced by man and is under the divine judgment upon sin—that is the meaning of hell. And Christ must descend into that hell in order to save and redeem man. He the Mediator must descend into the blackness of man's alienation from God to save him; he must unite in his own Person man and God and bear the guilt of man before the presence of God.[123]

It is in this context that Christ's cry of dereliction from the cross displayed both the reality of human guilt and the reality of divine wrath. He experienced those in order to save the human race by mediating in his forgiving grace the gulf that separates Creator and creature.

---

[121]   Torrance, *The Mediation of Christ*, p. 85.
[122]   Torrance, *The Doctrine of Jesus Christ*, p. 163.
[123]   Torrance, *The Doctrine of Jesus Christ*, pp. 163–4.

## Torrance's View of Justification

Having understood the depth of human sin in light of the incarnation, reconciliation and revelation of God in Jesus Christ, we may now see why the doctrine of justification is so central to all of Torrance's theology. For Torrance, it is not our faith as some autonomous action that saves us at all. Such an idea is but one more instance of human sin asserting itself. While faith certainly is our human decision, that human decision itself needs to be healed and was indeed healed in the person and work of Jesus Christ, the one Mediator. This is where atonement is central in its essential union with the incarnation. And this is where Christ's vicarious human activity is also decisive. In the Old Testament, Torrance believes, it is God's unswerving and steadfast love that surrounds his covenant people Israel in spite of their unfaithfulness. As especially emphasized in the prophet Hosea, God would not let his people go, but held on to them "throughout all their rebellion" and evoked faith from individual members of the community. In the incarnation Jesus himself stepped into this conflict.[124]

Keeping in mind Torrance's two key points—namely, that 1) we do not understand the real meaning of sin unless we understand it from the grace of God revealed in the incarnation, and 2) what we do understand from the incarnation is that God loves us more than he loves himself in that he was willing to sacrifice his own Son in order to overcome our enmity against him—it is easy to see what he means when he speaks of cheap and costly grace. In Torrance's words, "Grace is not cheap but costly, costly for God and costly for man, but costly because it is unconditionally free: such is the grace by which we are justified in Christ Jesus."[125] Without any constraint at all, God took the initiative and justified us by his free grace. Because of that everyone is put on the same level and that includes everyone: good and bad, those within the church and those outside the church, those who are religious and those who are secular. All "come under the total judgement of grace" because all that they are is called into question by the simple fact "that they are saved by grace alone".[126] That applies to every single aspect of human existence: human knowledge, human ethics, religion, philosophy and science. It is in this sense that Torrance unequivocally rejects the twin errors of "universalism" and "limited atonement", both of which ultimately are grounded

---

[124]    See Torrance, *The Mediation of Christ*, Chapter 2.

[125]    Torrance, *God and Rationality*, p. 56.

[126]    Torrance, *God and Rationality*, p. 56. "Justification," Torrance writes, "puts us in the right and truth of God and therefore tells us that we are in untruth … justification by grace alone does not mean that there is no natural goodness in man, but that man with his natural goodness is called in question. Jesus Christ died for the whole man (with his good and his evil) not for part of him, the evil part, but for the whole man. He died for all men, the good and the bad, and all alike come under the total judgment of his Death and Resurrection; all alike have to be born again in him, and made new creatures" (Torrance, "Justification", *Theology in Reconstruction*, p. 162).

in a "logical–causal" attempt to explain the atonement and both of which harbor elements of the Nestorian heresy. Logically, so the argument goes, if Jesus died for all, then both logically and causally all people must necessarily be saved. But if some in fact are not saved, then logically and causally Christ's atoning death does not apply to them.

There are, for Torrance, two fatal errors espoused here. First, such thinking arises from an attempt to project our own views from within fallen humanity on to the unique action of God in Jesus Christ and thus redefine soteriology in terms of human logic operating in a fallen world. Second, the argument for universalism and for limited atonement "involves a rationalization of evil in attempting to say why some men are finally saved and why some men are finally not saved, by resorting to an explanation in terms of a logico–causal continuity".[127] In other words, such thinking ignores the costliness of God's grace as evidenced in the cross of Christ. For Torrance, we simply cannot explain why some people do not believe in Christ and end up in hell—but even if they do, that does not mean that Christ did not die for them as well.

God's grace, therefore, is costly grace because it took place through the blood of Christ. In that sense it cost God his only Son to reconcile the world to himself in him. Here it is clear why the doctrine of atonement is intrinsically related to the doctrine of the incarnation. And these two doctrines are what they are precisely because the triune God has his life in himself as Father, Son and Holy Spirit, but nevertheless, in his free love, he elects to live a life with us and therefore for us. Here one also can see how important Torrance's doctrine of Trinity actually is: by making a clear and sharp distinction (but not separation) between the immanent and economic Trinity, Torrance can insist in each theological context that grace is identical with Jesus Christ and Jesus Christ is truly God himself, the eternal Son of the Father, present in history as our Savior, brother and friend. As God incarnate, he not only enables our true knowledge of God as an act of pure grace but he enables it in such a way that when God is truly known, we know that the truth of our theology never resides in our concepts themselves or in anything we can verify without faith in him in his activity here and now through his Holy Spirit.[128] This grace of God which is identical with the truth itself, namely, with Jesus as the Word of God incarnate, is, however, costly to us as well because it cuts the ground out from any and all forms of self-justification, from any type of self-reliance at all in any sphere, especially the sphere of religious achievement. That is why, for instance, in our knowledge of God, Torrance repeatedly stresses that we must think from a center in God or a center in Christ (which is the center in God made available to us in the incarnation and thus by grace and through faith alone) in order to know and verify our knowledge of the truth.

---

[127]    Torrance, "The Atonement: The Singularity of Christ and the Finality of the Cross", p. 249. See also Torrance's important discussion of Universalism and Election in relation to John A.T. Robinson's espousal of Universalism noted above.

[128]    See, for example, Torrance, *Theological Science*, pp. 200ff.

Since grace is identical with Jesus Christ, just as the gift of salvation is identical with the giver, and since he is the truth of God himself present among us, Torrance insists that

> Commitment in action *by itself* cannot be used as a pragmatic test of truth precisely because it is correlative to justification by Grace alone which insists that the true is the *real*, and which therefore summons us to cast ourselves entirely upon God, to reject reliance upon ourselves or our own works and to live constantly and entirely, not from a centre in ourselves, but from a centre in Christ.[129]

Torrance continues by asserting that whenever we allow ourselves to be thrown back on ourselves (in thought, word or deed) in order to verify the truth of theological statements, then and there we are attempting to live from a center in ourselves rather than from a center in Christ, and that very activity calls into question any theology that would claim to have the truth in itself.[130] Justification claims us and points us to the fact, the reality, that our lives are truly hidden with Christ in God and that therefore nothing we think can ever be true in itself but can only be true as it points beyond itself toward its true ground in Christ himself. Hence, for Torrance, justification has "the profoundest consequences for our life and thought and action for in it we are committed to a way of acting and thinking that affects the whole structure of our existence as human beings".[131]

That explains why Torrance believes that grace is so costly to us. Justification by grace alone is just as difficult, Torrance says, for people in their parish as it is for people in the university. That is why he notes that Luther once rightly stated that the reaction of the average person to the doctrine is "like a cow staring at a

---

[129]  Torrance, *Theological Science*, p. 201. It is precisely the doctrine of justification by faith that calls into question any thinking that would imply that the truth of Christology should be judged by the ethical behavior of Christians.

[130]  As we saw in detail in Chapter 2, it was precisely Arius' mythological thinking about God, and thus his projection of human experience into God to understand him, that constituted his attempt to think about God from a center in himself. It would not be inaccurate to say that Torrance's entire understanding of the Trinity is shaped by his view of justification, since his whole theology turns on his argument that we must think from a center in God and not from a center in ourselves. He repeats this theme with different emphases and in different contexts throughout his two books on the Trinity and elsewhere. See, for example, *Transformation & Convergence*, p. 211, where he writes, "we are unable to justify or verify our knowledge of God, for we cannot put ourselves in the right or truth with God. In faith, however, we rely ultimately on God himself to relate our thinking and knowing to the truth of his own Reality, and thus to make our human thinking and knowing of him terminate on God himself as their true ground beyond anything we can achieve of ourselves". See also Torrance, "Theological Education Today", *Theology in Reconstruction*, p. 26.

[131]  Torrance, *Theological Science*, p. 201.

new gate",[132] while the reaction of university students is sometimes one of anger and resentment since they find it hard to accept. It is in this sense that grace is costly to us: it calls into question all that we are and asks us to deny ourselves, to take up our cross and to follow Christ.[133]

> We need to learn and learn again and again that salvation by grace alone is so radical that we have to rely upon Christ Jesus entirely in everything, and that it is only when we rely on him alone that we are really free to believe: "Not I but Christ" yet "Christ in me". Because he came as man to take our place, in and through his humanity our humanity is radically transformed, and we become truly human and really free to believe, love, and serve him.[134]

The mystery of justification means that we can only be free when we surrender ourselves to Christ who alone can free us for God in truth (John 8). This is why Torrance insisted that grace is absolutely unconditional. Faith is not a work we do in order to be saved—it is not a justifying work. Faith is our human decision to abandon standing on ourselves in any way at all and give ourselves to Christ in and through the Spirit so that he may actually transform us. This is not a cooperative effort. Any such thought would simply express the "subtle Pelagianism of the human heart", that is, our self-will, which itself must come under judgment in Christ's unconditional forgiveness of sins. Because sin so deeply affects us, "we are trapped by our sin within the circle of our hearts which are turned in upon themselves, so that we cannot even repent of our faith or repent of our repentance, but are cast wholly and unreservedly upon the unconditional forgiveness of Christ Jesus".[135]

So the costliness of grace for us means that we must abandon ourselves, marked by sin as we are, to Christ himself in order to become free again and again. This is why Torrance excoriates those who think of salvation as conditional in any sense. People who are told that they can be saved only on condition that they believe are being given bad news and not good news because such a thought places the weight of salvation on what we do instead of on what God in Jesus Christ has done and wills to do for us here and now in and through his Holy Spirit. And, apropos our

---

[132]    Torrance, *God and Rationality*, p. 71.

[133]    Torrance, *God and Rationality*, p. 71. Torrance relates this to ecumenical theology in *God and Rationality*, pp. 118ff. See also Torrance, *Preaching Jesus Christ Today*, pp. 36–7. Torrance repeats this frequently. In his discussion of natural knowledge of God, for instance, he insists that we have natural knowledge just as we have natural goodness, but that all knowledge and goodness are called into question "by Christ who when he comes to us says: 'If any man will come after me, let him deny himself, take up his cross and follow me'" (Torrance, "Justification", *Theology in Reconstruction*, p. 163).

[134]    Torrance, *Preaching Jesus Christ Today*, p. 37.

[135]    Torrance, *Preaching Jesus Christ Today*, p. 36.

discussion of atonement, Torrance thinks that hidden in the Pelagian thinking[136] that espouses conditional salvation is a failure to take the New Testament teaching about Christ's "substitutionary role seriously, a reluctance to allow it to apply to the whole of their being and to all their human activity before God, even to their believing and praying and worshipping".[137] Because salvation is identical with the unconditional love of God (grace) expressed in the incarnate Word, Jesus Christ, the cross of Christ signifies that total forgiveness and total judgment must be proclaimed to all, irrespective of their response. For Torrance, both grace and judgment are unconditional—they have taken place in Jesus Christ on the cross and in his resurrection and apply to us all. While we are summoned to repent and believe, judgment means that even our believing and repenting can only be made good by Christ and not by us.

This is extremely important to realize, especially today when we are told by some that, in order to achieve liberation, women who have been subordinated to men need to tap into the power of their own experience in order to heal their imaginations with new conceptions of the deity. Searching for new conceptions of the deity in order to achieve liberation, however, amounts to what Torrance called a "conceptual letting go of God" that was evident in the so-called "new theology" offered by John A. T. Robinson, Paul Tillich and Rudolf Bultmann mentioned above in Chapter 1.[138] In his estimation, their thinking allowed language about God to become "detached from the Reality of God" so that "a conceptuality arising out of our own consciousness has been substituted for a conceptuality forced upon us from the side of God Himself".[139] Hence, Tillich's view of faith-knowledge as "symbolic and non-conceptual" represented his "romantic" approach to God such that the rationality he offered was "correlated with the question as to man, and the question that man puts to God is finally himself, the questioner", with the result that it becomes "difficult to see how the way of 'God' can avoid the way taken by man".[140] This opens the door toward a kind of "radical dualism" which will not

---

[136]  Thinking that, like the British monk Pelagius, supposes we can rely on our innate goodness to be in communion with God.

[137]  Torrance, *Preaching Jesus Christ Today*, p. 37. See also Thomas F. Torrance, *The School of Faith: The Catechisms of the Reformed Church* (hereafter: *The School of Faith*), trans. and ed with an intro. by Thomas F. Torrance, (Eugene, OR: Wipf and Stock, 1996), p. cvii, where Torrance traces this sort of thinking to those who detach the Holy Spirit from Christ. Torrance insists that our spiritual union with Christ is indeed our "carnal" union with him in his humanity; hence it is not an additional union because if it were then Christ's work of salvation would need to be completed by our actions in baptism and the Lord's Supper or by our actions of faith or conversion. In both of these ways we would be espousing some notion of conditional grace or conditional salvation which Torrance emphatically rejects.

[138]  Torrance, *God and Rationality*, p. 47.

[139]  Torrance, *God and Rationality*, p. 47.

[140]  Torrance, *God and Rationality*, pp. 47–8. See Torrance, "Theological Realism", pp. 176ff., for an astute critique of Edward Schillebeeckx for adopting a "non-conceptual"

allow God to be understood as actively present within our world in his Word and Spirit; thus God is understood as an interpretation of our own existence and not by reference to God at all. Then our statements about God become little more than statements about ourselves. "Their actual content is our own 'self-understanding'. You do not understand God out of Himself, but out of your own self. That was the fatal step taken by Bultmann in his famous essay of 1925 about the sense in which we can speak of God".[141] Once that step is taken, according to Torrance, then the word "God" "becomes not so much a cipher of your relations with God but a cipher of your relations with your fellow human beings", and what emerges is a complete secularization of Christianity and a "religionless Christianity" in which we are "flung" upon our own resources. Once this occurs, then, theological statements become not only anthropological statements but merely biographical statements and in that way they lack any scientific validity because they no longer refer to objective realities existing in their own right over against us. John Robinson and Rudolf Bultmann fit into this category, cutting us off from God and our neighbors by making theology little more than a "symbolic form of human self-expression". Robinson changes Jesus' question *"Who was neighbour* to him that fell among thieves?" to "How can *I get* a gracious neighbour?" By rejecting the fact that God acts *objectively* within our world, Bultmann claimed that God's love "is not a fact within our cosmic existence. Hence, the 'act of God' in the death of Christ is no different from the 'act of God' in a fatal accident on the street. Thus with one stroke he eliminates atonement as 'hodge-podge'".[142]

Finally, this thinking encourages us to separate Jesus from "the Christ" and "lets each man substitute himself in the place of Jesus" with the result that "He becomes a symbol which *we* have to fill with content from ourselves".[143] It is important to realize in this circumstance that atonement, Christ's death on the cross, has really destroyed human sin. But human sin is exposed by the cross of Christ as self-will. Hence, the way to human freedom will not be found and the solution to our social, cultural and political problems will never be solved, much less addressed, as long as it is thought that any of this can be achieved by relying on our own experience, with the result that we can and should re-define who God is in such a way that we no longer actually have to rely on Christ in everything but instead can rely on ourselves and use Christ to achieve our agenda. The problem here identified by Torrance in connection with the thinking of John Robinson, Rudolf Bultmann and Paul Tillich, with its far-reaching consequences, is still alive and well in contemporary theology. And this may simply be one more

---

approach to God. Torrance alertly sees the connection here between Schillebeeckx and others such as Blondel, Maréchal and Rahner; cf. Torrance, "Truth and Authority: Theses on Truth", *Irish Theological Quarterly* 38 (1972): 226–7.

[141]   Torrance, *God and Rationality*, p. 49.

[142]   Torrance, *God and Rationality*, p. 50. See also Torrance, "Epilogue", *Theology in Reconstruction*, pp. 277ff.

[143]   Torrance, *God and Rationality*, pp. 50–51.

confirmation of Colin Gunton's quite proper judgment that perhaps the favorite heresy of the twentieth century was Arianism.[144] It remains a popular temptation even now. By contrast, notice how Torrance's description of conversion is bound up completely with Jesus Christ:

> As fallen human beings, we are quite unable through our own free-will to escape from our self-will for our free-will is our self-will. Likewise sin has been so ingrained into our minds that we are unable to repent and have to repent even of the kind of repentance we bring before God. But Jesus Christ laid hold of us even there in our sinful repentance and turned everything round through his holy vicarious repentance, when he bore not just upon his body but upon his human mind and soul the righteous judgments of God and resurrected our human nature in the integrity of his body, mind and soul from the grave ... the Gospel speaks of regeneration as wholly bound up with Jesus Christ himself ... our new birth, our regeneration, our conversion, are what has taken place in Jesus Christ himself, so that when we speak of our conversion or our regeneration we are referring to our sharing in the conversion or regeneration of our humanity brought about by Jesus in and through himself for our sake. In a profound and proper sense, therefore, we must speak of Jesus Christ as constituting in himself the very substance of our conversion ... without him all so-called repentance and conversion are empty ... conversion in that truly evangelical sense is a turning away from ourselves to Christ ...[145]

It is easy to see the difference between the thinking of someone who recognizes and maintains the centrality of our justification by faith and someone who does not. The differences are stark. Conversion is tied to Christ's atoning sacrifice on the cross and frees us for and toward him alone. Ignoring our justification by faith will always mean attempting to redefine God and Christ in light of our self-experience which inevitably becomes not only the starting point but the norm for the truth of God himself.

## John Knox and the *Scots Confession*

We have seen the rough outline of what Torrance meant by justification. But let us look a bit more closely at some of his more technical explanations to see how profound and far-reaching his understanding really was. Torrance himself stressed that his conception of justification is in line with the thinking of John Knox who was a key contributor to the *Scots Confession* of 1560 and for whom

---

[144]    Colin E. Gunton, "And in One Lord, Jesus Christ ... Begotten, Not Made" in *Nicene Christianity: The Future for a New Ecumenism*, ed Christopher Seitz (Grand Rapids, MI: Brazos Press, 2001), pp. 35–48.

[145]    Torrance, *The Mediation of Christ*, pp. 85–6.

the Reformation debate with the Roman Catholic Church could be compared to the controversy of St Paul with the Judaizers in Galatia "in which the Gospel of grace was at stake". While Knox rarely used the expression "justification by faith" and preferred to speak of justification through the blood of Christ, Torrance notes that the whole matter of the Reformation is at stake in this doctrine and that justification should not be seen as a "principle in itself" but rather as a pointer to "Jesus Christ and his mighty acts".[146] He believes this is in accordance with the teaching of the *Scots Confession* of 1560.

Three important points converge here. First, instead of forming a separate article, justification belonged to the "inner texture of the Gospel and becomes evident as its cutting edge ... justification makes decisively clear the very essence of the Gospel of salvation by grace". Second, because Christ is at the center, it is our union with Christ, who himself is God in union with us, that is central. To be more precise: "What is absolutely central is Jesus Christ. Man's salvation is exclusively the work of God in Christ, God in union with Man, and therefore Man in union with God." Through union with him we "participate in his holy life". Knox stressed the importance of Christ's saving humanity with the result that it became clear that we were meant to share in his life of prayer and obedience so that by union with him "all that is his becomes ours". Third, the *Scots Confession* strongly emphasized the importance of both Christ's

> Resurrection and Ascension [as] part of the atonement [because] in the Resurrection and Ascension we have the affirmation of man by God, and his exaltation to be a partaker of a new humanity, a new righteousness, and a new freedom as a child of God, as a brother of Christ, as a joint-heir with him, as one who together with him has the same Father.[147]

In this sense, justification means not only forgiveness of sins but the conferral of a positive righteousness that comes from outside of ourselves and comes only through union with Christ. Because of this, justification cannot be construed as the start of some new "self-righteousness" but instead must be seen as "the perpetual end of it" because to become righteous means a "perpetual living in Christ, from a centre and source beyond ourselves".[148] This is a crucial point. Since Christ is risen from the dead and ascended into heaven, that means that he lives now as God and man representing us before the Father and enabling us to live the new humanity that took shape in him as he lived a life of perfect obedience for our sakes. Therefore, it is only as we participate in that new humanity through union with him that we live our justification by faith.

Because justification is rooted in the incarnation, there are Christological and eschatological overtones. The reconciliation that took place in the life of the

---

146  Torrance, "Justification", *Theology in Reconstruction*, p. 150.

147  Torrance, "Justification", *Theology in Reconstruction*, pp. 150–51.

148  Torrance, "Justification", *Theology in Reconstruction*, p. 152.

Mediator is real and complete but it awaits Jesus' return for its final implementation. Knox's distinct emphasis upon the ascension set him apart from the other Reformers and allowed him to stress the incarnation as well as Christ's second coming as the parameters within which genuine understanding of justification takes place. Important also is the fact that Knox's focus on Jesus Christ allowed him to stress the place of the doctrine of the Trinity in pointing us toward the one and only God to be confessed as the center from which theology moves. This is in contrast to the other Reformed Confessions such as the *Heidelberg Catechism* which tended toward a more anthropocentric starting point in a person's faith. According to Torrance, while Calvin was less anthropocentric than Luther, even he did not treat the doctrine of the Trinity until later because he followed the pattern of Lombard's *Sentences*. But Knox's starting point was clearly theocentric and trinitarian. And, according to Torrance, his theocentric starting point, as opposed to the anthropocentric starting points of Luther and Calvin, set him apart because it was within a trinitarian context that he stressed the centrality of Jesus Christ and his Gospel in a way that he made clear that "it is only through him and the Gospel he proclaimed that God's triune reality is made known". And he also underscored the significance of the Holy Spirit.[149]

Importantly, as we have been seeing in this book, Torrance's own theology shows the same emphasis upon the centrality of the doctrine of the Trinity. There could be no separation between the one God and the Triune God as took place in mediaeval theology and still takes place today whenever it is thought that knowledge of God can be attained without faith in Jesus Christ and therefore without the present action of the Holy Spirit uniting us to Christ himself who is our reconciler. Knox emphasized that the truth and reality of our justification was in Christ and in fact was Christ himself. For that reason, it could be in us only by faith as we seek it only in Christ and thus outside ourselves. Yet, this can happen only in and through the Holy Spirit uniting us to Christ. And this occurs in and through the sacraments of Baptism and the Lord's Supper.

For Knox, the truth of God is identical with Jesus Christ and comes to be present in us in faith and only through the action of the Holy Spirit. In baptism "we are ingrafted into Christ to be made partakers of his justice" and in the Eucharist "we are continually nourished through that union with Christ". Both of these sacraments point us away from ourselves and to Christ alone as the source of our righteousness which we may have only "through union and communion with him".[150] Justification means that we cannot rely on ourselves at all—not on our own righteousness or holiness but only on Christ himself.

Building on John Knox's thinking and the *Scots Confession* of 1560, Torrance maintains that there is an *objective* and *subjective* justification. The former takes place in Christ and before the Father and refers to the fact that our enmity with God

---

[149]    See Thomas F. Torrance, *Scottish Theology: From John Knox to John McLeod Campbell* (Edinburgh: T&T Clark, 1996), pp. 4ff.

[150]    Torrance, "Justification", *Theology in Reconstruction*, p. 152.

is overcome in the incarnation of the Son of God for our sakes as the Mediator. There are three implications. First, through the incarnation, the Father's Son has become our brother and has thus established our union with him. Second, through the Son's obedient life and through his brotherhood with us, "Christ is the active Agent who reveals God to us and reconciles us to God". He does this throughout his entire life of perfect obedience to the Father. Third, as truly divine and human, Jesus himself suffered the punishment due our transgressions in order to overcome death itself for us. Through the hypostatic union, then, there is a "conjunction" between divinity and humanity and out of this union issues our justification in the resurrection. This, Torrance says, is the doctrine that Reformed theology calls the *active* and *passive* obedience of Christ and Christ's "incarnational *Assumption* and *Sanctification* of our human nature". Active obedience refers to Christ's entire life of perfect obedience to the Father. It was "his own loving self-offering to the Father in our name and on our behalf and also his own faithful appropriation of the Father's Word and will in our name and on our behalf". Passive obedience refers to Christ's submission to the Father's judgment which he assumed when he became incarnate in our humanity under the law. He willingly accepted the divine verdict upon our sin and this was manifested mainly in the cross. But Christ's passion did not begin there; it began with his birth because, as Calvin himself believed, Christ's whole life "was in a real sense a bearing of the Cross, but it was in the Cross itself that it had its *telos* or consummation".[151] The important point to be noted here is that Christ's active and passive obedience do not differ with respect to time because both are real from the start of the incarnation and both stretch forward to their fulfillment in his death and resurrection. Their subject is also the same because both manifest the one activity of the Son of God acting humanly for our sakes. The active and passive obedience of Christ means that what is imputed to us is not only Christ's suffering God's judgment on the cross but also his active righteousness "in which he positively fulfilled the Father's holy will in an obedient life". Justification therefore means more than simply the non-imputation of our sins and the fact that we are pardoned in Christ; it also means our "positive sharing in his divine-human righteousness".[152] Hence, we are saved both by Christ's death for us and by the life he lived for us and which was raised by God from the dead so that we too may share in it through the action of the Holy Spirit. It is in this atoning and justifying life that we must understand the incarnation according to Torrance.

What, then, did Torrance mean by sanctification and how does this stand in relation to our justification in Christ? By sanctification he means to refer not only to Christ's active and passive obedience but also to "the *union* he established in his birth, life, death, and resurrection between our fallen human nature and his divine nature".[153] It is in this union of natures that he took our fallen humanity from the Virgin Mary and in that very act sanctified it from the beginning of his life to the

---

[151]   Torrance, "Justification", *Theology in Reconstruction*, pp. 153–4.

[152]   Torrance, "Justification", *Theology in Reconstruction*, p. 155.

[153]   Torrance, "Justification", *Theology in Reconstruction*, p. 155.

end. In this sense, the incarnation is from start to finish a redemptive event in which his nature "heals our nature".[154] By holding together Christ's active and passive obedience, Torrance stresses the fact that justification should not be seen merely as the "forensic non-imputation of sin", though it is that as well.[155] He wants to emphasize that in the incarnation a real union of divinity and humanity occurred in Jesus Christ and that we are to share in that saving union of divinity and humanity in him through faith. For Torrance, justification and sanctification are not to be seen as two stages in a process of salvation, that is, of an *ordo salutis*, but rather must be grasped in the perfect tense: "Christ has already consecrated or sanctified himself for our sakes, so that we are already consecrated or sanctified in him—therefore sanctification is imputed to us by his free grace just like justification".[156]

For Torrance, sanctification and consecration are terms used in the Johannine literature and in the Epistle to the Hebrews that can be considered the equivalent of Paul's language of justification. That is why sanctification cannot be separated at all from justification. Sanctification, or what Torrance terms *subjective justification* refers to the fact that both objective and subjective justification have already taken place for our benefit in Jesus himself. It especially suggests that what Christ does as a human subject to live a sinless life of obedience, which we are unable to do in ourselves, he does as our representative and therefore as the one who alone does what we cannot do, so that through the Spirit and united with Christ we are enabled to do it. That is to say, Jesus Christ lived a life of righteousness as our substitute and representative on our behalf. He responded to God's saving act; he accepted it and made it his own. But he did not do this for his own sake. What he did, he did for us. Objectively, he was the Word of God objectively incarnate justifying human existence. But, subjectively, he humanly lived that life from his birth to his death and resurrection as our representative. Justification therefore was fulfilled both objectively and subjectively in Jesus Christ himself on our behalf. In Torrance's words: "He was the Word of God brought to bear upon man, but he was also man hearing that Word, answering it, trusting it, living by it—by faith. He was the great Believer—vicariously believing in our place and in our name." Or again: "He was not only the will of God enacted in our flesh, but he was the will of man united to that divine will."[157] So, in Jesus Christ not only was God's justifying act embodied in the life of the man Jesus, but so also was our "human appropriation of it". It is in that unity that justification was fulfilled objectively and subjectively in Jesus Christ. Therefore, justification is seen both as an objective act of redemption on God's part and as a "subjective actualization of it in our estranged human existence" that has taken place once and for all in the life of Jesus himself.

---

[154]   Torrance, "Justification", *Theology in Reconstruction*, p. 156.

[155]   On this point see also Torrance, "The Atonement: The Singularity of Christ and the Finality of the Cross", pp. 253–4.

[156]   Torrance, "Justification", *Theology in Reconstruction*, pp. 157–8.

[157]   Torrance, "Justification", *Theology in Reconstruction*, p. 157.

Importantly, then, Torrance wished to hold together justification and sanctification in a way that would preclude any sort of Pelagianism, with the idea that somehow either or both of these could or should be understood to be left up to us to implement or complete by our own activities. Our actions of faith and hope are truly human actions that are what they are only because of who Jesus was and is as the risen and ascended Lord who empowers our new humanity through union with himself in the power of his Holy Spirit. Subjective justification, then, refers to the "translation" of God's mighty act of righteousness that took place in Christ into human life. Torrance thinks Calvin and Knox are one in this understanding of the matter by stressing that our regeneration comes about through our adoption into sonship through the Son. Therefore, it is only through union with Christ that any of this occurs. But this means that we share in his judgment and in his exaltation—we share in his active and passive obedience and thus also in his death, resurrection and ascension. None of this can take place, however, unless we are united to Christ through faith. What Torrance opposes with this thinking is the later teaching of the Church of Scotland in the *Westminster Standards*. They put justification first and then spoke of our union with Christ and of our sanctification as following that judicial act. Torrance wants to say that unless our union with Christ comes first, justification will be seen as a new form of works-righteousness or a new form of legalism which would obviate the joyous meaning of justification and its basis in Christ himself.

Once again, it is vital to stress that, for Torrance, the expression "justification by faith" does not mean that the weight of emphasis falls upon our own act of faith at any time. No. According to Torrance, following Knox, "We believe in Christ in such a way that we flee from ourselves and take refuge in him alone".[158] It is here that Knox and Calvin differed from Luther because they were not primarily concerned with our own assurance concerning our justification in Christ, and so the anthropocentric question of assurance did not assume undue prominence as it did in Luther. It is not that assurance was meaningless to Knox and Calvin. Rather, since our assurance was a reality in Christ himself, it was as unshakable as was the faithfulness of Christ himself. Like Knox and Calvin before him, Torrance wished to oppose any sort of legalism or self-righteousness that would naturally follow from a quest that might suggest that in some sense it is our faith that justifies us before God: "If it is upon our repentance and our faith that we have ultimately to rely, who can be saved, not to speak of being sure of his salvation?"[159] Any such thinking leads to our uncertainty about our salvation. But a faith that is exclusively focused on Christ himself as our assurance never looks toward itself but always away from itself and toward Christ's objective and subjective action on our behalf. It always confesses its unworthiness even in its own acts of obedience and repentance. Hence, in Torrance's understanding, "justification by faith alone"

---

[158]   Torrance, "Justification", *Theology in Reconstruction*, p. 160.
[159]   Torrance, "Justification", *Theology in Reconstruction*, pp. 160–61.

means "by the grace of Christ alone" and that "faith is but an empty vessel to be filled by the covenant mercies and faithfulness of God in Christ".[160]

It remains for us to mention briefly some of the radical consequences of the doctrine of justification. For Torrance, the expressions *sola fide*, *sola gratia* and *sola scriptura* all signify that we must look "exclusively to Christ" and "away from ourselves altogether in order to live out of him alone". This is the heart of Reformed theology, according to Torrance, and it is wholly in line with the *Scots Confession* which underscored the fact that "we willingly spoil ourselves of all honour and glory of our own salvation and redemption, as we also do of our regeneration and sanctification".[161] What this means in essence is that every form of self-justification, that is, every form of the Christian life that is not Christ-centered, already means that we are trying to live from a source other than Christ himself and that such an attempt is doomed to failure.

Specifically, this means that all goodness—our natural goodness as well as our goodness as Christians, including all good works as the expression of our sanctified existence—must be set aside because we recognize that Christ *alone* saves us and that even our best activities in response to him are the works of "unprofitable servants". We discover this only through the revelation of our justification in Christ himself. All works-righteousness is therefore completely excluded. This means that we can never advance beyond our justification in Christ as though "justification were only the beginning of a new self-righteousness, the beginning of a life of sanctification which is what we do in response to justification".[162] We are certainly called to live what we already are in Christ through his own "self-consecration and sanctification". But "sanctification" must not be seen as something we do *in addition* to what God has done in justification. Torrance here opposes the *Westminster Confession* with its return to the Roman Catholic notion of "infused sanctification" that then must be worked out "through strict obedience to legal precepts".[163] This is exactly what the *Scots Confession* opposed by insisting that we must be spoiled of any reliance upon our own activity for assurance. They challenge any notion of "co-redemption" which Torrance believed had become rampant in the theology of his time and is indeed rampant today not only in the Roman Catholic Church but in liberal and evangelical Protestantism with the idea that we must "'make real' for ourselves the *kerygma* of the New Testament". This can mean only that in the end "salvation depends upon our own personal or existential decision".[164] But that, for Torrance, is the exact antithesis

---

[160]   Torrance, "Justification", *Theology in Reconstruction*, p. 161.

[161]   Torrance, "Justification", *Theology in Reconstruction*, p. 161.

[162]   Torrance, "Justification", *Theology in Reconstruction*, p. 161.

[163]   Torrance, "Justification", *Theology in Reconstruction*, p. 162. For an especially clear explanation of why he rejects the Roman Catholic notion of "infused grace", see Torrance, *Conflict and Agreement I*, pp. 147ff. For his objections to aspects of the *Westminster Confession*, see Torrance, "The Deposit of Faith" and below, Chapter 7.

[164]   Torrance, "Justification", *Theology in Reconstruction*, p. 162.

of the Reformed doctrine of election because it conflicts with the Reformed view that salvation is based on God's prior objective decision to be for us in Jesus Christ. Within this context, it is easy to see why Torrance's theology rested on the covenant of grace, namely, God's unconditional free love for us exercised in Christ and through the Spirit, and why he would have objected to the concept of the covenant offered by the Federal theologians of the seventeenth century. His objection to the notion of the covenant as a contract that we must fulfill (one of the key elements of Federal theology) is based on the fact that our justification and sanctification are completed for us in and by Jesus Christ himself and thus our salvation in no way is contingent on our behavior, but only on our being in Christ.[165] He also objected to the idea that there was more than one covenant, that

---

[165]     Torrance's objections to aspects of the "Westminster theology" should be seen together with his objections to "Federal theology". His main objection to Federal theology is to the ideas that Christ died only for the elect and not for the whole human race and that salvation is conditional on our observance of the law. The ultimate difficulty here is that one could "trace the ultimate ground of belief back to eternal divine decrees behind the back of the Incarnation of God's beloved Son, as in a federal concept of *pre*-destination, [and this] tended to foster a hidden Nestorian dualism between the divine and human natures in the one Person of Jesus Christ, and thus even to provide ground for a dangerous form of Arian and Socinian heresy in which the atoning work of Christ regarded as an organ of God's activity was separated from the intrinsic nature and character of God as Love" (*Scottish Theology*, p. 133). This then allowed people to read back into "God's saving purpose" the idea that "in the end some people will not actually be saved", thus limiting the scope of God's grace (p. 134). And Torrance believed they reached their conclusions precisely because they allowed the law rather than the Gospel to shape their thinking about our covenant relations with God fulfilled in Christ's atonement. Torrance noted that the framework of Westminster theology "derived from seventeenth-century federal theology formulated in sharp contrast to the highly rationalised conception of a sacramental universe of Roman theology, but combined with a similar way of thinking in terms of primary and secondary causes (reached through various stages of grace leading to union with Christ), which reversed the teaching of Calvin that it is through union with Christ first that we participate in all his benefits" (*Scottish Theology*, p. 128). This gave the *Westminster Confession* and *Catechisms* "a very legalistic and constitutional character in which theological statements were formalised at times with 'almost frigidly logical definition'" (pp. 128–9). Torrance's main objection to the federal view of the covenant was that it allowed its theology to be dictated on grounds other than the grace of God attested in Scripture and was then allowed to dictate in a legalistic way God's actions in his Word and Spirit, thus undermining ultimately the freedom of grace and the assurance of salvation that could only be had by seeing that our regenerated lives were hidden with Christ in God. Torrance thought of the Federal theologians as embracing a kind of "biblical nominalism" because "biblical sentences tend to be adduced out of their context and to be interpreted arbitrarily and singly in detachment from the spiritual ground and theological intention and content" (p. 129). Most importantly, they tended to give biblical statements, understood in this way, priority over "fundamental doctrines of the Gospel" with the result that "Westminster theology treats biblical statements as definitive propositions from which deductions are to be made, so that in their expression

is, a covenant of works that could be equated with our natural human good works and also a covenant of grace. This, of course, had serious Pelagian overtones for Torrance.

Justification is so far-reaching that it affects both our natural goodness and our natural knowledge. It applies to the whole person and not just the evil part. This means that when God places us in the right in Jesus Christ, God himself tells us that we are in the wrong. This does not mean there is no natural human goodness. Rather it means that all our natural human goodness is called into question. Since we are entirely called into question and need to be born again and made new creatures in him, it is crucial to remember that the whole person, including all his or her good or evil, is questioned in Christ's death and resurrection and made new as well. This same thinking applies to our natural knowledge of God. The radical nature of justification does not mean that we have no natural knowledge of God, according to Torrance, but that any such natural knowledge is called into question "for man is summoned to look away from all that he is and knows or thinks he knows to Christ who is the Way, the Truth and the Life; no one goes to the Father but by him".[166] It is in this sense that Torrance accepts Barth's understanding of justification as applying to our knowledge of God: justification applies to the whole person and that includes all knowing and all of what we do. Torrance wants to apply the *Scots Confession* even to our Christian knowledge and insists therefore that if one were to substitute the word "verification" for "justification", then one would have to admit that "verification of our faith or knowledge on any other ground, or out of any other source, than Jesus Christ is to be set aside".[167] Justification means that Christ alone is the Truth toward which all our theological statements must point. But that means they have no truth in themselves and only do so as they point away from themselves toward Christ as *the* Truth. This thinking, which Torrance adopts from Karl Barth, affects Torrance's theology more than anything else because it allows him to hold consistently to his insistence that we must think and act from a center in God provided in the incarnation and atonement and therefore not from a center in ourselves. Any idea whatsoever that theological statements have their truth in themselves would necessarily mean that we had somehow turned back

---

doctrines thus logically derived are given a categorical or canonical character" (p. 129). For Torrance, these statements should have been treated, as in the *Scots Confession*, in an "open-structured" way, "pointing away from themselves to divine truth which by its nature cannot be contained in finite forms of speech and thought, although it may be mediated through them" (pp. 129–30). Among other things, Torrance believed that the Westminster approach led them to weaken the importance of the Doctrine of the Trinity because their concept of God formed without reference to who God is in revelation led them ultimately to a different God than the God of classical Nicene theology (p. 131). For Barth's assessment of Federal theology, which is quite similar to Torrance's in a number of ways, see *CD* IV/1, pp. 54–66.

[166]  Torrance, "Justification", *Theology in Reconstruction*, p. 163.

[167]  Torrance, "Justification", *Theology in Reconstruction*, p. 163.

toward a form of self-justification and thus implicitly or explicitly rejected our justification by faith and by grace alone. Torrance is not opposed to orthodoxy by any means—he is opposed to making orthodoxy an end in itself. We have to do our best to speak accurately about the Truth of God revealed in Scripture, but even when we have done so we must admit that "we are unfaithful servants, that all our efforts fall far short of the truth ... He who boasts of orthodoxy thus sins against Justification by Christ alone, for he justifies himself by appeal to his own beliefs or his own formulations of belief" and in that way is in conflict with the truth and grace of Christ.[168]

It is in this sense that Torrance claims that justification also calls into question all tradition because while tradition should not be "despised", it must always be subordinated to the Word and Spirit of God as the sole norm for theological truth. This calls for "repentant rethinking of all tradition face to face with the revelation of God in Jesus Christ".[169] This applies to all tradition including Reformed, Evangelical, Presbyterian and Roman Catholic. In his Presidential address to the Scottish Church Theology Society in 1960, Torrance claimed that "it is astonishing to find how close we have come to the Roman view even in the Church of Scotland".[170] What did he mean by this? He meant that instead of appealing to the Word of God in Scripture, appeals were being made to "Christian instinct" or the "mind of the Church". What he wanted to suggest was that all traditions, including the Reformed, the Lutheran and the Anglican, should allow their massive traditions to be called into question by the living Word of God mediated through the scriptural witness.

Because justification is by reference to Christ alone, Torrance believes that "conformity to Christ as the Truth of God" is "the one ultimate principle of unity".[171] The same applies to ecclesiastical order and polity. Torrance states that the main differences between the Reformed and Roman Catholic Church concern the centrality of Jesus Christ himself. These are obscured, he says, by the Roman doctrines of merit, tradition and especially by Mariology. But they are also obscured in the Church of England when it is thought that recognition of orders might have priority in discussion of the reconciliation of the churches. If this were to happen, then *de facto* Christ himself would not occupy the center and would no longer be the one who alone determines the unity of the churches. What is at stake in the ecumenical movement itself, then, is the doctrine of justification.

Justification applies as well to pastoral ministry, in that Jesus is the one who took our place by substituting himself for us in face of divine judgment. In our place he lived a life of obedience to God in worship, thanksgiving and praise. In these actions he opened a way to God the Father so that we may pray in his name. This has happened, of course, solely through him so that all of our worship,

---

[168]   Torrance, "Justification", *Theology in Reconstruction*, p. 164.
[169]   Torrance, "Justification", *Theology in Reconstruction*, p. 164.
[170]   Torrance, "Justification", *Theology in Reconstruction*, p. 164.
[171]   Torrance, "Justification", *Theology in Reconstruction*, p. 164.

thanksgiving and praise—our ministry—rests upon his substitutionary work. Torrance says that this means that Jesus' humanity "displaces" our humanity: "there takes place a displacement of our humanity by the humanity of Christ—that is why Jesus insists that we can only follow him by denying ourselves, by letting him displace us from a place of centrality, and by letting him take our place".[172] Is Torrance here advocating some sort of Christomonism or monophysitism which might imply that our humanity no longer has any real existence? It could sound that way if these words are taken out of context. But Torrance actually means the exact opposite. He means that we have our true humanity as intended by God only in and through the humanity of Christ, who as the eternal High Priest has once for all sacrificed himself through his entire life of obedience and finally on the cross.[173] He means that we live humanly as God intended only in and through him. And he means that whenever he is not seen and understood to be the one and only man who can mediate between us and God, and whenever his true humanity is depreciated or concealed by his divinity, then the need for some other human mediation slips in. This is why Torrance opposes what he calls "Roman sacerdotalism", as we will see in more detail when we consider the sacraments. According to Torrance, the Reformers certainly did not deny Christ's deity but they did attempt to overcome the tendency in the Dark and Middle Ages to stress the need for a human priesthood to mediate between our sinful humanity and the exalted Christ understood as King and Judge. They objected to

> the deep and subtle element of Pelagianism in the Roman doctrine of grace, as it emerges in its notion of the Church as the extension of the Incarnation or the prolongation of Redemption, or in its doctrine of the Priesthood as mediating

---

[172]    Torrance, "Justification", *Theology in Reconstruction*, p.166.

[173]    See, for example, how Torrance understands our union with Christ as participation which respects the Chalcedonian *homoousion* (not *methexis*—the Greek philosophical idea of participating in eternal realities), (Torrance, "The Roman Doctrine of Grace", *Theology in Reconstruction*, pp. 184ff). We have an ontological relation with Christ's human nature but we are never to be confused theoretically or practically with Christ himself in his unique divine–human existence. Our participation in Christ's new humanity means that "the human nature of the participant is not deified but reaffirmed and recreated in its essence as human nature, yet one in which the participant is really united to the Incarnate Son of God partaking in him in his own appropriate mode of the oneness of the Son and the Father and the Father and the Son, through the Holy Spirit" (Torrance, "The Roman Doctrine of Grace", *Theology in Reconstruction*, p. 186). Here Torrance insists that there is a limit: we cannot positively describe this participation any more than we can positively describe the hypostatic union. This does not mean that there is no ontological participation here, but that because our participation is governed by the mystery of Jesus Christ himself as truly divine and human, we must not resolve the mystery indicated in the Chalcedonian formulation by suggesting either that Christ is a "divine man" or a "human God" (Torrance, "The Roman Doctrine of Grace", *Theology in Reconstruction*, p. 184).

salvation not only from the side of God toward man but from the side of man toward God.[174]

And this they did by restoring the place of the humanity of Christ as depicted in the New Testament and the early church. He was the one

> who took our human nature in order to be our Priest, as he who takes our side and is our Advocate before the judgment of God, and who once and for all has wrought out atonement for us in his sacrifice on the Cross, and therefore as he who eternally stands in for us as our heavenly Mediator and High-Priest.[175]

What Torrance wants to emphasize is that it is Christ's continuing High-Priestly ministry that must be reflected in our ministry and worship as we are united to our heavenly head, namely, Jesus himself, the risen and ascended Lord. This is the significance of Christ's substitionary act. It is ongoing and he displaces us from the center in order that we may have our rightful place as those who act not in our own names but solely in his name and on the basis of what he has done for us. Justification therefore means that we must continually let him take our place as the only Priest who represents humanity: "Nothing in our hands we bring—simply to his Cross we cling."[176]

There is a critical side to this notion of substitution and it is this. Torrance wishes to oppose what he saw as a tendency for the worship and life of the community to center around the personality of the minister so that he or she becomes the one who offers its prayers and mediates the "truth" through his or her personality and through the way the minister conducts worship. Torrance regards this as a type of "*Protestant sacerdotalism*" which "involves the displacement of the Humanity of Christ by the humanity of the minister, and the obscuring of the Person of Christ by the personality of the minister". It is, he says, a psychological rather than a sacramental sacerdotalism, but it is "a sacerdotalism nonetheless, in which it is the personality of the minister which both mediates the Word of God to man and mediates the worship of man to God!" Torrance insisted that Protestantism is full of these psychological "priests" and that the church is harmed by their "psychological cult" and "psychological counselling" because it displaces "the truly pastoral ministry of Christ".[177] Whenever worship becomes focused on the minister's own prayers and personality, whenever the minister's sermon is not an exposition of the Word of God but a presentation of the minister's own views on

---

[174]   Torrance, "The Roman Doctrine of Grace", *Theology in Reconstruction*, p. 176. See also Torrance, "The Foundation of the Church: Union with Christ through the Spirit", pp. 192–208, "The Mind of Christ in Worship: The Problem of Apollinarianism in the Liturgy", *Theology in Reconciliation*, p. 206.

[175]   Torrance, "Justification", *Theology in Reconstruction*, pp. 166–7.

[176]   Torrance, "Justification", *Theology in Reconstruction*, p. 167.

[177]   Torrance, "Justification", *Theology in Reconstruction*, pp. 167–8.

a particular subject, and whenever a congregation so focuses on the personality of the minister that when that minister departs the congregation disintegrates, then those are the sure signs that Christ's High-Priestly mediation has been displaced as the sole factor that can, in reality, represent us before the Father. Jesus Christ must be seen as the sole Prophet, Priest and King so that the entire life of the congregation must be seen "as the Body of *Christ alone*".[178] That is the practical significance of justification for T. F. Torrance. Now we must consider the role of the Holy Spirit in Torrance's theology. To this we turn in the next chapter.

---

[178]    Torrance, "Justification", *Theology in Reconstruction*, p. 168.

# Chapter 6
# Torrance's Pneumatology

Like all Torrance's theology, his understanding of the Holy Spirit is patristically grounded. Therefore, he follows the thinking of the Nicene Council and of Athanasius, insisting that the Spirit is not just something divine that can be detached from the triune God and observed as a characteristic of world or human history, but rather is God himself acting directly upon us within the sphere of history as the Lord and Giver of life. This is why Torrance successfully avoids agnosticism, while duly acknowledging God's incomprehensibility, as well as pantheism and all forms of dualism in his thinking about creaturely relations with God. It is the Holy Spirit who both distinguishes us from the transcendent and sovereign God and unites us with him in a genuine relationship that requires that both God and creatures retain their distinctive existence as divine and human.

The factor that keeps the Holy Spirit from being confused either with our subjective experiences or with the church, which is somehow thought to "possess" the Spirit, is Jesus Christ himself. For the Spirit does not direct us to ourselves, whether in our own knowledge or spirituality, or to the church itself, but to Jesus Christ the Word of God incarnate who enables the church to be his witness on earth. Consequently, Torrance insists both that we know God in his inner essence as Spirit through the person of the Holy Spirit alone and that we need not and indeed cannot leave the limited sphere of human experience and conceptuality in order to accomplish this knowledge of God. It is nothing within our experience or our theology that allows this. This becomes possible only in and through the Holy Spirit, precisely as the Spirit enables us to hear and obey the Word of God spoken to us in Jesus of Nazareth and speaking to us now through the risen and ascended Lord and thus through the prophetic and apostolic witness.[1] All of this is possible

---

[1] In this regard, Torrance wanted to take very seriously the fact that "divine revelation is given to us not in a visual but in an *auditory* mode, that is through the *Word* to which people respond in the hearing of faith" (Torrance, *The Christian Doctrine of God*, p. 38). While the original disciples and apostles had visual and tactual contact with the incarnate Word, Torrance notes that those are blessed who have not seen and believed (John 20:29-30) and that "faith comes from hearing and hearing through the Word of Christ" (Romans 10:17). Also, in light of the incarnation, Torrance notes that there was a shift from "optical forms of thought to *auditive* forms of thought arising from direct acts of cognition in hearing God" (p. 39). We must therefore read Scripture and listen to the living voice of Christ not just through grammatical analysis of its words guided by a proper historical method (p. 39). See also Thomas F. Torrance, "The Hermeneutics of John Reuchlin, 1455–1522" in *Church, Word, and Spirit: Historical and Theological Essays in Honor of Geoffrey W. Bromiley*, ed

and real because that Word became incarnate in the man Jesus at a particular point in time. And Jesus rose from the dead so that we can see the power of the Spirit at work in the world as an event that is inexplicable from our side while nevertheless an event that took place in space and time in the particular life history of Jesus of Nazareth as an act of grace that cannot be demonstrated by observation but can only be grasped as grace through faith.[2] Torrance is quite consistent in holding that it is Christ's bodily resurrection from the dead that allows us to see the dynamic nature of God's unchangeable and constant love—an unchangeableness that is the very opposite of the immobility of death itself.[3] Death, of course, is the ultimate sign of immobility since it signifies our powerlessness to overcome it. But there is no such limit to God's dynamic ability to love us as in raising Jesus from the dead. Torrance is also emphatic and amazingly consistent in stressing that the Spirit brings no independent knowledge of God because the Spirit can never be detached in any way or at any time from the Word, precisely because the two are *homoousion* with the Father from all eternity.

Thus, as seen in Chapter 2, for Torrance, our knowledge of the Spirit is taken from and controlled by our knowledge of the Son in his unique oneness in being with the Father and with us. His thinking consistently demonstrates the theological and practical importance of this insight throughout each of his dogmatic excurses because his theology of the Spirit always is structured by his trinitarian understanding. In this chapter we will focus on the key elements of Torrance's Pneumatology that illustrate how and why his trinitarian thinking offers us a way of speaking intelligently about God's relations with us in creation without dissolving the differences between the Creator and creature, while underscoring the fact that true human freedom can only exist and be understood in and through the Holy Spirit. We will end with a brief discussion of how and why Torrance's doctrine of the Spirit provides a theologically plausible way to overcome the problems inherent in the *filioque*. Since this issue was already introduced in Chapter 2, there will be no need for an exhaustive discussion of the matter here. But the concept will help us see the connection between the Son and Spirit in Torrance's thought as we begin this chapter and again as we end it. In Chapter 8, on the church and sacraments, we will discuss how Torrance's doctrine of the Spirit enables him to state clearly

---

James E. Bradley and Richard A. Muller (Grand Rapids, MI: Eerdmans, 1987), pp. 107–22, 117–19.

[2] See, for example, Torrance, *The Christian Doctrine of God*, pp. 228–9. Hence, for Torrance, "our best cue for understanding the power of the Spirit must surely be taken from the bodily resurrection of Jesus Christ from the grave, which was at once a pure act of the Spirit and an event that took place in space and time" (p. 229). Theology thus begins with knowledge of faith which admits that *how* these two levels are coordinated cannot be explained any more than the virgin birth can be understood. These are miraculous acts of God within history establishing or re-establishing creation in its proper relation with God the Creator.

[3] Torrance, *The Christian Doctrine of God*, p. 244.

how and why the church is the sphere of God's new creation visible now within history between the time of Christ's first and second coming (advent). Because the Holy Spirit is the sovereign God freely acting within history in inseparable union and distinction with the eternal Father and Son, neither church nor sacraments can be regarded as ends in themselves. Were they to be so regarded, then one might mistakenly suppose that it is the church or the sacraments that bring salvation and eternal life when in reality it is God alone acting in and through the church's witness and sacramental actions who does this as the One who loves us more than he loves himself.[4]

## The Interrelationship between Incarnation, Atonement and Pentecost

In the last chapter we saw the importance of the doctrine of atonement for all of Torrance's theology. Here it is crucial to stress that just as that doctrine cannot be separated from the incarnation, so it cannot be separated from Pentecost either. This is an extremely important point that shapes Torrance's Pneumatology. In a discussion of the ecumenical relevance of the Holy Spirit, Torrance began by noting that, while the Western Church endorsed the *filioque*, it has tended to ignore it in practice, whereas the Eastern Church, while directly rejecting the *filioque*, has tended to uphold what was originally intended by the Western Church when it added the *filioque* to the Nicene–Constantinopolitan Creed, without, of course, ever agreeing that the Spirit proceeded from the Father *and* the Son. Nonetheless, while Torrance's thinking on the *filioque* certainly developed over the years, the point that he makes in this context is interesting and it is this: the *filioque* intended to stress the "Lordship of the Spirit" and "the propriety of the Spirit to the Son".[5] Torrance never wavered from this insight. Even in his later work he concluded his proposed resolution of the conflict between East and West over the *filioque* issue by expressing his belief that we can say both that the Holy Spirit proceeds from the Father *and* the Son and from the Father *through* the Son as long as Monarchy is not limited to the Father; as long as there is no distinction drawn between the underived Deity of the Father and the derived Deity of the Son and as long as the Holy Spirit is seen to belong "homoousially with the Father and the Son in their two-way relation with one another in the divine Triunity".[6]

In other words, for Torrance, the really important issue that will resolve this East–West conflict and many other theological issues as well is that we must maintain the "*homoousion* both of the Son and of the Spirit for they belong

---

[4]   See Torrance, *The Christian Doctrine of God*, p. 244.

[5]   Torrance, "The Relevance of the Doctrine of the Spirit for Ecumenical Dialogue", *Theology in Reconstruction*, pp. 229–39. A succinct version of these ideas is presented by Torrance in *The School of Faith*, where he insists that "The *filioque* is another way of saying *solo Christo, solo verbo, sola fide*" (pp. xcix, cii).

[6]   Torrance, *The Christian Doctrine of God*, p. 190. See also above, Chapter 2.

inseparably together".[7] Agreement on this key point would help lead to a common understanding of the church; a Christology which would not reduce the work of Christ to "timeless events", and finally a view of the Spirit that would not reduce the person of the Holy Spirit to "timeless processes".[8] It is here that Torrance's doctrine of the Trinity is decisive, for he insists that the proper understanding of the Spirit can only be thought out within a strict doctrine of the Trinity that maintains a close connection between the Spirit and the Son, so that with the early church fathers we would recognize "the Being of God in his Acts", and with the Reformers we would recognize "the Acts of God in his Being".[9] By this Torrance means that the Nicene theologians needed to stress the centrality of Christology by indicating, against Arius, that Jesus Christ is God himself acting in the incarnation, while the Reformation placed more emphasis on God's Act in his Being since they stressed Soteriology.[10] For Torrance, then, to take seriously the Lordship and Deity of the Spirit means to take seriously the Lordship and Deity of the Son in the incarnation, which then means we must take seriously the transcendent presence of God in his grace and condescension to us in the incarnation and again his direct personal and transcendent activity of self-giving to us at Pentecost. In this sense, Torrance explained that he wished to avoid substituting for the *filioque* any sort of "*ecclesiaque*", which he sees as the error of "Romanism", or any sort of "*hominique*", which he sees as the error of "Neo-Protestantism". In other words, Torrance thinks there is a danger in Roman Catholicism of confusing the Holy Spirit with the church and in Neo-Protestantism of confusing the Holy Spirit with the spirit of "religious man".[11] While it is certainly true today that one cannot merely accuse Roman Catholics of confusing the Holy Spirit with the church, it is equally true that it is not Protestants alone who are guilty of confusing the Holy Spirit with the human spirit.[12]

Torrance proceeds to diagnose what he then saw as a major affliction of the theology of the day, namely, that reason's normal capacity for objectivity had been damaged by a tendency to interpret the incarnation and atonement in terms of

---

[7]   Torrance, "The Relevance of the Doctrine of the Spirit", *Theology in Reconstruction*, p. 230. For a presentation of Torrance's theology of the Spirit that stresses this connection, see Gary Deddo, "The Holy Spirit in T.F. Torrance's Theology" in *The Promise of Trinitarian Theology*, pp. 81–114.

[8]   Torrance, "The Relevance of the Doctrine of the Spirit", *Theology in Reconstruction*, p. 230.

[9]   Torrance, "The Relevance of the Doctrine of the Spirit", *Theology in Reconstruction*, p. 230.

[10]   See Torrance, *Theological Science*, p. 344.

[11]   Torrance, "The Relevance of the Doctrine of the Spirit", *Theology in Reconstruction*, p. 231. See also *The School of Faith*, p. xcix.

[12]   See, for example, Molnar, *Divine Freedom*, for examples of the widespread confusion of the Holy Spirit with the human spirit in contemporary theology—both Protestant and Catholic.

human "self-understanding", thus reducing their objective meaning to descriptions of human spirituality and self-knowledge. To Torrance's mind, this meant that "modern religious man is afflicted with a deep-seated mental disease" which he characterized as the inability to distinguish between objective realities and subjective conditions. For Torrance, such a state of affairs indicated humanity's "desperate need of some kind of spiritual psychiatry".[13] But Torrance was not naïve enough to believe that some sort of "spiritual psychiatry" could solve the theological problems here denoted. He really believed the only solution could be an actual recognition of the Holy Spirit in his true eternal divinity through the miraculous action of that same Spirit enabling people to believe in Jesus Christ himself. But let us not get ahead of ourselves.

The point to be made here is that, for Torrance, there is an intrinsic connection between the doctrines of the incarnation, atonement and Pentecost. Hence, the only way to overcome "the kind of madness that has infected so much modern theology"[14] is to allow people to be reasonable in the proper sense, that is, to think objectively, not in some false objectivist sense—for that too would be irrational—but in the sense that they are willing and able to live as persons who love—to "behave in terms of the nature of the object". That means that we must not treat persons as things, for that too would be irrational. We must instead have strict respect "for the nature of what is other than ourselves", for that is "the very core of rationality".[15] All of this applies not only to our human relations and our relations with nature, but also to our relations with God. It is only when we learn to think of God "objectively", Torrance insists, that we will be able to act toward him as the Lord. Sounding almost as if he were giving in to a modified Pelagian position, Torrance claims we must "develop the capacity to relate ourselves objectively to him [God]". But then he quickly clarifies the matter, since, of course, he consistently rejects all forms of Pelagianism, claiming that we are incapable of doing this but that we must instead "let it happen to us". And this can happen, he says, only as

> we allow God in the sheer majesty and transcendence of his divine Being and Act to press upon us within the structured objectivities of things and other persons in which we have our human existence in space and time, and open us up for truly objective relation toward himself, in which we are reconciled to him and

---

[13]  Torrance, "The Relevance of the Doctrine of the Spirit", *Theology in Reconstruction*, p. 231.

[14]  Torrance, "The Relevance of the Doctrine of the Spirit", *Theology in Reconstruction*, p. 231.

[15]  Torrance, "The Relevance of the Doctrine of the Spirit", *Theology in Reconstruction*, p. 232. Torrance here is following the thought of Professor John Macmurray.

healed of our mental alienation and estrangement. That is not something we can achieve, but we can let it happen to us.[16]

How do the incarnation and atonement relate to God's objectivity in his free presence to us within space and time in the power of his Holy Spirit?

First, Torrance asserts that the incarnation is the objective presence of God for us within the sphere of history and thus within the sphere of space and time such that God does not hold himself aloof from us but loves us in such a way that he respects our human objectivity. Because God acts objectively toward us in the incarnation in this way, "we are enabled to relate ourselves objectively to him, in the divine love".[17] And what enables this action on our part is the "irreducible objectivity of the Holy Spirit" which cannot be separated from God's act of love in the incarnation and salvation since the Holy Spirit "enables us to act toward God in terms of his action upon us" in the incarnation and atonement.[18] Second, because the objectivity of God's action within history takes "concrete form in the historical humanity of Jesus Christ", we human beings are directly confronted with the "very Being and majesty of God himself, in all his ultimate Lordship".[19] This means that God really gives himself to us in the incarnation in the particularity of Christ's human existence as the one who lived, died, rose from the dead and is now our High Priest mediating between us and the Father through the Holy Spirit. "Face to face with Christ our humanity is revealed to be diseased and in-turned, and our subjectivities to be rooted in self-will."[20] Accordingly, our only hope is to renounce ourselves, take up our cross and follow him and thus come to know the Father through him. But none of this is under our control, since all of this only can occur through the activity of his Holy Spirit. Moreover, we can neither avoid nor remove this objectivity from history because it meets us within our own existence and indeed it is "backed up by God's own ultimate Being and Person". Here is where atonement relates to incarnation and Pentecost. Because God is present in person in the incarnation, God's objectivity "objects to, and resists, every attempt on our part to master or domesticate it, or to side-step or transcend it, or to ignore it". The incarnation is an unavoidable attack because it is present to us in "flesh and blood" in Jesus Christ and forces us to make a choice to accept or to reject him. As such it represents the "divine resistance on God's part to man's self-will". In this sense, it is only if the incarnation and atonement are taken seriously in

---

[16]  Torrance, "The Relevance of the Doctrine of the Spirit", *Theology in Reconstruction*, p. 233.

[17]  Torrance, "The Relevance of the Doctrine of the Spirit", *Theology in Reconstruction*, p. 234.

[18]  Torrance, "The Relevance of the Doctrine of the Spirit", *Theology in Reconstruction*, p. 234.

[19]  Torrance, "The Relevance of the Doctrine of the Spirit", *Theology in Reconstruction*, p. 234.

[20]  Torrance, *Theological Science*, p. 310.

their interconnection that a proper doctrine of the Spirit will become possible. Indeed, precisely because we are confronted with the very objectivity of God in the history of Jesus of Nazareth, "we are prevented from evaporating the Spirit into the immanent processes of nature or from confusing the Spirit with our own spirits".[21]

In this regard, Torrance emphasizes that our concepts are unfit in themselves for knowing God. But they are made capable of doing so, without reading back creaturely experiences into the Godhead, only because the Holy Spirit miraculously enables it.[22] Hence,

> The Father/Son relation is essentially a relation in the Spirit, and that does not allow us to read material images back into God. It was thus the central place given by Nicene theology to the doctrine of the Holy Spirit, as well as to the doctrine of the Son, that helped to cleanse the minds of the faithful from the Hellenic habit of thinking of God in mimetic, anthropocentric images.[23]

And this can happen objectively through our subjective experience exactly because the Holy Spirit enables us to hear the Word of God spoken in Jesus Christ himself—in fact, it is only by the Spirit that we can acknowledge Jesus' Lordship in the first instance.[24] In another context, Torrance expressed it this way: "theology does not know God by virtue of its own ideas and concepts or by the inner power

---

[21]  Torrance, "The Relevance of the Doctrine of the Spirit", *Theology in Reconstruction*, pp. 234–5.

[22]  See also *Theological Science*, pp. 310–11; *The Trinitarian Faith*, pp. 51–2 and 56; *The Christian Doctrine of God*, pp. 99–100, 107 and especially 158, where Torrance explicitly rejects forming analogies from our experiences of our fathers and sons and therefore projecting gender limitations into God. This is why Torrance repeatedly claims that knowledge of the triune God requires "repentant rethinking of what we have already claimed to know and a profound reorganisation of our consciousness" (*The Christian Doctrine of God*, p. 100).

[23]  Torrance, *The Trinitarian Faith*, p. 72. For a full discussion of this issue and how imageless thinking relates to our knowledge of God, see above, Chapter 2. See also Torrance, "Theological Education Today", *Theology in Reconstruction*, where he rejects J.A.T. Robinson's "mimetic or imitative" understanding of God because, if the basic relation between "sign and thing signified is a mimetic relation", then idolatry invariably follows (pp. 19–20). Torrance therefore insists that in theology we must *hear* the Word of God and not merely attempt to picture God (pp. 14, 20). Torrance also notes that Greek icons were not used mimetically but "spiritually and imagelessly to what they signify in the communion of saints" as this was clarified through the "iconoclastic controversy" (*The Trinitarian Faith*, p. 72, n. 69).

[24]  See Torrance, *The Trinitarian Faith*, pp. 56, 61, 64. See also, Torrance, "Spiritus Creator: A Consideration of the teaching of St Athanasius and St Basil", *Theology in Reconstruction*, p. 213; *The Christian Doctrine of God*, p. 65; and *God and Rationality*, p. 185.

of its own dialectic and spirituality, but only in response to God's Word, only in the recognition of His truth, and only under the leading of His Spirit".[25] Torrance insists that relations between subjects and objects within creation are not suspended by the activity of the Spirit for without these relations there would be no real natural world and we would have no real existence in relation to God. But, in accordance with God's atoning action in the incarnation, they must be modified "in accordance with the activity of God in his saving love". Hence, God's objectivity manifested in God's saving love in Jesus Christ himself objects to our human disobedience and this "leads to the re-establishment of true objectivity from the side of man toward God, in faith and love".[26]

In this sense, Torrance maintains that there is a difference between the Spirit's work in creation and providence and at Pentecost because at Pentecost the divine judgment takes place after reconciliation and peace are established. With the Fall, God's Spirit must encounter humanity in judgment.[27] This is why, according to Torrance, God mercifully withheld his full presence from us while still keeping us in being as his creatures. Once the world was reconciled, however, and the enmity between us and God was overcome in the history of Jesus himself, then the Holy Spirit could be poured out upon us without consuming us in judgment. That, for Torrance, illustrates the deep significance of the atonement in connection with the incarnation and Pentecost. Since Jesus vicariously experienced the divine judgment in our place out of love for us, therefore the church becomes the created sphere in which reconciliation is actualized and God is present among us in history. All of this happens as the Holy Spirit acts to apply the reconciliation that had taken place in Jesus' history to the history of those who lived before and after Jesus. In reality, the only way the Holy Spirit could be confused either with the church or with our own human spirituality is if the Holy Spirit is conceptually detached from Christ himself:

> unless we know the Holy Spirit through the objectivity of the *homoousion* of the Son in whom and by whom our minds are directed away from ourselves to the one Fountain and Principle of Godhead, then we inevitably become engrossed with ourselves, confusing the Holy Spirit with our own spirits, and confounding the one Truth of God with notions of our own devising.[28]

There is, perhaps, more in this statement than at first might meet the eye. Torrance is here simply applying the Athanasian insight that features prominently in his

---

[25]   See Torrance, *God and Rationality*, p. 181. Torrance insists: "By its very nature, therefore, theological activity has its objective basis not in itself but in God, and must never presume to find its truth in itself but only in Him" (p. 182).

[26]   Torrance, "The Relevance of the Doctrine of the Spirit", *Theology in Reconstruction*, p. 236.

[27]   See Torrance, *The School of Faith*, pp. ci-cvi.

[28]   Torrance, "Spiritus Creator", *Theology in Reconstruction*, p. 227.

trinitarian theology to the doctrine of the Spirit. He repeatedly stresses that because the Holy Spirit is wholly God[29] and is also inseparable from the Father and the Son both in eternity and in the economy, therefore it was right for the early church fathers to apply the *homoousion* not only to the Son's relation to the Father but also to the Holy Spirit's relation to the Father and Son.[30] This means that all knowledge of the Spirit must come from the Son or Word of God incarnate in Jesus Christ and must lead to the Father who reveals himself in his incarnate Word. But that is not the end of it. Just because the Spirit is *homoousion* in this way, it is impossible to understand the Holy Spirit at all if one begins with an analysis of "spirituality" or of some aspect of creation in general. There is, in other words, a methodological factor involved in affirming the *homoousion* of the Spirit and it concerns the fact that Athanasius rejected "an understanding of the Spirit beginning from manifestations or operations of the Spirit in creaturely existence, in man or in the world".[31] This is an enormously important point that is seldom heeded in contemporary theology.

Torrance unequivocally refuses to conflate the Holy Spirit into the incarnate Word, or to displace the Word with the Spirit by speaking, as some theologians do, of the Spirit's progressive *kenosis*. Speaking of a *kenosis* of the Spirit fails to take account of the distinction between the Son and Spirit and tends toward modalism and adoptionism—it is the Son or Word who became incarnate by the power of the Holy Spirit. The Spirit, as Torrance frequently notes, did not become incarnate,[32] and thus did not suffer and die for us; speaking of the *kenosis* of the Spirit could lead to an unmitigated ascription of suffering to the Spirit as well as to the Father in the sense of Patripassianism and thus could open the door to a type of modalism. While Torrance affirms that God suffers and dies for us on the cross in the Person of his incarnate Son, as we saw in the last chapter, and while he also affirms that the Father and Spirit are involved in the suffering and atoning death of Jesus, he also asserts:

> we cannot but say that both the Father and the Spirit participated in ways appropriate to their distinctive natures and properties in the birth of Jesus, in his servant ministry as Son of Man, in his atoning sacrifice on the Cross for sin, in his triumphant resurrection, in his ascension to the Father, in his heavenly intercession for us, and his rule over all things at God's right hand.[33]

---

[29]   See, for example, Torrance, *Trinitarian Perspectives*, p. 112.

[30]   See, for example, Torrance, *The Trinitarian Faith*, p. 212.

[31]   Torrance, *The Trinitarian Faith*, p. 201; cf. also Torrance, "Athanasius", *Theology in Reconciliation*, p. 231, and "Athanasius", *Divine Meaning*, p. 195.

[32]   See, for example, Torrance, *The Trinitarian Faith*, pp. 198, 212; *The Christian Doctrine of God*, pp. 66, 108, 146; *The School of Faith*, p. xcviii; and *God and Rationality*, p. 167.

[33]   Torrance, *The Christian Doctrine of God*, p. 199.

But what must be denied here is a *kenosis* of the Spirit and a dying of God the Father since any such beliefs confuse events in history with God's eternal being and activity before and within history in his Word and Spirit. Those who would subscribe to the *kenosis* of the Spirit also might speak of God's Spirit *becoming* the Spirit of Christ in the process of that *kenosis*. But any talk of the Spirit *becoming* the Spirit of Christ ignores the fact that from all eternity the Spirit is indeed the Spirit of the Son, that is, one in being with the Father and the Son. Any such thinking therefore tends to weaken the all-important fact that the Spirit directs us to Christ as the one in whom God the Father is known and loved by us. As Torrance notes, when Christ was baptized and received the Holy Spirit, it was not because he needed this since he was "eternally one in being with the Spirit in God", but because he vicariously was living out his life of obedience for our benefit.[34]

Torrance's thinking excludes also any attempt to understand the Holy Spirit from the movements of the world's evolutionary processes since such thinking would in fact separate the Spirit from the Father and Son and identify the Spirit with the cosmic spirit. Any such thinking would direct us to the cosmos for our knowledge of God instead of toward Christ where God has made himself known and continues to make himself known to us objectively through his Word and Spirit in their essential union, and thus through faith. Torrance will begin thinking about the Holy Spirit neither with the cosmos nor with our experiences because the Holy Spirit is the Spirit of the Father and Son from all eternity and therefore the Spirit acts in freedom toward us and within us in history by uniting us to Christ and through him to the Father. Recognizing this Spirit, however, can take place only in faith as one looks away from supposed experiences of the Spirit in creation and toward Jesus Christ himself as the one in whom the Spirit speaks to us and enables our union with Christ and thus with God in such a way that there is no confusion of God with the cosmos or with our experiences of him in the cosmos. Torrance, of course, insists that just as God crucified and risen is astonishing and "utterly new even for God", so too, when God "poured out his Spirit upon human beings in a way that he had never done before" some fifty days after at Pentecost, this was also "a really new event in the relations between God and the human race".[35] While the Spirit of God had always been present, sustaining God's creation from within, at Pentecost something quite new in the history of human experience took place and "something incomprehensibly new in the life and activity of the eternal God and the mode of his presence to all flesh" had occurred as well.[36] Because the God active here is the living God who eternally exists as Father, Son and Holy Spirit, Torrance insists that God is neither the "Unmoved Mover" of "Aristotelian scholastic theology" nor the "'Moved Unmover' of Whiteheadean

---

[34]  Torrance, *The Christian Doctrine of God*, p. 148. See also Torrance, "Come, Creator Spirit, for the Renewal of Worship and Witness", *Theology in Reconstruction*, p. 246

[35]  Torrance, *The Christian Doctrine of God*, p. 238.

[36]  Torrance, *The Christian Doctrine of God*, p. 238.

process theology".[37] Rejected here is any idea of God who is not active and who does not intervene personally in our changeable world of space and time as well as any pantheistic idea of a God "who is not detached from the ongoing process of this world and is not the transcendent Lord of space and time". For Torrance,

> Both these conceptions, the Unmoved Mover and the Moved Unmover, imply different forms of immobility or immutability, one of complete detachment from the world, and one of inextricable attachment to the world. Neither involves the biblical conception of the *freedom of God* who, while remaining constantly the one who he is, is also the one who is eternally new and constantly surpasses himself in all that he does.[38]

## Torrance's Understanding of *Theosis*

Just as creation and incarnation are new even for God, so Pentecost is something new and different. In fact, Torrance claims that Pentecost is as unique as the incarnation itself and that it must be seen together with Christ's birth, life, death, resurrection and ascension to make sense. Pentecost is a once-for-all event that cannot be undone and as such it has altered the relationship between God and creatures.[39] In Christ, therefore, the inner life of God was made to overlap with human life. Jesus became the bearer of the Holy Spirit and the Mediator of the Holy Spirit to the human race. "The inner life of the Holy Trinity which is private to God alone is extended to include human nature in and through Jesus."[40] As we have seen, this became possible only after the atonement took place in Jesus Christ, so that now the Holy Spirit, namely, God himself, dwells among sinners who are justified by grace. Thus, in Torrance's thinking, the prayer, *Come, Holy Spirit*, represents a commitment both to what God has done in Christ and to the fact that the Spirit lifts us up to participate in the divine nature in faith. This notion of participation is both important and easily misunderstood in Torrance's thinking.

As we have seen, there is one thing that needs to be avoided at all costs: any sort of confusion of the Holy Spirit with our human spirituality. According to Torrance, this is a danger that has been promoted from early in church history with various tendencies that emphasized the psychological and spiritual interiorizing of the Spirit's presence and of the human experience of salvation as in monasticism,

---

[37]   Torrance, *The Christian Doctrine of God*, p. 239.

[38]   Torrance, *The Christian Doctrine of God*, p. 239. Here Torrance appeals to Barth as one who saw clearly the fact that God is a living God who is free, self-moved and capable of doing new things and even "surpassing his own acts of love and grace" without ever ceasing to remain constantly the God he is, that is, the eternal Father, Son and Holy Spirit, Creator, Reconciler and Redeemer.

[39]   See Torrance, "Come, Creator Spirit", *Theology in Reconstruction*, p. 240.

[40]   See Torrance, "Come, Creator Spirit", *Theology in Reconstruction*, p. 241.

and later in Protestant pietism, and especially in the modern era with its stress upon psychology and personalist modes of thought. While it is absolutely correct to stress that God gives himself to us in his Spirit and lifts us up to participate not only in the new humanity of Jesus Christ but in the divine Being itself, the weight of emphasis, Torrance insists, must remain on "God giving" and not upon "man receiving".[41] It is with this in mind that he presents his interpretation of *theosis* or *theopoiesis*.[42]

"By *theosis* the Greek fathers wished to express the fact that in the new coming of the Holy Spirit we are up against *God* in the most absolute sense, God in his ultimate holiness or Godness."[43] But, as seen above, *theosis* "has nothing to do with the *divinization* of man any more than the Incarnation has to do with the humanization of God".[44] Even as Torrance notes that the word *theosis*, together with its cognate *deification*, is offensive to Reformed theologians,[45] he believes he can follow its original patristic intention, as long as it is taken to mean that creatures are not "divinized" but rather are made free for God through the power of God's Holy Spirit, because he wants to stress that the Spirit is not limited by our weakness and sin. Rightly understood, then, *theosis* actually expresses the sheer "Godness" of God the Holy Spirit.

Torrance thinks that both Catholics and Protestants have domesticated the Holy Spirit with ideas such as that the church "extends" the incarnation, authoritatively administers grace to all who will obey it, develops its worship and theology as expressions of its "own individuality and tradition", and subscribes to notions of co-redemption. Behind all of this, Torrance believes, lies "a confusion between the Creator Spirit of Holy God and the creative spirituality of Christian people, and therefore we think we can develop out of ourselves ways and means of translating the new coming of the Spirit and the new creation he brings into the forms of our own natural vitality".[46] While the terminology of Catholics and Protestants may differ, with Catholics speaking of "created grace" and Protestants speaking of "the Christian spirit", the reality is that the divinity of the Holy Spirit is undermined by falling under the disposal of creatures by thinking in these sorts of ways. "Protestantism may not have a legal centre and an articulated *magisterium* like Romanism, but it perpetuates in its own ways the same basic error, and therefore

---

[41]   Torrance, "Come, Creator Spirit", *Theology in Reconstruction*, p. 243.

[42]   See above, Chapter 5, for a discussion of *theosis/theopoiesis*.

[43]   Torrance, "Come, Creator Spirit", *Theology in Reconstruction*, p. 243.

[44]   Torrance, "Come, Creator Spirit", *Theology in Reconstruction*, p. 243.

[45]   Torrance says that "deification" is a misleading translation of the word *theosis* as it was used by Athanasius based on his understanding of John 10:35. This, because "there can be no suggestion that the nature of human being is deified through what might be called *theotic* activity in the renewing and sanctifying presence of God" (*The Christian Doctrine of God*, p. 95, n. 52). In this regard, Torrance maintained that we should translate 2 Peter 1:4 as "partners of the Deity" and not "partakers of divine nature".

[46]   Torrance, "Come, Creator Spirit", *Theology in Reconstruction*, pp. 244–5.

like the Roman Church is more and more imprisoned in its own developments."[47] What is it that must be done under these circumstances? Torrance says we must surrender to God's sovereignty, praying "*Come, Creator Spirit*". We must subject ourselves gladly "to the lordly freedom and majesty of God the Holy Spirit" and humbly open ourselves to the miraculous divine actions "that transcend all human possibilities and break through the limitations of anything we can conceive".[48] And when we do, we will see that because Christ is God himself, he gives us his Spirit, and because he is human as we are, he received the Spirit so as to mediate the Spirit to us. What this means above all is that the Spirit does not just proceed eternally from the Father, but is mediated to us through "the human nature and experience of the Incarnate Son. He came as the Spirit of Jesus ... not as isolated and naked Spirit, but as Spirit charged with all the experience of Jesus ... It is still in the Name of Jesus Christ that the Holy Spirit comes to us, and in no other name".[49]

This is why Torrance ultimately thinks of *Theopoiesis* or *Theosis* as the divine activity of Jesus Christ himself through which "we are adopted and made sons of God in him, as those who through union with Christ receive the grace and light of his Spirit, [and] are said to be *theoi* ..." We are united with Christ through his divine activity. Thus, he enables us to "partake of himself through grace and thus partake of God".[50] In this sense, we can only be saved by being united with Christ himself through the Holy Spirit. This is why, as we shall see in more detail shortly, Torrance insists that grace is no created intermediary between us and God but rather is God himself directly acting in his incarnate Son to overcome our self-will and restore us to communion with his Father. In this context, Torrance is quite consistent in rejecting any notion that grace be seen as "a detachable and transferable divine quality which may inhere in or be possessed by the human being to whom it is given in virtue of which he is somehow 'deified' or 'divinised'".[51]

Torrance spells out his understanding of how we share in the eternal communion of Christ with the Father through the Spirit in two important points. First, because he believes that the Holy Spirit is both mediated by Christ and that the Spirit mediates Christ to us, he argues that Christ was never without the Holy Spirit as the eternal Son. But, as the incarnate Son, he was given the Spirit for us, for his mission as the vicarious servant; this enabled him to come through the temptations

---

47   Torrance, "Come, Creator Spirit", *Theology in Reconstruction*, p. 245.

48   Torrance, "Come, Creator Spirit", *Theology in Reconstruction*, p. 245.

49   Torrance, "Come, Creator Spirit", *Theology in Reconstruction*, pp. 246–7.

50   Torrance, *The Trinitarian Faith*, p. 139.

51   Torrance, *The Trinitarian Faith*, p. 140. And again Torrance notes that *theosis* or *theopoiesis* should not be taken to mean that grace is somehow to be seen as a quality inherent in human being. This, Torrance says, is a debased way of understanding 2 Peter 1:4 which Athanasius clearly rejected. While Athanasius never actually used the word *theosis*, Torrance believes that the word *theopoiesis*, which he does use, expresses these insights when coupled with his stress upon the *homoousion*.

in the wilderness, to bring in the Kingdom and defeat the powers of evil, to pray and bear the burden of human evil and woe on our behalf. Thus,

> Since he is himself both the God who gives and the Man who receives in one Person he is in a position to transfer in a profound and intimate way what belongs to us in our human nature to himself and to transfer what is his to our human nature in him. That applies above all to the gift of the Holy Spirit whom he received fully and completely in his human nature for us.[52]

This means that the Holy Spirit has come to "dwell with human nature", just as human nature "has been adapted and become accustomed to receive and bear that same Holy Spirit". This is why the Holy Spirit must never be separated from Jesus himself. The Spirit came and comes "not as isolated and naked Spirit, but as Spirit charged with all the experience of Jesus as he shared to the full our mortal nature and weakness, and endured its temptation and grief and suffering and death".[53] Accordingly, it is only in the name of Jesus himself that the Spirit continues to come to us.

Second, the Holy Spirit is mediated to us only through the glorification of Christ. As we have seen, the Spirit could be received only after the atonement because, in Torrance's view, Jesus gained the gift of the Holy Spirit for us at great cost by receiving the Holy Spirit for us since he himself was both God the judge and the man who stood under God's judgment on our behalf. Thus, only after the atonement and "only with the taking up of the glorified Humanity of Christ our Brother into the unity of the Blessed Trinity, could the Holy Spirit be released in all his sanctifying and renewing agency to dwell with man".[54] Most important, it is the Spirit who, as it were, transmits the "energy of Christ's risen and glorified Humanity" so that he "comes in all the transforming power of the Saviour and Redeemer of men". In the Spirit, Christ "lifted up our human nature and worship and prayer and adoration to God" and thus he presented us to God as those who have been perfected in him. Hence, "the Spirit comes as the Spirit of a Manhood wholly offered to God in perpetual glorification and worship and praise".[55] What does all of this tell us about the renewal of the church's worship?

It tells us first that without Christ there is no answer to the will of God. We worship in Spirit and in Truth only as we partake of Christ's own worship.[56] In other words: "The Spirit which Christ breathes upon us ... becomes the Spirit of our response to him and through him to the Father."[57] This means that we may pray only in his name and that all true worship is both *epiclesis* and *paraclesis*,

---

52   Torrance, "Come, Creator Spirit", *Theology in Reconstruction*, p. 246.
53   Torrance, "Come, Creator Spirit", *Theology in Reconstruction*, pp. 246–7.
54   Torrance, "Come, Creator Spirit", *Theology in Reconstruction*, p. 247.
55   Torrance, "Come, Creator Spirit", *Theology in Reconstruction*, p. 248.
56   See Torrance, "Come, Creator Spirit", *Theology in Reconstruction*, pp. 249ff.
57   Torrance, "Come, Creator Spirit", *Theology in Reconstruction*, p. 249.

namely, "the invocation of the Paraclete Spirit and the coming of the Paraclete to help us. We come with empty hands and empty mouth, and he puts into our grasp the cross of Christ and into our mouth the prayer of the Lord. He assimilates us into the one all-sufficient worship of Christ, and the Father looks upon us only as we are found in him".[58] Here it is important to realize that the Holy Spirit does not act in place of the risen and ascended Christ, because it is precisely in his coming that the presence of Christ himself is with us, acting both from the side of God and from the side of humanity. In our worship, "the Holy Spirit comes forth from God, uniting us to the response and obedience and faith and prayer of Jesus, and returns to God, raising us up in Jesus to participate in the worship of heaven and in the eternal communion of the Holy Trinity".[59] Again, this is where Torrance's trinitarian theology shapes his doctrine of the Spirit in such a way that he is able to stress our human communion with the triune God in and through the humanity of Jesus Christ the incarnate Word exactly in such a way that our humanity is perfected, but given its meaning only in and through Christ's humanity which is what it is by virtue of its union with the eternal Word and in and through the power of the Holy Spirit himself. It is the Spirit who realizes in us the recreative power of the risen and glorified humanity of Christ. Just as Jesus was raised from the dead by the Spirit of holiness, so we in him can only be renewed by that same Spirit drawing us into the "self-consecration" of Christ and thus sanctifying us. While Torrance's language of assimilation and even absorption here could signal a warning about not confusing our humanity with the humanity of Christ and our human existence with the existence of the triune God, the fact is that Torrance makes clear throughout that by assimilation and absorption he means the kind of participation that suggests our conformity to the unique Person of the incarnate Son Jesus Christ and through him a genuine participation in the life of the Trinity which actually establishes and maintains our true humanity precisely in its distinction from and dependence upon the Father through the Son and in the Spirit.

### The Holy Spirit in the Life of the Trinity

Much energy today is expended attempting to find specific identifying features of the Holy Spirit in distinction from the Father and Son. Sometimes theologians expending this energy are simply looking for ways to identify the Spirit of God in all creation or in the world's different religions in a way that will avoid the scandal of particularity associated with the fact that the Holy Spirit is exclusively the Spirit of the Father and Son. At other times, theologians focusing on the specific features of the Spirit tend to place so much stress on the Spirit perfecting created being (which, of course, is an important insight that Torrance himself upholds) that they

---

[58]  Torrance, "Come, Creator Spirit", *Theology in Reconstruction*, p. 250.

[59]  Torrance, "Come, Creator Spirit", *Theology in Reconstruction*, p. 250.

tend to disregard the inseparability of the Spirit from the incarnate Word. In any case, a great deal of this energy is wasted because many theologians unwittingly ignore what is perhaps one of the most important insights to be gained from a proper understanding of the Holy Spirit, namely, that "In the nature of the case the Spirit hides, as it were, his own *hypostasis*, from us and reveals himself to us by revealing the Father through the Son".[60] Put another way, the Holy Spirit "is not approachable in thought or knowable in himself ... the Holy Spirit is not directly known in his own *hypostasis* for he remains veiled by the very revelation of the Father and the Son which he brings".[61]

In this regard, it is important to realize that the Spirit does not speak of himself but only of the Father and the Son and what he receives from them. Most importantly, then, in contrast to the incarnate Word, for instance, the Spirit does not show us himself but rather shows us the "face of the Father in the Son".[62] Following the thought of both Gregory Nazianzen and Basil, Torrance therefore insists that the Holy Spirit "hides himself from us behind the Father in the Son and behind the Son in the Father, so that we do not know him face to face in his own ὑπόστασις."[63] In this sense, while the Holy Spirit is personally present to us and within us, he is so in such a way that he points us toward the Father and the Son—but this means, of course, as Athanasius stressed in his letters to Serapion, that "When the Spirit is in us, the Word also who gives the Spirit, is in us, and in the Word is the Father".[64] Because the three Persons of the Trinity are so intimately connected in virtue of *perichoresis*, Gregory insisted on the inseparability of God's oneness and threeness.[65] One might even say, as Torrance does, following Didymus and Cyril of Alexandria that the three Persons are to be worshipped and glorified "as one Person".[66] Torrance even concludes that we must apply the notion

---

[60]    Torrance, "Come, Creator Spirit", *Theology in Reconstruction*, p. 226.

[61]    Torrance, *The Trinitarian Faith*, p. 211. See also Torrance, *God and Rationality*, p. 167, and *The Christian Doctrine of God*, p. 66.

[62]    Torrance, *The Trinitarian Faith*, p. 212. See also Torrance, "Come, Creator Spirit", *Theology in Reconstruction*, p. 253, where Torrance writes: "The office of the Holy Spirit in the Church is not to call attention to himself apart from Christ but to focus all attention on Christ, to glorify him, to bear witness to his deity, to testify to his mind and will, and in him and through him to lead us to the Father." Interestingly, Alasdair I.C. Heron, in his important book *The Holy Spirit: The Holy Spirit in the Bible, the History of Christian Thought, and Recent Theology* (Philadelphia: The Westminster Press, 1983), echoes these important insights by Torrance (p. 176), while Torrance refers to Heron to make the point that because the Spirit does not show us himself, "the world cannot receive him or know him" (*The Trinitarian Faith*, pp. 211–12). In Heron's words: "The Spirit mirrors Christ himself, but to the 'world' the mirror conveys no image" (Heron, *The Holy Spirit*, p. 56).

[63]    Torrance, *The Trinitarian Faith*, p. 212.

[64]    Athanasius, cited in Torrance, *The Trinitarian Faith*, p. 213.

[65]    Torrance, *The Trinitarian Faith*, p. 213.

[66]    Torrance, *The Trinitarian Faith*, p. 213. See also Torrance, *The Christian Doctrine of God*, p. 161, and *Trinitarian Perspectives*, p. 97.

of *consciousness* not only to the one nature of God common to the three Persons, but also to each of the three Persons in God. "Each divine Person in virtue of his distinctiveness shares in it [the divine nature] differently and appropriately, so that we would have to say that while Father, Son and Holy Spirit constitute one indivisible God they do so as three conscious Subjects in mutual love and life and activity". Here Torrance means that the notion of *perichoresis* or *coinherence* pertains to the "three divine Persons as conscious of one another in their distinctive otherness and oneness". But Torrance insists that this view can only be valid when held together with the idea that God must be thought of "as Person, but of this one Person as existing and meeting us in a triunity of Persons in one God".[67]

Very clearly, Torrance is aware of the dangers of modalism and seeks to avoid any hint of this by insisting that even when he thinks of God as Person this is only meant to suggest that "God is intrinsically personal" and not in any way to weaken the fact that God as Person exists precisely as three distinct persons eternally in relation, that is, "in their objective relations to one another".[68] Ultimately, then, what Torrance wants to say is that

> God is three Persons but he is the infinite and universal Person in three distinct substantive relations or hypostases, a fullness and communion of personal Being in himself who as such is essentially and creatively personalising, or person-constituting in his activities toward us through the Son and the Spirit.[69]

---

[67]  Torrance, *Trinitarian Perspectives*, p. 97. Torrance explicitly follows the thinking of Bernard Lonergan at this point claiming that to speak of God existing as Person and as three Persons does not imply any quaternity of persons in God. But he also notes in *The Christian Doctrine of God*, that Didymus the Blind and Cyril of Alexandria espoused this thinking as well. He believes we can speak of God as "the infinite and universal Person in three 'modes of existence'" as well, without implying modalism. It may be noted in this context that John Thompson, *Modern Trinitarian Perspectives* (New York: Oxford University Press, 1994), thinks there are "paradoxes and dangers" in thinking of three conscious subjects here (p. 148). But he thinks Torrance's reference to the "Person" of God "*simpliciter*" is yet more difficult and even "dubious". Yet all Torrance means by this is that God exists as one always only as three Persons. It is worth noting here that while Moltmann speaks of the "joint workings of three subjects, Father, Son and Spirit" (*Trinity and Kingdom*, p. 156) and claims both that "The Son is not identical with God's self" (*Trinity and Kingdom*, p. 86) and that "The Spirit acts as an independent subject" (*Creation*, p. 97), he deliberately rejects the idea that the triune God must be understood as a single subject. This is where Torrance and Moltmann differ. Torrance insists that in Christ and through the Spirit we meet the one Person of God; that the Spirit is not independent of the Father and Son at any time or in any way and that the whole Gospel hinges on the fact that the Son is indeed identical with God's self.

[68]  Torrance, *The Christian Doctrine of God*, p. 161.

[69]  Torrance, *Trinitarian Perspectives*, pp. 97–8. See also Torrance, *The Trinitarian Faith*, p. 230, where he insists that we are persons only in a dependent and contingent way "as *personalised persons*". Thus, "God alone is properly and intrinsically Person"

Torrance is well aware of the danger of tritheism that Rahner himself was attempting to avoid by adopting the expression "manner of subsisting" in place of an individualistic notion of person, and Torrance believes he has avoided that danger by emphasizing a deeper notion of *perichoresis*—deeper than Rahner, for instance, is willing to entertain since Rahner disallowed any mutual relation of love between Father and Son within the immanent Trinity and rejected the notion of a reciprocal "Thou" within the Trinity.[70] Torrance thinks this is evidence that Rahner has allowed his thought about the Trinity to be dictated by a logical necessity rather than by the economic trinitarian self-revelation at this point. What Torrance wants to stress is that the concept of person we meet in trinitarian doctrine is such that each Person is free to "go outside of himself while remaining in himself in relation to others what he distinctively is".[71]

It is here that Torrance insists upon his "onto-relational" understanding of the word "person" as discussed above[72] which essentially means to him that the persons of the Trinity exist in a relation within the one being of God that makes them who and what they are as persons. As he once put it in a Trinity Sunday sermon, "while God is three Persons, Father, Son, and Holy Spirit, they are not separated from one another like human persons. They are Three *in One*".[73] Thus no divine Person is who he is without the other two, but only in and with and through the other two. Ultimately, as seen above, what Torrance wants to stress by the expression "onto-relational" is that God is three Persons in the heart of his Being and that as such God is dynamic, relational and personal as the living God who loves *in se* and *ad extra*. And because God is relational in this way, we may actually know him in his inner being and relate with him in and through the Son and Spirit who are both equally God, graciously acting for us within history and thus within created time and space. For Torrance, this thinking builds into the concept of person "interpersonal relations", so that the concept of person is not understood in a static way as an "*individua substantia*" because such static

---

who is himself the "fullness of personal being" and thus also the creative source of "all other personal reality". "He alone" Torrance writes "is personalising Person, *persona personans*". Torrance means to stress two crucial insights here. First, in his deity as the Son of God become man God does not overwhelm and displace Jesus' human rationality and personhood but rather establishes it. Thus, "no human being has such a full and rich personal human nature as Jesus" (p. 230). But, second, this means that our humanity is not damaged but renewed precisely in its personal and creaturely existence by virtue of the incarnation and outpouring of the Holy Spirit. It is healed, restored and deepened as the Spirit comes to us and does not overwhelm our humanity but renews it by uniting us with Christ's glorified humanity in faith and by grace.

[70] See Torrance, *Trinitarian Perspectives*, p. 91, and Rahner, *The Trinity*, pp. 76 and 106.

[71] Torrance, *Trinitarian Perspectives*, p. 98.

[72] See above, Chapter 2.

[73] Thomas F. Torrance, "A Sermon on the Trinity" in *Biblical Theology*, Vol. 6, No. 2, January 1956: 40–44, at 40.

thinking is open to "logical manipulation" and "abstract formulation", whereas the onto-relational concept of person is not because it recognizes God's freedom to remain who and what he is while relating with us in the exercise of that freedom *ad extra*. Torrance saw his thinking as close to contemporary Orthodox theology. This is why he explicitly maintained, following Athanasius' important letters to Serapion concerning the Holy Spirit, against all forms of pantheistic confusion of Creator and creature, that

> The Spirit is the creative activity of God ... for he belongs to the unchangingly divine ... in contrast to the creatures who are changeable and alterable ... This is backed up by the place of the Spirit in the unity of the Trinity, for the Trinity is not a creature, and cannot be composed of both Creator and creature but is wholly Creator.[74]

And while Torrance does indeed closely follow Greek thinking in a number of ways in his trinitarian doctrine, he does not embrace the often mentioned idea that Greek theology (following the Cappadocians) begins with the three Persons and then moves toward God's unity whereas the West is said to begin with God's unity and then move towards some understanding of the three Persons. Torrance emphatically insists that the whole point of the doctrine is to say to us that God is simultaneously one and three and that we cannot begin with one (the three) or the other (the one) but must always begin our thinking with God's unity in Trinity and Trinity in unity. This is the revolutionary insight that led him to criticize the Cappadocians for opening the door to subordinationism within the immanent Trinity, as we shall see shortly. It also led to his brilliant solution to the *filioque* issue. But here we must note that, for Torrance, "the whole Being of God belongs to each divine Person as it belongs to all of them and belongs to all of them as it belongs each of them (*sic*), and thus does not detract from the truth that the Monarchy is One and indivisible, the Trinity in Unity and the Unity in Trinity".[75] For Torrance, then, one of the crucial elements of agreement that he helped to forge between the Orthodox and Reformed churches in their agreed statement regarding the Trinity[76] is that it offers an approach to the doctrine "which is neither from the Three Persons to the One Being of God, nor from the One Being of God to the Three Persons".[77] Each time this erroneous approach is adopted, then subordinationism, adoptionism, tritheism, Docetism and Ebionitism threaten in different ways and with different results. Torrance himself simply follows the thinking of Gregory Nazianzen who wrote:

---

[74] Torrance, "Spiritus Creator", *Theology in Reconstruction*, p. 215.
[75] Torrance, *Trinitarian Perspectives*, p. 125.
[76] See above, Chapter 1.
[77] Torrance, *Trinitarian Perspectives*, p. 126.

No sooner do I conceive of the one than I am enlightened by the radiance of the three; no sooner do I distinguish them than I am carried back to the one. When I think of any one of the three I think of him as the whole, and my vision is filled, and the greater part of what I conceive escapes me. I cannot grasp the greatness of that one so as to attribute a greater greatness to the others. When I contemplate the three together, I see but one luminary, and cannot divide or measure out the undivided light.[78]

## The Holy Spirit and God's Self-Communication

Here we must stress the connection between Torrance's doctrine of the Holy Spirit and his notions of God's self-communication and grace. For Torrance, the Holy Spirit functions not only to guard God's ultimate "unknowableness" but the Spirit also is the outgoing movement of God's inner triune life and so the Spirit takes us into communion with God himself and makes us open to his own self-revelation in faith. Thus, "since the Spirit is the Gift of God who is identical with God the Giver, it is God himself who is the living dynamic content of his self-revelation and self-communication in the Holy Spirit".[79] Everything here depends upon acknowledging both that the Father, Son and Holy Spirit exist in freedom internally and eternally without any need for us *and* that this self-same God graciously opens himself in love toward us in creation, reconciliation and redemption and so opens us toward himself in his Spirit. Torrance therefore means to stress that God gives himself to us in the incarnation and at Pentecost. It is the Spirit who comes to us and thus opens us to share in the mutual knowledge and love of the Father and Son. It will be recalled in this context that, for Torrance, Matthew 11:27 (and its parallel Luke 10:22) is a crucial scriptural text indicating that by grace we are enabled by God himself to participate in the Son's own knowledge and love of the Father.[80] This is our "personalisation" and it takes place as grace because what is given in the Son and Spirit "remains sovereign in its identity with the Giver" and indeed it "sets aside created intermediations between God and man".[81] This is a critical point for Torrance's theology of the Holy Spirit. Thus, "The Holy Spirit is no less than the Son the self-giving of God, for in him the divine Gift and the divine Giver are identical. This is why the *homoousion* was applied to the understanding of the nature and identity of the Holy Spirit ..."[82] This is why Torrance insists that, for

---

[78]  Torrance, *The Trinitarian Faith*, p. 213.

[79]  Torrance, *The Christian Doctrine of God*, p. 152.

[80]  See Chapter 2 above. See also Torrance, *The Trinitarian Faith*, pp. 58ff.; "Athanasius", *Divine Meaning*, p. 201; and "The Hermeneutics of Athanasius", *Divine Meaning*, pp. 229–288, 271.

[81]  Torrance, *Trinitarian Perspectives*, p. 100.

[82]  Torrance, *The Christian Doctrine of God*, p. 147. See also Torrance, *The Trinitarian Faith*, p. 225.

Reformed theology, the *homoousion* must also be applied to the doctrine of grace in such a way that any idea of created grace as a "detachable quality which could be made to inhere in creaturely being, thus assuming many forms within it while at the same time divinizing and elevating it" would be completely rejected as a type of "Arianism".[83] Because, for Torrance, the Gift and Giver are one in Christ; grace or God's self-communication cannot be detached from the action of the triune God himself in the history of his Word and Spirit. It is this that leads Torrance to repeat that what God is toward us, he is eternally in himself in this context—any attempt to detach grace from Christ acting in and through his Spirit amounts to making Christ an image of God detachable from his Being and thus somehow semi-divine.

> Grace is whole and indivisible because it is identical with the personal self-giving of God to us in his Son. It is identical with Jesus Christ. Thus it would be just as wrong to speak of many graces as many Christs, or of sacramental grace as of a sacramental Christ, or of created grace as of a created Christ.[84]

Torrance's insistence on this identity of Gift and Giver has wide-ranging implications for all aspects of theology. It means that knowledge of God ultimately is possible only as we acknowledge Jesus' Lordship by taking up our cross and following him in thought, word and deed—and that in itself means that we can think rightly about God only from a center in God and not from a center in ourselves, as we have seen more than once already. Hence, "we cannot go behind the back of Christ to find God, or know anything about Him apart from this God, for there is no other God than this God ... it is not some prior ontology, but Christology which is all-determining in our knowledge of God".[85] It means that all concepts of created grace are excluded as unfortunate attempts to control and domesticate God's salvific actions on our behalf—this excludes all forms of conditional salvation and certainly implies that grace cannot in any sense be equated with some moral quality of ours or some aspect of our religious consciousness.[86] It means the exclusion

---

[83] Torrance, "The Roman Doctrine of Grace", *Theology in Reconstruction*, p. 182.

[84] Torrance, "The Roman Doctrine of Grace", *Theology in Reconstruction*, p. 183.

[85] Torrance, *The School of Faith*, pp. lxxiii and xcviii. See also Torrance, *The Trinitarian Faith*, p. 23, and *The Christian Doctrine of God*, pp. 17, 24, 199.

[86] In analyzing the thinking of Ignatius of Antioch, who he believes is less moralistic in his thinking than the other Apostolic fathers, Torrance identifies and rejects just the kind of confusion that must not take place if the Holy Spirit is understood properly and the Gift is not separated from the Giver. He rejects the idea that God's love can pass over to us and work within us in such a way that it "practically becomes identified with [our] own nature" (Torrance, *The Doctrine of Grace*, p. 70). In Torrance's words: "This means that αγάπη passes over into a moral quality closely concerned with doing rightly, both in respect of actions and beliefs. It is easy to see how such a position leads to a subtle moralism" (p. 70). This is why Torrance insists that "Nicene theology rejected entirely the idea that grace

of any sort of natural theology as a foundation for understanding and relating to God the Father through the Son and in the Spirit.[87] It means the exclusion of all sacerdotalism and all forms of self-justification and self-sanctification.[88] And certainly all forms of self-justification and self-sanctification arise only because and to the extent that claims are made for our theological statements and formulations that suggest that they "have their truth in themselves" and not solely in Christ.[89] Here Torrance's doctrine of the Spirit is decisive because it is the Spirit alone who can "personalize" us; that is, only the Spirit can direct us away from ourselves and toward the truth itself. The Spirit delivers us from any sort of "impersonalizing objectivism and determinism" through establishing us in personal communion with the triune God himself precisely by uniting us to Christ and thus to the Father.[90] It means that our lives are indeed hidden with Christ in God and cannot be lived or understood in any way or at any time apart from him.[91] Grace means, to Torrance, God's utterly free but loving condescension to us to help us in the misery created by our own sinful self-will—a self-will of which we are completely unaware until we actually encounter God's grace in Jesus Christ as he makes himself known to us as our Savior, helper and friend.

---

is a created medium between God and man" (Torrance, *The Trinitarian Faith*, p. 140). For Torrance's explicit rejection of created grace, see "The Roman Doctrine of Grace", *Theology in Reconstruction*, p. 180.

[87] See, for example, Torrance's illuminating discussion of the thinking of the Shepherd of Hermas (from the mid-second century) which he thinks anticipates a Pelagian anthropology. In Torrance's estimation, the ultimate problem in Hermas' thinking is that he confuses the Holy Spirit with the human spirit: "While Hermas does not apparently think of the Holy Spirit as the third person of the Trinity, he does think of it in some transcendent relation to God, and yet it is regarded as existing immanently in man, as his spirit or goodness. In fact it belongs to man as a creature of God" (Torrance, *The Doctrine of Grace*, p. 121). In his earlier theology, Torrance actually maintains that it is the *filioque* which excludes any sort of natural theology because it ties the Spirit to the Word in such a way that it obviates any separation of our knowledge of the Father from our knowledge of the Son which comes to us through the Spirit of Christ alone. See, for example, *The School of Faith*, p. xcix, where Torrance writes: "The *filioque* clause implies the renunciation of a so-called natural revelation or natural theology".

[88] Regarding sacerdotalism, see above, Chapter 1 and Chapter 5. For Torrance, the church's priesthood and Christ's priesthood must not be conceived in univocal terms just as Christ's sacrifice and eucharistic sacrifice cannot be thought of in univocal terms. Hence, "the Church's priesthood cannot be thought of as having in any way control over Christ, any more than the body can control the head" (Torrance, "Eschatology and the Eucharist", *Conflict and Agreement II*, p. 195). See Chapter 8 for how this relates to the Eucharist.

[89] See Torrance, "Justification", *Theology in Reconstruction*, p. 163.

[90] Torrance, *God and Rationality*, pp. 188–9.

[91] See, for example, Torrance, *Theological Science*, pp. 200–201, for his understanding of the "logic of grace".

## The Holy Spirit Who Proceeds from the Father through the Son

T. F. Torrance understands the Spirit *absolutely* and *relatively*:

> Absolutely considered the Spirit is God of God … the Being of the Spirit is the Being or οὐσία of the Godhead. "God is Spirit", as Jesus said to the woman of Samaria [Jn. 4:24]. In this absolute sense "Spirit" refers to the Deity, without distinction of Persons, and is equally applicable to the Father, the Son and the Holy Spirit. Considered relatively, however, the Spirit is Person or ὑπόστασις who in distinction from and together with the Persons of the Father and the Son belongs with them to the one Being of God. The Holy Spirit is, then, like the Father and the Son, both *ousia* and *hypostasis*, and with the Persons of the Father and the Son is eternally in God and inseparable from him who is *one Being, three Persons*.[92]

Everything here depends upon the fact that our knowledge of the Spirit is grounded within the immanent Trinity in the sense that the Spirit is the Spirit of love uniting the Father and the Son within God himself. Without that inner trinitarian basis, the Spirit would not be seen as God's own self-communication but could be seen as a detachable entity that then could be described without acknowledging the Lordship of Jesus Christ and the love of the Father revealed in and through his incarnate Son. Any such thinking indeed would violate the fact that we have just stressed, namely, that the Father, the Son and the Holy Spirit really are, as Torrance insists, "*three Persons, one Being*",[93] and because of that, the Spirit in no way can be subordinated to the Father and the Son either in the immanent or in the economic Trinity. By drawing this important distinction between knowing God as Spirit absolutely and relatively, Torrance is able to maintain the simultaneous unity and Trinity of God while stressing all of the other important features noted above such as that our knowledge of God takes place only through God and that the Spirit must be known objectively and not reduced to some subjective element within human experience.

Having treated all of the main themes at work in Torrance's thought regarding the Holy Spirit, it remains for us to discuss briefly how and why Torrance's thinking about the Spirit is to be situated historically in relation to the thinking of certain key figures such as Athanasius, the Cappadocians and others, and how his thinking about the *filioque* simply carries forward his basic emphasis on the *homoousion* in such a way as to offer a plausible and indeed a helpful solution to the ancient controversies regarding this issue. We begin by noting that Torrance repeatedly cited 1 Corinthians 2:10f. to highlight the divinity of the Holy Spirit who is one in being with the Father and Son, in order to make sense of the fact that it is only through God that God can be known: "Only the Spirit of God who

---

[92]  Torrance, *The Christian Doctrine of God*, pp. 147–8.
[93]  Torrance, *The Christian Doctrine of God*, p. 147.

knows what is in God can reveal him to us, for he searches the very depths of God".[94] He also follows the thinking of Epiphanius (310–403) in order to argue against the semi-Arians and the *Tropici* who held that the Spirit was a creature of God.[95] He also opposed Eunomius and others who held that the Holy Spirit was an "impersonal creaturely force emanating from God and detachable from him" and not "God of God".[96] The issue of the divinity of the Holy Spirit arose in earnest between the Council of Nicaea (325) and the Council of Constantinople (381) with the rise of Macedonianism (after Macedonius who apparently had little to do with Macedonianism) which denied the full divinity of the Holy Spirit.[97] As did Athanasius before him, Torrance rejected the thinking of the *Tropici* and what he calls "tropical theology" because such thinking advances a kind of scriptural exegesis that does not offer a realist view of Scripture which is controlled by its witness to the incarnate Word and achieves meaning under the impact of the Holy Spirit. Instead, it offers a metaphorical or allegorical re-interpretation of Scripture which is oblique and which manifests the subjective and, one might even say, mythological whims of the interpreters rather than the truth of faith.[98]

---

[94]   Torrance, *The Trinitarian Faith*, pp. 214–15.

[95]   Torrance, "The Hermeneutics of Athanasius", *Divine Meaning*, p. 275. For an interesting and informative discussion of the *Tropici*, see *The Letters of Saint Athanasius Concerning the Holy Spirit*, trans. with intro. and notes by C.R.B. Shapland (London: Epworth Press, 1951), pp. 25ff. *Tropici* refers to those theologians who became prominent after 368 and who argued that the Spirit is in fact a creature differing from the angels only in degree and called the Spirit an angel, insisting that the Spirit is unlike the Son. While the Macedonians were "hesitant, confused and contradictory" regarding the Spirit's identity, not so with the *Tropici* (p. 28). Athanasius was quite direct in rejecting their thinking in his *Letters to Serapion*. Athanasius also rejected the thinking of Semi-Arians and Pneumatiomachi as well as Macedonians and Eunomius at a Council he presided over in 362 in Alexandria. All of this thinking was rejected again by the teaching of the Council of Constantinople (381) because each, in different ways, undermined the eternal divinity of the Holy Spirit and thus undercut the true meaning of justification by grace and sanctification. In fact, undermining the divinity of the Holy Spirit really meant cutting the ground out from under any true theological understanding of a genuine relationship between Creator and creatures and opened the door to Docetism, Ebionitism, adoptionism and all forms of self-justification. It undid the Trinity at root.

[96]   Torrance, *The Trinitarian Faith*, p. 216.

[97]   Shapland, *The Holy Spirit*, p. 24.

[98]   See, for example, Torrance, "The Hermeneutics of Athanasius", *Divine Meaning*, pp. 230–31. Rejecting allegorical or tropical interpretations of Scripture, Torrance writes: "the meaning is found in the real and creative activity of God's Spirit. That is not metaphor but reality" (p. 232). Interestingly, Torrance claims that, during the time of Athanasius, tropological exegesis "made the passion in the flesh an image of some passion in the Godhead" and says that this "was damaging both to the reality of the Incarnate Son and the reality of the eternal nature of the Godhead" ("The Hermeneutics of Athanasius", *Divine Meaning*, p. 263). Torrance links tropological exegesis with mythology on p. 264.

Torrance notes that the Cappadocians made important contributions to the development of the doctrine of the Trinity in refuting Eunomius. In fact, even though Basil was oddly reluctant to apply the *homoousion* to the Spirit, his important treatise on the Holy Spirit illustrates that the Spirit "has the same relation to the Son as the Son has to the Father, so that one Form of Godhead is beheld in the Father, Son and Holy Spirit".[99] Following Athanasius, he insisted that the Spirit was not some impersonal force but the living Lord who has real personal and objective subsistence in God and in fact is identical in being with the undivided Trinity even as he exercises divine functions in his own Person. Gregory Nyssen made similar arguments as did Epiphanius himself. But Torrance thinks there were problems in the Cappadocian understanding of the Trinity which were largely avoided by Epiphanius. For instance, Epiphanius did not refer to Father, Son and Spirit as "modes of existence" but instead insisted that they were enhypostatic because he applied the *homoousion* to the inner relations of the Trinity.[100] This had the effect of excluding any sort of subordinationism which would destroy the unity of the Trinity and thus the divinity of the Son and Spirit. He argued that the Spirit flows from the inner life of Trinity and abhorred "partitive thinking of God".[101] He insisted that it was the whole undivided Trinity, and therefore not just the Father, which is to be equated with the divine Monarchia.[102] As we shall see in a moment, this is an important insight that led to the definitions at the Council of Constantinople and to the agreement between Reformed and Eastern Orthodox theology in 1991.

Also important in the early church's development of trinitarian doctrine was the thinking of Didymus the Blind who also applied the *homoousion* to the Holy Spirit and adopted the phrase *One Being, Three Persons*, thus highlighting the importance of affirming that God is at once a unity in Trinity and Trinity in unity.[103] Didymus argued against any sort of Sabellian "unipersonalism" and tritheism. Cyril of Jerusalem made similar contributions to the development of the doctrine by refuting the idea that the Spirit was an impersonal cosmological force and insisting instead that the Holy Spirit is personally active in the world. Most importantly in all of this, these theologians rightly held that the Holy Spirit did not overwhelm creaturely being but actually sustained and perfected it.[104]

---

[99]   Torrance, *The Trinitarian Faith*, p. 218.

[100]   Torrance, *The Trinitarian Faith*, p. 221.

[101]   Torrance, *The Trinitarian Faith*, p. 222.

[102]   In a final chapter analyzing concerns about Torrance's theology, we shall consider Colin Gunton's criticisms of Torrance for adopting this viewpoint.

[103]   Torrance, *The Trinitarian Faith*, pp. 223ff.

[104]   Torrance, *The Trinitarian Faith*, pp. 225, 228.

## The Procession of the Holy Spirit and the *Filioque*

Torrance very deliberately adopts the thinking of Athanasius in order to stress two important facts: 1) our knowledge of the Holy Spirit "must be taken from our knowledge of the Son"[105] and 2) the *homoousios* must be applied to the Spirit just as it is applied to the Son. What this means is that while we certainly can say that the Holy Spirit proceeds from the Father and receives the Father as well as the Son, since the Son is of the proper being of God and the Spirit is said to be of God, therefore the Spirit must also be "proper to the Son in respect of his being".[106] Since the Spirit is one and is proper to the Word who is also one, Torrance quotes Athanasius' *Letters to Serapion* to assert that "he is proper to God who is one and ὁμοούσιον with him ... In nature and being he is proper to and not foreign to the Godhead and being of the Son and is thus of the Holy Trinity".[107] All of this is meant to underscore the truth that the basis for Athanasius' doctrine of the Spirit is the fact that the Spirit has an ontological relation with the Father and Son. Athanasius had already established this in his experiences with the Arians. Just as the Son is one in being with God, so too is the Holy Spirit. Because the Spirit is *homoousios* with God, "he cannot be divided from the Son, since the Holy Trinity is indivisible and of one nature".[108] Here Torrance is critical of both Basil of Caesarea and Cyril of Jerusalem for being "strangely hesitant" about affirming this particular consubstantiality of the Spirit. But he applauds Gregory Nazianzen for having no such hesitancy and notes that Epiphanius brought together two important concepts, namely, ὁμοούσιος and ἐνυπόστατος that formed the basis for a deeper understanding of both God's Triunity and of the procession of the Spirit from the *being* of the Father in a manner parallel to that of the Son in accordance with what was affirmed at Nicaea.

Affirming that the incarnate Son is one in being with the Father meant, of course, that "what God is toward us in his revealing and saving work in Jesus Christ he is inherently in his own eternal being as God". But it also meant that the Nicene theologians were claiming that he was from the very being of the Father, that is, he was "God of God, Light of Light, true God of true God".[109] Since both Father and Son are wholly God and simultaneously "enhypostatically" and personally related in the one being of God, it was imperative that the Holy Spirit would involve the same double movement of thought just because "there is a coinherent relation between the Holy Spirit and God the Son, just as there is a coinherent relation

---

[105]  Torrance, *The Trinitarian Faith*, p. 231. See also Torrance, "The Logic and Analogic of Biblical and Theological Statements in the Greek Fathers", *Theology in Reconstruction*, pp. 30–45, 37. This same piece is republished in *Divine Meaning*, pp. 374–91.

[106]  Torrance, *The Trinitarian Faith*, p. 231.

[107]  Athanasius, cited in Torrance, *The Trinitarian Faith*, pp. 231–2.

[108]  Torrance, *The Trinitarian Faith*, p. 232.

[109]  Torrance, *The Trinitarian Faith*, p. 232.

between the Son and the Father".[110] The upshot of all this is that since the Spirit is God himself acting *ad extra*, therefore he too must be acknowledged as being in himself what he is toward us, namely, one in being with the eternal triune God. For Epiphanius, "There never was when the Spirit was not".[111]

Torrance thus places great weight on Epiphanius' statement that "When you pronounce the ὁμοούσιον, you assert that the Son is God of God, and that the Holy Spirit is God of the same Godhead".[112] Since the Spirit belongs to the inner being of God in this way and is thus central to God's Triunity, there is no Father without the Son or Spirit and there is only one divine activity, namely, "that of the Father through the Son and in the Spirit".[113] It is only by keeping in mind, then, the intrinsic unity and identity of being of the three divine Persons that a proper understanding of the procession of the Spirit may be achieved. According to Torrance, the issue of the procession of the Spirit was first raised by Dionysius of Alexandria well before the Council of Nicaea. And Athanasius' response avoided both modalism and tritheism by asserting that the Spirit cannot be separated in any way from the communion of the Father as the one who sends him and Son as the one who conveys him. Because the Spirit is in the Word in this thinking, the doctrine of coinherence was greatly strengthened with this approach so that, for Athanasius, "the procession of the Spirit from the Father is inextricably bound up with 'the generation of the Son from the Father which exceeds and transcends the thoughts of men'".[114]

For this reason, Athanasius claimed that it would be irreverent "to ask *how* the Spirit proceeds from God" since that might suggest "an ungodly attempt to intrude into the holy mystery of God's Being".[115] Athanasius therefore would not even consider this question. Here we stand before the mystery of the Trinity that cannot be explained but only acknowledged—and when we acknowledge this mystery, we are led into the depths of dogmatic understanding which would remain otherwise completely inaccessible to human insight. But what is most important in this context is the fact that because Athanasius stopped his inquiry here, the whole problem of the "double procession", that is, the need to say that the Spirit proceeds from the Father *and* the Son, did not even arise for him. In any case, when Athanasius thought of the procession of the Spirit from the Father in accordance with the theology of Nicaea, he understood this to mean that the Spirit proceeds from the *being* of the Father, not from what came to be referred to as the Person of the Father seen in distinction from, although inseparable from, his being as God.[116] This, then, is the position Torrance wishes to recover today

---

[110] Torrance, *The Trinitarian Faith*, p. 233.

[111] Epiphanius, cited in Torrance, *The Trinitarian Faith*, p. 222.

[112] Epiphanius, cited in Torrance, *The Trinitarian Faith*, p. 233.

[113] Torrance, *The Trinitarian Faith*, pp. 233–4.

[114] Torrance, *The Trinitarian Faith*, p. 235.

[115] Torrance, *The Christian Doctrine of God*, p. 188.

[116] Torrance, *The Trinitarian Faith*, p. 236.

in the interest of settling the disputes between East and West over the *filioque*. We will discuss just what the disagreement involves in a moment. But first let us very briefly recount why Torrance is critical of the Cappadocians since that will shed light on his own view of the matter.

## The Problem with the Cappadocian Solution to the *Filioque* and Torrance's Solution

The Cappadocians took over the thinking just elaborated but in the process clearly distinguished between *ousia* and *hypostasis*, speaking of paternity, filiation and spiration, and also shifted the weight of emphasis on to the three Persons. They also were tempted to account for the unity and Trinity of the Godhead by appealing to what Torrance notes is the "dangerous analogy of three different people having a common nature".[117] The specter of tritheism led the Cappadocians to argue that the Father is the one principle or origin or cause of the Son and Spirit. They offered a unique notion of causality according to which the cause both comprised and was continuous with its effects. But it is just here that Torrance detects a serious problem that still is problematic for theology.

There are essentially two difficulties. First, the Cappadocians' attempt to avoid the charge of tritheism or the idea that there were "three ultimate divine Principles" caused them to advance a "damaging distinction between the Deity of the Father as wholly underived or 'uncaused', and the Deity of the Son and of the Spirit as eternally derived or 'caused'".[118] Second, the way in which they distinguished the Persons of the Trinity led them to

> cast the internal relations between the Father, the Son and the Holy Spirit into the consecutive structure of a causal series or a "chain" of dependence "through the Son", instead of conceiving them more, like Athanasius, in terms of their coinherent and undivided wholeness, in which each Person is "whole of whole".[119]

Thus the Cappadocians were misled by focusing on the notion of causality instead of paying attention to the "living will of God". Gregory Nazianzen differed from his fellow Cappadocians precisely by following Athanasius and stressing that the unity of the Godhead was to be found in each Person of the Trinity as well as in all of them, instead of in the Father only. This avoided the continuing threat of subordinationism attendant upon the notion of causality embraced by the other Cappadocians.

---

[117] Torrance, *The Trinitarian Faith*, p. 237.
[118] Torrance, *The Trinitarian Faith*, p. 238.
[119] Torrance, *The Trinitarian Faith*, p. 238.

Cutting through all the difficulties of this issue and taking into account all the proper distinctions, the main problem, then, concerns the fact that by shifting the emphasis from the *homoousios* as the key to identifying the oneness of the Trinity in its internal relations, the Cappadocians stressed the Persons as united through the Monarchy of the Father and through having one being in common. Thus, according to Torrance, they made "the first Person of the Trinity or the ὑπόστασις of the Father the sole Principle or Cause or Source of Deity".[120] This weakened the Athanasian insight "that whatever we say of the Father we say of the Son and the Spirit except 'Father'". Anything other than this Athanasian position would smack of Arianism, with the idea that the Father alone is the first principle of all things. For Athanasius, the Father, Son and Spirit together, and not just the Father, must be seen as the "originless αρχή of the Holy Trinity".[121] Torrance wishes to maintain the traditional order within the Trinity as embodied in the baptismal formula and so approves of the fact that the Spirit proceeds from the Father through the Son. But his objection is to the idea that the Spirit proceeds from the *person* and not the *being* of the Father because such a notion opens the door to subordinationism and then creates the need for what became the Western reaction to the "Eastern" understanding of the *filioque*.

With Didymus, Torrance wants to avoid any suggestion that the Son and Spirit derive their *being* from the Father because each Person of the Trinity is wholly God in themselves and together in the one being of God.[122] So while the persons of the Trinity do indeed derive their distinctive *identities* as Son and Spirit from the Father, they do not derive their *being* from the Father as Person. That is why Torrance insists that it is from the being of the Father that the Son and Spirit

---

[120]  Torrance, *The Trinitarian Faith*, p. 241.

[121]  Torrance, *The Trinitarian Faith*, p. 241. This is why Torrance insists that since each Person of the Trinity is "perfectly and wholly God" (*Trinitarian Perspectives*, p. 112), therefore "the fact that the One Being of God the Father belongs fully to the Son and the Spirit as well as to the Father tells us that the Holy Spirit proceeds ultimately from the Triune Being of the Godhead" (*Trinitarian Perspectives*, pp. 112–13) and thus from the "mutual relations within the One Being of the Holy Trinity in which the Father indwells the Spirit and is himself indwelt by the Spirit" (*Trinitarian Perspectives*, p. 113). This is what Torrance calls the "drastic and far-reaching implications" of maintaining that the Spirit proceeds from the *Being* of the Father and is thus of one and the same being as the Father. All subordinationism within the Godhead is thereby eliminated in one stroke. Here, Person cannot be played off against Being by suggesting that the Spirit proceeds only from the Person of the Father as though the Father could be separated somehow from the Persons of the Son and Spirit, which, of course, is impossible. This is further supported by the fact that, as we have seen, Spirit cannot be restricted to the Person of the Holy Spirit but must be applied to the entire Being of God who exists in communion as Father, Son and Holy Spirit.

[122]  Torrance, *The Trinitarian Faith*, p. 244.

proceed and not from the Person of the Father only.[123] By stressing that the Son and Spirit proceed from the being of the Father, Torrance is merely advocating the Athanasian concept that Father, Son and Spirit are so coinherently related that both the generation of the Son and the procession of the Spirit are constantly and dynamically taking place, so that there can be no thought of one Person causing the other or of being before or after another in being or of being subordinate to the other. All three Persons are wholly God and wholly God in the one being of God, that is, in the eternal communion of the Trinity. In other words, there is a unity in Trinity and Trinity in unity of the one eternal God. Ultimately, the Council of Constantinople, whose early sessions were presided over by Gregory Nazianzen, affirmed the position advanced by Athanasius and Epiphanius, according to Torrance.

Put even more pointedly, what Torrance objected to in the Cappadocian approach was their attempt to redefine οὐσία "as a generic concept".[124] This tended to undermine the specific sense of the being of the trinitarian Persons in their internal relations and made it difficult for theology to move from God's self-revelation in the economy to what God is "inherently in himself". There is in their position an "incipient subordinationism".[125] The whole of trinitarian theology is here at stake. For if God's Word and Spirit are not seen as "inherent" in the very being of God, then "we cannot relate what God is toward us in his saving revelation and activity to what he is in himself, or vice versa", as became clear in the position of pseudo-Dionysius that "mystical theology must reach beyond the notion of *Fatherhood* in its thought of God as a superessential undifferentiated *ousia* not nameable or knowable in its internal relations".[126] Hence, by grounding the unity of the Trinity in the Person of the Father alone as the ultimate principle of the Godhead, the Cappadocians really created the situation that led to the *filioque* and all the difficulties associated with it.

As history would have it, Western theologians reacted against this thinking and intended to avoid both Arianism and all forms of subordinationism by saying that the Spirit proceeds not just from the Father but from the Father *and* the Son. Naturally, Torrance's point is that there would have been no need for this reaction had the difficulties of the Cappadocian position not arisen—and they would not have arisen if they had kept more faithfully to the position espoused by Athanasius and later by Epiphanius, which applied the *homoousion* to the Holy Spirit as

---

[123] See also Torrance, *The Christian Doctrine of God*, p. 186. For a full discussion of these issues, see Molnar, *Divine Freedom*, pp. 328ff.

[124] Torrance, *The Trinitarian Faith*, p. 246.

[125] See Torrance, *Karl Barth*, pp. 131–2.

[126] Torrance, *The Trinitarian Faith*, p. 246. For anyone who might be tempted to think that this is a minor issue, it would be worth seeing the damage this can do to a theology like Rahner's which embraces the idea that God should be understood as the nameless and thus as the triune God. See Molnar, *Divine Freedom*, especially Chapters 4 and 6, for more on this and especially Rahner's idea that God is originally one as Father.

well as to the Son. Eastern theologians saw in this Western position the error of assuming that there are two ultimate principles of origin in the Godhead, which, of course, was not what Western theologians intended. Nonetheless, in their reaction to the *filioque*, Eastern theologians embraced the idea that the Spirit proceeds from the Father only. That situation would never have arisen, Torrance contends, if the church had stuck to the line of thought advanced by Athanasius and Epiphanius.

As seen above in Chapter 1, with his historical and theological position on the *homoousion* of the Holy Spirit along Athanasian lines, Torrance has not only offered contemporary theologians a way beyond the impasse created by the *filioque* but has himself initiated and helped to complete an important agreement between the Reformed and Orthodox churches on this issue, insisting that the churches may say that the Spirit proceeds from the Father *through* the Son or from the Father *and* the Son as long as the understanding advanced is that of Athanasius which we have just presented. Torrance's own preference is to say that

> the Spirit is from the Father but from the Father in the Son. Since the Holy Spirit like the Son is of the Being of God, and belongs to the Son, since he is in the Being of the Father and in the Being of the Son, he could not but proceed from or out of the Being of God inseparably from and through the Son.[127]

This is indeed a revolutionary development that, if embraced by the Roman Catholic Church as well, could lead to an historic agreement among the churches on what is perhaps the most important issue that at present still divides them both theoretically and practically with regard to trinitarian doctrine. It would affect all areas of theological inquiry, as we have been seeing, and would have the effect of pressing all theologians to think through every dogmatic inquiry on the basis of God's economic trinitarian self-revelation in a way that would always think from a center in God and never from a center in human experience, however important that experience may be and is in terms of the theological enterprise. This is an issue that will arise again in considering Torrance's theology of the church and the sacraments. But it is also an issue that plays itself out in detail in Torrance's view of the resurrection and ascension of Jesus Christ—two events without which dogmatic theology would be impossible from the start. To these doctrines and their trinitarian shape we now turn.

---

[127]  Torrance, *The Christian Doctrine of God*, p. 188.

# Chapter 7

# Resurrection and Ascension: Implications for Humanity in Light of Redemption and Eschatology

One of the striking things about Torrance's theology is the emphasis he places on Christ's resurrection from the dead. In its connection with the incarnation, the resurrection is so central to Torrance's theology that it is not too much to say that unless Christ has been raised bodily from the dead and unless that same risen Lord is alive and ascended into heaven, exercising his kingly, priestly and prophetic activity on our behalf, not only would we have no true knowledge of the triune God but we would be so utterly lost that our very humanity would lose its meaning.[1] Does this sound exaggerated? For those who might think so, consider this assertion by Torrance:

> *The raising of the Christ* is *the* act of God, whose significance is not to be compared with any event before or after. *It is the primal datum of theology, from which there can be no abstracting*, and the normative presupposition for every valid dogmatic judgment and for the meaningful construction of a Christian theology.[2]

This statement is meant to be taken with strict seriousness. Just because the resurrection is an act of God, therefore it really must be the starting point for all Christian theology. In other words, theology itself is impossible to the extent that it does not actually begin its deliberations with faith in the risen Lord himself—not some theory about the resurrection—but with the risen Lord himself. And that is why Torrance insisted that the resurrection really cannot be compared

---

[1]    Thus, "If there is no resurrection, human nature is no longer genuinely human. Since man is the concrete reality he is, resurrection of man in the nature of the case can be only *bodily resurrection*—any 'resurrection' that is not bodily is surely a contradiction in terms" (Torrance, *STR*, p. 82). In the present, we are united to the ascended Christ who is still to come—we do indeed communicate immediately with Christ in the Spirit, but he is mediated to us in our sense experiences through the sacramental elements involved in baptism, which signifies our justification, and the Eucharist, which signifies our sanctification. The veil of time actually stands between our present and our future. See Torrance, *STR*, pp. 153 and 150–51.

[2]    Torrance, *STR*, p. 74.

to anything before or after it. It is inimitable, just as Jesus, the incarnate Word, is utterly unique. Indeed, as Torrance notes more than once, the resurrection is unique in the same way as the original act of creation or the virgin birth itself.[3] It is in the resurrection that the order of redemption intersects with the order of creation. In a very real sense, the resurrection is the consummation and revelation of the meaning of the incarnation of God in creation. The resurrection would have "no material content apart from its inner connection with the incarnation, apart, that is, from the entry of the Creator himself into his creation in order to effect its redemption".[4] Moreover, the connection between redemption and creation at this point takes place, as Torrance insists, "on a wholly new basis".

> The resurrection of Jesus was not to a state of affairs in the old order of things but to a new state of affairs entailing the redemptive transformation of the old order ... the basic structure of what emerges in the Easter event is *absolutely new*: a reality which is not only *entirely unknown* to us but *entirely unknowable in terms of what we already know or think we know*, and only knowable through a radical reconstruction of our prior knowledge.[5]

Without question, Torrance means that we cannot rely on any *a priori* whatsoever to make sense of the resurrection because the risen Lord himself and the risen Lord alone discloses to us something completely new. This is the very basis of Torrance's rejection of any traditional independent natural theology. Because the incarnate Word is the primal datum of theology, we are up against an ultimate; indeed, we are up against *the* ultimate from which we cannot abstract for a moment without misconstruing who God is in himself and for us. This concept of the ultimate is something Torrance stresses in connection with the resurrection when he introduces the topic in order to show what kind of knowing is involved when it comes to making sense of the resurrection. But it is important to realize that just the same thinking applies to the incarnation because of the intrinsic connection between the two events and doctrines: "the incarnation and the resurrection really are *ultimates* which must be accepted, or rejected, as such, for they cannot be verified or validated on any other grounds than those which they themselves provide".[6] This is an enormously important point because it allows Torrance to emphasize that there is no authority outside or above Jesus himself which can validate our theological thinking. This is where the doctrines of justification, incarnation and resurrection hold together and structure the way we are to think if we are truly to understand the theological meaning of these events. Hence, "There

---

[3]    Hence, "The resurrection is a supernatural or miraculous event, quite inexplicable from the side of human agency or natural process. It is comparable only to the act of God in creation itself or in the incarnation" (Torrance, *STR*, p. 32). See also pp. 33–4 and 59–60.

[4]    Torrance, *STR*, p. 175.

[5]    Torrance, *STR*, p. 175; emphasis mine.

[6]    Torrance, *STR*, p. 22.

is no authority for believing in Jesus outside of Jesus himself",[7] and "Justification by grace alone tells us that verification of our faith or knowledge on any other ground, or out of any other source, than Jesus Christ, is to be set aside".[8] As we have already seen, Torrance stressed this same point in his Christology and doctrine of the Trinity, especially when he argues that we must think from a center in God (in the incarnate Word) and not from a center in ourselves.[9] It informs his theology of the resurrection as well as his view of the ascension and leads him to his distinctive view of the church and the sacraments which derive their essential meaning from this one crucial point, namely, that it is the risen and ascended Lord alone who remains the sovereign and loving head of his body on earth. He is the only one who leads the community as his witness on earth toward himself in his final advent. But because that is the case, we shall see that any and all attempts to understand our human priestly activity by confusing it with Christ's unique High Priestly activity obscures the all-important fact that there really is no authority outside of Jesus Christ himself for relating with and for understanding the triune God himself.

Just as in physics one has to presuppose that there is order in the universe for that science to function at all, and one cannot offer proof that there is such order without assuming it in the first place, so it is with theology that is based upon the resurrection. In each instance, we are, as Torrance notes, "committed to certain *ultimate beliefs* for which we can offer no independent demonstration, but without which the scientific system would not be possible at all".[10] Torrance does not use the notion of an "ultimate" to hide from reality, of course. Rather, he insists that "we can accept as ultimate only what is objectively forced upon us by the intrinsic intelligibility, truth and authority of the subject-matter (or of the reality in the field of our inquiry)".[11] This means we need to be responsibly critical of our own thinking in this sphere because of the constant danger of reading our subjective experiences back into the objective reality under discussion—in this case, the resurrection itself.

## Resurrection and Faith

The category of the ultimate also enables Torrance to explain just why it is so important to interpret the resurrection in *faith*. It is certainly not our faith which gives meaning to the resurrection. But faith is necessary to understand its true meaning because only in faith may we recognize the new creation that has

---

[7]  Torrance, "Questioning in Christ", *Theology in Reconstruction*, p. 121.

[8]  Torrance, "Justification", *Theology in Reconstruction*, p. 163.

[9]  See Torrance, *Theological Science*, pp. 216–17, and *The Christian Doctrine of God*, p. 88.

[10]  Torrance, *STR*, p. 16.

[11]  Torrance, *STR*, p. 16.

occurred in the life of Jesus as the risen Lord. Without faith, we simply try to grasp the reality of the risen Lord within the old order which Jesus himself came to redeem—an order which cannot disclose what is here made known. Important, then, to Torrance is the fact that the resurrection is not some isolated event but instead is an event in which we are already included, whether or not we know it. In this sense, the resurrection was

> a deed so decisively new that it affected the whole of creation and the whole of the future. The resurrection of Jesus Christ has creative and constitutive character, and as such cannot but transform our understanding of the whole relation of God to the universe of things visible and invisible, present and future.[12]

That, of course, is the point of preaching the Gospel: to inform people of their changed situation as it took place in Jesus' resurrection from the dead. Here is how Torrance puts it: "the risen Jesus Christ cannot be discerned within the frame of the old conditions of life which by his resurrection he has transcended, and cannot be understood except within the context of the transformation which it has brought about".[13] Consequently, the "evidence" for the resurrection can be properly grasped only within the "orbit" of our relationship with the risen Lord himself.

Torrance was not naïve. He recognized a problem here that was already mentioned in John 14:22 when Jesus was asked by Judas (not Iscariot): "Lord, how is it that thou wilt manifest thyself unto us, and not unto the world?" The answer is given in John 14:23f. where Jesus is said to be disclosed within the circle of love and of those who abide in the Word. It is in this sense that the resurrection can be appreciated only insofar as someone actually "dwells within it" by faith. That, for Torrance, explains why those who believe actually offer a very different explanation of the resurrection from those who do not participate in the "circle of knowing which it [the resurrection] sets up".[14] Outside this circle, the resurrection will appear only in a "mutilated" way unless and until those who hear the message allow themselves to "fall under its transforming impact".[15]

At this point, an important question arises. If the resurrection of Jesus already includes us, how is Torrance able to avoid the impression that somehow the resurrection is not a completed event in the life of Jesus that gave meaning to the lives of the disciples and gives meaning to our lives here and now? In other words, how can he avoid confusing Jesus' personal resurrection with the community's faith? This is certainly a crucial issue in contemporary theology.[16] Torrance's answer is clear, decisive and instructive. He follows St Paul to argue that Jesus' resurrection

---

[12]   Torrance, *STR*, p. 36. See also Torrance, *The Trinitarian Faith*, p. 183.
[13]   Torrance, *STR*, p. 37.
[14]   Torrance, *STR*, p. 38.
[15]   Torrance, *STR*, p. 38.
[16]   See, for example, Molnar, *Incarnation and Resurrection*.

did not take place for himself alone, but for us whom he had assumed into a unity of nature with himself, so that in a profound sense we have already been raised up before God in him: to what has objectively taken place in him there is a corresponding subjective counterpart in us which as such belongs to the whole integrated reality of the resurrection event.[17]

Taken out of context, this statement might seem similar to explanations that suggest that the objective reality of the resurrection is ultimately dependent upon and indistinguishable from the disciples' experience of faith and from ours. But Torrance is quick to explain that the objective reality of Jesus' bodily resurrection cannot "be identified with or resolved into that counterpart",[18] namely, into anyone's experience of faith. Here Torrance maintains that because the resurrection "has intelligible content as Word of God", it requires faith in order to be understood; accordingly, the New Testament writers would often present Christ's appearances to a disciple after stating that he rose from the dead. Nonetheless, "a clear distinction is drawn between the event of Christ's rising and its counterpart or coefficient in the believing community".[19] In 1 Corinthians 15, St Paul himself distinguishes between "objective events" and the "appearances"; indeed, the appearance by Jesus to Peter and the others was itself regarded by St Paul as an objective event. And yet it is distinguished from the event of the resurrection "in the same way as it is distinguished from the events of the crucifixion and burial of Christ" because the primal miracle attested here was not the appearances but the resurrection itself which was disclosed in and through the appearances.[20] So the resurrection is objectively true as an act of God in history

that presses for objective realization in the recognition and joy of faith, but there is nothing in the New Testament which allows us to resolve the reality of the resurrection itself into appearances to the believing community, as if the only real historical event here were what is called "the Easter faith".[21]

## Effects of Dualism on Understanding the Resurrection

The problem here, in Torrance's mind, is that "Cartesian–Kantian dualism" has led interpreters of the New Testament to separate the world into two realms: a physical realm open to investigation by discerning "causal connections" in a "mathematical and instrumentalist" scientific way and a "mental realm of internal reality" which

---

[17]  Torrance, *STR*, pp. 38–9.

[18]  Torrance, *STR*, p. 39.

[19]  Torrance, *STR*, p. 39.

[20]  Torrance, *STR*, p. 39.

[21]  Torrance, *STR*, pp. 39–40. Of course, Torrance has Bultmann's reduction of the Easter event to the Easter faith in mind here and elsewhere in his writing.

could be investigated historically. This dualism divided theoretical from empirical factors in human knowledge and led people to read the Bible in a "phenomenalist" way which assumed that things in themselves were unknowable, while all that was knowable was the way things appeared to people. But if the reports of Christ's resurrection are understood in this way, then the New Testament witness is necessarily distorted because such thinking imposes a dualist subjective attitude on to the New Testament texts, making any real grasp of its message impossible. For Torrance, while pure science had rejected this dualistic approach to reality, this problem continues in the split between "the sciences and the humanities".[22]

In German theology, this split made its appearance in the notion of two kinds of history: one based in objective and empirical reality and the other based in one's inner life and experience; importantly, however, the second type of history is not bound by time and space and so is only marginally related to actual historical events. Detaching these two kinds of events from each other, then, would mean that historical events could be interpreted "only in terms of symbols and metaphors" with the result that meaning could be seen only by thinking of an "occurrence *plus* meaning".[23] But, then, meaning is only based in one's interpretation of the facts and cannot be seen as "intrinsic" to the facts themselves. This allows interpretation or meaning to be separated from the facts and take on an independent life of its own "as some sort of spaceless and timeless 'event'".[24] According to Torrance, this is what happens when the meaning of the resurrection is separated from Jesus himself as God's revelation in history and thus from his "objective and personal reality as incarnate Son of God, the Lord of history and of creation".[25] It is here that Torrance spells out his approach to biblical interpretation.

This can be summed up very briefly by noting that, for Torrance, the resurrection accounts in the New Testament must be interpreted within their "native setting in Israel". And so the interpreter must be very self-critical to make sure that he or she does not impose an alien method or set of concepts on to the text from within a culture different from that in which the New Testament texts arose. That is what happened, of course, when the New Testament was interpreted in terms of "Graeco-oriental mysticism, gnostic cults and philosophies or later Hellenistic literature".[26] And, for Torrance, the most obvious difference between the New Testament, with its roots in Israel, and the Hellenistic and Oriental world is that the former has a non-dualist (but not monist) approach to reality, whereas the latter has a dualist approach which tended to give rise to all the difficulties just noted when it came to interpreting the resurrection in particular. While the former stressed Christ's

---

22    Torrance, *STR*, p. 40.

23    Torrance, *STR*, p. 41.

24    Torrance, *STR*, p. 41.

25    Torrance, *STR*, p. 41. In this regard, Torrance notes that he was disappointed with C.H. Dodd's later interpretation of the resurrection in his books *History and Gospel* and *The Founder of Christianity*.

26    Torrance, *STR*, p. 41.

bodily resurrection exactly because the New Testament wanted to "maintain the integrity and wholeness of the humanity of the Incarnate Son",[27] the latter tended to interpret the resurrection from a Docetic and adoptionist perspective, just because a practical and theoretical dualism was introduced into a non-dualist presentation of reality. Torrance himself believed that if we interpreted the resurrection from a merely historical point of view, it could appear to be only an absurdity, whereas if we interpret it from an exclusively theological point of view, it would represent no more than mythological projection.[28]

These were no mere theories for Torrance. His insights here are extremely powerful, with wide-ranging implications. When the message of Christ's resurrection was interpreted in a non-dualist way and therefore within its Hebraic setting then it had to mean the following: 1) "a radical revision of the concept of God himself"; 2) "he who was of the seed of David was declared to be the Son of God with power (Rom. 1:3f.)"; 3) "not only the justification and acknowledgment of Jesus by God the Father and his installation on the throne of divine Power (Acts 2:32f.; 5:30f.), but that God himself was directly present and personally active in the resurrection of Jesus" and that meant that God was personally active in Jesus' passion and death as well.[29] It is precisely here where Jesus, the crucified, was proclaimed to be raised from the dead and coming again to judge the living and the dead—this Jesus with the power of God himself standing at God's right hand (Acts 7:55f.)—that Judaism took such great offence. And it is here that Judaism "was unwilling to go forward with the Christian Church in accepting the full implication of the resurrection of Christ".[30]

Here, in Christ's physical death and bodily resurrection, dualism was once and for all destroyed because at this juncture in the incarnate Word, God was no longer to be seen as "namelessly and transcendentally remote or detached" from his creation and thus only able to operate through intermediaries, as happened in later Judaism. Now God was actually present to his creation by taking upon himself their nature and destiny in his Son Jesus Christ with the result that a whole "new understanding of the living God whose very being and life are accessible to human knowing and participating" was provided.[31] The resurrection, then, is the very basis for all that Torrance had to say about the Trinity, the incarnation, atonement and justification itself. Quite obviously, it was also the basis for what he had to say about the ascension and our eschatological relations with Jesus between the time of his resurrection and second advent, as we shall see. This is exactly why, for Torrance, the bodily resurrection of Jesus from the dead is so pivotal to all dogmatic theology and especially to the doctrine of the Trinity. In Torrance's

---

27  Torrance, *STR*, p. 42.
28  Torrance, *STR*, p. 94.
29  Torrance, *STR*, p. 42.
30  Torrance, *STR*, p. 43.
31  Torrance, *STR*, p. 43.

words: "Here we are at the very root of the doctrine of the Trinity, for through Christ we have access by one Spirit to the Father (Eph. 2:18)."[32]

Torrance's realist understanding of the resurrection, then, finds its basis in the Old Testament witness, Palestinian Judaism and the apostolic church—all of which were created as a frame of reference by the risen Lord himself. And because of this, the resurrection must be understood as an event within time and space as we know and understand them. Our efforts, again, must be to permit the resurrection itself to dictate meaning here and not allow other forms of thought to be imposed upon its reality in a manner similar to the way Christian theology transformed Greek thinking with its classical understanding of theology. Torrance believes we have an enormous advantage today because science itself has moved toward a non-dualist view of reality. This should help us avoid dualist views of space and time and may make it less likely that we might impose any sort of dualist view upon the resurrection itself, thus distorting its true meaning. Certainly, Torrance does not mean to suggest that modern science will enable us to grasp the meaning of the resurrection—he only means that we may be less likely to fall into the kind of problematic thinking advanced by D. F. Strauss and Rudolf Bultmann— thinking which, if followed, empties the resurrection of its real meaning at the outset by separating the reality of the risen Lord from history and faith and then imposing a purely "historical" or purely existential meaning upon the event.[33] And he also means that because science has developed relational notions of time and space that are more in accord with reality and are quite similar to classical Christian understanding of reality, this could be helpful as both approach their unique subjects.

## The Resurrection and the Person of Jesus

For Torrance, the resurrection cannot be separated from the incarnation in which the Son of God entered history and ultimately triumphed over the powers of evil. Consequently,

> The resurrection cannot be detached from Christ himself, and considered as a phenomenon on its own to be compared and judged in the light of other phenomena. Rather it must be considered in light who Jesus Christ is in his own Person … in the light of his divine and human natures.[34]

---

[32]   Torrance, *STR*, p. 43. See also Torrance, *STR*, p. 172.

[33]   For Torrance's appraisal of Bultmann's thinking, see especially *STR*, p. 89, n. 5, pp. 17–18, n. 25 and p. 19, n. 27; cf. also Torrance, *God and Rationality*, pp. 40, 49ff. Bultmann's "fatal step", according to Torrance, was to understand God not from God's Word which entered history in Jesus Christ but rather as the content of his own self-understanding. In this way, theological statements are converted to anthropological statements (p. 50).

[34]   Torrance, *STR*, p. 46.

This Jesus and not some other rose from the dead—thus, Torrance is not interested in any other resurrection but his. Two important points must be kept in view here. First, because it is the divine–human Person of Jesus of Nazareth who alone engenders a proper understanding of the resurrection, there can be no Nestorian separation of Christ's two natures and no Apollinarian displacement of his human nature by his divine nature; monophysitism is inherently ruled out as well. Second, because his actions on our behalf as the incarnate and risen Lord involve our salvation from corruption, decay and sin and thus our recreation, we must keep in view the fact that everything he does as one who has entered this fallen world for our benefit, involves both a real humiliation and a real exaltation since he is the Mediator who "has come to overcome our darkness and baseness" to enable us to reach "the light and glory of God".[35] In other words, as we have been emphasizing, there is an intrinsic connection between the doctrines of atonement, incarnation, resurrection and ultimately the Trinity that must be kept in view at all times.

## Resurrection, Incarnation and Atonement

When the Son of God became incarnate, he did this for our sakes in order to engage "with the forces of darkness", so that his entire life was "a redemptive operation in our human nature where the forces of evil have entrenched themselves and seek to enslave us".[36] He vicariously lived a life of perfect obedience to the Father and communion with the Father in order to provide for us "a way of saving obedience and communion with the Father". Because God entered into a sinful world in his Son, "the union effected in the incarnate person of the Son inevitably came under attack and strain". The forces of sin and evil worked to split that union of natures in the Person of the Son. And it is only by living a life of perfect obedience that Christ actually overcame that division and achieved genuine union between God and us "within our creaturely being".[37] That, as we have seen, is the heart of atonement. The important point to be noted here is that Christ's humiliation and exaltation are not two events that follow one another but rather two aspects of his one incarnate life—he is "God with us" in our lost existence marked by sin, but at the same time "if God is with us in Christ then in him we are with God."[38]

From within this perspective, the resurrection should not be conceived as "something that follows upon the crucifixion but as the other side of it".[39] This insight is confirmed, for Torrance, by the fact that the New Testament nowhere presents us with a "bare crucifixion" but only with the crucifixion "as seen and reported from the perspective of the resurrection". It is only in light of the resurrection

---

[35] Torrance, *STR*, p. 47.
[36] Torrance, *STR*, p. 47.
[37] Torrance, *STR*, p. 47.
[38] Torrance, *STR*, p. 47.
[39] Torrance, *STR*, p. 48.

that the actual meaning of the crucifixion could be discerned. Therefore, it is neither the resurrection alone nor the crucifixion alone nor the crucifixion with the resurrection as its finale that is the heart of the apostolic faith. Rather, the two are indissolubly connected and even may be said to be blended together, in Torrance's view. According to Torrance, Christ is always presented to us "clothed with his message and robed in his promises", for in him his word and saving actions are "indissolubly one".[40] Consequently, the Christ who is proclaimed to have died and risen for us by the New Testament "is clothed with the *kerygma* of his death and resurrection, for they are ontologically and structurally bound up with who he is in himself and in his relation to the Father".[41]

Thus, when the *Paschal Mystery* is proclaimed, what is conveyed is the fact that Jesus Christ *is* the lamb who was slain for our sakes and who now lives to intercede for us. Especially in Acts and First Peter, "Jesus Christ was regarded as constituting in himself the great Passover from death to life, from man-in-death to man-in-the-life-of-God, from damnation to salvation."[42] It was not, then, a case of presenting a message about Good Friday and then following that with a message about Easter. Rather, it was always a matter of presenting the Easter message "of Christ the crucified risen again". Christ himself is the Mediator, namely, "the bridge between man and God and between death and life", so that he atoned for our sin and guilt by condescending to experience our deepest misery and weakness, thus overcoming in his Person all that separates us from God. He literally resurrected "in himself our human nature in union and communion with the Father".[43] Accordingly, Christ's resurrection reveals that he has entered his office as Mediator; that the Father has accepted his sacrifice as full and sufficient for the world and that this finalized his eternal mediation between God and us. We thus participate in his atoning work by "sharing in his humanity in death and resurrection".[44] Moreover, "The risen and ascended Lord Jesus bears for ever the imprint of the Cross in his hands, feet and side—it is as such that he is enthroned as the Lamb of God" because it was the Father's own "self-sacrifice that lay behind and empowered the atoning passion and resurrection of Christ", and thus the fact that "in his ascension Christ offered himself through the eternal Spirit to the Father, means that the whole undivided Trinity was involved in the atoning passion of Christ".[45] Two other considerations are important to Torrance: understanding the resurrection in relation to 1) Christ's active and passive obedience and 2) the virgin birth.

---

[40] Torrance, *STR*, p. 48.
[41] Torrance, *STR*, p. 49.
[42] Torrance, *STR*, p. 49.
[43] Torrance, *STR*, p. 49.
[44] Torrance, *STR*, p. 49.
[45] Torrance, *The Christian Doctrine of God*, p. 255.

## Passive Obedience

Passive obedience signifies the fact that Christ was completely obedient to the Father's judgment. He truly experienced our weakness and powerlessness in death—so much so that the Father himself had to raise him from death. It was, says Torrance, "real and complete death"; a death he accepted and did not attempt to escape. Just as Christ refused to use his divine power to evade the temptations that he experienced, so too, in connection with his experience of death, he did not come down from the cross to prove his divinity (Matthew 27:40). He did not use his divine power to escape his vicarious mission which was to reconcile the world to God through his life of obedience. Passive resurrection is the "counterpart" to the "anhypostatic" element in the incarnation: Jesus experienced suffering and death and was raised by a "sheer act of Almighty God". Neither his suffering nor his humanity were redemptive in themselves but only insofar as God acted to overcome death and suffering in those activities on our behalf. But this passive obedience was also a positive and creative act of vicarious obedience on the part of Jesus and as such it corresponded to the "enhypostatic" element in the incarnation and the priestly aspect of redemption since we are saved through "the human mediation of the incarnate Son".[46] Connecting the resurrection with justification, Torrance insists that the cross indicates Christ's experiencing judgment in our place and the resurrection signifies our emancipation from sin and death. The resurrection, then, means both that the Father justified the Son and that through Christ's sacrifice sin has been destroyed and human life placed on a completely new basis (Romans 4:25):

> If the Cross is God's *No* against us in judgment on our sin which Christ endured for our sakes—"My God, my God, why hast thou forsaken me?"—the resurrection is God's *Yes* to us in his affirmation of Jesus as Son of Man and all that he has done for us in our nature and on our behalf.[47]

Here Torrance proposes a proper doctrine of satisfaction within the doctrine of atonement. Instead of understanding this in a legalistic sense of meeting "the demands of justice", Torrance proposes that we see it as the manifestation of God's "good pleasure" in not allowing his incarnate Son to see corruption in death, so that just as the Father said, "Thou art my beloved Son in whom I am well pleased" at Jesus' baptism, so at his resurrection the words "Thou art my beloved Son, this day have I begotten thee" are translated into fact, since in him God "made us accepted according to the good pleasure of his will ... the act of the Son is manifested to be the act of God himself. In Pauline language, Christ was raised for our justification".[48] Therefore, satisfaction does not refer to God's satisfaction in

---

46  Torrance, *STR*, p. 51.
47  Torrance, *STR*, p. 52.
48  Torrance, *STR*, p. 52.

Jesus' death as recompense for a law which was violated; nor does it simply refer to God's satisfaction in the "fulfilment of divine righteousness, but satisfaction of the Father in the Son who has fulfilled the Father's good pleasure in making righteous atonement".[49]

## Active Obedience

Connecting Christ's active obedience in justification with his resurrection is unusual within the contours of contemporary theology, since most theologians present the resurrection either as the Father's act upon Jesus or the Spirit's act or a combination of both. But Torrance argues that the Son offered his human life of "holiness and filial love" to his Father so that now the resurrection should be seen "as his own act in taking again the life that he had laid down".[50] Torrance notes that, historically, Hilary of Poitiers most fully integrated Christ's active and passive obedience.[51] Because Christ assumed "fallen and corrupt humanity" and yet lived a life of perfect union and fellowship with his Father, overcoming "our impurity through his purity" and destroying sin and death in his life of holiness, death and sin could not control him. Instead, he triumphed over them. In his resurrection, one can see that death is no more natural to human life than sin is. Torrance goes further to say that the hypostatic union itself

> survived the descent into hell and Christ arose still in unbroken communion with the Father. The resurrection is thus the resurrection of the union forged between man and God in Jesus out of the damned and lost condition of men into which Christ entered in order to share their lot and redeem them from doom.[52]

This thinking stresses the enhypostatic element in the incarnation as it relates to the resurrection because it sees "the fullness and integrity of [Jesus'] human life and agency in the saving work of God".[53] But it also leads Torrance to criticize Barth for playing down this aspect of Christ's resurrection in his *Church Dogmatics* with his desire to stress the fact that the resurrection was a "free pure act of divine

---

[49]   Torrance, *STR*, p. 53.

[50]   Torrance, *STR*, p. 53

[51]   Torrance, *STR*, p. 53, n. 6. See Hilary, *De Trinitate* IX, 9–14, pp. 38ff. Torrance refers to Heinrich Vogel, *Gott in Christo* (Berlin: Lettner, 1951), pp. 739ff., as a more modern view of this matter. Torrance refers to Mark 8:31, 9:9, 31; 10:34; Luke 18:33 and John 5:27ff. as texts which support the view of Jesus' *active* resurrection by connecting his designation as the Son of Man with "his triumphant judgment of the forces of darkness and evil".

[52]   Torrance, *STR*, p. 54.

[53]   Torrance, *STR*, p. 54.

grace".[54] Torrance adopts the thinking of Cyril of Alexandria who believed that Jesus actively rose from the dead and that this view "is essential to the unity of his person as Mediator".[55] Torrance is forceful and consistent in connecting the resurrection with atonement. He argues that the resurrection itself is the completion of what his entire life was about, namely, utterly abolishing any enmity between human beings and God himself. Hence,

> Atonement without resurrection would not be reconciliation and without reconciliation atonement had not reached its proper end in union with the Father, in peace. It is thus the resurrection of our human nature in Christ into communion with the life of God that is the end and goal of atonement.[56]

Resurrection thus means that God's steadfast love has triumphed over all evil and judgment itself, and that in his obedience the Son of Man himself remained faithful to God

> in the midst of judgment, death and hell, and in spite of them, so that he raised himself up from the dead in perfect Amen to the Father's Will, acquiescing in his verdict upon our sin but responding in complete trust and love to the Father. The resurrection is the goal of the steadfast obedience of the Son of Man in answer to the steadfast love of the Father.[57]

Applying the notion of active obedience to the resurrection, then, leads Torrance to maintain that Christ's Amen on the cross was not an act of resignation but a positive act fulfilling the Father's will, while the resurrection was not just his Amen to the Father but the Father's Amen to the Son. In this sense, Christ's substitionary and representative work of "obedience unto death" was "perfectly efficacious and sufficient, both from the side of God and from the side of man".[58] This is exactly the point that enables Torrance to avoid even a wisp of conditional salvation, as we have already seen. In and through Christ's resurrection from the dead, our human nature *now* and *forever* is "set within the Father–Son relationship of Christ" so that when Jesus said, "I am the resurrection and the life", this statement was meant to convey the fact that the truth of our humanity is permanently and eternally real in him. "Reconciliation is identical with the living and personal Being of the Mediator and as such marches through the ages and is present in the midst

---

54    Torrance, *STR*, p. 32, n.7. See *CD* IV/1, pp. 303ff.

55    Torrance, *STR*, p. 32. He also thinks that while Calvin did not deny that Jesus was raised by the Father, "he has no hesitation in stating also that He rose again Himself as the Conqueror" (Torrance, *The School of Faith*, pp. lxxvi–lxxvii). He also notes that the *Larger Catechism* states unambiguously that he rose by his own power.

56    Torrance, *STR*, p. 67.

57    Torrance, *STR*, pp. 67–8.

58    Torrance, *STR*, p. 68.

of all world affairs …"[59] Jesus is the eternal High Priest who enables us to share in his union with the Father. Here it is important to realize that, for Torrance, the resurrection cannot be separated from the ascension. In the ascension, "our human nature in Jesus Christ is exalted to the right hand of God", while in the resurrection we are "assumed into the divine life embodied in him".[60]

Torrance thus interprets 2 Peter 1:4 to mean that we become partakers of God's life and love through the atonement, resurrection and ascension of Jesus himself. In Torrance's words:

> The relation of Jesus Christ to God is unique, for he is God the Son in the unity of the Holy Trinity, but the resurrection of our human nature in him implies a reconciliation or oneness with God which is not identity, yet a real sharing in the union of the incarnate Son with the Father, through a sharing not only in his human nature but in the life and love of God embodied in him.[61]

Torrance, of course, is very careful to distinguish divine and human being and activity in his explication of *theosis* or *theopoesis*, as we have already seen.[62] But he does want to emphasize that we are not really saved or renewed in our lives "without being united to him and partaking of him".[63] When the Nicene theologians interpreted Christ's statement in John 10:35 that Scripture "called them gods (θεοί) to whom the Word of God came", they referred "to those who, while created become partakers of the Word through his creative impact upon them".[64] This implies that only Christ is God and Lord and it is only through his divine activity that we are adopted and made sons and daughters of God and receive "the grace and light of his Spirit". Rejected completely was any idea that Jesus was a "created intermediary" because in reality he was both fully divine and fully human as the Mediator. Nicene theology also rejected completely any notion that grace was some "created medium between God and man". It is rather God's own self-giving which is "governed by the oneness of the Father and the Son".[65] It is no divine quality that can be detached from God the giver and transferred to human beings so that they then can be said to be deified or divinized.

Torrance's presentation of the resurrection and atonement, together with his view of the Trinity and our knowledge of and participation in the life of the Trinity, represents a major theological accomplishment. The resurrection means that we must understand Jesus himself as "the Truth—'I am the Truth'". And it is as the

---

[59]   Torrance, *STR*, p. 69.

[60]   Torrance, *STR*, p. 70.

[61]   Torrance, *STR*, p. 70.

[62]   See above, Chapter 5 and Chapter 6.

[63]   Torrance, *The Trinitarian Faith*, p. 139. For a full treatment of how our union with Christ shapes Torrance's theology, see Lee, *Living in Union with Christ*.

[64]   Torrance, *The Trinitarian Faith*, p. 139.

[65]   Torrance, *The Trinitarian Faith*, pp. 139–40.

*incarnate* Son who is risen from the dead that Jesus himself "remains Truth, uncreated Truth and created truth in one." He is neither just God nor just a man, but God become flesh so that his Word is not just addressed *to* us, but he himself humanly is the "answering word of man addressed to God in the unity of his one Person".[66] This means that the Truth is now accessible to us because Christ is the Truth. In other words, "Jesus Christ constitutes the bridge between the reality of God and the realities of our world, the connection between the transcendent Rationality of God and the created rationalities of this world".[67] Because of this, Jesus Christ is the very center within history where we may actually know God and speak of God "without having to transcend our creaturely forms of thought and speech. It is in and through Jesus Christ therefore that we creatures of space and time may know God the Father, in such a way as to think and speak truly and validly of him ..."[68]

It is an interesting fact that here, at the heart of his theology of the resurrection, Torrance finds the very center that allows us to think accurately about God, using our limited and broken human concepts in such a way that we may actually speak truthfully, that is, without projecting our concepts and experiences back into God. It would be hard to find a contemporary theologian who was more consistent than Torrance in thinking of the triune God and his actions for us from that center in God rather than from a center in ourselves.[69] And, for Torrance, the only thing that makes this possible is the resurrection of Jesus, the incarnate Son, from the dead. Without Christ's resurrection, Torrance insists that not only would God's own being and act be divided but our knowledge also would be divided from the reality of God himself. Yet, "in and through Jesus Christ we may yet know God in his reality beyond ourselves. The whole epistemic function of the incarnation thus comes to its complete fruition in the resurrection of Christ in the fullness of his humanity".[70] Translation: because Jesus Christ is *homoousion* with the Father and with us in the incarnation, his bodily resurrection from the dead and his ascension into heaven mean that he alone, as the risen and ascended Lord, now personally enables us to know God in Spirit and in Truth. This happens through the very power of his Holy Spirit which he pours out upon us, and thus through faith and union with him. In particular, this takes the form of our life in the church and thus in the shape of participation in preaching and sacraments as we shall see in Chapter 8. That is why Torrance insists that "In the doctrine of the Church as the Body of Christ everything turns upon the fact of the resurrection of Jesus Christ in Body and His ascension in the fulness of His humanity".[71] Here, then, is where the

---

66  Torrance, *STR*, pp. 70–71.
67  Torrance, *STR*, p. 71.
68  Torrance, *STR*, p. 71.
69  See above, especially Chapter 2.
70  Torrance, *STR*, pp. 71–2.
71  Torrance, *Royal Priesthood*, p. 43.

heart of Torrance's trinitarian theology, which we have already discussed in detail in Chapter 2, begins. That is why he can say:

> The resurrection is therefore our pledge that statements about God in Jesus Christ have an objective reference in God, and are not just projections out of the human heart and imagination, objectifying forms of thought in which we fashion a God in terms of the creaturely content of our own ideas.[72]

But, of course, everything depends upon our constantly thinking from a center in God and not from a center in ourselves. And that requires prayer and hard scientific theological investigation. It does not, however, require any dualistic attempt to escape this world of space and time because God himself has entered that sphere to enable us to know him and to love him. The importance of keeping together the incarnation and resurrection for Torrance, then, allows him to claim that we may not interpret anything Jesus said and did in abstraction from "the spatio-temporal structures and conditions of concrete human existence".

> Cut away from Jesus Christ the fact of the incarnation of the Son of God in this world, and everything becomes fragmented, and paradoxical, and empty of decisive significance. This applies above all to the resurrection of Jesus Christ from the dead, for it would be quite unintelligible and nonsensical if the consummation of God's work in space and time were not of the same tissue as all the rest of it.[73]

### Resurrection and Virgin Birth

Like Barth, Torrance held Christ's birth and resurrection inseparably together as miracles that conflicted with the existing world views and forced themselves on the community against the current or prevailing beliefs. Accordingly, they can be properly understood only in light of each other. The resurrection actually unveiled the mystery of the incarnation. And, in the incarnation, as we have already seen, God himself had entered our fallen world and, without ceasing to be the divine Son or Word, he was hidden in the sphere of creation which is not only unlike God but at enmity with his grace. Here God utters his *No* against human sin and evil in order to speak his *Yes* which is identical with Jesus' resurrection from the dead. Referring to 1 Corinthians 15:17–20, Torrance says God's *No* would have been to no avail without Christ's resurrection—without the resurrection we would, in other words, still be in our sins. Here "*redemption and creation come completely*

---

72    Torrance, *STR*, pp. 72–3.
73    Torrance, *STR*, pp. 178–9.

*together*, in such a way that they gather up all the past and proleptically include the consummation of all things at the end".[74]

The unveiling which took place in the resurrection was not absent from Jesus' birth to his resurrection either—it was in evidence in the transfiguration, his healing miracles and all other manifestations of his power. For Torrance, "the crucifixion represents the nadir of the hiddenness, the resurrection represents the high point of the revelation of Jesus as the Son of God become man".[75] That is why, as we saw at the start of this chapter, the resurrection is comparable only to the original act of creation, even though it transcends that act in importance, since it discloses the nature of the Creator as the very Word who became present as Savior within history in the incarnation itself. So it is the resurrection itself that discloses to us "that the Virgin Birth was the act and mode of the Creator's entry into his own creation as Man among men".[76] The virgin birth is not to be understood biologically since it intends to convey a theological message and biological investigations can only yield biological answers.[77] Rather, it must be understood in faith in the same way the resurrection is understood only in faith, as an act of God within history that does not abrogate the historical process but gives it its true meaning as a new creation within the old sinful order of things. Without the ambiguity associated with those who say that apart from his resurrection Jesus would not be the Word of God incarnate, Torrance insists that *"what Jesus Christ is in his resurrection, he is in himself. The resurrection was not just an event that happened to Christ, for it corresponded to the kind of Person he was in his own Being"*.[78] This means that the resurrection discloses that Christ's whole life, together with his resurrection, is the manifestation in time and space "of the ultimate and original and final creative activity of God". And this clearly illustrates that any attempt to understand Jesus from a merely human or historical point of view would ignore the fact that this

---

[74] Torrance, *STR*, p. 58.

[75] Torrance, *STR*, p. 57.

[76] Torrance, *STR*, p. 59.

[77] See Torrance, *STR*, p. 60, n.16.

[78] Torrance, *STR*, p. 60. Importantly, then, when Torrance claims that "The Deity of Christ is the supreme truth of the Gospel, the key to the bewildering enigma of Jesus" (*The Christian Doctrine of God*, p. 46), he does not think this is a view that was imposed upon historical events but rather it was "inherent in them, belonging to the necessity of their inner reality which forced itself upon the disciples, and now continues to force itself upon our minds" (p. 46). In light of the resurrection, Torrance insisted that the facts of Jesus' life are not undermined in any way or discounted but are seen in their true and proper sense. The resurrection does not cut Jesus off from his historical being and activity but "gathers it all up and confirms its concrete factuality by allowing it to be integrated on its own controlling ground, and thereby enables it to be understood in its own objective significance and intelligibility ... It is indeed the resurrection that really discloses and gives access to the *historical* Jesus, for it enables us, as it enabled them [the evangelists], to understand him in terms of his own intrinsic *logos*, and appreciate him in the light of his own inherent truth" (pp. 46–7). See also Torrance, *The Christian Doctrine of God*, pp. 52–3.

man himself was and is "God manifest in the flesh, the Creator in our midst as human creature, come to effect the recreation of human nature ..."[79] Indeed, it is the virgin birth that signifies, for Torrance, both the continuity and discontinuity of the church's connection with Israel: "The Virgin Birth tells us that we cannot understand Christ simply by placing Him in the continuity of the history of Israel, for at the Virgin Birth that continuity was broken by an invasion from above."[80] Nonetheless, the virgin birth also signifies that in Jesus "we have the true Israel of God continuous with the Messianic Remnant of the Old Testament ... the New Israel is not founded upon a priestly continuity on the stage of history but precisely upon the continuity of the prophetic-apostolic witness".[81] The continuity between the church and Israel must therefore be understood in light of the ascension, because it is itself a new creation that is real and visible only to faith as the church awaits Christ's second advent and is gathered by Christ himself as his body on earth. But this means the church is gathered from history as we know it and becomes a new creation within the limits of eschatology in the sense that it is already what Christ intended it to be in him. But it will not be fully that new creation until Christ returns to complete the redemption. The resurrection itself tells us that

> we cannot find Christ to-day simply by placing Him in the continuity of history as we know it. To do so would be to by-pass the Resurrection. Jesus Christ has withdrawn Himself from sight that we may know Him by concentrating through the witness of the apostles upon the Life, Teaching, Death, and Resurrection of Christ, so that it is only in history and in this particular history that He gives Himself to be known.[82]

In this sense, the resurrection and ascension together tell us both that Jesus is risen and that he is God and man and that "In Him the new creation is already a fact, and it is in Him that its continuity is a living dynamic reality".[83]

Torrance sees the virgin birth as an important part of the Apostolic faith and of the faith of the Church of Scotland. It means that Jesus "was conceived miraculously in the womb of the Virgin Mary through a direct act of the Holy Spirit". This signifies both that he was a man born of a woman like all others and that he was born in a manner different from others, namely, without a human father and "through a creative act of God". His unique birth corresponded to his unique being as God and man—it was in this unity of God and man in his Person that Jesus was conceived by the Holy Spirit and born of the Virgin Mary. Torrance therefore strongly opposes any separation of Jesus' two natures "before or after

---

[79]   Torrance, *STR*, p. 60.

[80]   Torrance, *Conflict and Agreement I*, p. 212. See also Torrance, *Incarnation*, pp. 94–104.

[81]   Torrance, *Conflict and Agreement I*, p. 212.

[82]   Torrance, *Conflict and Agreement I*, pp. 212–13.

[83]   Torrance, *Conflict and Agreement I*, p. 213.

his birth, before or after his baptism". And against those who think John's Gospel said nothing of the virgin birth, Torrance declares that John's Gospel explicitly refers to it in the following words: "who *was* born not of human stock, by the physical desire of a human father, but of God" (John 1:13). Torrance notes that in the second century Tertullian claimed that "it was gnostic heretics who changed the text to the plural because of their dislike of the virgin birth!" and insists that the text as cited here was the original form of the Gospel for the first three and a half centuries; it was affirmed by Harnack and established by contemporary New Testament scholars.

Torrance clarifies his understanding of the virgin birth, noting that it does not mean that the Holy Spirit was the father of Jesus because "there was no marriage between the Holy Spirit and Mary".[84] Jesus simply did not have a human father. That is what is implied in the creedal affirmation of the virgin birth. Nor did he have some prior "embryonic existence in the womb of Mary which was then taken up by God and adopted to be the Son of God".[85] Torrance is thus consistent in firmly rejecting any form of adoptionism—Jesus was not adopted into divine Sonship "in the womb, at the same time as his conception or his birth, or after his birth". Instead, with the incarnation from the Virgin Mary there took place "a new creation within a humanity estranged from God through sin and guilt".[86] It was for our salvation and redemption that this took place. Accordingly, any bracketing of the virgin birth from the death and resurrection of Jesus leads to a "deficient understanding of the atonement as only an external transaction expressible merely in legal terms. Incarnation and atonement cannot be separated from one another".[87] With the early church and Calvin, Torrance maintains that the root of our redemption is traceable to Jesus' very conception and not simply to the cross and resurrection. And this, he says, is precisely what led Christians to reject abortion and infanticide as early as the first century.[88]

Torrance even sees a connection between the virgin birth and the Eucharist because the church cannot exercise any authority over the Eucharist, just as Joseph

---

[84]    Torrance, "The Truth of the Virgin Birth", unpublished manuscript in the Library of Princeton Theological Seminary: 1–3, 1.

[85]    Torrance, "The Truth of the Virgin Birth": 1–2.

[86]    Torrance, "The Truth of the Virgin Birth": 2.

[87]    Torrance, "The Truth of the Virgin Birth": 2.

[88]    Torrance, "The Truth of the Virgin Birth": 2. See Torrance's interesting pamphlet, *The Soul and Person of the Unborn Child* (Scottish Order of Christian Unity, Handsel Press, 1999), for an important discussion of the fact that a foetus is soul of his or her body and as such is personally related to the mother, father and others as an embryonic human being and is ultimately to the Trinity through whom we all become truly personal. Torrance's insights are firmly grounded in his onto-relational notion of persons and his opposition to abortion is grounded also in the fact that we cannot think mechanistically of persons or of embryos precisely because they are created by God as body and soul and not simply bodies without personal relations.

could not "exercise his authority over the virgin birth". This, because it is the Lord's Supper and does not belong to the church in such a way that the church could exercise any sort of Lordship in relation to the real presence of Christ himself. Just as Joseph could only be a witness to the miracle of the incarnation, so too the church must "stand aside even in the Eucharist where it is ordained to serve. The Church can never manage the Eucharist or exercise any lordship over it". That is how the virgin birth also connects with the Eucharist in Torrance's mind: "Inasmuch as the mystery of the virgin birth is sacramentally present in the Eucharist, it belongs to the Church in the Eucharist humbly to *receive* (*Take ye, eat ye*) the eternal Word as the ground of the Church's being, and to be entirely subordinate to Him as Word."[89] Just as the Eucharist itself means the exercise of Christ's own authority as Lord of the church and Head of his body on earth, so the "Resurrection is sacramentally present in the Eucharist, it belongs to the Church in the Eucharist to acknowledge that its outward historical form which partakes of the fashion of this passing world is made the empty tomb out of which the new creation is raised up to enter the Kingdom of God".[90] In sum, for Torrance, the virgin birth is a sign of the mystery of the union of divinity and humanity in the Person of Christ. As such, the outward sign and the inward reality belong together. "Thus the Virgin birth attests and corresponds to the nature of what it signifies. The mystery of the birth and the mystery of the Person of Christ cannot be separated."[91] This runs parallel to the mystery of the resurrection and the empty tomb as its sign.[92] And it has implications for the existence and being of the church between the ascension and second coming of Jesus as in its proper ministerial function in subordination to Christ in Word and Sacrament.

---

[89]    Torrance, *Conflict and Agreement II*, p. 190.

[90]    Torrance, *Conflict and Agreement II*, p. 190.

[91]    Torrance, "The Truth of the Virgin Birth": 2. See also Torrance, *Conflict and Agreement I*, p. 212, for how the virgin birth connects with the resurrection and ascension and relates to our understanding of the church. This will be discussed in detail in Chapter 8.

[92]    Torrance insists that we can no more conceive of the resurrection of Jesus without the empty tomb than we can conceive of the incarnation as the union of "true God and true man apart from the virgin birth". In this sense, the virgin birth "as an article of credal faith has played a very important role in the history of the church in rebutting Docetism, and Ebionism, Eutychianism or Sabellianism and Nestorianism"; here too "we have a powerful force keeping the church faithful to the basic doctrine of salvation and justification by the grace of God alone. It proclaims that in Christ there is created in our humanity the possibility of salvation, a possibility which does not arise from man but which is anchored from the side of God" (Torrance, *Incarnation*, p. 104).

## The Nature of the Resurrection

There are two important aspects Torrance wished to stress when considering the nature of the resurrection. First, the resurrection was an actual historical event in the life of Jesus himself—an event comparable to his birth and death on the cross: "it is an event datable in history".[93] Second, it was also an event of "fulfilled redemption" that issued in a "new creation" beyond the processes of this world that involve corruption, death and decay. As an historical event understood as an act of redemption, the resurrection meant that Christ himself experienced death and hell and destroyed their power in his bodily resurrection so that our lives have been fully restored to a "new being". Take away the resurrection as a fully historical event and then, according to Torrance, "atonement and redemption are empty vanities, for they achieve nothing for historical men and women in the world".[94] Indeed, as already noted at the start of this chapter, Christ's bodily and historical resurrection is so decisively important that Torrance insists:

> If there is no resurrection, human nature is no longer genuinely human. Since man is the concrete reality he is, resurrection of man in the nature of the case can be only *bodily resurrection*—any 'resurrection' that is not bodily is surely a contradiction in terms.[95]

And this is why he so strongly stresses the importance of the empty tomb. In light of Christ's actual resurrection, which could not be reduced to the rise of faith in the disciples as Bultmann did, Torrance emphasizes that

> Everything in the Christian Gospel, now regarded in the light of Easter, was seen to pivot finally upon the *empty tomb* — that Jesus arose in body, arose as very man in the fullness and integrity of his human nature, but human nature which through the Spirit of holiness had been stripped of corroding forces of corruption and clad in the incorruptible garment of deathlessness.[96]

---

[93] Torrance, *STR*, p. 87. The historicity of the event is absolutely central to the Christian faith, Torrance insists, and must not be called into question for any reason. It is "a real historical event occurring in the same sphere of reality to which we human beings belong" (Torrance, *Theological Science*, p. 335).

[94] Torrance, *STR*, p. 87.

[95] Torrance, *STR*, p. 82.

[96] Torrance, *STR*, p. 83. See also *Reality and Evangelical Theology*, where Torrance writes: "If, then, we consider the gospel at its decisive point, in the resurrection of Jesus Christ from the grave, it must be insisted that we empty it of any real or final significance when we think or speak of the resurrection without an empirical correlate in space and time such as the empty tomb" (p. 37).

This explains why Torrance so robustly contests any Docetic understanding of the resurrection; any such view would mean that the message of the resurrection would have nothing to offer to men and women of flesh and blood as they actually exist. Any eschatology therefore minus the actual resurrection would have no relevance to on-going world history. For Torrance, "Everything depends on the resurrection of the body, otherwise all we have is a Ghost for a Saviour".[97] And Torrance wants to say that the risen and ascended Jesus Christ now interacts with us both in his humanity and in his divinity as the one Mediator. Unless that is true, eschatology will be undercut by the church's substitution of itself for the one Mediator. As we shall see, this is something that must not happen because it would undermine the fact that it is Christ alone who validates Christian faith and hope and thus enables us to live as part of his new creation.[98]

While Torrance was very aware of the fact that the empty tomb could not be equated with the miracle of the resurrection, he did insist that it is inseparable from the Gospel message and that it is that aspect of the message which points us toward history. The empty tomb speaks against any spiritualizing of the Gospel message of Christ's bodily resurrection. Spiritualizing the resurrection, he thinks, seems to stem from a modern aversion to the idea that God himself is active within the structures of space and time; in other words, it stems once more from the kind of dualism we noted above that Torrance adamantly and rightly opposed.[99] If one were to marginalize the testimony to the empty tomb, one would make the resurrection nonsensical.[100] Indeed, "It is *the empty tomb that constitutes the essential empirical correlate in statements about the resurrection of Christ*".[101] Torrance insisted that if this particular "empirical correlate" is in any way ignored or removed, then the resurrection itself "becomes nonsensical".[102]

---

[97]  Torrance, *STR*, p. 87.

[98]  See Torrance, *The Doctrine of Jesus Christ*, p. 191. Torrance connects this to the fact of our justification and ties this to the ascension following the thinking of John Knox in "Justification", *Theology in Reconstruction*, pp. 152–3. "Justification is not the beginning of a new self-righteousness, but the perpetual end of it, for it is a perpetual living in Christ, from a centre and source beyond us. To be justified is to be lifted up above and beyond ourselves to live out of the risen and ascended Christ, and not out of ourselves."

[99]  Torrance actually thinks St Augustine's comparison of the bodies of the saints to "the ethereal bodies of the stars" shows more the influence of Plato than of revelation which demands what he describes as a "proper theological reserve at the boundary of the eschatological" (*STR*, p. 140). What Torrance insists upon is that our "spiritual bodies" are not to be thought of as any less human because "To be a spiritual man is to be not less than man but more fully and truly man" (*STR*, p. 141). That is why the empty tomb is so important. Jesus' body really was raised. It was a "spiritual body" only in the sense that it was raised by the Spirit and healed of all corruption and decay.

[100]  Torrance, *STR*, p. 90.

[101]  Torrance, *STR*, p. 141.

[102]  Torrance, *STI*, p. 90.

Before the resurrection Jesus lived on earth but "not 'in the form of God'", and thus he did not call upon his divine power to overcome the weakness and humiliation that he made his own in the incarnation for our sakes. At this time he did not live "in the condition of his transcendent glory as eternal Son of God which he had with the Father before the world was, but after the manner of man and in the form and existence of the humble servant he had become in subjection to law". But after his resurrection he did live among us on earth "in the mode of the exalted Son of God, yet in his nature as man, now victorious and triumphant man, in the midst of history".[103] After Easter, Jesus lived as the "New Man" who was no longer subject to the forces of corruption, suffering and death but who nevertheless lived among the people, even talked and ate with them, to show that he was no ghost but a real and physical human being. Torrance cites John of Damascus and Cyril of Alexandria to support this idea that Jesus did not eat because he was hungry or to nourish his body but only in order to strengthen the faith of the disciples.

Torrance does not wish to see the resurrection as an interruption of the laws of nature because such thinking does not take into account Jesus' unique person and the fact that the incarnation and resurrection were miracles related to who he was as the Creator God who became man. In Christ's resurrection we have at work the final and ultimate creative activity of God himself destroying sin and death for our benefit. That is why it is so mysterious or, as Torrance would say, "baffling". Just as science cannot explain the event of creation by getting behind the processes of creation to observe the act of God creating the world itself, so any idea that the resurrection can be described as an interruption of the natural order of things presupposes that both creation and resurrection as acts of God, establishing, maintaining and restoring the created universe to its proper order, could be understood by observing nature itself. That is impossible because here we are thinking of an act of God that establishes nature in existence. Simply to describe nature and think that one had described the acts of creation and redemption misses this important fact. In that sense, Torrance insists that natural laws simply do not apply to those processes by which nature came into being or by which it is restored, but only to those processes of nature that already exist and therefore are observable. Consequently, "Far from being an interruption of the processes of nature, creation is the manifestation of the creative source of created reality and its immanent order. It is creative activity itself breaking through and manifesting itself within the events of the created world".[104] And it is this creative power that breaks through in the resurrection, according to Torrance. Therefore, while we cannot observe the resurrection any more than we can observe the act of creation, "it is just as factual and real as creation".[105] And in the resurrection itself we are concerned with what Torrance calls "new creation". Because the resurrection is also God's redeeming act, it is "not something that can be caught

---

[103] Torrance, *STR*, p. 84.
[104] Torrance, *STR*, p. 78.
[105] Torrance, *STR*, p. 78.

within the framework of those structures [that needed redemption—the old order] or interpreted by the secular historian who can only work within it".[106] History, as it occurs in this world, "decays and is so far illusory" because it falls into "the darkness and forgetfulness of the past". Since the resurrection occurs within this particular kind of history, it

> resists and overcomes corruption and decay, and is therefore a *new kind of historical happening* which instead of tumbling down into the grave and oblivion rises out of the death of what is past into continuing being and reality. This is temporal happening that runs not backwards but forwards, and overcomes all illusion and privation or being. This is fully real historical happening, so real that it remains real happening and does not slip away from us ... That is how we are to think of the risen Christ Jesus. He is not dead but alive, more real than any of us. Hence he does not need to be made real for us, because he does not decay or become fixed in the past. He lives on in the present as real live continuous happening, encountering us here and now in the present and waiting for us in the future.[107]

Hence, while the occurrence of the resurrection itself is neither described in the Gospels nor open to historical verification, it is "linked with facts at least theoretically provable within the historical framework—the resurrection appearances and the empty tomb".[108] Nonetheless, because it is the Holy Spirit who alone makes the being of God immediately present to us and enables us to understand both the meaning of Christ's resurrection and our hoped for resurrection, none of this can be understood without faith.[109]

Torrance gives a very interesting explanation that is quite helpful in understanding what he means here and elsewhere when he insists upon the historicity of Jesus' human life as the life of the incarnate Son and of his bodily resurrection. He says that historians are sometimes deluded into thinking that we must conceive historical events in terms of causal necessity. This happens because once an event has actually occurred, then it is seen to be necessary in the sense that it cannot be undone—it is, in other words, factually necessary. It has happened and nothing can change that. It cannot be other than what it is. The mistake here

---

106   Torrance, *STR*, p. 88.

107   Torrance, *STR*, pp. 88–9.

108   Torrance, *STR*, p. 88.

109   See Torrance, *STR*, pp. 141–2, and *STI*, p. 85. The resurrection will always be a "stumbling block" if we fail to see that it is not just one phenomenon among others but the act of God who became incarnate to redeem the world. Holding the incarnation and resurrection together allows Christ himself through his Spirit to speak to us in and through space and time and therefore obviates any attempt to impose some sort of alien phenomenology on to these unique events which supply a wholly different meaning under the impact of the Holy Spirit.

is to think that because an event has happened and is therefore "necessary" in the sense just described, that therefore "it had to happen".[110] But, for Torrance, historical events take place through "a free happening, by means of spontaneous human agencies" and so that while there are "elements of causal determination in historical happening", still "historical events are not by any means merely natural physical factors relating to the kind of patterns of space and time in which we live and work".[111] This must be recognized and respected so that we do not (as often happens) confuse temporal relations with logical relations so that events will be considered necessary in such a way that their free spontaneity is denied or ignored. This is why Torrance advocates what he calls "kinetic thinking" or thinking "in which we penetrate into the living happening behind the factual necessity"[112] in order to understand events from within their own movement, and thus do not impose a logical necessity of thought upon a factual necessity.

Applying this distinction between logical and factual necessity to the resurrection, Torrance proposes that events are rightly understood only when one allows them to be "determined by the nature of the subject of the happening". Thus, the eruption of a volcano is different from the killing of Julius Caesar because in the former instance we have to do only with "determinate objects", whereas in the latter we have to do with "personal agents".[113] Since these subjects differ, explanations of the events will differ. Applying this thinking to the resurrection, Torrance argues that because the subject of incarnation and resurrection is Jesus Christ himself in his uniquely divine–human being and action, therefore the resurrection is a unique historical happening that must be understood in light of this unique subject. That is why, as already seen, Torrance insists that these are miracles and that they can only be appreciated both historically *and* theologically. Since the agent here is the Son of God acting within history, any mere theological interpretation would end in mythology, while any mere historical explanation would reduce Jesus once more to a historical figure who is no longer allowed to function as the Son of God incarnate. Such thinking would obscure the fact that the risen Jesus is more real and more historical because he is no longer subject to decay, passing away and death. When understood through the Spirit as a "free happening, as the sovereign act of its Subject",[114] then the resurrection must be seen as an act of God within history but also as a free action that cannot be explained by history divorced from theology nor by theology divorced from history; in other words, an interpretation of the resurrection in faith respects the free action of the Holy Spirit as the one who enables understanding of this event for us.

Torrance applies this same thinking to the time-form of this world as characterized in the New Testament by referring to our "*nomistic form of human*

---

[110] Torrance, *STR*, p. 91.
[111] Torrance, *STR*, p. 92.
[112] Torrance, *STR*, p. 92.
[113] Torrance, *STR*, pp. 93-4.
[114] Torrance, *STR,* p. 95

*existence*", that is, by our fallen existence under the law which takes one form in nature and another in history. It is this nomistic existence or the necessity of our deeds and lives marked by sin that is overcome because we are justified in Christ "under the law" yet "apart from the law" (Romans 7:8f.). The resurrection itself is that act that redeems time since it occurs "within the nomistic character of our existence, and yet emancipates us from it into a new relationship with God the Father".[115] Because of sin, Torrance thinks, we became prisoners of "an ethical or legal order from which [we] could not extricate [ourselves]". In other words, as human beings we were made for fellowship with God and still sense our obligations toward God both ethically and legally; yet we could not be the people God intended us to be because of our fallenness. This is the "tyranny and curse of the law", namely, "the 'necessity' or inescapable 'nomistic form' of his existence" that Christ redeemed in order to "lift him up into living fellowship and loving communion with God the Father".[116] We live in time that is marked by sin and death and yet not allowed to fall into utter chaos by God; this preservation takes the form of our lives under the law. The significance of the resurrection in this context is such that the risen Jesus

> broke through the nomistic form of our existence, rising again no longer in the form of a servant under the law, but in the form of the life-giving New Man, entirely and fully human, yet man no longer confined to the kind of limits that are imposed on us in our fallen world by the time-form of law or by the nomistic form of time. However, far from violating or abrogating time, he redeemed it. Just as in justification the law was not destroyed but established, so in the resurrection time is not annihilated but recreated ...[117]

All of this means that it is in the hypostatic union that time and eternity are joined in such a way that we are actually exalted—our human existence in time is sanctified in the risen Lord—and taken up into God: "In Christ the life of human being is wedded to eternal life".[118] Yet, the ascension tells us that this time of the new creation established in Christ is "hidden from us". It is actually "held back until in the mercy of God Jesus Christ comes again to judge and renew all his creation".[119] Here we see the importance of eschatology in Torrance's thinking about the resurrection within a trinitarian context. While we genuinely participate in the new creation here and now by faith in the risen Lord in whom this new creation is already real, our lives, as they will be, remain hidden from view and can be seen and understood only within faith and hope until the ascended Lord returns. It is the church, Torrance claims, that participates both in history, which

---

[115]   Torrance, *STR*, p. 96.
[116]   Torrance, *STR*, p. 97.
[117]   Torrance, *STR*, p. 98.
[118]   Torrance, *STR*, p. 98.
[119]   Torrance, *STR*, p. 98.

now decays and passes, and yet also lives in the time of the new creation of the risen Lord "through the *koinōnia* of the Spirit", so that the church, which is shaped by the entrance of the "end-time" active within it, continues to live on earth by being "crucified with Christ to the time-form of this world", while still being sent to fulfill its mission in the world by virtue of its union with Christ. Thus,

> though risen with Christ and already a partaker through the Spirit in the new creation, the Church is sent like Christ into the world as the servant of the Lord, humbling itself and containing itself in *kenōsis* within the limits and laws of this world in order to proclaim the Gospel of reconciliation and to live out reconciliation within conditions of fallen human existence.[120]

This, then, is the realm of apocalyptic in which we speak of the new world and new time "by using language culled from the old world and the old time".[121] Practically speaking, then, we speak, live and know of our lives as those who already participate in the new creation in Christ only as we participate in communion with the Father through his incarnate, risen and ascended Son and therefore only through the Spirit and in faith. It is here that Torrance's view of the sacraments is crucial; for it is through the sacraments of Baptism and the Eucharist that we live in the age that is passing away and yet also live in the "new age" that is coming upon Christ's return. Hence, "as often as the Church partakes of Holy Communion in the *real* presence or *parousia* of Christ it becomes ever anew the Body of the risen Lord".[122]

Here we are at the very limits of what human beings can say about their new life in Christ because they still live in the two worlds—the one that is redeemed and coming and the one that is passing. Torrance provides a glimpse of how things really do appear differently to individuals in light of Christ's resurrection and ascension: when they die they are with Christ "in his immediate presence, participant in him and made like him. That is to each believer the *parousia* of Christ to him".[123] Yet Torrance claims that when viewed from the perspective of this fallen world, all that we see is each believer's body "laid to sleep in the earth, waiting until the redemption of the body and the recreation of all things at the final *Parousia*". When seen from the perspective of the "new creation there is no gap between the death of the believer and the *parousia* of Christ, but looked at from the perspective of time that decays and crumbles away, there is a lapse in time between them".[124] For Torrance, the only way to think of these together is to think of them in Christ.

---

[120]  Torrance, *STR*, p. 99.

[121]  Torrance, *STR*, pp. 99–100.

[122]  Torrance, *STR*, p. 102.

[123]  Torrance, *STR*, p. 102. Here Torrance follows the thinking of Emil Brunner in his book *Eternal Hope*, trans. Harold Knight (Westminster Press, 1954), while yet noting that Brunner's view of the resurrection is "rather docetic".

[124]  Torrance, *STR*, p. 102.

It is in his Person that "human nature and divine nature are hypostatically united and in whom our human existence and history are taken up into his divine life".[125] Here eschatology is crucial. For if we are to live in this world, which is crumbling and passing away, as servants of the Gospel and therefore as those already risen from death with Christ, then we must reject any attempt to fix the Kingdom of God "within the old structures" as easily happens when biblical eschatology is mythologized. All millenarian thinking therefore fails to recognize the nature of the resurrection as a completed act of reconciliation. It fails to see that Christ has already effected the new creation of all things and that this is what remains to be finished and revealed when he comes again. But even now he is working "in and under and with all world-events". The church lives between the times of Christ's resurrection and Pentecost and his final advent and therefore must not seek "to force his hand, or to force upon the world the consummation before its time".[126] Eschatology therefore plays a very decisive role in Torrance's thinking about the resurrection and is dictated to a large extent by his view of the ascension and how that event is connected with Christ's incarnation, death, resurrection and final advent. Let us briefly explore the importance of the ascension and of eschatology in Torrance's thought.

**The Ascension and Eschatology**

Because Torrance's theology is dictated by who Jesus was and is, it is inherently eschatological in the sense that he deliberately maintains an "eschatological reserve" both with regard to our knowledge of God and of the church, the sacraments and the Christian life itself.[127] He stresses that our lives which are given us now by the grace of God are lived out in time and space between the events of Christ's death and resurrection and his second coming. But they are not lived in a vacuum. They are lived in prayer, thanksgiving and joy as we rely upon the risen and ascended Lord himself to enable every aspect of our lives from

---

[125]  Torrance, *STR*, p. 102.

[126]  Torrance, *STR*, pp. 103–4. See how Torrance applies this thinking to history in *Theological Science*, p. 336.

[127]  Torrance therefore maintains that "just as we cannot comprehend *how* God created the world out of nothing, or *how* he brought Jesus Christ forth from the grave, so we are unable to grasp *how* his redemptive and providential activity makes all things, material as well as spiritual, to serve his eternal purpose of love" (*The Christian Doctrine of God*, p. 226). Ever since the resurrection and ascension, we must realize that our lives take place "in the eschatological reserve created by the ascension" (*STR*, pp. 157, 152, 156). This means that our work for the Kingdom is always our fallible work that takes place from a center in Christ and looks forward to his ultimate renewal of all things. It can never claim to be more than an ambiguous work within history because history is not yet fully redeemed. The same holds true of the church, as we will see.

the simplest daily tasks to the worship of the community in which we renew our baptismal vows and are renewed by the real presence of Christ himself until he comes again to consummate the redemption. Torrance's eschatology is, as it were, set in motion by Christ's ascension because it is in and through Christ's ascension that he definitively assumes his position as the one Mediator once and for all. And he does this as he enters upon his role as King, Prophet and Priest. Torrance wished to emphasize the fact that while Christ is now at the "right hand of the Father", this is not to be understood in a spatial sense so that he is conceived as "contained in heaven" and thus separated from us here on earth. Such misunderstanding follows from imposing a "receptacle view" of space and time on to the event of the ascension; this is something, as we have already seen, that Torrance strongly and rightly rejects.[128] Quite the contrary: as the divine–human Lord of heaven and earth, he is hidden from us who live within the sphere of space and time. But he is also present to us as King, Prophet and Priest through the power of his Holy Spirit. We will postpone much of our discussion of how Torrance thinks of this *triplex munus* of Christ until Chapter 8, when we will explore his views of the church and the sacraments which are essentially dictated by his understanding of the ascension in its connection with the resurrection and incarnation. For now we simply note that Torrance relies quite heavily on the theology of John Calvin who gave special emphasis in his theology to the ascension in its essential connection with the incarnation and resurrection. What is perhaps most important here is that just as Torrance's thinking is marked by the actual incarnation of the Word in our human flesh and Jesus' bodily resurrection from the dead, so it is marked by his view of Christ's bodily ascension. Thus, Torrance even can say, "If in a previous generation we had to battle for the Humanity of the historical Jesus, today we have to do battle for the Humanity of the risen Jesus ascended to the right hand of God the Father Almighty."[129] Without Jesus' bodily resurrection, there is no salvation within history for us, and without Jesus' bodily ascension "in the fulness of His Humanity, then we have no anchor within the veil and there is no hope for us men and women of flesh and blood (Heb. 6.19f; Col. 1.27)".[130] That is why Torrance so adamantly opposed any attempt to demythologize the ascension. Any such attempt would, in effect, dehumanize Christ and make the Gospel itself irrelevant to us—any depreciation of Christ's humanity, Torrance insisted, leads to an inhuman institutional church, as we shall see.[131]

Torrance's eschatology, then, bears the imprint of his view of Christ's ascension. Christ's ascension involves a veiling of his divine power and majesty—a holding back of these so that the resurrection and ascension are, in a certain sense, fused together in Jesus Christ and his continuing ministry as King, Prophet and Priest. In this sense, Christ's kingly power is exercised through his sacrifice and priestly

---

[128] See above, Chapter 4.
[129] Torrance, *Royal Priesthood*, p. 43.
[130] Torrance, *Royal Priesthood*, p. 43.
[131] Torrance, *Royal Priesthood*, p. 44.

mediation even now. He is the Royal Priest who did not attempt to manipulate the divine will but actually endeavored to force the priestly and scribal authorities back to a true priestly relation to God's Word. He criticized hardened traditions and confronted them with the Kingdom of God in forgiveness and with healings. As our High Priest (Hebrews 3:1f.), Christ fulfilled both sides of the Old Testament revelation: he was and is the Word of God present in the midst of space, time and history, and he was and is the perfect human response to God in his life of obedient self-offering. It is in the ascension that both of these aspects fully and completely come together. Jesus does not merely bear witness to what God does here. Rather, as the Son of God himself, he comes as the Priest to sacrifice himself for us. But he does not do this in some legal sense. He does it as the Royal Priest, as the "Apostle–Priest", as the only one qualified to act for us in his priestly solidarity with sinners, and thus in a sovereign way "on the ground of his own endless Life. He is Priest in final reality, and his sacrifice actually bears away our sins and cleanses us from guilt, and takes us into the presence of the Father".[132]

Unlike the Aaronic priesthood, Christ makes a true atonement once and for all. In Christ, kingly and priestly activity become one because he acts with a finality and effectiveness that are fulfilled with power to which all other priesthood can only bear witness or symbolize. The ascension means therefore the "coincidence of grace and power which makes [Jesus' priestly ministry] Royal or Sovereign Priesthood".[133] As already noted, we will discuss how Christ's heavenly priesthood is actualized on earth between the time of his resurrection, Pentecost and his second coming in Chapter 8. Here it is enough to note that the risen and ascended Lord now represents us before the Father as those who are incorporated into him and perfected in him. As his incarnate life was both the fulfilled intervention of God in history on our behalf and our perfect human response, he is to be understood as our personal advocate who makes himself the true content of our worship and prayer. He not only represents us eternally but he substitutes himself for us by vicariously offering worship and prayer to the Father on our behalf. What he does in worship, prayer and obedience issues from our human nature and this in a very real way becomes our worship and prayer as we pray in his name.[134] Through the Holy Spirit, Christ's own prayer and intercession "are made to echo in our own".[135] It is in this context, as we shall see, that Torrance understands the Eucharist. He rejects any Pelagian idea that the community offers an "immolated Christ" to the Father or that in offering ourselves in addition to Christ in his personal sacrifice we somehow complete his work. No. For Torrance, Christ stands in for us as the Mediator and Advocate beside whom there is no other. Consequently we "take shelter" in his sacrifice and not in our own. By sending the Holy Spirit at Pentecost, Christ actualized his High-Priestly blessing. That was indeed the point of the

---

[132]  Torrance, *STR*, p. 114.

[133]  Torrance, *STR*, p. 114.

[134]  Torrance, *STR*, pp. 116–17.

[135]  Torrance, *STR*, p. 117.

ascension—he ascended to the Father in order to fill all things with his personal presence and blessing. "It is this image of Christ the Royal Priest that occupies such a central place in the *Apocalypse*, not least in the opening chapters but also at the end in the consummation and fulfilment of Christ's blessing, in the New Jerusalem that descends from above."[136] Torrance refused to equate the priesthood of the church with the existence of all believers but rather insists that the church's priesthood exists only as a reflection of Christ's Royal Priesthood. Through the Spirit, it is Christ's own priestly ministry that is at work in and through the church which is his body.[137]

Just as the concepts of King and Priest are radically changed by reference to Christ who makes himself both their subject and their content, so the concept of Prophet is changed to refer to the fact that he is the prophet in a unique sense,

> for he is in himself the Word he proclaims just as he is himself the King of the Kingdom and the Priest who is identical with the Offering he makes. Christ ascended, then, as the Word made flesh, as he is both Word from God to man and word from man to God. He is God's own Word translated into human form and reality and returning back to the Father as answering Word in perfect fulfilment of his Will. It is in that identity of Word of God and Word of man that Christ's prophetic ministry is fulfilled.[138]

Therefore Christ's own self-proclamation takes place through the Spirit and is echoed in and heard through the church. In and through the church's own preaching, it is Christ himself, the incarnate and risen Word, who is mightily at work summoning people to believe in him. Repeatedly stressing the fact that, as the ascended Word, Christ is present now in the history of the church's activities of witness, Torrance showed how his view of the incarnation and of the Trinity shaped his thinking even here.

> The Lord Jesus Christ, in whom human nature and divine Nature while not confused are indissolubly united in his one Person, is taken up in his ascension into the very heart of the Godhead. Hence the incarnate Truth of Jesus Christ as our Lord and Saviour now belongs for ever to the ultimate Truth of the one Triune God—and that includes the whole of his atoning mediation on our behalf from his birth to his crucifixion and resurrection. It is in and through him in whom we believe, and whom we worship as true God of true God, that the doctrine of

---

[136] Torrance, *STR*, p. 118.

[137] In Torrance's understanding, this means that "The form of priesthood in the Church derives from the Form of Christ as the Form of the Suffering Servant" (*Royal Priesthood*, p. 82). Hence, "Only as it [the Church] learns to let the mind of Christ be in its mind, and is inwardly and outwardly shaped by His servant-obedience unto the death of the Cross, can it participate in His Prophetic, Priestly, and Kingly Ministry" (*Royal Priesthood*, p. 87).

[138] Torrance, *STR*, p. 119.

the Blessed and Undivided Trinity has its material content—the crucified Jesus, risen again, is now for ever lodged in the heart of the Triune Being of God.[139]

It is because the man Jesus is at the right hand of the Father but present in history now as the incarnate Word through the very human activities of the church in its preaching, teaching and sacramental activity, that we can be united to Christ through these very human actions as Christ prophetically acts to unite us to himself through the Holy Spirit's own personal activity.[140] Christ is thus to be understood as himself the actual living content of his prophetic ministry "in which Christ effectively ministers himself to us".[141] Following Barth, Torrance insists that the church is the "bodily and historical form of Christ's existence on earth through which he lets his Word be heard", so that in and through the church's proclamation and witness "he himself through the Spirit is immediately present validating that Word as his own, and communicating himself to men through it".[142] It is through the church's proclamation of the Gospel that the risen and ascended Christ rules the world until his return to judge and renew all creation. While people are sacramentally united to Christ in and through the church's ministry, the important point to be noted here is that he himself is immediately present. Hence, the church in no way attests itself but must always direct people's attention away from itself and toward the risen and ascended Lord who is coming again. This, as we shall see in the next chapter, is a crucial insight that is dictated by Torrance's strictly trinitarian understanding of the church and the sacraments and thus also of his view of priestly power subordinated to the power of the one eternal High Priest himself. In this thinking, Torrance deliberately follows Irenaeus, Athanasius, Gregory Nazianzen and Hilary.

### The Nature of the Ascension

As with the resurrection, the ascension must be understood from within the "whole movement of the incarnation and the saving acts of God within it".[143] Apart from this, the ascension, like the resurrection, can only appear to be quite enigmatic. The forty days between the resurrection and ascension remind us of the fact that we are not dealing with some sort of "progressive spiritualization or immaterialization of

---

[139]  Torrance, *The Christian Doctrine of God*, pp. 109–110.

[140]  See Torrance, *STR*, p. 120.

[141]  Torrance, *STR*, p. 120.

[142]  Torrance, *STR*, p. 120. Torrance explicitly refers to Barth's understanding of the church as "the earthly-historical form of the existence of Jesus Christ" (Barth *CD* IV/1, p. 643) in order to stress that the church has both an empirical historical existence and a spiritual existence in and through the Holy Spirit that cannot be separated in any way (*The Trinitarian Faith*), p. 276.

[143]  Torrance, *STR*, p. 123.

the body of Christ", but rather with the training of the disciples in their union with Christ through his own self-manifestation so that their understanding of suffering and glory as well as humiliation and exaltation "were bound together in his own Person in indissoluble union".[144]

Torrance intended to think relationally about the ascension in such a way that all false kenoticism (kenoticism that would strip Jesus of his true divinity while incarnate) and all demythologizing (that would reduce the ascension to the experience of those who encounter Jesus) are avoided. Just as in the incarnation, Jesus as the Word of God incarnate must be understood relationally and not in terms of any sort of receptacle notion of space and time; unless this happens, Jesus will mistakenly be seen as merely divine or merely human but not the way he really is: God acting for us *as* man within time and space as we know and experience these. Consistent with his earlier views, Torrance emphatically rejects the receptacle or container notion of space in this context because he believes such thinking ultimately would lead to some sort of monophysitism by conceptualizing Jesus' humanity as having to be extended as a receptacle to contain the divine.[145] Torrance describes the differences between the Lutherans and Reformed, claiming that Luther tended to undermine history by thinking of the divine being relating to Christ's physical being as a "mathematical point"; this Torrance links to the existential views of Jesus' history advanced later by the demythologizers which detached faith completely from time and space because they conceptualized the incarnation merely as an "objectifying form of thinking".[146] While Luther certainly wished to present a proper view of the incarnation which upheld both Jesus' divinity and humanity, whenever the receptacle view held sway, then the Word tended to be "resolved into Jesus without remainder" and the problems of false kenoticism and demythologizing developed.[147]

With the Lutherans, Torrance wants to say that no part of the Logos was excluded from the incarnation. In fact, the Logos was totally incarnate. But, with the Calvinists, Torrance also intends to stress that the Logos remained wholly himself as the Creator, Preserver and Ruler of the universe even while living out his incarnate life on earth. In other words, "He became man without ceasing to be God".[148] Thinking of Christ's divine and human natures together and relationally becomes an even more pronounced difficulty in relation to the ascension because Jesus ascends from our human place to God's place. That means that he ascended from our fallen space which, along with our fallen time, he had healed in his resurrection from the dead. We say that space and time were resurrected in him and we speak this way in apocalyptic language that tends to break down and must point toward the new reality beyond. As the ascended Lord, Christ's humanity

---

144   Torrance, *STR*, p. 123.
145   See Torrance, *STR*, p. 125.
146   Torrance, *STR*, p. 126.
147   Torrance, *STR*, p. 126.
148   Torrance, *STR*, p. 126.

was "fully and truly human".[149] In this sense, Torrance intends to think through the relation of the risen Jesus, who confirmed space and time in their reality, to the ascended Jesus, who exists beyond all notions of space and time, while continuing to relate with us in space and time which are both healed in him and yet remain to be transformed at the second coming. This cannot be enclosed within our categories of space and time. Following Calvin, Torrance insists that Jesus' ascension is an ascension beyond the heavens conceivable to us. Because God transcends the created heavens and earth, he is everywhere. Therefore, to say that Christ has ascended to the right hand of God means that God's power is not limited by time and space. God's omnipresence consequently is defined by God's nature.[150]

Turning to the incarnation, Torrance maintains that Jesus himself is the place in space and time where God and humanity meet and have genuine communion. In light of the ascension, the question becomes how to think of Jesus as this place within space and time while yet acknowledging that he has ascended to God in heaven and then attempting to understand just what that means for us here and now. Following Karl Barth, Torrance understands heaven as that side of created reality that is inaccessible and incomprehensible to human insight. As part of the created world, it must be distinguished from God and seen as "the creaturely correspondence to his glory, which is veiled from man, and cannot be disclosed except on his initiative".[151] We must think of Christ, then, as ascended beyond all space and time without in any way undermining his full humanity as the risen Lord.

> In the incarnation we have the meeting of man and God in man's place, but in the ascension we have the meeting of man and God in God's place, but through the Spirit these are not separated from one another (they were not spatially related in any case), and man's place on earth and in the space–time of this world is not abrogated, even though he meets with God in God's place.[152]

In Torrance's thinking, it would be a monumental misunderstanding either to project our limited time and space into God or to deny that God himself has his own unique time and space. Here is where the doctrine of the Trinity is particularly decisive in connection with the ascension. Space "concretely considered is place" but place has content because it involves certain ends and purposes. As already noted, time and space must be understood relationally and this decisively excludes any application of the receptacle or container notion of space because that would either limit God to his own place or constrain him by containment within our place. Space and time, of course, cannot be separated any more than location

---

[149]   Torrance, *STR*, p. 127.

[150]   See Torrance, *STR*, p. 128.

[151]   Torrance, *STR*, p. 129. See Barth, *CD* III/1, p. 453, III/3, pp. 418–76 and IV/2, pp. 153–4.

[152]   Torrance, *STR*, pp. 129–30.

can be separated from time because, as Torrance makes clear, "temporal relation belongs to location".[153] Consequently, when we speak of "God's place" and of "man's place" we have to be very clear that since place and time are defined by "that *for which* they exist or function", divine and human place and time must be clearly distinguished and interrelated on the basis of God's own gracious activity as Creator, Reconciler and Redeemer.

Hence, our human place is defined by the room we make in our lives and movements, while "God's 'place' is defined by the nature and activity of God as the room for the life and activity of God as God".[154] For Torrance, "we must speak of the 'place' and 'time' of God in terms of his own eternal life and his eternal purpose in the divine love, where he wills his life and love to overflow to us whom he has made to share with him his life and love".[155] God's "time" is defined "by the uncreated and creative life of God, and 'place' for God can only be defined by the communion of the Persons in the Divine life". That is the place where "*perichorēsis*", which refers to space or room (from the word *chora*), enters the discussion. For *perichoresis*, as seen above, refers to the "mutual indwelling of the Father, Son and Holy Spirit in the Triunity of God".[156] And, for Torrance, this would make no sense at all if one tried to think of God in some timeless or spaceless way. Any such way of thinking would immediately call into question God's ability to act as the one who loves us within our time and space in the exercise of his divine activity as our Creator, Savior and Redeemer. God's place is boundless and so when we speak of the ascension of Christ from our place to God's, then our statement is "bounded" by our nature and space on the one side and by God's "boundless nature" on the other; it is limited "only by the limitless room which God makes for himself in his eternal life and activity".[157] From our side, then, statements about the ascension are "closed"; but from God's side they are "infinitely open". In any case, Torrance follows Calvin and holds that the ascension, like the incarnation, must not be espoused in such a way as to enclose Christ within the limits of our space and time or within our limited thought and speech.

## God's Time

It must be remembered that, for Torrance, God's life "is not immobile but continually self-moving" and carries its purpose within itself. Thus, "while it is

---

[153]   Torrance, *STR*, p. 131.

[154]   Torrance, *STR*, p. 131.

[155]   Torrance, *STR*, p. 131. There is "a 'before' and 'after' in God's activity, which calls for a consideration of the unique nature of 'time' in the eternal Life of God" (*The Christian Doctrine of God*, p. 209).

[156]   Torrance, *STR*, p. 131.

[157]   Torrance, *STR*, p. 131.

from everlasting to everlasting without beginning and end, it is continually new and carries within it the eternal purpose of God's love ... The eternal life of God has *direction*".[158] This is evident in God's act of creation, as we have already seen. While God was always Father, he became Creator out of love for us so that even as creation is a new act even for God, God himself was not different after creation than he was before because God is, always was and always will be the eternal Father, Son and Holy Spirit. While Torrance was very clear that our time relations must never be read back into God,[159] he also maintained that God's eternal life, including his constancy (his unchanging triunity as the one who is self-moved and loving) is "characterised by time". This is not created time with a beginning and an end, with a past, present and a future, but "God's kind of time which is the time of his eternal Life without beginning and end".[160] God created our time, but without "any temporal movement in himself". God holds our time "within the embrace of his divine time".[161] Thus, following Augustine, Torrance insists that God's uncreated time must be sharply distinguished from our created time as its basis and enabling condition. God's time is not an eternal timeless *now* that would devalue our time. Rather it is God's real eternal life as the triune God. This loving God enables our contingent existence through his own movement which itself is essentially dynamic and constant.

Further, Torrance claims that the limitations of our past, present and future do not apply to God's time. Still, there are "moments" in God's eternity, such as his life before and after creation and incarnation, in which the purpose of God's free love is expressed and is fulfilled for us in Christ himself and through the actions of his Holy Spirit. Torrance stated, with Barth, therefore that God "has a 'history'"[162] in the unique sense that God is and remains the subject of this particular history. Because God's unique time at once totally transcends our created time, while embracing it and healing it in the incarnation, resurrection and ascension of Jesus Christ, "There is and can be no conflict between the unchanging constancy of God's eternal time and the movement and activity of God toward the fulfilment of his eternal purpose of love".[163]

Consequently, it is the incarnation that discloses to us that at that point in our time "the eternal *became* time". Because God became this man without ceasing to be God, we may understand that God's very nature "is characterised by both repose and movement, and that his eternal Being is also a divine *Becoming*".[164] Yet God's becoming too is unique because it is never a becoming that is on the

[158]   Torrance, *The Christian Doctrine of God*, p. 240.
[159]   See, for example, Torrance, *The Trinitarian Faith*, pp. 88ff. and *The Christian Doctrine of God*, pp. 108–9.
[160]   Torrance, *The Christian Doctrine of God*, p. 241.
[161]   Torrance, *The Christian Doctrine of God*, p. 241.
[162]   Torrance, *The Christian Doctrine of God*, p. 242.
[163]   Torrance, *The Christian Doctrine of God*, p. 242.
[164]   Torrance, *The Christian Doctrine of God*, p. 242.

way toward being or toward the "fullness of being", but rather it "is the eternal fullness and the overflowing of his eternal unlimited Being. Becoming expresses the dynamic nature of his Being".[165] In God's own becoming, our space and time are included in a way that we can never fully express so that our space and time now and forever have a reality in our relations with God "throughout all history". All of this is real because the triune God is himself self-moving and ever-living—this God is essentially dynamic rather than static and yet is constant as the very God who is revealed and active in Jesus Christ himself.[166] This is where Torrance's often repeated insight, that what God is toward us he is eternally in himself, pays dividends. Because God loves us by sacrificing himself for us in his Son, we know that God will be absolutely faithful to us just because he cannot deny himself or go back on his own promises. Torrance is thinking of Hebrews 6:12ff., 1 Corinthians 10:13 and 1 Peter 4:19 in this context. This, Torrance thinks of as the "irreversibility of God's eternal time in its forward movement toward the complete fulfilment of his eternal purpose of love in creation and redemption".[167] In fact, since "God really is like Jesus", therefore we know that there is no hidden Deity behind Jesus who is unreliable and before whom we can only cower. Rather,

> it is in the bodily resurrection of Jesus Christ from the dead, in which the final immobility of death, or the immobility which is death, was utterly vanquished, that we may clearly discern the essentially dynamic nature of God's unchangeableness or constancy. This is the living immutability of his eternal Being which is the very antithesis of all inertial immutability or immobility. This is the triumphant freedom of the divine constancy revealed and enacted in Jesus: "I am the resurrection and the Life".[168]

For Torrance, then, Christ has both ascended to "God's place" and is present to us in our place just as God himself is omnipresent. "The ascension of Christ is thus an ascension to fill all things with himself, so that in a real sense he comes again in the Ascension."[169] The ascension thus reveals to us that there is a gap between the time of the new creation and the time of the old—in other words, there is a "gap between the resurrection reality of our humanity in Jesus Christ and the corruptible existence which we still wear and in which we are fully implicated".[170] Yet the ascension also refers to our human exaltation so that "our humanity in Christ is taken up into the full Communion of Father, Son and Holy Spirit in

---

165  Torrance, *The Christian Doctrine of God*, p. 242.
166  Torrance, *The Christian Doctrine of God*, p. 242.
167  Torrance, *The Christian Doctrine of God*, pp. 242–3.
168  Torrance, *The Christian Doctrine of God*, 243–4.
169  Torrance, *STR*, p. 132.
170  Torrance, *STR*, p. 133.

life and love".[171] Here Torrance wishes to stress that we are fully human and so we exist with our own "place" as human beings and with the "room" that we have been given to live our lives, but that as such we are enabled by God himself to participate in God's own "place" and the "room" he has created for us in the "fulfilment of his divine love".[172]

Moreover, because Christ is now ascended and is thus "withdrawn from our sight", it is Christ himself who "sends us back to the historical Jesus Christ as the *covenanted place* on earth and in time which God has appointed for meeting between man and himself".[173] It is precisely because it is the historical and risen Jesus who is the Word of God incarnate that we know from the ascension that

> to all eternity God insists on speaking to us through the historical Jesus. Just because it is the historical and risen Jesus who is ascended, what Jesus says to us, the Jesus whom we meet and hear through the witness of the Gospels, is identical with the eternal Word and Being of God himself. *Jesus speaks as God and God speaks as Jesus.*[174]

The ascension also tells us that we really cannot know God by transcending time and space. We encounter God within time and space and thus within our actual physical existence. For Torrance, then, the ascension is the exact opposite of any sort of demythologizing which would demean time and space as something to be left behind because it is conceived only as a projection of our own thinking that must be transcended to reach God in some timeless and spaceless way. No. For Torrance, the ascension directs us firmly back to the incarnation as the place within space and time where God wills to have communion and actually does have communion with us in his reconciling and redeeming love for us. Here once more Torrance emphasizes the importance of not trying to "go behind the back of Jesus Christ" to find some sort of direct knowledge of God in the form of some sort of *theologia gloriae.*[175]

How, then, are we to think of Christ as ascended to God's place and at the same time as the one who establishes us in our place within space and time? It is through the Holy Spirit that Christ is present to us in the church, so that the church is to be understood as the place where God and creatures now meet and have communion in Christ. This certainly does not mean that the church takes the place of Christ. Rather, the church is the place where Christ continues to be present within history. His very presence is a presence whose reality takes place in the power of his Spirit.

---

[171]   Torrance, *STR*, p. 133. Here Torrance relies on Irenaeus who speaks of the risen and ascended Christ as manifesting himself from heaven in order to "gather together all things in one" and "to raise up anew all flesh of the whole human race".

[172]   Torrance, *STR*, p. 133.
[173]   Torrance, *STR*, p. 133.
[174]   Torrance, *STR*, pp. 133–4.
[175]   Torrance, *STR*, p. 134.

The Spirit enables our proper knowledge of the ascension as a historical event as described above. Through the Spirit, Christ is actually present and can be said to be "nearer to us than we are to ourselves" because while we live on earth, we are, in the Spirit, "made to sit with Christ 'in heavenly places', partaking of the divine nature in him".[176] This, of course, is the goal of the incarnation: to enable us to share in Christ's new risen and ascended humanity and thus "to partake of the divine nature".

Our exaltation to share in Christ's "self-presentation before the Father", however, does not mean the dissolution of our true humanity in any sense but rather its intensification by being exalted in Christ "to share in God's life and glory".[177] Thus, it is through the Holy Spirit that even now we experience "communion in the consummated reality which will be fully actualized in us in the resurrection and redemption of the body".[178] There is, of course, "the danger of 'vertigo'", Torrance says, in thinking this through because people tend to conceptualize this participation in the divine nature by identifying their own being with God's being in mystical or pantheistic fashion. Torrance adamantly opposes any such thinking because it would destroy the historical connection between the resurrection, ascension and the historical Jesus as the one point in history where we have communion with the triune God. Torrance will say that "we share in the life of God while remaining what we were made to be";[179] but this must be understood in and from the revelation of God in Jesus Christ and through his Holy Spirit. And when it is thus understood, it clearly does not imply identity between divine and human being but only that we live our renewed human lives from a center in Jesus Christ alone as the one person in history who is both divine and human and so can enable us to be one with God in a union that upholds our distinction from him and our own unique human existence as well. This is the point of the hypostatic union after all.

And this relationship between us and the risen and ascended Christ is not merely an individual relation (though it is that too); it has cosmic implications because it is not only our humanity that is saved in Christ, but the "whole universe of things, visible and invisible" is upheld and fulfilled through what he did on the cross and by rising from the dead: "The resurrection of Christ in *body* becomes the pledge that the whole physical universe will be renewed, for in a fundamental sense it has already been resurrected in Christ".[180] The ascension also involves a

---

[176] Torrance, *STR*, p. 135.

[177] Torrance, *STR*, p. 135. Torrance refers to Matthew 22:30 in this context, where the text says that in the resurrection there will be no marriage for we will be as angels in heaven, and insists that this does not mean that we will take on some "bodiless angelic nature" because resurrection does not mean we will be transformed into another nature. Rather, it means that human nature will become "imperishable".

[178] Torrance, *STR*, p. 136.

[179] Torrance, *STR*, p. 136.

[180] See Torrance, *STR*, p. 155.

corporate dimension in that the relation between the church as Christ's body and Christ himself requires that the church press forward toward meeting the coming Lord throughout its history. But this means to Torrance that our thinking must be "governed also by the *distance* of the ascension and the *nearness* of the advent".[181] Primarily, this means that the church must never attempt to identify its structures in this world with what it will be in the eschatological consummation. The church must really respect the "eschatological reserve" created by the risen and ascended Lord himself. Finally, there is an individual aspect to eschatology in which each of us lives in that "eschatological reserve" in such a way that we realize that all that we do is done within the ambiguities of this world which is passing away and the new world which will finally come only with Christ's second advent. All our work will involve a mixture of good and evil so that we will only be able to "live eschatologically in the judgment and mercy of God, putting off the old man and putting on Christ anew each day" and always conscious that in doing all that we must do we are still "unprofitable servants" summoned to look away from ourselves and toward Christ in whom "our true being is hid with Christ in God".[182]

The ascension also establishes the church in history on the foundation of the apostles and prophets; it "finalizes the grounding of the Church on the historical Jesus Christ, and its confirmation on that foundation through the Baptism of the Spirit at Pentecost".[183] By his ascension, then, Jesus establishes the church in history with its mission, its foundation in Scripture and its unique form of prayer and worship that is in no way spaceless and timeless but rather involves our life in this world which is passing as we participate in the love of God made real within these structures. This has eschatological implications because Torrance insists we must never identify the life of the church in its worship or ministry "with the real inner forms of its being in the love of God" because these only are "temporary forms which will fall away when with the advent of Christ the full reality of the new humanity of the Church as the Body of Christ will be unveiled".[184] In a very real sense, the ascension teaches us that while the historical Jesus is no longer visible in history between the resurrection and his second advent, nonetheless because our lives are truly "hid with Christ in God", we are "summoned to look away from [ourselves] to Christ, remembering that [we are] dead through the cross of Christ but alive and risen in him".[185] We live now in and through his Word and the sacraments as those who have been baptized into Christ and have been "justified once and for all". But we therefore live as those who belong to Christ and not to ourselves and so we feed upon Christ in the Eucharist and do not feed upon our

---

[181]   Torrance, *STR*, p. 156.

[182]   Torrance, *STR*, pp. 157–8.

[183]   Torrance, *STR*, p. 136.

[184]   Torrance, *STR*, p. 137.

[185]   Torrance, *STR*, p. 158. See also Torrance, "The Ministry: The Meaning of Order", *Conflict and Agreement II*, pp. 13–30, 24.

"own activities or lives" and thus "out of our own capital of alleged spirituality".[186] Nourished by Christ's body and blood at the Eucharist, we now live and work in the strength of that communion "until Christ comes again". Indeed, "As often as he partakes of the Eucharist he partakes of the self-consecration of Jesus Christ who sanctified himself for our sakes that we might be sanctified in reality and be presented to the Father as those whom he has redeemed and perfected (or consecrated) together with himself in one".[187] When Jesus himself comes again, then Scripture and sacrament will no longer be necessary.

Thus, while, in Torrance's mind, there is a kind of apocalyptic strife within history as the Kingdom of God establishes itself through the preaching and teaching of the church, the ascension teaches us that it is this very Jesus Christ himself (who is the Kingdom of God in its realization and future coming) who remains the secret meaning of all history.[188] The genuine work of Christians is to pray. That is the church's most important service for the state because in prayer and through the Spirit "the heavenly intercessions of the risen and enthroned Lamb are made to echo in the intercessions of mankind and the people of God are locked with Christ in the great apocalyptic struggle with the forces of darkness".[189] It is thus in faith that those who recognize that the ascended Lord is the real mystery of world history that we can see that even the darkest moments of history can be seen as reactions to the initiative of God's grace. The God who made the cross serve his purposes of love will do the very same with history even now. At present, of course, we can only glimpse the risen and ascended Lord through a glass darkly. But when we are fully redeemed, we will see him in his fully transcendent glory.[190]

## Christ's Second Coming

Before closing this chapter, let us very briefly consider Torrance's understanding of Christ's *parousia*. The *parousia* refers to "the *real presence* of him who was, who is, and who is to come".[191] Because this refers to the incarnate life of the risen Lord, it cannot be understood merely in some spiritual sense that excludes Christ's historical presence on earth. Hence, "the presence of the historical Jesus is eternally fused into the presence of the risen Jesus and as such constitutes the one indivisible *parousia* of the ages. 'Behold I am with you all the days until the consummation of time' (Matt. 28:20). 'I am the first and the last, and the living one; I was dead and behold I am alive unto the ages of the ages' (Rev. 1:17)".[192]

---

186    Torrance, *STR*, p. 158.
187    Torrance, *STR*, p. 158.
188    Torrance, *STR*, p. 138.
189    Torrance, *STR*, p. 138.
190    See Torrance, *STR*, pp. 139–40.
191    Torrance, *STR*, p. 143.
192    Torrance, *STR*, p. 144.

It is important to realize that for the New Testament there is only "*one parousia*" which, Torrance contends, "is applied equally" to the first and second advent. While we tend to separate time and space in our ordinary experience, this *parousia* binds them together so that here we have a presence that "is neither spaceless nor timeless but which determines the whole invisible structure of history and is ultimately regulative of the shape and mission of the Church and indeed of the new creation inaugurated by the resurrection of Jesus Christ from the dead".[193] Yet this particular *parousia* also reaches forward to the time when Christ will come again in a *parousia* that will have "the same texture as that of the historical Jesus in the incarnation and the risen Jesus of Easter and the ascension".[194] It is in fact the consummation of the incarnation and of what happened on the cross.

While the *parousia* is essentially one, the ascension created an interval between the first and second advents of Christ which Torrance calls "*an eschatological pause* in the heart of the *parousia*".[195] This leads us to speak of a first and second advent instead of just referring to the *parousia* as the one happening that it is. Christ's Kingdom was fully inaugurated with his crucifixion and resurrection as that very Kingdom which "will be openly manifested at the end of time when the veil will be taken away".[196] This is what is traditionally called the *parousia*. But Torrance will have none of that kind of thinking which suggests that this aspect of the *parousia* was developed because, unbeknownst to Jesus, there was a longer delay than expected after his death and resurrection. No. Here Torrance applies his positive knowledge gained from the ascension. Jesus' withdrawal from history meant that he himself has created this eschatological interval. The church living by the Spirit awaits Christ's final return and lives and works in light of that coming— that is what God has established by giving the world time to repent and believe the Gospel preached by the church. Hence, Torrance himself states that he finds

> it difficult not to accept the fact that Jesus envisaged a considerable lapse in time between his first and final advents—and that, so far as the Church's communion with him was concerned in that long interval, he gave them the Holy Supper that they might eat and drink sacramentally in his presence, proclaiming his death, till he should come again.[197]

Since the ascension has indeed created an "eschatological reserve or eschatological time-lag"[198] we must not confuse our existence as those who really live here and now and those who will be what Christ intends as part of his new creation when he returns. We have immediate relations now with Christ in and through his Spirit.

---

[193]   Torrance, *STR*, p. 144.
[194]   Torrance, *STR*, p. 144.
[195]   Torrance, *STR*, p. 145.
[196]   Torrance, *STR*, p. 146.
[197]   Torrance, *STR*, p. 147.
[198]   Torrance, *STR*, p. 152.

But our relations take place mediately through his Word and the sacraments of Baptism and the Eucharist. But because this is so, we must think of the second advent of Christ as "always and inevitably imminent" and we must not suppose that New Testament expectation ever resulted in "disillusionment".[199]

When this is not seen and when our eschatological relation with the risen and ascended and coming Lord is not respected, then this could mislead people to unduly stress the idea of a "'delayed advent' which allegedly forced the early Church to alter its whole eschatological outlook and to adjust its life and mission accordingly".[200] This kind of thinking, however, merely reflects our inability to keep together Christ's first and second *parousia* because of the limitations of our own existence within space and time. We are tempted to use "artificial devices" to account for the interval between the two advents instead of recognizing that this is what the risen and ascended Christ actually intended. Torrance believes there is exiguous support for this thinking in the early church and none at all in the New Testament itself. While he admits of different emphases in Paul's letters to the Thessalonians and to the Philippians, for instance, Torrance nonetheless claims that Paul's thinking "still falls within the 'all is present, yet all is future' orientation of the basic outlook of the New Testament".[201] In this sense, both realized and future eschatology must be seen as held together in Christ himself. Torrance actually goes so far as to say that the idea of a delayed *parousia* seems to be more "a legend of the critics" than a reflection of the genuine eschatology of the New Testament which holds together the beginning and the end of all things in Christ, while this thinking tears them apart and then reads that division back into the New Testament. For Torrance, with St Paul, our "'salvation is nearer to us now than when we first believed' (Rom. 13:11)".[202]

It is the ascension itself, then, that actually determines the pattern of the church and its mission in space and time. In fact, Torrance argues that the ascension constitutes the church in a threefold relation to Jesus. First, the ascended Christ refers us back to the Gospels and to the witness of the historical Jesus as the place where we meet God within history. But Jesus also sends the Spirit and so he is really present in a different way, even though he has personally withdrawn from history. Thus we have a horizontal relation with Jesus which is mediated through the historical Jesus and the apostolic and prophetic witness to him, and we have an immediate and vertical relation to him through the Spirit.[203] Second, we have a sacramental relation with the risen and ascended Jesus that takes place through Word and sacrament. We will consider this in the next chapter in detail. Here we simply note, for example, that with the bread and wine of the Eucharist, Christ uses these signs of the new order which point to the cross and resurrection in

---

[199]   Torrance, *STR*, p. 153.

[200]   Torrance, *STR*, p. 153.

[201]   Torrance, *STR*, p. 154.

[202]   Torrance, *STR*, p. 154

[203]   Torrance, *STR*, p. 147.

order to continue to forgive and seal our lives with the Gospel. So the sacraments become the normal way for Christ to mediate himself to us within history during this time between his first and second advent.

While God may still answer payers for direct miraculous healings, Torrance believes that with the withdrawal of Christ's resurrected body in the ascension there really is "no appointed *programme* of anything like 'faith healing' or miraculous activity of a kindred sort".[204] This is an extremely important point because it means that Christ held back the physical transformation of creation until the time when he actually returns to "make *all things new*". In the meantime, he sends the church to live and work "in the form of a servant within the measures and limits of the on-going world of time and space".[205] Like Jesus who refused to turn stones into bread with the miraculous power that belonged to him, the church is called to serve him not by triumphantly imitating the state but by each Christian taking up his or her cross and following Christ from his cross to his resurrection and on toward the consummation of all things in the new creation. Christ's miracles were indeed signs of the Kingdom. But he never used them in order to help himself. Rather, he lived and worked within history, experiencing all the weakness and limitations of the creature, and he did so right to the end when he refused to come down from the cross. But he did in fact institute the sacraments as "miraculous signs" of the church's forgiveness and healing and of its own death and resurrection in Christ.

One final word remains to be said about our eschatological relation with the risen and ascended Lord. Eschatology, of course, refers to the "last Word and final Act of God in Christ".[206] It points us toward the end or the consummation of world history in Christ's final *parousia*. This final Word of God, however, also takes place within time and space and therefore must be contrasted with Bultmann's view which sees the *parousia* taking place when history has ended. According to Torrance, the New Testament view is just the opposite. It speaks of the eschatological "within the temporal".[207] God's eschatological acts therefore "run throughout time to their end at the consummation of time". These are not just acts of God that end time but rather acts of God that gather time up in order to fulfill God's purposes for history. By referring eschatology to Christ in the first instance, Torrance is able to speak of eschatology not by referring us away from time and space but toward them as the sphere where God acts and will act to bring history to its fulfillment. Christ himself is both the first and the last since he is the one who fulfilled the covenant and reconciled us to the Father, and it is he who will come again to bring this "to its final manifestation and consummation at his coming again".[208] After Christ's ascension, his eschatological activities are "veiled from our sight" because we live within the time and space of this world and "communicate with the new creation

204   Torrance, *STR*, p. 149.
205   Torrance, *STR*, p. 149.
206   Torrance, *STR*, p. 150.
207   Torrance, *STR*, p. 151.
208   Torrance, *STR*, pp. 151–2.

only through the Spirit in Word and Sacrament". Torrance believes that we should understand the final *parousia* of Christ more as his unveiling of what he has already accomplished for us in his life history than as "the consummating of what till then is an incomplete reality".[209] When he comes again it will, of course, be in the "fullness of his humanity and deity to judge and renew his creation". But, for Torrance, that is not another work in addition to what he finished on the cross and through his resurrection. Rather, it will be a "gathering together of what the cross and resurrection have already worked throughout the whole of creation and the unveiling of it for all to see, and therefore an unfolding and actualization of it from our point of view".[210] Torrance also insisted, however, that this does not mean that nothing new will be manifested at the end. He simply wished to stress that there is a relation between the old and the new which we experience through the Spirit here and now, and yet there is also a relation between the present, past and future as we are indeed united to the risen and ascended Lord who is coming again to finally make all things new. None of these distinctions can be eliminated without falsifying theology. And each of these distinctions derives from the very activity of the triune God as the Father sent his Son for the reconciliation of the world, and the Spirit, sent by the Son, gathers together those who now live by faith and hope into his fulfilled creation and toward the final consummation of all things in Christ. Now we must explore Torrance's view of the church, sacraments and ministry as the particular form that Christ's presence takes in history in the time between his first and second advents. That will be the subject of the next chapter.

---

[209]   Torrance, *STR*, p. 152.
[210]   Torrance, *STR*, p. 152.

# Chapter 8

# Torrance's Trinitarian Understanding of the Church, Sacraments and Ministry

Torrance's view of the church, sacraments and ministry is at once ecumenically and theologically grounded in such a way that he is able to stress how the church is the visible presence of Christ on earth and in history, while at the same time avoiding any idea which would reduce the church's reality to its institutional structures. What enables Torrance's profound thinking in this area is precisely his trinitarian view of the matter. This is made clear at the outset in his consideration of Vatican II, when he wrote:

> One of the immense gains of the second Vatican Council was the recovery of the Greek patristic insight that *the Church is grounded beyond itself* in the divine–human nature of Christ and through Christ *in the transcendent communion of the Holy Trinity*, from which it derives its essential intelligible structure to which all its visible institutional structures in this world are subordinate.[1]

It is Torrance's great merit as a theologian that he maintains the logic of this insight by illustrating exactly how and why the church's true meaning can only be found in the triune God acting for us within history in his Word and Spirit and therefore in faith. This is especially apparent in his view of apostolic succession when he insists that this is not something that can be demonstrated historically but can only be understood within faith.[2] It is also apparent in his understanding of Christ's

---

[1]   Torrance, "Ecumenism: A Reappraisal of its Significance, Past, Present and Future", *Theology in Reconciliation*, pp. 15–81, 64; emphasis mine. This has serious ecumenical implications because the church must allow the Trinity alone to question its theology and practice. Scientific theology enables us to sort out whatever social and psychological conditioning has affected our theology (Torrance, *God and Rationality*, p. 118). This is important because, for Torrance, the reasons for church disunity "are more non-theological than theological" (p. 121). He also relies on the doctrine of justification: "The Church can never justify itself, therefore, by claiming historical succession or doctrinal faithfulness, by reference to its own place and time on earth and history, but must cast itself upon the justification of Christ's grace alone" (Torrance, "The Meaning of Order", *Conflict and Agreement II*, pp. 28–9). See also Torrance, *Royal Priesthood*, pp. 41 and 70.

[2]   For Torrance, disagreement among the churches regarding apostolic succession was traceable to the receptacle idea of space as discussed above (Chapter 4), together with Cyprian's conception of Peter's role and a "pre-Christian notion of succession taken from Roman law but quite foreign to Biblical thought" (*God and Rationality*, p. 128). Eventually,

real presence in the Eucharist, as we shall see. Additionally, he demonstrates with clarity and consistency why divisions among Christians regarding ministry and the sacraments could be overcome if and to the extent that all of those who confess the Nicene–Constantinopolitan Creed allowed Jesus Christ himself, through his Spirit, really to exercise his Lordship over and within the church and all its practices. This thinking shapes Torrance's view of the church, sacraments and ministry and gives it immense ecumenical significance because, in reality, Eastern Orthodox, Roman Catholic and mainstream Protestant Churches all accept the authority of this creed and already stand together in that sense. In this chapter I hope show how Torrance's thinking is shaped by allowing Jesus himself to exercise his Lordship over and within the church; this will become especially apparent when we consider the Lord's Supper.

## The Church Grounded in the Trinity and its Existence in Israel

For Torrance, the church is already present in Israel in a hidden way but it becomes visible in connection with Christ's own resurrection and ascension:

> It is important to remember that this Church was already in existence as Church when Christ died and rose again. The Church was not founded with Pentecost; nor indeed was it first founded with the Incarnation. It was founded with creation, with the establishment of the One Covenant of Grace … although that was proleptically conditioned by the Incarnation and Redemption.[3]

Torrance consistently contends that it is the church that is grafted on to Israel and not the other way around. Consequently, he insists that there is one community that includes Israel and the church and that this has both theological and ecumenical implications for the church today.[4] And when Torrance says that the church was founded with creation, he does not mean to equate God's establishing the covenant with his act of creation; rather, he wishes to state that the church

---

this led to the idea that grace was transmitted "by means of ecclesiastical vessels and offices" in a mechanistic way (p. 129). Torrance believed that receptacle notions of time and space made it difficult for Roman Catholic theologians to see that the church's apostolicity could not be controlled or handed on legally but could only develop spiritually as the visible church remained faithful to Jesus himself who was "the Apostle in the absolute sense" (*The Trinitarian Faith*, p. 286; this is explained in Torrance, *Royal Priesthood*, pp. 11–12 and 41–2). See also Torrance, "The Meaning of Order", *Conflict and Agreement II*, pp. 21–6, and *Conflict and Agreement I*, pp. 131–2.

[3]   Torrance, *The School of Faith*, pp. cxix–cxx.

[4]   See Torrance, "The Foundation of the Church", *Theology in Reconstruction*, pp. 192ff.

did not come into being automatically with the creation of the world ... The Church was formed in history as God called and entered into communion with his people and in and through them embodied and worked out by mighty acts of grace his purpose of love which he brought at last to its fulfilment in Jesus Christ.[5]

For Torrance, then, there are three stages to the church's existence: its preparatory form in Israel, its new form in Christ and its eternal form when Christ comes again.[6] While Torrance therefore has no hesitancy in referring to the church in Israel,[7] he does believe that the Christian church takes shape through a "change in the economy or dispensation of the Covenant". Therefore, it must be distinguished "from the Church in old Israel". But "the Covenant remains the same" and God's purposes remain the same because God indeed made a covenant of grace with creation. In the old Covenant, God elected one people in order to bless all and that is what was fulfilled in the incarnation and is communicated to the world through the church. The church's life in its new form takes place through the Holy Spirit enabling Christians to "share in the New Humanity of Christ and therefore in the new creation". Indeed, "This union of Christ and His Church in the Spirit, is the mystery hid from the ages but now revealed in the Gospel. But through the Communion of the One Spirit of God the mystery of Christ and His Church presses out toward universal fullness in all creation".[8] For Torrance, there is an essential connection between the Spirit and the Word within the Godhead, and thus when the Holy Spirit acts for us in the economy, we are united with Christ because the Holy Spirit does not act independently of Christ himself.[9] Ultimately, "The Church is grounded in the Being and Life of God, and rooted in the eternal purpose of the Father to send his Son, Jesus Christ, to be the Head and Saviour of all things".[10] Yet the church has no independent existence, as we shall see, because its existence only has meaning as it finds that meaning again and again in its heavenly head, the risen and ascended Lord. Following Athanasius, Torrance insists:

---

[5]  Torrance, "The Foundation of the Church", *Theology in Reconstruction*, pp. 192–3.

[6]  Torrance, "The Foundation of the Church", *Theology in Reconstruction*, pp. 193ff.

[7]  Thus, "It was with the redemption of Israel out of the bondage of Egypt and its establishment before God as a holy people in the ratification of the covenant at Sinai that Israel stood forth as the *Ecclesia* or Church of God" (Torrance, "The Foundation of the Church", *Theology in Reconstruction*, p. 194). See Torrance, *Royal Priesthood*, where he speaks of a parallel between "the worship in the Old Testament Church and in the New Testament Church" (p. 19). Cf. also Torrance, *The Trinitarian Faith*, p. 280.

[8]  Torrance, *The School of Faith*, p. cxx–cxxi.

[9]  Following the catechism of John Craig, Torrance writes: "the work of the Spirit must be thought of in inseparable unity with the work of the whole Trinity, although it is regarded as especially related to Christ ... [hence] the Church itself [is] 'the good work of the three Persons'" (Torrance, *The School of Faith*, p. c).

[10]  Torrance, "The Foundation of the Church", *Theology in Reconstruction*, p. 192.

the Church really is the one Church of Christ when it looks away from itself to its objective source and ground in the Godhead, and dwells in the Holy Trinity, for it is in the Father, Son and Holy Spirit that the Church and its faith are rooted and founded.[11]

Aside from John Craig's catechism of 1581, Torrance finds the basis for this grounding of the church in the Trinity in the Cappadocians and in Hilary, who himself relied on the teaching of Irenaeus as well as Athanasius and the Cappadocians.[12] Throughout his writings on the church, Torrance was careful to state that the church's oneness, holiness, catholicity and apostolicity could not be directly equated with the visible structure of the community without falling into a kind of legalistic understanding that would actually undermine the true nature of the church as the Body of Christ in union with its heavenly head, understood in a strictly Pauline sense.

> The Christological understanding of the Church teaches us that the being and reality of the Church, and therefore of the continuity of the Church as Church, are not to be found in the earthly-historical forms of the Church as such, but in Jesus Christ Himself who loved the Church and gave Himself for it, who graciously assumed it into oneness with Himself in the New Covenant and who by His quickening Spirit ever renews it as His Body.[13]

Adopting Karl Barth's view that the church is the "earthly-historical form of the existence of Jesus Christ, the one holy catholic and apostolic Church",[14] Torrance stressed that there is an empirical church on earth that actually is Christ's Body within the sphere of space and time.

---

[11]   Torrance, *The Trinitarian Faith*, p. 268.

[12]   Torrance, *The Trinitarian Faith*, pp. 268–70. Torrance, however, notes that already in Hilary there is a trace of that understanding of the church that distinguishes between an "external fellowship of believers, and the Church as a mystical body", which he thinks was influenced by Origen and which became "characteristic of the Roman doctrine of the Church"; he criticizes this for a number of reasons but mainly because it tends to equate the church's oneness, holiness, catholicity and apostolicity with its historical and legal structures in such a way as to actually confuse the Holy Spirit with the church and reverse the relations between Christ as the head of his body and the community itself.

[13]   Torrance, *Conflict and Agreement I*, p. 132.

[14]   Torrance, *The Trinitarian Faith*, p. 276. In "The Foundation of the Church", *Theology in Reconstruction*, p. 193, Torrance writes: "Because Jesus Christ through the Spirit dwells in the midst of the Church on earth, making it his own Body or his earthly and historical form of existence, it already partakes of the eternal life of God that freely flows out through him to all men."

## Rejection of Dualism and Legalism

Precisely because he grounded his view of the church in the Trinity, Torrance rejected any sort of dualist view which might imply that the true church could be equated with some mystical reality behind or above time, space and history; for that would undercut the realities of the incarnation and atonement. Yet, as just noted, he also rejected any reduction of the church to its historical form of existence; for that would imply the legalistic view that ignores our justification by faith. Instead, Torrance wishes to present a "unitary doctrine of the Church" based on the Nicene *homoousion* so that he could say the church really is the Body of Christ on earth without confusing it with either its juridical existence or some mystical and timeless—spaceless—reality. Because Torrance never confuses the church with Christ, he would never say or imply that the only body Christ needs is the church. Such a statement overlooks the fact that Christ is in his place, and his time is the time of his eternity, even as we are here in time and space (in our place), so that while he has reconciled the world to the Father through his life of atonement on our behalf within our fallen time, space and history, the church still must recognize that it lives in a situation of eschatological reserve in which it is not yet what it will be until Christ actually returns to complete the redemption of the world. This is the time of Christ's patience in which people are given time and space to decide to repent and believe in Jesus himself. And that patience allows genuine human freedom and love to be exercised by us within the sphere of creation. Thus, Torrance regularly insists that while the church is indeed Christ's Body on earth, it is so only because it participates in the humanity of the Lord who rose bodily from the dead and now is actively involved with us as the ascended and coming Lord through his Holy Spirit. But this risen and ascended Christ is not merely present to and for the church; rather, he is present to and for the church in order to be known and loved by the whole world as the one who has reconciled and intends to redeem all of creation. And we do not merely participate in Christ's humanity, according to Torrance. We also share in the inner life of the eternal Trinity in and through our union with Christ. That is our eternal life. It is not just a life in which we have a "vision" of God, for that would imply that there is no genuine resurrection of the body. Rather, it is a life that includes our new and glorified bodies and thus includes a full relationship of vision, hearing and all that goes with our full humanity as it will be when Christ comes again.

Torrance sees the beginning of a problematic view of the church already in the work of Tertullian, who envisioned the church's unity in terms of "discipline" and who viewed the "deposit of faith ... as a fixed set of formal propositions constituting the *regula fidei*".[15] In Torrance's view, Tertullian should have seen the church's unity, with Irenaeus, as the apostolic teaching through which the Truth, in its identity with the risen, ascended and advent Lord, continually renews and

---

[15] Torrance, *The Trinitarian Faith*, pp. 270–71. See also Torrance, *Karl Barth*, pp. 221, 223.

reforms the church as his Body on earth. Seen in that way, the church is called to conform both in its order and structure to him who was crucified and who thus exercised his power on earth in the form of a servant.[16] Whenever the truth of the Gospel was detached from the living Christ, as it was when it was detached from its foundation in the New Testament faith and "organised into a system of truth on its own",[17] then the evangelical faith of Irenaeus and of Nicene theology was exchanged for the legalistic and anthropocentric views espoused by Tertullian early in church history and by the Westminster confessions later on. Then one's understanding of the church is impoverished not only by a dualistic understanding but by an understanding that undercuts our active and real union with Christ in and through the present activity of the Holy Spirit.

Torrance notes that Cyprian tended to trace the unity of the church to its foundation in Peter as it is held together among the bishops united with Peter, although Cyprian did not suggest that Peter's leadership in any way meant that he had any "primacy of authority" or that this was to be understood in terms of "any succession in office".[18] Torrance believes that the episcopate is indeed apostolic in origin but he maintains that a proper conception of a bishop

> did not carry with it the idea that the Church over which he presided was endowed with the grace of the Holy Spirit as a possession to be dispensed under his authority, far less the idea that the bishop himself constituted the link between Christ and the faithful. Rather was the Church regarded as wholly subject to the sovereignty of the Spirit, while its bishops were but servants … of Christ called

---

[16]   See Torrance, *The Trinitarian Faith*, pp. 286–7. See also Torrance's superb article "The Deposit of Faith" for a clear, concise and revealing presentation of how and why the "deposit of faith" must be understood as a sacred deposit of faith entrusted to the Apostles and thus "enshrined" in the Apostolic foundation of the church in such a way that the deposit itself was understood "as the whole living Fact of Christ and his saving Acts in the indivisible unity of his Person, Word and Life, as through the Resurrection and Pentecost he fulfilled and unfolded the content of his self-revelation as Saviour and Lord within his Church" (2). What this means, above all, is that the Word and Spirit could never be resolved into the church or into the apostolic deposit and used in some legal way to define the church's oneness, holiness, catholicity or apostolicity. It thus could never be resolved into "a system of truths or a set of normative doctrines and formulated beliefs" because the truths, doctrines and beliefs in question "could not be abstracted from the embodied form which they were given in Christ and the Apostolic Foundation of the Church" (3). Ultimately, the truth of the deposit, for Irenaeus and for Torrance, must be seen as grounded within the Trinity in such a way that our knowledge of God is completely governed by the unique oneness in being between the Father and Son in eternity and in time (8–10). See also Torrance, *Reality and Evangelical Theology*, pp. 122–3.

[17]   Torrance, "The Deposit of Faith": 15.

[18]   Torrance, *The Trinitarian Faith*, p. 271.

to act like deacons ministering to others as good stewards of the manifold grace of God.[19]

Once again, the problem of interpreting authority in the church is traceable, for Torrance, to various dualisms (epistemological, anthropological and cosmological) which opened the door to Gnosticism and to Arianism and to other heresies within the church. The Nicene view of the church, however, remained consciously grounded in the Trinity:

> the Church regarded itself as wholly centred in the Lordship of Christ, and his reign as the enthroned and exalted Κύριος Χριστός who was and is and ever will be coequal and coeternal with the Father and the Holy Spirit in the supreme sovereignty and power of the Holy Trinity.[20]

This trinitarian basis of the church's historical existence means that the very shape and structure of the visible church on earth takes its origin and continues in virtue of the incarnation and "economic condescension of God in Jesus Christ to be one with us in the concrete realities of our human and social life, and his saving activity within the structures of our creaturely existence in space and time".[21]

It was therefore in the very perception of the finality of Jesus' saving Lordship that the church finally actualized its own perception of itself as the Body of Christ on earth and thus as the

> dwelling-place of the Spirit of the Father and the Son, the "place" (χώρα and τόπος) where the one God, Trinity in Unity and Unity in Trinity, brings us into union with himself in such a way that we may partake of the eternal communion of Father, Son and Holy Spirit in the Godhead. As united to Christ in his incarnate reality the Church constitutes the sanctified community within which we may

---

[19]   Torrance, *The Trinitarian Faith*, pp. 272–3; cf. 1 Peter 4:10. See Torrance, *Royal Priesthood*, Chapter 5, for his presentation of a biblical doctrine of the episcopate. It must be governed by three principles: 1) that "Christ alone is the Head of the Church, and presides over it in all things (Col. 1:18; 2:10; Eph. 1:22; 4:15; 5:23)"; 2) "The ministry is a gift of the ascended Head to the Body, and as such is placed within the Body. It is essentially a subministration which by its very place and nature must not seek to dominate or lord it over the Body, i.e. to usurp the place of the Head. As placed within the Body the ministry is essentially corporate, and must manifest a unity in the Body corresponding to its One Head"; 3) "All members of the Body are joined together by the One Spirit in such a way that they are ordered by the Head according to a diversity of function and in a mutual subordination of love" (*Royal Priesthood*, p. 88).

[20]   Torrance, *The Trinitarian Faith*, p. 273

[21]   Torrance, *The Trinitarian Faith*, p. 274

draw near to the Father through the Son and in the Spirit and share in the eternal life, light and love of God himself.[22]

It is just this trinitarian understanding of the church that forced theologians to contest all sorts of dualisms in order to present a view of the "empirical church" as Christ's Body in such a way that room was made to allow for the fact that the structure of the church was tied to Christ himself and could only be lived out in "union and communion with the risen, exalted and advent Lord whose kingdom will have no end".[23] While theologians were relatively successful in this venture prior to and immediately after Nicaea and Constantinople, dualist forms of thought, stemming mainly from Alexandrian theologians, led to difficulties. Clement and Origen, for instance, made a detrimental distinction between "a physical or sensible Gospel ... and a spiritual or eternal Gospel ..." This led to the idea that only the spiritual and not the physical Gospel would endure since it was only a "shadowy representation" of the spiritual one. This erroneous thinking led to the idea of the visible church "as a passing similitude of the real thing, and the invisible Church of enduring spiritual reality, which Origen spoke of as the mystical 'bride of Christ'".[24]

It is important to see how this erroneous ecclesiology, with its dualist presuppositions, leads to a distorted view of the incarnation. While the Nicene church intended to affirm the *homoousion* of the Son with the Father, so that they could uphold the church as the actual physical body of Christ on earth as it was united to its heavenly head, theology indebted to this Origenistic approach tended to equate the real church "with a spiritualised timeless and spaceless magnitude", while the on-going life and mission of the empirical church was "regarded as subject to the laws that control human society in this world".[25] This led to a dualistic view of the church as a juridical society and a mystical body which undercut the fact that through the power of the Holy Spirit it is in reality the empirical church that is the Body of Christ. Because his view of the church as the Body of Christ is essentially Christological and thus trinitarian, Torrance adamantly opposes any sort of Docetic ecclesiology. That is why his ecclesiology is ecumenical at root. For him, the doctrine of the church demands that the church's unity be more than a mere spiritual unity, just as acknowledging that Jesus is the Son of God incarnate requires awareness that he had a real physical human body that he assumed in order to redeem it for our sakes. Further,

> because the Church is rooted and grounded in the bodily incarnation of Christ and lives by His atoning death in our flesh and blood and by His physical resurrection, the Church can be content with nothing short of physical and

---

22    Torrance, *The Trinitarian Faith*, p. 275.
23    Torrance, *The Trinitarian Faith*, p. 275.
24    Torrance, *The Trinitarian Faith*, pp. 275–6.
25    Torrance, *The Trinitarian Faith*, p. 276.

visible unity in Christ. To be content with a "spiritual unity" is to transfer the menace of Docetic heresy to the Doctrine of the Church.[26]

This insight has implications also for the church's ministry because it implies that ministry is corporate in nature, and that this is expressed in the collegiality that is visible in church synods and councils; it also implies that the nature of the church's continuity is mediated through baptism into Christ, through actions of Word and sacrament and through the episcopate rightly understood as a sign of these. A Christological view of the church's continuity, Torrance believed, would undercut false notions of "apostolic succession". Finally, because the church's form must correspond to Christ himself who lived his life in the form of a servant, "all notions of worldly power, lordly rule, disparity, and pomp, etc., can have no place at all in it". Torrance insisted that if the doctrine of the "*Suffering Servant*" is central to Christology and is held as normative for understanding the form and order of the church, "then most of the major differences between the Churches can be cut clean away".[27] Needless to say, Torrance's ecclesiology is shaped not only by a rigorous Chalcedonian Christology but by a profound Pneumatology, a rich doctrine of the Trinity and most importantly by an application once again of the Nicene *homoousion*. Just as all Christian doctrine hinges on Christ's internal relation to the Father as his eternal Son, so too does the very being of the church,

> for it is in him that the very being of the Church is rooted. Thus through the communion of the Holy Spirit imparted to it by Christ, the Church is united to Christ as his body, but in such an interior ontological and soteriological way that Christ himself is both the Head and the Body in one.[28]

## The Spirit and the Church

Torrance believes that the failure to think through the relation of the Holy Spirit, precisely as the Spirit of the incarnate Word, to nature leads to the error of confusing the Spirit with nature. This has not been thought through adequately in

---

[26] Torrance, *Conflict and Agreement I*, p. 138. See also Torrance, *Royal Priesthood*, where Torrance thinks of apostolic succession in terms of the church's continuing historical existence as it "ever becomes the Body of Christ through Word and Sacrament", and insists that while the church is neither the "continuation" of Christ nor the incarnation, it must be seen as a historical entity just as was Jesus himself. "To cut the link between the Church and the historical particularity of the Incarnation is to transubstantiate the Church into some docetic and timeless *corpus mysticum*, and to sever the Church from any saving act of God in our actual flesh and blood historical existence" (p. 69).

[27] Torrance, *Conflict and Agreement I*, pp. 138–9.

[28] Torrance, *The Trinitarian Faith*, p. 277.

Reformed theology, according to Torrance.[29] For Torrance, the work of the Spirit must be considered from the side of Christ as the application of his finished work to us and from the human side as we are enabled to receive the fruits of that work. The former relates to Christ's threefold office as Prophet, Priest and King, while the latter relates to the Spirit who calls forth our faith and thanksgiving in prayer and worship. In connection with understanding the church as the Body of Christ, however, Torrance insists "that the doctrine of the Spirit has Christology for its content (John 14:17, 26; 15:26; 16:13f.), so that the doctrine of the Spirit is really Christology ... applied to the Church as the Body of Christ".[30] It was after all the Spirit who uttered the eternal Word in the birth of Jesus from the Virgin Mary. And it was the entire Godhead who dwelt bodily in Jesus (Colossians 2:9) who was the

> new Man, the Last Adam, the Head of a new race gathering up all humanity in Himself (Eph. 1:10; Rom. 5:15f.; 1 Cor. 15:21f., 45), and in Him that new humanity pressed toward its universalistation ... in the resurrection of Christ and His ascension to fill all things (Eph. 1:23; 4:10). It was as such that He sent out His Spirit upon the Church begetting it and assuming its existence in space and time into communion with His own existence in the Body which He assumed for Himself in the Incarnation, and determining its form and course in space and time in accordance with His own life and work in the Body.[31]

---

[29]   See Torrance, *The School of Faith*, p. ciii. Torrance notes that at the Reformation there was a renewed emphasis on the doctrine of the Spirit that stressed the fact that the acts of God must be seen together with his Being as Father, Son and Holy Spirit. Without this, he says, there could be no doctrine of the church. He notes that, up to the Council of Trent, the Roman Catholic Church had produced no authoritative statement on the church and that there was no major monograph on the church between Cyprian's *De Unitate* and Wycliffe's *De Ecclesia*. It was at the Reformation, he says, that "the doctrine of the Church as the community of believers vitally united to Christ as his Body through the Spirit received its first great formulation since patristic times" (Torrance, "Epilogue" *Theology in Reconstruction*, p. 266). But most importantly here Torrance insists that for Protestants, who reacted to the static conceptions of Roman Catholic theology and stressed God's saving acts and the dynamic aspect of God's activity as opposed to the ontological, they detached God's acts from his being and lost contact with patristic theology and historical dogma. This resulted in "the loss of the doctrine of the Spirit. Detached from the Being of God, the 'Spirit' became swallowed up in the spirit of man or the consciousness of the Church, and detached from the Being of the Son the saving acts of God became dissolved into 'eschatological events' indistinguishable from man's own existential decisions" (Torrance, "Epilogue", *Theology in Reconstruction*, p. 267). Torrance hoped for a new "Reformation" based on a theology that held together God's being and act in all areas, including Christology, the Trinity and Ecclesiology. He saw this taking place at least in part at Vatican II.

[30]   Torrance, *Royal Priesthood*, p. 25

[31]   Torrance, *Royal Priesthood*, p. 25.

Torrance believed that Karl Barth's reference to the church as the repetition of the incarnation in history in *CD* I/2 was unfortunate, but observed that he later wisely rejected the idea of "repetition" in favor of analogy.[32] Torrance repeatedly stressed that the church, which is Christ's Body on earth, must never be confused with Christ himself.[33] When the church is seen as an extension of or continuation of the incarnation, then the church usurps Christ's place as the Head of his Body and presents itself as another Christ; the church then attempts to "stand between men and Christ arrogating to itself what belongs to Christ alone".[34] But in reality

> The Church is only the Body of Christ, an alien body graciously assumed by Him into unity with Himself, but it remains other than He, a purely human Church, a communion of human believers who are marvelously given to share in His divine Life and Love because He loved the church, gave Himself for it on the Cross, bought it with His own Blood and appropriated it to Himself as His own.[35]

Yet, as the Body of Christ, the church actually exists in a real union and communion with the risen, ascended and coming Lord and thus genuinely communicates with him in his body and blood through the Holy Spirit. This means that the church can rely upon the fact that Christ "remains faithful and will not break His Covenant". Under no circumstances and at no time, then, can the church be separated from him.[36]

## The Church as a Body of Justified Sinners

But this does not mean that the church is sinless. The church is a body of justified sinners. The church of those who are justified by faith and grace still awaits

---

[32]    The references are to Barth *CD* I/2, pp. 135–6 and 302, and IV/1, pp. 857ff., and III/2, pp. 531ff.

[33]    See Torrance, *Conflict and Agreement I*, p. 111.

[34]    Torrance, *Conflict and Agreement I*, p. 111. Torrance spells out in detail exactly what this looks like by tracing the differences between the Roman Catholic and Reformed ideas of grace ultimately to a "subtle element of Pelagianism in the Roman doctrine of grace as it emerges in its notion of the Church ... as an extension of the Incarnation or the prolongation of Redemption, or in its doctrine of the Priesthood as mediating salvation not only from the side of God toward man but from the side of man toward God" (Torrance, "The Roman Doctrine of Grace", *Theology in Reconstruction*, p. 176). For Torrance, Reformed theology holds that while the ministry indeed "represents" Christ by acting on his authority, "it does not represent the people, for only Christ can take man's place, and act for man before the Father. In other words, it rejects the notion of created grace or connatural grace".

[35]    Torrance, *Conflict and Agreement I*, p. 111.

[36]    Torrance, *Conflict and Agreement I*, p. 111.

redemption "when Christ will change the body of their humiliation" and make "it like unto His glorious Body". That is why, according to Torrance, the church is given the two sacraments of Baptism and the Lord's Supper (Holy Communion). The former signifies that the church is completely justified and made perfect in Christ and yet also needs to be forgiven each day; the latter signifies that it "needs to have its feet washed, as it were, as Jesus so dramatically showed at the Last Supper, and that as often as the Church has communion in the Body and Blood of the Saviour so often is it renewed in its cleansing and sanctification through participation in Christ and His Self-sanctification on its behalf".[37] As the body of Christ, then, the church has a multi-faceted relationship with the crucified, risen, ascended and advent Christ.

First, as the "body of sin", which Jesus incorporated into himself in the incarnation in order to judge our sinful fallen humanity and sacrifice himself vicariously for us on the cross so that we might actually be made righteous in him, the church must recall that Christ fully identified himself with the church "in its body of sin and death, and broke His Body and shed His Blood to cleanse and heal the Church, that is, all people who take refuge in His name and receive Him as Lord and Saviour". That is exactly what the church recalls when it celebrates Holy Communion. Second, the church is the Body of the risen Lord and thus is his "spiritual body" in the sense that we are already risen with him. In the risen Christ the church has "both the first-fruit and the pledge of its own resurrection" so that "The Church is even now the Body of the risen Christ, and therefore shares already in the risen Body of Christ" in that through the Spirit it is commanded to live as having died to the past and having been raised with Christ. This means that the church should live in the freedom that comes from the risen Lord and never be bound in legal fashion to its past mistakes. Third, because the church is the Body of the ascended Christ, it realizes that its Head has "withdrawn Himself from sight, and ascended to the right hand of God the Father almighty, who from there pours out his Spirit upon the Church". From the ascension we know decisively that the church is *distinct* from Christ. But because Christ gives us his Holy Spirit, we know that Christ "refuses to be separated from His Church". The ascension therefore both directs us back to the historical Jesus as the very place where the risen and ascended Lord chooses to meet us and maintain his covenant with us, and forward to the coming Jesus who will judge the living and the dead and reign in glory. Finally, the church is the Body of the advent Christ. This means that it is "directed to look ahead, beyond all history, to find the fulness of its life in the coming Lord and in the unveiling of the new creation". As the church awaits its coming judge, it must therefore cast itself upon his judgment and bring "all that it has done and failed to do before God in humble confession that it may be cleansed and forgiven, and all its wrong may be put away". The church is thus called to

---

[37]   Torrance, *Conflict and Agreement I*, p. 112.

hope in the advent Christ who will not only judge the church but will renew all creation and present the church to the Father as his "spotless bride".[38]

> It is the advent which reminds the Church that although it is already one Body with Christ through the Spirit, it has yet to be made one Body with Him in the consummation of His Kingdom. Until then the Church is the Bride of Christ waiting for the great Marriage Supper of the Lamb, and can only live in that expectation and hope.[39]

When Christ returns, there will no longer be a need for the institutional ministry, for the Bible or for the Sacraments, "for the Word and the Lamb Himself will be in the midst of His Church, and He will be its Light and Glory, and His servants shall serve Him day and night".[40]

Torrance offers a very realistic view of the church on earth as the Body of Christ himself and deliberately ties this understanding to the Lord's Supper. In a sense, Christ's real presence in the Eucharist is a simple and complex notion for Torrance. It is simple in that

> Through the consecrated elements the Church partakes of the very body and blood of Christ, and there is enacted a *true and substantial union* [this is Calvin's normal way of expressing the nature of that union], an ontological union, between Christ and His Church. Christ has become bone of our bone and flesh of our flesh, but in the Eucharist we become bone of His bone and flesh of his flesh. No union, save that of the Persons of the Holy Trinity, could be closer, without passing into absolute identity, than that between Christ and His Church as enacted in the Holy Eucharist.[41]

It is somewhat more complex in that this presence of Christ is a living presence that is both spiritual and bodily and takes the form of the community actually gathering and worshipping in Christ's name only as the Holy Spirit enables his body to appear on earth in each of its gatherings.

> The Church is the point or the sphere in human flesh where the personal union in Christ between God and man creates for itself a corresponding personal fellowship between man and man, within which the relation between the Father and the Son and the Son and the Father is folded out horizontally in history, or (to put it the other way round) within which men in their relations with one

---

[38]   Torrance, *Conflict and Agreement I*, pp. 113–15. See also Torrance, *Conflict and Agreement II*, pp. 172–3.

[39]   Torrance, *Conflict and Agreement I*, p. 115.

[40]   Torrance, *Conflict and Agreement I*, p. 115.

[41]   Torrance, "Eschatology and the Eucharist", *Conflict and Agreement II*, pp. 188–9.

another in creation are given to share in the life and love of the Father and Son
and the Holy Spirit, that is in the Communion of the Spirit.[42]

Thus, this takes place in faith and hope and in the power of his Holy Spirit in
such a way that the church, as the presence of God's Kingdom in the world,
never can be directly observed and can only become apparent at the end "in the
judgement and consummation of the world".[43] In Torrance's view of the Eucharist,
there can be neither any sort of Nestorianism nor any sort of Eutychianism in the
doctrine of "sacramental union" because his understanding of the sacrament is
Christologically dictated and it is indeed dictated by the teaching of Chalcedon
itself. Thus, for Torrance, there can be no

> separation or fusion between the elements of bread and wine and the reality of the
> body and blood of Christ. Just as the humanity of Christ remains true humanity
> even after the resurrection and ascension and so is no docetic phantasm, so the
> bread and wine remain true bread and wine and are no mere species, though by
> consecration they are converted into instruments of the real presence.[44]

But that does not mean it is not real here and now. This reality, however, is
discernable only in faith and by hope as the Holy Spirit enables it. Christ effects
his "carnal union" with all people through the Holy Spirit which is poured out
"on all flesh" and which operates "on all flesh". Objectively, then, all are already
grafted into Christ. But that does not mean that some might not ultimately break
themselves off from this life-giving source of eternal existence. Here the problem
of damnation can be seen in what Torrance calls the "enigma of Judas". Yet even
those who suffer damnation cannot escape the love of God active and revealed in
Jesus Christ because

> His love refuses to allow the sinner to escape being loved and therefore resists
> the sinner's will to isolate himself from that love. His being in hell is not the
> result of God's decision to damn him, but the result of his own decision to
> choose himself against the love of God.[45]

None of this can be properly seen or described in purely juridical terms because
the church is not an "extension of the Incarnation".[46] We have an ontological
relationship with the body and blood of the risen Christ. But it is an ontological
relationship that is established, maintained, shaped and upheld only by the Holy
Spirit and thus it can never be directly equated with the institutional church or its

---

[42]   Torrance, *The School of Faith*, p. cxviii.

[43]   Torrance, *The School of Faith*, p. cxvi.

[44]   Torrance, "Eschatology and the Eucharist", *Conflict and Agreement II*, p. 188.

[45]   Torrance, *The School of Faith*, pp. cxiv–cxv.

[46]   Torrance, *The School of Faith*, pp. cxii–cxiii.

juridical and structural existence and activity. Torrance believes that the church as the Body of Christ is one because Christ and his Spirit exist as a unity in the one being of God himself. Because of that, any division in the church on earth represents a tearing asunder of that oneness already effected in Christ's own life, death and resurrection and in which all are included.

But Torrance insists that union of churches is not something that can be achieved or maintained by any sort of "will to power".[47] The church cannot use temporal power to achieve these ends because that would undermine the reality of the church's existence as the Body of Christ who suffered and died for the church. Its own historical form can only be one of taking up its cross and following Christ and of allowing the living Lord to build his Kingdom on earth as it is in heaven through the Holy Spirit. What Torrance opposes, then, is the "use of political theology as a basic hermeneutic to interpret the Gospel and the mission of the Church in the world today" because in doing this they "become trapped in an ecclesiastical will to power".[48] He opposes using temporal power to attain spiritual ends because this is not the way the church as the Body of Christ exists as the Kingdom of God on earth between the time of Jesus' resurrection, ascension and second coming. The determination to use temporal power to attain unity or universality will always mean that the positive evangelical and spiritual forces at work in the church will be suppressed. Torrance's call back to the Gospel is important because the unity of church already exists by virtue of its union with its heavenly Head as his Body on earth. On the strength of this real union, the church must work tirelessly to see that there is no division in the life of the church on earth. While this cannot be achieved through the "will to power", it certainly can be achieved, at least provisionally prior to Christ's second coming, through prayer for the Holy Spirit, through worship and through our obedience to the Word of God calling us away from all forms of self-reliance and toward union with Christ through faith and in hope.

## The Church as a Community of Reconciliation

The church is also a community of reconciliation. "That is what the Church is meant to be as the Body of Christ, a community of reconciliation bringing to men the healing of the Cross, and living out in their midst the reconciled life, drawing

---

[47]  Torrance, "Ecumenism", *Theology in Reconciliation*, p. 78.

[48]  Torrance, "Ecumenism", *Theology in Reconciliation*, p. 79. On a very practical level, Torrance would oppose using economic and political pressure to oppose evils such as racism because such activities ultimately "play into the hands of the secular will to power". He also opposed the Roman Catholic Church's use of canon law "to build up its own internal power and to impose its will upon the temporal order" ("Ecumenism", *Theology in Reconciliation*, p. 78). See also Torrance, *The Mediation of Christ*, pp. 30–31.

them into its own fellowship of peace with God and with all men."[49] Torrance believes that it is tragic that the church has allowed division which disrupts creation to enter the church itself, creating division where there should be unity. The church, meant to live as a community of love and reconciliation in union with Christ, actually displays to the world division, and to that extent it is in conflict with itself as the community that should be one as a communion of love and faith "in the One Lord". In spite of this, God still makes use of the church, just as he made the cross itself serve the purposes of his love.

It is Holy Communion that requires the church to work to overcome all division and to seek reconciliation with those "from whom it is estranged". Unity is, in Torrance's view, a "holy gift" from God and is to be seen as "the very essence of its salvation in Christ" and thus it cannot be ignored or rejected. It must be embraced and lived out even in the sphere of sinful history just because the church is a community that is one by being united with Christ. The church suffers as it works to serve the Gospel and awaits Christ's own manifestation of himself because the church takes up its cross to follow him not as "co-redeemer with Christ"[50] but as a community that exists in solidarity with a world gone astray and prays and intercedes for the world before God himself. Torrance's goal of reconciliation among the churches can be reached only by starting from the "central fact that Jesus Christ loved the Church and gave Himself for it, and by His Spirit made it His own Body. From the oneness of Christ we will try to understand the unity of the Church in Him".[51] The practical connection, then, between Christ's reconciling death and the lives we are to live as those who are reconciled in him implies that we are actually called to live out the oneness among ourselves that has been created by the communion we have with Christ in his body and blood: "by feeding upon the Body and Blood of Christ [the community] must live out in its own bodily existence the union and communion in which it participates in Christ".[52]

Practically speaking, this means, to Torrance, that the Christian church is called above all to "Intercommunion". Because our communion in the body and blood of Christ is actually our sharing in the atoning grace of the cross and resurrection of Jesus himself, we must work toward visible unity as a community of reconciliation. This means that "To eat the Body and drink the Blood of Christ sincerely is to resolve to act out that Communion in the body; to engage in Intercommunion obliges the Churches to work out their reconciliation, seeking how unity in faith and order may be achieved between them".[53] In this context, Torrance specifically refers to unity between the Church of Scotland and the Church of England and to the fact that the latter seems to understand the Eucharist as an expression of prior

---

[49] Torrance, *Conflict and Agreement I*, p. 118.

[50] Torrance, *Conflict and Agreement I*, p. 119

[51] Torrance, *Conflict and Agreement I*, p. 123.

[52] Torrance, *Conflict and Agreement I*, p. 119. See also *Conflict and Agreement II*, p. 187.

[53] Torrance, *Conflict and Agreement I*, p. 125.

unity residing in the episcopacy, whereas the former sees the Eucharist as the "Lord's Supper" so that "He invites to it whom He will".[54]

Such a church will be marked by "steadfast continuity in the teaching of the Apostles, fellowship or sharing together in a common life of faith, eucharistic communion, prayer and worship, and common Christian aid to the poor and needy in the world (cf. Acts 2:42ff.)".[55] As noted above in Chapter 1, Torrance himself has done much to bring Reformed and Orthodox churches together by focusing on their common faith in the Trinity. It is precisely by his appeal to the thinking of Athanasius and Cyril of Alexandria that Torrance hopes his presentation of a "non-dualist" vision of the church grounded beyond itself in the triune God will bring together Evangelical, Catholic and Orthodox churches to affirm the substance of the faith and move away from those dualistic presentations of the past that have divided them.[56] Significantly, Torrance also insists that Israel cannot be left out of this ecumenical movement because his goal is for "the reconciliation and unification of the whole people of God".[57]

For Torrance, however, there are barriers to intercommunion associated with differing views of priestly power. For instance, he believes that the Roman Catholic view of priesthood implies that the priest has the power over the Eucharist, while the Evangelical view respects the fact that it is the Holy Spirit alone, over whom no one has control, who

> makes Christ present in its [the church's] midst ... [so that] at the holy Eucharist the minister obeys the will of God and celebrates according to the institution of Christ; but in the miraculous presence of the Word made flesh he can exercise no control, for it is the Lord's Supper ... and not his own ... ; *it is the subjection of the Eucharist to the control of the priesthood here which lies behind all denial of Intercommunion.*[58]

Once again, because Jesus Christ, the Son of Man, is *Lord* of the Eucharist—it is the *Lord's* Supper not the church's or the priest's—therefore

> In the presence of the Son of Man the barriers to intercommunion are thrown down ... the Son of Man reserves the right to dispense His own Supper to whom He will, and to distribute the holy bread to the outcasts and the hungry, in spite

---

54 Torrance, *Conflict and Agreement I*, p. 124.
55 Torrance, "Ecumenism", *Theology in Reconciliation*, p. 70.
56 See especially Torrance, "Ecumenism", *Theology in Reconciliation*, p. 75.
57 Torrance, "Ecumenism", *Theology in Reconciliation*, p. 75.
58 Torrance, *Conflict and Agreement I*, p. 161; emphasis mine. In this context, Torrance expresses his belief that the doctrine of the assumption actually leads to this misunderstanding.

of all priestly protestations. In the presence of the eschatological Christ, the Son of Man, all barriers to intercommunion are broken down.[59]

Torrance sees all misunderstanding of the function of priesthood as rooted in a failure to acknowledge Christ's unique high priestly function within the church. This is particularly evident, he thinks, in the Roman Catholic teachings regarding Mary's assumption into heaven.[60] One of the by-products of this teaching, he believed, was the belief that at Mass

> the priesthood gives birth to the Eucharistic Christ, and joins Him to the Church in one body ... the priesthood also extends the work of Christ, repeating and perpetuating in time His propitiatory sacrifice ... the priesthood exercises such controlling power in and over the Church that it becomes a unique and divine order.[61]

Torrance opposes any notion that the church prolongs or extends the incarnation as a kind of Pelagianism.[62] Torrance rejected this thinking because he believed the church had power neither over Christ nor over the Holy Spirit.

## Torrance's View of Grace in Relation to the Roman Catholic View

Specifically with regard to the Roman Catholic Church, Torrance notes that dialogue is made more difficult by the fact that this church "does not acknowledge anything within its own tradition greater or higher than its own tradition". This makes it difficult, if not impossible, for it to "transcend itself".[63] Behind this very serious difficulty lies the problem in the Roman Catholic conceptions of grace and sin. In Torrance's view, grace, for Roman Catholics, "is construed in essentially ontological and causal categories, and is therefore assimilated to the language of nature". This, for Torrance, represents a radical departure from the apostolic tradition. And behind this notion there lurks a view of grace shaped more by "heathen literature, piety and mysteries of the ancient Mediterranean world" than of the Bible. Under the influence of thinkers such as Tertullian, with his tendency to assimilate the Christian view of the Spirit with the Stoic, and Augustine, with his tendency toward elements of Neo-Platonism, and mediaeval theology, with its Aristotelian categories, "'grace' became something very far removed from what

---

[59]   Torrance, *Conflict and Agreement II*, p. 192.

[60]   See Torrance, *Conflict and Agreement II*, p. 160.

[61]   Torrance, *Conflict and Agreement II*, p. 161. This was referred to above as "sacerdotalism".

[62]   Torrance, "The Roman Doctrine of Grace", *Theology in Reconstruction*, p. 176.

[63]   Torrance, *Conflict and Agreement I*, p. 146.

was meant by St. Paul and St. John".[64] Divine grace came to be conceptualized as flowing "from the divine nature into human nature where it can be spoken of as created grace".

> Grace is thus assimilated to the concept of being and there is a graduated infusion of grace corresponding to the grand hierarchy of being. In this way the whole of Roman soteriology and sacramentalism is built up round the basic conception of the deification of creaturely man.[65]

For Torrance, it is because God communicates himself to us that, when it comes to understanding the meaning of God's grace, we must always remember that "The Gift and the Giver are one".[66] Therefore,

> Grace is not something that can be detached from God and made to inhere in creaturely being as "created grace"; nor is it something that can be proliferated in many forms; nor is it something that we can have more or less of, as if grace could be construed in quantitative terms. This is the Reformation doctrine of *tota gratia*. Grace is whole and indivisible because it is identical with the personal self-giving of God to us in his Son. It is identical with Jesus Christ.[67]

All of this means that the basic differences concerning both grace and nature and ministry and sacrament stem from what he sees as a fundamental form of monophysite Christology operating in Roman Catholic thought; this is certainly not something intended, Torrance insists, but it does unfortunately occur.[68] Put

---

[64]  Torrance, *Conflict and Agreement I*, p. 147. See also Torrance, "The Roman Doctrine of Grace", *Theology in Reconstruction*, pp. 169–91. Torrance opposes thinking of grace as a "supernatural quality" that is "infused into the soul". Such thinking is more Hellenistic than biblical and detaches grace from the personal activity of Christ himself, thus leading to a "lapse into the Hellenistic notion of pneumatic potency". There can be no associating grace with the Holy Spirit unless the Spirit is seen to be *homoousion* with the Son. Torrance also opposed thinking of grace as a means that was "dispensed and controlled through institutional structures" because this would always lead to the idea that we can *use* grace for our own purposes. Finally, Torrance objected to the idea of "irresistible grace" which saw grace as a "divine mode of causation at work in the universe, in nature as well as in supernature, and leading from one to the other" (Torrance, "The Roman Doctrine of Grace", *Theology in Reconstruction*, pp. 172–3). See also Torrance, *The Doctrine of Grace*, pp. 31ff.

[65]  Torrance, *Conflict and Agreement I*, p. 147.

[66]  Torrance, "The Roman Doctrine of Grace", *Theology in Reconstruction*, p. 182. See also Torrance, *Royal Priesthood*, p. 66, *The Trinitarian Faith*, pp. 24, 140–41, and *The Christian Doctrine of God*, p. 147.

[67]  Torrance, "The Roman Doctrine of Grace", *Theology in Reconstruction*, pp. 182–3.

[68]  See Torrance, "The Roman Doctrine of Grace", *Theology in Reconstruction*, p. 186.

another way, he opposes what he sees as a "transubstantiation of human nature into the divine or any commingling of the divine with the human".[69]

In other words, Torrance opposes a notion of deification of human nature that would in any way go beyond the *"inconfuse, immutabiliter, indivise,* and *inseparabiliter"* of Chalcedon in its teaching regarding the relation of the divine and human in Christ himself.[70] Instead, he interprets "deification" as Athanasius did, to mean that we participate in Christ's divinity through our union and communion with Christ in his human nature. It is only because divine and human natures are hypostatically united in Christ that, when we are really united with him in his humanity, we "partake of all his benefits, such as justification and sanctification and regeneration … in him we really are made partakers of the eternal Life of God himself". This, however, can take place only through the action of the Holy Spirit and through the power of his resurrection as we actually participate in his new humanity as the risen and ascended Lord.[71] While Torrance accepts the fact that those who embrace the idea of "created grace" might intend this same reality, he nonetheless believes that such an idea is misleading, because "created grace" goes beyond the mystery disclosed in Christ and recognized at Chalcedon by attempting to flatten out the mystery that there is a genuine union of divinity and humanity in him but not a confusion of the two. Classically, the monophysite error sins against the *inconfuse* of Chalcedon by presenting Christ as a "divine man" or a "human God". This is expressed sacramentally, in Torrance's thinking, in the idea of "transubstantiation in the Mass" which points to "some docetic error in Christology," namely, "to a transubstantiation of the human nature of Christ, leaving only a *species* to remain".[72] And where Christ's humanity as the risen, ascended and advent Lord is eradicated in this way, room is created for other mediators than Christ himself. And this opens the door to what Torrance sees as the distorted Roman Catholic teaching on Mary and the priesthood.

For Torrance, the whole church must be seen as both justified in Christ and yet sinful because redemption has not yet occurred. But he notes that Roman Catholic theology holds that "the Church as a whole is perfect and without spot or stain" and yet "they are forced to acknowledge that its members are not without sin".[73] This thinking, he believes, is a rather convoluted attempt to maintain the doctrine of justification by grace alone and yet it falters precisely because it attempts to preserve the church "as a whole" as sinless while attributing sins to its members. This makes no sense except on the ground of the doctrine of the immaculate conception, which Torrance sees as the apex of how sin really is misunderstood by Roman Catholic theologians. This doctrine, for Torrance, undercuts the patristic principle that what was not assumed was not saved because it teaches that Mary

---

[69]   Torrance, *Conflict and Agreement I*, p. 148.

[70]   Torrance, "The Roman Doctrine of Grace", *Theology in Reconstruction*, p. 184.

[71]   Torrance, "The Roman Doctrine of Grace", *Theology in Reconstruction*, p. 184.

[72]   Torrance, "The Roman Doctrine of Grace", *Theology in Reconstruction*, p. 184.

[73]   Torrance, *Conflict and Agreement I*, p. 148.

was without original or actual sin before the incarnation took place. The crucial difference here concerns the fact that in the incarnation Christ assumed our sinful, fallen humanity in order to heal and redeem it.[74]

Torrance believes that the Roman Catholic teaching on the immaculate conception and the assumption undercuts full belief in the incarnation because of this refusal to accept the fact that the Son assumes our fallen humanity; in effect, this means refusal to accept the fact that the church actually is his "earthly historical body" which he has justified and sanctified. It is in the doctrine of the assumption that the church confuses itself with Jesus Christ who alone is risen and ascended into heaven. And it is this doctrine, Torrance insists, that gives rise to the idea that somehow the priesthood "which continues to beget the Church from age to age as the body of Christ" is substituted for the Royal Priest.[75] This problem, for Torrance, arises exactly because Christ's true humanity is overshadowed and ignored when it is thought that Mary and not Christ alone was assumed bodily into heaven. This is the monophysite problem in Christology that he believes entraps the Roman Catholic position on Mary, the priesthood and church unity. Conceptualizing the church as "full of grace", as Mary is "full of grace", makes it

---

[74] See Torrance, *Conflict and Agreement I*, pp. 148–9. See the important discussion in Torrance, *Royal Priesthood* about the role of the ascension here. See also Torrance, *Karl Barth*, pp. 231–2, and "Athanasius", *Theology in Reconciliation*, pp. 228, 230. This thinking stems from the "Latin Heresy", that is, a form of dualistic thinking that refuses to take seriously the full incarnation of the Word within our sinful humanity in order to heal us from within. See also T.F. Torrance, "Scientific Hermeneutics according to St. Thomas Aquinas", *The Journal of Theological Studies*, October 1962, Vol. XIII, Part 2: 259–89. In an otherwise very sympathetic treatment, Torrance maintains that Thomas Aquinas ultimately would not say that "what the word is in the humanity of Christ he is antecedently and eternally in God, for the incarnate form does not apply eternally", and then asks: "Does this not mean that the incarnation of the *word* is ultimately only an episode in the life and activity of God?" (276). In Torrance's view, it is Thomas's very notion of God that is the problem because "his Aristotelian preconceptions prevented him from thinking through fully the implications of the incarnation for the Christian understanding of God" (281).

[75] Torrance, *Conflict and Agreement I*, p. 151. Christ's Royal Priesthood is utterly unique. Only he exercises this. As his Body on earth, the church participates in his priesthood by faith and by grace. That is why Torrance insists that "Christ's ministry is absolutely unique. *Sacerdotium Christi non est in genere*" (Torrance, *Royal Priesthood*, p. 36). Here is where Torrance's insistence that the church as the Body of Christ cannot be confused with Christ himself is important. It means ultimately that the church's ministry cannot be seen as the continuation or extension of the incarnation. Such a view "by-passes the resurrection and the ascension and seeks to ground the ministry of the Church entirely on the historical Jesus". This damages the fact that for the New Testament the church participates in the "whole ministry of Christ". He alone is the Prophet, Priest and King, while the church's ministry is "prophetic, priestly and kingly" but only in dependence on Christ himself. "The ministry of the Church is in no sense an extension of the ministry of Christ or a prolongation of certain of his ministerial functions" (Torrance, *Royal Priesthood*, p. 37).

impossible to conceive of the unity of the church in a way that "allows a distinctive place for the will of God and for the will of man".[76]

A further difficulty concerns the relation of history and tradition. No longer is Christ himself seen as the ultimate and ongoing judge of our reading of Scripture and our understanding of tradition, but rather the Roman Catholic Church makes itself the "master of all tradition", thus identifying "Truth with its own Subjectivity".[77] This is particularly problematic because it allows the doctrine of the physical assumption of Mary, for instance, to be held without the slightest bit of historical evidence for it in the apostolic tradition.[78] Its evidence is instead traced to popular piety and to a view of doctrinal development that does not acknowledge the eschatological reserve mentioned above. This thinking actually is epitomized in the *analogia entis* which makes the Roman Catholic Church, in its own self-consciousness, "the ultimate criterion of the truth".[79]

The same problem is in evidence in the doctrine of papal infallibility which also identifies the "spirit of the Roman Church with the Holy Spirit" and "the historical consciousness of the Roman tradition with the Mind of Christ".[80] On a practical level, the doctrine of the assumption asserts, firstly, that Mary does not belong to the church waiting for the coming of its Lord and for the redemption of the body. Secondly, somehow Jesus' uniqueness is transferred to Mary by some sort of *communicatio idiomatum* so that she can be referred to not only as "*Maria Mediatrix et Corredemptrix* and even as *Filia Dei* and *Dea*" but as ascended into heaven like Christ himself.[81] This teaching can only lead to a final denial of the second coming of Christ himself with its fully realized eschatology, at least in the case of Mary. Thirdly, all of this leads to a concept of the church and the priesthood that is thought to miraculously continue to give birth to the church in history as Mary gave birth to Jesus himself. This in turn gives rise to the ideas that the priest not only "extends the work of Christ", but that the priest

---

[76]    Torrance, *Conflict and Agreement I*, p. 151.

[77]    Torrance, *Conflict and Agreement I*, p. 152.

[78]    Torrance points out that not only is there no scriptural authority for this dogma, but that the idea of Mary's physical assumption is "contrary to the unique eschatological character of Christ's Resurrection and Ascension ... [and] it turns the assumption of Mary into one of the saving acts of God alongside the salvation-events of Christ Himself" (*Conflict and Agreement I*, p. 157). Indeed, Torrance notes that after the sixth century in the liturgy there was no talk of a physical assumption of Mary. He notes also that even as late as 1568 the church officially said it did not know what happened to Mary's body after her death. The most problematic difficulty here for Torrance, however, is not that there is no historical evidence for the dogma, but that the Roman Catholic Church claims to produce "apostolic tradition ... at will ... out of itself" (p. 157).

[79]    Torrance, *Conflict and Agreement I*, p. 152.

[80]    Torrance, *Conflict and Agreement I*, p. 153. See also Torrance, *God and Rationality*, p. 129.

[81]    Torrance, *Conflict and Agreement I*, p. 160.

repeats and perpetuates Christ's sacrifice in the Mass and even "gives birth to the Eucharistic Christ, and joins Him to the Church in one body".[82] All of this thinking, for Torrance, undercuts Christ's actual uniqueness as well as his actual historical and eschatological mediation of us to the Father as the eternal High Priest and as Prophet and King.[83]

## Prophet, Priest and King and the Sacraments of Baptism and the Lord's Supper

A proper understanding of the relation between Christ's ministry as the Royal Priest, described in the letter to the Hebrews, and the church's ministry must be conceptualized in connection with the relation of the Head and members of the Body because it is a relation of service to Christ on the part of the church. The most important point to be made in this regard is that "it is always Christ Himself who is at work, nourishing, sustaining, ordering, and governing His Church on earth" *through* the church's obedient ministry.[84] It is through his Spirit that he enables the church to minister by preaching Christ crucified and risen; he enables the church to "declare forgiveness of sins, and call all men to be reconciled to God". But, most decisively, "it is the Lord Himself who is present in the midst of His Church as the Word made flesh making the preaching of the Gospel effectual as Word and Power of God".[85] This, of course, is his prophetic activity, in which the church is included in a genuine relation with him and thus with the entire Trinity in history without losing its humanity but rather gaining its true humanity through participating in his new humanity. It is also through the Spirit that the church is commanded and enabled to administer both Baptism and the Lord's Supper. Yet again, it is Christ himself "who is present in the midst of this Church as our High Priest who cleanses the Church in His own Blood, feeds it with Himself, blesses it with His Spirit, renews it in the power of His resurrection and presents it as His own Body to the Father".[86]

This realistic imagery conveys the kind of real presence Torrance has in mind when he speaks of the sacrament of the Lord's Supper within the perspective of Christ's own High Priestly ministry; this is a unique ministry that enables the ministry of those in the church who are in his service. To celebrate the Lord's Supper means above all, for Torrance, that the church is renewed in faith, in that

---

[82] See Torrance, *Conflict and Agreement II*, pp. 150–51 and 156–62, for his account of the assumption of Mary.

[83] As we shall see below, this does not mean that Torrance's own theology of the Eucharist might not be used to further an ecumenical understanding of eucharistic sacrifice.

[84] Torrance, *Royal Priesthood*, p. 37.

[85] Torrance, *Royal Priesthood*, p. 38.

[86] Torrance, *Royal Priesthood*, p. 38.

Christians, by virtue of their baptism, literally share in the body and blood of the new humanity of the risen, ascended and coming Lord. In this sense, faith does not refer to a relation that is somehow less than real on the human and historical level. No. It is a genuine *ontological* renewal; ontological because it is real sharing in the new humanity of the risen Lord himself who acts as Priest, Prophet and King in and through these specific historical activities of the church between the time of his first and second coming.[87] And Christians do not just do this in some spiritual way that ignores the body because it is the incarnate Lord with whom they are in union. They do it rather by eating his flesh and drinking his blood in the eucharistic celebration itself. This is a theme Torrance frequently repeats in many of his writings. The Holy Spirit, who is inseparable from the Son and Father within both the immanent and economic Trinity, enables us to feed on the body and blood of Christ himself without having to conceptualize bread and wine as something other than they are and without having to conceptualize our new humanity as something more or other than genuine human being existing in relation to the risen Lord himself and awaiting his return and the final redemption of the body.

Torrance's thinking about the Lord's Supper actually has a bearing upon his notion of ministry within the church as well. He believes that while the church is sent out into the world which still exists "under the law as servant of Christ", it is nonetheless "joined in One Body and One Spirit with Christ risen from the dead". Hence, the church cannot be tied to the world and patterned by its historical limitations. It must rather use these to proclaim God's Word.

> As through the fraction of the bread the Church ever becomes one Body in the Lord's Supper, so the Church that dares to proclaim that death till He come and to enact that proclamation in the mortification of its members on earth, finds itself ordered according to the new humanity after the image of the Creator.[88]

Torrance therefore believes that it is in the Lord's Supper especially that the two important aspects of the church's order are held together: there is the "*nomos*-form of historical succession on the stage of this world" and there is the "aspect that derives from the new being of the Church in the risen Lord"[89] which must be conceptualized together with Paul's emphasis on "the *charismata* and their relation to the real presence of Christ". They are, for Torrance, the "means by which the ascended Christ who sends down His Spirit upon the Church orders it in the love of God". Hence the *charismata* are valid "only in the real presence of Christ to the Church".[90] It is here that Torrance expresses his view of ministry by asserting that he does not deny tradition or "even juridical succession", but rather wishes to subordinate these

---

87    See, for example, Torrance, *Royal Priesthood*, p. 29.
88    Torrance, *Royal Priesthood*, p. 71.
89    Torrance, *Royal Priesthood*, p. 71.
90    Torrance, *Royal Priesthood*, p. 71.

to the presence of the living Lord, and to give outward successions in ministerial orders their place as signs of *charismata* in the Church, signs of the divine New Order which in the Gospel and Sacraments is ever breaking through the Church into the world and ever being realised afresh in our midst.[91]

Thinking this way, Torrance insists that Christ is present precisely as the risen Lord of the church as he makes use of the sacraments. But he is not bound by these forms. That is why succession is not to be seen as a "closed succession". In fact, it is in his view of the Eucharist that ministry is most clearly expressed. In this sacrament, "Church order is seen to be only *in actu*. At the Eucharist Christ is fully present, present bodily, and it is there that in the profoundest sense the Church becomes the Church as Body of Christ".[92] Hence, the church receives its form as it exists in communion with "the Body and Blood of Christ". As it carries out this ordinance, it is his body. In obedience to the Word, the church assumes its true form in the Eucharist—this is something, however, that is dynamic rather than static and thus, "It cannot be abstracted from the Real Presence of the Risen Lord and then used as a criterion to judge the Church or to establish the validity of ministry. That would be the essence of self-justification".[93]

This means, of course, that misunderstanding will arise if the meaning of Christ's presence is sought and found in the church and its continuity instead of in Christ as the risen, ascended and coming Lord present in his Spirit.[94] Christ's real presence in the Eucharist "stands above the institutional continuity of the Church, and can never be made relative to it, for that would make the Church the master of Christ's presence and not Christ the Master of the Church".[95] It is in this sense, when we consider the fact that it is the *Lord's* Supper and not the product of the church's activity and consciousness, that Torrance stresses once more that there are important reasons for intercommunion: the Lord's Supper could be and should be seen as the place where our disorders are healed. And Torrance supports this position in this context insisting, firstly, that no ecumenical council has ever made agreement regarding the Lord's Supper "a prerequisite for unity or reunion". The Nicene Creed mentions one baptism and is normative here, says Torrance. Secondly, the unity presupposed by the Lord's Supper, Torrance says, is the unity of baptism into the one body of Christ. To refuse the Eucharist to those who are baptized into Christ "would seem to amount either to a denial of Baptism or to attempted schism within the Body of Christ". Thirdly, behind all of this lies the meaning of atonement through Christ's blood. For churches to refuse to unite at the Lord's Table "is surely to deny the sacrifice of Christ, for He loved the Church

---

[91]  Torrance, *Royal Priesthood*, pp. 71–2.
[92]  Torrance, *Royal Priesthood*, p. 72.
[93]  Torrance, *Royal Priesthood*, p. 72.
[94]  See Torrance, *Royal Priesthood*, p. 106.
[95]  Torrance, *Royal Priesthood*, p. 106.

and died for it to make it one in Him".[96] To proclaim reconciliation and atonement and then not to live as those reconciled "in the Communion of the Body and Blood of Christ" is to really limit the efficacy of Christ's atoning death.[97]

One further point regarding ministry needs to be made here very briefly. Because ministry, including priesthood, means witnessing to the Royal Priesthood of Christ himself, Torrance insists that both sides in the debate about ordaining women seem to misunderstand the real issues. Those who favor ordination of women and those who reject such ordination both tend to focus on the idea of "power", in which priests are given the power to celebrate the Eucharist and to give absolution. In Torrance's thinking, this misses the point of a priesthood shaped by the suffering, death and resurrection of Christ himself because it neglects the fact that "Christ himself … is the real Celebrant" and thus ministers and priests must "retreat before the presence of Christ".[98] Torrance links this to a Christology which emphasizes Christ's divinity at the expense of his humanity and thus searches for other human mediators than Christ because the divine Christ could no longer be approached from the human side. This led to the idea of a priesthood that could stand in for Christ. There is, however, no need for this because Christ himself is the High Priest who is active even now in the witness and actions of those who are obedient to him. When priesthood is seen in this light, then, Torrance insists that there is no problem in ordaining women as well as men because both share in Christ's humanity and all are one in him. To restrict ordination to males in effect would be to misconstrue the incarnation itself. In the incarnation, the Word assumed human nature into unity with his divine nature and so overcame any inequality between men and women and so it would be a mistake to focus on Christ's maleness to exclude women from the priesthood.[99]

Christ continues to mediate himself and to act as our High Priest before the Father so that ministry means service of him in the church. That is why ministers and priests cannot be said to represent us before the Father—that would impinge on the

---

[96]   Torrance, *Royal Priesthood*, p. 105.

[97]   Torrance, *Royal Priesthood*, p. 106.

[98]   Torrance, *Royal Priesthood*, pp. xi, xiii.

[99]   Torrance makes a persuasive case for his position in *The Ministry of Women* (Edinburgh: The Handsel Press, 1992). And in fact his case is made with specific reference to the Eucharist where he insists that the minister does not act in his own name but in the name of Christ and thus "yields place to Christ, lets Christ take his place, never in such away that he takes Christ's place or acts in his stead" (p. 11). Torrance believes that "there are no intrinsic theological reasons why women should not be ordained to the Holy Ministry of the Word and Sacrament; rather, there are genuine theological reasons why they may be ordained and consecrated in the service of the Gospel" (p. 12). Among those are: the incarnation and new order of creation; the virgin birth, which exposes male sovereignty as sinful and sets it aside; the hypostatic union of divine with human nature in Christ (and not simply maleness); the fact that Christ is one in being with the Father and this being is both beyond gender and governs our view of ministry; the healing of our human nature in Christ; and his atoning sacrifice for all.

living Christ and on his real presence as the subject of the sacraments of Baptism and the Lord's Supper. That would end in a type of sacerdotalism that would place the ministers and priests between us and Christ. And that is the self-justification Torrance opposes. In Torrance's thinking, the ascension plays an important role here because Christ is not visibly present and so we cannot discern his body as we shall be able to when he comes again. We have no control in this matter and thus no church order can be directly read off from the Lord's Supper because Revelation is concealed in the creaturely reality of our fallen world and is disclosed only by God himself. Torrance agrees with Albert the Great, Peter Lombard, Bonaventura and Thomas Aquinas that while priesthood or the presbyterate "is ordained to celebrate the Eucharist within the corporate priesthood of the whole Body, the order of priesthood is itself ordered by the Sacrament of the Eucharist".[100] To Torrance, this means that since the Eucharist is the *Lord's* Supper, he alone is the one who orders "His own Table, and graciously grants us to serve as deacons or waiters at it". This means the priesthood "cannot be managed".[101] Thus, there is "a doctrine of the priesthood of the whole Church through its participation in the substitutionary Self-consecration of Christ our High Priest".[102] Christ himself, for Torrance, "is the one Priest, and men are ordained only in the sense that He gives them to share in His Priesthood ... in a mode appropriate to those who are but stewards and servants".[103]

Moreover, Christ is also present "through the One Spirit as King governing the Church and using it as the instrument of His Gospel in the extension of His Kingdom and the renewal of the world". Hence, "Throughout the whole prophetic, priestly, and kingly ministry of the Church, it is Christ Himself who presides as Prophet, Priest and King, but He summons the Church to engage in *His* ministry by witness (μαρτυρία), by stewardship (οἰκονομια), and by service (διακονία)".[104] What all of this means is that the church's ministry of reconciliation is to be seen as a participation in the movement of the Head of the Body downward, enabling the church to participate in the movement of God's grace "within the irreversible relationship of Lord and servant, Head and Body, in subordination, and in entire conformity, to the Kingdom of Christ".[105] Ministry in the church that reflects this movement never attempts to represent the church before God, supposing that the church's ministers could act on behalf of others before God. Rather, because ministry is witness to the unique activity of Christ in the midst of the church as Priest, Prophet and King, the church is not democratically grounded as though it was built up from the members of the church toward God. It is the other way

---

[100] Torrance, *Royal Priesthood*, p. 77.

[101] Torrance, *Royal Priesthood*, p. 79.

[102] Torrance, *Royal Priesthood*, p. 80. Torrance here relies on the letter to the Hebrews and John 17.

[103] Torrance, *Royal Priesthood*, p. 81.

[104] Torrance, *Royal Priesthood*, p. 38.

[105] Torrance, *Royal Priesthood*, p. 38.

around. Ministry represents the Head of the Body for the members, but not the members, because it is only the instrument of the Head actively uniting the members to himself. They receive their commission from the risen and ascended Lord and not from the church. In everything, it is always Christ himself who is the enabling condition of the church's witness. And this happens from above and not from below.[106]

Clearly, then, Torrance understands Christ's prophetic, priestly and kingly offices in relation to the Holy Spirit who proceeds from the Father through the Son. This is in keeping with his belief that the Spirit must be understood both in terms of Christ applying his finished work to us and of humanity receiving the fruits of that work. With regard to Christ's prophetic office, "the Spirit is indeed the prophetic Spirit who continues to utter Christ the Word and utters the Word with all the quickening, life-giving power of God".[107] As we have noted, it is imperative that the Spirit in its "quickening power" not be separated from the Word because "the Spirit is correlative to Christ's Prophetic Office ... as Advocate".[108] In other words, all that Torrance said in connection with the doctrine of atonement is brought to bear in his thinking about Christ's prophetic office to mean that Christ actively is present to us, with us and in us now as our advocate. He is, as Torrance so often says, not only "the Word of God to man, but the Word of man to God in perfect response and obedience, and in that two-fold capacity He is our Advocate".[109] Yet he is this as one of us just because of the incarnation. Incarnation must be held together with Christ's activity in his prophetic office or else his work may be divorced from his person and then false notions of atonement as something purely judicial, moral or conditional will follow. Here Christ's prophetic and kingly work as the unique Mediator are inseparably united. Failure to make these particular distinctions will open the door to ideas of mystical identity with the divine or a collapse of divine into human subjectivity, and these ideas, of course, obliterate a true relational understanding of humanity and divinity in Christ. For Torrance, our salvation depends upon the very being of Jesus as God incarnate who continues to represent us as the risen, ascended and coming Lord. That is his prophetic office and it cannot be separated for a moment from the action of the Spirit or from his person as the King who is one in being with the Father from all eternity.

Torrance also insists on keeping together Christ's priestly office as the one who sacrifices himself for us once and for all with his prophetic and incarnational activities as well, because that keeps it from degenerating "into a legal and cultic fiction with no basis in actual existence and reality" so that it becomes irrelevant "to our actual humanity".[110] Beyond this, all of these activities would be meaningless without their connection to Jesus as the Son of God who is the divine King, who

---

106    Torrance, *Royal Priesthood*, pp. 40–41.
107    Torrance, *The School of Faith*, p. ciii.
108    Torrance, *The School of Faith*, p. ciii.
109    Torrance, *The School of Faith*, p. lxxxix.
110    Torrance, *The School of Faith*, p. xc.

became incarnate to save us from sin and death out of pure love. Without this, Christ's priestly activity in atonement "would degenerate into a pagan notion of placating an angry God, and dwindle into a ritualistic superstition".[111] Unless we see clearly that in Jesus' priestly act of sacrifice for us "it is God Himself condescending to provide the sacrifice in His own free act of Incarnation", then "it becomes a Pelagian sacerdotalist conception of appeasing an angry God through human mediation and human sacrifice".[112] This activity must be seen, then, as already noted, as both an act of God *as God* and an act of God *as man* so that *we* do not need to do anything to complete this work or to enable it; we only have to receive it gratefully as the very gift of grace, that is, of God himself enabling our lives as those who are no longer his enemies but his friends, who are now able to live as part of the new creation inaugurated by Christ's own life, death, resurrection and ascension and thus as the fully human beings God intended us to be. This is what Torrance means when he speaks of Christ's advocacy: "He bestows upon us what He in our Humanity has received in the fulness of the Spirit".[113] In this sense, Christ's personal mediation of the Spirit is an integral part of his priestly office, and Pentecost itself

> is the mighty act of the risen and ascended High Priest who has opened the Kingdom of Heaven for all believers, opened a new and living way in His flesh to the Father, and opened the door for the pouring out of the riches of the divine Life and Love upon men.[114]

Regarding Christ's kingly office, Torrance is equally emphatic that Christ's role as *Christus Victor* cannot in any way be separated from his other two offices without serious misunderstanding. In this context, Torrance repeats his belief, noted above in Chapter 5, that it would be a serious mistake to regard our deliverance from the oppression of sin and death through Christ's atoning and expiatory death as a "ransom to the devil". It is rather to be understood in analogy to the Exodus. Redemption means "the expiation of guilt" that "brings justification" and "not only renders man free from the law but thereby also emancipates him from the thraldom of evil". Evil is here seen to have no right or power over us because it is exposed as having "usurped the right of the law of God and through that right to have robbed God of His inheritance in His people and His people of their inheritance in God". This way of thinking eliminates the very idea of understanding expiation and redemption as some sort of ransom paid to the devil.[115] It is imperative, then, that Christ's victory over the powers of sin, evil and death be seen in connection

---

[111]  Torrance, *The School of Faith*, p. xc.

[112]  Torrance, *The School of Faith*, p. xci. One can easily see how Torrance's thinking here relates to his developed view of atonement presented above in Chapter 5.

[113]  Torrance, *The School of Faith*, p. xci.

[114]  Torrance, *The School of Faith*, p. xci.

[115]  Torrance, *The School of Faith*, pp. xcii–xciii.

with his own personal suffering and death on our behalf that culminated on the cross. God's mighty actions for us took place in the weakness of the cross; by Jesus' submission "to all that evil could do to Him", he "broke its power by a meekness and obedience unto the death of the Cross".[116] This is the true and decisive overcoming of the power of sin and death because it is his holiness lived out in our human existence and his submission to the Father's will that freed us from the power of the law "in which evil seeks to clothe itself". In the justification wrought by Jesus, "we are no longer under the judgement or power of the law and are free from its tyranny, and from the evil that usurps its authority". In this way, humanity is stripped of any "claim to the price of ransom". Thus, Christ opens an entirely new way of existence in the freedom of the Spirit.[117]

Again, however, it must be remembered that Christ's kingly office cannot be isolated because if Christ's act of redemption is detached from the fact that he is redeemer precisely as the incarnate Lord, then his redemptive actions dissolve into "mere events, into the *beneficia Christi*, or into the timeless repetition of a mystery".[118] In each of these cases, the focus will be on an aspect of human behavior that opens the door to some form of self-justification and human alienation from God once again. But Torrance does not want to place undue emphasis upon God's transcendent action either because this would only lead to self-justification in the form of undue focus on our human response or some "sacerdotalist notion of ministry", with the necessity of some form of human response substituting for the mediation of Christ himself. This thinking is fatal to true theology because it fails to integrate properly Christ's work as *Victor* with the very being and obedience of Jesus himself. Integrating these three offices, then, will allow us to see that Christ the King must be understood as the "Royal Son of God" who expressed the Father's will to enter history and effect our salvation from within that history and yet also to enable salvation to arise out of our humanity and return back to God the Father. Jesus, the Son, literally brings us back to the throne of God in and through his resurrection and ascension.

It is the Holy Spirit, of course, working as the "power and operation of God", who applies Christ's victory over sin and death to us and thus enables our deliverance from evil here and now. "Through the Spirit Christ clothed with His victory and power is present to us, so that His triumphant work is ever operative and bearing fruit in us."[119] It is through the Spirit that Christ both gives himself to us and at the same time does not come under our control. He remains the Lord and Giver of life and the Savior of the world. Grace therefore is the grace of Christ and not the Spirit. Torrance opposes those strains of tradition in both Protestant and Catholic circles that associated grace with the Spirit because this association, he believes, led theologians to detach grace from Christ and conceptualize it as

---

116   Torrance, *The School of Faith*, p. xciii.

117   Torrance, *The School of Faith*, pp. xciii–xciv.

118   Torrance, *The School of Faith*, p. xciv.

119   Torrance, *The School of Faith*, pp. civ–cv.

"'something' communicable and transmissible" and thus as something that could be "infused". This at once undercuts the ontological connection between Giver and Gift already discussed and opens the door once more to forms of self-justification and Pelagianism. This problem never would have arisen, Torrance thinks, if the Lordship of the Spirit had never been separated from Christ's activity in his kingly office.

## Torrance's Understanding of the Sacraments

We have already touched upon the meaning of Baptism and the Lord's Supper in connection with Torrance's understanding of the Church and ministry, since these sacraments are precisely the way the church is constituted in and by God's Word and Spirit within space and time. Here we need to spell out exactly how Torrance understands Baptism and the Lord's Supper in order to see how his view of the sacraments is specifically grounded in the Trinity and why it is for that very reason a profound and even revolutionary understanding that cuts through the errors of dualism and monism that threaten whenever the sacraments are considered in a context that is not fully trinitarian in nature.

Perhaps the most important factor determining Torrance's view of Baptism and the Lord's Supper is the fact that he sees them determined by their relation to the "whole historical Jesus Christ from his birth to his resurrection and ascension". For this reason, Torrance sees their content not only as God's actions of salvation toward, for and in us, but as those divine actions fulfilled in the humanity of Christ in such a way that Jesus Christ himself is to be seen as the "primary *mysterium or sacramentum*".[120] By this he means that since the Son of God has "incorporated himself into our humanity and assimilated the people of God into himself as his own Body", therefore the sacraments "have to be understood as concerned with our *koinonia* or participation in the mystery of Christ and his Church through the *koinonia* or communion of the Holy Spirit".[121]

## Baptism

For Torrance, there is a depth dimension to the sacrament of baptism that cannot be ignored. And that dimension concerns the fact that, important as the baptismal rite may be (and it is important for Torrance), its meaning can neither be identified with the Church's act of baptizing nor with the response, faith or attitude of the person who is baptized. Why? Because baptism, though an act of Christ *and* his church, is primarily to be understood as an act that God does and will do for us in

---

[120]  Torrance, "The One Baptism Common to Christ and His Church", *Theology in Reconciliation*, pp. 82–105, 82.

[121]  Torrance, "The One Baptism", *Theology in Reconciliation*, p. 82.

his Spirit.[122] In other words, the meaning of the rite of baptism must be found "in the living Christ who cannot be separated from his finished work and who makes himself present to us as such in the power of his own Reality".[123] But Torrance does not want to emphasize Christ's divine action in such a way that it undermines the all-important point that it is his human activity as the eternal Word incarnate in our flesh that actually reverses our sinful inheritance from Adam. He follows Irenaeus, whose view of baptism he considers one of the finest in the early church, to say that through baptism we participate "in the new humanity of Jesus Christ. Hence, the reality of our baptism is to be found in the objective reality of what has already been accomplished for us in Jesus Christ and is savingly operative in us through union and communion with Christ effected by the Spirit".[124]

This is why Torrance contrasts *baptismos* and *baptismas* in order to advance his view of this sacrament. The former was used in Greek to signify "a rite of religious ablution". But the latter was deliberately adopted by Christians in opposition to the Greek notion in order to express the depth dimension that gives meaning to the baptismal rite. The intention, Torrance notes, was to refer us through the rite to "the objective reality in Jesus Christ himself".[125] Jesus is thus to be seen as both the "material content" and the "active agent", since it is the risen Lord himself who is alive and who actively effects a genuine union of those who are baptized with him acting as their Savior. He is present now, sanctifying his church through the power of his Spirit. He does not have to be made present because he is

> actually present with us to the end of the world ... It is Christ in His life-act, Christ with His mighty acts wrought out for us, who is always present with us to the end of the world; so that when we in His Name proclaim the *kerygma* and administer the *baptisma* it is actually Christ Himself, really and fully present, who acts savingly in His Church, revealing Himself and baptizing with His Spirit.[126]

While the baptism of John gave the church its ritual form, that was "transformed and filled with content through Jesus' submission to John's baptism and his fulfilment of it in the whole course of his vicarious obedience".[127] Jesus humbled

---

[122]   Torrance, "The One Baptism", *Theology in Reconciliation*, p. 84.

[123]   Torrance, "The One Baptism", *Theology in Reconciliation*, p. 84.

[124]   Torrance, "The One Baptism", *Theology in Reconciliation*, p. 94.

[125]   Torrance, "The One Baptism", *Theology in Reconciliation*, p. 83. In *Conflict and Agreement II*, pp. 110ff., Torrance offers a clear explanation of these issues and why he thinks *baptisma* relates to the *kerygma* because it is not meant to call attention to the preacher or the preaching but only to Christ; *baptisma* also calls attention only to Christ and what he has done on our behalf and not to the rite itself or to the person who administers it (p. 111).

[126]   Torrance, *Conflict and Agreement II*, pp. 111–12.

[127]   Torrance, "The One Baptism", *Theology in Reconciliation*, pp. 84–5.

himself and, by receiving baptism from John, "identified himself with sinners in obedience to the Father's will that he should make righteousness available for 'the many'".[128] When, at his baptism, he was declared by the Father to be his beloved Son, this was not understood in the early church to mean that Jesus was adopted "to be the Son of God" but rather this was seen as "a public proclamation of his divine Sonship, pointing back to his birth from above of the Spirit, to be the Saviour of the world, and pointing forward to his death on the Cross when he was to fulfil the whole work of atoning redemption".[129]

Beyond this, the early church interpreted the Spirit's coming upon Jesus at his baptism as "his endowment with divine authority" as the one who would open the "Kingdom of Heaven to all baptised in his Name and pour out upon them the fulness of his Spirit".[130] In his resurrection, Jesus was "declared Son of God" and he was given "all power in heaven and earth" by his Father and "installed ... at his right hand". He exercised this power when he commissioned the Apostles and sent them "to make disciples of all nations". After his ascension, Jesus "endowed the Church with power from on high by baptising it with his own Spirit at Pentecost".[131] Pentecost was the counterpart in the church of Jesus' own baptismal experience. The Holy Spirit was sent by the Father in the Son's name and descended upon the apostolic church, thus "sealing it as the people of God redeemed through the blood of Christ, consecrating it to share in the communion of the Father, the Son and the Holy Spirit, and sending it out into the world united with Christ as his Body to engage in the service of the Gospel".[132]

This is the sense in which the commission of the risen Lord to baptize in the name of the Father, Son and Holy Spirit is to be understood. It refers back to Jesus' own baptism in the Jordan and forward to "its complement" in the church's baptism at Pentecost. Jesus lived his entire life experience as incarnate for our sake and certainly not for himself and so this is what forms the basis for both baptisms, in Torrance's thinking. It is important to realize that Torrance accepts Matthew 28:19 as an "authentic utterance of Christ" when Jesus says to go into the whole world and baptize in the name of the Father, Son and Holy Spirit and teach what Jesus himself commanded, remembering that he is with them always even to the end of the world.[133] Moreover, it is exactly here that one can see how the sacrament

---

[128]  Torrance, "The One Baptism", *Theology in Reconciliation*, p. 85.

[129]  Torrance, "The One Baptism", *Theology in Reconciliation*, p. 85.

[130]  Torrance, "The One Baptism", *Theology in Reconciliation*, p. 86.

[131]  Torrance, "The One Baptism", *Theology in Reconciliation*, p. 86.

[132]  Torrance, "The One Baptism", *Theology in Reconciliation*, p. 86.

[133]  See Torrance, *Conflict and Agreement II*, pp. 115–16, and *STR*, p. 7. Torrance notes that the "textual authorities" for this verse are "overwhelmingly strong" so that one could doubt its authenticity "only on purely *a priori* grounds, in a refusal to believe that the name of the Father, Son, and Holy Spirit could be brought together like that on the lips of Jesus. But hesitation in that way must arise from a myopic reading of the Gospels ... for all through them we have to do with the relation of the Son to the Father and with the presence

of baptism is rooted in the Holy Trinity. We are not, Torrance insists, baptized in the name of Christ alone but also in the name of the Father and the Spirit. Since the Father was not crucified and the Spirit did not become incarnate, it would be a mistake to think of baptism "exclusively as Baptism into the death of Christ".[134] We are in fact baptized into that "threefold Name" and that indicates that baptism is a rite "essentially appropriate to the trinitarian character of the baptismatic event, which includes throughout it the relation of the Son to the Father through the Spirit".[135] Baptism, then, involves the fact that the Father's eternal love was given to us in the incarnation of his Son so that we were enabled to have fellowship with the Father through him; it also concerned

> the work of the Spirit through whom Jesus was born of the Virgin Mary, by whom He was anointed as the Christ at His Baptism, through whom He cast out demons and brought the Kingdom to bear redemptively upon the needs of men, through whom again He offered Himself without spot to the Father, and according to whom He was raised from the dead by the Father.[136]

Indeed, this was the Spirit the ascended Christ "poured out upon the Church", thus renewing people "in the power of the resurrection". Since we are baptized into the name of the triune God and since therefore baptism is "ultimately grounded upon the fact that in Jesus the Son of God incorporated Himself into our humanity", it is this union with Christ and thus with the Trinity that gives the sacrament its meaning. Without this link with the incarnation, baptism all too easily might degenerate into "the sacramental mystery of a timeless dying and rising known also to the Semitic and Hellenistic religious mysteries". This, according to Torrance, is what the early church resisted by grounding baptism in the incarnation and not in Romans 6 alone. So while we are baptized into Christ's death and resurrection, we must also realize that baptism "is the Sacrament of the Incarnation, the Sacrament of the Nativity, as it was sometimes called".[137]

Hence, Jesus' baptism of repentance was for our sakes and "in him it was our humanity that was anointed by the Spirit and consecrated in sonship to the Father".[138] It is just here that one can see that Torrance's understanding of baptism is indelibly marked by the actions of the triune God and so is trinitarianly conceived: he was born of the Virgin, lived a life of obedience as the Son for us, sacrificed

---

and power of the Spirit" (*Conflict and Agreement II*, pp. 115–16). Torrance thinks people may have difficulty with the authenticity of this verse just to the extent that they do not give Jesus' own baptism by John its proper place in Christian baptism and so they abstract baptism "from the whole course of Christ's ministry from the Jordan to the Resurrection".

[134]   Torrance, *Conflict and Agreement II*, p. 116.
[135]   Torrance, *Conflict and Agreement II*, pp. 116, 128ff.
[136]   Torrance, *Conflict and Agreement II*, p. 116.
[137]   Torrance, *Conflict and Agreement II*, pp. 116–18.
[138]   Torrance, "The One Baptism", *Theology in Reconciliation*, p. 86.

himself on the cross for us and offered himself "through the eternal Spirit to the Father". None of this was done for his own sake but "for us men and for our salvation".[139] Humanly, Jesus experienced judgment for us. He made atonement for us and in our human nature he rose from the dead. Thus, for Jesus, baptism meant that he took upon himself our unrighteouness and made us righteous. For us, baptism means that

> we become one with him, sharing in his righteousness, and that we are sanctified in him as members of the messianic people of God, compacted together in one Body in Christ. There is *one baptism* and *one Body* through the *one Spirit*. Christ and his Church participate in the one baptism in different ways—Christ actively and vicariously as Redeemer, the Church passively and receptively as the redeemed Community.[140]

This explains why the Nicene creed speaks of one baptism and not of one Eucharist, though one might have expected such a reference. Consequently, baptism is an ordinance whose primary focus is neither upon what we do nor upon what the church does but upon "what God has already done in Christ, and through His Spirit continues to do in and to us ... Baptism is administered *to* us in the Name of the Triune God, and our part is only to receive it, for we cannot add anything to Christ's finished work".[141] Torrance thinks we should understand baptism "stereoscopically". By that he means that we must continually keep in mind the fact that Jesus' baptism with water and the Spirit in the Jordan, his baptism with blood on the cross and the baptism of the church with the Spirit at Pentecost all together give meaning to the church's baptismal action and thus impart to it a dimension of depth. Accordingly, when we are baptized we partake of Christ's baptism and thus of a redemption that "has already been accomplished for us in Christ".[142] It is here that Torrance repeats his all-important point, namely, that in baptism

> we have to look away from ourselves, and look through the administration of the rite, into the crucified and risen Jesus. Hence ... what happens in our baptism into Christ and what happened once and for all in his vicarious baptism are so polarised together into an inseparable unity, that it is quite impossible for us to entertain the idea of rebaptism, for that would be to crucify to ourselves the Son of God afresh, and put him to an open shame.[143]

---

[139] Torrance, "The One Baptism", *Theology in Reconciliation*, p. 86.

[140] Torrance, "The One Baptism", *Theology in Reconciliation*, p. 87. Torrance stresses that, for Athanasius, "it is in baptism that 'the fullness of the mystery ... is lodged, for it is given in the name of the Father, Son and Holy Spirit'" (*The Trinitarian Faith*, p. 290).

[141] Torrance, "The One Baptism", *Theology in Reconciliation*, p. 88.

[142] Torrance, "The One Baptism", *Theology in Reconciliation*, p. 89.

[143] Torrance, "The One Baptism", *Theology in Reconciliation*, p. 89.

Whenever this "stereo-understanding" was not maintained, then all of the problems relating to sacramental practice began to arise and did indeed arise. The whole issue of rebaptism only emerged when the rite was disjoined from the dimension depth in the life of Christ himself as the Lord who must continually give meaning to the rite for it to have objective validity. For it is only if he is not seen as the objective guarantee of our repentance that the whole question of whether or not baptism washes away *only* original sin could arise in the first instance. When the unrepeatability of baptism was tied only to this fact, namely, that it only washed away original sin, then it was thought that other sacraments were needed to supplement baptism in order for those who sinned after baptism to be forgiven. Torrance, of course, rejects any idea that there could be more than two sacraments because Baptism and the Eucharist are the only two sacraments actually instituted by Christ himself. And thus these are the only two sacraments that can explicitly find their dimension of depth in the life, death and resurrection of Jesus and in his continuing intercession for us in the power of his Spirit. Any attempt to find them in the church conceived as a sacrament itself would simply mean that the unique mediation of Christ had been confused with the church and that would mean that the church had displaced Christ and substituted itself for Christ.

## Water Baptism and Spirit Baptism

Torrance believes that there is a deep unity in distinction between water baptism and baptism with the Spirit. The former is grounded in the latter and receives its meaning from the latter. While water baptism is not something that is "dispensable", we must not look to that but rather through that action and toward the action of the Spirit which is mediated to us on the basis of Christ's passion. Thus,

> Apart from him nothing is of any avail, not even the invocation of his Name, for in the last analysis it is not so much our confession of Christ that counts but his confession of us. Thus the whole significance of baptism was seen to be lodged, not in the due administration of the rite as such, mandatory though that was, but in him unto whom we are baptized and by whose blood we have been redeemed.[144]

It is here that Torrance states once more the damaging effect that dualism has had in theology, specifically in relation to an understanding of the sacrament of baptism that then leads away from what he calls a properly stereo-understanding. It caused

---

[144]  Torrance, "The One Baptism", *Theology in Reconciliation*, p. 93. Here it is easy to see why Torrance opposed the idea that sacraments work *ex opere operato*, albeit he would admit that this misguided notion at least originally expressed an evangelical concern for "salvation by grace alone" (*Theology in Reconciliation*, p. 124). See also Torrance, *Conflict and Agreement II*, p. 166: "the mediation of the divine act is not through the element as such but in its particular use in the action of the Church".

Origen to look for the reality of Christ who gives meaning to the sacrament and his redemption "beyond history" instead of within history in the sense described above. In Torrance's view, it is just this dichotomy between "the spiritual and the physical, the eternal and the temporal, that lay at the root of gnosticism" and opened the door to Arianism.[145] Although Gnosticism was successfully opposed in the early church, it left its mark on the sacrament because it led to the popular view that included "a mystical notion of redemption, combined with mythico-ritualistic modes of initiation and participation in the divine"[146] which were quite antithetical to understanding the sacrament in a stereo fashion. One of Torrance's great contributions to contemporary theology, then, rests in his own attempt, following Irenaeus, to think through the sacrament of baptism on the ground of a "dogmatic re-thinking of the doctrine of the saving act of the one Triune God in baptism".[147]

In Torrance's view, it was the specter of dualism and legalism that caused Tertullian to adopt a "rather naturalised" notion of regeneration so that his focus was more on what happened in us than on what happened in Christ for us. Hence, "Tertullian tended to think of salvation as saving discipline in which the healing processes of divine grace and the penitential merit of men cooperate to effect man's cleansing and renewal".[148] This was coupled with a "psychological turn" that tended to focus more on our faith than on what Christ did and does through the Spirit to enable our faith. With this stress upon our human action, instead of on Christ's promise of forgiveness, Tertullian once even advised that infants' baptisms should be postponed until they could take on the requirements of baptized life and acquire the faith necessary for salvation. It is just this thinking that led to the Donatist crisis, Torrance believes. Augustine, Torrance notes, took the opposite approach, following Irenaeus, by grounding our subjective faith in the objective events of Christ's incarnate life. Augustine thus was able to offer "a profound theological account of infant baptism".[149] Yet Augustine's dualistic conception of the intelligible and sensible worlds led him to think of grace as a "healing medicine" poured into a wounded humanity. This facilitated an understanding of salvation as a "spiritual process at work in human life and history" and then tended to shift the focus from the actions of God in Christ to something happening in the human soul. This thinking led to the twin ideas that baptism only meant a washing away of past sins and that it mediated grace needed to heal any damage sin had caused, as well as giving the baptized the ability to obey the law of God.[150] Eventually, this Augustinian emphasis led to the ideas that the sacraments contained grace as well

---

[145] Torrance, "The One Baptism", *Theology in Reconciliation*, p. 93.

[146] Torrance, "The One Baptism", *Theology in Reconciliation*, p. 94.

[147] Torrance, "The One Baptism", *Theology in Reconciliation*, p. 95.

[148] Torrance, "The One Baptism", *Theology in Reconciliation*, p. 96.

[149] Torrance, "The One Baptism", *Theology in Reconciliation*, p. 97.

[150] See Torrance, "The One Baptism", *Theology in Reconciliation*, p. 98.

as caused grace in the recipients. And it was precisely this emphasis that led to the reactions of the Reformers.

It is worth noting here that it is precisely Torrance's opposition to sacramental dualism that led him to criticize Karl Barth's view of baptism because he thought Barth made much too sharp a distinction between water and Spirit baptism.[151] This led Barth to oppose applying the term "sacrament" to baptism altogether because he believed that Christ was the only sacrament and that our ethical response was called for but was not in itself to be regarded as a sacrament. Torrance sees this thinking as a return to the kind of dualism that Barth himself rejected in the early parts of the *Church Dogmatics*, and thus he believes that Barth's later thinking was

> deeply inconsistent with his dynamic doctrine of the Trinity and the *opera ad extra* in creation and redemption as well as with his doctrine of the Incarnation according to which God himself has come to us within the space–time structure of our worldly existence and communicated himself personally to us there in his own living being and reality as God.[152]

This was just the kind of thinking that Torrance's stereo-understanding elaborated above was designed to protect against.[153] And Torrance's thinking stood opposed to Barth's rejection of infant baptism as well.[154]

For Torrance, it is just because baptism is our sharing in Christ's own life of obedience and of faith that the sacrament "tells us in unmistakable terms that it is not upon our own faith or our own faithfulness that we rely, but upon Christ alone and upon His faithfulness".[155] In and through the sacrament we are sealed by way of covenant "to a life of faith and obedience to the Father in Him". Whoever is baptized, then, "flees from his own weakness and faithlessness to the everlasting faithfulness of God" but also "renounces reliance upon himself and his own works

---

[151]   See Torrance, "The One Baptism", *Theology in Reconciliation*, p. 99, and Torrance, *Karl Barth*, pp. 134–5.

[152]   Torrance, "The One Baptism", *Theology in Reconciliation*, pp. 99–100.

[153]   For more on these matters, see Molnar, *Karl Barth and the Theology of the Lord's Supper*, pp. 303ff. See also James J. Buckley, "Christian Community, baptism, and Lord's Supper", pp. 195–211, and Alasdair I. C. Heron, "A personal engagement", pp. 296–306, especially p. 303, in *The Cambridge Companion to Karl Barth*, ed. John Webster (Cambridge: Cambridge University Press, 2000).

[154]   For Barth's extensive arguments against the Reformer's views on infant baptism and against the idea itself, see *CD* IV/4, Fragment, pp. 165–95.

[155]   Torrance, *Conflict and Agreement II*, p. 124. This is why Torrance insists that baptism does not attest our faith and decisions but God's prior decision to save us in Christ (p. 129). "Even if my salvation depends on God for ninety-nine per cent of its efficacy and only one per cent on me, my salvation is nevertheless as uncertain as my own frailty and weakness" (p. 130).

of obedience or faithfulness to God's Will".[156] It is into that faith and faithfulness, Torrance contends, that "we baptize our children, for the promise is not only to us but to them also in the faithfulness of Christ who commands us to present them to him".[157] Torrance therefore insists that if we stick to this biblical perspective, then infant baptism is not a problem because through it we are acknowledging at all times that "God has bound Himself to us and bound us to Himself before ever we bind ourselves to Him".[158] For Torrance, "infant-baptism is ... the clearest form of the proclamation of the Gospel and of a Gospel which covenants us to a life of obedience to the Father".[159] Both in doctrine and form, the very same baptism is administered to adults and to children, according to Torrance, because "it is only as little children that we enter into this inheritance of the Kingdom freely bestowed upon us in the New Covenant", and this takes place by relying only upon "Him who has already laid hold of us by His grace".[160] Even though Barth himself insisted that the meaning of water baptism is to be found in Jesus Christ alone and not at all in our human responses (ethical or otherwise), Torrance opposed Barth's ethical interpretation of baptism because he believed, for Barth, "the meaning of baptism is found not in a direct act of God but in an ethical act on the part of man made by way of response to what God has already done on his behalf".[161] Here is where Torrance believes that a properly understood doctrine of the Trinity can overcome all dualism and deism by enabling us to hold an even stronger unity between water and Spirit baptism as "objectively determined by the saving act of God in the incarnate Son and by his direct act now through the Spirit".[162] The only viable way he believes this can be achieved is to develop an understanding of baptism that allows us to see it as a direct act of God which is part of the "economic activity of the Holy Trinity, from the Father, through the Son and in the Holy Spirit".[163]

*Trinity and Baptism*

For Torrance, it is exactly the doctrine of the Trinity that impels us to think of God as the one "*who really acts*" in such a way that he not only created the universe but that he can and does interact with us "in such a way that he creates genuine reciprocity between us and himself within the space–time structures of existence in which he has placed us".[164] Because God does not remain hidden and

---

[156] Torrance, *Conflict and Agreement II*, p. 124.

[157] Torrance, *Conflict and Agreement II*, p. 124.

[158] Torrance, *Conflict and Agreement II*, p. 125.

[159] Torrance, *Conflict and Agreement II*, p. 125.

[160] Torrance, *Conflict and Agreement II*, p. 125.

[161] Torrance, "The One Baptism", *Theology in Reconciliation*, p. 99.

[162] Torrance, "The One Baptism", *Theology in Reconciliation*, p. 99.

[163] Torrance, "The One Baptism", *Theology in Reconciliation*, p. 100.

[164] Torrance, "The One Baptism", *Theology in Reconciliation*, p. 100.

inaccessible to us but has stepped out of himself, as it were, without surrendering his transcendence, he has done this,

> as Karl Barth expressed it, in order to open his inner life and being to communion with us. Here the grace of God is not simply the relation between God and the creature construed in terms of efficient causality but the out-going of God himself towards the creature, and the personal self-giving of God to man which takes place by way of Incarnation.[165]

By this very self-communication of God to us in the incarnation, we are in fact given access to God's inner life as Father, Son and Holy Spirit. Here is where Torrance very clearly maintains that the self-communication of God is not something that can be detached from its objective embodiment in Jesus Christ where God hypostatically assumes our very being into a "binding relation with his own being" and in the Spirit actually "creates in us the capacity to receive it and lifts us up to participate in the union and communion of the incarnate Son with the heavenly Father".[166] These actions *ad extra* of God in his Word and Spirit are not "emanations" from God that "somehow pass over into 'created mediations' other than God"; nor are they "'economic modalities' in which the being of the Godhead is not really committed" because in the incarnation God has really and inseparably united himself in his inner being to us in these historical events. Here Torrance refers to the thinking of Karl Rahner, assuming that he and Rahner are really saying the same thing.[167] Although Torrance was indeed hopeful that a genuine agreement on these issues could be reached between Reformed and Roman Catholic theology based on a properly formulated doctrine of the Trinity, the fact is that Torrance and Rahner actually stood a good deal further apart than Torrance himself suspected in the mid-1970s, exactly because Rahner understood grace in terms of "quasi-formal" causality and thus detached grace from its identity with Christ himself and located it within the experience of creatures in almost exactly the manner that Torrance so carefully rejected, as noted above. Years later, Torrance became more skeptical of Rahner's approach when he suspected that his having possibly introduced a "logical necessity" into his trinitarian doctrine might possibly also lead to a certain reversibility between creature and Creator in other areas of his thought.[168]

---

[165]  Torrance, "The One Baptism", *Theology in Reconciliation*, p. 100.

[166]  Torrance, "The One Baptism", *Theology in Reconciliation*, p. 100.

[167]  Torrance, "The One Baptism", *Theology in Reconciliation*, p. 101.

[168]  See also, Torrance, *The Christian Doctrine of God*, where he writes of Rahner: "That is why he insisted so strongly that the economic Trinity *is* the immanent Trinity [to avoid implying that there is a God behind the God revealed in Jesus Christ], although as we have noted that 'is' may not be construed in a logically necessary or reversible way" (p. 200).

It is not too much to say that Torrance's trinitarian understanding of baptism is both profound and full of ecumenical promise. Just as in his doctrine of the Trinity proper we saw that our knowledge of and full human participation in the communion of the Father and Son through the Spirit is grounded in the mutual knowledge and love of the Father and Son indicated in Matthew 11:27 and Luke 10:22,[169] so here in baptism Torrance insists that we are enabled by the Holy Spirit to participate in the Son's own incarnate relation with the Father:

> Through the Incarnation of the eternal Son the mutual relation between the Father and the Son has penetrated into our human existence in space and time, overlapping with it and actualising itself within our human condition ... in Jesus Christ the mutuality between the Son and the Father has been given a basis in our earthly existence and given incarnate form within human history, where it is accessible to us here and now.[170]

This does not just occur on the level of knowledge. Torrance insists that it also involves our human lives and activities as a whole, exactly because objectively Jesus himself provides our subjective human response to the Father for us, and through the Holy Spirit we are enabled by God himself here and now to share in that new humanity by grace. That is why Torrance insists that, dogmatically speaking, we are baptized in the name of the triune God and that this occurs in the name of Jesus who now has universal authority in heaven and on earth so that "what is then done in his Name and at his command on earth is valid for the one eternal God, Father, Son and Holy Spirit in heaven".[171] There is, then, a "genuine reciprocity" between God's own self-giving and our human response which both respects and is upheld by God who remains transcendent and free. This, for Torrance, is the nature of God's grace. It is because there is a unique hypostatic union of divine action and human response in the incarnate Son which can never be undone that the Spirit "unites us with Christ in such a way that his human agency in vicarious response to the Father overlaps with our response, gathers it up in its embrace, sanctifying, affirming and upholding it in himself".[172]

In this circle there is a genuine reciprocity between divine and human activity. But it occurs continuously in such a way that "God's saving act is not taken captive within the circle as though it could be validated, legitimised or assured in terms of man's activity in response to God". This, because all of this activity rests completely upon "the free ground of God's being and grace in Jesus Christ". Because the triune God himself is active in giving himself to us in Christ, even when he creates a genuine reciprocity between himself and us through Christ

---

169   See above, Chapter 2.
170   Torrance, "The One Baptism", *Theology in Reconciliation*, pp. 101–102.
171   Torrance, "The One Baptism", *Theology in Reconciliation*, p. 102.
172   Torrance, "The One Baptism", *Theology in Reconciliation*, p. 103. See also Torrance, *Conflict and Agreement II*, pp. 122–3.

and in his Spirit, "his act of grace remains sovereignly free and is not trapped within a reciprocity between man and God that begins with man and ends with man".[173] All of this means that we are not the ones who baptize ourselves. Rather are we baptized in the name of the Father, the Son and the Holy Spirit. We are thus "initiated into a mutual relation between the act of the Spirit and the response of faith". Indeed, faith itself arises as the very gift of the Holy Spirit and it is in this way, through the Spirit, that we are united with Christ and thus to the Father. Baptism therefore is a sacrament that refers us to what God in Christ has done for us. It does not refer us to what we do but to Christ as the one in whom God "has bound himself to us and bound us to himself, before ever we could respond to him". Yet it also is a sacrament "of what God now does in us by his Spirit". Baptism tells us, Torrance says, "that it is not upon our act of faith or on our faithfulness that we rely, but upon Christ alone and his vicarious faithfulness". It also tells us that, in a free act of his Spirit, God binds us to himself by making himself present to us so that in our free, spontaneous act of faith, as we respond to the grace of God in Christ, our faith itself is "undergirded and supported by Christ and enclosed with his own faithfulness, and thus grounded in the mutual relation between the incarnate Son and the heavenly Father".[174] It is precisely this trinitarian understanding of the sacrament that Torrance believes avoids all sacramental monism and dualism because it is anchored in the dimension depth which alone gives a properly theological meaning to the church's activity in the sacrament of baptism. Properly understood, then, baptism must be seen "within the saving operation of the economic Trinity" so that our attention is focused "upon Jesus Christ himself", because "it is only *in him* that God is incarnate and it is *through him* alone that the saving operation of God takes concrete form in our creaturely existence, and therefore it is only through *our union with him* that we share in all that God has done for us".[175]

## The Lord's Supper

If baptism is the sacrament of our incorporation into Christ, the Eucharist is the sacrament of our renewal in Christ. Hence,

> we who are incorporated into Christ through Baptism as members of his Body are commanded by him to celebrate the Eucharist, doing this as often as we eat the bread and drink the wine in *anamnesis* [memory] of him and showing forth his death till he come, that the bread which we break may be the communion in

---

[173]   Torrance, "The One Baptism", *Theology in Reconciliation*, p. 103.
[174]   Torrance, "The One Baptism", *Theology in Reconciliation*, pp. 103–104.
[175]   Torrance, "The One Baptism", *Theology in Reconciliation*, p. 104.

the body of Christ and the cup of blessing which we bless the communion in the blood of Christ.[176]

And it is to be noted that Torrance's understanding of the Lord's Supper (Eucharist) is strictly trinitarian in nature. Hence, he insists that when the church celebrates the Eucharist in Christ's name

> it is Christ himself who is really present pouring out his Spirit upon us, drawing us into the power of his vicarious life, in death and resurrection, and uniting us with his self-oblation and self-presentation before the face of the Father where he ever lives to make intercession for us.[177]

In both sacraments, Torrance's thinking is marked by his profound understanding of the pervasive nature of our justification by faith. At times it can sound Christomonistic to those unfamiliar with his approach, as when he says, "justification calls for a radical self-renunciation, a displacement of the self by Jesus Christ". [178] Yet he explains that what is thus called for is

> a relentless objectivity in which you do not love your neighbour because love is a form of your self-fulfilment, in which you do not think out of your own self-centredness but out of a centre in the incarnate Word who summons you to leave all and follow Him, and in which you do not pray or worship God in your own name or in your own significance but only in the name and significance of Jesus Christ ... in which you do not feed upon yourself but feed only upon the Body and Blood of the Lord.[179]

But what this then means is that our true selves are realized only in and through Jesus himself. We are not, of course, absorbed into him as in Christomonism. Rather, as we live from him and in him by faith, he actually enables us to be the people he intended us to be—those who love God and neighbor and thus those who have eternal life in and through faith and thus through Christ alone and by grace alone. This is how Torrance applies the doctrine of justification here. While both Baptism and the Lord's Supper are human responses to the proclamation of God's Word, it is important to realize that they are

> above all the divinely appointed and provided ways of response and worship. They are not sacraments of what we do, but Sacraments of the vicarious obedience of

---

[176] Torrance, "The Paschal Mystery of Christ and the Eucharist", *Theology in Reconciliation*, pp. 106–38, 107.

[177] Torrance, "The Paschal Mystery of Christ and the Eucharist", *Theology in Reconciliation*, p. 107.

[178] Torrance, *God and Rationality*, p. 70.

[179] Torrance, *God and Rationality*, p. 70.

Christ once and for all offered in His finished work and for ever prevalent before
the Face of the Father in the heavenly intercession and mediation of his Son.[180]

Just as we do not baptize ourselves but are baptized out of ourselves and into
Christ, so

we do not come before God in the Eucharist on the ground of what we have done
even by way of response to his Word, for we come with nothing in our hands but
the bread and wine, to feed upon Christ's Body and Blood and find shelter in His
sacrifice and oblation on our behalf.[181]

In this context, Torrance makes the all-important point that, in both Baptism and the
Lord's Supper, "the emphasis is undoubtedly on the human response vicariously
fulfilled for us in Christ" so that even the form of the sacraments "is determined
for us by dominical appointment". Even our responses of faith and repentance,
however, are not actions upon which we are supposed to rely "but solely on that
which Christ has already done and continues to do". This, according to Torrance,
is what is made available to us through the sacraments.

Interestingly, Torrance insists that it is just because we "are called to rely entirely
upon the steadfast and incorruptible response of Christ made on our behalf" that
we are thus freed "from the anxieties begotten of ulterior motivation" and thus may
experience "genuine freedom and joy in responding to God".[182] Because liturgical
language and action derive "their true form through assimilation to the vicarious
life and work of Jesus Christ", their validity is always determined by the extent
to which they actually conform to Christ's own human actions of worship and "in
so far as they make room for Him and direct us to Him as the actualized essence
and core of man's true worship of God". For that reason, "it is the Eucharistic
celebration in union with the proclamation of the Word that gives shape to the
Christian liturgy and mission".[183] For Torrance, our faith "corresponds more to the
activity of the Word as Word" while sacramental action "corresponds more to the
activity of the Word as Event" since sacraments concern both our physical and our
spiritual existence. Hence, "we are baptized in body as well as in soul, and it is
into our bodies that we take the bread and wine, feeding upon the Body and Blood
of Christ and not just upon His Word and Spirit".[184] Through Word and sacrament,
Jesus Christ enables us to "participate in Him" through the power of his Spirit.

---

[180]   Torrance, *God and Rationality*, p. 158.

[181]   Torrance, *God and Rationality*, p. 159.

[182]   Torrance, *God and Rationality*, p. 159. See also Torrance, "The Mind of Christ in
Worship", *Theology in Reconciliation*, p. 211. This is why the mind of Christ himself in
worship is so central—without the mind of Christ, that is, without Jesus worshipping before
the Father for us and with us and in us, there is no true worship.

[183]   Torrance, *God and Rationality*, p. 159.

[184]   Torrance, *God and Rationality*, p. 160.

He, the crucified and risen Lord, continually sustains our existence in relation to God. As the word "Eucharist" implies, the Lord's Supper or Eucharist must be understood as our act of "prayer, thanksgiving and worship" and simultaneously as an "act in which through the Spirit we are given to share in the vicarious life, faith, prayer, worship, thanksgiving and self-offering of Jesus Christ to the Father, for in the final resort it is Jesus Christ himself who is our true worship".[185] For Torrance, the Eucharist should not be seen as an "independent act on our part in response to what God has already done for us in Christ" because it is not the Church's supper, he says, but the "*Lord's* Supper".[186] And, most importantly, it is our act "towards the Father already fulfilled in the humanity of Christ in our place and on our behalf, to which our acts in his name are assimilated and identified through the Spirit".[187] Indeed, following the thought of John McLeod Campbell's idea that the Eucharist takes place "within the circle of the life of Christ", Torrance maintains that it is "a form of the life of Jesus Christ ascending to the Father in the life of those who are so intimately united to him through the Spirit, that when they pray, it is Christ the incarnate Son who honours, adores and glorifies the Father in them".[188]

Seen in this context, then, the function of the sacraments is directed "to the tension between the physical and the spiritual that continues to characterize a world waiting for the redemption of the body and to the tension between the state of the world already redeemed by Christ and its state in the future consummation when He will return to make all things new".[189] Torrance thus sees the sacraments of the Lord's Supper and Baptism as "prophetic signs that have to do with the saving of creation ... they are the counterparts in our ongoing life to the deeds of grace and power in the historical life of Jesus" in which Jesus himself took the burden of our sin and sickness upon himself and thus took responsibility for us. In this light, sacraments, according to Torrance, "both call for and provide a response in which the interaction of the spiritual and physical is exhibited here and now in anticipation of the new creation". That is why we cannot simply respond to the Word in some intellectual or spiritual way; our response must be both a physical and spiritual activity since we "are upheld by Christ from within our existence and are enfolded in His one all-embracing response to the Father on our behalf".[190]

---

[185] Torrance, "The Paschal Mystery of Christ and the Eucharist", *Theology in Reconciliation*, p. 109.

[186] Torrance, "The Paschal Mystery of Christ and the Eucharist", *Theology in Reconciliation*, p. 109.

[187] Torrance, "The Paschal Mystery of Christ and the Eucharist", *Theology in Reconciliation*, p. 109.

[188] Torrance, "The Paschal Mystery of Christ and the Eucharist", *Theology in Reconciliation*, p. 109.

[189] Torrance, *God and Rationality*, p. 161.

[190] Torrance, *God and Rationality*, p. 161. See also Torrance, "The Paschal Mystery of Christ and the Eucharist", *Theology in Reconciliation*, pp. 110–11.

For Torrance, Jesus' own interpretation of his passion is "perpetuated in the eucharistic liturgy" and it is this that formed the early church's view of atonement.[191] When Jesus instituted the "Holy Supper" on the night of his betrayal, "he gave his supreme revelation of the meaning of his life and death, and provided the Church with a permanent centre of reference to which it could return in proclaiming his death until he returned. 'The Son of Man came not to be served but to serve, and to give his life as a ransom for many'".[192] Torrance, of course, follows the Reformation understanding of the Lord's Supper by allowing his view to be normed by the teaching of Holy Scripture.[193] The origins of the Lord's Supper can be found in the Passover or Covenant meal. Torrance gives a detailed presentation of this relation in his important chapter "The Sacrament of the Lord's Supper" in *Conflict and Agreement in the Church II*,[194] noting that Jesus used bread and wine "with the significance of the Passover and with the deliberate intention of founding the New Covenant in His Body and Blood".[195] Also important is the fact that since Torrance emphasizes the whole life and ministry of Jesus in connection with his saving work, he believes that Jesus' parables about the wedding feast, his feeding the thousands, his eating with publicans and sinners and the lost of the house of Israel, and his justification of this action by referring to the Messianic banquet, where all would sit down with Abraham, Isaac and Jacob in God's Kingdom, must all be seen as part of a full understanding of the meaning of the Lord's Supper. Most importantly, however, just as the risen Lord himself gave the command to baptize, so the risen Lord's appearances to the disciples in the upper room where they had their last meal together prior to his death was important. Following Luke's account, Torrance notes that Jesus first returned to the disciples "at their Easter Evening meal".[196] Also, he was made known to his disciples in the breaking of the bread at Emmaus, and there is the Johannine account of their meal with the risen Jesus by the lake. Torrance acknowledges that one could argue that these events are not directly related to the Lord's Supper, but

---

[191]   Torrance, *The Trinitarian Faith*, p. 168.

[192]   Torrance, *The Trinitarian Faith*, p. 169. Cf. Mark 10:45; Matthew 20:28, Mark 8:55f.; Matthew 16:25f.; Luke 9:24f.; Job 33.24 and 28; Psalm 49:8f. Of course, as seen above in this chapter and in Chapter 5, Torrance rejects the idea that in the atonement a ransom was paid to the devil on our behalf, as held by Origen and by Gregory Nyssen. "There is not the slightest trace here [in Athanasius' view] of Origen's notion of ransom to the devil, for the very idea that the powers of darkness have any inherent right over man to which deference is to be paid was quite impossible for Athanasius" (*The Trinitarian Faith*, pp. 175–6). Torrance finds this idea "morally repugnant" because Jesus sacrificed his life in place of all and on behalf of all as a substitute.

[193]   See Thomas F. Torrance, "The Sacrament of the Lord's Supper", *Conflict and Agreement II*, p. 133.

[194]   See Torrance, *Conflict and Agreement II*, pp. 134–7.

[195]   Torrance, *Conflict and Agreement II*, p. 135.

[196]   Torrance, *Conflict and Agreement II*, p. 136.

the resurrection inevitably modified the character of the meal ... so that the Lord's Supper as celebrated in the Church was not just the prolongation of the Last Supper ... but was a 'sacramental' continuation of the acts of Christ in the miraculous feeding of the multitudes ... and entailed the 'sacramental' extension into the Church of the resurrection meals of the risen Lord with his disciples.[197]

For Torrance, the Reformers recovered this scriptural view of the Lord's Supper and reacted against Pelagian conceptions of both the atonement and the priesthood which they saw in the Roman Catholic Mass. They opposed "a repeated sacrificial immolation of Christ even in a propitiatory sense" because, according to Torrance, this "gave the Church control over men's salvation".[198] This, of course, does not mean that there is no proper notion of sacrifice that can be used to explain what happens in the Mass, in Torrance's thinking. In fact, George Hunsinger utilizes a particularly interesting presentation of this matter in Torrance's book *Space, Time and Resurrection,* arguing that there is "one sacrifice common to Christ and his Church—that is the highpoint of Torrance's teaching".[199] Hunsinger sums up Torrance's views by stressing that there are three modes to Christ's one sacrifice: 1) "the once-for-all and historical mode in which the work of expiation was completed"; 2) "the ascended and eternal mode by which its efficacy never ends"; and 3) "the daily and eucharistic mode through which the faithful come to dwell in Christ and he in them as his sacrifice continually becomes theirs and theirs his".[200] All of this is predicated upon Torrance's strong emphasis on the fact that the risen and ascended Christ "*is* the Son of God, God himself come to us as Priest, Priest sent from God, Apostle-Priest, as well as Priest qualified to act for

---

[197]   Torrance, *Conflict and Agreement II*, p. 136.

[198]   Torrance, *Conflict and Agreement II*, p. 137.

[199]   Hunsinger, *The Eucharist and Ecumenism*, p. 155. In Chapter 4, Hunsinger relies on T.F. Torrance and Max Thurian to present a proper view of eucharistic sacrifice in a truly ecumenical way that maintains the unique work of Christ, together with the sacramental action of the church in a way that eschews false notions of priesthood and instead sees the priestly activity of the church as belonging to the community "and only through the community to its eucharistic ministers (cf. 1 Pet. 2:5, 9)" (*The Eucharist and Ecumenism*, p. 168). Because Christ's priestly office did not terminate with his death and because neither the community nor its ministers are equal to Christ, Christ himself continues to exercise his priesthood through the obedient activity of the church. Priests are never to be seen as "secondary saving agents alongside Christ" (p. 168) so that he believes that "Christ in his Spirit works *through* the priest but not (causally) *by* the priest" (p. 170). Hunsinger wisely notes that what Torrance says about the Eucharist runs parallel to what he says about baptism, namely, that, as noted above, there is "one baptism common to Christ and his church". See Torrance, "The One Baptism", *Theology in Reconciliation*, pp. 84ff.; Torrance, *STR*, pp. 112–22.

[200]   See Hunsinger, *The Eucharist and Ecumenism*, p. 156.

us through his incarnational solidarity with sinners".[201] It is this priestly office that
led the Reformers to oppose any notion of "sacerdotal control" over the church
as the Body of Christ "which through the words of consecration fetched it down
from heaven and brought it to rest upon the altar".[202] Torrance admits that the best
Roman Catholic theologians of the time never held these views in such a crude
formulation, but he also observes that they did not repudiate them either. And
these views were indeed given doctrinal formulation at the Council of Trent "in a
way that has for ever involved the Roman Church in excommunion from the rest
of Christendom".[203]

What, then, are the key issues Torrance wishes to stress? According to the
Roman Catholic view, the priest is seen "as one who builds a bridge and so mediates
between God and man", and he does so in the case of the Mass by "re-enacting the
sacrifice of Christ". But, for the Reformers, "the Incarnation had radically altered
the whole conception of priesthood"[204] because, in light of this event, Jesus Christ
himself is seen as the bridge between God and man.

> In the humanity of the ascended Christ, there remains for ever before the Face
> of God the Father the one, perfect, sufficient Offering for mankind. He presents
> himself before the Father as the Redeemer who has united himself to us and
> has become our Brother. He represents us before the Father as those who are
> incorporated in him and consecrated and perfected together with him in one for
> ever.[205]

For Torrance, the Roman Catholic teaching here opposed the apostolic teaching,
especially as it was presented in the Letter to the Hebrews. The Priesthood of the
incarnate Son "opened up in Himself a new and living way to God" and he did this
"once and for all" in his perfect priestly work.[206] And behind all of this there was a

---

[201] Torrance, *STR*, p. 114. The key to grasping the sacrament of the eucharist, then, is
to be found only in the *"vicarious humanity of Jesus, the priesthood of the incarnate Son.*
Eternal God though he was, he condescended to be our brother, and since we are children
sharing in flesh and blood, he partook of the same, made like unto his brothers in every
respect, so that he might be a merciful and faithful High Priest in the affairs *towards God*
to make expiation for the sins of the people" ("The Paschal Mystery of Christ and the
Eucharist", *Theology in Reconciliation*, p. 110).

[202] Torrance, *Conflict and Agreement II*, p. 137.

[203] Torrance, *Conflict and Agreement II*, p. 137.

[204] Torrance, "Toward a Doctrine of the Lord's Supper", *Conflict and Agreement II*,
pp. 133–54, p. 137.

[205] Torrance, *STR*, p. 115. See also Torrance, *Conflict and Agreement II*, for how
Torrance's thinking about this matter is eschatologically structured in relation to Christ's
absolutely unique sacrifice (pp. 178–86).

[206] Torrance, "Toward a Doctrine of the Lord's Supper", *Conflict and Agreement II*,
p. 137.

change in the concept of God, a stress upon Christology and its relation to faith as well as a recovery of the doctrine of justification by faith and grace through Christ alone. Torrance became more hopeful that there could be ecumenical agreement on these issues between the time he wrote *Conflict and Agreement II* and *Theology in Reconciliation*, especially in light of the fact that, at Vatican II, the Roman Catholic Church sought to recover "the human priesthood of Jesus Christ [and] a deeper understanding of the humanity of Christ as the sacrament *par excellence*". This emphasis, Torrance hoped, could lead Roman Catholic theologians to think through the implications of "the vicarious priesthood of Christ for the hierarchy of the Church", as it had already done for the liturgy, and he also hoped that Reformed theologians would think through their conception of ministry "in terms of the consociation with the one priesthood of Jesus Christ".[207] This is no minor point in Torrance's thought.

In his magisterial piece "The Mind of Christ in Worship: The Problem of Apollinarianism in the Liturgy",[208] Torrance spelled out exactly what a proper emphasis on the humanity of Jesus Christ in the liturgy means. If we neglect the mind of Jesus in its oneness with the mind of the Father in meditating our worship of the Father, then the whole nature of worship is undermined by what Torrance calls Apollinarianism in the liturgy. If justification is seen simply as the "non-imputation of sin in which we believe", then one might suppose that we are justified by *our* faith. But, according to Torrance, justification really should mean our "feeding upon Christ, a participation in his human righteousness, so that to be justified by faith is to be justified in him in whom we believe, not by an act of our faith as such". That is why Torrance insists we rely on Christ's *vicarious* prayer.[209] Avoiding Apollinarianism or monophysitism in the liturgy, then, meant, to Torrance, that our eucharistic prayers took place not only *in* and *through* Christ but *with* him. Apollinarianism eliminates Jesus' full humanity and supposes that because the divine mind is changeless and sinless, it replaces Jesus' human mind in order to save us. But this eliminates from Jesus the full range of human experience and ultimately destroys his mediation from the human side toward the Father. It also severs Christ's *homoousios* with us.[210] This opens the door to other sources of

---

[207]   Torrance, "Ecumenism", *Theology in Reconciliation*, p. 63.

[208]   Torrance, "The Mind of Christ in Worship", *Theology in Reconciliation*, pp. 139–214. See also Paul D. Molnar, "The Eucharist and the Mind of Christ: Some Trinitarian Implications of T.F. Torrance's Sacramental Theology" in *Trinitarian Soundings in Systematic Theology*, ed Paul Louis Metzger (New York and London: T&T Clark/Continuum, 2005), pp. 175–88.

[209]   Torrance, "The Mind of Christ in Worship", *Theology in Reconciliation*, p. 141, and "Toward a Doctrine of the Lord's Supper", *Conflict and Agreement. II*, pp. 133–53, 147.

[210]   Torrance, "The Mind of Christ in Worship", *Theology in Reconciliation*, pp. 173ff. Torrance follows Cyril to stress the importance of Jesus' human mind for our lifting of our minds in and through and with him to the Father.

mediation and compromises the true nature of eucharistic worship. Here is where Torrance's view of the sacrament hinges on his trinitarian doctrine.

*Eucharistic Real Presence*

Therefore, the fact that the doctrine of God and Christology are intimately related to Torrance's view of the Eucharist is important. This is what leads him consistently both to emphasize Christ's real presence in the Eucharist and yet to reject any notion of transubstantiation.[211] The issue is both Christological and sacramental. For Torrance, transubstantiation rests ultimately upon an Ebionite or Docetic Christology because such thinking can only envision the incarnation to mean that divinity was transformed into the humanity of Jesus or that his humanity was transformed into his divinity. The parallels with the sacrament are obvious: applying transubstantiation to the bread and wine must mean that these created elements are no longer seen as bread and wine, but somehow (docetically) they become something else.

Torrance rejects this because he wants to understand Christ's real presence in his body and blood *relationally* so that he is present *miraculously* (in a way we cannot explain and by means of an act of God similar to the virgin birth itself). But Christ is present in a way that does not destroy the sacramental sign (bread and wine), while Christ himself, through the Spirit, enables us to feed upon his own body and blood as the ascended and coming Lord and thus through faith precisely by engaging in communion with him through these created elements.[212] Holding the resurrection together with the Last Supper within a properly eschatological perspective and conceiving them as a "sacramental whole" enables Torrance to

---

[211]    While Torrance sees the mediaeval doctrine of transubstantiation as an objective attempt to understand Christ's real presence in the categories available at the time, that does not mean he accepts it as a view that accords with a truly scriptural understanding of Christ's real presence. In fact, he believes that transubstantiation fails to do justice to the union and distinction of Christ's humanity and divinity in Christology, and to the union and distinction between the risen and ascended Christ and the community, and between the bread and wine as sacramental signs and the reality of Christ's real and spiritual presence at the Eucharist. Cf. Torrance, "Truth and Authority: Theses on Truth", *Irish Theological Quarterly* 38 (1972): 237–8.

[212]    For an illuminating view of these matters, see Thomas F. Torrance, "Predestination in Christ" in *The Evangelical Quarterly*, 13, (1941): 108–31, 128ff. and 140f. "Christological heresies have generally taken the form of transubstantiating, as it were, one side of the Person of Christ into the other. Thus for example the ancient docetic heresy transubstantiated the humanity into the divinity, while the ancient ebionite heresy transubstantiated the divinity into humanity. In other words, these heresies amount either to a divinising of humanity or a humanising of divinity" (128). And Torrance notes that "the doctrine of transubstantiation in the sacrament … means the presence of Christ there is docetic. To transubstantiate the worldly symbols into something they are not, is virtually to deny the humanity of Christ, and to say that God has not come all the way to our world" (140).

hold a theologically realist view of Christ's eucharistic presence. While Jesus has withdrawn his visible historical presence from us, "there is such an intervention by the risen Lord as the invisible reality behind each celebration of the Lord's Supper". Indeed,

> Jesus Christ is as really present in the Eucharist as He was on that Easter day ... As surely as in the Eucharist we handle bread and wine, we put our fingers into His wounds and He breathes upon us His peace and forgiveness in answer to the prayer: 'Lamb of God who takest away the sins of the world, grant us thy peace.' The Eucharist then is the sacramental enactment of the real presence of Christ.[213]

Hence, Torrance believes that "while we can only eat and drink the body and blood of Christ through faith, yet, by the power of the eternal Spirit, the Church is given through the Eucharist a *relation in being* to Christ, beyond its relation to Him through faith".[214]

Much of Torrance's understanding regarding Christ's real presence in the incarnation and thus in Jesus' life, death and resurrection, together with his ascension and second coming, centers around his firm rejection of the receptacle or container notion of space, which, as we saw above,[215] tended to think in exclusive terms of Christ's real presence as either confined within the bread and wine or confined in heaven as the ascended Lord. Torrance rejects a receptacle notion of space "which cut off spatial from temporal relation" and tends to make real presence "timeless, i.e. a purely spatial presence unconditioned by time".[216] The problem with such thinking is that it posits a spatial relation "without extension in time" and makes it "impossible to discern any difference between the real presence of Christ in the days of His flesh, in the Eucharist, and at the Last Day". This, unfortunately, "is equivalent to making the historical foundation of faith irrelevant".[217]

Christologically, the receptacle notion of space led to views of the incarnation as "the self-emptying of Christ into the receptacle of a human body".[218] Eucharistically, this led the idea that Christ's real presence in the host meant that he was somehow contained within and conditioned by the host. In Torrance's view, the receptacle notion tends to imperil Christ's full human nature. Dropping the receptacle view and adopting a more relational view, one can see that Christ's real presence is his own *personal* presence as "Priest and King over His Church".[219] And this means at

---

[213]   Torrance, "Eschatology and the Eucharist", *Conflict and Agreement II*, p. 186.

[214]   Torrance, "Eschatology and the Eucharist", *Conflict and Agreement II*, p. 187.

[215]   See above, Chapter 4.

[216]   Torrance, *STI*, p. 32.

[217]   Torrance, *STI*, p. 35.

[218]   Torrance, *STI*, p. 35.

[219]   Torrance, "Toward a Doctrine of the Lord's Supper", *Conflict and Agreement II*, p. 138.

once that we must focus on the historical events in which the triune God has made himself present as our representative and savior, that is, in the historical events of Christ's own life, death, resurrection and, most importantly, his ascension to the right hand of the Father where he exercises his priestly and kingly functions within the church on earth. Here is where eschatology also plays an important role in Torrance's thought as he follows the thinking of Calvin:

> The Lord's Supper is a communion with the risen and ascended Christ through the Spirit which he pours upon His Church, and in it He who was crucified comes to show us His wounds in His hands, feet, and side, to give us peace and forgiveness ... and to quicken us again by the breath of His Spirit that we may go from the Supper to fulfil our calling in obedience to His sending ...[220]

In this way, the church actually experiences the new creation which overlaps with the old creation and is therefore "veiled" and only sacramentally "unveiled in anticipation of the great unveiling of the Kingdom of Christ at the final Parousia".[221]

So Christ's real presence in the Eucharist is just as real as his presence on earth as the incarnate Word and his presence when he comes again in his final Parousia. Yet his real presence in each form must be distinguished but not separated. Hence, for Torrance, "Jesus Christ is really present under the veil of the bread and wine, but in such a way that He holds back the full power and majesty of His presence to give us time on earth and in history to fulfil His Will before He comes again".[222] That is why, following Calvin, Torrance insists that we pray at the Eucharist, "Thy Kingdom come; thy will be done on earth, as it is in heaven". Torrance therefore rejects any idea that the Eucharist is: 1) merely a memorial of the historical event of the Last Supper or 2) "a timeless rite of mystical repetition".[223] In Torrance's words:

> The one involves an un-Christological separation between the sign and thing signified, and treats the sign as the sign of what happened historically in the past alone; and the other involves an un-Christological confusion between the sign and the thing signified through a doctrine of transubstantiation ... transubstantiation

---

[220] Torrance, "Toward a Doctrine of the Lord's Supper", *Conflict and Agreement II*, p. 138. See also Torrance, *Royal Priesthood*, pp. 37 ff. See especially Torrance's treatment of this in *STR*, pp. 114ff.

[221] Torrance, "Toward a Doctrine of the Lord's Supper", *Conflict and Agreement II*, p. 139. See also *Conflict and Agreement II*, p. 195.

[222] Torrance, "Toward a Doctrine of the Lord's Supper", *Conflict and Agreement II*, p. 139.

[223] Torrance, "Toward a Doctrine of the Lord's Supper", *Conflict and Agreement II*, p. 139.

destroys the whole analogical relation of participation and conformity to Christ, and so disrupts the basic Christological nature of the Sacrament.[224]

Sign and thing signified are related analogically so that there is neither a relation of identity nor difference between the two but rather one "involving something of identity and something of difference". But this relation is completely determined by the humanity of Jesus Christ "who is the substance of the matter signified".[225] The matter can be put succinctly as follows. Christ's *real presence* is the "whole Christ, not just the presence of his body and blood, nor just the presence of his Spirit or Mind, but the presence of the actual Jesus Christ ... as Gift and Giver".[226] Important conclusions follow. First, Christ's real presence is his personal and creative presence among us, his "self-giving to us"; we have no "ecclesiastical, liturgical or intellectual" control over it. Second, the whole Christ is present "in the fulness of his deity and in the fulness of his humanity, crucified and risen ... Jesus Christ clothed with his Gospel and clothed with the power of his Spirit, who cannot be separated from what he did or taught ..."[227] Third, "he creatively effects what he declares ... 'This is my body broken for you', 'This is my blood shed for many for the remission of sins'".[228] Fourth,

> the Eucharist is the dominically appointed place ... where we meet with Christ and have communion with him in his real presence, as he is the one place appointed by God within our space–time existence where heaven and earth, eternity and time, God and man fully meet and are for ever united, and the only place where God and man are reconciled.[229]

We are "gathered up through communion with Christ into the living presence of God in the eternal communion of the Holy Trinity". Hence the real presence "is objectively grounded in *the presence of God to himself,* and as such is the profoundest and most intensive kind of presence there could ever be." Fifth, we cannot construe Christ's real presence in the Eucharist "in terms of anything we can analyse naturally in this world", but, because Christ is really present, there

---

[224]  Torrance, "Toward a Doctrine of the Lord's Supper", *Conflict and Agreement II*, pp. 139–40.

[225]  Torrance, "Toward a Doctrine of the Lord's Supper", *Conflict and Agreement II*, p. 141.

[226]  Torrance, "The Paschal Mystery of Christ and the Eucharist", *Theology in Reconciliation*, p. 119.

[227]  Torrance, "The Paschal Mystery of Christ and the Eucharist", *Theology in Reconciliation*, p.120.

[228]  Torrance, "The Paschal Mystery of Christ and the Eucharist", *Theology in Reconciliation*, p. 120.

[229]  Torrance, "The Paschal Mystery of Christ and the Eucharist", *Theology in Reconciliation*, p. 121.

are indeed "spatial and temporal ingredients in a proper understanding of the real presence".[230] Many of the serious problems that have arisen in the Western understanding of the Incarnation and real eucharistic presence have taken different forms in Catholic and Protestant thought. But, for Torrance, all are traceable to Platonic dualism and Aristotelian phenomenalism.

## Dualism and Phenomenalism

If attention is directed "*at* the Eucharist itself rather than *from* or *through* the Eucharist to its real ground in the paschal mystery of Christ", it is phenomenalized "as something enshrining a hidden meaning or mystery in itself".[231] This shift resulted when theology moved from a Christocentric to an anthropocentric starting point.[232] The Neoplatonic distinction between the real and the transient worlds "laid the foundation for a dualist understanding of the relation between God and the world"[233] and also of the sacraments by inhibiting "a serious consideration of a real *becoming* of the intelligible in the sensible, or of the eternal in the contingent".[234] Following Augustine, "sacraments came to be defined as outward and visible signs of inward and invisible grace".[235] This led to a symbolic understanding of the sacraments, which threatened to lead to "a merely spiritual interpretation of the real presence". But by assimilating grace to causality, this tendency was restrained by what Torrance calls an "instrumentalist notion of sacramental grace". Catholic understanding of the real presence, interpreted in terms of *transubstantiation*, restricted Christ's real presence, "defined in this phenomenalist, physico-causal way".[236] But this points to "some docetic error in Christology", namely, "to a transubstantiation of the human nature of Christ, leaving only a *species* to remain".[237] With the causal connection between grace and the experience of the participants came the *ex opere operato* which inevitably depersonalized real

---

[230] Torrance, "The Paschal Mystery of Christ and the Eucharist", *Theology in Reconciliation*, p. 121.

[231] Torrance, "The Paschal Mystery of Christ and the Eucharist", *Theology in Reconciliation*, p. 122.

[232] See Torrance, "The Deposit of Faith" for how this applies to doctrine, pp. 7 ff., 15 ff.

[233] Torrance, "The Paschal Mystery of Christ and the Eucharist", *Theology in Reconciliation*, p. 122.

[234] Torrance, "The Roman Doctrine of Grace", *Theology in Reconstruction*, p. 175.

[235] Torrance, "The Paschal Mystery of Christ and the Eucharist", *Theology in Reconciliation*, p. 122.

[236] Torrance, "The Paschal Mystery of Christ and the Eucharist", *Theology in Reconciliation*, p. 123.

[237] Torrance, "The Roman Doctrine of Grace", *Theology in Reconstruction,* p. 184. See also "Eschatology and the Eucharist", *Conflict and Agreement II*, p. 188. For Torrance, after Christ's resurrection and ascension, his true humanity excludes any "docetic

presence, and implied that the priest was "given the power to do what Christ does, in *re-enacting his sacrifice*".[238] This led to the ideas that Christ as the victim in the Eucharist is effected by the liturgy and that "*something is done to Christ* in the Eucharist".[239] Eucharistic sacrifice seen as "a cultic repetition of the immolation or propitiatory sacrifice of Christ is not far off".[240] Consequently, just as Torrance opposed transubstantiation, he also opposed any sort of dualist interpretation. Epistemological and ontological dualism led people to focus on the eucharistic rite itself "with a serious loss in objective depth in the paschal mystery of Christ and a foreshortening of its meaning".[241] Whenever the Eucharist is set within an Augustinian dualistic framework,

> its meaning tends to be found either in the rite itself and its performance or in the inward and moral experience of the participants, for then the Eucharist is regarded either as a holy mystery in itself enshrining and guaranteeing the divine mystery of the Church in the host, or as the appointed ordinance which occasions and stimulates deeper spiritual consciousness and awareness in believers.[242]

As we have seen more than once, for Torrance, God gives himself to us in Jesus Christ; the Gift is identical with the Giver. If our understanding of God's relation with the world is "damaged" because of a dualistic perspective, then we will assume that God has not actually given himself within created time and space "but only something of himself through a created mediation".[243] A dualistic perspective actually divides the Gift from the Giver. The Catholic tendency focuses on the Gift in its concern for real presence, thought of "as inhering in the Eucharist as such".[244] The Protestant tendency focuses on ourselves as receivers over against the Giver. Torrance insists, against both of these tendencies, that because the Gift is identical with the Giver, God is immediately present in his own Being and life

---

phantasm". Thus bread and wine are not just "species" but instruments of Christ's real presence ontologically uniting himself with his church.

[238] Torrance, "The Paschal Mystery of Christ and the Eucharist", *Theology in Reconciliation*, p. 124.

[239] Torrance, "The Paschal Mystery of Christ and the Eucharist", *Theology in Reconciliation*, p. 124.

[240] Torrance, "The Paschal Mystery of Christ and the Eucharist", *Theology in Reconciliation*, p. 124.

[241] Torrance, "The Paschal Mystery of Christ and the Eucharist", *Theology in Reconciliation*, p. 130.

[242] Torrance, "The Paschal Mystery of Christ and the Eucharist", *Theology in Reconciliation*, p. 131.

[243] Torrance, "The Paschal Mystery of Christ and the Eucharist", *Theology in Reconciliation*, p. 131.

[244] Torrance, "The Paschal Mystery of Christ and the Eucharist", *Theology in Reconciliation*, p. 132.

through Jesus Christ; this self-giving "takes place *in the Holy Spirit* who is not just an emanation from God but the immediate presence and activity of God in his own divine Being, the Spirit of the Father and the Son ... this is a real presence of Christ to us".[245]

With respect to eucharistic sacrifice, the Offerer is identical with the Offering: what "the Incarnate Son offers to the Father on our behalf is his own human life which he took from us and assumed into unity with his divine life, his *self*-offering through the eternal Spirit to the Father". Because the historical offering of his body on the cross is inherently one with himself as the Offerer, it is a once-and-for-all event which remains eternally valid. Understood dualistically, the Offerer and Offering are not finally one; "neither is his offering once and for all nor is it completely and sufficiently vicarious".[246] He becomes only a created intermediary and the offering is seen as a merely human offering so that no real mediation between God and creatures has taken place. Torrance insists that if Christ's human priesthood is seen within a Nestorian or Apollinarian framework, "then it becomes only a representative and no longer a vicarious priesthood, for it is no longer unique but only an exemplary form of our own";[247] thus it is no longer uniquely substitutionary.

This directs us to rely on ourselves "to effect our own 'Pelagian' mediation with God by being our own priests and by offering to him our own sacrifices". Even if this is done "for Christ's sake" and motivated by him, if it is not done "*with him*, and *in him* we have no access *through him* into the immediate presence of God". If, however, "Jesus Christ is himself both Priest and Victim, Offerer and Offering", who has effected atoning reconciliation and so forever "unites God and man in his one Person and *as such* coinheres with the Father and the Holy Spirit in the eternal Trinity", then "we participate in his self-consecration and self-offering to the Father and thus appear with him and in him and through him before the Majesty of God in worship, praise and adoration with no other sacrifice than the sacrifice of Christ Jesus our Mediator and High Priest".[248] When the Church

---

[245]   Torrance, "The Paschal Mystery of Christ and the Eucharist", *Theology in Reconciliation*, p. 132. See also Torrance, *The Ground and Grammar*, p. 164.

[246]   Torrance, "The Paschal Mystery of Christ and the Eucharist", *Theology in Reconciliation*, pp. 133, 209.

[247]   Torrance, "The Paschal Mystery of Christ and the Eucharist", *Theology in Reconciliation*, p. 133. This is why Torrance so insistently opposes Apollinarianism in worship. Take away Christ's human mind as the one who worships the Father with us and on our behalf, "then his priestly ministry becomes absorbed in the majesty of his Godhead, and we are left without an effective mediation from mankind towards the Father. Then Christ himself, in the identity of Offerer and Offering, is not central to the liturgy ... he himself is not our worship ... so that we are inevitably thrown back upon ourselves to offer our own worship to the Father ... of our own devising" (p. 204).

[248]   Torrance, "The Paschal Mystery of Christ and the Eucharist", *Theology in Reconciliation*, p. 134. Torrance is adamant that what makes Christ's sacrifice for us unique

worships, praises and adores the Father through Jesus Christ, it is the self-offering and self-consecration of Jesus Christ

> in our nature ascending to the Father from the Church in which he dwells through the Spirit he has poured out upon it, uniting it to himself as his Body, so that when the Church worships, praises and adores the Father through Christ and celebrates the Eucharist in his name, it is Christ himself who worships, praises and adores the Father in and through his members, taking up, moulding and sanctifying the prayers of his people as they are united to him through communion in his body and blood.[249]

T. F. Torrance's achievement here is massive. By focusing on "*God as Man* rather than upon God in Man", Torrance embraces a high Christology which concentrated on the *humanity* of the incarnate Son of God and a view of eucharistic worship and life in which "the primacy is given to the priestly mediation of Jesus Christ himself".[250]

> It is in fact the eternal life of the incarnate Son in us that ascends to the Father in our worship and prayer through, with and in him, in the unity of the Holy Spirit. While they are our worship and prayer, in as much as we freely and fully participate in the Sonship of Christ and in the whole course of his filial obedience to the Father, they are derived from and rooted in a source beyond themselves, in the economic condescension and ascension of the Son of God. The movement of worship and prayer ... is essentially correlative to the movement of the divine love and grace, from the Father, through the Son and in the Spirit.[251]

This leads to a more unified soteriology which views Incarnation and atonement as a single continuous movement of God's redeeming love and accentuates Jesus Christ's "*God–manward* and his *man–Godward* activity". Focusing on

---

is the fact that he is *God* himself acting *as man* in our place. See above, Chapter 1, pp. 12–13, and "Eschatology and the Eucharist", *Conflict and Agreement II*, p. 184.

[249] Torrance, "The Paschal Mystery of Christ and the Eucharist", *Theology in Reconciliation*, p. 134. See also "Eschatology and the Eucharist", *Conflict and Agreement II*, p. 182, where Torrance insists that "the eucharistic sacrifice is only the *anamnesis* or *proclamation* of that lonely sacrifice [of Christ for us which is 'absolutely unique'], and does not involve any identity between a sacrifice of our own and His". Thus there can be no "identity between the bread and wine of the Eucharist with the glorified Body in the heavenly places, identity between the action of the Church on earth as it celebrates the sacrifice of Christ, and perpetual Self-Offering of Christ Himself before the Face of the Father" (p. 183).

[250] Torrance, "The Paschal Mystery of Christ and the Eucharist", *Theology in Reconciliation*, p. 135.

[251] Torrance, "The Mind of Christ in Worship", *Theology in Reconciliation*, p. 212. Torrance follows John McCleod Campbell in this.

Jesus' vicarious humanity emphasizes that Christ has put himself in our place, experiencing our alienated human condition and healing it. Eucharistic *anamnesis* is no mere recollection of what Christ has done for us once for all, but a memorial which "according to his command" and "through the Spirit is filled with the presence of Christ in the indivisible unity of all his vicarious work and his glorified Person".[252]

Earlier in this chapter we noted that Torrance's important espousal of intercommunion was based on the fact that the Eucharist is the *Lord's* Supper and thus it does not belong to the church but to the risen Lord himself, into whom we are incorporated at baptism and whose body and blood we feed upon in the Eucharist. We have now seen that because it is Christ himself, Prophet, Priest and King, who mediates himself to us in Baptism and in the Eucharist, no human priesthood can take his place but can only minister in his name in witness to his own active mediation of himself and of our salvation. Since baptism recalls that "Christ dwells in us corporeally, independently of the Supper", it thus indicates that the continuity of the Body of Christ cannot "be sought on the plane of historical relativity but in the continuous act of God, which in the Resurrection is continuous temporal fact".[253] Consequently, for Torrance, to refuse the Eucharist to the baptized, namely, to those "incorporated into His resurrection-body amounts either to a denial of the transcendent reality of holy Baptism or to attempted schism within the Body of Christ".[254] Because all are baptized into Christ, therefore it is the Son of Man himself who has broken down all "barriers to intercommunion" so that "sinners are freely invited to eat and drink with the Lord".[255] There is enormous theological and ecumenical potential in Torrance's thought on this subject, to say the least, precisely because "In the presence of the eschatological Christ, the Son of Man, all barriers to intercommunion are broken down".[256] For Torrance, it is just because the Son of Man is really present in the Eucharist that the bread and wine we drink "spills over freely to all who hunger and thirst after righteousness". Anyone who truly realizes this real presence of Christ, as the one "to whom all judgment has been committed", will see that "it is the Lord's Supper … and not our own … and that we cannot send any Church or any sincere baptized believer away, without sinning against the majesty and grace of the Son of Man".[257]

Here is where we conclude by noting that ecumenical agreement concerning the unity of the church in the Eucharist is a necessity that will only be real wherever and whenever the church allows Jesus Christ himself, risen from the dead, ascended into heaven and coming again, to be the sole Lord of his church and of his supper,

---

[252] Torrance, "The Paschal Mystery of Christ and the Eucharist", *Theology in Reconciliation*, p. 136.

[253] Torrance, "Eschatology and the Eucharist", *Conflict and Agreement II*, p. 191.

[254] Torrance, "Eschatology and the Eucharist", *Conflict and Agreement II*, p. 191.

[255] Torrance, "Eschatology and the Eucharist", *Conflict and Agreement II*, p. 192.

[256] Torrance, "Eschatology and the Eucharist", *Conflict and Agreement II*, p. 192.

[257] Torrance, "Eschatology and the Eucharist", *Conflict and Agreement II*, p. 193.

so that he alone will be the one who unifies Christians again and again in the power of his real presence. It is just because Christ's real eucharistic presence is genuinely creating the unity of the church here and now that the refusal of intercommunion suggests that we are standing in the way of Christ's own priestly and prophetic ministry, to the detriment of the church itself.[258]

---

[258] See Torrance, "Eschatology and the Eucharist", *Conflict and Agreement II*, pp. 200–202.

# Chapter 9

# Considering Some Criticisms of
# T. F. Torrance's Theology

As with any great theologian, there have been and always will be critics. T. F. Torrance is no exception. In this chapter I will identify and explore some criticisms of Torrance's work with a view toward seeing more clearly where theological decisions regarding key issues must be made. My goal is to assist readers in sorting through various criticisms of Torrance's thought in order to understand his position and decide for themselves whether and to what extent the various criticisms are valid and helpful.

At a more extreme end of the spectrum, there are those who claim that Torrance, following Barth, had misrepresented the history of the church and done a disservice to theology because he embraced the idea that God's being is his act and insisted that the gift and giver (grace and Christ) cannot be separated. In this perspective it is thought that Barth had collapsed God's being into his revelation, that Torrance was mistaken to apply the *homoousion* to the doctrine of Christ's person, that Torrance's description of and rejection of what he called the "Latin Heresy" was wrong, that Torrance and Barth were Christomonists and that Torrance actually fabricated an Athanasius who really did not exist in order to base his Barthian thinking on a solid historical foundation.[1] This is clearly an extreme characterization of both Torrance and Barth and it seems to flow from a perspective that has great difficulty understanding exactly why theologians such as Barth and Torrance were more than a little ambivalent about introducing traditional natural theology into their understanding of God, Christ, revelation, faith and grace. In fact, it was precisely to the extent that Barth and Torrance allowed their thinking to take shape from a center in God provided by God himself in the incarnation and outpouring of the Holy Spirit that they were not only Christocentric theologians (without being Christomonists) but also were theologians whose trinitarian theology was tied to God's actions within history in his Word and Spirit without in any way collapsing the immanent into the economic Trinity or separating the immanent from the economic Trinity in some dualist fashion.[2] Reading Torrance

---

[1]   See, for example, Richard A. Muller, "The Barth Legacy: New Athanasius or Origen Redivivus? A Response to T.F. Torrance", *The Thomist*, October, 1990, Vol. 54, No. 4: 673–704.

[2]   For a much more positive reading of Torrance's Christology, see Andrew Purves, "The Christology of Thomas F. Torrance", *The Promise of Trinitarian Theology*, pp. 51–80.

with an open mind, it would be difficult to draw the conclusion that he simply was inventing an Athanasius to support a series of prior judgments. While there are some who might find occasional historical inaccuracies in Torrance's appraisal of Athanasius, much of what Torrance presents is carefully researched and accurately presented. One gets the impression that Torrance's scientific theology is historically and theologically grounded in a way that truly allows the unique object of faith to dictate what he thinks and says; moreover, he seems quite open to revising his thinking and to being self-critical in light of ongoing interaction with the risen and ascended Lord himself. All of this would seem to speak against these rather extreme criticisms of his work.

Other critics raise questions about whether or not Torrance has grounded his understanding of revelation in an intuitive experience, contrary to his own assertions that revelation always remains self-grounded.[3] While showing great respect for Torrance's theological achievement in his attempt to maintain both the sovereignty of God's grace and our full human inclusion in relationship with God by grace alone, this view actually propounds the notion that in the end Torrance's theology is foundationalist. That is, Torrance attempts to justify Christian beliefs (and thus his theology) by appealing to human experience in the form of an intuition. Accordingly, those who criticize Torrance from this vantage point do so by claiming that his thinking is caught in an irreconcilable conflict. On the one hand, it is suggested that if Torrance maintains the sovereignty of grace, then there can be no truly reciprocal relationship between the knowing subject and the God who graciously reveals himself in his Word and Spirit. On the other hand, it is then supposed that since Torrance does indeed ground the validity of our knowledge of revelation in our human intuitions, therefore there must be a genuinely reciprocal relation between knower (human persons) and known (God) that is characteristic of all human inquiry. This, then, would undermine Torrance's espousal of the sovereignty of God's grace as the sole determinant of our knowledge of God. Put simply, according to this view, the essential weakness of Torrance's theological enterprise consists in the fact that he must either deny that human rationality has a reciprocal relationship with God in order to affirm the sovereignty of God's grace or he may affirm that human rationality has a genuine place in the knowledge of God via revelation, in which case he must then deny the sovereignty of grace.

Those who bring this criticism against Torrance generally have not paid sufficient attention to the fact that it is precisely the doctrine of justification by faith and by grace alone that has structured Torrance's understanding of our knowledge of God through revelation. This is a pivotal point, because while Torrance certainly insists that human rationality is not suspended in our knowledge of God, and while he also claims that in knowing God the human subject is actively involved in such knowledge, he simultaneously insists that the basis of that knowledge always lies outside our concepts and experiences and can be found

---

[3]     See Ronald F. Thiemann, *Revelation and Theology: The Gospel as Narrated Promise* (Notre Dame, Indiana: University of Notre Dame Press, 1985), pp. 32–46.

only in Christ and thus only in faith and by grace. This is exactly what he means when he repeatedly insists that we must think from a center in God and not from a center in ourselves. For Torrance, there is a reciprocal relationship between us and God. But it is a relationship that has its reality in the movement of God toward us in the incarnation and in our movement toward God through faith by participating in the new humanity of Jesus himself as he vicariously represents us before the Father. In other words, for Torrance, our knowledge is quite real but it is real only as a sharing in the mutual knowledge and love of the Father and Son through the power of the Holy Spirit by means of our participation in Christ's new humanity.

Torrance himself reacted very strongly against the charge of foundationalism.[4] And this is perhaps quite understandable when the reader considers how very consistent Torrance's thinking on this subject actually is. In each of the dogmatic areas considered in this book, it is easy to see that Torrance expends a great deal of time and energy explaining how and why he believes that our knowledge of God could never be grounded in our own knowledge, experience or intuitions because it is governed exclusively by its relationship with the triune God who alone enables us to know him through what he calls repentant thinking. The very notion of repentant thinking clearly points in the direction of justification as the factor that alone allows us really to know God without projecting our intuitions or images on to God and without grounding that knowledge in our own intuitions or experiences. Here it is important to recall Torrance's main theological point, namely, that such experience is possible only in faith, by grace and through a present miraculous action of the Holy Spirit.[5] In other words, as Torrance often says, we cannot ultimately explain *how* our knowledge is related to the unique object that establishes the possibility and actuality of that knowledge of God

---

[4]  See Thomas Torrance Responds, *The Promise of Trinitarian Theology*, p. 331.

[5]  It is worth noting here that Ronald Thiemann actually misreads Torrance in *Theological Science*, claiming that Torrance equates revelation and intuition (*Revelation and Theology*, p. 39). Thiemann writes: "'Through that process [of allowing thought to conform to its object] the theologian finally gains 'an intuitive apprehension of the whole pattern of faith... . In natural science this is spoken of as *discovery*, in theology this is spoken of as *revelation*'" (*Theological Science*, pp. 129–30, quoted in Thiemann, p. 39). But Torrance continues by saying that "The interrogative form of inquiry must always reckon with the fact that in the last analysis it cannot say just how it has come to learn the truth. In natural science this is spoken of as *discovery*, in theology this is spoken of as *revelation*; the difference between discovery and revelation being determined by the nature of the object with which each has to do" (*Theological Science*, p. 131). This last statement by Torrance is important because for him revelation itself disallows any sort of foundationalism. Elmer Colyer, *How To Read T.F. Torrance*, also rejects Thiemann's idea that Torrance is a foundationalist because of the way he uses the concept of intuition (p. 344, n. 97), although in his book *The Nature of Doctrine in T.F. Torrance's Theology* (Eugene, OR: Wipf and Stock Publishers, 2001), Colyer characterizes Torrance as possibly a "soft foundationalist" (p. 50).

because in knowing God in Christ we are up against an ultimate.[6] That means we cannot find any authority to validate that knowledge outside of Jesus Christ who is himself God actually empowering us to know the Father through his Holy Spirit; this understanding would call into question claims that Torrance has confused revelation with human intuition.

From yet another perspective, Torrance has been criticized for reading Barth in a way that is so scientific and objective that Barth's theology, on which he relies in many ways, loses both its revolutionary character and its actualistic dynamism. According to this perspective, one has more of a subtle sense of being in a physics lab when reading Torrance and this too tends to obscure Barth's actualism and particularism.[7] Torrance even has been criticized for a kind of reductionism that actually advances the very existential understanding of revelation and the dualism he believed he had overcome in his theology.[8] In the end, according to this criticism, it is assumed that it is precisely Torrance's reliance on Barth and even on Kierkegaard that leaves God ultimately detached from history and from the human situation. This then places Torrance in the position of advocating a kind of mysticism that finally keeps the Word of God beyond our reach within our historical situation.[9] Part of the reason for this apparent dualism is traced to Torrance's supposed lack of engagement with Scripture and ultimately to his reading Scripture within what is sometimes referred to as an "incarnation–resurrection framework".[10] This is said to cause Torrance to fail to stress the activity of the Holy Spirit and even to detach the Holy Spirit from the event of revelation itself, with the result that Torrance's own view of the Spirit is finally judged to be "subordinationist".[11] Thinking in these sorts of ways leads Torrance actually to impose his own theological realism on the texts he reads, whether they be scriptural texts, patristic texts or the texts of Calvin.

---

[6]   See Torrance, *God and Rationality*, p. 36. For Torrance, "If you think you can reduce to statements how statements are related to the Truth of God you have resolved everything without remainder into statements alone" (p. 36). Torrance notes that this is a perennial problem and that it lies at the "heart of rationalist fundamentalism" (p. 36). Of course, Torrance equally opposes reducing statements about being and about God to expressions of our "inward moral states or attitudes of soul" (p. 37) because that would end in liberalism or what he calls modernism.

[7]   For examples of such criticism, see John Douglas Morrison, *Knowledge of the Self-Revealing God in the Thought of Thomas Forsyth Torrance* (New York: Peter Lang, 1997), p. 291, and George Hunsinger, *How To Read Karl Barth: The Shape of His Theology* (New York: Oxford University Press, 1991), pp. 10–11.

[8]   See Morrison, *Knowledge of the Self-Revealing God*, pp. 285–6 and 316ff.

[9]   See John Morrison, *Has God Said? Scripture, the Word of God, and the Crisis of Theological Authority* (Eugene, OR: Pickwick Publications, 2006), pp. 231–3.

[10]   See, for example, Morrison, *Knowledge of the Self-Revealing God*, p. 287.

[11]   Morrison, *Knowledge of the Self-Revealing God*, p. 337.

Torrance's attempt to develop a new natural theology also has been criticized from a number of perspectives. On the one hand, it is said that there is a residue of the old natural theology embedded in some of what Torrance has to say on the subject, even though his main dogmatic teaching shows no such influence.[12] On the other hand, it is claimed that Torrance's own understanding of God from the human level to the eternal Trinity makes the divine movement itself sound all too similar to "Platonic emanations". [13] Others find Torrance's new natural theology appealing since it indicates that he forged his own position independently of Barth and thus it provided a touchstone for broad theological discussion that Barth was unable to do.[14] The key issue to consider regarding Torrance's new natural theology is this: why is it that in his main works on the Trinity and his other dogmatic treatises he never explicitly advances an argument for any natural theology, old or new? This book offers a perspective that suggests that the reason may be that Torrance's belief that knowledge of God takes place as we know the Father through his Son and in the Spirit rules out any approach to God other than through faith in God's revelation, and that his "new natural theology" was simply his attempt to offer a theology of nature based on the knowledge of God that is gained through revelation. And, as noted above, in his dialogue with scientists he did seem to embrace some residual elements of the old natural theology that did not in fact come into play when he was thinking in a strictly dogmatic context.

Apart from the question of natural theology, there is a vital issue at stake in these other criticisms as well and it concerns the fact that Torrance, like Barth, wished to affirm God's continuing freedom even in his relations with us in history. Like Barth before him, Torrance was skeptical of mysticism. He himself noted that he rarely used the term[15] and that when he did, it was meant precisely to affirm that God is "infinitely greater than we can ever conceive or express".[16] Nonetheless, Torrance very firmly stresses that he did not want to work with any sort of "mystical tradition" or mystical theology and that all references to mysticism could be omitted from his thinking without in any way jeopardizing his theology.[17]

---

[12]   See Molnar, "Natural Theology Revisited".

[13]   Morrison, *Knowledge of the Self-Revealing God*, p. 293.

[14]   See, for example, McGrath, *An Intellectual Biography*, pp. 176ff. See also Alister E. McGrath, *A Scientific Theology: Volume I Nature*, pp. 279–305, where McGrath attempts to secure his own "natural theology" by appealing to Torrance's "new natural theology". One might well wonder, however, whether Torrance himself would countenance all that McGrath claims, especially when he asserts that natural theology has apologetic importance that would enable the Christian evangelist to "have a number of 'points of contact' for the gospel within the created order" (p. 299). On these issues, see above, Chapter 3.

[15]   See, for example, Torrance, *Reality and Scientific Theology*, p. 93.

[16]   Torrance Responds, *The Promise of Trinitarian Theology*, p. 328.

[17]   See Torrance Responds, *The Promise of Trinitarian Theology*, p. 329.

It is particularly imperative to realize that Torrance never argues that we are lifted up beyond the sphere of history and humanity by leaving these spheres behind in order to relate with and know God himself; rather, Torrance's constant insistence, as seen throughout this book, was on the fact that because of the incarnation we actually find God in the humanity of Jesus and only in him since he is that point in history where God has acted to enable us to know him precisely without leaving history and our own humanity behind. That is why Torrance maintained that the incarnation and resurrection must be held together to avoid any sort of Docetism; it was specifically because of the resurrection, in Torrance's view, that we could know God humanly without projecting concepts into God and without leaving the sphere of human experience and insight. Moreover, Torrance does not believe that Scripture is not the Word of God as some have suggested. Rather, for Torrance, Scripture is not the Word of God *as* Jesus is. Scripture is thus holy because that is the historical witness the triune God uses to continue to reveal himself to us. But the authority and significance of Scripture reside not in themselves but only as they point to Jesus Christ, the Word made flesh and "cohere in him".[18]

There are several crucial factors in Torrance's theology as it is shaped by the doctrine of the Trinity that need to be considered in relation to the criticisms just discussed. First, Torrance grounds his theology quite explicitly in the risen Lord himself and not at all in our ideas or experiences and certainly not in any kind of framework, whether it is incarnational or not. He is unequivocal about this, as he insists, and his thinking bears out the fact that all dogmatic theology whatsoever must begin and end with the incarnate, risen and ascended Lord.[19] Second, the criterion of Torrance's dogmatic thinking is the ascended and advent Lord who in reality is the same incarnate Word who forgave sins during his ministry and who is the same yesterday, today and tomorrow in virtue of his unique relationship with the Father and the Spirit within the immanent Trinity and in the economy. That is why Torrance repeatedly insists that atonement was not something that took place

---

[18]   Torrance, "The Place of Christology in Biblical and Dogmatic Theology", *Theology in Reconstruction*, pp. 144 and 142. See also Torrance, "The Deposit of Faith". Torrance insists that "we cannot take our feet off the ground or seek any kind of meaning or knowledge through detachment from the actualities of our life on earth" (Torrance, "Early Patristic Interpretation of the Holy Scriptures", *Divine Meaning*, p. 114) because in the incarnation, according to Scripture, we are given true knowledge of God the Father through his Son and in his Spirit. See Torrance, "Early Patristic Interpretation", *Divine Meaning*, pp. 114ff. and 128–9.

[19]   This is why Torrance insists that the raising of Christ as the act of God is the "*primal datum of theology, from which there can be no abstracting*, and the normative presupposition for every valid dogmatic judgment" (*STR*, p. 74). See also above, Chapter 7. For this reason, Torrance also insists that what is known from the risen Lord simply cannot be derived from either empirical reflection or from any religious a priori; it is utterly unique and as such it can only be known as a new creation within the old order and from itself (*STR*, p. 78).

"outside" our humanity but within it.[20] Third, Jesus Christ therefore continues to exercise his high priestly ministry even now and so remains forevermore both fully human and fully divine and as such the one and only mediator.[21] Everything here depends, for Torrance, as I noted above in the chapters on the Trinity, incarnation and atonement, on our understanding of the incarnate Word both enhypostatically and anhypostatically; his vicarious humanity is the historical locus for thinking from a center in God and not from a center in ourselves. When these points are not given their proper place in Torrance's overall theological perspective, then perhaps charges of an existential, dualist or mystical separation of God from history might arise. But, for Torrance, God meets us precisely *as* the man Jesus and not in some mystical existential experience. That, for Torrance, would lead to a symbolic view of Jesus' uniqueness, which he rejects. We have seen that, although the immanent and economic Trinity must not under any circumstances be separated, a clear distinction is still required because God always remains who he is even in his relations with us. That is why Torrance actually asserts the *enhypostatic* aspect of the incarnation:

> Far from the presence of the Deity of the Son overwhelming or displacing the rational human person in Jesus, his human mind and human soul, the exact opposite took place. And so it must be said that no human being has such a full and rich personal human nature as Jesus.[22]

Furthermore, Torrance asserts the *anhypostatic* aspect of the incarnation by maintaining that Christ's humanity has no existence apart from the Word and that there is

> unconditional priority of the Truth as Grace and the irreversibility of the relationship established between the Truth and us. The Logic of Grace is the way the Truth has taken in His disclosure to us. Because He does not cease to be Grace in our knowing Him, all our thoughts and their interrelations must reflect the movement of Grace.[23]

Those who would criticize Torrance for embracing dualism need to explain why it is that Torrance applies the *homoousion* not only to the Son's relation with the Father in eternity but also to the incarnate Word so that he frequently argues, as

---

[20]   See above, Chapter 7.

[21]   See above, Chapters 2 and 5, and *The Trinitarian Faith*, pp. 143–4, where Torrance rightly insists that the incarnation remains to all eternity; that is the basis of Christ's continuing kingly, prophetic and high priestly ministry, as we saw in Chapter 8.

[22]   Torrance, *The Trinitarian Faith*, p. 230.

[23]   Torrance, *Theological Science*, p. 214.

seen above, that Christ is one in being with us and that it is therefore through *his* humanity that we actually participate in the new creation.[24]

Fourth, Torrance's eschatological thinking bears out the fact that while he does indeed wish to maintain a proper distinction in union between humanity and divinity as this is revealed and real in the person and work of Christ, he still repeatedly insists upon a genuine union that excludes all dualism, especially any Nestorian separation of humanity and divinity.[25] This is why Torrance insists that it is Jesus Christ himself (and not some mystical experience of ours) that is

> the bridge between the reality of God and the realities of our world … He is thus the centre in our midst where the Reality and Word of God are translated into human reality and word and where we human beings may know and speak of God without having to transcend our creaturely forms of thought and speech. It is in and through Jesus Christ therefore that we creatures of space and time may know God the Father, in such a way as to think and speak truly and validly of him … Apart from the resurrection we could not say this.[26]

Those who would charge Torrance with dualism, then, would have to explain this important aspect of Torrance's theology which cannot be ignored or subverted in any complete appraisal of his work.

It is my hope that this book will offer support for the view that it is specifically Torrance's trinitarian understanding of the incarnation, resurrection, atonement and eschatology that enables him to maintain the authority of Scripture without falling into fundamentalism or liberalism;[27] it enables him to claim that God is present and directly active within space and time, but without being merged into space and time; it enables him to insist that the Holy Spirit binds us to the man Jesus himself precisely through the very human witness of the scriptural writings; it enables him to insist repeatedly and convincingly that our knowledge of the

---

[24]    See above, Chapter 3, and *The Trinitarian Faith*, p. 203.

[25]    Some have even charged Torrance with a Nestorian understanding of the Person of Christ. See, for example, Morrison, *Knowledge of the Self-Revealing God*, p. 320.

[26]    Torrance, *STR*, p. 71. The point here concerns the *vicarious humanity* of Christ which, as Torrance notes, Ray Anderson expressed very well. Thus, "revelation and reconciliation operate together". Self-revelation therefore includes "a corresponding movement from below to above … by which humanity is vicariously represented in the personal life, death, and resurrection of Jesus Christ". Torrance mentions that this truth was always a source of strength for him because "in and through [his] stumbling words and acts, [he relies] on the crucified and risen Lord Jesus himself who is present fulfilling his own ministry, undergirding mine in his name from below and above" (Torrance Responds, *The Promise of Trinitarian Theology*, p. 322).

[27]    See especially Torrance, *Reality and Evangelical Theology*, pp. 15ff. and Chapter 8. See also Torrance, "The Place of Christology in Biblical and Dogmatic Theology", *Theology in Reconstruction*, pp. 140ff., and "The Deposit of Faith".

immanent Trinity takes place within the realm of humanity and history and that we neither can nor should seek to escape this realm when knowing God on the higher level, that is, in his inner triune relations; it finally enables him to present a view of the church and sacraments that meticulously accentuates the significance of our humanity as it is actualized in and through the Spirit uniting us to Christ in his real presence as High Priest and empowering us to live as participants in the new creation.

But, for Torrance, all of this means that we cannot forget the depth dimension of the sacraments or of the Scriptures themselves since the meaning of both is determined by God's dynamic actions empowering these media with their significance as signs and human activities, denoting, indeed participating in, the real presence of God's Word and Spirit.[28] These are opened to us precisely where we are. But *that* they are opened to us always remains an *act* of the triune God and must never be confused with our knowledge in and through which this takes place. Torrance always was extremely careful to avoid prescriptive views of Scripture and doctrine because they tend to be legalistic by abstracting the words of Scripture and doctrinal teaching from their proper foundation in the Truth which is and remains identical with God's own triune activities within history on our behalf.[29]

Torrance's use of Scripture was most forcefully criticized by James Barr. Yet, as Kye Won Lee indicates, Torrance regarded Barr's thinking as a kind of "linguistic formalism" or nominalism that equates reality with linguistic usage when it should realize that reality is what it is and can only be understood *through* language.[30]

---

[28]   See above, Chapter 8.

[29]   See above, Chapters 2 and 8, and Torrance's important article "The Deposit of Faith".

[30]   See Lee, *Living in Union With Christ*, p. 47. See T.F. Torrance, "Scientific Hermeneutics According to St. Thomas Aquinas": 259, where Torrance himself characterizes James Barr's position espoused in *The Semantics of Biblical Language* (Oxford, 1961) as an "outstanding example of ... nominalist scepticism". Torrance's scientific approach to theology, as we have seen, requires that interpretation should provide "reasons ... for the significations established" (259). And, as noted above in Chapter 2, Torrance insists, against Barr, that we must not neglect "the fundamental principle of hermeneutics advanced by the Greek Fathers that we do not subject realities to the terms referring to them, but subject terms to the realities to which they refer. The Latin Fathers followed suit with their axiom, *non sermoni res, sed rei sermo subiectus est*" (Torrance, *Royal Priesthood*, p. x). Torrance directly responded to Barr's criticism of his use of biblical terms because he followed Kittel's *Theological Dictionary of the New Testament*, noting that Barr was rather hostile to Kittel's work. He called Barr a "brilliant philologist whose ideas cannot be ignored, although they are often rather exaggerated" (*Royal Priesthood*, p. x). And he indicated that he accepted some of Barr's criticisms of his use of biblical language but definitely not all of them, claiming that Barr's criticisms did not touch the heart of his work on Christ's royal priesthood. Instead, Torrance asserted that Barr's approach mistakenly "treated language independently as something having significance in itself ... and not primarily by reference to the realities beyond which they are meant to direct us" (*Royal Priesthood*, p. x). For

Torrance rejected both "subjectivist existentialism" and any such nominalism with his scientific realism, as discussed throughout this book. As seen above, Torrance was quite consistent in arguing that "The truthfulness of theological statements ... depends not on the truthfulness of their intention but on a participation in the Truth which God alone can give".[31] In Torrance's view, Barr changed statements about being to statements about statements.[32] Barr himself does not really address Torrance's rejection of nominalism and his insistence that terms must be subjected to realities rather than realities to terms when he claims that theologians such as Torrance who argue for the scientific character of theology are really only arguing for the superiority of their own theology and nothing more.[33] Torrance insists that theology stands or falls by the fact that God alone is the one who justifies and sanctifies all that is said and done in prayer and thanksgiving. He described even the best theology as the work of unprofitable servants. As such, it must always look to God for its justification.

Torrance also has been criticized for his style; such criticisms mainly focus on his brevity, which has led some to conclude that certain of his theological accounts of his own and others' work are actually unintelligible. He has even been criticized for espousing theological positions that are "private" and thus "publicly inexpressible".[34] In other words, since Torrance believes that knowledge of God is only possible based on the fact that we are included in God's own self-knowledge by grace, this seems to privilege some in relation to others who do not have this experience. They wonder whether or not the human apprehension of the truth really places human beings beyond the human and in the sphere of angels.[35] Along

---

Torrance, this is a "peculiar form of nominalism which rejects the relation of language to knowledge and culture, and which to get any kind of sense out of theological language treats it as some kind of description of religious phenomena ... [Barr] fails by his conflation of semantics with syntactics to deal faithfully with their [biblical] language in accordance with their intention in using it" (*Royal Priesthood*, p. x). See also Torrance, "Theological Education Today", *Theology in Reconstruction*, p. 19, where Torrance concludes that "It is not surprising that by denigrating the objective reference of language Barr should find so many people 'obscure', for he fails to deal faithfully with their language in accordance with their intention in using it".

[31]   Torrance, *Reality and Evangelical Theology*, pp. 147, 142. This thinking, for Torrance, is clearly dictated by the doctrine of our justification by faith and by grace alone (pp. 148ff.).

[32]   Torrance, *Reality and Evangelical Theology*, p. 73.

[33]   James Barr, *Biblical Faith and Natural Theology* (Oxford: Clarendon Press, 1993), p. 181.

[34]   See Daniel W. Hardy, "T.F. Torrance" in *The Modern Theologians: An Introduction to Christian Theology Since 1918*, Third Edition, ed David F. Ford *with* Rachel Muers (Oxford: Blackwell Publishers, 2005), pp. 163–77, 173. Elmer Colyer thinks the critique of Torrance offered by Daniel Hardy represents "the most serious criticism of Torrance's theological position to date" (Colyer, *How To Read T.F. Torrance*, p. 358).

[35]   See, for example, Hardy, *The Modern Theologians* (2005), p. 174.

with this set of criticisms, there is also included the idea that Torrance is both an "exclusivist" and that there is an "occasionalist tendency" in his thinking that stems from his engagement with Barth's "actualism". His thinking is said to be exclusivist because those who have not properly responded to the truth do not have genuine knowledge of reality and are thus excluded in some sense from genuine knowledge; this narrow vision seems therefore to exclude whatever does not conform to the reality which alone enables proper understanding. Torrance also has been criticized for not offering a full account of history because he focused too much on the knowledge of truth as explicated within history.[36]

Within the context of these criticisms, it is worth calling attention to two crucial features of Torrance's trinitarian understanding of dogmatics. First, as already noted, the doctrine of justification by faith must be taken into account when it comes to our knowledge of God. Moreover, for Torrance, the Holy Spirit is pivotal in our knowledge of God so that none of us can claim surety for our knowledge but must always refer to God himself as the only one who ultimately decides its truth value. It is because the object of theological inquiry is the truth of God as incarnate in Jesus that when the nature of that object prescribes the manner in which it is known, the doctrine of justification applies. Thus, "What the nature of this Truth requires, then, is *justification by Grace*, and *demonstration of the Spirit*, that is, verification and action by the Truth Himself".[37] Among other things, this implies that "human forms of thought and speech have all to be taken seriously and strictly honoured, but Truth who is by His very nature Grace and Spirit, and therefore His nature must be taken seriously and strictly honoured".[38] This thinking stresses the human and limited character of our knowledge of God and does not locate our knowledge of God beyond the sphere of history and experience, perhaps in some angelic realm. Second, it is important to recognize Torrance's view of sin and of the fact that, as sinners, we know God and the meaning of other doctrines in a way that will always be inaccurate unless and until we engage in repentant thinking. Even so, as seen above, repentant thinking itself is not at all under our control but takes place as God's grace enables it.[39] That is why Torrance speaks of theology as

---

[36]   See, for example, Hardy, *The Modern Theologians* (2005), p. 175.

[37]   Torrance, *Theological Science*, p. 198. Torrance also insists that "justification by the Grace of God in Christ applies not only to our life and action, but to our knowledge and is essentially relevant to epistemology" (p. 198).

[38]   Torrance, *Theological Science*, p. 198.

[39]   See above, Chapters 4 and 5, and see especially Torrance, *The Christian Doctrine of God*, pp. 99–100. Torrance writes: "In some ways the situation is rather more difficult in theology than in natural science, for due to our deep-rooted sin and selfishness we are alienated from God in our minds [Col. 1.21], and need to be reconciled to him. Hence, as we have seen, a repentant rethinking of what we have already claimed to know and a profound reorganisation of our consciousness are required of us in knowing God, as was made clear by Jesus when calling for disciples he insisted that they must renounce themselves and take up their cross in following him."

circular. It is not a vicious circle only because and to the extent that it begins and ends from a center in God and a center in history provided by God himself in the incarnation.[40] The fact that true theological knowledge is circular does not mean it is wrong; it simply means that theology must always begin and end in faith. Then theology can be certain of its truth. But because Torrance insists on the doctrine of justification by faith, here he also invariably, and very consistently, maintains that none of our knowledge is true in itself; it is true only as God actually enables us to know him through our views and concepts.[41]

Is this exclusivist? Yes. It is exclusivist in the sense that God can only be known with certainty through God alone, in accordance with Athanasius' famous dictum that it is more godly and accurate to know the Father through the Son than to name God the unoriginate through the works he has made. But it is fully inclusive since Torrance repeatedly contends that Christ died for the sins of everyone and so salvation (which includes our ability to think correctly about God) is in no way conditional. Therefore, while knowledge of God certainly includes our active knowing, its truth is not conditional on our acts of knowledge; rather, our obedient actions of faith spring from the fact that true knowledge of God and right ethical behavior have become real in Christ's vicarious humanity on behalf of all. No one is excluded from this. But people may exclude themselves for some inexplicable reason. And that is the problem of sin and evil discussed above. This sheds light on the charge of occasionalism.

Was there an occasionalist tendency in Torrance's thought in the sense that he so emphasized divine action that he eliminated human action and attributed to such human action no importance at all? What I have tried to show in this book is that Torrance's trinitarian theology, tied as it is to Christology and Pneumatology, represented his concerted effort to explain exactly why it is imperative to see that our humanity has its true and full meaning only in Jesus Christ. His constant assertion that what God is toward us in his Word and Spirit, he is eternally in himself is one of the ways this can be seen. By this he meant, among other things, that human being and action must be taken with strict seriousness just as we must take Jesus'

---

[40]    Since it is only through communion with God and therefore only through God that we know God, Torrance insists "that formulation of the Christian doctrine of God must be *intentionally circular*" because it is constrained by the very nature of God revealed in Christ (*The Christian Doctrine of God*, p. 28). Thus, "In this circular procedure we are not operating with a vicious circle, begging the question, or falling into the fallacy of a *petitio principii*. On the contrary, we are avoiding the grave mistake of retreating from the reality of God's trinitarian self-revelation, and moving outside of it in order to argue from some starting point of our own choosing or some alleged ground above or beyond the Holy Trinity from which the truth and validity of the doctrine of the Trinity may be judged. That would be in fact to deny that God is God, that he constitutes in himself the transcendent ground which we cannot know or understand in any way except in and through himself. It would be just as fallacious as attempting to justify ultimates in terms of what is not ultimate" (*The Christian Doctrine of God*, p. 27).

[41]    See, for example, Torrance, *Theological Science*, p. 201.

humanity with strict seriousness because humanity itself has been assumed into union with God in him. As we have seen already, the *homoousion* applied not only to the eternal Son in relation to the Father but to the fact that in the incarnation Jesus is one in being with us so that our humanity finds its reality, meaning and purpose in, through and with him. Through the Holy Spirit we actually participate in Christ's new humanity. But more than that—Torrance insisted that we must therefore share in the mind of Christ and that meant that since he shared fully our human experiences, we must realize that our full humanity is included in our relationship with God in Christ. Torrance rejected Apollinarianism in worship[42] precisely because he wanted to take with full seriousness Christ's humanity and ours.[43] And the fact that he did indeed give humanity its proper place within the theological enterprise is apparent throughout his theology and especially by his refusal to think of justification in a merely forensic sense. Perhaps Torrance's words best summarize his thinking here:

> It is the miraculous nature of the Spirit's activity that while He creates in us the ability to know God beyond all creaturely and human capacities this does not involve any suppression of our rational and critical powers. If we are enabled to apprehend God in His own divine nature, it is without having to take our feet off the ground, so to speak, or without having to transcend our human nature in its setting in space and time. In no way are we asked to take leave of our senses or to take irrational leaps—precisely the opposite is the case.[44]

Another question concerns whether or not Torrance's idea of science can be applied to all sciences. Here I think one should consider the fact that, for Torrance, the scientific method is simply meant to stress that all thinking—whether theological, biological, social or other, if it is to be scientific—must take place in accordance with the nature of the object being investigated.[45] This is the very factor that drives his particular theological realism. Once again, Torrance's theological realism strictly adheres to the doctrine of justification. Hence he refuses to build a logical bridge from reality as we may experience it to the reality of God in some form of an *analogia entis*. His realism is meant to stress that we must let God in Christ

---

42 See above, Chapter 8.

43 Elmer Colyer, *How To Read T.F. Torrance*, addresses the "occasionalist" charge by noting that for Torrance revelation and reconciliation are not "timeless and spaceless". They are not "conceived exclusively in terms of an 'event,' provoking the charge of 'occasionalism' (a noninteractive relation between the human mind and God in revelation), but rather a pattern of continued interaction between God and the time-space structures of this world in God's historical dialogue with Israel" (p. 65).

44 Torrance, *God and Rationality*, p. 168. See also Torrance, *Reality and Scientific Theology*, pp. 189–90.

45 See, for example, Torrance, *Theological and Natural Science*, pp. 120–21.

actually shape what we think and say about God and ourselves. And this can take place only in faith and by grace and revelation.

It is fairly common to see criticisms of Torrance's style. Many admire his succinctness. Still, Torrance does cover immense amounts of material in brief sweeping presentations. He presumes a great deal of background knowledge in early church history, mediaeval history and even modern history, and frequently presents his thinking about dualism or the sacraments, for example, in the context of wide historical developments. He is not materially incorrect in this. But there is so much in such a short space that it does sometimes make the reader's task a bit more difficult to decipher exactly what is going on. This does not make his presentations "unintelligible". Even Torrance himself noted the difficulty of his style and hoped that his repetition of theological themes would alleviate this. Yet it might be worth noting that he went on to say that "the difficulty of my style is sometimes due to the difficulty of the subject-matter!"[46]

What about the criticism that Torrance's position verges on the private and publicly inexpressible? From within the context of what has been presented in this book, one would have to judge Torrance's position in this regard in relation to the Gospel that drives his thought and enables him to formulate all his doctrinal *loci* from within the trinitarian self-revelation. This self-revelation, of course, is as public as was Christ's crucifixion and resurrection. And even though the risen Lord did not appear to everyone, the fact that he rose from the dead and sent the disciples out to preach the Good News associated with that event into the whole world clearly suggests that the truth of the Gospel was not meant to be and is not a private matter. The knowledge of who God is and what God has done in his Word and Spirit and is doing even now as the ascended and advent Lord is certainly not public knowledge if by that one means that it can be understood and presented without faith. But the fact that theological knowledge is indeed faith knowledge and thus knowledge of the truth does not make it publicly inexpressible. Still, the truth expressed in Torrance's theology will never be understood without faith which is not under our control because faith itself comes from the Holy Spirit. That is one reason why Torrance frequently stressed the need for prayer and humility when engaging in theology.

With regard to Torrance's treatment of history, one would have to assess Torrance's achievement by his own stated intentions. By that I mean that his interest with history was always one that was dictated by his quest for theological truth. What attracted Torrance to history was his own quest for a scientific theology, which he found in the early church fathers and also in Thomas Aquinas, Calvin, Luther and Barth. Of course, Torrance did not simply repeat the theology of Calvin or Barth. Rather, he took from them the theological truth they recognized and presented it within a modern scientific context and was able to avoid "the 'scholasticizing' tendency of most commentators"[47] so that Torrance could

---

[46]   Torrance, *The Christian Doctrine of God*, p. xi.
[47]   See Hardy, *The Modern Theologians* (1993), p. 75.

distinguish Calvin from Calvinism and Barth from Barthianism. Torrance's lifelong concern with patristic theology led him to the fourth-century fathers in order to present an ecumenical theology that is both evangelical and apostolic. Torrance intended to let the fathers speak for themselves. But he also brought them into conversation with contemporary theology. This is especially true with regard to his trinitarian theology, as seen throughout this book. But again Torrance's interest in the fathers was motivated by his concern to present the truth of the Christian faith. He is clearly interested in history but not in history without theology. Thus, his historical quest is guided by his search for the truth of God revealed in Christ and through his Spirit—he was always after that depth dimension that ultimately gave meaning to history itself. This does not invalidate his presentation of history which is often marked by his own reading of the fathers in their original Greek and Latin. It simply means that he refuses to allow an abstract view of history to dictate the task of theology.

Some have raised questions about Torrance's fundamental emphasis on the *homoousion* to the effect that while Barth stressed revelation for understanding the Trinity, Torrance, by contrast, stressed the *homoousion*.[48] Here it would be important to realize that Torrance believed that it was precisely the *homoousion* that reinforces a proper understanding of God's self-revelation in the incarnation in space and time.[49] For Torrance, one should not stress one of these categories over the other since both are equally important. Without revelation we would know nothing of the *homoousion*, and without the *homoousion* we would have an incorrect view of revelation. Holding these two categories together enables Torrance to understand three levels in our theological understanding of God's self-revelation in Christ as attested in Scripture, beginning with our experience of the Gospel, leading to a scientific and conceptual attempt to understand that experience and finally to a "metascientific" level where we integrate the knowledge gained on the first two levels.[50]

While Torrance himself notes that it is dangerous to have a single term carry the entire weight of conveying the central belief of the Gospel, he nonetheless insists that it is not the term that is of central significance; rather, the central issue is the Gospel itself which the term was meant to express.[51] He therefore insists that the fathers at Nicaea did not impose "an alien meaning upon the evangelical witness" but instead allowed their thinking to be shaped by God's own self-revelation in order to express the message of the Gospel. This term, however, did

---

[48] See Colin Gunton, "Being and Person", p. 118. See also Molnar, *Divine Freedom*, pp. 321ff., for a discussion of some differences between Gunton and Torrance regarding the Trinity.

[49] See also Torrance's response to Colin Gunton, *The Promise of Trinitarian Theology*, pp. 314–18.

[50] For Torrance's own detailed argument, see *The Christian Doctrine of God*, pp. 82–111.

[51] See Torrance, *The Incarnation*, p. xii.

function heuristically to help the early church understand the "ontic nexus in the relation of Christ to God the Father" which gave meaning to the entire scriptural witness.[52] Torrance admits, however, that the term itself is not "sacrosanct and beyond reconsideration", since "all theological terms and concepts fall short of the realities they intend"; accordingly, it too must be assessed continually "in the light of what it was coined to express in the first place".[53] And that is the point here. The term was meant to express the heart of the Gospel, namely, that what God is toward us in Jesus Christ he is eternally in himself. As seen above and throughout this book, each and every doctrine depends upon the unbroken oneness in being between Jesus and his Father and between the Holy Spirit and the Father and Son. Take away that unity of essence, and a proper understanding of atonement, knowledge of God, justification, the church's sacramental practice, among many other things, collapses.[54] All of this is meant to underscore Torrance's often repeated insight that "There is in fact no God behind the back of Jesus, no act of God other than the act of Jesus, no God but the God we see and meet in him".[55] As Torrance sees it, everything depends on whether or not one is willing to think from a center in God and in history provided by God himself in the incarnation, since the only other alternative would be to rely on one's own self-understanding and human culture to fashion God in terms of one's own myths and symbols as the Arians had done.[56]

The *homoousion* therefore, in Torrance's view, safeguards Christology from both Arianism and Nestorianism and thus helps us see that the economic Trinity is indeed the immanent Trinity without separating or collapsing the latter into the former. Any attempt to relate the economy to the eternal being of God which smacks of Arian or Nestorian tendencies misses the heart of the Gospel, namely, that Christ is capable of saving us from sin exactly because he is God (one in being with the Father) present among us acting as our mediator (against Arianism of all stripes) and there is a real hypostatic union of divine and human natures in the one Person of Christ (against Nestorianism of all stripes, including the idea that there was merely a moral union of two persons—one who was divine and one who was human) so that in the end no real incarnation would have taken place. The errors of Arianism and Nestorianism both lead to the same empty cistern: the separation of the immanent and economic Trinity and thus the idea that we must rely on ourselves both to know God in truth and to save ourselves from sin, suffering, evil and death. As seen throughout this book, any self-reliance in knowing God and in attempting to escape from sin simply misses the essential meaning of revelation which discloses to us that all of this has been enabled by the very fact that Jesus himself is God present and acting for us as the Savior of the world.

---

[52]   Torrance, *The Incarnation*, pp. xii–xiii.

[53]   Torrance, *The Incarnation*, p. xiii.

[54]   See especially Torrance, *The Incarnation*, pp. xvi–xvii.

[55]   Torrance, *The Incarnation*, p. xvii.

[56]   See Torrance, *The Incarnation*, p. xix.

When Torrance is criticized for overemphasizing the *homoousion*, it is usually because it is thought that this emphasis undermines a proper focus on the economy; when one stresses the equal divinity of the Father, Son and Spirit, it is thought that the particular characteristics of the persons of the Trinity are understated and thus flattened out. In addition, an emphasis on the *homoousion*, it is sometimes said, leads Torrance to locate the divine Monarchy in the entire Trinity rather than only in the Father. This line of criticism amounts to a rather subtle charge of something like a modalist tendency in Torrance's thought, which obscures the kind of "commanding and obeying" and "superordination and subordination" Barth saw not only in the economic Trinity but also within the immanent Trinity.[57] From this perspective, Torrance is said to underemphasize specific scriptural texts in his treatment of the Trinity, especially those texts in the Fourth Gospel and in 1 Corinthians 15 that stress the subordinationist elements of the economic Trinity.

It is further suggested that perhaps this under-emphasis is due to Torrance's reading Athanasius through "Augustinian eyes", so that even Athanasius' stress on "the particular being of the three persons of the Godhead" is stronger than Torrance's own presentation allows. When, for example, Torrance says that, for Athanasius, "the fullness of the Father's Being is the Being of the Son and of the Spirit",[58] this is said to undermine the fact that there is a real economic subordination of the Son within the economy. Yet, this criticism implies that problems arise because Torrance insists that this cannot be read back into "the eternal Godhead unless one operates with the altogether dubious idea that the Father is the 'cause' of the being of the Son, as both Basil and Gregory Nyssen held, a notion which Gregory of Nazianzus rightly rejected in line with the teaching of Athanasius".[59] It will be remembered here that Torrance had also criticized Barth for residual elements of subordinationism in his doctrine of the Trinity.[60] Here the real issue concerns whether or not the Father is known through the Son or through some aspect of creation. That is the context within which Torrance made his assertion that the fullness of the Father is the Son and Spirit. He wanted to stress that there was no access to the Father except through the Son and by the Spirit, as we have seen repeatedly.

What exactly is at stake in this notion of causality which Torrance so firmly rejects? Put simply, as seen above, one of the primary tasks of the theologian is to recognize that what God is toward us in his Word and Spirit he is eternally in himself, but that the anthropological ingredient in that recognition cannot be read back into the immanent Trinity indiscriminately without actually collapsing the immanent into the economic Trinity or separating the former from the latter. This

---

[57]   See, for example, Gunton, "Being and Person", p. 121. See also pp. 130–31.

[58]   Gunton, "Being and Person", pp. 130-31. See Torrance, *The Christian Doctrine of God*, pp. 116–17.

[59]   Torrance responding to Gunton, *The Promise of Trinitarian Theology*, p. 316. See also above, Chapter 2, for how this affects Torrance's trinitarian thinking.

[60]   See above, Chapter 1, and Molnar, *Divine Freedom*, pp. 323ff.

means that because all three Persons share equally as the one ultimate principle of the Godhead, there can be no room at all within the immanent Trinity for any kind of subordinationism; such thinking would open the door to the notion of degrees of Deity "such as that between the 'underived Deity of the Father', and the 'derived Deities of the Son and the Spirit'".[61] In Torrance's view, this actually would weaken the recognition that it is God himself who is active in his Word and Spirit as our Savior and Redeemer.[62]

Torrance believes that the use of "*aitia*" (causality) by Basil and his brother Gregory to describe the relations of the trinitarian Persons is unfortunate because it implies a "chain of causality" which is further complicated by the Greek position on the *filioque*. In Torrance's view, causality undermines the full Deity of the Persons because, for him, the Father is not to be seen as the cause of the divine being but only as first in the order of the Persons.[63] Hence, "there can be no thought of one Person being ontologically or divinely prior to another or subsequent to another".[64] Since each Person is fully God, the order within the Trinity does not apply to the Being of the divine Persons or to their Deity; "they are distinguished by position and not status, by form and not being, by sequence and not power, for they are fully and perfectly equal".[65] The order of the Persons, that is, Father, Son and Holy Spirit, is important because any change in order actually could suggest that God is different in his eternal essence from who and what he is when acting for us in Christ and the Spirit; it therefore could open the door to modalism, tritheism and to subordinationism, which indeed destroy the saving significance of the Gospel because modalism or tritheism would strip Jesus of his divine power and the Spirit of his divinity by suggesting God is ultimately one or ultimately three different divinities and not three Persons, one Being; the latter also would strip Jesus of his divine power along Arian lines while opening the door to identifying the Holy Spirit with the human spirit. The order of the Persons of the Trinity is a most serious issue that is often overlooked in contemporary theologies of the Trinity with dire consequences.

In addition to criticism for not offering the same amount of scriptural exegesis as is found in the fathers or in Barth, Torrance has been criticized for paying little attention to the details of Jesus' life as recorded in Scripture.[66] In Torrance's defense, one could note that his propensity toward brevity often took the form of very brief references to Scripture.[67] And Torrance overtly made his own the

---

[61]   Torrance, *Trinitarian Perspectives*, p. 112.

[62]   See above, Chapter 2.

[63]   Torrance, *The Christian Doctrine of God*, p. 180.

[64]   Torrance, *The Christian Doctrine of God*, p. 180.

[65]   Torrance, *Trinitarian Perspectives*, p. 136.

[66]   See, for example, Gunton, "Being and Person", p. 132.

[67]   See, for example, *The Christian Doctrine of God*, pp. 150–51 and all of Chapter 3, "The Biblical Frame". And, when citing the fathers, Torrance was certainly aware of their own extensive reliance on Scripture. But, of course, the most important issue concerns

approach to Scripture used by early church fathers such as Irenaeus, Athanasius and Hilary.[68] And it might also be noted that in his books *Space, Time and Resurrection* and *Reality and Evangelical Theology*, Torrance pays a good deal of attention to the way Scripture functions for our understanding of God. Moreover, Torrance's *Incarnation: The Person and Life of Christ* is replete with references to Scripture throughout in support of his understanding of the Person and work of Jesus Christ. With regard to the criticism that Torrance paid little attention to the details of Jesus' life as recorded in Scripture, one could say in his defense that Torrance often adopts as his own a patristic reference such as that of Basil in his work on the Holy Spirit who refers to Luke 2:52 to indicate that Jesus' human

> growth in wisdom was regarded as opening up a way for man to rise to true knowledge of the Father. Jesus Christ is not only the Truth who has accommodated himself to us ... not only the Word become flesh, but he is also Man hearing and obeying that Word, apprehending that Truth throughout his life on earth, so that he provides for us in his own obedient sonship within our human nature the *Way* whereby we are carried up to knowledge of God the Father.[69]

Torrance also believed that focusing on the details of Jesus' human life without seeing the depth dimension of that life was problematic; it was not Jesus' religious experience that was of interest to the biblical authors and to Torrance, but the fact that he himself was and is God's Word acting toward us and for us within history.

Other criticisms of Torrance relate directly to his understanding of the Trinity. For instance, Torrance has been criticized for using the term "Father" as a name for the relation that exists between the Father and the Son. Those who make this criticism generally want to avoid naming the Persons either "modes of being" or "relations" because that would take away their particularity, and if that is taken away, then the door is opened to modalism which all theologians, including Barth and Torrance, theoretically reject. This criticism is based on Basil of Caesarea's view that persons are not relations but that they are instead actually "constituted" by their relations to one another.[70] So the question to Torrance would

---

whether or not Torrance's thinking about the triune God was faithful to the scriptural witness or not. This book clearly demonstrates, I think, that it was and is.

[68] See, for example, "The Complex of Biblical Interpretation", pp. 5–14, "Early Patristic Interpretation of the Holy Scriptures", pp. 93–129, and "Transition to the West: the Interpretation of Biblical and Theological Statements according to Hilary of Poitiers", pp. 392–427, in *Divine Meaning*. These are just three important instances of how Torrance adopts a biblical hermeneutic that avoids any sort of fundamentalism or liberalism in his own work.

[69] Torrance, "The Logic and Analogic of Biblical and Theological Statements in the Greek Fathers", *Theology in Reconstruction*, p. 38. See also above, Chapter 5, for how Torrance integrates this thinking into his own view of the incarnation and atonement.

[70] See, for example, Gunton, "Being and Person", p. 126.

concern whether or not the three Persons were allowed by him to be distinctly themselves in a manner similar to the way the Cappadocians understood their distinctiveness.[71] According to this view, Torrance is thought to have shown little concern for the distinctiveness of the Persons within the Trinity, and, like many Western theologians, he tended to lose their particularity.[72] Further, it is claimed by those who assess Torrance's thought in this way that Torrance relies on Augustine to support the idea that persons are relations and that this is a Western and not an Eastern way of stating the matter.

This leads to further criticisms. For instance, Torrance is faulted for his understanding of the relation between person and *ousia* within the Trinity because it is thought that he believes that *ousia* refers to the being of the immanent Trinity, while *hypostasis* refers to being in its reference outwards. And this thinking, it is claimed, uses the notion of being (*ousia*) to describe God's unity, while *hypostasis* is then used to describe to describe God's "threeness". Accordingly, the terms *ousia* and *hypostasis* are used to denote the fact that the three Persons are the very triune being of God himself and thus they simply refer to aspects of the one divine Being. Within this line of thinking, Torrance then is said to undermine the particularity of the Persons and actually end up with a type of thinking that suggests that God actually might exist one way within the immanent Trinity and another way in the economy, even though it is clear that Torrance himself opposes this modalist idea.[73]

Torrance might respond to this criticism by noting that when he was referring to inner and outer in the use of the categories *ousia* and *hypostasis*, he was not referring to the immanent and economic Trinity (in terms of inner and outer) but to the fact that God exists *as* three Persons in the very being of God. The outward reference in this context then refers to the fact that the Persons of the Trinity exist in objective otherness in relation to each other within both the immanent and economic Trinity. Hence, Torrance himself writes:

> The main point that should be taken from this account is that while both *ousia* and *hypostasis* describe 'being' as such, in the trinitarian formulation 'one Being, three Persons', Being or οὐσία is being considered in its internal relations, and Person or ὑπόστασις is being considered in its otherness, i.e. in the objective relations between the Persons. In the case of the Father, this would amount to a distinction between the Father considered absolutely, as he is in himself, and the Father considered relatively to the Son, although of course it is one and the same Fatherly Being that is being considered absolutely *in se* as *ousia* and relatively *ad alium* as *hypostasis* … *ousia* is, in fact, identical with the personal Being or intrinsic Communion that the one God is in himself.[74]

---

[71]   See Gunton, "Being and Person", pp. 126–7.

[72]   See Gunton, "Being and Person", p. 127.

[73]   See, for example, Gunton, "Being and Person", p. 127.

[74]   Torrance, *The Christian Doctrine of God*, p. 131.

Torrance therefore envisaged no division of *ousia* from *hypostasis*. And since each Person of the Trinity, for Torrance, is fully and completely divine, one cannot restrict the concept of *ousia* to God's being generally and equate that with God's oneness, because there is no being of God outside or alongside the oneness of God that subsists in the Persons of the Trinity as they exist in relation to each other (their otherness). For Torrance, therefore, the connotation of these categories does not undermine the distinct characteristics of the Persons but rather underscores the fact that their distinctness must not be understood in any tritheist sense that might divide the Persons from their perichoretic relational coinherence. That is why, as seen above especially in Chapter 2, Torrance insisted upon the onto-relational nature of the Persons within the Trinity—their relations "belong to what they essentially are in themselves in their distinctive *hypostases*". Since God is thus three Persons in the heart of his being, God is dynamic, relational and personal as the living God who loves *in se* and *ad extra*. It is from the doctrine of the Trinity, then, that Torrance believed that a previously unknown concept of persons developed "according to which the relations between persons belong to what persons are".[75] By distinguishing our understanding of the Father absolutely and relatively, Torrance recognizes and preserves the unique understanding of person and being as articulated in the formula "One Being, Three Persons" expressed at the Council of Alexandria in 362 under the leadership of Athanasius.[76]

Torrance could respond to these criticisms by noting that he is not uninterested in the particularity of the Persons of the Trinity but that such interest must not be allowed to *define* and *delimit* the Persons of the Trinity.[77] In addition to following Athanasius here, Torrance also followed Karl Barth who resolutely insisted, following Augustine, that we may indeed denote the generation of the Son and procession of the Spirit, but this "cannot be comprehended".[78] This means, to Barth and to Torrance, that we are unable to

> establish the How of the divine processions and therefore of the divine modes of being. We cannot define the Father, the Son, and the Holy Ghost, i.e., we cannot delimit them the one from the other. We can only state that in revelation three who delimit themselves from one another are present, and if in our thinking we

---

[75]  Torrance, *The Christian Doctrine of God*, p. 102. See above, Chapter 2.

[76]  See Torrance, *The Christian Doctrine of God*, p. 112. Torrance insists that we cannot begin with God's "threeness" or God's "oneness" but only with God's self-revelation in which God is known as fully three and one simultaneously. See above, Chapter 2. The fact that this cannot be done is well made by Lewis Ayres in his important book *Nicaea and its Legacy: An Approach to Fourth-Century Trinitarian Theology* (New York: Oxford University Press, 2004). Ayres also maintains, against those criticisms just mentioned, that for Augustine persons are not just relations and there is no divine substance prior to or apart from God's existence as Father, Son and Holy Spirit (*Nicaea*, pp. 374–80).

[77]  See above, Chapter 2.

[78]  Barth, *CD* I/1, p. 476.

are not to go beyond revelation we must accept the fact that these three who delimit themselves from one another are antecedently a reality in God Himself. We can state the fact of the divine procession and modes of being. But all our attempts to state the How of this delimitation will prove to be impossible.[79]

Here there is a certain apophatic reserve which led Barth to assert that

> What has to be said will obviously be said definitively and exclusively by God Himself, by the three in the one God who delimit themselves from one another in revelation. Nor can there be any repetition of this by us ... The *ignoramus* which we must confess in relation to the distinction that we have to maintain between begetting and breathing is thus the *ignoramus* which we must confess in relation to the whole doctrine of the Trinity, i.e., in relation to the mystery of revelation, in relation to the mystery of God in general. If we could define this distinction we could define the Son and the Spirit and then we could define the Father as well, and therewith God Himself. For God Himself is the Father, the Son and the Spirit. Only if these were not God could we achieve a definition here ... there could be a successful definition of these three only on the assumption that the Father, the Son, and the Spirit are not God.[80]

Why must there be no definition here? Because God is, as Torrance rightly stresses, *ineffably* three Persons, one Being. This is a fact beyond which we cannot go and from which we may know God as he truly and eternally is, namely, as Father, Son and Holy Spirit. Any definition here would necessarily result in a dissolution of the doctrine of the Trinity into a definition such that God would now be under our control. Thus, if someone were to ask Torrance what it means to say that the Persons of the Trinity really subsist, that is, what the Persons really are, Torrance would likely respond, following Barth, by saying that such a question goes beyond the very limit set by revelation itself and moves toward a definition that, if achieved, will eventually lead in the direction either of modalism or tritheism or perhaps even subordinationism, but not toward an understanding of the eternal Father, Son and Holy Spirit. That is one of the chief reasons Torrance objected to the Cappadocian introduction of causality into their understanding of the trinitarian relations in the first place.

Closely tied to this issue are criticisms of Torrance's view of *perichoresis*. Some theologians believe that Torrance uses this term mainly to affirm the divine unity when in fact they believe that term should be used to indicate that the three Persons "constitute" the one God.[81] According to this view, Torrance supposes not only that *perichoresis* led to a new concept of persons in which their relations belong to what they are, but that he mainly derives the meaning of the term from

---

[79] Barth, *CD* I/1, p. 476.

[80] Barth, *CD* I/1, p. 477.

[81] See, for example, Gunton, "Being and Person", pp. 124–5.

the economy instead of from reflection on the eternal Persons, since, for Torrance, *perichoresis* depicts the revelation of the one God.[82] Those who make this criticism claim that Torrance's error is to move from *perichoresis* to person instead of from person to *perichoresis*, so that Torrance actually argued that *perichoresis* rather than the Persons of the Trinity gave us the new concept of persons. And this illustrates once more that Torrance has read the Eastern fathers through Western eyes with the result that his notion of the *homoousion* flattens out the distinct particularities of the Persons.[83]

With this criticism of Torrance's thought, too, one could ask whether or not those who make it do so because they want to move beyond the limit recognized by Barth and Torrance. Moreover, one needs to consider in this context whether or not Torrance actually has recognized a genuine limit here such that any movement beyond it could lead to a rationalizing of the mystery of the Trinity itself. For Torrance, *perichoresis* is a term that is intimately connected with the term *homoousion* and therefore its meaning is strictly governed "by the mutual indwelling of the Father and the Son and the Spirit".[84] Torrance rejects the idea that the meaning of the term *perichoresis* is derived mainly from the "economy" since this idea illustrates "the error that attributes it to Gregory of Nazianzus" who used the term to speak of Christ's divine and human natures and not of the trinitarian Persons. Torrance claims that *perichoresis* was first used to refer to the Trinity by John of Damascus in *De Fide Orthodoxa* who appropriated it from Pseudo-Cyril's *De Sancta Trinitate* without acknowledgment. It thus came to refer to "the complete mutual containing or interpenetration of the three divine Persons, Father, Son and Holy Spirit, in one God".[85] Further, Torrance insists that while it is through revelation that we know of the "coinherent relations within the one being

---

[82]     Gunton, "Being and Person", p. 125.

[83]     It is indeed ironic that Torrance would be accused of reading Eastern fathers through Western eyes and thus distorting their views since Torrance himself made every effort to avoid this and did indeed avoid this as when he himself criticized the great Patrologist, Berthold Altaner, for misunderstanding the important thinking of John Philoponos when Altaner claimed that Philoponos tried to reconcile Christian teaching with Aristotelianism. According to Torrance, it was exactly opposite: Philoponos criticized Aristotelianism in light of Christian teaching. Thus, for Torrance, "we cannot understand the language of the Greek Fathers, far less their thought, by reading back Latin Aristotelianism into it, as evidently happened with the influential Boethius" (Torrance, *Theological and Natural Science*, p. 86). Torrance himself was taking a courageous stand here by defending Philoponos, who had been condemned as a "monophysite" and "tritheist" precisely because he was read incorrectly through "western eyes" in such a way that Latin terms such as *substantia* were mistakenly equated with *hypostasis* or *essentia* with *ousia*.

[84]     Torrance, *The Christian Doctrine of God*, p. 102. See also Torrance, "The Relation of Incarnation to Space", *Divine Meaning*, p. 367.

[85]     Torrance, *The Christian Doctrine of God*, p. 102.

of God",[86] still the meaning of this concept was grounded upon the relations within God's being made known in revelation. This is why Torrance insists that

> Just as we take our knowledge of the Father from our knowledge of the Son, so we must take our knowledge of the Spirit from our knowledge of the Son, and in him from our knowledge of the Father: that is, from the inner relations which the Father, Son and Holy Spirit have with one another in the one indivisible being of the Holy Trinity.[87]

Indeed, Torrance argues that "It is on that inner divine basis, and not on any creaturely basis outside of God, that the life and work of Christ the incarnate Son of God are to be understood as that of the One Mediator between God and men, who is himself God and man".[88] Those who suggest that *perichoresis* is understood by Torrance mainly from the economy and not from the relations of the eternal Persons must deal with these statements by Torrance himself. It certainly appears that it is not *perichoresis*, thus understood, that is Torrance's theological criterion, but, by his own reckoning, that criterion is the inner trinitarian relations of the Father, Son and Spirit. Indeed, if *perichoresis* had been his criterion here, Torrance would have violated his own oft-repeated insistence that concepts are subject to realities rather than the other way around!

Torrance is sometimes criticized for not engaging more with John Zizioulas, in spite of their disagreements, since both theologians agreed that the fathers contributed to a new notion of person. Those who make this criticism want to retrieve the notion that persons are not relations but have their being precisely in relation to others. This insight, it is suggested, would allow theologians to give proper weight both to the one and the many within the Trinity and would enable theologians today to overcome the weaknesses of individualism and collectivism.[89] Torrance, therefore, is said to have failed to stress adequately how we may understand human personhood better from our new understanding of the divine Persons within the Trinity. With reference to this criticism, we may refer the reader to Chapters 5 and 6 above for how Torrance works out his own understanding of the incarnation by referring to Jesus as the "Personalising Person" who enables us to overcome individualism. Torrance, like Barth, understood good dogmatics as ethics since both theologians rigorously applied the doctrine of justification to the theological enterprise itself. One might even say that Torrance's entire theological anthropology, which is based on the doctrines of the Trinity, incarnation and atonement (as well as the doctrine of justification), bear out his ethics in a particularly striking way since he steadfastly refuses to base his understanding of

---

[86]  Torrance, *The Trinitarian Faith*, p. 305.
[87]  Torrance, *The Trinitarian Faith*, p. 306.
[88]  Torrance, *The Trinitarian Faith*, p. 308.
[89]  See, for example, Gunton, "Being and Person", pp. 131–2.

our personal relations anywhere else but in Christ himself as the "personalizing person".[90]

Finally, we may mention very briefly the fact that while Torrance has been praised for his attempts to deal creatively with *filioque* issue, he also has been criticized because it is thought that any version of the *filioque* leads toward some sort of modalism. In other words, if the Spirit comes from the Father *and* the Son, one will always be led to ask what it is that ultimately gives the Father and Son their underlying unity, and with that question one will ineluctably be led toward modalism by moving beyond the Trinity to find a deeper cause for the meaning of existence.[91] Those who make this criticism are careful to stress that neither Barth nor Torrance actually are modalists in their thinking. Nonetheless, it is suggested that neither Barth nor Torrance paid sufficient attention to the particular Persons of the Trinity as experienced within the economy and this lack of attention fails to eliminate the underlying causes of modalism.[92]

As seen above, Torrance's goal in presenting his innovative understanding of the *filioque* was to eliminate any hint of subordinationism within the Trinity and also avoid any suggestion that there is more than one source of the divine Being.[93] That precisely was the importance of the agreed formula that God is one Being, three Persons. And that is why Torrance so adamantly opposed introducing causality into the Trinity either in a Western or an Eastern style. Those theologians who believe that the Monarchy is to be sought in the Father rather than in the whole Being of the Trinity, as understood by Torrance, need to consider Torrance's substantive proposal that if the divine Monarchy is found in the Being of the Father, Son and Spirit, then one could say that the Spirit proceeds from the Father through the Son or even from the Father and the Son as long as no subordinationism or modalism was implied. While Torrance would freely admit that modalism is a serious issue, he might also point out that the underlying issue is whether or not our thinking begins and ends with Jesus Christ and thus with the fact that God is one Being, three Persons and not with any other "original one". Torrance's solution to the *filioque* undercuts modalism, tritheism and subordinationism root and branch. And that is, or at least should be, the appeal of his Athanasian and Epiphanian solution to the problem of the *filioque*.

---

[90] For more on Torrance's ethics, see Molnar, *Incarnation and Resurrection*, pp. 100–104 and 144–51.

[91] See, for example, Gunton, "Being and Person", pp. 133–4.

[92] See, for example, Gunton, "Being and Person", p. 134.

[93] See above, Chapters 1, 2 and 6. See also Torrance, *The Promise of Trinitarian Theology*, p. 317.

# Conclusion

We have completed our exploration of the main dogmatic *loci* of T. F. Torrance's theology and we have seen that his thinking is rigorously and consistently structured by his patristically and Reformed appreciation of the doctrine of the Trinity. Torrance therefore can legitimately be called the theologian of the Trinity. As one of the truly great theologians of the twentieth century, T. F. Torrance has consciously and consistently presented a fully developed understanding of the Trinity as the single intelligible and ecumenically viable way to understand not only inter-church relations but all serious theological issues regarding Christology, Pneumatology, theological method, creation, atonement, sacramental theology, knowledge of God, nature and grace, church practice, ministry, worship and much else besides, including very technical questions such as the *filioque*. Here, then, it is appropriate to conclude this work with the words Torrance himself used to conclude his monumental first book on the Trinity, the Collect for Trinity Sunday:

Almighty and everlasting God, who has revealed thyself as Father, Son, and Holy Spirit, and dost ever live and reign in the perfect unity of love: Grant that we may always hold firmly and joyfully to this faith, and, living in the praise of thy divine majesty, may finally be one in thee; who art three Persons in one God, world without end.

# Selected Bibliography

Achtemeier, P. Mark, "Natural Science and Christian Faith in the Thought of T.F. Torrance" in *The Promise of Trinitarian Theology: Theologians in Dialogue with T.F. Torrance*, ed Elmer M. Colyer, pp. 269–302 (Lanham, Maryland: Rowman & Littlefield Publishers, Inc., 2001).

Ayres, Lewis, *Nicaea and its Legacy: An Approach to Fourth-Century Trinitarian Theology* (New York: Oxford University Press, 2004).

Barr, James, *Biblical Faith and Natural Theology* (Oxford: Clarendon Press, 1993).

Barth, Karl, *Church Dogmatics*, 4 vols. in 13 pts.

Vol. I, pt. 1: *The Doctrine of the Word of God*, ed G.W. Bromiley and T.F. Torrance, trans. G.W. Bromiley (Edinburgh: T&T Clark, 1975).

Vol. I, pt. 2: *The Doctrine of the Word of God*, ed G.W. Bromiley and T.F. Torrance, trans. G.T. Thomson and Harold Knight (Edinburgh: T&T Clark, 1970).

Vol. II, pt. 1: *The Doctrine of God*, ed G.W. Bromiley and T.F. Torrance, trans. T.H.L. Parker, W.B. Johnston, H. Knight, J.L.M. Harie (Edinburgh: T&T Clark, 1964).

Vol. III, pt. 1: *The Doctrine of Creation*, ed G.W. Bromiley and T.F. Torrance, trans. J.W. Edwards, O. Bussey, H. Knight (Edinburgh: T&T Clark, 1970).

Vol. III, pt. 2: *The Doctrine of Creation*, ed G.W. Bromiley and T.F. Torrance, trans. H. Knight, G.W. Bromiley, J.K.S. Reid, R.H. Fuller (Edinburgh: T&T Clark, 1968).

Vol. III, pt. 3: *The Doctrine of Creation*, ed G.W. Bromiley and T.F. Torrance, trans. G.W. Bromiley and R.J. Ehrlich (Edinburgh: T&T Clark, 1976).

Vol. IV, pt. 1: *The Doctrine of Reconciliation*, ed G.W. Bromiley and T.F. Torrance, trans. G.W. Bromiley (Edinburgh: T&T Clark, 1974).

Vol. IV, pt. 2: *The Doctrine of Reconciliation*, ed G.W. Bromiley and T.F. Torrance, trans. G.W. Bromiley (Edinburgh: T&T Clark, 1967).

Vol. IV, pt. 4: *The Doctrine of Reconciliation*. Fragment. *Baptism as the Foundation of the Christian Life*, ed G.W. Bromiley and T.F. Torrance, trans. G.W. Bromiley (Edinburgh: T&T Clark, 1969).

Barth, Karl, *Fides Quaerens Intellectum: Anselm's Proof of the Existence of God in the Context of his Theological Scheme*, trans. Ian W. Robertson (London: SCM Press, 1960).

Bauman, Michael, *Roundtable Conversations with European Theologians* (Grand Rapids, Michigan: Baker Book House, 1990).

Buckley, James J, "Christian Community, Baptism, and Lord's Supper", *The Cambridge Companion to Karl Barth*, ed John Webster, pp. 195–211 (Cambridge: Cambridge University Press, 2000).

Colyer, Elmer M., *How to Read T.F. Torrance: Understanding His Trinitarian & Scientific Theology* (Downers Grove, Illinois: InterVarsity Press, 2001).

Colyer, Elmer M., *The Nature of Doctrine in T.F. Torrance's Theology* (Eugene, Oregon: Wipf and Sock Publishers, 2001).

Colyer, Elmer M., (ed.), *The Promise of Trinitarian Theology: Theologians in Dialogue with T.F. Torrance* (Lanham, Maryland: Rowman & Littlefield Publishers, Inc., 2001).

Deddo, Gary, "The Holy Spirit in T.F. Torrance's Theology", *The Promise of Trinitarian Theology: Theologians in Dialogue with T.F. Torrance*, ed Elmer M. Colyer, pp. 81–114 (Lanham, Maryland: Rowman & Littlefield Publishers, Inc., 2001).

DiNoia, J.A., O.P., "Karl Rahner", *The Modern Theologians*, Vol. 1, ed David F. Ford, pp. 183–204 (Oxford: Blackwell, 1989).

Godsey, John D., (ed.), *Karl Barth's Table Talk* (Richmond: John Knox Press, 1962).

Grenz, Stanley J., *Rediscovering the Triune God: The Trinity in Contemporary Theology* (Minneapolis: Fortress Press, 2004).

Gunton, Colin E., "And in One Lord, Jesus Christ … Begotten, Not Made", *Nicene Christianity: The Future for a New Ecumenism*, ed Christopher Seitz, pp. 35–48 (Grand Rapids, Michigan: Brazos Press, 2001).

Gunton, Colin E., "Being and Person: T.F. Torrance's Doctrine of God", *The Promise of Trinitarian Theology: Theologians in Dialogue with T.F. Torrance.* ed Elmer M. Colyer, pp. 115–37 (Lanham, Maryland: Rowman & Littlefield Publishers, Inc., 2001).

Gunton, Colin E., *The Promise of Trinitarian Theology, Second Edition* (Edinburgh: T&T Clark, 1997).

Hanson, Revd Canon A.T., "Two Consciousnesses: The Modern Version of Chalcedon", *Scottish Journal of Theology* 37.4 (1984): 471–83.

Hardy, Daniel W., "Thomas F. Torrance", *The Modern Theologians: An Introduction to Christian Theology in The Twentieth Century, Volume I*, ed David F. Ford, pp. 71–91 (Oxford: Blackwell Publishers, 1993).

Hardy, Daniel W., "T.F. Torrance", *The Modern Theologians: An Introduction to Christian Theology Since 1918*, Third Edition, ed David F. Ford with Rachel Muers, pp. 163–77 (Oxford: Blackwell Publishers, 2005).

Haught, John F., *The Revelation of God in History* (Wilmington, Delaware: Michael Glazier, 1988).

Heron, Alasdair I.C., *A Century of Protestant Theology* (Philadelphia: The Westminster Press, 1980).

Heron, Alasdair I.C., *The Holy Spirit: The Holy Spirit in the Bible, the History of Christian Thought, and Recent Theology* (Philadelphia: The Westminster Press, 1983).

Heron, Alasdair I.C., "A personal engagement", *The Cambridge Companion to Karl Barth* ed John Webster, pp. 296–306 (Cambridge: Cambridge University Press, 2000).

Hesselink, I. John, "An Interview with Thomas F. Torrance", *Reformed Review* 38.1 (Autumn 1984): 47–64.

Hunsinger, George, "The Dimension of Depth: Thomas F. Torrance on the Sacraments of Baptism and the Lord's Supper", *Scottish Journal of Theology* 54.2 (2001): 155–76.

Hunsinger, George, *The Eucharist and Ecumenism: Let Us Keep the Feast* (Cambridge: Cambridge University Press, 2008).

Hunsinger, George, *How To Read Karl Barth: The Shape of His Theology* (New York: Oxford University Press, 1991).

Imhof, Paul, and Hubert Biallowons (eds.), *Karl Rahner in Dialogue: Conversations and Interviews 1965–1982*, trans. and ed Harvey D. Egan (New York: Crossroad, 1986).

Johnson, Elizabeth A., *She Who Is: The Mystery of God in Feminist Theological Discourse* (New York: Crossroad, 1992).

Kaiser, Christopher B., "Humanity in an Intelligible Cosmos: Non-Duality in Albert Einstein and Thomas Torrance", *The Promise of Trinitarian Theology: Theologians in Dialogue with T.F. Torrance*, ed Elmer M. Colyer, pp. 239–267 (Lanham, Maryland: Rowman & Littlefield Publishers, Inc., 2001).

Kimel, Alvin F., Jr (ed.), *Speaking the Christian God: The Holy Trinity and the Challenge of Feminism* (Grand Rapids: Eerdmans, 1992).

LaCugna, Catherine Mowry, *God For Us The Trinity and Christian Life* (San Francisco: Harper San Francisco, 1991).

Lauber, David, *Barth on the Descent into Hell: God, Atonement and the Christian Life* (Aldershot: Ashgate, 2004).

Lee, Kye Won, *Living in Union With Christ: The Practical Theology of Thomas F. Torrance* (New York: Peter Lang Publishing, Inc., 2003).

Mackey, James P., *Jesus the Man and the Myth: A Contemporary Christology* (New York: Paulist Press, 1979).

McCormack, Bruce L., *Karl Barth's Critically Realistic Dialectical Theology: Its Genesis and Development 1909–1936* (Oxford: Clarendon Press, 1995).

McGrath, Alister E., *A Scientific Theology: Volume I, Nature* (Grand Rapids, Michigan: William B. Eerdmans Publishing Company, 2001).

McGrath, Alister E., *Thomas F. Torrance: An Intellectual Biography* (Edinburgh: T&T Clark, 1999).

Molnar, Paul D., *Divine Freedom and the Doctrine of the Immanent Trinity: In Dialogue with Karl Barth and Contemporary Theology* (New York/London: T&T Clark/Continuum, 2002/2005).

Molnar, Paul D., "The Eucharist and the Mind of Christ: Some Trinitarian Implications of T.F. Torrance's Sacramental Theology", *Trinitarian Soundings in Systematic Theology*, ed Paul Louis Metzger, pp. 175–88 (New York and London: T&T Clark, 2005).

Molnar, Paul D., *Incarnation and Resurrection: Toward a Contemporary Understanding* (Grand Rapids: William B. Eerdmans Publishing Company, 2007).

Molnar, Paul D., *Karl Barth and the Theology of the Lord's Supper: A Systematic Investigation* (New York: Peter Lang, 1996).

Molnar, Paul D., "Love of God and Love of Neighbor in the Theology of Karl Rahner and Karl Barth", *Modern Theology* 20.4 (October 2004): 567–99.

Molnar, Paul D., "Natural Theology Revisited: A Comparison of T.F. Torrance and Karl Barth", *Zeitshrift für dialektische Theologie* 20.1 (December 2005): 53–83.

Moltmann, Jürgen, *God in Creation: A New Theology of Creation and the Spirit of God*, trans. Margaret Kohl (New York: Harper and Row, 1985).

Moltmann, Jürgen, *The Trinity and the Kingdom, The Doctrine of God*, trans. Margaret Kohl (New York: Harper & Row, 1981).

Morrison, John Douglas. *Has God Said? Scripture, the Word of God, and the Crisis of Theological Authority* (Eugene, Oregon: Pickwick Publications, 2006).

Morrison, John Douglas, *Knowledge of the Self-Revealing God in the Thought of Thomas Forsyth Torrance* (New York: Peter Lang, 1997).

Muller, Richard A., "The Barth Legacy: New Athanasius or Origen Redivivus? A Response to T.F. Torrance", *The Thomist* 54.4 (October 1990): 673–704.

Palma, Robert J., "Thomas F. Torrance's Reformed Theology", *Reformed Review* (Autumn 1984) vol. 38/no. 1: 2–46.

Peters, Ted, *God as Trinity: Relationality and Temporality in Divine Life* (Louisville: Westminster/John Knox Press, 1993).

Purves, Andrew, "The Christology of Thomas F. Torrance", *The Promise of Trinitarian Theology: Theologians in Dialogue with T.F. Torrance*, ed Elmer M. Colyer, pp. 51–80 (Lanham, Maryland: Rowman & Littlefield Publishers, Inc., 2001).

Rahner, Karl, *Foundations of Christian Faith: An Introduction To the Idea of Christianity*, trans. William V. Dych (New York: Seabury, 1978).

Rahner, Karl, *The Love of Jesus and the Love of Neighbor*, trans. Robert Barr (New York: Crossroad, 1983).

Rahner, Karl, *Theological Investigations*. 23 vols.

Vol. 5: *Later Writings*, trans. Karl-H. Kruger (Baltimore: Helicon Press, 1966).

Vol. 6: *Concerning Vatican Council II*, trans. Karl-H. and Boniface Kruger (Baltimore: Helicon Press, 1969).

Vol. 9: *Writings of 1965–1967*, trans. Graham Harrison (New York: Herder and Herder, 1972).

Vol. 11: *Confrontations 1*, trans. David Bourke (New York: Seabury Press, 1974).

Vol. 19: *Faith and Ministry*, trans. Edward Quinn (New York: Crossroad, 1983).

Rahner, Karl, *The Trinity*, trans. Joseph Donceel (New York: Herder and Herder, 1970).

Schaff, Philip and Henry Wace (trans. and ed.) *A Select Library of Nicene and Post-Nicene Fathers of the Christian Church Second Series* (Edinburgh: T&T Clark, 1987).

Shapland, C.R.B. (trans), *The Letters of Saint Athanasius Concerning the Holy Spirit* (London: Epworth Press, 1951).

Stanley, Timothy, "Returning Barth to Anselm", *Modern Theology* 24.3 (July 2008): 413–37.

Thiemann, Ronald F., *Revelation and Theology: The Gospel as Narrated Promise* (Notre Dame, Indiana: University of Notre Dame Press, 1985).

Thompson, John, *Modern Trinitarian Perspectives* (New York: Oxford University Press, 1994).

Torrance, David W., "Thomas Forsyth Torrance: Minister of the Gospel, Pastor, and Evangelical Theologian", *The Promise of Trinitarian Theology: Theologians in Dialogue with T.F. Torrance*, ed Elmer M. Colyer, pp. 1–30 (Lanham, Maryland: Rowman & Littlefield Publishers, Inc., 2001).

Torrance, Iain R., Review of *Thomas F. Torrance. An Intellectual Biography* by Alister McGrath, *The Evangelical Quarterly* 73.3 (2001): 285–88.

Torrance, Thomas F., "The Atonement: The Singularity of Christ and the Finality of the Cross: The Atonement and the Moral Order", *Universalism and the Doctrine of Hell: Papers presented at the Fourth Edinburgh Conference in Christian Dogmatics, 1991*, ed Nigel M. De S. Cameron (Grand Rapids, Michigan: Baker Book House, 1992).

Torrance, Thomas F., *Calvin's Doctrine of Man* (Eugene, Oregon: Wipf and Stock, 2001).

Torrance, Thomas F., "The Christian Apprehension of God the Father", *Speaking the Christian God: The Holy Trinity and the Challenge of Feminism*, ed Alvin F. Kimel, Jr, pp. 120–43 (Grand Rapids: William B. Eerdmans, 1992).

Torrance, Thomas F., *The Christian Doctrine of God, One Being Three Persons* (Edinburgh: T&T Clark, 1996).

Torrance, Thomas F., *Conflict and Agreement in the Church, Vol. I: Order and Disorder* (Eugene, Oregon: Wipf and Stock, 1996).

Torrance, Thomas F., *Conflict and Agreement in the Church, Vol. II: The Ministry and Sacraments of the Gospel* (Eugene, Oregon: Wipf and Stock, 1996).

Torrance, Thomas F., "The Deposit of Faith", *Scottish Journal of Theology* 36.1 (1983): 1–28.

Torrance, Thomas F., *Divine and Contingent Order* (Edinburgh: T&T Clark, 1998).

Torrance, Thomas F., *Divine Meaning: Studies in Patristic Hermeneutics* (Edinburgh: T&T Clark, 1995).

Torrance, Thomas F., *Incarnation: The Person and Life of Christ*, ed Robert T. Walker (Downers Grove, IL: InterVarsity Press, 2008).

Torrance, Thomas F., *The Doctrine of Grace in the Apostolic Fathers* (Pasadena/ Eugene, Oregon: Wipf and Stock, 1996).

Torrance, Thomas F., *The Doctrine of Jesus Christ* (Eugene, Oregon: Wipf and Stock, 2002).

Torrance, Thomas F., *God and Rationality* (London: Oxford University Press, 1971; reissued Edinburgh: T&T Clark, 1997).

Torrance, Thomas F., *The Ground and Grammar of Theology* (Charlottesville: The University Press of Virginia, 1980).

Torrance, Thomas F., *The Hermeneutics of John Calvin* (Edinburgh: Scottish Academic Press, 1988).

Torrance, Thomas F., "The Hermeneutics of John Reuchlin, 1455–1522", *Church, Word, and Spirit: Historical and Theological Essays in Honor of Geoffrey W. Bromiley,* ed James E. Bradley and Richard A. Muller, pp. 107–22 (Grand Rapids, Michigan: William B. Eerdmans, 1987).

Torrance, Thomas F., *The Incarnation: Ecumenical Studies in the Nicene-Constantinopolitan Creed* (Edinburgh: The Handsel Press, 1981).

Torrance, Thomas F., *Karl Barth, Biblical and Evangelical Theologian* (Edinburgh: T&T Clark, 1990).

Torrance, Thomas F., *Kingdom and Church: A Study in the Theology of the Reformation* (Eugene, Oregon: Wipf and Stock, 1996).

Torrance, Thomas F., Letter to Brand Blanshard of April 11, 1952, published in *The Scotsman*, April 14, 1952 and forthcoming in *Theology in Scotland* in 2009.

Torrance, Thomas F., *The Mediation of Christ* (Colorado Springs: Helmers & Howard, 1992).

Torrance, Thomas F., *The Ministry of Women* (Edinburgh: The Handsel Press, 1992).

Torrance, Thomas F., "My Interaction with Karl Barth", *How Karl Barth Changed My Mind*, ed Donald K. McKim, pp. 52–64 (Grand Rapids, Michigan: William B. Eerdmans, 1986).

Torrance, Thomas F., *Preaching Christ Today: The Gospel and Scientific Thinking* (Grand Rapids, Michigan: William B. Eerdmans, 1994).

Torrance, Thomas F., "Preaching Jesus Christ", *A Passion For Christ: The Vision that Ignites Ministry*, ed Gerrit Dawson and Jock Stein, pp. 23–32 (Edinburgh: The Handsel Press and PLC Publications, 1999).

Torrance, Thomas F., "Predestination in Christ", *The Evangelical Quarterly* 13.2 (April 1941): 108–141.

Torrance, Thomas F., "The Problem of Natural Theology in the Thought of Karl Barth", *Religious Studies* 6 (1970): 121–35.

Torrance, Thomas F., *Reality and Evangelical Theology* (Philadelphia: The Westminster Press, 1982).

Torrance, Thomas F., *Reality and Scientific Theology* (Eugene, Oregon: Wipf and Stock, 2001).

Torrance, Thomas F., *Royal Priesthood: A Theology of Ordained Ministry* (Edinburgh: T&T Clark, 1993).

Torrance, Thomas F., "Scientific Hermeneutics according to St. Thomas Aquinas", *The Journal of Theological Studies* XIII.2 (October 1962): 259–89.

Torrance, Thomas F. (trans. and ed.), *The School of Faith: The Catechisms of the Reformed Church* (Eugene, Oregon: Wipf and Stock, 1996).

Torrance, Thomas F., *Scottish Theology: From John Knox to John McLeod Campbell* (Edinburgh: T&T Clark, 1996).

Torrance, Thomas F., "A Sermon on the Trinity", *Biblical Theology* 6.2 (January 1956): 40–44.

Torrance, Thomas F., *The Soul and Person of the Unborn Child* (Scottish Order of Christian Unity, Handsel Press, 1999).

Torrance, Thomas F., *Space, Time and Incarnation* (Edinburgh: T&T Clark, 1997).

Torrance, Thomas F., *Space, Time and Resurrection* (Edinburgh: T&T Clark, 1998).

Torrance, Thomas F., "The Truth of the Virgin Birth", unpublished manuscript in the Library of Princeton Theological Seminary, 1–3.

Torrance, Thomas F., *Theological and Natural Science* (Eugene, Oregon: Wipf and Stock, 2002).

Torrance, Thomas F., "Theological Realism", *The Philosophical Frontiers of Christian Theology: Essays presented to D.M. MacKinnon*, ed Brian Hebblethwaite and Stewart Sutherland, pp. 169–96 (Cambridge: Cambridge University Press, 1982).

Torrance, Thomas F., *Theological Science* (New York: Oxford University Press, 1962).

Torrance, Thomas F., *Theology in Reconciliation: Essays towards Evangelical and Catholic Unity in East and West* (London: Geoffrey Chapman, 1975).

Torrance, Thomas F., *Theology in Reconstruction* (London: SCM Press Ltd, 1965).

Torrance, Thomas F., *Transformation & Convergence in the Frame of Knowledge: Explorations in the Interrelations of Scientific and Theological Enterprise* (Grand Rapids: William B. Eerdmans, 1984).

Torrance, Thomas F., *The Trinitarian Faith: The Evangelical Theology of the Ancient Catholic Church* (Edinburgh: T&T Clark, 1988).

Torrance, Thomas F., *Trinitarian Perspectives: Toward Doctrinal Agreement* (Edinburgh: T&T Clark, 1994).

Torrance, Thomas F., "Truth and Authority: Theses on Truth", *The Irish Theological Quarterly* 38 (1972): 215–42.

Webster, John. *Word and Church: Essays in Christian Dogmatics* (Edinburgh: T&T Clark, 2001).

Wiles, Maurice, *The Remaking of Christian Doctrine* (Philadelphia: Westminster Press, 1978).

Wright, David F. and Badcock, Gary D. (eds), *Disruption to Diversity: Edinburgh Divinity 1846-1996* (Edinburgh: T&T Clark, 1996).

# Name Index

Achtemeier, P. Mark 2, 29
Albert the Great 291
Altaner, Berthold 347
Anderson, Ray 332
Anselm 6, 23, 34–5, 96
Apollinaris 138
Aquinas, Thomas 6, 285, 291, 333, 338
Aristotle 24, 39, 50–1, 81, 126, 132–3, 135
Arius 33, 38, 43–4, 49, 56–7, 86, 99,
    170, 190
Athanasius 6, 8, 18, 21–2, 31, 33, 36, 38,
    40–4, 46, 50–3, 55, 57–8, 60, 62,
    64–70, 73–5, 77–9, 81–3, 85–7, 89,
    99, 108, 122, 125, 127, 132, 134–5,
    138 142, 149–50, 153, 155–8,
    187, 193, 195, 198–9, 202, 205–6,
    209–17, 250, 267–8, 281, 284, 299,
    310, 325–6, 336, 341, 343, 345
Athenagoras 85
Augustine 6, 33, 65, 90, 144, 162, 240,
    254, 282, 301, 318, 344–5
Ayres, Lewis 345

Badcock, Gary 15–16
Baillie, Donald 5
Baillie, John 2, 5, 7, 14
Barr, James 35, 333–4
Barth, Christoph 7
Barth, Karl 1, 4–9, 13–14, 21, 23, 34–5,
    40–1, 43–4, 47, 52, 60, 68–70, 73,
    85, 93–4, 96–8, 105, 115–16, 121,
    129, 140, 146, 159–60, 162, 165,
    182, 197, 216, 230, 234, 250, 252,
    254, 268, 275, 302–4, 325, 328–9,
    335, 338–9, 341–3, 345–9
Basil of Caesarea 53, 64–6, 193, 202,
    211–12, 341–3
Basileides 74
Bauman, Michael 3, 7
Blanshard, Brand 23

Blondel, Maurice 173
Bonaventura 291
Bouillard, Henri 98
Bromiley, Geoffrey 13, 187
Brunner, Emil 13, 23, 113, 123 166, 245
Buckley, James 302
Bultmann, Rudolf 23, 30, 130, 172–3, 223,
    226, 239, 262

Calvin, John 1, 6, 8–9, 13, 34–5, 47, 76,
    127, 159–60, 162–4, 176–7, 179,
    181, 231, 237, 247, 252–3, 277,
    316, 328, 338–9
Campbell, John McCleod 176, 309, 321
Chalmers, Thomas 15
Clement of Alexandria 272
Colyer, Elmer 1, 29, 95, 158, 327, 334, 337
Congar, Yves 20
Craig, John 267–8
Cullman, Oscar 14
Cyprian 265, 270, 274
Cyril of Alexandria 8, 62, 65, 150, 155,
    202–3, 231, 241, 281, 313
Cyril of Jerusalem 211–12

Dawson, Gerrit 11
Deddo, Gary 190
Didymus the Blind 202–3, 211, 215
DiNoia, J. A. 68
Dodd, C. H. 224
Duns Scotus, John 81

Einstein, Albert 22–6, 99
Epictetus 138
Epiphanius 64, 67, 210–13, 216–17
Eunomius 150, 210–11

Farrer, Austin 9
Fergusson, David 16
Florovsky, Georges 157

Gregory Nazianzen 8, 57, 62, 64–5, 74,
    143, 149–50, 155, 202, 205, 212,
    214, 216, 250, 341, 347
Gregory Nyssen 58, 79, 138, 143, 150,
    155, 211, 310, 341
Grenz, Stanley J. 1, 71–2
Gunton, Colin E. 70–1, 174, 211, 339,
    341–9

Haight, Roger 117
Hanson, Revd. Canon A T 156–7
Hardy, Daniel 2, 334–5, 338
Harnack, Adolf von 45, 237
Haught, John 107
Hegel, G. W. 131
Heim, Karl 98
Herod the Great 102
Heron, Alasdair I. C. 3, 22, 28, 202, 302
Heron, John 22
Hesselink, I. John 3–4, 7, 9
Hilary of Poitiers 33–6, 49, 62, 73, 125,
    230, 250, 268, 343
Hodges, H. A. 11
Hooker, Richard 127
Hosea 168
Hume, David 3
Hunsinger, George 1, 311, 328

Ignatius of Antioch 207
Irenaeus of Lyons 33–4, 36–7, 39–40, 86,
    2250, 255, 268–70, 296, 301, 343

John of Damascus 62, 74, 82, 241, 347
Johnson, Elizabeth 51

Kaiser, Christopher 22–3
Kant, Immanuel 3, 24, 43, 99, 121, 129,
    223
Kennedy, H. A. A. 7
Kierkegaard, Søren 328
Kilbansky, Raymond 9
Kittel, Gerhard 333
Knox, John 174–6, 179, 240
Küng, Hans 27

LaCugna, Catherine 62
Lamont, Daniel 4–5, 11
Lauber, David 146

Lee, Kye Won 1–2, 232, 333
Lessing, G. E. 129–30
Lewis, John Wren 29
Lombard, Peter 35, 176, 291
Lonergan, Bernard 203
Luria, Isaac 80
Luther, Martin 116, 127–30, 170, 176, 179,
    251, 338

Macedonius 210
Mackey, James 15
MacKinnon, D. M. 48
Mackintosh Hugh Ross 4–5, 7, 13–14, 103,
    148
Macmurray, John 191
Major, John 35
Maréchal, Joseph 173
Martin, Alexander 4
Mascall, Eric L. 9
Maxwell, James Clerk 25
McCormack, Bruce L. 6, 16
McGrath, Alister E. 1–15, 29, 95, 329
McIntyre, John 2, 14–16
Melito of Sardis 143, 146
Molnar, Paul D. 8, 70, 82, 93, 115–17, 129,
    145, 190, 216, 222, 302, 313, 329,
    339, 341, 349
Moltmann, Jürgen 79–82, 84, 87, 145, 149,
    203
Morrison, John 328, 332
Muller, Richard 325

Newbigin, Lesslie 71
Newton, Isaac 129–30

Origen 33, 36, 40, 42–3, 60, 74, 85–6, 99,
    124, 127, 133–4, 268, 272, 301,
    310, 325
Ott, Heinrich 14

Palma, Robert 3
Pannenberg, Wolfhart 95
Pelagius 172
Peters, Ted 131, 149
Philoponos, John 24, 87, 91, 347
Photius 24
Plato 3, 24, 39, 74, 91, 132, 240
Polanyi, Michael 25–6

Pope John XXIII 37
Purves, Andrew 325

Rahner, Karl 20–1, 68–71, 84, 105–7,
 114–15, 128, 173, 204, 216, 304
Reid, J. K. S. 12
Reuchlin, John 187
Robinson, John A. T. 29–30, 71, 125, 140,
 169, 172–3, 193

Schillebeeckx, Edward 27, 172–3
Schleiermacher, Friedrich 3–4, 30, 105
Schmidt, Karl Ludwig 7
Schmidt, Martin 7
Serapion 58, 202, 205, 210, 212
Shepherd of Hermas 208
Smith, Norman Kemp 3
Spear, Margaret Edith 7
Spinks, Bryan 22
Stanley, Timothy 6
Strauss, D. F. 226

Taylor, A. E. 3
Tertullian 37, 237, 269–70, 282, 301
Thiemann, Ronald 326–7
Thompson, G. T. 5
Thompson, John 203
Thurian, Max 311
Tillich, Paul 30, 130, 172–3
Torrance, David W. 4
Torrance, Iain R. 14–16, 22
Torrance, Thomas F. 1–30, 31–72, 73–100,
 101–36, 137–86, 187–218, 219–64,
 265–324, 325–51

Vogel, Heinrich 172

Webster, John 71
Wiles, Maurice 30, 71
Wollebius, Johannes 6
Wycliffe, John 274

Zizioulas, John 348

# Subject Index

Advent Lord/advent of Christ (*see second coming, parousia*) 16–17, 150, 189, 221, 225, 236, 246, 258–63, 269, 272, 276–7, 284, 330, 338

Agnosticism (agnostic) (*see Knowledge of God, agnostic views*) 38, 44, 46, 52–54, 74, 108, 122, 152, 187

Aitkin Fellowship 6

Alyth Barony Parish Church 9, 13

Analogy (see *analogia entis*) 6, 51, 97, 117, 122, 155, 164, 214, 275, 293
  *Analogia entis* (analogy of being) 286, 337

Anthropology 13, 62, 157
  Pelagian 208
  philosophical 64, 165
  theological 13, 163, 348–9

Apollinarianism /Apollinarian 101, 137–8, 150, 227, 185, 313, 320, 337

Apologetic (apologetics) 4, 95, 116, 329

Arianism 33, 38–9, 44–8, 54–5, 66, 74, 110, 132, 174, 207, 215–16, 271, 301, 340

Ascension 8, 18, 119, 126–8, 132, 149, 175–6, 179, 195, 197, 217, 219, 221, 225, 228, 232–3, 236, 238, 240, 244–62, 266, 274, 276, 278–9, 285–6, 291, 293–5, 297, 315–16, 318, 321
  Ascension and Eschatology 246–50
  Christ's Second Coming (*see second coming, parousia, advent Lord*)
  God's Time 253–9
  The Nature of the Ascension 250–3

Atonement 8, 12–13, 16, 59, 70, 85, 106, 118–20, 135, 137–86, 189–97, 200, 225, 227–34, 237, 239, 248, 269, 289–90, 292–3, 299, 310–11, 321, 330–32, 340, 343, 348, 351

abasement (condescension, self-humiliation) 10, 47, 104, 118, 131, 139, 190, 208, 227, 271, 321

active obedience 177, 230–4

assumption of our fallen humanity 16, 119, 138, 143, 146, 150–1, 163, 167, 174, 177, 227, 230, 234, 243–5, 251, 276, 285

atonement as a personal act 142–7

atonement as satisfaction 229–30

cross (*see crucifixion*) 10, 12–13, 57, 76, 117, 120, 122, 138, 140–1, 146–8, 151–7, 159–67, 169, 171–4, 177, 184–5, 192, 195, 201, 207, 228–9, 231, 237, 239, 249, 257–63, 275–6, 279–80, 294, 297–9, 320, 335

dereliction 146, 152, 155, 161, 167

despair 159, 161

devil 98, 143, 159, 293, 310

divine impassibility 109, 140, 147–55

evil 75, 87–8, 98, 106, 118, 120, 140, 143, 146, 149, 159, 163, 166, 168–9, 182, 200, 226–7, 230–1, 234, 258, 279, 293–4, 336, 340

exchange 141, 154

expiation 293, 311–12

forgiveness 11, 18, 118, 120–1, 147, 153, 171–2, 175, 247, 262, 287, 301, 315–16

guilt 118, 150, 152, 155, 159, 161, 165, 167, 228, 237, 248, 293

Jesus' death (*see Death*) 13, 30, 57, 70, 109, 119–20, 140, 146–9, 154, 159, 169, 173, 177–9, 182, 200, 225, 228–31, 236–7, 246, 249, 255, 260, 262, 272, 276, 279, 280, 288, 290, 293–4, 297, 298, 300, 306–7, 310–11, 315–16, 332

judgment 11, 58, 120, 140, 146, 148, 151–2, 154, 160, 166–8, 171–2, 174, 177, 179, 183, 185, 194, 200, 229–31, 258, 276, 278, 294, 299, 322

justification (*see justification by faith*) 10, 17–19, 75–6, 81, 124, 141, 147, 151, 156, 161, 168–86, 210, 219–21, 225, 229–30, 238, 240, 244, 265, 269, 284, 289, 293–4, 307, 310, 313, 326–7, 334–7, 340, 348

forensic 178, 337

misery 159, 208, 228

passive obedience 177–9, 228–30

punishment 159, 161, 177

ransom 143, 293–4, 310

reconciliation 53, 98, 101, 117, 120–1, 137, 143, 145, 147, 154, 164, 168, 175, 183, 194, 206, 231–2, 245–6, 263, 279–81, 289, 291, 321, 332, 337

redemption 36, 54, 57–8, 80, 84–5, 88, 90, 103, 142–3, 146, 150, 178, 180, 198, 206, 220, 229, 234, 236–7, 239, 241, 245–6, 255, 257, 267, 269, 275–6, 284, 286, 288, 293–4, 297, 299, 301–2, 309

sacrifice (*see eucharistic sacrifice*) 13, 84, 138, 143–4, 146–8, 161, 168, 174, 184–5, 195, 208, 228–9, 247–8, 276, 282, 286–7, 289–93, 298, 308, 310–12, 319–21

salvation (*see conditional salvation*) 4, 10, 18, 36, 42, 54, 57–9, 66, 68, 72–3, 76, 84, 102–3, 108–9, 112, 114–16, 122, 126, 131, 137–8, 140–3, 149–50, 156, 163, 170–2, 175, 178–81, 185, 189, 192, 197, 207, 227–8, 231, 237–8, 247, 261, 275, 280, 286, 292, 294–5, 299, 300–302, 311, 322, 336

sanctification 119, 159, 177–81, 210, 219, 276, 284

self-justification (*see Righteousness, self-will*) 75, 147, 151, 169, 180, 183, 208, 210, 289, 291, 294–5

sin 13, 60, 88, 90, 106, 117–20, 137–50, 152–6, 159–68, 171–4, 177–8, 195, 198, 227–31, 234, 237, 241, 243–4, 276, 282, 284, 292–4, 300–1, 309, 313, 335–6, 340

original sin 162, 300

soteriology 14, 27, 110, 154, 169, 190, 283, 321

unassumed is unredeemed (unhealed) 150

works-righteousness (*see Righteousness, self-righteousness, self-will*) 179–80

Auburn Theological Seminary 7

Auburn Lectures 60, 102, 112, 124

Baptism (*see Sacraments*) 22, 65, 107, 154, 172, 176, 215, 219, 229, 237, 245, 247, 258, 261, 273, 276, 287–90, 291, 295–309, 311, 322

Beechgrove Church, Aberdeen 13–14

Biblical interpretation (scriptural interpretation) 25, 224, 328, 332, 339, 341–2

allegorical/metaphorical 125, 210

exegesis 210, 342

fundamentalism 4, 328, 332, 343

historical criticism 25

liberalism 4, 328, 332, 343

symbolic (*see Symbol*) 43, 124–5, 128, 172–3, 331

*Tropici* (tropical interpretation of scripture) 125, 210

Blackie Fellowship 6

Cappadocian doctrine of the Trinity 8, 64–6, 77, 205, 209, 211, 214–17, 268, 344, 346

Chalcedon (*see Christology*) 32, 156, 278, 284

Chalcedonian 22, 184, 273

Christ (*see Atonement, Christology, homoousion, incarnation, resurrection, ascension*)

*homoousion* with the Father and with us 54ff., 101–136

*homoousion* with the Spirit 189–213

incarnation 101–135, 137–186, 187ff.
incarnation and creation 73–99
Reconciler and Redeemer 137–85
resurrection and ascension 214–263
Christology 9–10, 14, 20–1, 24–7, 54, 69,
    99, 101, 105–11, 124, 126–30,
    142, 156, 163, 170, 190, 207, 221,
    273–4, 283–5, 290, 313–14, 318,
    321, 325, 336, 340, 351
adoptionist (adoptionism) 101, 195,
    205, 210, 221, 237
*a priori* 220, 297, 330
centrality of Christ 4, 19, 190
centrality of Christology 190
Chalcedonian (*see Chalcedon*)
Christ as personalizing person 144–5,
    159, 203, 348–9
Christocentric (Christocentricity) 18,
    112, 116, 318, 325
Christomonism (Christomonist) 184,
    307, 325
*communicatio idiomatum* 286
crucifixion (*see cross*) 102, 151, 160,
    223, 227–8, 235, 249, 260, 338
Docetic (*see Docetic Christology*) 39,
    63, 78, 99, 101, 105–11, 124, 138,
    225, 240, 245, 284, 314, 318
Easter event 220, 223
Ebionite (Ebionitism) (Ebionism) (*see
    Ebionite Christology*) 25, 39, 99,
    101, 105–11, 124, 205, 210, 238,
    314
Eutychianism (*see Eutychian*) 238, 278
from above 101, 108–9, 236, 292
from below 101, 107–9, 113,
    155–6, 292, 332
Incarnation (*see Incarnation*)
Jesus' vicarious activity (*see
    Incarnation, Jesus' vicarious
    activity*)
Monophysitism (monophysite) 24, 184,
    227, 251, 283–5, 313, 347
Nestorian (Nestorianism) 153, 169,
    181, 227, 238, 278, 320, 332, 340
Resurrection 10, 18, 30, 60, 69–70,
    76, 85, 90, 92, 110–11, 117–18,
    119–20, 130, 132, 141, 149, 151,
    152, 154, 157, 159, 161, 166, 168,

    172, 175, 177–9, 182, 188, 195,
    197, 218–51, 254–5, 257–8, 260–3,
    266, 269, 270, 272, 274, 276,
    278–80, 284–7, 290, 293–4, 295,
    297–8, 300, 307, 311, 314–16, 318,
    322, 328, 330, 332, 338
Theocentric (Theocentricity) 112, 116,
    176
Creation 8, 24, 28–9, 40–3, 49–50, 59,
    73–100, 101, 105, 107, 118, 126,
    131–7, 149–50, 164, 188–9, 194–8,
    201, 203, 206, 220, 222, 224–5,
    234–5, 241, 244, 250, 253–5,
    262–3, 266–7, 269, 276–8, 280,
    290, 302, 309, 316, 341, 351
and *homoousion* 54
as contingent 17, 25, 27, 39, 79–83,
    86–90, 92–3, 95–6, 98, 118, 123,
    134, 254
contingent freedom 29, 90–3
contingent intelligibility 29, 50, 88–9
*creatio ex nihilo* 79–80, 85
free creation 79, 90–3
new act for God 42, 82–3, 137, 197
new creation 119, 189, 198, 221,
    235–41, 244–6, 255, 260, 262, 267,
    276, 293, 309, 316, 330–1, 333
panentheism (*see Panentheism*)
pantheism (*see Pantheism*)
priest of creation 28
understanding creation *through*
    incarnation 85–93
zimsum (zimzum) 80

Death (*see Atonement, Jesus' death*) 80, 88,
    90, 117, 140–1, 165, 168, 177, 188,
    195, 197, 200, 236, 238, 241–5,
    255, 292, 340
Demythologize (demythologization,
    demythologizing) 130, 247, 251,
    256
Divine freedom 41–2, 47, 52, 56, 78–9,
    82–4, 90, 114, 129, 139–40, 145,
    148–9, 162, 181, 196–7, 199, 205,
    206, 255, 294, 329
Docetic Christology (*see Christology,
    Docetic*)
Docetic ecclesiology 272–3, 278

Docetism 109, 205, 210, 238, 330
Dogmatic theology 2, 29, 64, 98, 124, 217,
   225, 330
Dualism (dualist) (Augustinian and
   Newtonian) (Platonic) (Cartesian
   and Kantian) (Greek) (*see legalism,
   moralism, self–justification,
   phenomenalism, cosmological,
   epistemological, Greek*) 5, 8, 25,
   27, 38–43, 46, 54–5, 66, 69, 80,
   89, 92, 99, 107, 129–30, 146, 172,
   181, 187, 223–6, 240, 269–73, 295,
   300–3, 306, 318–23, 328, 331–2,
   338

Ebionite Christology (Ebionite) (*see
   Christology, Ebionite*)
Election 8, 17, 28, 140–1, 169, 181
Eschatology (eschatological) (*see Hope,
   eschatological reserve*) 16–17, 126,
   130–1, 149, 175, 219, 225, 236,
   240, 244–7, 258, 261–2, 269, 274,
   281–2, 286–7, 312, 316, 322, 332
   and ascension 246–50
   and the Lord's Supper 314, 316, 318
   apocalyptic 17, 245, 251, 259
Eternity 20, 38, 50, 53, 57–9, 61, 81, 83,
   105–6, 108, 111, 116, 124, 131,
   188, 195–6, 244, 254, 256, 269–70,
   292, 317, 331
   eternal life 120, 149, 157–8, 189, 244,
   253–4, 268–9, 272, 284, 307, 321
Ethics 102, 151, 168, 348–9
   conditional salvation (*see salvation,
   Pelagianism*) 172, 207, 231
   good Samaritan 115
   justification by faith (*see justification*)
   75, 170, 174–5, 179, 183, 269, 307,
   313, 326, 334–6
   legalism (moralism, self-justification)
   (*see Dualism*) 141, 151, 179,
   269–73, 301
   love of God 9–10, 65, 84, 112, 113–15,
   118, 120, 148, 153, 172, 232, 258,
   272, 278, 288
   love of neighbor 113–15, 119, 173, 307
   natural law 89, 241

   self-justification (*see Atonement,
   Righteousness, self-will*)
Eunomian heresy 65, 150, 210–11
Eutychian/Eutychianism (*see Christology*)
   62, 238, 278
Evolution (evolutionary) 107, 196

Faith 10, 12, 15–16, 18, 23, 25–7, 32–40,
   46–7, 51–2, 70, 75–6, 87, 93–5,
   98–9, 102, 107–8, 111, 113, 116,
   119–21, 123, 130, 138–9, 144–6,
   154, 159, 162, 164, 166, 168–80,
   182–3, 187–8, 194, 196–7, 201,
   204, 206, 210, 219, 221–3, 226,
   228, 233, 235–6, 238–45, 251,
   259, 262–3, 265, 268–70, 274–5,
   278–81, 285, 287, 295, 301–03,
   306–09, 313–15, 325–7, 329,
   334–9, 351
   Deposit of Faith 36–8, 270
   Resurrection and Faith 221–3
Fideism 94

Gnostic (Gnosticism) 17, 39, 74, 109, 271,
   301
God (*see Christology, Holy Spirit, Trinity,
   knowledge of God*)
Godliness (piety) 6, 21, 36, 58, 68, 282,
   286
Gospel 33, 36–7, 39, 43, 54, 56–60, 62,
   75–6, 91, 95, 101–2, 109–10,
   116–17, 141, 150, 155, 174–6, 181,
   203, 222, 235–7, 239–40, 242, 245,
   247, 250, 256, 260–1, 267, 270,
   272, 279–80, 287, 289–91, 297,
   303, 317, 329, 338–42
Grace (*charis*) 7, 9–11, 18, 30, 35, 41,
   47, 57–8, 60, 70, 75–6, 78, 81,
   84–7, 90, 92, 94, 97, 104–5, 112,
   114–18, 120–1, 126, 128, 135, 139,
   141, 145, 147, 152, 155, 158, 160,
   162–72, 175, 178, 180–4, 188,
   190, 197–9, 204, 206–8, 210, 221,
   231–2, 234, 238, 246, 248, 259,
   265–7, 270–1, 275, 280, 282–5,
   291, 293–4, 300–307, 309, 313,
   318, 321–2, 325–7, 331, 334–5,
   337, 351

cheap grace 112, 168
costly grace 11, 168–71
created grace 20, 78, 198, 207–8, 275,
    283–4
  identity with Jesus Christ 10, 207, 294
  logic of grace 104, 145, 152, 331
  oneness of Gift and Giver 10, 46, 57–8,
    78, 170, 206–7, 232, 283, 294–5,
    317, 319, 325
  Torrance's view in relation to the
    Roman Catholic view 20, 175, 180,
    183, 190, 265–6, 274–5, 282–7

Hellenic thought (Hellenism) 44–6, 49, 51,
    89, 193
Historical Jesus 26, 36, 104–5, 129–30,
    141, 156, 235, 247, 256–61, 276,
    285, 295
Holy Spirit (Pneumatology) (*see Trinity,
    Filioque*) 8, 17–18, 22, 32, 35,
    37–8, 46–8, 50, 52–61, 63–7, 73,
    76–9, 82, 85, 93, 99, 102–3, 107,
    114–15, 117–18, 121–24, 135,
    141–2, 151, 153–4, 158, 162, 169,
    171–2, 176–7, 179, 184, 187–217,
    233, 236–7, 242–3, 247–8, 250,
    256–7, 267–82, 284, 286, 288, 292,
    294–5, 297, 303, 305–6, 319–21,
    325, 327–8, 332, 335, 337–8, 340,
    342–3, 351
  Pentecost 32, 82, 153–4, 159, 189–97,
    206, 246, 248, 258, 266, 270, 293,
    297, 299
  procession (*see Filioque*) 8, 22, 44,
    65–7, 212–17, 345–6
  self-communication (*see Grace,
    Revelation, self-revelation*)
  *Theosis* (*see Theopoiesis, Theosis,
    deification, divinization*)
Hope 70, 120, 130, 179, 192, 240, 244,
    247, 263, 277–9
  eschatological reserve 67, 120, 246,
    258, 260, 269, 286
Human freedom 78, 90, 105, 129, 145,
    162, 173, 175, 188, 196, 269, 276,
    294, 308

Incarnation 9, 12–13, 18, 20, 30–2, 35, 39,
    41–4, 47, 49, 52, 54, 57–8, 68–70,
    75–6, 78, 82–92, 99, 101–35,
    137–86, 187, 189–92, 194, 197–8,
    204, 206, 219–20, 225–7, 229–30,
    233–5, 237–8, 240–3, 246–7,
    249–57, 260, 267, 269, 271–6, 282,
    284–5, 290, 292, 298, 304, 312,
    314–15, 325, 327–8, 330–2, 336–7,
    339–40, 343, 348
  *anhypostasis* (anhypostatic,
    *anhypostasia*) 104, 139, 229, 331
  container concept of space and time
    (receptacle concept of space and
    time) 24, 33, 89, 99, 111, 114–35,
    247, 251–2, 265–6, 315
  *enhypostasis* (enhypostatic,
    *enhypostasia*) 55, 103–5, 139,
    211–12, 229–30, 251–2, 315, 331
  *homoousion* (*see Christ, homoousion,
    Creation, homoousion, Trinity,
    homoousion*)
  hypostatic union 63, 78, 177, 184, 230,
    244, 257, 290, 305, 340
  Jesus' vicarious activity (*see
    Christology, Jesus' vicarious
    activity*) 118–20, 135, 138–9, 146,
    151, 153–9, 168, 174, 178, 194,
    196, 199, 227, 229, 248, 276, 296,
    299, 305–9, 312–13, 320–2, 327,
    331–2, 336
  kenosis (*see Atonement, abasement,
    condescension*) 118, 123–4, 134,
    138, 156, 195–6, 245
  logos 49–50, 89, 235
  Scotist view 118
  virgin birth 188, 220, 228, 290, 314
    resurrection and virgin birth 234–8

Kerygma 180, 228, 296
Kingdom of God (Christ, Heaven) 17, 58,
    115, 132, 200, 238, 246, 248–9,
    249, 259–60, 262, 272, 277, 279,
    291, 293, 297–8, 303, 310, 316
Knowledge of Christ (Christ's deity) 5, 25,
    39, 58, 64–7, 102, 104, 122, 140–2,
    146, 149–50, 158, 184, 189–90,
    203–4, 235, 255, 263, 331, 341–2

Knowledge of God (*see Trinity, imageless
     thinking, internal relations*) 4–5,
     25–7, 32, 36, 38, 44–5, 49–52, 54,
     58, 64, 66, 68, 70, 74–5, 77, 86, 94,
     96–9, 121–2, 124–5, 147, 157, 159,
     163–4, 169–71, 176, 182, 187–8,
     193, 196, 207, 209, 246, 256, 270,
     326–7, 329–30, 334–6, 340, 343,
     351
   *a priori* 70, 91, 97, 220, 297, 330
   agnostic (views) (agnosticism) (*see
     Agnosticism*)
   dualistic (views) (dualism) (*see
     Dualism*)
   imageless thinking (knowledge) (see
     through knowledge) 48–54, 132,
     193
   knowledge of the Father through the
     Son 18, 36, 40, 57, 69–70, 76, 99,
     202, 204, 272, 336, 341
   mystery 42, 53, 67–8, 79, 107, 114,
     167, 171, 184, 213, 259, 267, 284,
     295, 299, 319, 346–7
   nameless 69, 74, 89, 216, 225
   natural theology (*see Natural
     Theology*) 6–8, 12, 23, 75, 86,
     93–9, 127, 152, 163, 208, 220, 325,
     329
   new natural theology (*see New natural
     theology*) 7, 86, 93–9, 329
   nominalism 26, 35, 181, 333–4
   non-conceptual (non-objective) 33–4,
     124, 172
   pre-understanding 95
   significative or signitive knowledge
     124–6, 131
   symbolic knowledge 30, 43, 124–5,
     128, 172–3, 331
   *theologia* 26, 36, 50
   *theologia gloriae* 256
   ultimates 110, 220, 328, 336

Mariology 19, 183
McCormick Theological Seminary 9
Method (methodological) (*see Theological
     science, scientific method*) 34, 69,
     97–8, 195

Ministry (ministerial priesthood) 16,
     19, 184, 208, 238, 248–50, 271,
     273, 275, 281–2, 283–6, 287–91,
     311–13, 320, 322
   priestly power 250, 281
   sacerdotalism 19–20, 184–5, 208, 282,
     291
   women ministers (women's ordination)
     19, 290
Miracle 30, 79, 97, 104, 110, 149, 223,
     234–5, 238, 240–1, 243, 262
Moderator of the Church of Scotland 22
Mystery (*see Knowledge of God*)
Myth (mythological, mythical, mythology,
     *mythologia*) 32–3, 36, 38–9, 45–6,
     49–50, 52, 57, 109, 116, 126, 130,
     135, 138, 170, 210, 225, 243,
     246–7, 251, 301, 340

Natural science 7–8, 14, 23–4, 27–9, 93–5,
     110, 327, 335
Natural Theology (*see Knowledge of God*)
Neoplatonism (Neoplatonic) 24, 89, 318
Neo-Protestant (Neo-Protestantism) 113,
     190
New Natural Theology (*see Knowledge of
     God*)
Nicaea (Nicene, Nicene-
     Constantinopolitan, Nicene
     Council, Nicene Creed, Nicene
     faith, Nicene theology) 5, 15, 18,
     32–3, 37–8, 40–1, 43–6, 49, 51–2,
     55–6, 58–60, 65, 67, 73–4, 77,
     108, 110, 124–33, 138, 182, 187,
     189–90, 193, 207, 210, 212–13,
     232, 266, 269–73, 289, 299, 339

One Mediator 16, 27, 114, 143, 149, 155,
     168, 240, 247–8, 348
Oneness of God's Act and Being
     (*see Trinity, homoousion,
     consubstantiality*) 54, 190
Oriel College, Oxford 9
Origenist thought (Origenism) 36, 40,
     42–3, 66, 74, 85–6, 89, 99, 124,
     127, 133–4, 268, 272, 301, 310

Panentheism (*see Creation*) 41, 80, 139

Pantheism (*see Creation*) 41, 78, 80, 82, 92, 187

*Parousia* (*see Advent Lord, second coming*) 127, 132, 245, 259–63, 316

Pelagianism (Pelagian) (*see Ethics, conditional salvation*) 11, 171–2, 179, 182, 184, 191, 208, 248, 275, 282, 293, 295, 311, 320

Phenomenalism (phenomenalist) (*see Sacraments*) 26–7, 99, 224, 318–23

Pneumatology (*see Filioque, Holy Spirit, Procession, Trinity*) 187–217, 273, 336, 351

pneumatic potency 282

    grace and the Holy Spirit 199, 210, 232, 327, 335

    Macedonianism (Macedonian) 66, 210

    Holy Spirit absolutely and relatively considered 53, 209

Political theology 279

Prayer (liturgy, worship) 20, 27, 32, 36, 46, 68, 123–4, 139, 143, 172, 175, 183, 185, 197–8, 200–1, 234, 246, 248, 258–9, 267, 274, 277, 279, 281, 286, 307–10, 313–15, 319–21, 334, 337–8, 351

Princeton Theological Seminary 14, 22, 237

Princeton University 9

Rationalism (rationalizing) 4, 23–4, 33, 36, 63, 122, 140, 169, 181, 328, 347

Realist theology 3–4, 31–2, 99, 210, 226, 277, 287, 315

    doctrine of the Holy Spirit 66

    understanding of the resurrection 226

    view of church 277–8

    view of eucharistic presence 287, 315

    view of Scripture 210

Revelation (self-revelation) (trinitarian self-revelation) (*see Self-communication*) 19, 26, 34–8, 45–7, 50–7, 63–4, 67–70, 73–6, 79, 89, 92–9, 101, 103–4, 107, 111, 113, 120–2, 124, 127, 131, 153–4, 157, 159–60, 164, 168, 180, 182–3, 187, 202, 204, 206, 208, 216–17,

220, 224, 235, 248, 257, 270, 291, 310, 325–9, 332, 336–40, 345–8

    Jesus as revealer in his humanity as such 104, 123, 343

Righteousness 10, 18, 152, 155, 161, 175, 177–80, 230, 296, 299, 313, 322

    self-righteousness (*see Atonement, works-righteousness*)

    self-will (*see Atonement, self-justification*) 11, 75, 138, 142, 145, 151, 155, 160–1, 167, 171, 173–4, 192, 199, 208

    unrighteousness 76

Sacraments 1, 8, 14, 16–17, 20, 126, 128, 132, 135, 176, 184, 188–9, 217, 221, 233, 245–7, 250, 258, 260–3, 265–323, 333, 338

    Baptism (*see Baptism*)

        Spirit Baptism and Water Baptism 299–03

        Trinity and Baptism 303–6

    Church as a community of Reconciliation 279–82

    Church as a Body of Justified Sinners 275–9

        Body of Christ 186, 233, 251, 258, 268–9, 271–7, 279, 285, 289, 307, 312, 322

    Church grounded in the Trinity and in Israel 147, 168, 224, 236, 266–73, 281, 310

    Dualism and legalism (*see Ethics, moralism*) 269–73, 301

    Dualism and phenomenalism 318–23

    Intercommunion 16, 280–2, 289, 322–3

    Jesus as King 184, 186, 247–9, 274, 285, 287–8, 291–2, 294, 315, 322

    Jesus as Priest 19, 185–6, 221, 247–9, 274, 285, 287, 291, 311, 315, 320, 322

        High Priest 8, 19, 132, 149, 184–6, 192, 221, 232, 247–8, 250, 282, 287, 290–1, 293, 312, 320, 331, 333

    Jesus as Prophet 137, 187, 219, 247, 249–50, 274, 285, 287–95

Lord's Supper (Eucharist, Holy
Communion) 1, 16–17, 19–20,
127–8, 143, 172, 176, 208, 219,
237–8, 245, 248, 258, 260–1,
266, 276–8, 280–2, 287–91, 295,
299–300, 306–23
epiclesis 200–1
eucharistic real presence 126–7,
238, 245–6, 259, 266, 277–8,
287–90, 314–18 eucharistic
sacrifice (*see Atonement,
sacrifice*) 208, 287, 311,
319–21
transubstantiation 284, 314, 316,
318–19
Scottish Church Theology Society 13, 17,
183
*Scots Confession* 174–86
*Scottish Journal of Theology* 12–13, 22
Second coming (*see Advent Lord,
parousia*) 176, 189, 238, 246, 248,
252, 259–63, 279, 286, 288, 315
Self-communication (*see Revelation*) 18,
21, 31, 50, 68–9, 106, 206–7, 209,
304
Society for the Study of Theology 13
Space and time (*see Incarnation, container
concept or receptacle concept*) 24,
28, 30, 39–42, 51, 53, 55, 81–9,
91, 99, 102, 105–08, 111–12, 116,
123–35, 141, 145, 157, 177, 188–
92, 197, 204, 219, 224–7, 234–5,
239–63, 268–74, 279, 282, 288,
294–5, 298, 302–3, 305, 315–17,
319 332, 337, 339
God's time (*see Eternity*) 253–9
Subjectivism 5, 38, 46, 54
Symbol (symbolic) (*see Biblical
interpretation*) 30, 43, 54, 80, 124,
172–3, 224, 248, 314, 318, 331,
240
self-expression 128–9, 173

Templeton Foundation Prize for Progress
in Religion 22–3, 28
Theological science (scientific theology,
scientific method) 2, 4–5, 23–4,
26–30, 33, 71, 75, 87, 90, 94, 96,

125, 145, 173, 221, 223, 234, 265,
326, 334, 337–9
*Theopoiesis* 157–8, 198–9
deification 78, 128, 158–9, 198, 283–4
divinization 78, 129, 158, 198
*Theosis* 157–8, 197–201, 132
Time (*see Space and time*)
Transcendental method (transcendental
experience) 69, 70, 115, 225
Trinity 2–3, 8–10, 14, 17–18, 20–2, 26,
29–30, 31–72, 74–5, 77, 82, 84–5,
93, 97–9, 101, 103, 110, 112, 121–
2, 128, 131, 135, 137, 139, 142,
147, 149, 153, 169–70, 176, 182,
190, 197, 200–205, 208–16, 221,
225–28, 232, 237, 249–50, 252,
265–71, 273–4, 277, 281, 287–88,
295, 298, 302–304, 306, 317, 320,
325, 329–33, 336, 339–49, 351
appropriation, doctrine of 122
Arius/Arianism (*see Arianism*) 33,
38–9, 43–9, 54–7, 66, 74, 86, 99,
110, 129, 132, 170, 174, 190, 207,
215–16, 301, 340
Cartesian/Kantian Dualism (*see
Dualism*)
centrality of the Doctrine in Torrance's
Theology 31–72, 121, 176
constancy 91–2, 141, 254–5
cosmological dualism (*see Dualism*)
deposit of faith (*see Faith*) 18–19,
36–8, 180, 270, 333
derived and underived deity 21, 67,
189, 341–2
Dualism (*see Dualism*)
economic 18, 21, 26, 31, 42, 56, 59,
64–70, 84, 139, 149, 169, 209, 288,
304, 306, 325, 331, 340–1, 344
epistemological dualism (*see Dualism,
Knowledge of God*)
external relations 41–3, 84, 86
*Filioque* (*see Holy Spirit,
Pneumatology, Procession*) 8, 22,
38, 65–7, 188–90, 205, 208–9,
212–17, 342, 349, 351
glory 59, 115, 138, 162, 164, 180, 227,
241, 251–2, 257, 259, 276–7
Greek Dualism (*see Dualism*)

*homoousion* 5, 20–2, 38, 40–1, 48,
52–9, 61, 63, 65–6, 92, 101, 103,
124, 131, 184, 188–9, 194–5, 199,
206–7, 209, 211, 216–17, 233, 269,
272–3, 283, 325, 331, 337, 339–41,
347
    consubstantial (consubstantiality)
        55, 103, 212
*hypostasis* 41, 55–6, 139, 202, 209,
214, 344–7
imageless thinking of God (*see*
    *Knowledge of God, imageless*
    *thinking*)
immanent 18, 26, 40–1, 55–6, 59–60,
64–71, 84, 92, 103, 139, 149, 169,
204–5, 209, 288, 304, 325, 330–1,
333, 340–2, 344
immutability 109, 148, 197, 255
incomprehensibility (*see Knowledge*
    *of God, mystery*) 44, 53, 83, 167,
187, 252
    ineffable reality of God 138
    ineffable trinitarian relations 45, 53
    ineffable self-naming of Yahweh
        to us 52
internal relations 41, 43–4, 48, 52,
55–6, 78, 84, 214–16, 273, 344
Modalism (modalist) 41, 55, 78, 147,
152, 195, 203, 213, 341–4, 346,
349
Monarchy 21, 64–5, 67, 189, 205, 215,
341, 349

omnipotence 70
ontological 18, 26, 42, 70, 84
onto-relational understanding of Person
    59–61
*ousia* 41, 55–6, 66–7, 75, 189, 209,
214, 216, 344–7
*Perichoresis* (coinherence)
    (coindwelling) 22, 38, 61–5, 128,
    202–4, 213, 253, 346–8
Sabellianism (Sabellian) 39, 55, 65,
110, 211, 238
self-moved 197, 254
Subordinationism (subordinationist) 8,
22, 64–5, 77–8, 110, 152, 205, 211,
213–6, 328, 341–2, 346, 349
Tritheism (tritheist) 41, 55, 149, 152,
204–5, 211, 213–14, 342, 345–7,
349
triunity 21, 67, 189, 203, 212–13,
253–4
Unitarian (Unitarianism,
    "unipersonalism") 55, 211
Truth 5, 11, 17–19, 26, 30–1, 33, 35–41,
46, 54, 56–7, 60–1, 75–6, 91,
102–6, 108–11, 117, 120–22,
124–6, 144–6, 157, 159, 161–2,
165, 167–71, 174, 176, 182–3, 185,
194, 200, 205, 208, 210, 212, 221,
232–3, 235, 249, 269–70, 286,
327–8, 331–6, 338–40, 343
Westminster Confession 19, 180–1, 270
World-view 17, 234